AF531192

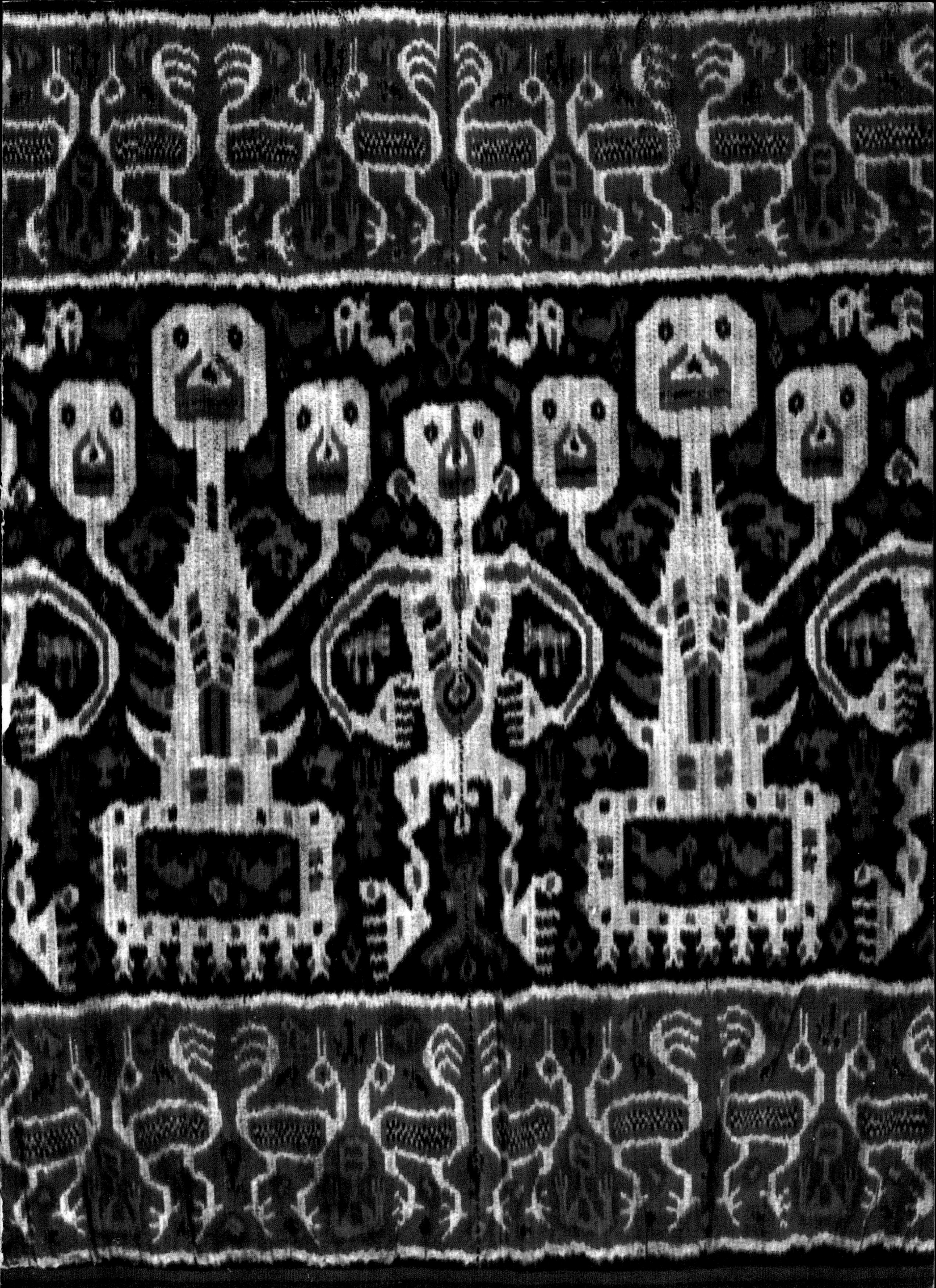

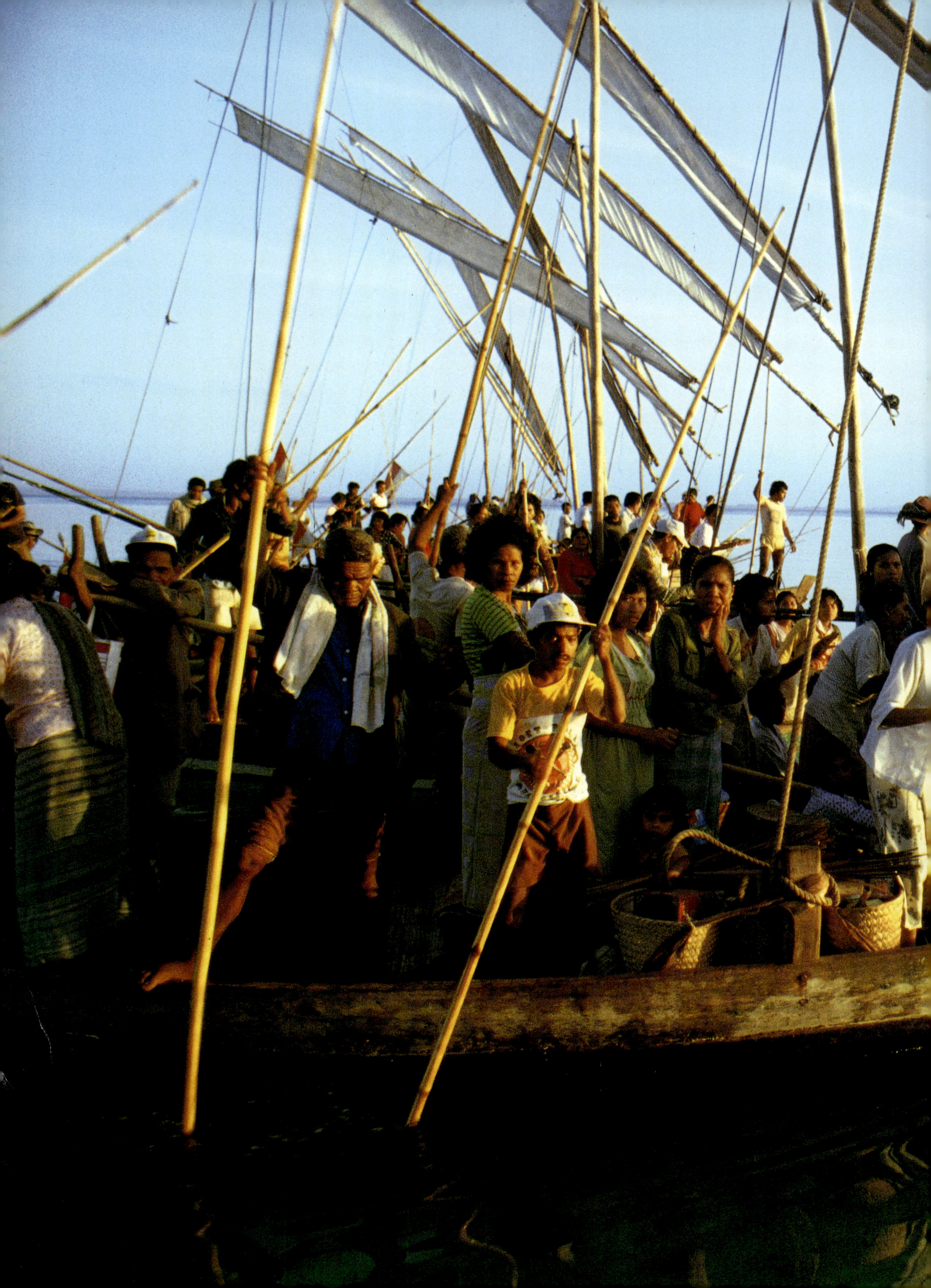

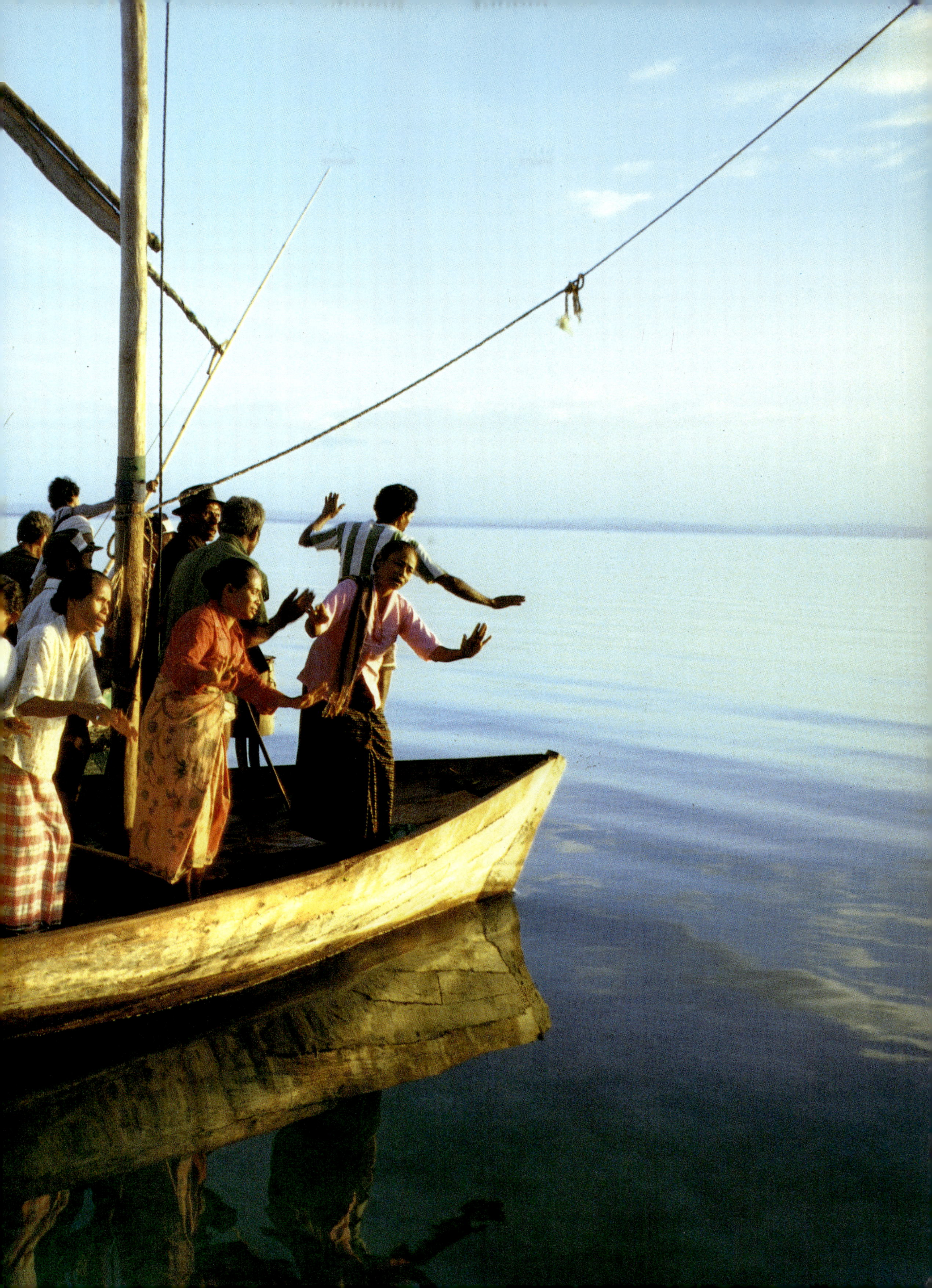

BEYOND

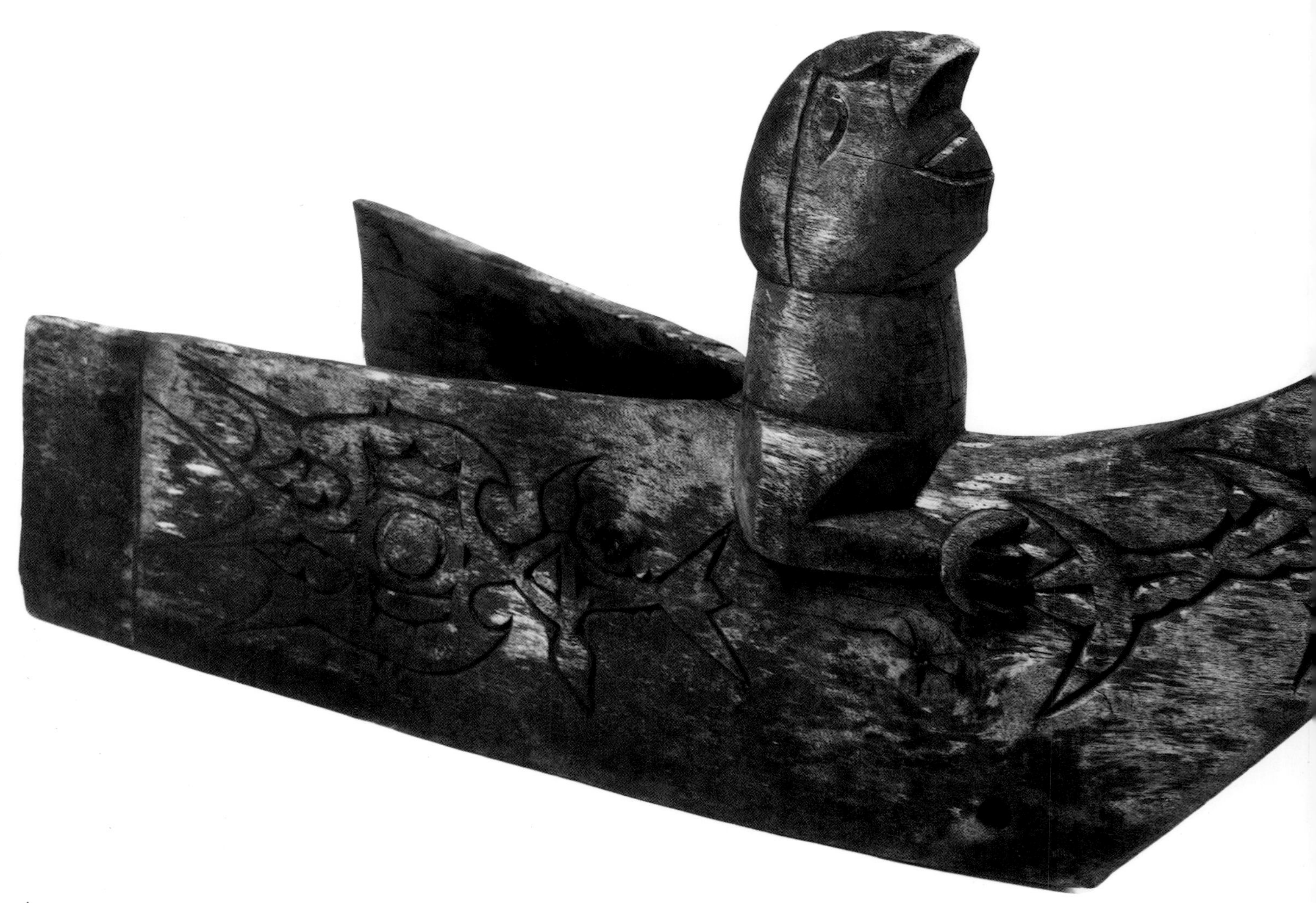

THE JAVA SEA

Art of Indonesia's Outer Islands

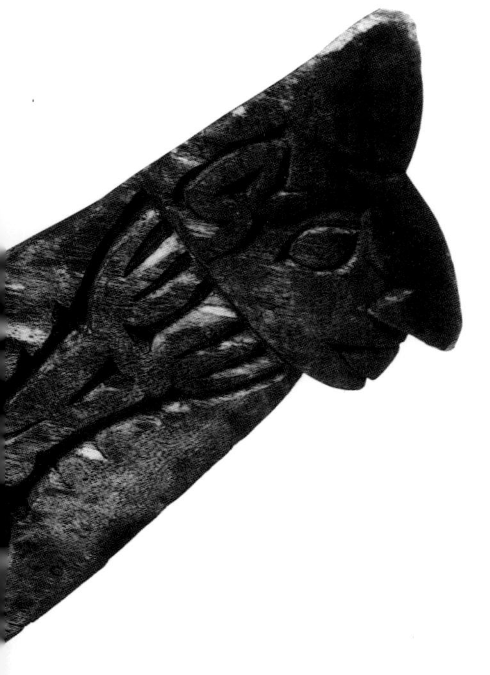

by Paul Michael Taylor
and Lorraine V. Aragon

with assistance from Annamarie L. Rice

THE NATIONAL MUSEUM OF NATURAL HISTORY,
Smithsonian Institution,
Washington, D.C.

in association with

HARRY N. ABRAMS, INC.
New York

Published on the occasion of
Beyond the Java Sea: Art of Indonesia's Outer Islands
an exhibition organized and circulated by
The National Museum of Natural History,
Smithsonian Institution, Washington, D.C.

Exhibition itinerary:
Houston Museum of Natural Science, Houston
November 21, 1990–February 17, 1991

National Museum of Natural History, Washington, D.C.
April 19, 1991–July 14, 1991

M. H. de Young Memorial Museum, San Francisco
September 28, 1991–January 5, 1992

Copyright © 1991 by the Smithsonian Institution

All rights reserved. No part of this publication may be reproduced or transmitted in any form or by any means, electronic or mechanical, including photocopying, recording or any other information storage or retrieval system without permission in writing from Office of Special Exhibits, National Museum of Natural History.

Library of Congress Cataloging-in-Publication Data

Taylor, Paul Michael.
Beyond the Java Sea : art of Indonesia's outer islands/by Paul Michael Taylor and Lorraine V. Aragon, with assistance from Annamarie L. Rice.
p. cm.
Catalog of an exhibition.
Includes bibliographical references and index.
ISBN 0-8109-3112-5 (hardcover : Abrams)
1. Ethnic art—Indonesia—Exhibitions. I. Aragon, Lorraine V., 1954. II. Rice, Annamarie L. III. National Museum of Natural History (U.S.) IV. Title
N7326.T89 1991
709'.598—dc20 90-28241
CIP

The clothbound edition of this book is published in 1991 in association with Harry N. Abrams, Inc., New York. A Times Mirror Company

ISBN: 0–8109–3112–5 (cloth)

Published by the National Museum of Natural History, Washington, D.C.

A paperbound edition of this book is available from the Smithsonian Institution Museum Shops, SKU #1444397.

Project coordinator: Marjory G. Stoller, Office of Special Exhibits
Editor: Letitia Burns O'Connor, Perpetua Press
Copyeditor: Brenda Johnson-Grau
Designer: Dana Levy, Perpetua Press
Assistant Designer: D. J. Choi

Typeset in Sabon by Andresen Typographics, Tucson
Printed and bound by Toppan Printing Company, Tokyo

Author's note: Measurements for objects in the exhibition are given in centimeters. A single measurement indicates diameter or maximum length; otherwise the information on the dimensions is ordered height by width by depth.

Cover: Altar (Fig VIII. 6)

Back cover: Ceremonial cloth, *tampan* (Fig IV. 20)

P. 1: Detail of man's cloth (Fig. VII.39)

Pp. 2–3: Tanimbar villagers departing for a ceremony (Fig. VIII.4)

Pp. 4–5: Canoe-prow ornament (Fig. IX.25)

Manufactured in Japan

Contents

Lenders to the Exhibition

Barbier-Mueller Museum, Geneva
Bernisches Historisches Museum, Switzerland
Christensen Fund, Palo Alto, California
The Julius and Dorette Fleischmann Collection, Cincinnati Museum of Natural History
Field Museum of Natural History, Chicago
Collection of Anita E. Spertus and Robert J. Holmgren, New York
Mark and Kathy Johnson
Jerome L. Joss
Dr. and Mrs. Robert Kuhn
Thomas Murray
Museum Nasional Indonesia, Jakarta
Museum Negeri Nusa Tenggara Barat, Mataram
Museum Negeri Siwa Lima, Ambon
UCLA Fowler Museum of Cultural History
Department of Anthropology, National Museum of Natural History, Smithsonian Institution
Rijksmuseum voor Volkenkunde
Collection of John and Anne Summerfield
Royal Tropical Institute, Tropenmuseum, The Netherlands
University Museum, University of Pennsylvania
Anonymous lender

Beyond the Java Sea has been made possible by grants from Chevron U.S.A., Inc., Texaco Foundation, and the Smithsonian Institution Special Exhibition Fund. Travel and support within Indonesia provided by Yayasan Nusantara Jaya Foundation, Jakarta; transportation between Indonesia and the United States provided by Garuda Indonesian Airways.

FOREWORD

WE SHOULD KNOW MORE ABOUT INDONESIA, because it is a country of developing importance. It lies on the other side of the Earth from the United States, and is formed from an arc of over 13,000 islands, 3,200 miles (5,120 kilometers) in length and 1,100 miles (1,760 kilometers) from north to south. Its land area is five times that of California and its population is more than two-thirds that of the United States. It contains a rich pattern of different cultures, traditional but dynamic, as our authors show, but it also has a strongly developing modern industrial culture.

The Festival of Indonesia, which has provided impetus for a great set of exhibitions including "Beyond the Java Sea" is timely, opening our eyes to a hardy people of increasing importance in the world.

In this book Paul Taylor, assisted by Lorraine Aragon, draws on his fifteen years of study of the language and culture of Indonesia. The exhibit on which it is based has been done with open access to national collections within Indonesia, and Indonesian scholars and conservators have been thoroughly involved in its planning and production.

Many masterworks in this exhibition have never been seen outside Indonesia, and the results are stunning. This wonderful art is shown in its social and cultural contexts, and a world of extraordinary artistic richness unfolds. We can respond strongly to the sophisticated and stylized patterns, the strong forms and the rich yet disciplined colors. My personal favorites are the textiles, but there is very great diversity and something for all tastes. Art pervades every activity in many of the islands. It may provide the "essence" of an everyday object to enable it to perform its function well; it may express marriage alliances, kin relationships, status, or rank; help with healing the sick or ensuring fertility; honor ancestors; or link daily life with the supernatural. Art is integral to normal living, it is vitally important. No wonder the work is so careful, and the use of symmetry or asymmetry so deliberate, the patterns often following basic forms of a strong tradition even where innovation is present.

This art is from the outer islands, where the great impact of a rapidly developing nation is less felt. But as this book shows, the cultures have been dynamic and have changed with the impact of new ideas. As the authors relate, in recent times even museum exhibits on Java have had their impact on visiting artists who have carried new ideas back. New materials have also become incorporated into traditional designs.

A vital aspect of the mission of the National Museum of Natural History is "to increase understanding and to share knowledge of cultural diversity." The working partnership between Indonesians and Museum staff has been richly rewarding to us, and we are proud of the results.

FRANK H. TALBOT
Director
National Museum of Natural History
Smithsonian Institution

Acknowledgments

PRODUCING A MAJOR EXHIBITION requires a great deal of what Indonesian villagers call *gotong royong,* or cooperation among many people to attain a shared goal. Initial impetus and continuing support for this book and the accompanying exhibition came from the organizers of the Festival of Indonesia, a coordinated program of activities throughout the United States that included this exhibition as one of its core components. Within Indonesia, the festival was spearheaded from its inception by the Yayasan Nusantara Jaya, a dynamic cultural foundation headed by Dr. Mochtar Kusumaatmadja. While serving as Foreign Minister of Indonesia, Dr. Kusumaatmadja had cosigned the bilateral agreement for this cultural festival with then-Secretary of State George Schultz. In the United States, the Festival's executive coordinator Ted M. G. Tanen rendered much assistance. This encouragement from government and cultural leaders made possible the unprecedented access to Indonesia's museum facilities and loans from those museums, which made this exhibition possible.

Many thanks also go to Drs. Bambang Soemadio, Director of the Directorate of Museums, and Dra. Suwati Kartiwa, Director, Museum Nasional Indonesia, and to that museum's former director, Teguh Asmar, M.A. Many helpful officials of Indonesia's great cultural institutions, including Minister of Education and Culture Dr. Fuad Hassan, Director General of Culture G.B.P.H. Puger, Minister Dra. Haryati Soebadio, Director General Joop Ave, Pak Adenan Rahmad, and Pak H. Boediardjo, advised us, arranged access to research facilities, invited us to give public lectures and progress reports, and encouraged direct collaboration with technical and research staff of Indonesian institutions.

The expert staff at the Yayasan Nusantara Jaya kindly helped with everything from suggesting travel arrangements to pioneering bilateral loan and photo-sharing agreements with the Smithsonian. Our thanks to Ibu Judi Achjadi, Ibu Raya Sumardi, Pak Erman Soehardjo, S.H., Ibu Anggrek May Koetin, S.H., and many others. The directors and staffs of Indonesia's provincial museums visited in 1987 and 1988 were uniformly hospitable; we especially appreciate the willingness of the Siwa-Lima Museum in Ambon and the Museum Nusa Tenggara Barat in Mataram (Lombok) to lend to this exhibition. The staff of the Museum Nasional Indonesia under Dra. Suwati Kartiwa was thoroughly helpful and interested in our work, and we thank them all. The Indonesian Museum Staff Training Program organized by the Ford Foundation with the Asian Cultural Council (coordinated by Maureen Liebl) helped make the research, design, and production of this exhibition truly collaborative. We thank the following Indonesian museum counterparts who worked with us in Washington at various times: Basrul Akram, I Wayan Suanda, Arifin Pramono, Mohammadin Razak, Gagi Soepono, Himawan, Hans Rijoly. Mohd. Ansar Sudirman S.E., the President of Sarinah Department Store (Jakarta) kindly sponsored a series of museum lectures given by Paul Taylor and others at the Museum Nasional Indonesia. Drs. Bambang Soemadio and his assistant, Mr. Basrul Akram, of the Directorate of Museums were respectively the Indonesian organizer of the training program and the program's first participant; both have been tremendously helpful through every phase of the exhibition as well.

For their encouragement, we thank the Smithsonian's Assistant Secretary for Museums Thomas Freudenheim, Director Frank Talbot of the National Museum of Natural History, Acting Deputy Director Stanwyn Shetler, and Associate Director for Public Programs Robert Sullivan, as well as former Director Robert S. Hoffmann, former Acting Director James Tyler, and Secretary Emeritus S. Dillon Ripley. Among the many who assisted in the exhibit's production, we thank Rick Yamada (art-packing); Carol Grissom (conservator during packing in Indonesia), and Charles Bessant (bracketmaker); as well as the exhibition's designers at Staples and Charles, Inc.; our registrar, Rosemary De Rosa; the coordinators at the National Museum of Natural History's Office of Exhibits Central, Marjory Stoller, Cissy Anklam, and Maggi Jackson; the staff of the Natural History Museum's Education Department, L. McKie, Debbie Rothberg, and Carolyn Sadler; ethnographic conservators Edith Dietze and Cathy Valentour; and the production staff of the Smithsonian's Office of Exhibits Central under Walter Sorrell and Karen Fort, especially the Fabrication Unit under the supervision of Kenneth Clevinger (cases, shipping crates); Ben Snouffer of the Model Shop (manikins); Pat Burke of the Graphics Lab (label silkscreening, photo mounting); and Script Editor Rosemary Regan (exhibit script, gallery brochure). This book and the exhibition are much enriched by the illustrations, all done by Marcia Bakry, except Fig. I.2 drawn by Margaret Davidson. We are grateful to photographer Diane Nordek, who with the assistance of Harold ("Doc") Dougherty is responsible for all photographs of objects in the exhibition, except as follows: Dennis Anderson (Figs. VIII.34, VIII.36, IX.40), Pierre-Alain Ferrazzini (Fig. V.19), Roy Hamilton (Figs. VII.4–6), Linda Turner (Fig. III.20), and The University Museum, Philadelphia (Fig. V.26).

For invaluable collaboration with other exhibits and activities in the Festival of Indonesia we wish to thank Helen Jessup and Osa Brown ("Court Arts of Indonesia"), Jan Fontein ("Sculpture of Indonesia"), Joseph Fischer ("Modern Indonesian Art"), Richard Kurin and Richard Kennedy (Folklife Programs, Smithsonian), Ellen Wells (Dibner Library), Janet Solinger (Smithsonian Resident Associate Program), and Eric Crystal (Program Coordinator, Center for Southeast Asia Studies, University of California, Berkeley). Much other help has been provided by James Wallace, Mary Ellen McCaffrey, Annelore Aceto, Mary Kay Davies, Mayda Riopedre, Roger Magazine, Karen Moran, Jennifer Salkin, Michelle Roberto, Jeanne Helldorfer, Georgia Reilly, Ramin Javedan, Ruth V. Taylor, Barbara and Benjamin Lockett, Mary Zurbuchen, Sarah Bradley, Jacqueline Beeckman, Victor Krantz, Michael Sorafine, Thomas Murray, Richard Strauss, Ambaryatun Pramono, Mrs. Suhardini, J. D. Rubinstein, Joseph Goulet, Paula Fleming, Joyce Sommers, and many others.

The funding sponsors and the lenders are listed separately; we not only appreciate their sponsorship and generosity but also the pleasure of working with people who share our enthusiasm for the subject. Though we are unable to list the names of helpful staff at all lending museums, let alone the names of equally helpful staff at museums we visited but from whom we did not borrow for this exhibition, we thank them all.

The many scholars who provided information or field photographs are cited throughout the text, but we especially acknowledge the help of regional and topical specialists who have given valuable information or read prior drafts of exhibit script or sections of this manuscript: Ian Glover, Patrick Kirch, Peter Bellwood, Bennet Bronson, Arifin Pramono (Prehistory); Jerome Feldman, Y. Miko Yamamoto (Nias), Susan Rodgers, Rita Smith Kipp, Kathryn Bovill, Sandra Niessen, Edward M. Brunner, P. Voorhoeve (Batak), Mattiebelle Gittinger (Indonesian textiles and Lampung), Robert J. Holmgren, Anita Spertus (Lampung), George Appell, Herbert L. Whittier, Richard A. Drake, Bernard Sellato (Dayak), Clementine H. Nooy-Palm, Eric Crystal, Kathleen Adams, Elizabeth Coville, Toby Volkman (Sulawesi), James J. Fox, Joel Kuipers, Laurence Moss, Clark E. Cunningham, Ruth Barnes, Webb Keane (Lesser Sundas), Roy Hamilton (Borneo, Indonesian textiles, and Lesser Sundas), Susan McKinnon, Nico de Jonge, Jacques Pierret, Hans Rijoly (Southeast Moluccas), Stuart Kirsch, Jacques Hoogebrugge, Susan Meyn, Robert Welsch (Irian Jaya), Helen Jessup, George Attiyeh, George Acciaioli, Lucy A. Whalley, Raymond Hebert, Wheeler Thackston, F. K. Lehman (Courts), Anne Summerfield (textiles). Our gratitude for the help we have received should in no way imply that responsibilities for errors are due to anyone but ourselves.

Both authors express their special thanks to curatorial assistant Annamarie L. Rice, who shepherded the various drafts through to completion and helped scour libraries and archives for photographs and information used throughout the book. Ms. Rice is also the sole author of the catalog chapter on Irian Jaya. We gratefully acknowledge the help of the book's editor, Letitia O'Connor, and its designer, Dana Levy, both of Perpetua Press, Los Angeles, who considerably polished and then produced the final product. Finally both of us thank our respective spouses and families for everything from their patience to their enthusiasm, which helped us see the project through to completion.

Part One

Appreciating Outer-island Art

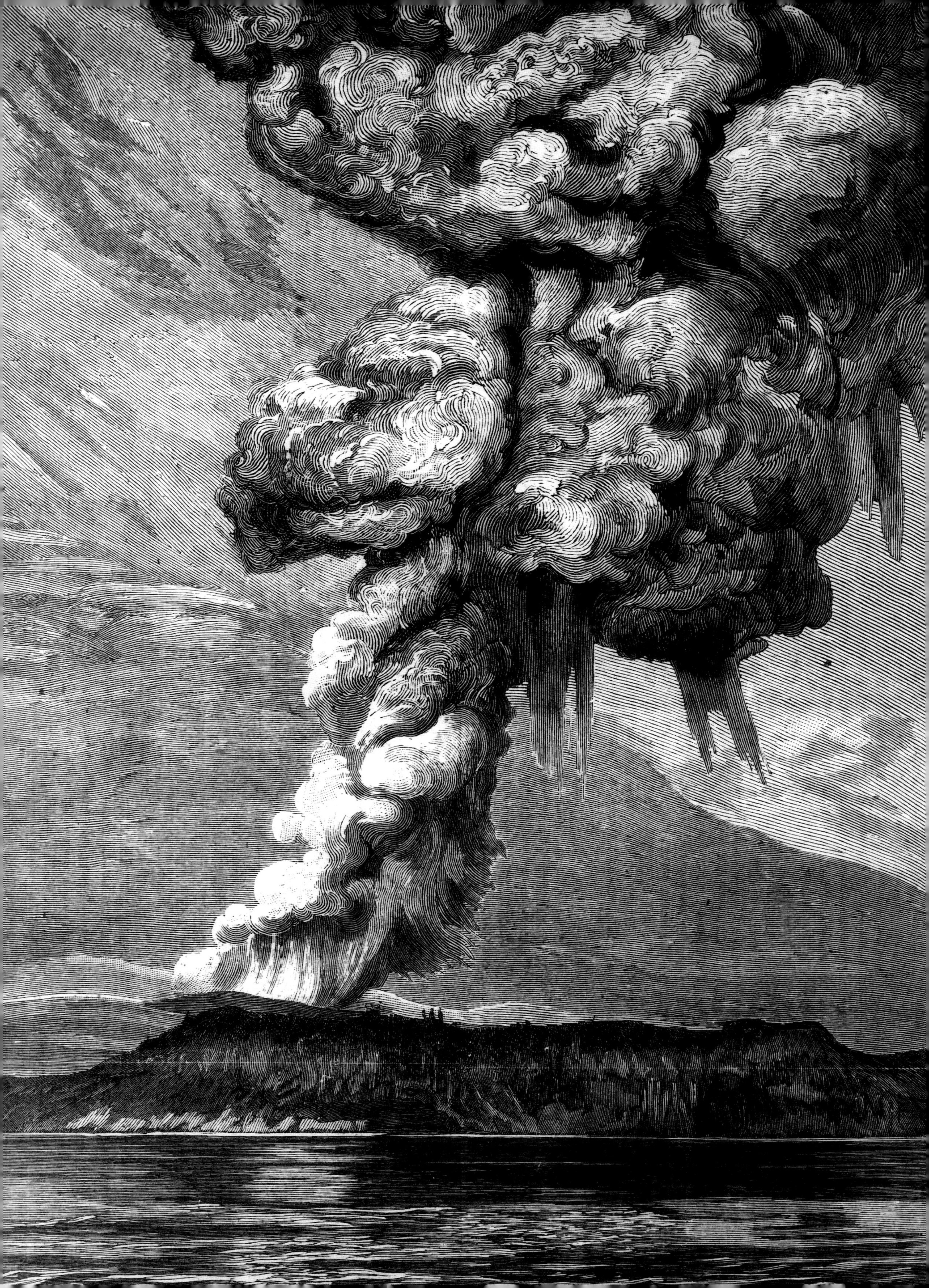

The Indonesian Archipelago and Its Art

In the aftermath of World War II, the founders of modern Indonesia emerged from Japanese occupation and began their four-year struggle for independence from Dutch colonial rule. They resurrected for the purpose an old Sanskrit motto coined during the Majapahit Empire, which had in the fourteenth century briefly unified most of Indonesia. *Bhineka Tunggal Ika*, the national motto now emblazoned across the talons of the mythical *garuda* bird on Indonesia's seal, means "Unity in Diversity."

The motto poses a continual challenge because more than 13,000 islands and three hundred ethnic groups make up the politically unified, modern Republic of Indonesia. *Beyond the Java Sea* explores the traditional art of eight regions in the so-called outer islands: Nias, the Batak and the Lampung regions of Sumatra, Sulawesi (Celebes), Kalimantan, the Lesser Sundas (Nusa Tenggara), the Southeast Moluccas, and Irian Jaya (West Irian). Relatively unknown in the West, the outer islands include all of Indonesia's islands *except* Java (including nearby Madura) and Bali, the better-known inner islands that border the Java Sea.

Through the chapters of this book, the reader will travel from Nias in the far west to Irian Jaya in the east, encountering artworks that are exemplars of indigenous Indonesian aesthetics as well as masterpieces as defined by a Western collector's aesthetic. These works and the accompanying discussions will also introduce the peoples who produced them. Throughout this region, art links village life with the supernatural; it honors ancestors, cements alliances, affirms political power, social rank, and kin relationships, and, of course, it simultaneously surrounds with beauty the peoples who create it. Yet each regional style presents topics and problems peculiar to it. The format of this presentation will allow readers to understand the similarity as well as the diversity, finding in the art of each region recurring themes and styles that reflect the closely related histories of the peoples and the similar purposes for which all Indonesians create art.

Because the objects discussed and illustrated here represent a vast range of peoples and art traditions within the outer islands, available information about them, and about the cultures of the peoples who produced them, is often incomplete. For example, the creators of these works of art are generally anonymous to us, but that anonymity is itself an artifact of the way these objects were acquired by Western collectors and museums (Price 1989:56–67). In their own societies, Indonesian artists played central roles, often also acting as ritual or political leaders. Thus the Batak staff (Fig. 2) carved by a Toba shaman is a work of art whose creator made and used it to contact spirits of the deceased, call back wandering souls of the sick, repel evil forces from the village, or divine

Fig. 1 Engraving of the Krakatau eruption on May 27, 1883, published in *The Graphic*, August 11, 1883 (after photograph taken on that date, reproduced in Simkin and Fiske 1983:fig. 2).

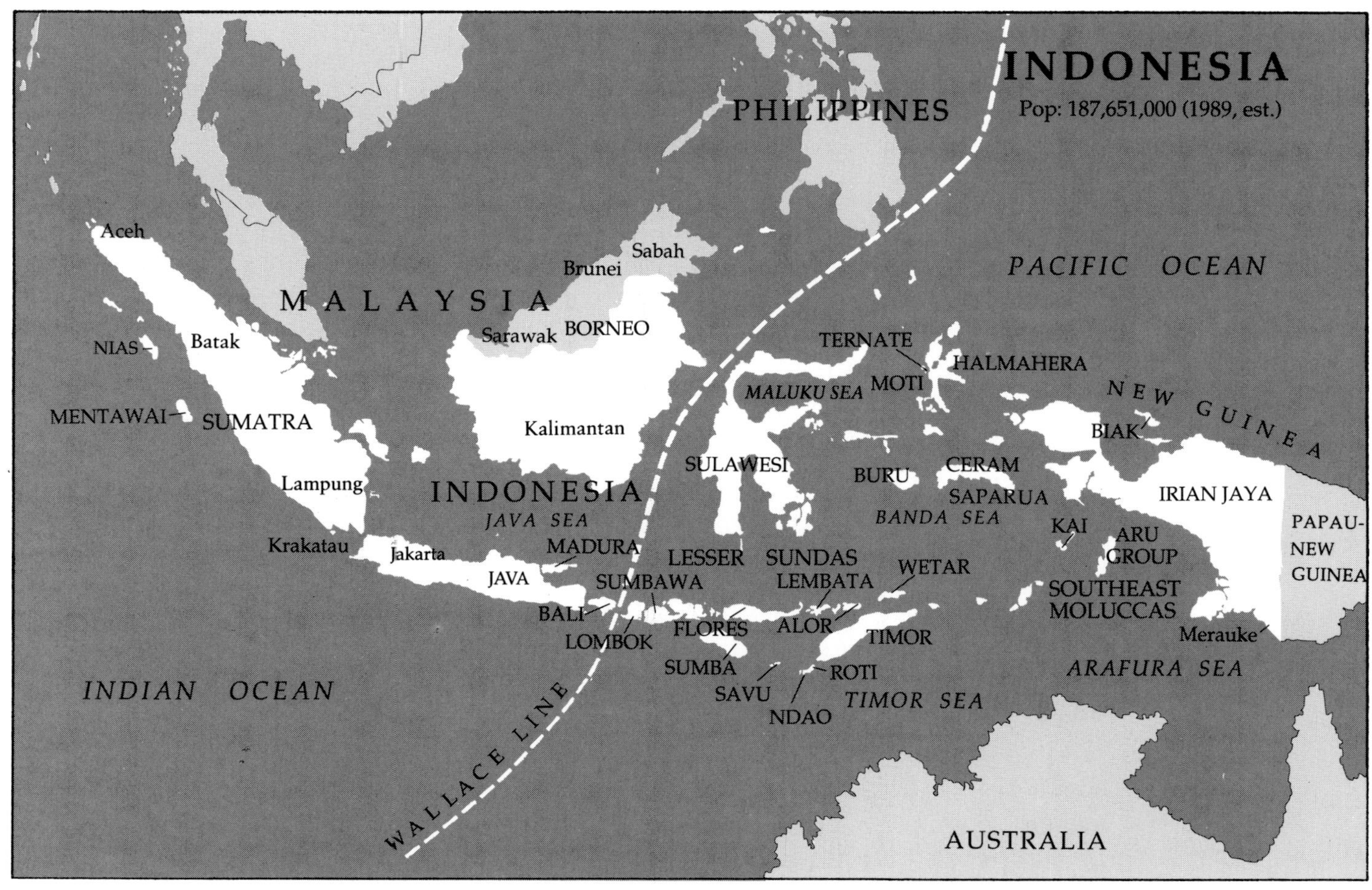

promising times for travel or ceremonies. It is clearly not an anonymous work created by a "culture"—it is a highly individual masterpiece of Batak art. Though we are ignorant of their names, we are sometimes able to recognize individual sculptors, as in the case of a nineteenth-century master sculptor of Bawömataluo village on Nias. Two of his works are brought together again here for the first time (Figs. II.19, II.20), one from a museum in Bern, Switzerland, and one from the Museum Nasional Indonesia in Jakarta. The individual sculptor's mark is visible in the soft curvature of limbs, muscles, and headgear, as well as details of the facial features on the two sculptures (including the distinctive upturned tip of the nose on both figures).

Even though the names and life histories of individual artisans remain unknown, ethnographic accounts from visitors, as well as the indigenous historical accounts of literate peoples throughout the region, can provide a cultural context for understanding these objects. Most such accounts, like virtually all artworks discussed here, date from the nineteenth or very early twentieth century, following an accelerated period of exploration and information gathering about remote areas and preceding a distinct breakdown or transformation of many traditional forms of social organization and beliefs as a result of continuing incursions of those same contacts.

Some early scholars and amateur collectors were admirably meticulous in their fieldwork—superior in some ways to many present-day researchers owing to the length of time they spent as missionaries, colonial officials, and so forth. Yet their impressions and writings inevitably had a colonial perspective. Many shared a European epistemology that treated people, cultures, and the products of those cultures, as objects for studies of social evolution and thus as interesting examples of the primitive. Despite our recognition of these biases, today's scholarship builds on those traditions, and nineteenth- and early twentieth-century

OPPOSITE

Fig. 2 Priest's staff, Toba Batak (see Fig. III.37).

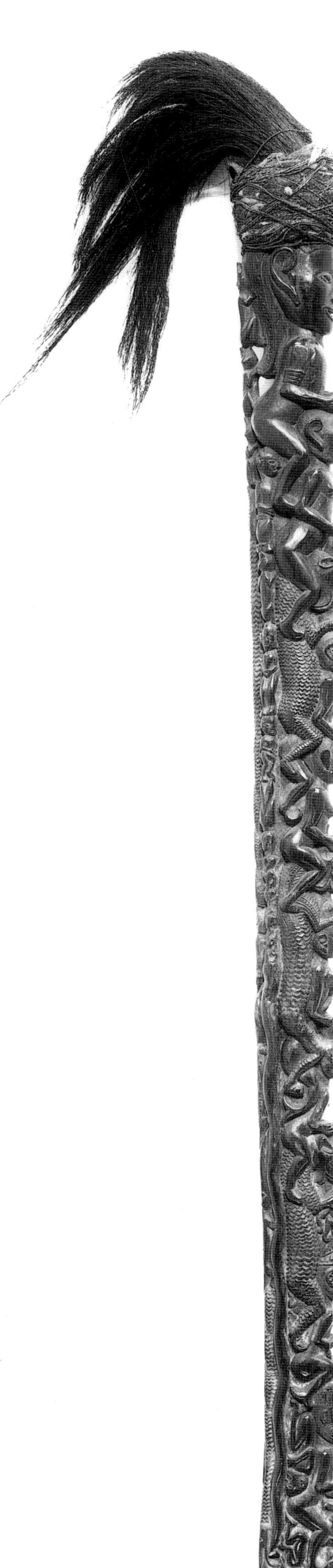

accounts will necessarily dominate museum and scholarly presentations of Indonesian art, until Indonesian and other scholars apply different approaches to produce more informed accounts of this artwork. Some of these objects are no longer made, nor are they clearly remembered. In such cases these old accounts and descriptions provide the only direct evidence we may ever have on their use and meaning. But for most of these objects, much information will come out of the continuing efforts of researchers and from contemporary artisans themselves.

In addition, many Indonesian art forms are made of fragile, impermanent media (wood, textiles, and other plant fiber), and many earlier examples have completely disappeared. So it is difficult to develop a historical understanding of some outer-island traditions. Today outer-island artists look to traditional arts as sources of inspiration. Some traditions have continued or been modified; some (such as Toraja art traditions) are undergoing a renaissance; others (some traditional arts of Lampung or the Southeast Moluccas) became extinct with the transformation of the cultures that produced them.

Outer and Inner Islands

> If ever there was a tail which wagged a dog, Java is the tail, Indonesia the dog.
> (Geertz 1966:13)

The compelling and beautiful art forms that survive and prosper in the outer islands reflect the richness and diversity of those cultures, which have been preserved by their relative isolation in the past. The area is vast, even if only the land is counted; its population is often sparse. Fifty-eight percent of all Indonesia's population clusters on the inner islands of Java, Madura, and Bali, which account for only seven percent of the nation's land area. The inner islands form the indigenous home of only a handful of populous ethnic groups (including the Javanese, Sundanese, Madurese, and Balinese). By contrast, almost all of Indonesia's three hundred linguistic/ethnic groups inhabit the outer islands, including peoples whose traditional levels of social organization ranged, in the recent past, from tiny bands to tribes, chiefdoms, and kingdoms. Those peoples now often continue their traditions within the modern Indonesian nation state.

The distinction between the outer and inner islands has an ecological and historical basis, as pointed out by Geertz (1966). Outer-island societies have relied (with few exceptions) on "slash-and-burn," or swidden, agriculture for their starch staple crops (Fig. 3), whereas the inner-island populations have been wet-rice agriculturalists (Fig. 4). The former technique requires a shifting form of agriculture that supports a low population density. Wet-rice agriculture (or *sawah* in Indonesian) requires intensive agriculture on stable plots and can thus support high population densities. Its dependence on irrigation and controlled distribution of water also frequently led to a complex form of intervillage coordination.

Virtually all Indonesian peoples practice agriculture; the few remaining ethnic groups who practice preagricultural forms of subsistence, as "hunter-gatherers," are scattered in heavily forested interior areas of the outer islands and have the lowest population densities. Fox (1977), however, has demonstrated that a subsistence system based on palm gathering is not only persisting but also gaining ground in southeastern Indonesia (Fig. 5). Ethnic groups from the islands of Roti and Savu, who rely on wild lontar palm juice as their starch staple, have been steadily expanding and taking over seasonally dry regions of Timor, which had formerly been farmed by slash-and-burn methods that exhausted the soil (cf. Ormeling 1955). Thus hunting and gathering as a way of exploiting the environment, which is used by a small minority of outer-island peoples, is not just a "living fossil," but an actively expanding means of subsistence.

Various combinations of historical and ecological factors have been suggested to explain today's disproportion in population density between the inner and outer islands of Indonesia. Pelzer (1963) points to the fact that wet-rice

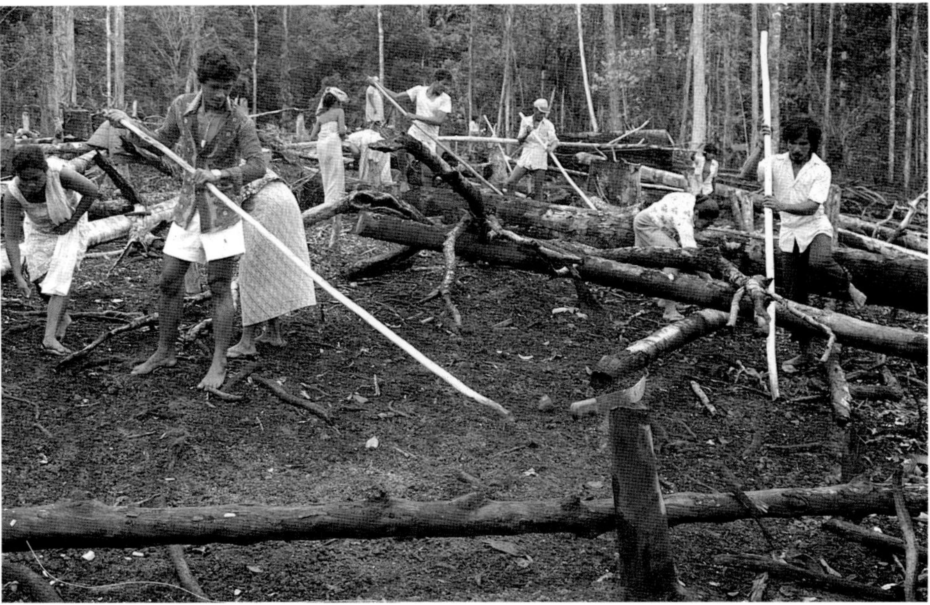

Fig. 3 Sowing rice in a swidden, or slash-and-burn, plot on Halmahera in the Moluccas (1981). Longer-term crops such as coconut, manioc, and banana plants are also planted along with the rice soon after the forest on this plot has been cut and burned. Those crops will mature and dominate the field after the rice has been harvested. Paul M. Taylor

agriculture was introduced very early on Java. He explains Indonesia's striking population disparity as the product of a very long, incremental population growth in the inner islands. Indeed, as Geertz (1966) points out, wet-rice agriculture has the potential for large increases in yields as labor inputs increase, so that an increasingly dense population can live off the same amount of land by putting greater and greater amounts of labor into even a small plot. Nutrients are not depleted because they are brought into the system with continuous highly regulated irrigation. When a forest is cleared for wet-rice agriculture, a miniature ecological aquarium is created, whose productivity continues as long as nutrient-bearing irrigation water flows through it. Swidden agriculture, by contrast, quickly depletes the soil's nutrients, requiring long fallow periods for the nutrient layer of the soil to regenerate, until so-called second-growth forest grows up to resemble the primary forest that had been cut for the swidden farm. Thus swidden agriculture, the predominant form of agriculture throughout the outer islands, only temporarily displaces the tropical forest then allows it to regenerate, given adequate fallow periods. Yet it is incapable of providing food for dense populations and thus limits population growth.

On Java and Bali, Geertz (1966) also emphasizes, the widespread implementation of such labor-intensive high-yield farming was, however, accelerated by historical factors, particularly Dutch colonial introduction—on the inner islands only—of improved medical care and such colonial land-use policies as in-kind taxation, which required increased crop yields and thus increased labor inputs and increased numbers of children (who become a family's laborers) on farms.

Such geographical and ecological demarcations provide background, and a more accurate geographical focus, for the study of art forms such as those of Nias, the various Dayak groups, the Toraja, and others. Such art forms have sometimes been grouped together as "primitive" art, "tribal" art—or even, as Stöhr et al. (1982) called it, "archaic" Indonesian art. Each of these appellations invites misunderstanding. The chorus of scholarly complaints about the concept of "primitive" art has grown quite loud (Clifford 1988; Cole 1985:280–285; Price 1989), for good reasons, as the sophisticated (even cosmopolitan) art in this exhibit will illustrate. Recognizing the complexity of art forms like those included here, many authors refer to the art of small-scale societies as "tribal" (rather than "primitive") art. One could certainly limit the discussion of a category of Indonesian art to the art forms of "tribal" peoples. However, those peoples would have to be defined *negatively*, rather than positively, as pre-

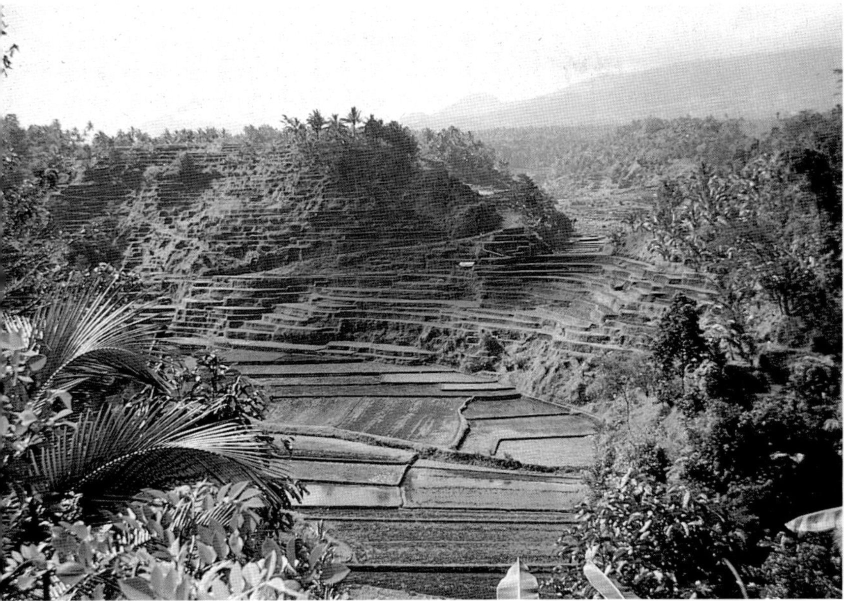

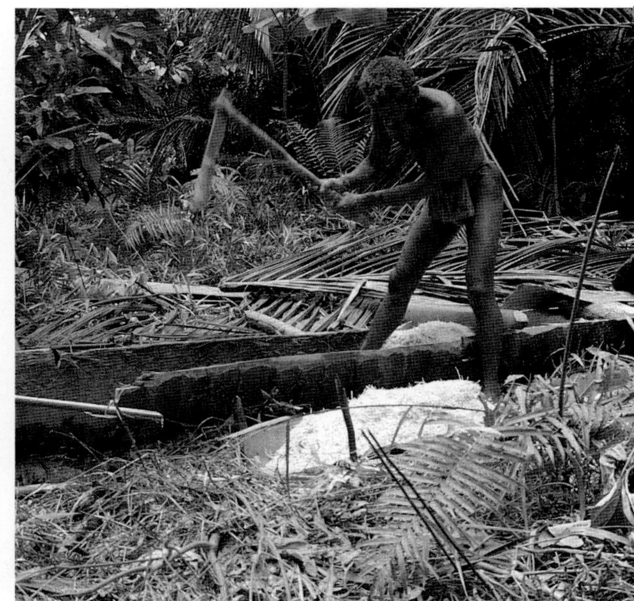

Fig. 4 Rice monocropping in a wet-rice field on Bali, 1984. Lorraine V. Aragon

Fig. 5 A Tugutil tribesman of upriver Dorosago, in the interior of Halmahera, gouges the edible pith of a sago palm (*Metroxylon*), 1981. Today's small populations of hunter-gatherers carry on trade with agricultural peoples, often providing valuable forest products such as resins, processed sago, rattans, or medicinal plant products. Paul M. Taylor

industrial, non-court, and so forth. Such a definition would deter us from including the very influential art forms of trade emporia and courts within walking or boating distance of the centers of "tribal" art production. Moreover, the continued use of terms such as "primitive," "tribal," and "archaic," no matter how qualified with favorable adjectives, perpetuates a post-colonial view of this art as evolutionarily antecedent to, rather than just different from, Western art forms.

Classifying such art forms is a problem for museums or art dealers, not for Indonesian artists. A far more dynamic picture of traditional Indonesian society and art can be formed if the basis for our study is a regional one, rather than one defined by levels of socioeconomic development. Such a view allows us to see the art of the interior peoples of Kalimantan on Borneo or the Lesser Sundas in the context of coastal trade emporia that developed into courts; it also allows us to see that the court arts, though much influenced by foreign contacts, were also enriched by long and continuous contacts with the peoples in the interiors of their own islands.

Trade was essential to outer-island courts, which generally were located in coastal areas with good harbors, especially near the mouths of rivers. An estuarine location allowed participation in the interisland trade in resins, spices, medicinal forest products (brought from upriver to the coastal court), as well as beads or precious jewelry and metal products, imported and locally produced ceramics, and textiles (van Leur 1960, Hall 1985). Such ancient trade continues today, dwarfed however by Indonesia's modern agricultural and industrial trade in products such as timber, minerals, and petroleum.

The Indonesian Archipelago

Geographically, the Indonesian nation is entirely an archipelago. The world's largest island complex, it stretches from the Indian Ocean in the west, straddling the equator between the Philippines to the north and Australia to the south, eastward to the island of New Guinea, whose western half forms Indonesia's easternmost province of Irian Jaya. The islands that make up this archipelago are commonly divided into four major geographical groups. The Greater Sunda complex includes the major islands of Sumatra, Java, Borneo, and Sulawesi, and the many smaller islands around them including the small but well known and densely populated island of Bali. These islands lie atop the Sunda shelf, a suboceanic extension of the Asian continent. The Lesser Sundas (or Nusa Tenggara) is formed by the chain of volcanic islands that continues through

Fig. 6 Double-outrigger canoe, upriver from Kampung Dorosago, Halmahera, 1981. Paul M. Taylor

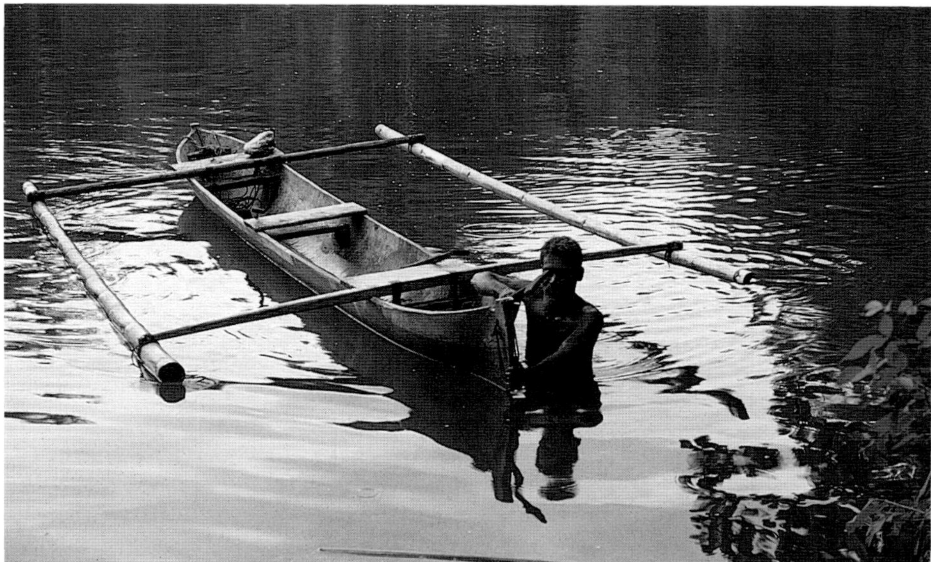

the deep oceans eastward of Bali, from Lombok to Timor, including the province of East Timor (formerly Portuguese Timor), annexed by Indonesia in 1976. The third group of islands constitutes the islands of the Moluccas (or Maluku), lying north and east of the Lesser Sunda chain and east of Sulawesi. The Moluccan region consists of deep seas interspersed with volcanic islands and uplifted blocks at the shifting border of the Asian and the Australian continental plates. The fourth area is Irian Jaya, the western half of the island of New Guinea. Along with the Aru group in the southeastern Moluccas, New Guinea is a continental island that sits atop the Sahul continental shelf, which links it to Australia and forms the bottom of the shallow Arafura Sea.

Viewed geologically, the archipelago is one of the most structurally complicated regions in the world, comprising relatively stable blocks of great age (such as the Sunda shelf and the Sahul shelf) as well as highly unstable areas, with deep sea basins, and large plates of oceanic crust colliding on boundaries to the southwest, south, southeast, and east, which have risen to form long arcs of islands. It is traditional to discern two majestic, parallel arcs that form many of Indonesia's major islands, linked along an undersea path through the Andaman and Nicobar Islands to the Arakan Yoma mountains of Burma and the Himalayas. The inner arc is formed by the islands of Sumatra, Java, Bali, and the line of islands in the Lesser Sundas that includes Lombok, Sumbawa, Flores, and Wetar. The outer arc forms the chain of islands off Sumatra's west coast, from Nias through the Mentawai Islands, then mostly undersea south of Java into the Lesser Sundas, where the arc rises above sea level to produce the islands of Sumba and Timor, then continues in the Moluccas running east to Tanimbar then turning sharply north and back west to include Ceram and Buru.

The islands of the outer arc are a nonvolcanic, largely submarine ridge, while the inner arc is dominated by volcanoes. Extinct or active volcanoes dominate the views in every landward direction in most places on islands of the inner arc. The very large islands of Borneo and Sulawesi, which do not lie on the double-arc system, consist of highlands with large areas of alluvial plains. New Guinea's highland regions are also very substantial. On the western half of that equatorial island, Irian Jaya's Mount Sukarno (elev. 5,029 meters) remains covered with snow throughout the year.

The large number of still-active volcanoes in this chain include the one that gave history its most famous eruption. In August, 1883, the islet of Krakatau, a long-familiar nautical landmark in the strait between Sumatra and Java, erupted with a thunderous noise that remains the loudest sound known to have been heard by man. The mountain poured forth ash and floating pumice and unleashed sea waves cresting as high as thirty-six meters, causing the death of more than 36,000 people and the complete destruction of 165 coastal villages, as well as temperature and atmospheric changes throughout the world that lasted for several years afterward (Fig. 1). Indonesia is home to many active volcanoes, and some part of the country experiences daily slight tectonic earthquakes—but large, destructive earthquakes are rare. Indonesia has by far the world's highest number of active volcanoes—132 eruptions in the last 10,000 years. The United States is a distant second with fifty-five (Simkin and Fiske 1983:23). Because many of Indonesia's volcanoes are in highly populous areas, 33 percent of the world's known fatal volcanic eruptions have occurred in Indonesia. Because new ash revitalizes soil that would otherwise quickly be leached by the heavy rainfall, population density, however, is related to volcanic activity. For example, agricultural yields and population soon increased remarkably in the areas of southern Sumatra initially devastated by Krakatau (Simkin and Fiske 1983).

There are large and populous areas of alluvial plains in the outer islands, particularly along the coasts of the Java Sea, the relatively shallow sea bordering the eastern coast of Sumatra and along the northern coast of Java. Alluvial plains rarely develop along the deeper Indian Ocean coastlines off western Sumatra or off Java's southern coast.

The seas that separate these landmasses vary from the deep waters of the Pacific and Indian oceans to the relatively shallow waters of the Sunda shelf, including the coral-dotted Java Sea. Indonesia's seas have maintained the isolation and separateness of its 13,000 islands but have also united them. A long history of interisland communication has tended to make the coastal populations of all the islands more similar to each other, exchanging ideas and products that helped them adapt to the coastal environment. This pattern has also left interior or highland peoples on each island more isolated from each other, except through contact with the downriver coastal peoples who remain in contact with other parts of the archipelago. By preventing mass migrations of people, the seas (along with difficult-to-traverse interior terrain) have undoubtedly made it possible for small ethnic groups to survive and maintain their cultural distinctiveness with less interference. In the same way that these geographical factors have promoted cultural diversity, they have diminished central political control throughout Indonesia's history.

Indonesia's many sandy, palm-lined beaches often make landings difficult because of strong currents and tidal movements. The resplendent coral reefs that flourish along Indonesia's coasts can also be treacherous and are most easily navigated in traditional crafts by sailors familiar with passages through them or in light double-outrigger canoes of shallow draft that could be dragged over the reefs (Fig. 6). Chinese junks and similar foreign vessels were never a successful means of trade in this region, and indigenous peoples have always dominated maritime as well as intraisland trading systems of the archipelago (Patannè 1971). Coastal trading peoples, such as the Bugis of South Sulawesi, regularly sailed large wooden sailing ships throughout the archipelago (X. 42) and even as far as the coasts of Australia (Cense 1952; MacKnight 1969; Collins 1937; Horridge 1979). The much smaller double-outrigger canoe is common throughout Indonesia for fishing and for local or intervillage transportation. Prow ornaments (see Figs. VIII.3–5, IX. 22–25) of such canoes now grace art museums around the world (Horridge 1978, 1987). An outrigger, like the floating timber or bamboo rigged out from the side of the single-outrigger canoes found throughout Polynesia and Micronesia, helps to stabilize a craft. The double-outrigger canoe, having one outrigger on each side (Fig. 6), is prevalent only in Indonesia because of its relatively protected seas, of the stability of the crafts in navigating coral reefs, which are absent further north on Asia's coastline, and of the outrigger's usefulness in dragging the crafts up to dry on mud flats or rocky substrates to prevent the soaked wooden hulls from being eaten by marine worms.

The predominant natural vegetation over the archipelago's landmass is tropical rain forest, a forest whose climatic requirements are suggested by its name: consistently warm (not high) temperatures with little seasonal variation and heavy rain without a marked dry season. A walk through Indonesia's rain forests affords some of the world's most impressive sights. The huge trees, supported by trunks whose bases flare out into buttresses much taller than a man, rise up over one hundred feet before branching off and creating an interwoven canopy of leafy branches filtering almost all light and letting little penetrate (see photographs, e.g., in Griffiths 1989). Unlike temperate forests, rain forests have no single dominant tree type. Hundreds of species grow together, their trunks like columns in a dimly lit, silent cathedral, draped with lush lianas and epiphytic ferns and clusters of orchids.

In some other parts of the archipelago, especially the Lesser Sunda Islands, close to Australia, monsoonal forests predominate. An annual dry season is one important effect of the monsoons—especially in the long arc of island regions near Australia, from easternmost Java through the Lesser Sundas—because hot dry air flows away from high-pressure areas over Australia at the end of the southern hemisphere's summer (the northern hemisphere's winter), in a northwesterly direction across Indonesia. This phenomenon brings a dry season, and even desertlike conditions on some parts of Timor, during the northern hemisphere's spring. As this air becomes increasingly humid passing over the seas of the archipelago, the drying effects of the monsoon become less and less marked. In the northern hemisphere's late summer, by contrast, warm air flows from high-pressure areas over Asia, picking up moisture as it crosses the Indian Ocean, then flows through the archipelago in a southeasterly direction, bringing heavy rains. The monsoon winds are keys to the indigenous long-range interisland trading systems (Collins 1937), for merchants use them to navigate westward in one season and eastward in the next.

Yet as Neill (1973:41) notes, nature only proposes Indonesia's vegetation; man disposes. Almost all Indonesian peoples practice agriculture, and in the past two centuries population growth has virtually wiped out primary forests on Java, much of Sumatra, and most of Bali, and the rain forest is now being cut down at an alarming rate in all the other islands as well.

Many generalizations have been offered about the effects of ecology and habitat on the formation of cultures in particular areas of Indonesia—including the many differences in population density and settlement patterns associated with swidden agriculture as opposed to wet-rice agriculture. The ecological diversity of the archipelago has often been offered to explain its cultural diversity. Not only does the archipelago consist of islands separated by seas but also New Guinea and the islands of the volcanic arcs consist of mountainous areas separated by valleys and lowlands—providing many refugia, or regions protected by their isolation, for very great numbers of plant and animal species. By this explanation, there are large numbers of cultures (as measured by the more than three hundred languages spoken) partly owing to the same physical isolation (which historically prevented some migrations, conquests, etc.) and also owing to the great variations in fauna and flora. Though such generalizations are appealing, they are difficult to test and counterexamples abound. Perhaps one-third of Indonesia's languages are spoken in Irian Jaya, but its geographical and environmental diversity is not much greater than that of other more linguistically homogeneous areas of the archipelago.

Some forms of artistic production are obviously dependent upon geographic factors. Pottery, for example, must be made near clay deposits because the raw material is heavy and difficult to transport. Throughout the archipelago, regional trade in ceramics has developed outward from such deposits. The Moluccas in eastern Indonesia has just three centers for the manufacture of pottery, each at the center of a local trading network: Moti Island in the northern Moluccas, Saparua Island in the central Moluccas, and Kai Island in the Southeast Moluccas.

In fact, however, artistic production has been one of the most important

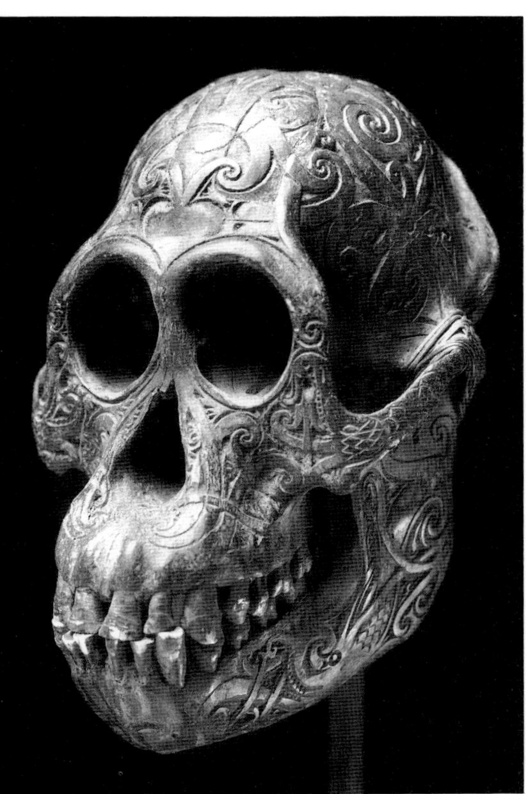

Fig. 7 Incised skull of an adult female orangutan, Dayak, Kalimantan, Borneo. Private collection

means by which Indonesian peoples overcame the limits that their environment would seem to place on other activities. In the Lesser Sundas, for example, the inhabitants of some villages on the same island practice weaving, while those of other villages do not. Lower fertility of the soil or unreliable rainfall in the villages that develop weaving traditions may provide an explanation for the importance of weaving there (Adams 1969:58, Barnes 1989b, Hamilton 1990). Cloth can be traded for food from other villages. On the tiny, densely inhabited, agriculturally rather unproductive island of Ndao, off southwestern Timor, gold and silversmithing is the occupation of all the male inhabitants. As documented by Fox (1977), this dry, poor island could never support its population otherwise. With the favorable winds of the dry season, the men leave Ndao to make and sell their magnificent gold and silver jewelry (see Fig. VII.38) on the big islands of Timor, Savu, Sumba, Flores, and Roti, bringing back payment of rice and small animals.

The flora and fauna provide artistic inspiration as well as the organic raw materials. The raw materials used in Indonesian art need much more study and fieldwork. De Hoog's (1959) unique and intriguing study of the types of wood used to make Nias ancestor figures, and his suggestions about the symbolic associations of those types of wood, was based only on items in museum collections. Such studies beg for testing and replication among Indonesia's artists in the villages where they work. Peoples of the outer islands are intimately familiar with their fauna and flora. Halmahera's lush rain forests are relatively poor of terrestrial fauna, for it does not lie on any continental shelf and was never connected by land bridge to any continent; yet, Taylor's (1990) study of folk biological classification among the Tobelo of Halmahera in the northern Moluccas includes detailed data on local conceptualizations about 1,122 locally named classes of plants and 596 locally named classes of animals.

Within Indonesia's rich forests dwell some of the world's most fascinating land animals, from Komodo dragons and birds of paradise to flying foxes, flying snakes, and sun bears. Most play important roles as inspiration for human legend and have long histories of interaction with human forest-dwellers (McNeely and Wachtel 1988). Elephants with long tusks have been selectively killed by hunters for so long that only short-tusked elephants remain (van Heurn 1929). Rhinoceroses are close to extinction, their horns used as a medium of sculpture and as a medicinal export to China. Hornbill birds and orangutans (whose name means "people of the forest") are among Borneo's animals that the Dayak peoples associate with ancestors or creators (Harrisson 1972, Sumnik-Dekovich 1985) and are so represented in their art (V.18, Fig.7). For Nias islanders the tigers of nearby Sumatra, though unknown on Nias, became powerful symbols of nobility (see Fig. II.33). The distribution of animals (especially mammals) on the islands of Indonesia is due partly to the western islands' orientation along the Sunda shelf, which in the past has allowed land passage to the Asian mainland, while New Guinea and some southeastern Moluccan islands lie on the Sahul shelf, which allowed passage to Australia in prior ages. Between the two continental shelves is a transitional area through which naturalist Alfred Russell Wallace in 1864 drew the "Wallace Line"—bisecting the archipelago, between Bali and Lombok in the south and Borneo and Sulawesi in the north, with a posited demarcation line between Asian and Australian fauna.

Wallace actually drew two lines bisecting the archipelago (Wallace 1962: esp. Chapter 9 and Physical Map in Chapter 1), the first (now famous) line separating what he called "Indo-Malayan" (=Asian) and "Austro-Malayan" (=Australian) faunal regions, and the second line, further east, separating the "Malayan" from what he called "Papuan" (or sometimes more erroneously "Polynesian") peoples. He based this distinction on characteristics of physical type, culture, language, and even "intellect." In fact the boundaries between physical races, language phyla, and key cultural traits do not all precisely coincide, but they do collectively determine an ethnologically crucial transition zone between Island Southeast Asia and Melanesia.

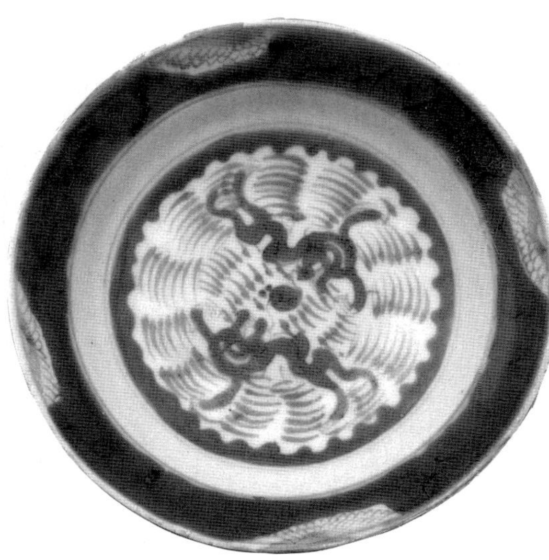

Fig. 8 Ching dynasty blue-and-white porcelain dish depicting two dragons circling a jewel or pearl.

Island Southeast Asia and Melanesia as Culture Areas

When the Netherlands recognized Indonesia's independence in 1949, the new nation did not include its present easternmost province of Irian Jaya. This island's incorporation into the Republic of Indonesia was only recognized in 1969. *Dari Sabang ke Merauke!* ("From Sabang to Merauke") became a slogan for the republic, which would stretch from the tiny islet of Sabang (northwest of Sumatra) in the far west to the town of Merauke in the southeastern corner of Irian Jaya, near the Papua New Guinea border. Prior to Indonesia's independence, Dutch and other scholars had long recognized fundamental differences between the peoples of Island Southeast Asia and those of Melanesia (including New Guinea and islands to its east). These differences between so-called world culture areas were emphasized during the Netherlands' struggle to retain western New Guinea and thus politicized and partly discredited within Indonesia.

Nevertheless, the concept of culture areas is still widely used in introductory textbooks (to organize highly disparate cultures into understandable groupings), in museum anthropology (to do the same thing with artifacts), and in professional affiliations—even of those scholars who no longer use the concept or ascribe to it any explanatory value. Many have questioned the usefulness of the standard five-part division of Oceania (Pacific islands) into Indonesia, Melanesia, Polynesia, Micronesia, and Australia (see, e.g., Oliver 1989:15), although it remains standard. Meanwhile a persistent anthropological trend, particularly in the Netherlands, emphasizes the usefulness of comparative studies within a clearly defined region or culture area, known as a "field of ethnological study," of which Indonesia has proved to be a fruitful example (de Josselin de Jong 1984).

In the broadest sense, the word "Indonesia" itself (or more often its equally outdated synonym "Malaysia") has long been used by anthropologists to distinguish a major world culture area that is more accurately called Island Southeast Asia. This older usage of the term includes the modern nations of the Philippines, Indonesia (except Irian Jaya), Brunei, and the eastern part of Malaysia (Sarawak and Sabah on Borneo). This definition differentiates Indonesia as a world culture area distinct from Melanesia (including Indonesia's Irian Jaya, Papua New Guinea, and nearby islands), Micronesia (including Guam and the Micronesian islands), Polynesia (from Hawaii to New Zealand to Easter Island), and Australia.

This five-part division of Oceania (which was itself the "fifth part" of the world after Europe, Africa, America, and Asia) appears to have been introduced in 1831 by Grégoire Louis Domeny de Rienzi, in a lecture delivered to the Geographical Society of Paris, and later elaborated by him in his book *Océanie, ou cinquième partie du monde . . .* (Domeny de Rienzi 1836:11–14). Domeny de Rienzi noted that parts of the Malay Peninsula and Formosa, as well as parts of Madagascar, should be associated with "Malaysia" (or "Western Oceania") as "Malay colonies." This association reflects the presence of indigenous Austronesian-language speakers among the aborigines of Taiwan, Madagascar, and present-day Western Malaysia. The use of the term "Malaysia" or "Malaisia" for this entire area was quickly adopted, and used by Horatio Hale in his 1846 report on ethnology and philology of the U.S. Exploring Expedition's Pacific voyages (1838–1842) under the command of Charles Wilkes (Hale 1968[1846]:3–4). Pickering (1872:44–138) went on to suggest that the Malaysian culture area was also populated by a distinctive Malayan racial type, which had spread through Polynesia (especially Hawaii) into the northwest coast of the United States, though his racial typology has been discredited. This interest in the Island Southeast Asian culture area persisted into the twentieth century, both for museum studies (e.g., Mason 1908) and ethnographic overviews (e.g., Cooper-Cole 1945), though increasingly the term "Indonesia" came to be used instead. An influential field of comparative customary law studies also focussed on legal systems of the wider "Indonesian" (i.e., Island Southeast Asian) area, again including present-day Malaysia and the Philippines but excluding Irian

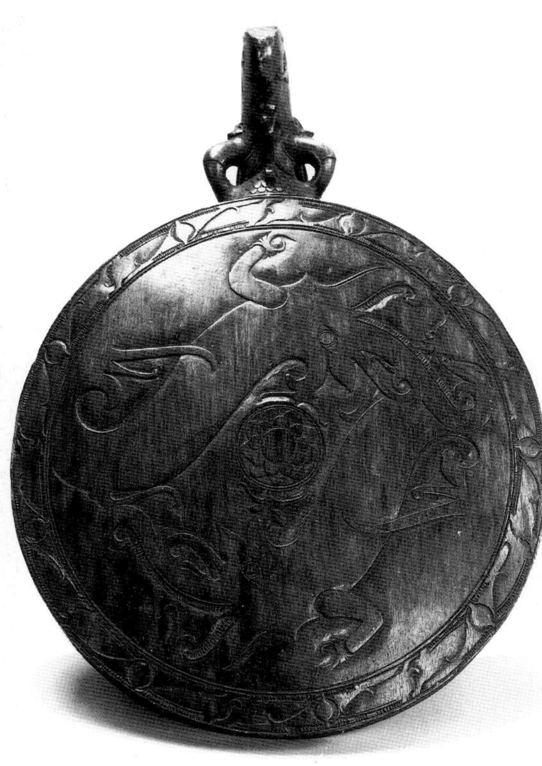

Fig. 9 Seat. Top view of Fig. V.32.

Jaya (van Vollenhoven 1918–1933, ter Haar 1948). Now, since both names have become the names of independent nations, Island (or Insular) Southeast Asia is more common (see, e.g., Lebar 1972).

Island Southeast Asia's distinguishing traits included weaving, metallurgy, grain-crop staples as foods, and the long presence of world religions, such as Hinduism, Buddhism, and Islam, especially in coastal regions. Island Southeast Asia also developed large population densities, bureaucratically organized kingdoms, and other complex forms of sociopolitical organization.

Melanesia, by contrast, was noted for small-scale political organization led by nonhereditary charismatic leaders (known as "big men"), tuberous-crop staple foods, and the division of domestic residence into communal men's houses and separate, or more individualized, women-dominated domestic house units.

Though anthropologists and scholars of customary law often emphasized such differences between "Melanesian" New Guinea (including Irian Jaya) and "Indonesia," the various criteria of distinction noted above do not all coincide in any single border between Indonesia and Melanesia. There was widespread historic trade in textiles between the Moluccas and Irian (Gittinger 1979:25; Elmberg 1968:83.), and continuing metallurgical exchanges between Ternate in the Northern Moluccas and Biak and other coastal areas of Irian (Kamma and Kooijman 1973). Generally, the spread of grain-crop staples has been moving historically eastward through Island Southeast Asia (Spencer 1966:110–122, figs. 4, 5). Some have even claimed early influences of Hindu-Buddhist religions on the indigenous religions of parts of Irian Jaya (Horst 1893).

Such boundaries between world culture areas often do not coincide with political boundaries, and trade has long united peoples and art traditions across the boundaries drawn on maps by scholars, colonial governments, or politicians—as examples in this book document. The varied art styles of Indonesia reflect contact with and migrations of "foreign" peoples throughout this region over the centuries. Throughout Indonesia's history, objects from overseas often became prized heirlooms, their design motifs copied and adapted into local forms. During the past two thousand years there has been active trade with Chinese, Indian, Mainland Southeast Asian, and Middle Eastern populations. Since the 1500s, starting with the Portuguese and Dutch colonial period, contact with the West has also been important.

"Foreign" influences never, however, compromised the distinctiveness of local aesthetics. The dragon or *naga*, originally from India, came to the coast of Borneo in a very Chinese-looking form, as seen on the figurehead of a ship used in Banjarmasin, one of Borneo's most splendid courts (see Figs. X.22, X.23; see also Jessup 1990:61–69, fig. 41). But Chinese dragons have for centuries been making their way upriver, to Dayak groups of Borneo's interior, as relatively common motifs on Ming and Ching dynasty blue-and-white porcelain trade goods like the eighteenth- or nineteenth-century dish (Fig. 8), probably from a kiln in China's Fujian province (Ho 1988). The dish (purchased in 1988 at a shop on Ternate in the Moluccas) shows two "fish dragons" circling a jewel or pearl, a relatively common motif since at least the fifteenth century on Ming and Ching dynasty exportware traded throughout the outer islands of Indonesia. Among the Dayak these mythical animals of East Asian art have become distinctively different, tendril-laden, elongated zoomorphs called *aso'* ("dog" in some Borneo languages), as seen in a similar design format, carved atop a Dayak wooden seat (Fig. 9). On Alor, in the Lesser Sundas, the introduced dragon image is transformed again into a delightful, seahorselike openwork wooden sculpture (Figs. VII.21–22). Such transformations of this and many other forms show the vitality of each art tradition. Each region's artists find models in designs from around the world, yet make of them something that takes on a distinctive local form.

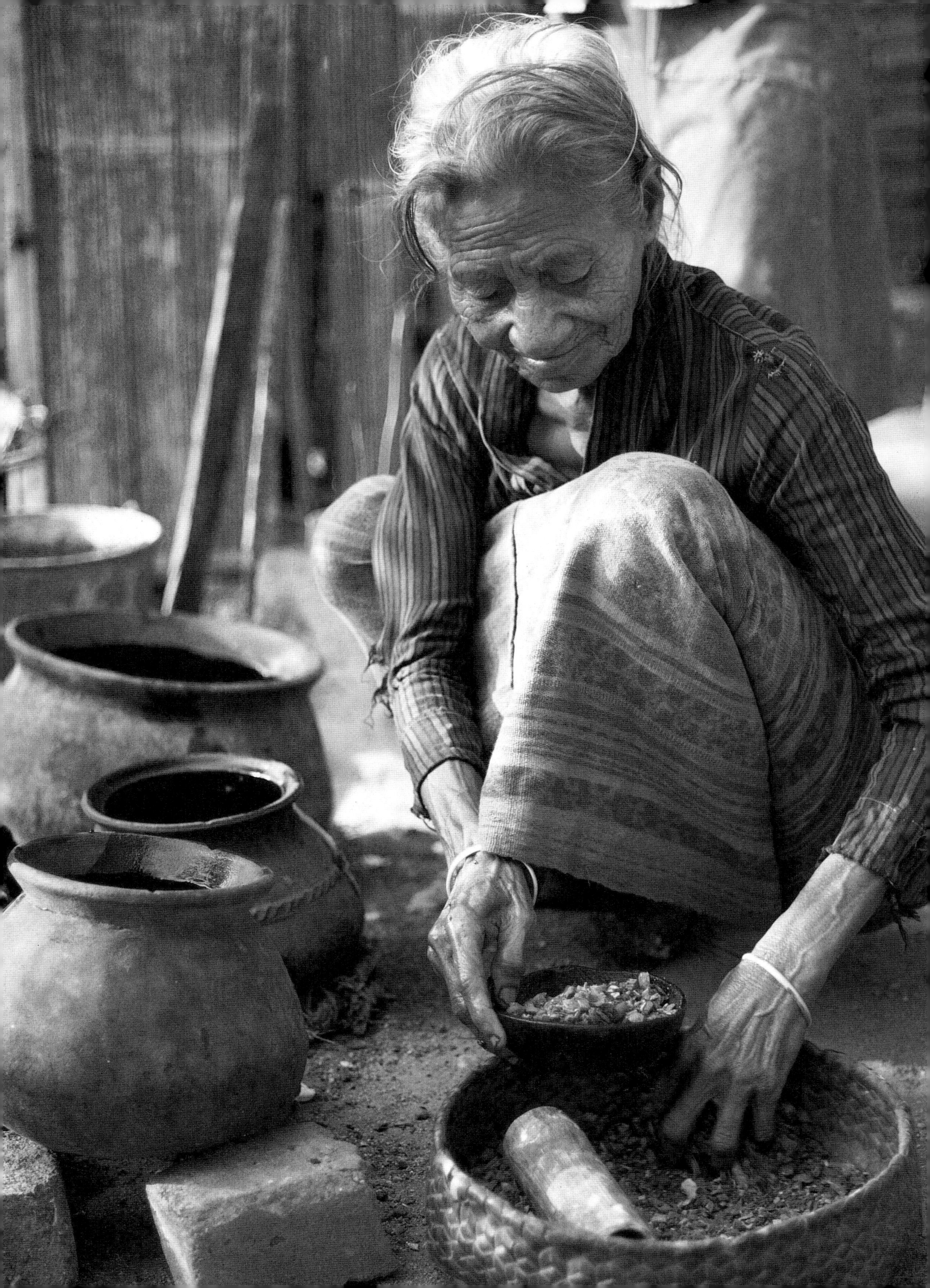

Traditional Indonesian Aesthetics and Design

Two centuries ago the German philosopher Alexander Baumgarten first used the Greek word *aesthetikos* ("pertaining to sense perception") to designate the appreciation of art and beauty. Much self-reflective and useful critical prose has since been written about our aesthetic response to objects—both objects created to elicit an aesthetic response ("art by destination") and objects created for other purposes that nevertheless elicit an aesthetic response ("art by metamorphosis"). This emphasis on the aesthetic response produced by art permits a useful cross-cultural basis for studying art, since "art" can then be defined as a human creation that produces an aesthetic response, and the aesthetic responses of people in different cultures can be compared. As Jacques Maquet notes, all known societies "recognize and actualize the human potentiality for aesthetic perception and appreciation." (1986:64).

Aesthetics and Function

The objects illustrated here were selected with canons of Western connoisseurship in mind. However, even if we had no other sources of information about Indonesian cultures, we could infer that the makers of these pieces had their own aesthetic intentions. An exploration of Indonesian aesthetics, including statements artists make about their intentions, reveals the canons that Indonesian artists used, in cultures throughout the archipelago, to create objects that were intended to produce an aesthetic response. Artists often imbued functional objects with aesthetic value; however, no Indonesian art object in the selection presented here or found in the course of our research was, according to evidence we have, made solely for the purpose of eliciting an aesthetic response. Yet each object shown here clearly represents (among other things) a remarkable aesthetic use and modification of materials.

Throughout Indonesia, areas in close proximity to each other may share frequent contact but often develop very different aesthetic approaches to the same material, in choice of colors as well as organization of design elements. In discussing this phenomenon in the Lesser Sundas, Ruth Barnes has explored an example noted by Ernst Vatter, the German ethnographer who visited the Lamaholot region of East Flores in 1928–29. Vatter compared exquisite *ikat* cloths like those produced by Lamaholot people of Lembata (Fig. VII.50) to the beautiful *hinggi* textiles of Sumba (Fig. VII.39):

> One would be tempted to proclaim the Solor Islands as one of the least artistic and in their material culture most unimaginative areas of Indonesia, if there were

Fig. 10 The chopped roots of *Morinda citrifolia* are added to the bath used for dyeing threads. Lamaholot, Lamalera village, Lembata. Ruth Barnes

Fig. 11 The warp threads used to produce an *ikat* textile are set up on the *ikat* frame and the pattern is "tied" (*ikat*) before immersion in the dye bath. Only the untied portions of the threads are dyed in each immersion. Lamaholot, Lamalera village, Lembata. Ruth Barnes

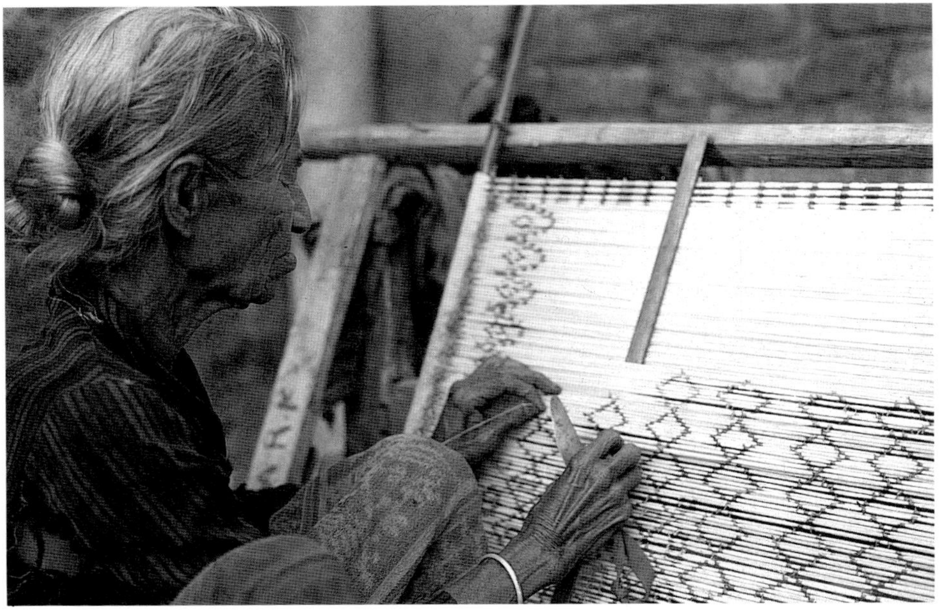

> not at least one field of craft activity . . . that is the *weaving*, and related to it, the *ikat*. . . . The ornaments are simple, but their simplicity is here an aesthetic advantage. Design and color are reserved and calm; the textiles produced in East Flores, on Solo and on Lomblen [Lembata] lose out in a first comparison to the cloths of Sumba, with their vivid animal ornaments, or to the decorative products of the small islands Savu and Roti, with their brilliant colors, but in the long run they exert the stronger artistic effect. One never grows tired of them, but appreciates to an increasing degree the reserved gentility which speaks through the calmly organized surface, through the unpretentious patterns and the muted colors (Vatter 1932:217; quoted and trans. Barnes 1989b:2).

The "reserved and calm" design and color, and the "unpretentious patterns and the muted colors" that so impressed Vatter when he observed textiles of the entire Lamaholot region, seemed to reflect local aesthetic canons, which Barnes studied at one weaving village, Lamalera on Lembata. Barnes found, however, that Lamalera weavers expressed aesthetic canons quite different from those inferred by Vatter. The Lamalera weavers expressed an aesthetic consideration based on the laboriousness of the process required to create a work. For example, Lamalera weavers prefer to dye with morinda (*Morinda citrifolia*), which requires a difficult extraction of dye material from morinda roots (Figs. 10, 11), followed by a lengthy process of repeated immersing and drying of the threads over a period of days until the threads change from light pink to deep red. The bark of an unidentified tree locally called *tenor* can also be used to produce a similar red color. *Tenor* is easier to extract, requires only a few immersions, is more colorfast, and is locally recognized for its higher color intensity. Yet many women consider *tenor* unsuitable for making important textiles, such as those used in the traditional bridewealth sarong (tube-skirt). The quick results obtained with *tenor* are precisely what makes it unsuitable (Barnes 1989b:27–31).

In other areas the lush look and color mattered more than the material used in manufacture. On Nias, for example, fake gold was traditionally considered as good as real gold for use in the creation of important artifacts. The use of the gold color is reserved for the nobility, because it is a symbol of their status. Nias commoners were not entitled to wear heavy gold ornaments. According to Loeb (1972[1935]:136), goldsmithing and carving was carried out only by nobles. In the color symbolism and hierarchy followed in Nias ceremonial clothing and ornaments, each color is associated with categories of excellence or greatness. According to Feldman (1989:205), yellow colors (reserved for the highest-ranking members of society) indicate wealth; red indi-

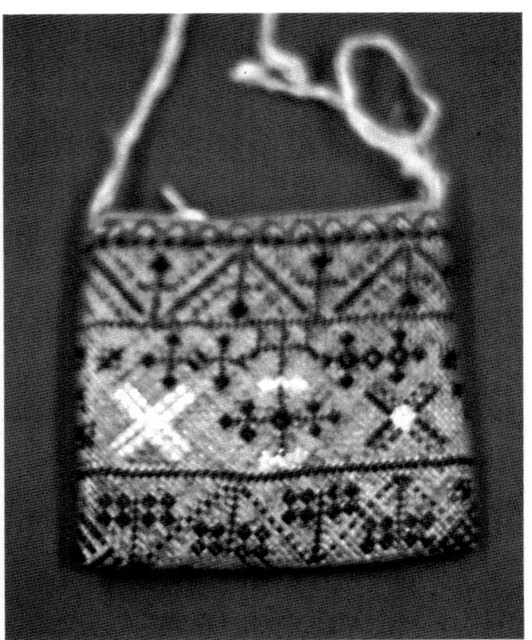

Fig. 12 The silver-colored cigarette wrapper strips used in this tobacco pouch are modern substitutes for thin sheets of silver used in the past. Kahumanaun, Saluan, Central Sulawesi, 1988. Y. Miko Yamamoto

cates great knowledge of *adat* (traditional law and custom); blue represents victory or success; white represents peace and purity; black, as on a Nias warrior's soot-darkened armor (Fig. II.37), indicates fierceness. The color can be more symbol-laden than the composition or surface quality of the material. For example, in Sulawesi, the silver-colored paper from cigarette packages is considered a perfectly valid substitute for the silver foil bands woven into basketry (Fig. 12).

Some Western scholars have searched for the most traditional forms of aesthetics in the same way they searched for the most primitive forms of social organization. Those societies least influenced by Indian, Chinese, Islamic, European, and even indigenous Indonesian court traditions may be direct descendants from more archaic forms of Indonesian society, yet even the most isolated peoples and cultures everywhere are constantly changing. For example, Nias and the chain of islands reaching south from Nias along the west coast of Sumatra were considered by many writers, including Heine Geldern (Loeb 1972[1935]:305–331), to represent an earlier form of Indonesian social organization, which had formerly existed on Sumatra as well. People who use an archaic type of technology are not, however, necessarily also archaic in any particular aspect of their ideological systems. Nevertheless, the aesthetic concepts of an Indonesian people at the most simple stages of socioeconomic development (the stage Heine Geldern claimed to have found on Sumatra and neighboring islands) provide one glimpse of an aesthetic system that may have been largely supplanted by different aesthetic canons associated with more advanced chiefdoms and kingdoms that later spread throughout the region.

The Mentawai islanders, who inhabit a group of islands south of Nias, are a fascinating tribal people whose means of subsistence and settlement size are similar to those posited for the earliest or most technologically simple forms of Indonesian society. Mentawaian artistic productions, and the aesthetic sense behind them, express their conviction that traditional design is the "fulfillment of an object's essence" (Schefold 1988:12–21). Ethnographer Reimar Schefold writes that Mentawaians lavish a great deal of attention on the manufacture of their relatively few items of utilitarian technology, far beyond the technical requirements of producing these pieces. Bows and arrows, for example, must be given the traditional artistic shape of such objects; otherwise, "the object would not 'match its essence' (*mateu*), and such an object cannot be relied upon" (1988:16). A Mentawaian bow maker explained that arrows shot with a carelessly decorated bow (not just a poorly shaped one) could never hit monkeys, because the inadequately decorated material would not "feel" itself to be or perform as the functional object (a bow) it was to become.

Such phrasing of aesthetic concerns reflects animism, the belief that, as among Mentawaians, "everything, man, animal, and plant, but also every object, lives and has a soul. And a living being such as a bow can only be put to good use . . . if its appearance expresses the bow's essence. . . .; this appearance [includes] traditional shape, and its decorations and colours, as these were handed down from the ancestors" (Schefold 1988:16). Rather than creating a functional object and then adding decorations, the maker included the decorations as fundamental elements of an object—the absence of which would impair its ability to function. Schefold met only "utter incomprehension" when he suggested to his Mentawaian informants that perhaps the decoration involved magical images or that it gave an object supernatural powers. To the contrary, they insisted, the beauty of an object was quite simply a prerequisite for its "soundness from within."

Many taboos and behavioral prescriptions are associated with aesthetic productions throughout the outer islands, which suggests that aesthetics have a divinely regulated or moral aspect. For example, Vergouwen (1964:58) says that the Toba Batak weaver had to conform to very specific length specifications for *ulos* cloths used in marriage ceremonies (Figs. III.23, III.24). Otherwise, it was thought that misfortune would come to the weaver of the cloth.

Terms used in Indonesian languages to describe beauty usually include a moral component. The modern Indonesian term *halus* has an aesthetic component ("finely made, meticulously crafted, delicate") and a moral one ("refined, well-mannered, polite"). This integration of moral and aesthetic concepts is found in outer-island Indonesian languages as well. For example, in the Uma language of Central Sulawesi, the terms *lompe'* or *belo'* (depending on the dialect) mean morally righteous as well as physically beautiful. The Tobelo of the northern Moluccas (who speak a West Papuan language) use the verb root *-hailoa* ("to be [visually] beautiful, [visually] pleasing") to describe the character of a person with the qualities of kindness, fairness, and empathy. Those qualities, as well as "visual beauty," are expressed by the abstract noun *muhailoa* formed from that verb. Of course, Tobelo can recognize different applications of the term. Some people are *-hailoa* ("kind, fair") even though their face (that is, outward appearance) is *-torou* ("ugly"). For some others, the reverse is said to be true.

Detailed studies of the aesthetics of the outer islands are rare, but information about aesthetics in ethnographic accounts helps us to interpret the tendency of some societies (such as the various Dayak groups of Kalimantan) to decorate surfaces of virtually every object with meaningful—and beautiful—designs. The remarkable intricacy of carvings on such objects as the Dayak blow-dart quivers (Figs. V.36, V.37) or the aristocrat's walking stick or staff (Fig. V.8) certainly constitute especially pleasing and well-elaborated examples of this cultural tendency to embellish. But such objects were more than just containers for quivers or aids to walking. The talismanic effects of the animal images carved into the quivers are aesthetically and literally powerful. The staff or walking stick (both terms translate the single Indonesian word *tongkat*) clearly serves as a marker of the owner's high status. This staff was also probably intended to provide a more pervasive protection for the person who used it, including the invocation of the ancestor figures carved in its handle.

Our discussion of aesthetics has to this point primarily considered its relation to the explicit functions of objects (as bows, blow-dart quivers, or walking sticks), and particularly how aesthetic qualities of an object contribute to, or may even be required for, the proper carrying out of their explicit functions. Some of the more implicit functions of these objects will be considered in the next chapter, because they relate to many fundamental characteristics shared by Indonesian cultures, including the use of objects to express reciprocity in the treatment of ancestors, in marital alliances, and in the maintenance of harmonious relations among spirits and persons inhabiting the cosmos, as well as among persons in social hierarchies. People in traditional Indonesian societies use their art to express these rich ideas, even though (like people everywhere) they often cannot easily express such basic notions in words.

Accuracy of Duplication and Individual Variation

Appropriate decoration, so that an object may fulfill its function, is one example of a widespread and frequently noted aesthetic criterion in Indonesian art: *accuracy of duplication*, according to traditional procedures, rather than artistic innovation. Even today throughout the archipelago, this criterion continues to be applied—in revealing ways as new materials, new technologies, and new markets provoke modifications of traditional art. Such circumstances can sometimes reveal what Indonesian peoples themselves consider the necessary and unchangeable components of their art. For example, Ruth Barnes's (in press) article, "Without Cloths We Cannot Marry," describes some effects of the disappearance from Lembata, as a result of the international primitive art market, of most heirloom *ikat* cloths used in exchanges associated with marriage ceremonies (Fig. VII.50). In the 1980s, new artificial dyes made weaving easier, but the labor-intensive weaving profession was still declining as other opportunities for women's employment increased and Indonesia's rapidly developing national school system gave girls other things to learn than traditional arts. As a result, the necessary symbolic colors of the traditional bridewealth cloths were retained, as well as their size and format, but more easily dyed indigo threads were used, without the laboriously decorated *ikat* center panels and with coarser, more quickly produced weaves. The essentials of a traditional bridewealth cloth thus illustrate the essentials of their artistic canon: size, format, and combination of colors.

The essential elements of manufacture that make art valuable locally can still be modified for nontraditional uses or for sale. Thus a ceremony consecrating *tau tau*, wooden sculptures of deceased ancestors used by the Toraja (Fig. VI.5), is an essential component of their manufacture. Yet today unconsecrated versions are made for sale to foreigners and as replacements for consecrated images stolen for sale in the international art market. Sacredness is not appropriate for these new uses.

Although the traditional procedures that require duplication vary throughout Indonesia, continuity is always justified by reference to ancestors who provide a charter for proper and appropriate ways of acting in many fields. Ancestors are the universally perceived repositories of spiritual and magical as well as practical knowledge, the source of established traditions of behavior and systems of knowledge that continue today. Connection to such ancestors includes following not only general rules about appropriate aesthetic canons but also detailed and secret instructions for the production of particular, ritually important objects. Like magical formulae, instructions for producing ritually important objects constitute a form of esoteric knowledge from the ancestors, known only to a few people who are both ritual leaders and artists (see Fox 1988 and Taylor 1988 on esoteric knowledge in Indonesian speech and ritual). Sometimes this knowledge—like that required to carve sacred Batak staffs (Tichelman 1939) or to decorate the sacred bamboo container of the Dayak with elaborately incised figures from both the seen and unseen, human and otherworldly, Dayak cosmos(Fig. V.6–7)—is acquired through apprenticeship. In the case of the beautifully woven *ikat pua'* cloth of the Ibanic groups of Borneo, the knowledge arrives in the weaver's dream, and she cautiously and laboriously creates the cloth to match the dream, seeking help—if she is inexperienced—from older, stronger women to weave the most powerful and dangerous motifs revealed to her (Drake 1988; Vogelsanger 1980).

There is considerable variation in the ways that individual artists interpret a style or template in any particular medium. No two staffs, no two *pua'* cloths, are alike. In these and all other examples of ritual objects produced in traditional ways, there is ample room for variation in the arrangement and shape of components, in the materials or techniques used, and in the care and quality of the workmanship.

Indonesian Design Formats and the Organization of Meaningful Design Elements

Preferences for particular design formats are widespread; that is, characteristic arrangements of design elements are found in many kinds of artwork—the two-dimensional surfaces of textiles, the cylindrical surfaces of decorated bamboos, or even the many wooden, metal, and mixed-media sculpted shapes. The design formats that are used across a wide area of the archipelago can be analytically separated from the aesthetic canons of any particular people who might arrange design elements in accordance with that format. Such design formats can also here be heuristically distinguished from the content of the design—for instance, whether the motifs or colors or materials used are symbolic or connote royalty, femininity, or power. Parallelisms between these design formats and more general characteristics of Indonesian culture can also be posited.

One frequent characteristic of design formats throughout Indonesia (though Dayak art of Borneo presents some interesting exceptions) is an avoidance of symmetry. Some kinds of partial symmetry are common, however, particularly radial symmetry around a central point on the top of objects that are otherwise asymmetric sculptures (e.g., Figs. V.9, V.32, X.25). Two-dimensional textiles or surfaces are often symmetric along one axis (longitudinal or horizontal), but asymmetric along the other, as illustrated by the *hinggi* cloth of Sumba (Fig. VII.39) or the Central Sulawesi barkcloth headscarf (Fig. VI.43).

In traditional Indonesian architecture—as exemplified by the Nias chief houses mentioned above (Fig. II.23), the Toraja kindred house (Fig. VI.4), and houses of the Atoni on Timor (Figs. VII.12, VII.13)—the main pole or main beam does not divide the house equally into halves: one side is larger than the other. Many investigators have pointed out (Cunningham 1964; Robert Barnes 1974) that architectural asymmetric design mirrors the common opposition between superior families of the bride and inferior families of the groom in a so-called asymmetric marriage-alliance system (see "The Arts of Marriage" section below). Certainly some association between asymmetric design elements and characteristics of wife-giving and wife-taking groups are clearly recognized, and locally discussed, in societies that have such marital-alliance patterns. The Indonesian preference for such asymmetric architecture and design patterns is, however, far more widespread than is this particular type of asymmetric marital alliance, for it is found in places like Sulawesi where asymmetric marital-alliance systems are not practiced. In the Lesser Sundas and the Southeast Moluccas, particularly, the asymmetry of the house is strongly associated with dualism, complementarity, and contrasts that are expressed in other areas of the culture (see Waterson 1990:175ff and catalog chapters VII and VIII).

An interesting manuscript by Iban Dayak artist Augustine Anggat Ganjing has been translated by Gana Ngadi into English with the title *Basic Iban Design: An Introduction* (Ganjing 1988). The artist/author, a former illustrator for the journal *Nandai* (published by the Borneo Literature Council in Sarawak), has filled the book with the curved and complex designs with which Dayak artists cover the surfaces of most objects. The designs are the subject matter of his text but also thoroughly cover the surfaces of objects in his images of Dayak village scenes. Ganjing explains the designs as elaborations of five elementary curves, called by the letters they approximate (the J, C, V, W, and S curves), then applies them to the production of the tendril designs, leaf designs, and others found in Dayak art. He also distinguishes between two main types of designs, the "balanced type," or bilaterally symmetric, and the "unbalanced type (irregular)," or the nonsymmetric (Ganjing 1988:23ff). Bilaterally symmetric depictions of figures in Dayak art seem not to be encumbered by an ideology in which asymmetry is the norm. Those who ascribe norms of asymmetry to asymmetric alliance systems (or preference for unilineal descent groups) will undoubtedly note that Borneo societies have cognatic forms of social organization, without asymmetric alliance patterns of marriage.

In many parts of Indonesia a careful avoidance of even numbers and a preference for odd numbers is expressed in the production of artworks. Such avoidance paradoxically is often strongest in societies, like those of the Lesser Sundas, where dualism and contrasting pairs are emphasized, probably because of their emphasis on complementarity (that is, inequality) as well as duality in their symbolic systems (see catalog chapter VII). Such prohibitions can also be attributed to the strict, divinely regulated nature of aesthetic production in the outer islands. For example, Barnes (1989a:52) describes restrictions on weaving and decorating the women's cloths of Lamalera, which prescribe that the number of warp stripes and the number of *ikat* bands in each panel always be uneven. The Lamalera three-panel bridewealth cloth, like the fine example from the Tropenmuseum (Fig. VII.50), is "made up of two symmetrical outer panels, which makes the combined number of ikat bands even. However, with the addition of the central panel, the uneven number is again established." (Barnes 1989a:52). She also cites Gregorius Keraf, a linguist born in Lamalera, who describes how an odd number of components is also the norm in Lamalera boat-building. Because practices may deviate while norms are upheld, mere observation or counting of parts (on objects in museum collections, for example) may not accurately reflect the local understanding of asymmetry:

> Odd numbers express a form of life, a continuous dynamic. This situation represents an important factor in the attitude of life of the people of Lamalera. Even numbers indicate that everything has been finished, is complete. Thus there is no living dynamic, there is no life. Because of that, whenever a boat of the form *uak nalã* (i.e., "section missing") does not possess an odd number of sections, it is nevertheless still thought to possess an odd number, through the description as a *boat lacking a section*. In other words, it is "a boat whose sections are not complete," i.e., odd in number. By this method . . . no violation of the prevailing norm occurs (Keraf 1983:6).

Thus even though many kinds of even numbers and some partially symmetric designs can be found, norms about avoiding symmetry and even numbers are widely held. Geirnaert (1989a:65–67) discusses techniques for assuring that the two halves of the traditional man's cloth of West Sumba are woven so that one side is larger than the other. The warps are set up separately for the two halves so that one half is wider and longer than the other. Each border is twined in a single long strip, then cut in half to be placed on the edges of the cloth. In order to produce a more asymmetric look, one half is reversed, so that it shows the mirror image of the other. This technique, called "reversal of symmetry," constitutes a method of making bilaterally symmetric patterns more asymmetric, and often has associations with symbolism of dualism and complementarity (Lévi-Strauss 1963:245–268). Indeed, Indonesians eschewed absolute symmetry but, paradoxically, do this to achieve a balance based on complementarity (see also Niessen 1985:169–228).

A design frequently encountered in two-dimensional forms (including surfaces of cylinders that could be imagined to be opened out into two-dimensional patterns) repeats elements within boxes or bands. Geometric motifs are arranged in bands around the cylindrical sides of the earliest piece illustrated here, the Dongson period drum (Figs. I.5–11). Indeed, such arrangements occur in textiles, sculpture, and in other media in the art of many Indonesian regions, such as the ship cloths of Lampung in southern Sumatra. For example, the long *palepai* ship cloth from Lampung (Fig. IV.6) depicts repeated identical ships in rectangles divided by bands featuring ceremonial poles or trees. The stylized trees and ships are created out of innumerable squared-off scrolls, a widespread motif familiar from Dongson drums. Because similar geometric patterns were used in bronze drums, some early authors considered these patterns evidence of an early, Dongsonian substratum in Indonesian art that had been preserved in tribal areas (see catalog chapter I). Textiles and bamboo cylinders provide the preeminent two-dimensional decorative formats in which Indonesians created their artworks. Textile design generally involves the arrangement of elements within boxes (including a central box framed by the border of the cloth) and bands. The same arrangement is found on the surfaces of many bamboo containers (Fig. VI.6).

These design formats can be widely observed, and each element of the design generally has a meaning that is understood in the community or at least by the artist (in the case of esoteric designs). In addition, there are some widespread meaningful Indonesian methods of organizing design *elements* into varying design formats. For example, a tripartite organization in a particular work of art often clearly indicates a reference to the tripartite cosmology of upper world, middle world, and lower world, which sometimes corresponded to a traditional division of human society into nobility, commoners, and slaves. In such cases, the design elements are arranged to reflect such a division, regardless of the particular design format. Feldman (1979) has documented how the chief's house of Bawömataluo village, South Nias, is locally recognized to be divided into three parts: the lower level of poles upholding the house (providing shelter for pigs and domesticated animals), the middle level where the occupants sleep and live, and the upper level of rafters for storage of heirlooms. This tripartite division corresponds to local concepts about the division of society (slaves, commoners, and nobility), as well as the division of the universe (lower world, middle world, upper world). Any set of three can represent another (see catalog chapter II).

One of the most intriguing and elaborate examples of such meaningful design is the Ngaju or Ot Danum Ḍayak bamboo container (Fig. V.7). In this piece, human and animal forms inhabit the upper as well as the middle world, but the standard imagery is also given a unique inversion. Like many Southeast Asian tribal peoples, the Ngaju consider otherworldly inhabitants to resemble folk of this world—farming, living in houses, and so on—but with some important characteristics that are the *opposite* of familiar ones. Thus spirits are cold rather than warm-blooded, and they cast no shadows. On this bamboo container, another inversion is introduced: the lower world, middle world, and upper world are each depicted with their mirror image. The esoteric or ritual knowledge required to depict the structure of the cosmos on a sacred ritual object such as this was dangerous and therefore mastered by few people. The artist who created this ritual container has not only depicted invisible worlds that are like ours but different in crucial ways but also conjured up another permutation of the invisible worlds, in which each component of the tripartite cosmos has a mirror image.

In these cases, a tripartite design division clearly relates to a tripartite view of the cosmos. Nevertheless, elements of such tripartite designs are found in areas of Indonesia where notions of the cosmos are not tripartite and are used in places where tripartite divisions of the universe are not part of the cosmology. Likewise, asymmetric designs become metaphors of asymmetric marriage-alliance systems where such marital traditions occur, but the preference for asymmetric design is far more widespread. In such cases, a commonly used design pattern can take on particular meaning in a society which draws on it to create a metaphor for some characteristic of that society or its view of the universe. The carved altar plank from the Southeast Moluccas, for example (Fig. VIII.31), bears some elements of a characteristic tripartite design division, marked by the presence of birds and other heavenly beings at the top and by fish and similarly appropriate lower-world creatures at the base, but it has an ambiguous or mixed middle area. Ethnographers report that this tripartite conception of the universe is not pervasive among the cultures of the region, as it is, for example, on Nias or Kalimantan. Instead, dualism is foremost, stressing oppositions between older and younger, male and female, wife-giver and wife-taker groups, and so on. The specific meaning of such altar planks is unknown because the traditional religions that inspired them are now extinct. Of course, a tripartite division can also be interpreted by observers in dualistic terms. For example, the cosmos might be divided into this world and the other world, with the latter further subdivided into upper and lower. Similarly, the ambiguous divisions represented on the altar plank might refer to an opposition between sea and land and to an opposition between land and sky. These dualistic oppositions are filled with symbolic significance in myths and rituals of the Southeast Moluccas.

As design formats are either borrowed or independently developed and elaborated throughout the archipelago, they take on new meanings. Valid parallels between the designs used in a culture and other characteristics of that culture may be identified, but design elements and design formats are adopted by people of different cultures in other regions—where they may be reinterpreted or lose their meaningfulness entirely. Much remains to be studied, for example, about the origins and links between design elements of Indonesian art and ostensibly related elements from foreign sources. Some observers claim to find the so-called tree-of-life motif, for example, in widely disparate representations of treelike objects and motifs throughout Indonesian art (Jessup 1990:69–71), though no evidence has been found that such images are historically related. Indeed the similarities are not locally recognized; one of the archetypal tree-of-life forms frequently presented is the *gunungan*, or mountain figure, used in Javanese shadow puppet theaters, though in fact the local terms for the figure emphasize "mountain," not "tree." Other motifs such as buffalo horns, by contrast, have different symbolic associations throughout Indonesia but are generally recognized as buffalo horns (Hough 1932). Minimally, there may be an association between trees or growing things with life, but there is no proof that all such images are related. Many Indonesian cultures have, perhaps independently, developed symbolic associations with particular types of trees, often associated with medicinal, magical, or other uses of their parts, vegetative appearance or behavioral characteristics of the plants (seasonality, soil preferences, etc.), or other associations (see examples catalogued in Heyne 1950, Burkill 1966 [1935]).

Some Indonesian cultures do, however, use the tree as a metaphor of the cosmos, with roots as the under world, trunk (with tree houses built into the lowest branches) constituting the middle world, and upper branches constituting the upper world. Indeed the Ngaju (Dayak) example studied by Schrärer (1963) is among the best-known and best-documented examples of such a tree image and is heavily laden with images from local symbolism. A particularly elaborate and powerful example of such imagery from the Ngaju (or nearby Ot Danum) people is depicted way on the etched bamboo container noted above (Fig. V.7).

The expression "tree of life" (which does not translate any Indonesian term) is most applicable in cases where the tree image is central to the arrangement of design elements on the artwork and where evidence can be found that it has come to symbolize life, that is, fertility or prosperity. These are in fact the associations claimed for the so-called tree-of-life motifs found on Lampung textiles of southern Sumatra (see catalog chapter IV). The beaded ceremonial textile (Fig. IV.11), which was perhaps used as a component of gift exchanges at the marriage of a Lampung aristocrat, depicts a Lampung mythological tree of life. The image has also been associated with the Buddhist "wishing tree" and is thought to symbolize fertility or gratification of desires through community prosperity (Randhawa 1963). Similar tree images can be seen in the ship cloths from Lampung (e.g., Figs. IV.7, IV.20).

The term "ship cloth," given to Lampung's elaborate supplementary weft and embroidered textiles produced prior to the twentieth century, refers to another well-known image in Indonesian art. Sometimes imaginatively associated with ship-of-the-dead motifs found in Mesopotamia, ancient Egypt, and other distant lands, the image of the ship does present an obvious metaphor for passage from one stage of existence to another. On Borneo, model ships hung in rafters represent vehicles for the passage of the deceased to spirit worlds. In Lampung, fine textiles like those referred to above have been called ship cloths because many of them depict ship images. Yet field research supports the view that the ship motif appearing on most Lampung ceremonial textiles symbolizes a general life-cycle transition, not a ship of the dead specifically (Langewis and Wagner 1964:33–34; Gittinger 1972:137; 1976:219). Just as ships indicate transition, they can also represent a vehicle in which some object is sent or by means of which contact takes place. That is the more probable component of the ship metaphor in the so-called boat altars on Tanimbar, in the Southeast Moluccas (see catalog chapter VIII), which are shaped like boats and associated with boats. Ships have also often been used as symbols for the community (Manguin 1986). Myths about Batak and Toraja houses, for example, describe them as ships, and observers have noted their shiplike forms, with curved roofs and tall, outward-thrusting façades at "prow" and "stern" (Fig. VI.3–4).

The sumptuous textiles, incised mats, and other artworks of Lampung present a rich and challenging mixture of indigenous Lampung motifs and Hindu-Buddhist mandalas, Chinese-style dragons, peacocks, and floral patterns. This mixture of elements reflects the long tradition of continuous contact between the coastal people of Lampung and the Indian- and Chinese-influenced kingdoms of Sumatra, Java, and mainland Asia. Holmgren and Spertus (1980, 1989) document Indian and especially West Javanese influences in Lampung textile imagery, and Gittinger (1989) traces the resemblances of Lampung designs to motifs of the Tai-speaking peoples of mainland Southeast Asia. The image of the ship that frequently appears on Lampung textiles may be an indigenous metaphor appropriate to textiles used for rites of passage, but centuries of foreign borrowing have greatly enriched the design vocabulary of Lampung and of many other regions.

Some Principles for Interpreting the Selection of Design Elements

Some principles of interpreting design elements found in Indonesia's art (or principles used in adopting and reinterpreting foreign elements in Indonesia's art) are themselves characteristic of Indonesian culture. They can be inferred from the ways Indonesians have reinterpreted the design elements of foreign cultures or from the design formats in which those elements appear. For example, a foreign design element may be adopted because it is associated with the prestige of a distant place or with the prestige accorded to objects from distant places. In northern Sumatra, for example, Hindu influences may be found in the elephant mount accorded a Toba Batak ancestor figure (Fig. III.18). The rider is Toba (not Indian), and the Hindu elements are added to indicate prestige. Similarly, the ceremonial cloth from Lampung in southern Sumatra (Fig. IV.12), which illustrates a wedding aboard a ship, depicts a bridal couple riding an elephant beneath an umbrella. Both the parasol and the elephant are Hindu symbols of royalty, used by the Lampung artisan to indicate the honored status of the bridal pair.

Islamic influences are apparent in the artwork of coastal Sumatra, especially Aceh (at Sumatra's northernmost tip). Such influences are evident in the fine filigree of jewelry manufactured by the Karo of Sumatra, close neighbors of the Toba Batak. The Karo used Acehnese-like filigree to give a piece a look of higher status or prestige, as shown in the *sertali* necklace or the exquisitely formed Karo ring (Figs. III.10, III.11). This is in marked contrast to the very thick and heavy look that is the preferred aesthetic for fine Toba Batak jewelry, such as the *singa* bracelet (Figs. III.2, III.3) or the Toba waist chain (Fig. III.4). Hinduism and Islam subtly influenced the ideational, as well as material, culture of tribal peoples. Batak traditional religion, for example, shows clear signs of Hindu influence that may have entered directly from Indian trade or contacts with Hindu-Buddhist kingdoms on coastal Sumatra or Java (see catalog chapter III). The Batak term *debata* ("higher god") is of Sanskrit origin, and several Batak deities have clear Indian parallels (Loeb 1972[1935]:72–78). Dravidian clan names are found among the Pakpak and Karo Batak (Loeb 1972[1935]:21), while the Toba Batak traditionally wrote their sacred knowledge in accordion-folding bark books (*pustaha*) using an indigenous Batak script derived from the Sanskrit alphabet (Fig. III.25).

Studies of the adoption of foreign items in Indonesian art have often emphasized that the criteria of selection come from the receiving culture. As Visser (1989:81) notes, for example, "Textiles are not chosen at random but rather . . . deliberately, for their colors and motifs or patterns, in order to fit the value system of the receiving culture." Many of the canons of art associated with noble classes and the development of outer-island courts might be considered an intentional result of the careful selection of foreign symbols and their associated ideologies, which emphasize a hierarchically organized, rank-stratified society. Objects came to symbolize authority, and accession to office was represented by the acquisition of such symbols of authority.

For example, visits by Lampung chiefs to the Bantam courts were supposedly the inspiration for the Lampung "throne," or *pepadon*, system. Lampung nobles, impressed by the Javanese court etiquette and its trappings, sponsored expensive feasts with buffalo sacrifices, competing to acquire titles and symbols of power such as carved wooden thrones (*pepadon*), gates (*lawang kori*), chariots (*rata*), and other prized possessions that could be purchased from the descendants of clan chiefs who had been authorized to use them by the

Bantam sultans of West Java. The floral and dragon motifs carved on such wooden artworks (Fig. IV.3) were imported from Java. This *pepadon* system may simply have been a local Lampung elaboration of indigenous methods of increasing status through the construction of monuments built in association with the sponsorship of public feasts. Nineteenth-century Lampung presents an example of a rank-stratified, pre-court society, which might have developed full courts and sultanates if allowed to continue imitating the Javanese courts without the interference of colonialism or modern republican ideas (see catalog chapter IV).

Often design elements from many sources are used in the same contemporary tradition. On Toraja textiles, wood surfaces, and etched bamboos made today, some design elements are identical to those pan-Southeast Asian motifs also seen on Bronze-Age kettledrums (Waterson 1988:44–45). Others are Hindu motifs, deriving from Indian textiles that came to the Toraja through trade. Whatever their origins, carved motifs are assigned specific local meanings, referring to local plants, animals or artifacts, and are used to indicate the status of the owners of the ornamented building or to commemorate an elaborate funeral.

Today "foreign" ideas, or ideas from elsewhere in the archipelago, are sometimes adopted by remote outer-island peoples from prestigious museum exhibitions in Jakarta. Geirnaert (1989a:64) notes that the West Sumbanese began incorporating metallic threads into their locally made *lambelekko* skirts in approximately 1985—the direct result of interest in Indian silver and gold thread after a number of exhibitions held in Jakarta around 1980 showed *songket* textiles from Sumatra (like that shown in Fig. X.15) as well as ordinary Javanese cloths (*lurik*) into which metallic threads had been woven (see Kartiwa 1982, 1983). Analysis of materials and colors should only be taken so far. Even today weavers in small villages of West Sumba, who rely on machine-spun thread, are often at the mercy of whatever inexpensive threads traders bring to them: "Towards the end of 1983, the shelves of Waikabubak's shops were laden with unusually bright orange and red skeins. About three months later, one could observe these two colors combined in *lambelekko* skirts on the streets" (Geinaert 1989a:64). Similarly, new technologies can introduce new techniques and materials or remove technical constraints on production.

One pervasive principle of interpretation frequently noted in the catalog of objects that follows is often applied to design elements and especially to objects as a whole—that is, the commonly reported identification of some objects as male goods and other objects as female goods, particularly those objects used in marriage-alliance gift exchanges (Niessen 1984; McKinnon 1989; MacCormack and Strathern 1980; Strathern 1988).

A long history of trade and contact has brought Indonesian peoples together, with intermarriage one result. As ter Haar (1948) observed, in cases of traditional marriage between ethnic groups, where each group has its own ceremonies (including gift exchange), the ceremonial system of the bride's group always prevails. This predominance reflects the universal notion that the wife-giving family is ritually superior to the wife-taking family. Perhaps intermarriage, and particularly the confusion or misinterpretation that might result if gifts associated with marital exchanges were too different from one place to another, has contributed to a general standardization of the gender of objects. That standardization is also undoubtedly related to the fact that smiths and jewelry-makers are usually male, whereas weaving is almost universally a female specialty. Consequently, textiles are generally considered female, and metal objects such as weapons are generally considered male.

Nevertheless, it is an oversimplification to refer to an object in its entirety as female or male, even those objects called "male" and "female" and used in marital exchanges. Male goods—especially the most important ones used in the marriage ceremonies—often have a female component, and female goods have a part that is clearly considered (even called) male. See, for example, an archetypal pair of objects that could be used in marital exchanges among the Batak:

the *piso*, or knife (Figs. III.29, III.30), which is a male good given from the family of the groom to the family of the bride, and the *ulos*, or sacred cloth, given from the family of the bride to the family of the groom (Fig. III.24). The knife, though a male good, has both a male and a female figure adorning its double handle. Similarly, each *ulos* textile, though as a whole the object constitutes a female good, has one supplementary weft end panel that is considered the male component (Niessen 1985).

This characteristic joining of male and female elements in some artworks has been interpreted as a technique for creating pieces that are ritually more powerful (Rodgers 1985; de Zwaan 1922, 1930:132–134, 1955). Rodgers infers that the joining of male and female elements in Indonesian jewelry is an indication that the piece was considered especially powerful, although there is no clear ethnographic evidence to show that this interpretation was shared by her informants for the particular objects she mentions. The headdress ornament (Fig. III.10) is an example of the kind she discusses. Such ornaments were used by Karo traditional ritual specialists to call back the soul of an ill villager. In such cases, the *sertali* is paired with a bridegroom's *bura layang-layang* necklace and swung through the air, the combined male and female forces being used to contact helpful spirits (Rodgers 1985:320). The triangular segments that rise from each separate pendant of the men's headdress, *sertali ruma-ruma*, represent the roofs of Karo *adat* houses.

Similarly, de Zwaan (1922, 1930, 1955), in his studies of Nias art, devotes a great deal of attention to the hermaphroditic qualities of some Central Nias ancestor figures. Central Nias *adu* figures are primarily male, but some are female or display a combination of male and female sexual characteristics. Ancestor figures with both male and female features were sometimes tied together in a row along with other figures that only show male features (Fig. II.14). Such rows of figures, according to Feldman (1985b:57) were attached to, and sometimes fully covered, house walls. De Zwaan speculates that such hermaphroditic figures must be related to, or invoke, fertility. If the association of male and female elements in the same object is associated with fertility, McKinnon (1989) provides an exception from Tanimbar. She states that male valuables do not include images of both male and female elements, whereas female valuables do (1989:39), though a footnote (N. 9) summarizes some exceptions. She concludes that male productivity involves death (hunting and fishing, for example, being quintessential male activities, as are warfare and headhunting). By contrast, female activities (gardening, child-rearing) are associated with life. Growth and fertility explicitly require the complementarity of male and female; death involves the denial or absence of sexual complementarity. McKinnon writes:

> The process that is productive of death always turns in on itself: it pits heat against heat, man against man. The process that is productive of life always turns toward an other, which is complementary in nature: it requires the union of male and female, the union of objects generated out of heat and death with objects generated through coolness and growth. (1989:41)

If this magical power is associated with fertility, then there would indeed be a logical association between the joining of male and female elements, on the one hand, and notions of fertility and reproduction, on the other hand. The ritual act of bringing together representations of male and female deities (sun and moon, for example, in the Southeast Moluccas) is an essential component of rituals designed to ensure fertility.

If marital-alliance gifts represent the families being united by the marriage, then it not surprising that male and female components occur both in goods designated male and in those designated female. A family that gives its daughter or sister in marriage to another family is giving away its most valuable female good. Among the Tobelo of Halmahera, the entire family of the groom considers itself "male" relative to the family of their new in-laws, who in turn consider themselves "female" relative to the groom's family. Just as the "male" family includes many female members (the groom's mother, sisters, and so on), so too the male goods that represent it contain female elements. Just as the "female" family includes many male members (the bride's father, brothers, and so on), so too the female goods that represent it contain male elements.

By eschewing absolute symmetry, Indonesians thereby achieved a balance based on complementarity, as with the pairing of patterns at both sides of an asymmetrically designed Batak *ulos* textile (Fig. III.24), for example (see Niessen 1985:169–228). Traditional Indonesian artists have often expressed notions of complementarity in answer to inquiries about the reasons for placement of design motifs, explaining that balance between male and female elements within a design (not only on gifts associated with marital exchanges) dictated placement of those elements. A house door made by the Tetum of Timor (Fig. VII.14) and decorated with both a preeminently male symbol (the buffalo-horn motif of a warrior's headdress) and a preeminently female symbol (a woman's breasts) is a clear example of complementarity. Hicks (1988) presents ethnographic evidence that such a door symbolically invokes two concepts most closely associated with the domestic domain—(male) protection *and* (female) fertility. What does such a statement mean? Certainly, men can protect the household and women can reproduce (to populate it and to bring forth children who start new households), but each role contains or complements the other. The man's protective role is always phrased in terms of protecting the household, including women; and women require men to reproduce. The unification of male and female components in Indonesian art often carries this joint association of protection and fertility.

As illustrated by the last examples given above, the arts of people throughout the archipelago exhibit a remarkable and simultaneous exploration of presentations that are both abstractivist and naturalistic. Naturalism here does not refer to verisimilitude or the attempt to make an exact, holographic depiction of the ancestor. Indeed, the *tau tau* figures of the Toraja people represent rare examples of the development of versimilitude as an aesthetic standard. But naturalistic depictions of the human form, characterized by the representation of details approximating the physical features or the adornment of particular individuals represented in art, developed from Nias in the far west to the Moluccas in the east. Detailed ornamentation and signs of status (especially jewelry) were sometimes used to make a general form represent an individual. Some examples from Nias (Figs. II.19–20, II.26) come from areas that also produced highly abstract, very reduced and stylized depictions of ancestors (Figs. II.10, II.31). Similarly, the artists of the Southeast Moluccas produced elaborately ornamented figures (Figs. VIII.6, VIII.18), as well as abstract sculptures akin to those of the modern artist Brancusi (Fig. VIII.25), to depict their ancestors.

Many highly abstract or stylized forms can only be interpreted in the light of the more naturalistic depictions of the same kind. Thus the sleek, abstract depictions on the handle of a Batak knife used as a male good in marital exchanges (Fig. III.29) might not even be recognized as male and female human figures. Only by comparison with numerous other examples of such knives (Fig. III.30) can the the similarity of subject matter be discerned.

The juxtaposition of male and female elements in the Tetum door, which indicates both the protection and fertility of the household, recalls an abstract design frequently occurring in Indonesian art, especially along borders of textiles (e.g., Figs. IV.2, IV.21). Known as *tumpal*, the design consists of interlocking wedges, often colored so that wedges pointing in one direction are all one color and those pointing in the other direction are contrasting. The design is most often reported to indicate both fertility *and* protection (e.g., Langewis and Wagner 1964:23). Based on the degree of abstraction found in the representation of other design elements, this *tumpal* form could well represent, in the most abstract way, the interlocking or association of opposites, male and female. The association of these opposites in one design visually portrays Indonesian cultural concepts of complementarity and balance.

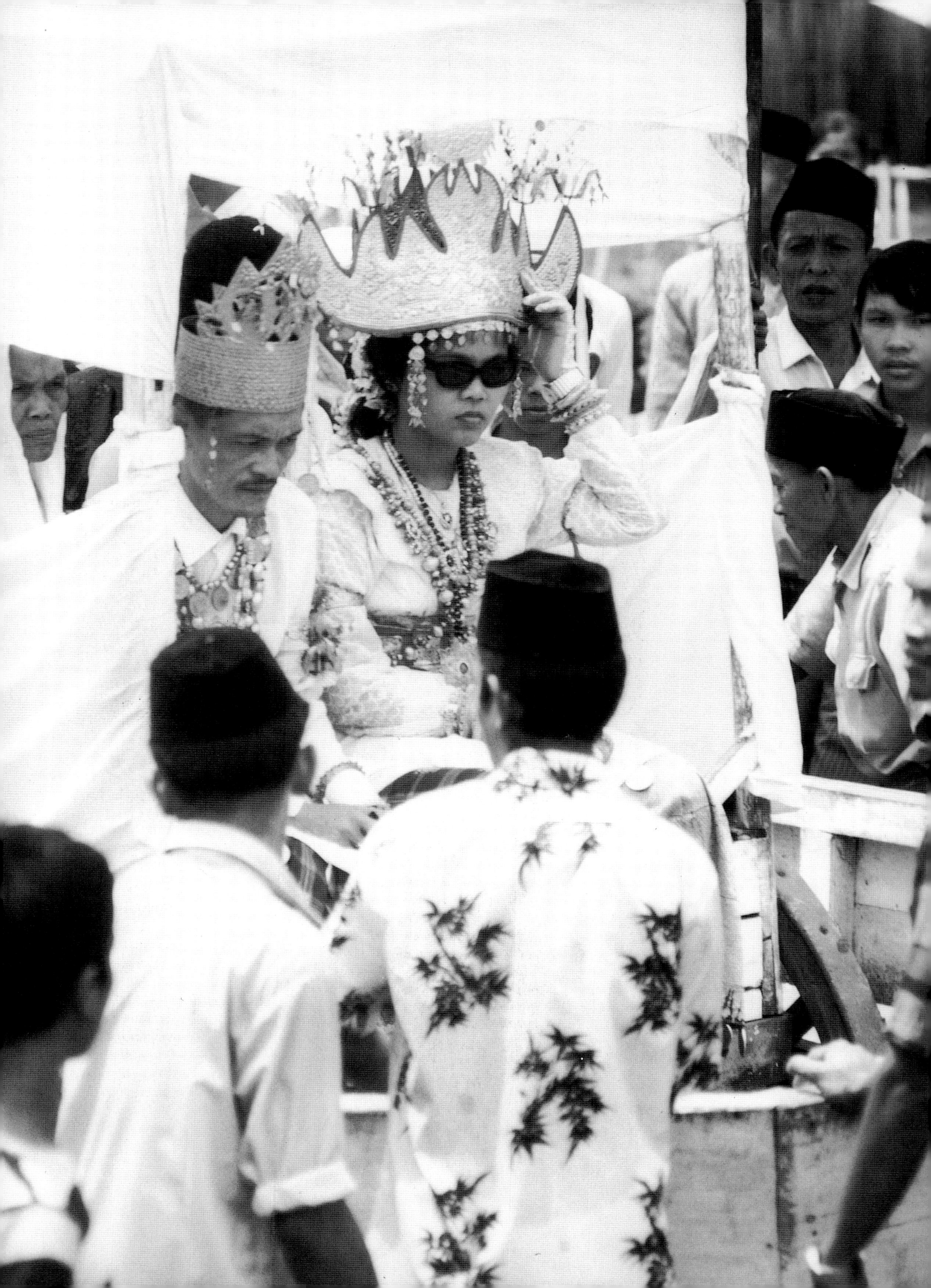

Purposes and Functions of Art in the Outer Islands

In Indonesian aesthetics and design, an artwork is meaningful, partly because the object as a whole and elements of its design or the arrangement of those elements convey meanings. A fine Batak *ulos* cloth given by the bride's family to the groom (Fig. III.21) conveys many things—the affection of the bride's parents for their daughter, the creation or maintenance of an alliance between families and clans (not just individual spouses); the ritual blessing of the "wife-giving" family necessary for prosperity, fertility, and offspring; and the highly public and ceremonial beginning of a series of exchanges reflecting that alliance. In these exchanges female goods (like the *ulos*) are given by the family of the bride to the family of the groom, and male goods are given by the groom's family in return. In the social functions of the art of the outer islands, recurring themes include the role of ancestors in establishing the family or kin group and providing its members with a special identity, the importance of marital alliances, which unite those families or kin groups in addition to uniting the bride and groom, and the relationship of humans to the spirit world through ritual life.

In all these areas of life, Indonesians emphasize the importance of reciprocity and exchange in maintaining harmony in relationships as well as in the cosmos. Relations with long-deceased ancestors or with spirits, between nobles and commoners, between spouses, or between in-laws—all are based on concepts of complementarity and reciprocity that are reflected in Indonesian art. Indeed much of the finest art from the outer islands of Indonesia serves as currency in the reciprocal exchange of complementary male and female goods in marriage alliances or as emblems of the relationships of reciprocity that unite the living with their dead ancestors.

People use their art to express visually relations with ancestors, with other persons in families those ancestors founded, with families united by marriage, and with the spirit world. Through these relationships with others, people perceive their identity as individuals, families, and ethnic groups, and they also explore their place in society and in the cosmos. The interpretation of each of these paradigmatic themes is also central to anthropological theory. Theories of Indonesian kinship, descent, and alliance, for example, are the basis for differing schools of thought in anthropology (van Wouden 1968 [1935], Needham 1962, J. Barnes 1971, Scheffler 1973, de Josselin de Jong 1984, Singarimbun 1975, Koentjaraningrat 1975:145–165).

Fig. 13 Bride and groom arrive at marriage ceremony in a modern-style chariot (*rato*), Abung, Gunung Sigill, South Sumatra, 1971. Mattiebelle Gittinger

Role of Ancestors

Departed ancestors are the foci of the family, and ancestors are sometimes founders of entire ethnic groups. They are integrated into everyday life through many magnificent art forms including carved stone ancestral altars, wooden free-standing sculptures, demonic ancestor imagery on carved polychrome shields and incised bamboo utensils, and (especially in Borneo and Irian Jaya) artistic and ritual treatment of the corpses or skulls of the deceased. Ancestors define the clans and other groups descended from them. Ancestors join other spirits and continue to interact with the living. Yet every person's path through life brings him eventually to death, the point at which he joins the ancestors, a passage in which he is aided by those who survive him. The continuous interaction between the living and the dead begins with the funeral ceremonies.

In most outer-island societies, funerary rituals are extensive. Pre-Christian or pre-Islamic Batak funerary ceremonies, for example, served to pacify the deceased and to elevate his or her rank among the ancestors in the upper world. The expected reciprocity in relationships among the living continued in a modified form after death. The funerary ceremonies particularly served to mollify the deceased, to satisfy his or her needs, and therefore to encourage the deceased to aid living relatives.

Literature on Indonesian societies often uses the word "ancestor" to describe the spirits of the deceased, because that English word seems best to translate indigenous words. Yet "ancestor" is misleading because it implies the necessity for procreating descendants. Many Indonesian societies do emphasize the importance of bearing children who will honor a person after his or her death, and some artworks serve to put to rest peacefully the spirits of people who die without offspring. Among the Batak, for example, persons who possessed no descendants to honor them were considered pitiful, and life-sized moveable puppets called *si gale-gale* (Fig. III.33) were used to console the deceased by acting the part of descendants.

All Indonesian kinship systems classify some collateral relatives of a parent's or grandparent's generation as parents or grandparents. Thus a parent's brother or sister is often a classificatory parent (that is, classified and referred to as a parent); and the brother or sister of a person's grandparent is often a classificatory grandparent. Reciprocally, one does not need to have biological children to have classificatory children. Which nieces and nephews are considered "children" and which aunts and uncles are considered "parents" depends upon the ethnic group and can vary by locality and dialect within a single ethnic group. Indonesia's cultural diversity is reflected in a wide array of different kinship terminologies used by its more than three hundred ethnic groups. Yet all of them consider some collateral relatives (a grandparent's brother, for example) to be lineal relatives (that is, a grandparent, in the same example). Such a linkage of kin types often implies expectations about behavior, so that a father's brother who is classified as a father would be treated as a biological father in many contexts.

This association of direct ancestors with collateral kin comes quite naturally to Indonesians and may help explain why many so-called ancestor figures are carved or honored for people without offspring. In fact, infant and child mortality has always been high by modern standards, and many people who survive to adulthood have no children. Yet all who die are treated as ancestors. The small, relatively unformed ancestor figures in groupings of Nias ancestor images, for example (Fig. II.10), were probably placed alongside other ancestor figures to commemorate the deaths of less important individuals, often representing infants or stillborn children (cf. Feldman 1985b:52). Because collateral kin are associated with direct ancestors and direct descendants, the children of a stillborn infant's brothers or sisters are that infant's classificatory children too. Nias villagers of all ages include such infants in their rituals like parents or other ancestors. Nias people honor these childless antecedents as true ancestors. Personality, or individuality, is developed through the lifetime of an individual and celebrated in a series of rites of passage recognized by peoples throughout the archipelago. The rudely carved sticks of wood, or even pieces of root or coral, sometimes tied in with rows of ancestor figures, are therefore appropriate representations of the unformed personhood of deceased children.

Distant ancestors are honored as the founders of families or ethnic groups. In the Lesser Sunda Islands and in the Moluccas, such first ancestors function as culture heroes—mythical personages who established an ethnic group and taught it the practical and ritual knowledge it needs to survive. They define the descent group, such as a clan or lineage, and often give that group a mythical charter, or justification and explanation for the status quo. Throughout the outer islands, those who have authority claim that their ancestors provided it and set up the rules for its transmission. One of the most important links to that authority is through the transmission of heirlooms, often artworks that recall a founding ancestor in imagery or in stories. The Batak sword (Fig. III.5), for example, was a chief's prestigious heirloom passed from father to son among the Toba Batak, a patrilineally organized society. The human figure on the hilt probably represents a clan ancestor to the man who first made or commissioned the sword. Its status as an heirloom, enhanced by the figure depicted on it, makes this artwork a visible symbol of the transmission of traditions.

The possession of heirloom objects may be strictly prescribed. The long *palepai* textiles owned by Lampung aristocrats, for example (Figs. IV.2, IV.6, IV.7) were hung on a wall behind participants in life-cycle ceremonies (such as circumcision and marriage) for aristocrats (Gittinger 1972:45). They were inherited by the eldest males descended from the community's founder in the male line (Gittinger 1972, 1976), and were said to have been inherited from a community's founder, usually from father to eldest son in noble families. Younger brothers expressed their slightly more distant links to ancestors by borrowing the pieces for their own rites of passage. Other *palepai* were arranged in sequences to represent the relationships of other kin groups to the key participant of the life-cycle ceremony. In short, artworks are called upon to summarize the relationships among the individuals attending the ceremony, by reference to relationships among their ancestors.

Indonesian court traditions from throughout the archipelago emphasized the importance of true regalia. That term may be applied to a special heirloom that is a symbol of office and that is perceived as establishing authority within a court or kingdom. Possession of the object itself—a crown, staff of office, or other official heirloom, provides the authority for that office (Jessup 1990; catalog chapter X).

Not only the line of inheritance of heirloom artworks but also the strictly regulated procedures for producing some artworks are means by which social inequality is maintained by reference to the ancestors, who are believed to have laid out the proper procedures. Niassans, for example, had clear rules about types of artistic production to which only the nobility had access. Those rules emphasized not only that the nobles had ancestral authority for their distinctiveness but also that the distinction between nobles and commoners was a complementary one, that the two classes were mutually dependent, and that this system of fixed social inequality was based on reciprocal obligations. For example, only Nias nobles could commission, own, or inherit particular items of gold jewelry, headdresses, weapons, and other regalia (see Figs. II.33, II.36, II.40, II.44). The Nias aristocracy proclaimed their authority by the manufacture and use of these gold items, which established links to prosperous ancestors and community founders. In conjunction with the manufacture of valuables, aristocrats were required to host a series of feasts displaying the gift-giving and generosity required for them to accede to the high status to which they were qualified by birth.

People of all social strata throughout the outer islands traditionally turned to ancestors as protectors, but often the most lavish monuments to ancestors were erected by aristocracy, partly because of their greater control of wealth and partly because the founding ancestors gave them the charter for their superiority. People of all classes still stress the importance of the interaction between the living and the ancestors by displaying and invoking ancestor images. The Nias wooden ancestor sculptures (*adu*), which are attached to posts or wall altars inside the houses of commoners as well as chiefs, function as intermediaries for contact with spirits. Through the medium of these figures, new births and marriages are reported to the ancestors. Offerings of food on the altars serve to request the ancestors' help in times of illness or misfortune. From Nias in the west to Sumba and the Moluccas in the east, large megalithic stones serve as altars or monuments to the ancestors. Their central position in the villages' public spaces reflects the centrality of ancestors in everyday life.

A distant ancestor becomes a symbol of the group of people who share that line of descent; more closely related ancestors define smaller groups. In their art, Indonesians depicted lineages or chains of ancestors, or the groups defined by ancestors, in several ways. The Nias ancestor statue (Fig. II.13), for example, has other small ancestor images tied in his headdress, possibly symbolizing the parents or other ancestors of the main figure depicted. Inside their houses, Niassans display long rows of ancestor figures tied together (Fig. II.11), in which each figure depicts a different deceased member of the house. A child growing up sees those images in his house not only as artworks but also as embodiments of the descent group to which he belongs and as symbols of the trajectory of his own life.

Ancestor images evoke ancestors, but images also often act as intermediaries or altars—the ancestor figures of the virtually extinct Southeast Moluccan traditional religions (Figs. VIII.12, VIII.13, VIII.18–20) were foci of a continuing interaction of dead ancestors (through their images) with the living. Actions performed by the living on images of the deceased are often considered to be performed on the deceased's spirit. Thus offerings made to the image of an ancestor are offerings made to the ancestor. Sir James Frazer gave examples from Indonesia's outer islands in *The Golden Bough* to establish that such magical or spiritual effects of human acts imply a theory of causality, which he termed "sympathetic magic": "One of the principles of sympathetic magic is that any effect may be produced by imitating it" (Frazer 1890, vol. 1:9). The object so treated (for example, the ancestor figure) must in some way be like the object being imitated (the ancestor). Throughout the outer islands, ancestor figures display some individuality, sometimes distinctive ornaments or positions, and sometimes even verisimilitude—as in the Toraja *tau tau* carved to resemble the deceased or the Dayak *temadu* ancestor figures described by Bertling (1927).

Wherever descent from an ancestor determines the right to inhabit a clan or descent-group house, the houses themselves become symbols of the family and also of the ancestor who founded it (Waterson 1990:138–166). Feldman (1985b:64) has described the South Nias chief's house as "symbolically represent[ing] a clan ancestor dressed in full regalia. The house pillars are said to be the legs, the façade is the face, and the tall roof represents the chief's crown." Descent groups among the Batak and Nias are patrilineal; that is, membership is determined by descent in the male line. The nearby Minangkabau people of Sumatra, by contrast, have matrilineal descent groups and inheritance patterns. Membership in a "house" passes from a man to his sister's son, rather than his own son, as does the inheritance of his land or possessions. Such societies have unilineal descent groups, in which any person knows that membership in a descent group is clearly derived from either the father (as among the Batak or Nias) or the mother (Minangkabau).

In cognatic descent groups, the criterion for membership is descent from a common ancestor through either the male *or* the female line. Often people have rights to join any group founded by one of their ancestors but must fulfill additional requirements to become members of a descent group, such as residence in the descent group's house or participation in its ceremonies. For example, if each of an individual's paternal grandparents and each of his or her maternal grandparents belonged to different cognatic descent groups (each founded by a different ancestor), that individual could join any of these four groups. In order to activate an affiliation with one group or another, the person might have to take up residence near the clan house and will always have to participate in ceremonies associated with that house. For cognatic descent groups also, special houses are associated with founding ancestors. The Toraja, for example, center their ritual life on the kindred house (*tongkonan*; Fig. VI.4), whose elaborate decoration provides an image of the descent group's status. The building itself becomes a symbol of family identity and tradition, precisely because it is perceived as a link to a founding ancestor (Kis-Jovak et al. 1988; Crystal 1989). Toraja individuals make claims of affiliation through either male or female genealogical lines to particular *tongkonan* houses and validate those claims through contributions to ceremonial feasts sponsored by the household. The *tongkonan* members collectively own such ancient sacred treasures as the textiles (Figs. VI.15, VI.27) that are displayed at major rituals. The origin of those sacred cloths is also associated with sacred powers of ancient ancestors (see catalog chapter VI).

Not only do the living create images of ancestors and monuments to their ancestors but they also intend to become ancestors. Aristocratic rulers in outer-island Indonesia always honor their own ancestors and refer to their ancestral charters to rule their people. Yet many of those rulers also created artworks with some foresight, preparing themselves to become mythical ancestors of the future. So life imitates art. Nias aristocrats, for example, took up the pose of the ancestor figures that decorated their walls in order to assert their authority during ceremonies, announcements of decisions or verdicts, and the formal receipt of gifts. A photograph of a South Nias ruler named Ndöuzatarö, obtained on Nias by Jerome Feldman in 1988, depicts the nobleman in this position (Fig. 15). The black-and-white photograph had been retouched with gold paint over the Ndöuzatarö's gold headdress, metal moustache, necklaces, bracelet and sword, to emphasize his noble status. On Sumba, in the Lesser Sundas, aristocrats build their own megalithic monuments like the *penji* (Fig. VII.20), in preparation for becoming ancestors. Such monuments are important visual symbols of the families they founded; erecting them is an important duty of an aristocrat's family life.

In addition to providing protection, the deceased ancestors can serve as sources of advice, inspiration, and information about magical or other esoteric knowledge. Images and motifs used in art can either be passed down from ancestors to an individual through the line of descendants or communicated directly by ancestor spirits—for example, in dreams. Among the Iban of Borneo, dreams are the vehicle by which spirits, including ancestral spirits, communicate with the living. Iban weavers who are old enough and strong enough to weave the most sacred Iban textile, known as the *pua'* (Fig. V.26), have a dream in which Kumang, a deity who taught the Iban how to weave and dye, teaches them a new design and even an individual honorific or "praise name" uniquely given to that design. One of the functions of the *pua'* cloth is to induce communication with ancestors—through dreams—in those who sleep wrapped in it (Heppel 1989).

Though it is possible to explore the traditional religious meanings of ancestor images and other artworks, a visitor to the outer islands of Indonesia in the 1990s will quickly observe, near places where ancestral religions are strong, ancestral images produced by people converted to Christianity or Islam who maintain the images without their original religious or ritual uses. The social function of those images has been transformed. In the past, they were key components of traditional religions; now, they are symbols of ethnic or family identity, artworks of traditional style for sale to outsiders, or as some Christian Toraja describe the *tau tau* sculptures of their ancestors "three-dimensional photographs" to remember their deceased family. Though rituals honoring ancestors may have been more dramatic and elaborate in the past, in many areas they are now subdued as a result of conversion to world religions. With their relatively simple funerals and their emphasis on beseeching God rather than pre-Christian or pre-Islamic antecedents, such religions do not easily assimilate the traditional roles for ancestors. Yet they do encourage and sanctify another custom that traditional outer-island societies have always taken seriously: marriage.

Fig. 14

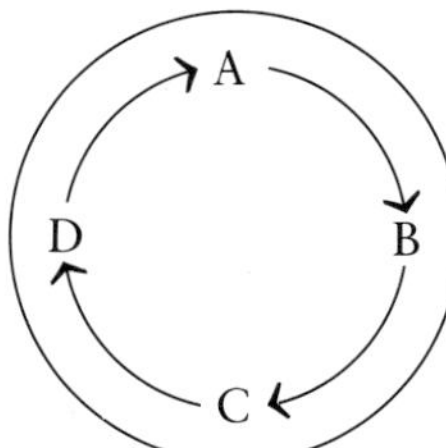

The Arts of Marriage

Indonesia is a heartland of structuralism in anthropology, a metatheory about societies that attempts to analyze social relations, or symbols, or other components of a society and its culture into structural elements and to predict how the diversity of social customs could be derived from underlying structures. Since the time of the early Dutch structuralist tradition of F.A.E. van Wouden, marital alliances have been considered the key to understanding the underlying structures of Indonesian social organization. In *Types of Social Structure in Eastern Indonesia*, van Wouden (1968 [1935]) posited an original eastern Indonesian social organization based upon descent groups whose member intermarried in prescribed ways. In a society consisting of patrilineal clans A, B, C, and D, for example, the women of clan A would be expected to marry the men of clan B; the women of B to marry the men of C; the women of C to marry into clan D; and the women of clan D to marry into clan A. This circular pattern of marriage prescriptions can be considered a continuing marital alliance among the clans A through D, each of which was founded by a different ancestor. Just as ancestors define families, marriage unites them (see Fig. 14).

Following van Wouden, Dutch anthropologists of the Leiden school gave this system of expected marriages between clans the delightful name "circulating connubium" and described some of the most striking and pervasive features of asymmetric alliance within Eastern Indonesian society as resulting from it. From the perspective of a man or woman in clan A, for example, one immediately sees from the diagram in Fig. 14 the opposition between a clan from which people in A take their wives (D) and one into which they give their women as wives (B). Throughout Indonesia, the wife-giver family is ritually superior to the wife-taker family, but that kind of ritual superiority in circular connubium is not the basis for social classes or ranks. A is superior to B, B to C, and C to D, but D is also ritually superior to A. Such alliances between families are asymmetric because there must be at least three families exchanging women—the simple (or symmetric) exchange between two families or clans is excluded. Furthermore, the relations between individuals in different clans are unequal, because of the ritual superiority of the wife-givers. As noted in the previous chapter, this has sometimes been invoked as a means of explaining the Indonesian preference for asymmetry in art and architecture. Some Indonesian groups themselves consciously make the association between their marital-alliance pattern and their architecture—for instance, representatives of the wife-giving group may sit on the right (larger) side in the host's traditional house during ceremonies.

The same structural patterns have been invoked to explain the predominance of paired contrasts in speech and activities of people in such places as the Lesser Sundas and the Moluccas. This duality is also observed in Timor, where the Atoni, the Mambai, and other peoples practice so-called diarchic political organization (van Wouden 1962[1935]:25–84, Schulte Nordholt 1971, Traube 1986), in which paired rulers divide power between complementary ritual functions and jural functions, and where the ritual leader is also often considered metaphorically female and older in contrast to the jural leader who is considered male and younger. Van Wouden argued that one can consider dualism a fundamental organizing principle of a society with clans arranged like that in the simple diagram above. Whether or not the people in clans A through D know it, he thought their society was effectively divided into moieties, or halves, of society that cannot intermarry. Members of clans A and C effectively can never intermarry, nor can the members of clans B and D. That complementary dualism is one source that is posited for more pervasive dualisms in society. Furthermore, every individual is faced with the paired contrast between wife-givers and wife-takers, who also have complementary functions. Such simple contrasting pairs function as hooks onto which many other contrasts in society can be hung. Wife-givers may be associated with femaleness, female goods, domesticity and feminine activities, ritual superiority, and related concepts;

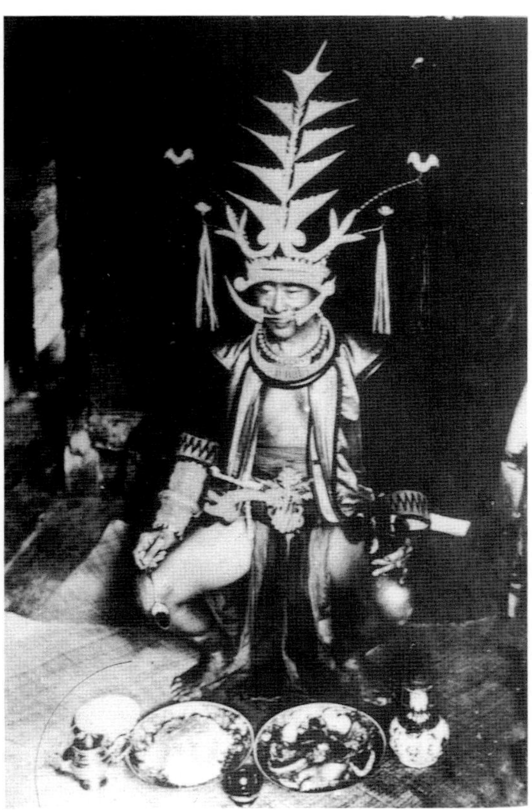

Fig. 15 Ndröuzatarö, a South Nias ruler, posing as an ancestor figure for photograph, Bawömataluo village, 1920s. Black-and-white photograph overpainted with gold paint. Obtained on Nias, 1988. National Anthropological Archives, Smithsonian Institution.

wife-takers with maleness, male goods, hunting, fishing, or other male activities, ritual inferiority, and related concepts.

Such associations are common throughout the areas of Indonesia that have asymmetric marriage systems. Yet the actual situation of kinship and marriage relations is far more complex than any diagram that tries to summarize the idealized structural principles of the clans with a few letters—and is a continuing area of debate within anthropology (see, for example, Bovill 1986, McKinnon in press). Scholars who build models of society from intermarrying clans (or smaller units of alliance like groups of families) also debate how much information those models explain. For van Wouden, his model of eastern Indonesian society (double-unilineal descent and circulating connubium) was presented as a posited original form of society, which has broken down everywhere and is visible only in parts in each location. Patrilineal societies kept part of the original double-unilineal system, and matrilineal societies also kept only part of that system. No society maintained the original social structure intact. Furthermore, van Wouden considered the marriage system to be the primary component of social organization. Others have theorized that no single component of the society is primary or should be called upon to explain all the others. For them, the underlying principles themselves are primary, and marriage patterns are but one way in which those principles are realized in any particular society. Many other scholars deny that the simple explanatory models derived today accurately explain original Indonesian societies that existed in the past. Instead, such models are idealized pictures of how marital alliance works; these ideal models differ from practice to some extent today and probably always have.

For example, every Batak must select a spouse from a patrilineal family unit other than the one into which he or she was born. Ideally, a young man in family B should renew the alliance created by the marriage of his parents by marrying a girl from his mother's family (family A). His sister, also in family B, should do the same by marrying into family into which her father's sister married (family C). Thus ancestral marriage alliances continue through the generations. This is the rule in an asymmetric marriage system. Because a man marries a woman of his mother's patrilineal family unit, this system is sometimes called a "mother's brother's daughter marriage" system. If the exchange were symmetric (between only two families), then a woman in B could also marry her mother's brother's son in A, and her brother in B could freely marry his father's sister's daughter in C. The reason such marriages are strictly forbidden is that they would confuse the fundamental principles of alliance by ignoring the distinction between wife-giving and wife-taking groups.

In theory, these alliances continue through the generations and are cemented through a ritual exchange of gifts, symbolizing the fertility and good fortune that come to the groom's family from his wife-givers and the material well-being from the wife-takers. In practice, however, young Batak men and women frequently marry into families that were not previously allied, thus regularly creating new alliances that also, ideally, should be continued through the generations that follow (Singarimbun 1975).

In asymmetric alliance systems, the universal distinction between male and female goods is sometimes based on which gender manufactures the good, thus women weave and textiles are female, and so on. But the distinction itself, and its association with behavior expected from particular in-laws, can be applied differently to the same object in different places and is related to differences in the gender division of labor. Barnes notes, for example, that basket-weaving is a male activity in Lamalera but a female activity in other Lamaholot regions of the Lesser Sundas (1989b:4). Van Wouden (1968[1935]:25–84) noticed that some male goods such as pigs or certain weapons in some areas of Timor are considered female goods in other areas of the same island, perhaps for similar reasons. Whatever the placement of particular objects in these categories, a man in an asymmetric alliance system who is in need of something frequently goes to his in-laws for help—and the kind of thing he needs determines to whom he directs his request. He obtains male goods from the husbands of his sisters or daughters and female goods from his son's wives or from the brothers or father of his own wife.

Art and the Spirit World

A final pervasive theme of Indonesian art is the relationship of persons to spirits. The contact between persons and ancestral spirits often takes place through the medium of art; similarly, visual and other arts are used to contact deities and to express fundamental beliefs about the cosmos and man's place in it relative to spirits, deities, plants, and animals.

Spirits and deities are not necessarily the same as ancestors (individual humans who have died), though there is overlap because some of the deceased—especially important ancestors—can become deified spirits. Those who die suddenly or violently, those who do not receive proper funeral ceremonies, and women who die in childbirth, can all become harmful spirits. Sometimes an image that looks very much like an ancestor image is used as intermediary to a deity or spirit that was never a living human. For example, the *adu höro* figures of Nias (Fig. II.17) are images of a generalized ancestor, not any particular known individual. Because moral norms were collectively set down by ancestors in the distant past, offerings to atone for violations are made to the *adu höro* image, perhaps as a representation of the collective ancestors whose wrath enforces social norms and whose benevolence protects society.

Toraja funerals help move souls of the recently deceased away from the village to a land of the dead (*puya*) somewhere southwest of Torajaland (see catalog chapter VI). After a series of expensive rituals, high-ranking nobles may actually move on to the upper world and become a kind of deity (*deata*)—located somewhere alongside the major Toraja gods (Nooy-Palm 1986:3)—who can assist their descendants (Coville 1988). The distinction between humans, animals, and spirits is sometimes ambiguous in Dayak representations. The *tenyalang*, or hornbill figure, of Borneo is sometimes considered a founding deity, who was never a human, and sometimes considered the representation of a human ancestor. Despite boundary-crossing examples like these, the distinction between spirits who were ancestors and other spirits is usually clear.

Spirits of the deceased were appropriated as the symbolic justification and the cause of headhunting, which took place in the past in many of Indonesia's outer islands. Loeb (1972[1935]) records that Niassans presented enemy heads to deities in order to sanctify important events; they were taken as part of rituals required for blood revenge, major building construction, the death of a chief, the ceremonial production of gold jewelry, to strengthen an oath, as part of bridewealth payments, or to cure particularly serious illnesses. The Nias ancestor image (Fig. II.18) was used to request success in the hunt for heads. The thick legs of the figure represent strength required in the hunt, while the enlarged breast may represent the fertility that would result from a successful hunt. Similarly, among the Dayak of Borneo, headhunting was a highly ritualized activity deemed an essential male activity to ensure fertility and prosperity—a counterpart to the female activities of rice growing (Sutlive 1990) or weaving (Vogelsanger 1980).

Performance art, as well as just visual art, functions to contact ancestral spirits or deities. The anthropomorphic figures on the *hasapi*, or lute (Figs. III.39, III.39a), probably depict the beneficial spirits invoked with the instrument's music. Such instruments formerly accompanied dancing at religious rituals during which shamans would become possessed by the spirits of ancestors and speak for them (Loeb 1972[1935]:27). Similarly, the Batak waist ornament (Fig. III.4) has a fringe of tiny pellet bells, providing the ringing sound often used for the same purpose in religious ceremonies throughout the outer islands. Today, however, *hasapi* are more likely to be played for the leisure entertainment of courting teenagers.

Indonesians call on the power of art at transitional times in the human

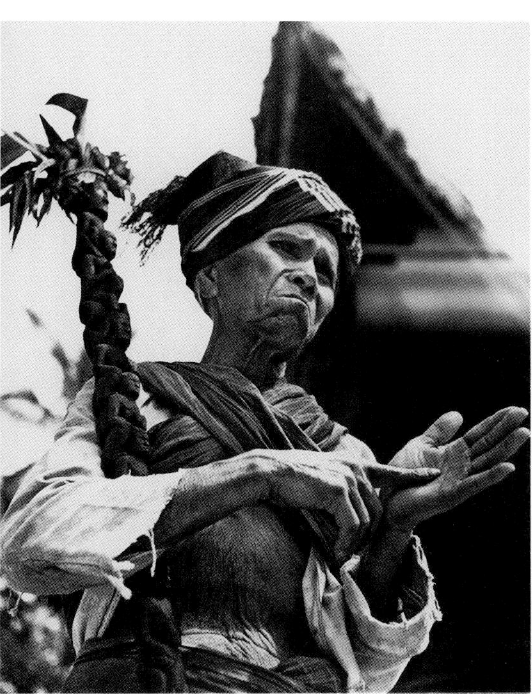

Fig. 16 Traditional Toba Batak priest with magical staff, North Sumatra, circa 1938. Schuh 1943, Royal Tropical Institute, Tropenmuseum, The Netherlands

life-cycle such as birth, circumcision, marriage, various stages of adulthood, accession to offices, and death. The power of objects ritually given during these critical transitions can be called upon and even increased later. For example, the power of a Batak *ulos* cloth (Figs. III.23, III.24) was increased on each occasion that it was used in a blessing ceremony. The special cloth given to bless and protect a Toba Batak woman pregnant with her first child can be used later to cure herself or her children with the power of the original blessing (Vergouwen 1964:59).

Many artworks were presented as gifts at times of transition. For example, the ceremonial *tampan* and *palepai* textiles (Figs. IV.2, IV.6, IV.7, IV.11–13) were displayed by noble familes of Lampung (southern Sumatra) as banners at ceremonies or used as wrappers for gifts exchanged. Such cloths were used for births, tooth-filing ceremonies, engagements, marriages, house-building feasts, and funerals (Gittinger 1972; van Dijk and de Jonge 1980; Holmgren and Spertus 1989). Ritual advice is also important for selecting auspicious times for life-cycle events. Such artworks as the Batak priest's "calendar" and bark books (Figs. III.43, III.44, III.25) served this important function, providing auspicious dates. Artworks were also commissioned to commemorate the feasts (opportunities for the display of generosity) that accompanied the celebration of life transitions, such as the simple commoner's ancestor figure from the Maenamölö region of South Nias (Fig. II.30), built to commemorate a community feast given by the sponsor whose ancestor is depicted, in order to fulfill the sponsor's status as an adult citizen. In short, life's transitions were met with ritual or celebration, in which visual art objects and performance art have always played a role.

Finally, shamans or spirit-mediums—humans who have contact with individual helper-spirits—required tools, amulets, and magically powerful paraphernalia. Batak ritual leaders, for example, made a number of painstakingly carved divining tools and amulets. These objects helped the priest or shaman to contact spirits of the deceased, call back wandering souls of the sick, repel evil forces from the village, or divine promising days for travel, warfare, or ceremonies. The powerful Batak staffs (see Fig. 16) were carved by priests following a careful series of sacrifices and procedures then activated with *pupuk*, or magical substances made of parts of plants or animals and often placed in hollow areas within the staff itself (Loeb 1972[1935]:86).

Throughout the outer islands, the preparation of magical and medicinal substances, and the knowledge of magical formulae (Taylor 1988), were and still are strictly esoteric knowledge. Without detailed information from the individuals who created them, it is impossible to interpret completely the ritual objects such as the Dayak view of the *tiwah* ceremony shown on the etched bamboo (Fig. V.7) or to understand the use of Dayak magical paraphernalia (Fig. V.23). The so-called calendars of the Batak (Figs. III.43, III.44) are actually oracles, which only the *datu* or priest who use them can fully interpret. Ritual knowledge, magical or medicinal knowledge, and aesthetic knowledge were closely linked in traditional Indonesian societies.

The guardians of esoteric knowledge are the leaders of traditional communities, and the upholders of *adat*, or custom. The deep respect for traditional ideas about reciprocal relations with ancestors, about marriage and the reciprocities it entails, and about relationships with the spirit world, are at the heart of the respect for custom that members of every outer-island society proclaim. Even more than the English word "custom," *adat* (and its translations in other Indonesian languages) has an ethical and normative connotation. Traditional respect for ancestors and ancestral ways is therefore closely linked to a thoroughgoing respect for reciprocity and mutual support in an individual's relationships with other people and with other inhabitants of the the natural and supernatural worlds.

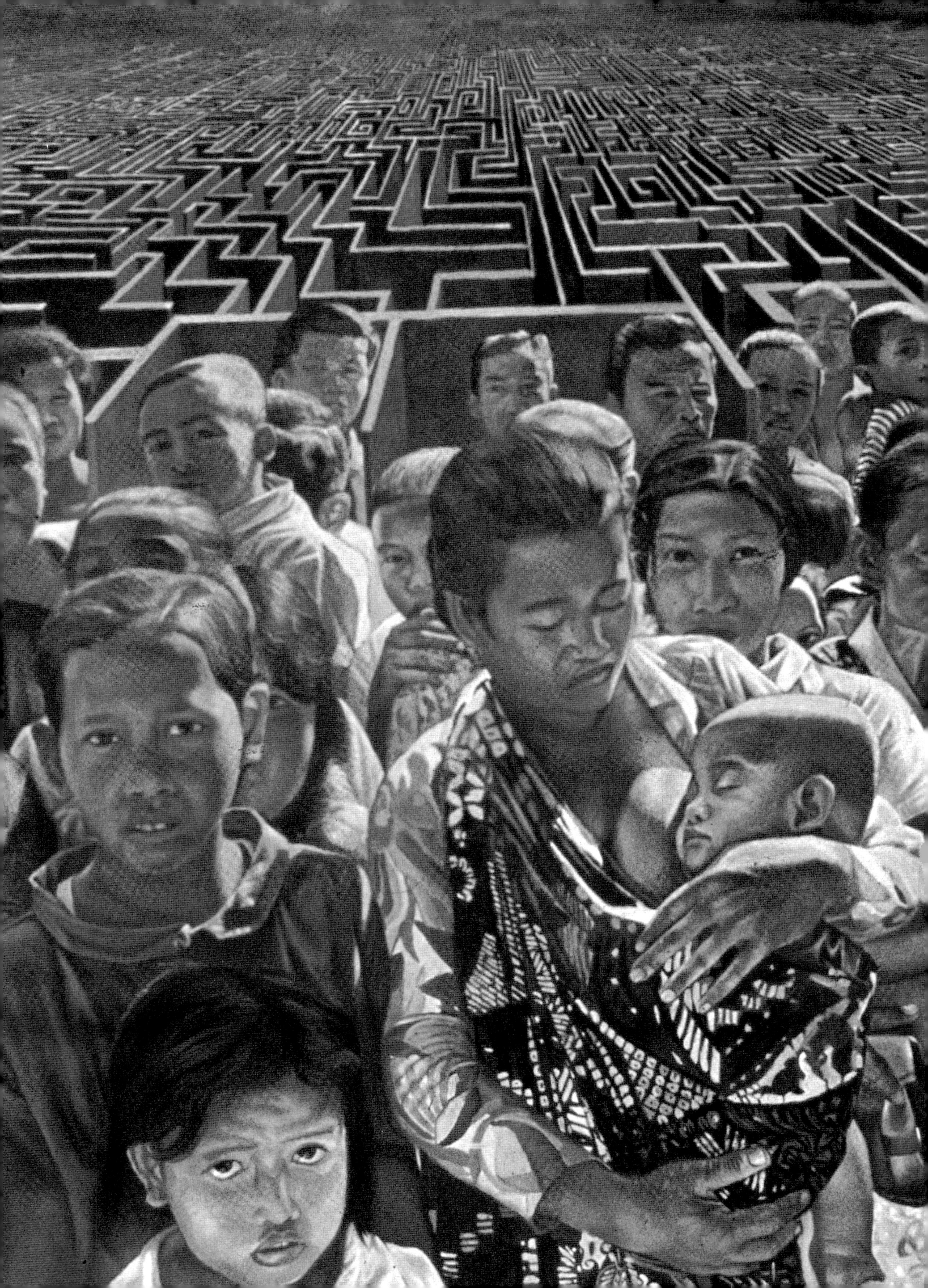

Outer-island Art and Artists Today

Because art in Indonesia's outer islands is closely linked to traditional social customs and to religions or concepts of the spirit world and ritual life, the traditional arts have to some extent only fared as well as the traditions themselves. Widespread conversion of tribal peoples to Christianity or Islam has led to the extinction of some major art forms, such as ancestor figure sculpture in the Southeast Moluccas (Figs. VIII.6–8, VIII.12–21, VIII.25–26). The production of *palepai* and related ship cloths in the Lampung region of South Sumatra has virtually ceased because of the decline of the *pepadon* system of aristocratic ranks that used those textiles in accession ceremonies.

Some art forms and the traditional religions that inspired them have continued to flourish, recognized by the Indonesian government in a climate of freedom of belief. For example, most Toraja people of Sulawesi practice Christianity, but many others continue to follow their ancestral beliefs, which have now been formally organized into a government-recognized religion called *aluk to dolo* ("way of the ancestors"). In areas where conversion to Christianity or Islam has been thorough, art forms that were consistent with the new religions (such as the arts associated with marital exchanges in the Southeast Moluccas) have continued. Other art traditions (particularly those tied to ancestor worship) have disappeared or been converted to new forms suitable for a national craft industry and an international tourist market.

Handicraft industries now produce for sale to tourists forms of traditional arts that had previously been made only for local use. In Lembata, for example, weavers produce a minimalist bridewealth cloth for use in marriage exchanges to substitute for the more elaborate traditional cloths purchased by outsiders for sums too great to refuse (Barnes in press). Recent changes in Indonesia's traditional arts are not purely reactive, the result of traditional systems of artistic expression inexorably breaking down, buffeted by modernism into being either abandoned or transformed into marketable tourist art. The transformation of art forms is also an accommodation by Indonesian peoples to their changing culture.

As Errington (in press) notes, the availability of traditional artworks attracts tourists, as seen in the advertisement from Indonesia's national carrier Garuda Indonesia Airways (Fig. 17), despite concerns about the removal of antiquities from the country. Because collectors value more highly objects that are old and that are made for indigenous use, not sale, outer-island communities have, as a result, lost, and continue to lose, clan heirlooms, antiquities, and funerary objects. Until the early 1980s, for instance, it was possible to see

Detail of *Kaum Urban*, Fig. 24

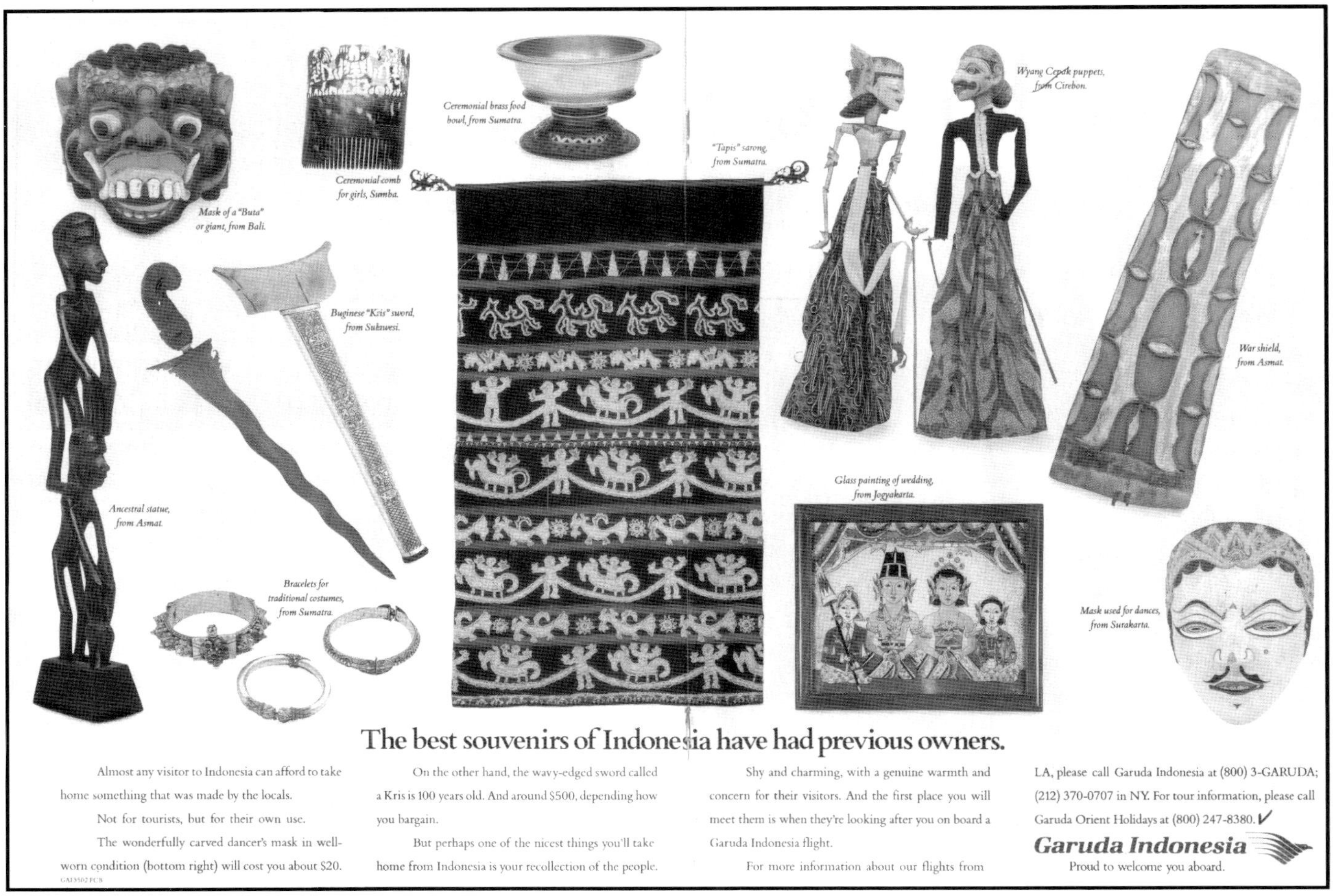

The best souvenirs of Indonesia have had previous owners.

Almost any visitor to Indonesia can afford to take home something that was made by the locals.

Not for tourists, but for their own use.

The wonderfully carved dancer's mask in well-worn condition (bottom right) will cost you about $20.

On the other hand, the wavy-edged sword called a Kris is 100 years old. And around $500, depending how you bargain.

But perhaps one of the nicest things you'll take home from Indonesia is your recollection of the people.

Shy and charming, with a genuine warmth and concern for their visitors. And the first place you will meet them is when they're looking after you on board a Garuda Indonesia flight.

For more information about our flights from LA, please call Garuda Indonesia at (800) 3-GARUDA; (212) 370-0707 in NY. For tour information, please call Garuda Orient Holidays at (800) 247-8380.

Garuda Indonesia
Proud to welcome you aboard.

Fig. 17 Advertisement for Garuda Indonesia Airways.

To make sure their ancestors get to heaven, the people of Torajaland carry them halfway there.

On the Indonesian island of Sulawesi there lies a mysterious mountain plateau, Torajaland.

Isolated from the outside world, the customs and rituals of the Torajan people have changed little for hundreds of years.

According to legend, the first Torajans descended from heaven, on a great ladder which reached down to earth.

So now, when someone passes on, their relatives help them make it back to heaven again.

After an elaborate funeral ceremony, they climb swaying bamboo ladders, and place the coffins in caves, high up on the limestone cliff faces.

Halfway to heaven.

Then a carved wooden effigy (or *tau tau*) of the deceased is placed in a balcony, so the spirit can forever watch over the village.

Today, it is possible to visit the lost world of the Toraja.

A journey through time itself.

For information about our flights, call (800) 3-GARUDA. For tour information, call Caruda Orient Holidays (800) 247-8380.

Garuda Indonesia
Proud to welcome you aboard.

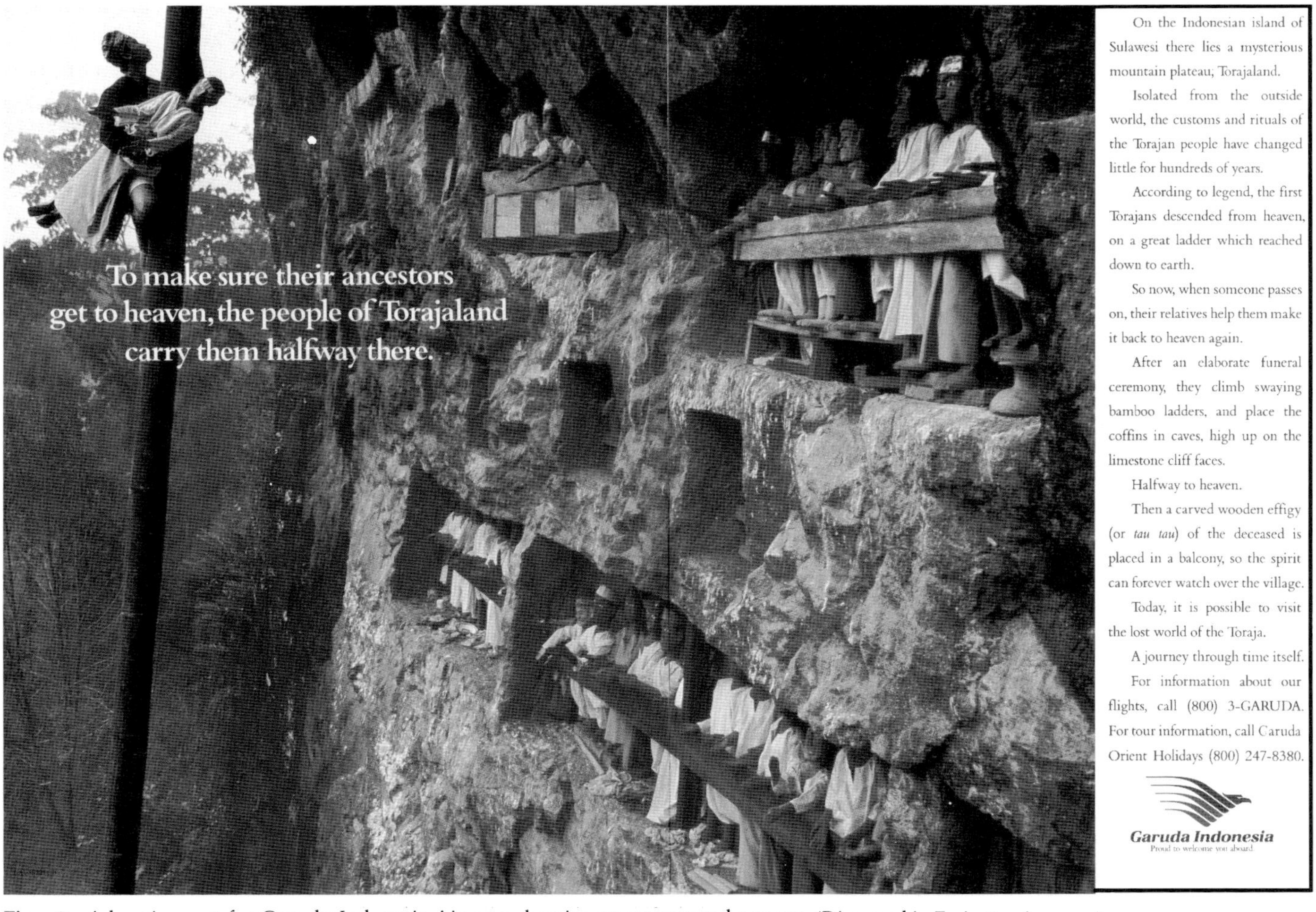

Fig. 18 Advertisement for Garuda Indonesia Airways showing unconsecrated *tau tau*. (Discussed in Errington in press.)

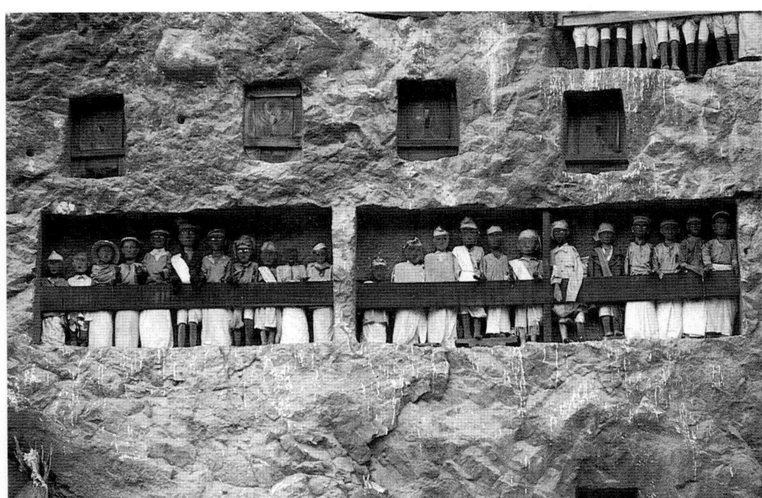

Fig. 19 Toraja *tau tau* balconies, before theft of *tau tau*, Lemo village, 1977. Michael Zerner

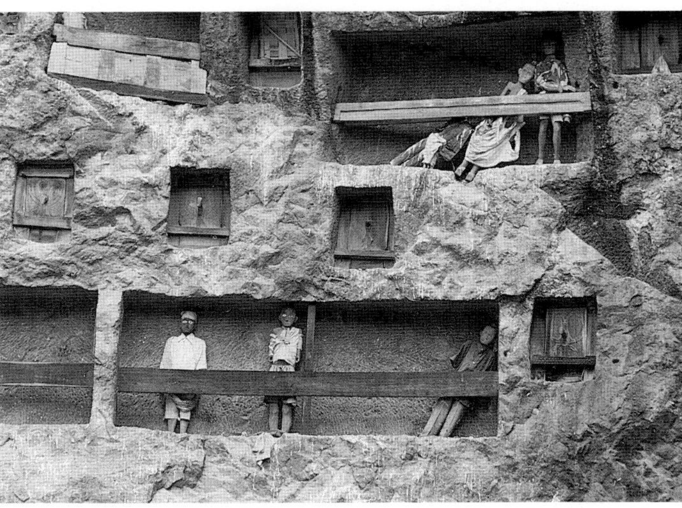

Fig. 20 Toraja *tau tau* balconies, after theft of *tau tau*, Lemo village, 1988. Danielle Hayes

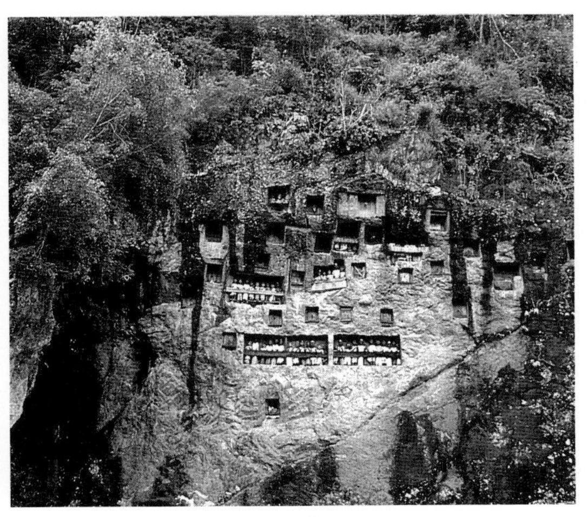

Fig. 21 Toraja *tau tau* balconies, after replacement *tau tau* statues were added, Lemo village, 1989. Toby Volkman

consecrated portrait statues of the deceased called *tau tau* in specially prepared balcony-like vaults in the limestone cliffs high above Toraja villages in Sulawesi. The sculptures became popular in the international primitive art market, however, and many were stolen and sold to art dealers (Figs. 19–21). Toraja were forced to remove the consecrated images that remained to protect them from thieves. Many funerary sculptures are now hoarded in secret, difficult-to-reach caves, huddled together, as Crystal (in press) has noted, like people in a bomb shelter. Today's tourists will see picturesque *tau tau*, like those shown in another Garuda advertisement (Fig. 18), but these *tau tau* are modern reproductions. Such figures are made by the Toraja (often with help from their local government) for the sake of encouraging tourism. The figures shown in the advertisement have not been consecrated nor have they been used in funeral ceremonies. Ironically, the custom of placing *tau tau* high in limestone cliff faces was itself a reaction to grave plundering by Bugis warriors from southern Sulawesi in the seventeenth century, when the Toraja dead were placed with valuable goods in coffins at the bases of cliffs.

This booming market in Indonesian artworks has also resulted in the increased production of replicas that can be sold by middlemen as authentic old pieces. Although exasperating to the curator and collector, the production of forgeries for the primitive art market is a growing industry (see Vion 1987). These forgeries usually imitate artworks from the late nineteenth and twentieth century, often being copied from illustrated books about Indonesian art. Such forgeries do reduce some of the pressure on the people to sell their clan and heirloom treasures, which are Indonesia's artistic patrimony, given that the buying power of villagers in Indonesia's outer islands is minuscule compared to that of collectors. The continued presence of heirloom valuables throughout the region is testimony to those people unwilling to part with them, even at prices far beyond their ability to earn, whereas their increased presence in the marketplace shows that many villagers understandably have other priorities in a changing society (see Barbier in press).

To attract buyers while preserving their heirlooms and discouraging the production of fakes, Indonesian local and private museums, craft retailers, tourism promoters, and the craftspeople themselves throughout the archipelago have sought to garner greater recognition and acceptance for the modern artworks that have descended from traditional arts, particularly in areas where new art forms are emerging from the reinterpretation of tradition.

The traditional artistic productions for the tourist art market neverthe-

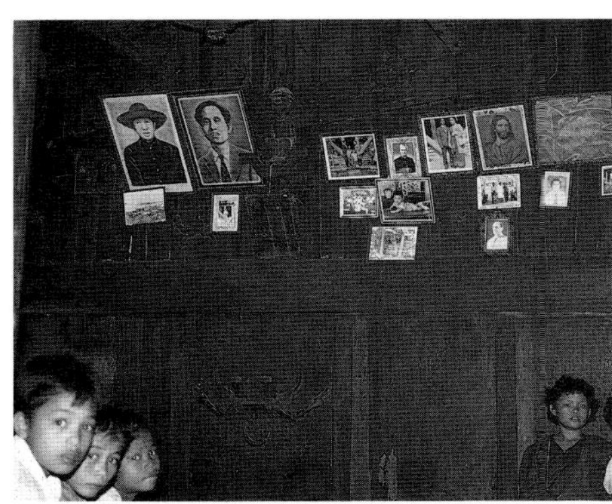

Fig. 22 Recently carved ancestor figures made for sale, alongside photographs of ancestors, missionaries, and Jesus Christ, on the wall of the chief's house at Bawömataluo village, South Nias, 1988. The chief and his wife, like most Nias nobles, are Roman Catholic. Most commoners are Protestant. Paul M. Taylor

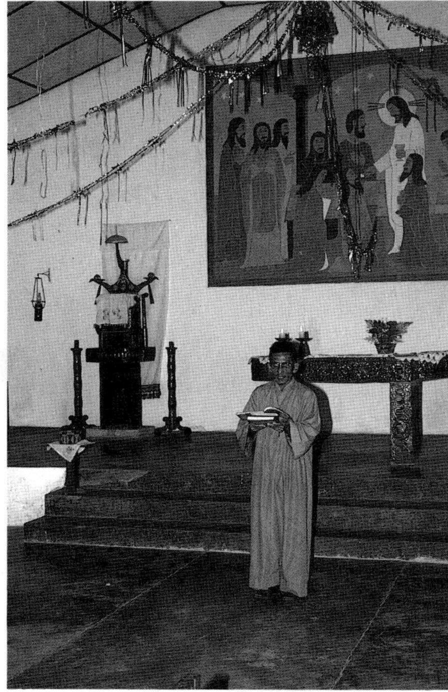

Fig. 23 Roman Catholic layman leading Sunday prayer service in the absence of a priest, Bawömataluo village, South Nias, 1988 Paul M. Taylor

less take on new local functions. Nias warrior's costumes (Figs. II.35, II.37), for example, are often worn by male dancers at major rituals in times of peace. Holt (1971:8) records that southern Nias islanders perform warrior's dances at weddings, funerals, and harvest rites, presumably with the intention of driving harmful spirits away from such major life-cycle events or rites of passage. The performances are still spectacular, as tens of thousands of those who disembark from tour boats in southern Nias to view them can attest.

Many have argued that since Indonesia's independence in 1945, government-promoted nationalism and centralized development are wiping out local artistic and cultural traditions and creating a homogenous culture. Yet in some areas, such as the West Sumba region of the Lesser Sundas studied by Geirnaert, the homogenization of Indonesian life has forced people to create new textile designs to express village as well as ethnic group identification more strongly:

> [D]ress plays a prominent part in expressing identity, both ethnically and in the social hierarchy. In a region that used to be intensely divided into small rival kingdoms, textile production may be a mild reaction to the necessity of complying with the norms of modern Indonesia whose goal is unification. Cultural identity is maintained in dress behavior. (Geinaert 1989a:77)

Conversion to world religions requires abandoning ancestor worship and the ancestral religion, but the exact terms of this social transformation are negotiated differently in each region. The respect for ancestors and ancestral ways that are represented by care of ancestral images is usually retained. The Batak populations have undergone a virtually complete religious conversion to Protestantism or Islam, and so one might expect that the production of stone ancestor figures (Fig. III.18) would become much less important. Yet Barbier (1983) points out that the new, more easily worked medium of concrete has given new life to the production of megalithic ancestor figures. Bruner (1972) also notes that many Toba Batak who have migrated to cities sponsor the construction in their homelands of concrete monuments to clan founders, along with the appropriate feasting and rituals. Such sponsorship helps both the city dweller and his rural kindred.

Christian Toraja on Sulawesi also use *tau tau* funerary statues in their funeral ceremonies, as do those who follow *aluk to dolo*. Toraja Christians do not consider these *tau tau* sculptures to be receptacles for souls of the deceased but consider them portraits, like the photographs that are also displayed on funeral biers.

On Nias, the walls of the chief's house at Bawömataluo village display recently carved Nias ancestor figures made purely for sale (see Feldman in press), with photographs of the chief's own ancestors and family alongside images of their new religious fathers, that is, Roman Catholic missionaries and Jesus Christ (Fig. 22). In the Roman Catholic church at Bawömataluo, South Nias (Fig. 23), the altar resembles an ancestral stone monument and bears a conglomeration of motifs found on several of the ancestor stones around the village, as well as displaying Catholic iconography. (Virtually all South Nias's noble class converted to Catholicism while commoners became Protestant, reflecting even in their choice of Christian sects the continuing division between the classes.)

Another approach to reproducing traditional art is exemplified by the efforts of Sumarah Adhyatman, a founder of the Ceramic Society of Indonesia, who has organized exhibitions and catalogs of recent ceramics (frankly presented as such) carefully done in unmodified antique style (Adhyatman 1983). Hers is an attempt to encourage Western and other collectors to abandon their criterion of age in judging a piece's authenticity and value.

Finally, many artists actively participate in the production of cosmopolitan modern art forms, including oil-on-canvas paintings marketed internationally as modern art. A few examples will only begin to illustrate the range of

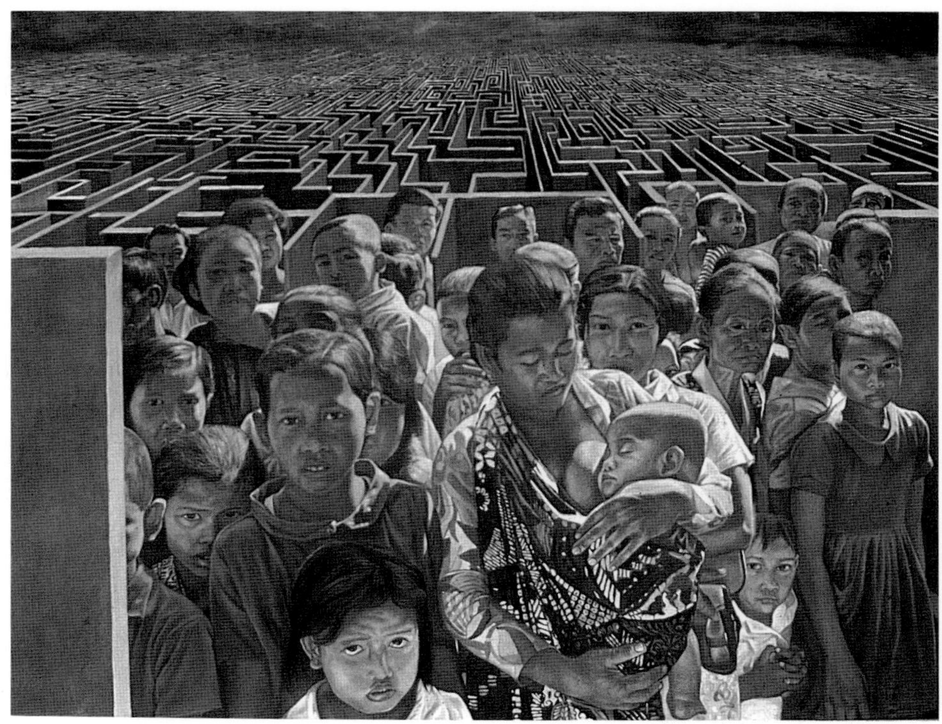

Fig. 24 *Kaum Urban* ("Urban Crowd"), painting, oil on canvas, circa 1980, by Dede Eri Supria (Acehnese, b. 1956 in Jakarta). Joseph Fischer

participation by these artists from the outer islands in modern art forms (see also Moerdowo 1958; Fischer 1990). Most Indonesian modern artists work in cities on Java and Bali. Sumatran painters dominate contemporary painting by artists of the outer islands, because Sumatra is geographically close to such international emporia as Singapore and to Indonesia's national emporia of "new art" (*seni rupa baru*) on Java. The internationally acclaimed Acehnese painter Dede Eri Supria, for example, presents a Norman Rockwell-like version of contemporary Indonesian life—often about city life in the capital city of Jakarta (in western Java) where he works. Some of his paintings depict everyday scenes of Jakarta's urban poor or its young middle class. Other paintings—like *Kaum Urban* ("Urban Crowd")—depict confusion, sometimes near-hopelessness, but always a dignified striving on the part of Indonesia's desperate so-called little people (Fig. 24).

Though he is of Acehnese descent, Jakarta-born Dede Eri Supria seems never to use traditional Acehnese motifs or even refer to Acehnese-inspired ceremonies or traditions. Supria is a leader in a field of contemporary Indonesian art whose symbols, metaphors, and audience all come from a modern urban Indonesian setting. Nevertheless, several of his paintings express a critique and skepticism of the anonymity and displacement caused by that urban setting. Yet amid the images of pervasive modern malaise are references to fundamental human values, which the artist seems to associate with Indonesia's villages. For example, the nursing mother in *Kaum Urban* ("Urban Crowd") wears garments that suggest a Javanese village setting in contrast to clothes of the city dwellers that surround her.

Still, simplicity rather than traditionalism—especially simplicity amid urban confusion—is a key element of Supria's more endearing subjects, and traditional village life is just one metaphor for that simplicity. Rural life and other images of simplicity are ironically placed in ultra-urban settings. Entitled *Jalan Thamrin* ("Thamrin Avenue"), one painting (illustrated in Bujono 1979:16) depicts an aerial view of the skyscrapers lining both sides of that major Jakarta thoroughfare, along which government agencies often place signs with exhortative or patriotic slogans. In the painting, massive scaffolds hold an immense sign across several buildings, bearing the ironic slogan *Kesederhanaan adalah Pola*

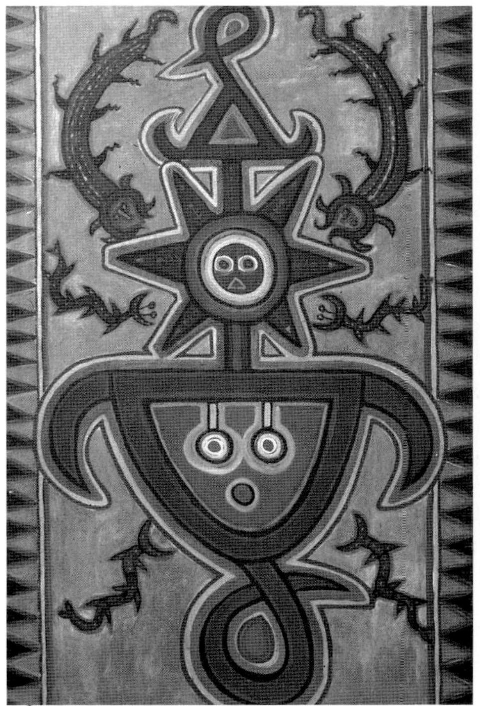

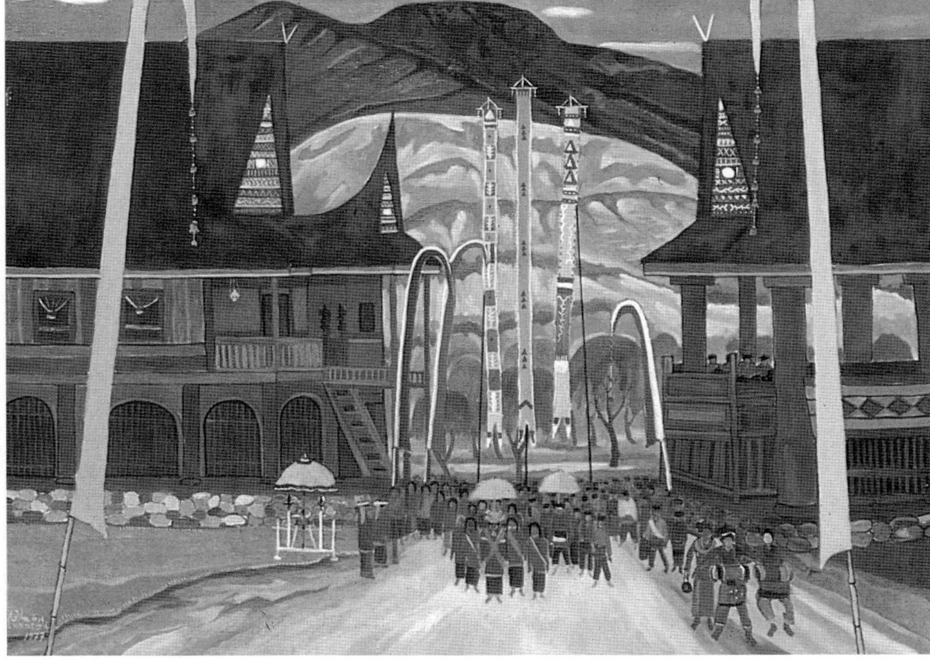

Fig. 25 *Pustaha Batak* ("Batak Book"), painting, oil on canvas, 1977, by Batara Lubis (Toba Batak, b. 1927 in Tapanuli), 102 x 70. Collection of the Indonesian Ministry of Education, Directorate of Culture.

Fig. 26 *Pesta Adat* ("Traditional Festival"), painting, oil on canvas, by Batara Lubis. Collection of the Adam Malik Museum.

Fig. 27 *Rumah Tetangga Kita* ("Our Neighbor's Home"), sculpture, wood, 1985, by Amrus Natalysa (Sumatran Malay, b. 1933 in Medan), 89 x 45 x 22. Tunggal Siagan

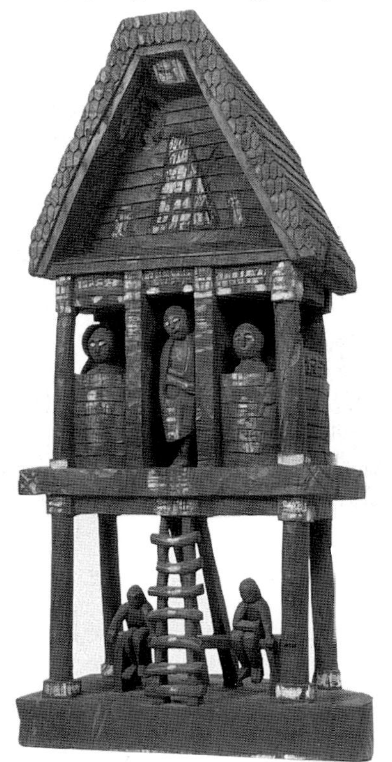

Hidup Masyarakat Kita ("Simplicity is a fundamental principle of our society"). Many of Dede Eri Supria's political paintings can be understood in terms of the inhibiting effects of urbanism on people of the outer islands, which are perhaps more extreme than those on the Javanese he more frequently depicts. One painting depicts an imposing bronze statue cast in the Russian-influenced socialist style used along Jakarta's monumental avenues in the early 1960s. *Disekitar Patung Pembebasan Irian Barat* ("Around the Statue Commemorating the Liberation of West Irian") depicts in the foreground the monumental statue of a powerful man with arms stretched upward, his shackles broken and dangling—but in the background the tilted gridlike frame of a city skyscraper surrounds him like a cage.

Many outer-island artists producing artworks for the cosmopolitan modern art marketplace are more deeply grounded in regional traditions and consciously refer to and reinterpret traditional themes. Compare, for example, the traditional Batak manuscript (Fig. III.25) with a 1977 painting by Batak painter Batara Lubis (Fig. 25), entitled *Pustaha Batak* (which has been translated as "Batak Motif" but is better translated as "Batak Book"). Another painting of the same year (Fig. 26) depicts an unspecified traditional ceremony. The emphasis instead is on the idea of tradition, the *adat*, a reference to the ethical and moral basis of traditional society made contemporary.

The house in traditional Indonesian society is a metaphor for the cosmos and for society, a symbol of the family that derives from its founding ancestors and also of the ethics of reciprocity among family members and between that family and others. The Sumatran Malay artist Amrus Natalysa calls up these images to the Indonesian viewer with his sculpture *Rumah Tetangga Kita* ("Our Neighbor's House" or "Our Neighbor's Home"), made in 1985 (Fig. 27). In Indonesian, *kita* is the pronoun translated "we (inclusive)" and thus the addressee is included. The viewer is included as a member of the family, looking on with the artist at "our" neighbor's home.

Part Two

Outer-island Art: A Catalogue

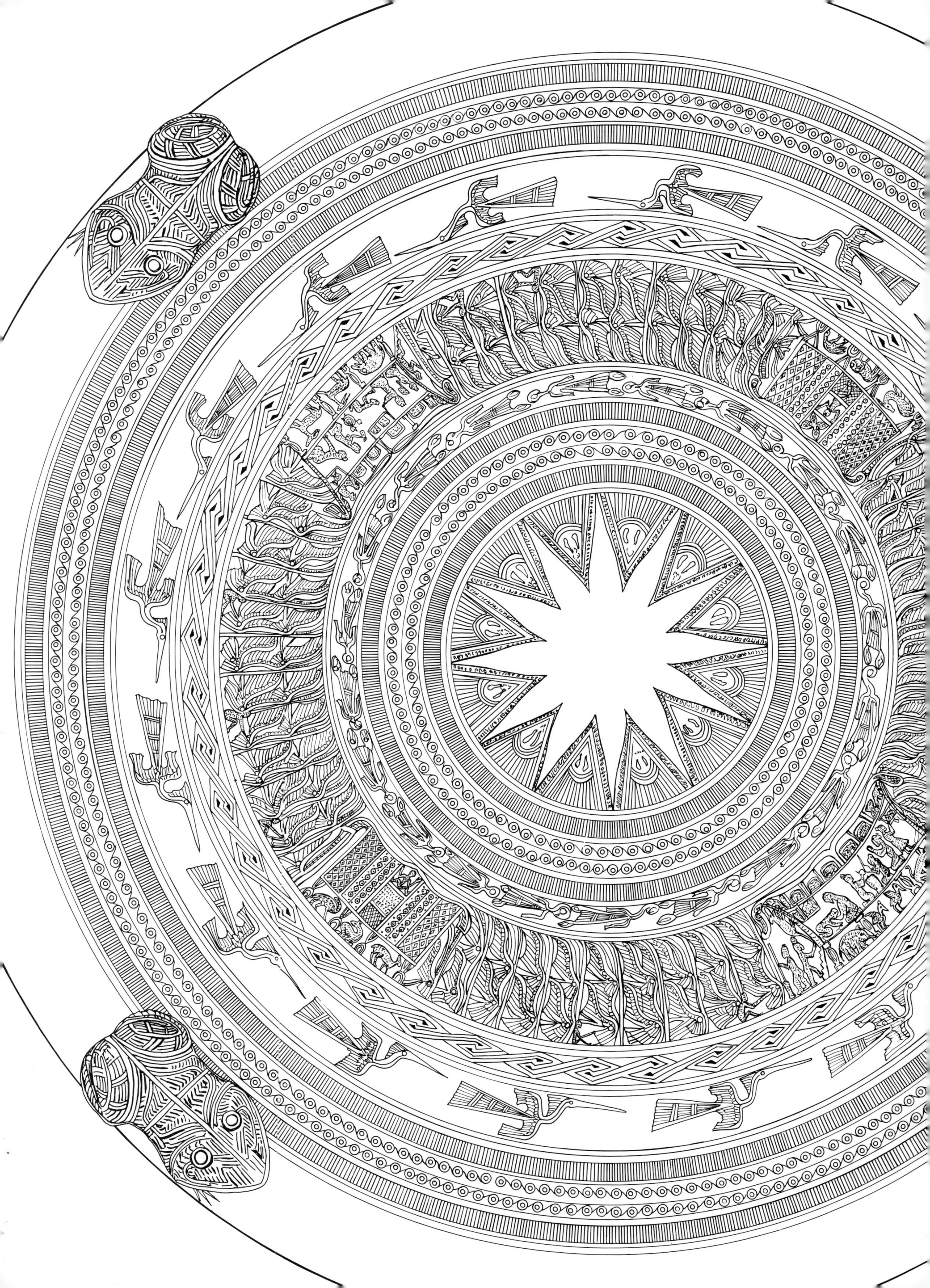

I

Prehistory

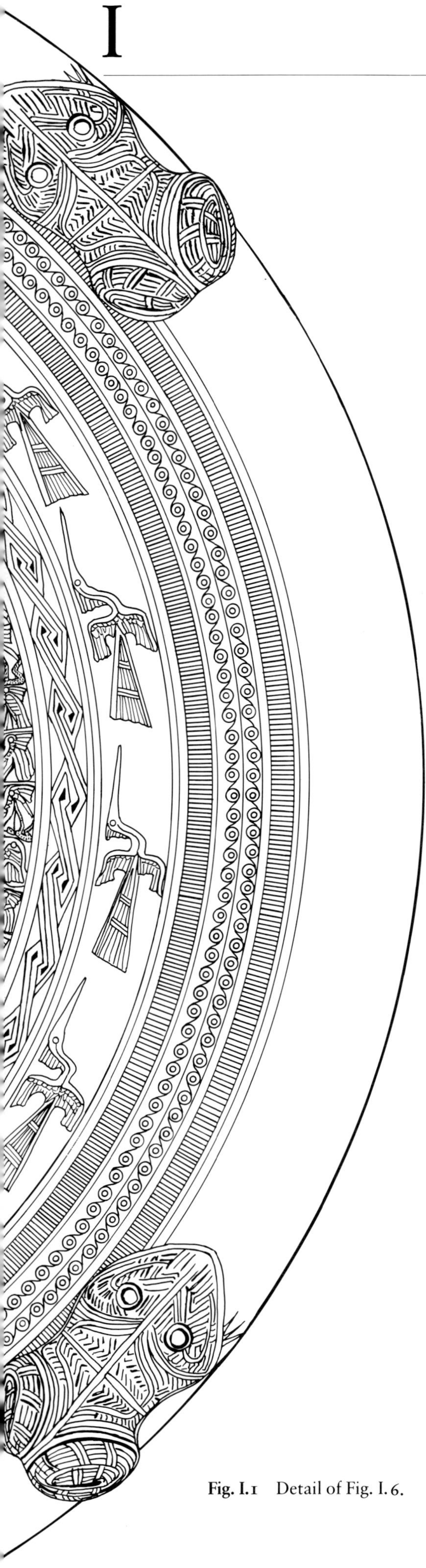

THE ARTS OF INDONESIA'S OUTER ISLANDS reveal some motifs and designs that may be attributed to a common prehistoric Southeast Asian and Pacific island culture and others that are attributed to later foreign influences from mainland Asia, the Middle East, and Europe. Many authors have attempted to find a prehistoric substratum of Indonesian art by identifying Asian, Middle Eastern, or European elements within Indonesian art and then making suppositions about what existing art traditions might have been like prior to those influences. A more reliable method of obtaining data on the earliest forms of Indonesian art is through archeological investigations. The most ancient objects excavated in Oceania are pottery from the Lapita Pacific island cultures (1500–500 B.C.) and bronzeware from Vietnam's Dongson culture (600 B.C.–A.D. 100). These finds indicate that persons were actively traveling and trading throughout the archipelago as early as the second millennium B.C. The designs on the prehistoric artworks described in this chapter have inspired generations of indigenous artisans and still appear on Indonesian art today.

Archaeological and linguistic evidence supports the idea that a common prehistoric Austronesian protoculture existed in Southeast Asia and the Pacific. Even though descendants of the early Austronesian speakers have now populated a vast region of the Pacific, including most of Indonesia, they actually supplanted earlier peoples whose non–Austronesian-speaking descendants are found today in the New Guinea area and also on some islands of Indonesia. On the basis of linguistic evidence, Bellwood (1985:102–129) concluded that the earlier non-Austronesian speakers whose languages included prototypes of some of the present-day Papuan and Austro-Asiatic languages were displaced by a prehistoric expansion of Austronesian speakers through Southeast Asia, the Philippines, and eventually into Indonesia. He considers the origin of the Austronesian groups that moved throughout the Pacific to have been a group of Proto-Austronesian–speaking migrants from the mainland of southern China

Fig. I.1 Detail of Fig. I.6.

Map 1 Range of Austronesian, Papuan, and Austro-Asiatic languages in Southeast Asia. Bellwood 1985:104. Redrawn by Marcia Bakry, Smithsonian Institution.

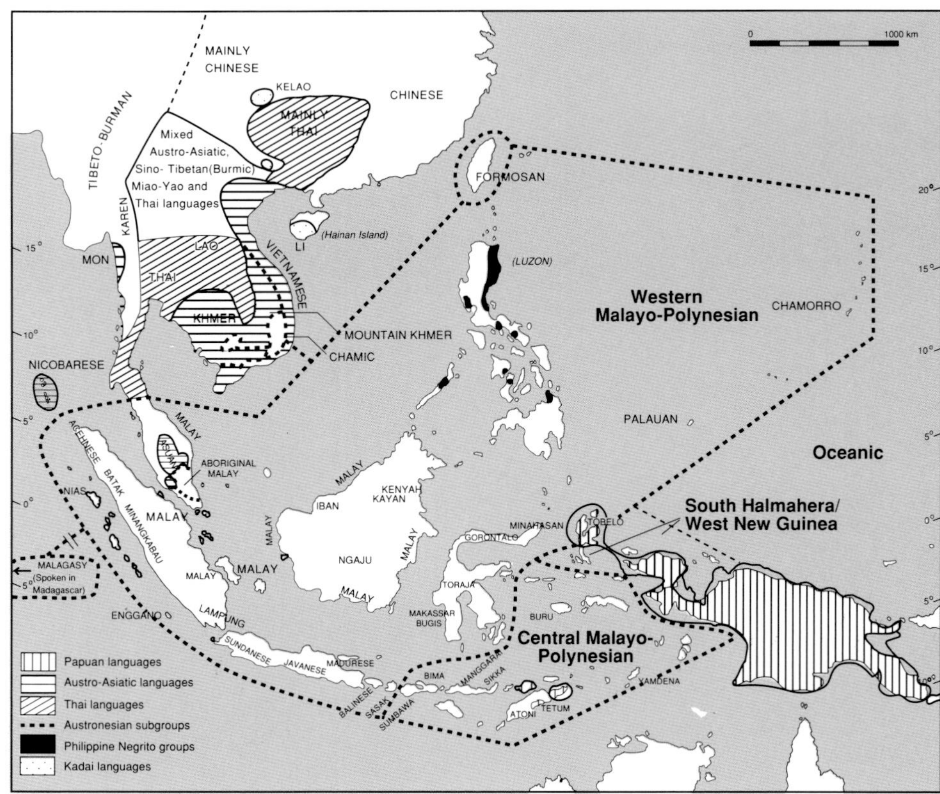

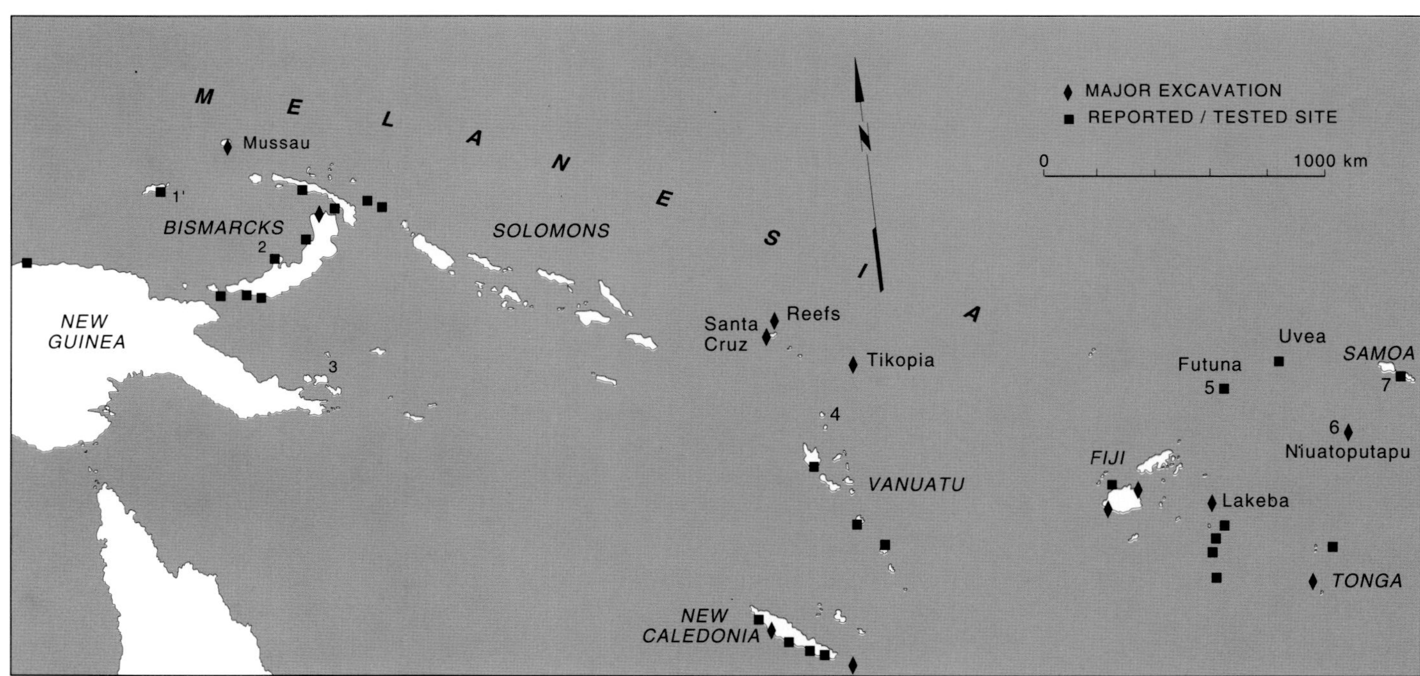

Map 2 Map of Lapita sites in the southwest Pacific. Kirch and Hunt 1988:10

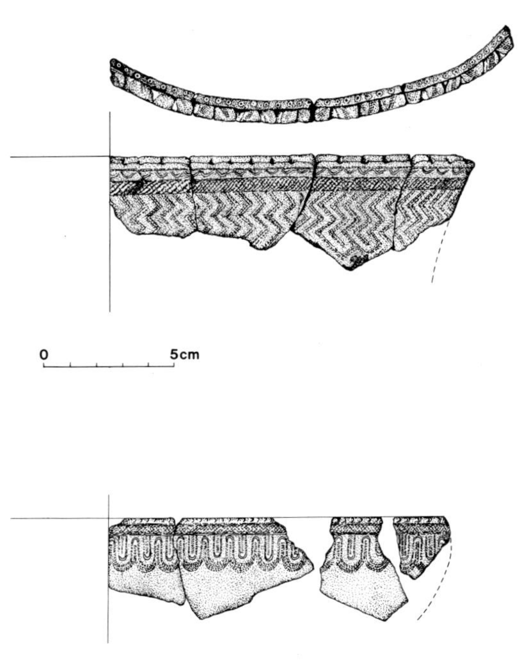

Fig. I.2 Lapita sherds from Talepakemalai site in Mussau. P. Kirch 1988:337. Drawn by Margaret Davidson.

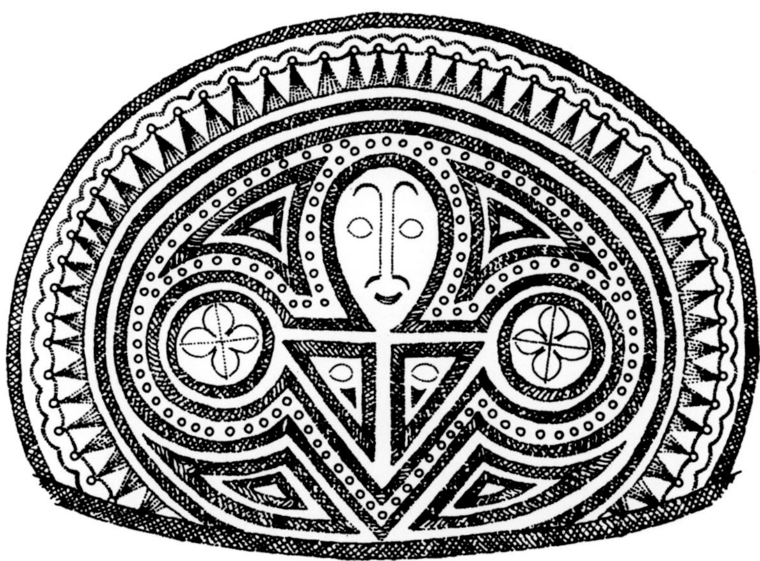

Fig. I.3 Lapita pottery with design motif that resembles a human face. Green 1979:22

that migrated to Taiwan and developed a language Bellwood terms "Initial Austronesian." Bellwood suggests that Proto-Austronesians settled on Taiwan by circa 4000 B.C., then their Initial-Austronesian–speaking descendants moved into the Philippines by 3000 B.C. and by 2500 B.C. were headed southward into the Indonesian archipelago. The Austronesians spread so thoroughly through the archipelago that today almost all of its ethnic groups speak Austronesian languages (Map 1).

The only non-Austronesian languages spoken in Indonesia today are the so-called Papuan languages of Irian Jaya, Halmahera and Morotai, Timor, Alor, and Pantar—all presumably spoken by the descendants of ethnic groups that were not supplanted by Austronesian speakers during waves of Austronesian migrations (Wurm 1983:28–34), including the migrations of Austronesian speakers along the north coast of New Guinea and into the Pacific islands, which Wurm (1983) dates to circa 5,000 years ago. The term "Papuan" has been applied to all non-Austronesian languages of this region, on the grounds that they might originally have been related, even though there are now insufficient similarities among these languages, as measured by currently available methods, to consider them all descendants of a single protolanguage.

This linguistic record reveals that the various Austronesian cultures that make up the vast majority of Indonesian peoples developed from one primary cultural substratum, which in turn has long been in contact with a second cultural substratum, that of the Papuan-speaking peoples in eastern Indonesia and New Guinea. Knowledge of the prehistoric migrations of Indonesians, and of their earliest contacts with other groups, is useful for understanding the history of Indonesian arts, and this short summary of the linguistic evidence for an Austronesian substratum is sufficient to show that it should be possible to seek in the archeological record some evidence for the art forms of early Austronesians as they might have looked prior to indigenous innovations and foreign introductions.

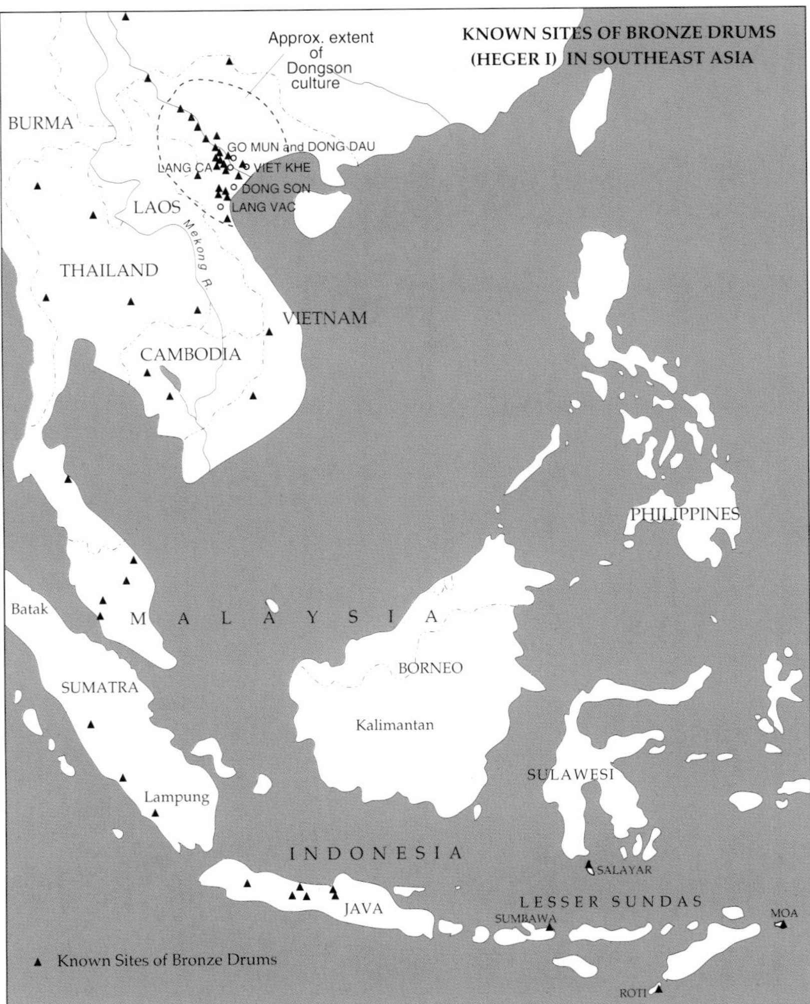

Map 3 Distribution of Heger I type kettledrums throughout Southeast Asia. Marcia Bakry, Smithsonian Institution.

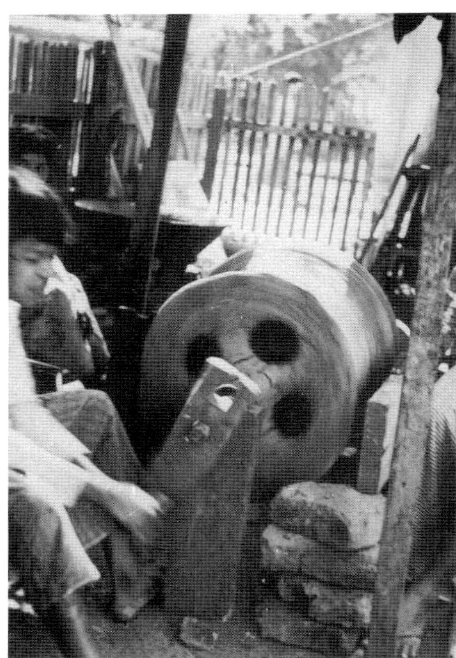

Fig. I.4 Person of Karin ethnic group turning a clay mold of locally produced kettledrum, Tampawaddi district, Burma, late 1970s. Sylvia Fraser-Lu

OPPOSITE
Fig. I.5 DONGSON DRUM
Sumbawa region, Sangeang
Bronze, 90 x 122
Museum Nasional Indonesia, Jakarta, 3364

Information about human contact and migration, trade, social stratification, and the origin of design styles continue to be sought by scholars in the archaeological record. Pacific archaeological research during the last two decades has greatly increased knowledge of an ornamented pottery style called Lapita after an archaeological site in the Melanesian region of New Caledonia. The Lapita-pottery–making cultures (Map 2), known primarily through their finely decorated pottery and related obsidian finds, are dated roughly 1500–500 B.C. The recurrence of similar ceramic decoration styles over widely scattered islands in the western Pacific, also in association with traded obsidian flakes, has led archaeologists to posit a wide prehistoric trading and colonization network.

The stamped and incised designs on Lapita pottery are mostly geometric (Fig. I.2) but include spiral forms and some human faces (Fig. I.3) that resemble those found on later Indonesian Dongson-style bronzeware (Fig. I.14). Although prehistoric links between Lapita and later bronze-using cultures of Southeast Asia, including Dongson, are not yet documented, items produced by these cultures display similar elemental design motifs that can still be seen on Indonesian artworks. Materials produced by both the Lapita and the later Bronze Age cultures provide evidence of long-distance trade, suggesting prehistoric antecedents for the systems of ritual gift exchange still operant in Indonesia and other areas of Oceania today. Moreover, remains found at the Talepakemalai site along with pottery sherds indicate that people lived then much as they do today in outer-island Indonesia. They built stilt-houses and, for subsistence, fished, gathered shellfish, and cultivated a wide variety of trees and plants. Shell knives and scrapers offer indirect evidence that they cultivated tubers (Kirch 1988:336–339).

The Lapita peoples may have been the early Austronesian speakers who expanded from the Southeast Asian mainland eastward through the Pacific islands and then into Indonesia, Melanesia, and Polynesia (Bellwood 1985). Or, the Lapita cultures may have developed independently in the Pacific, possibly

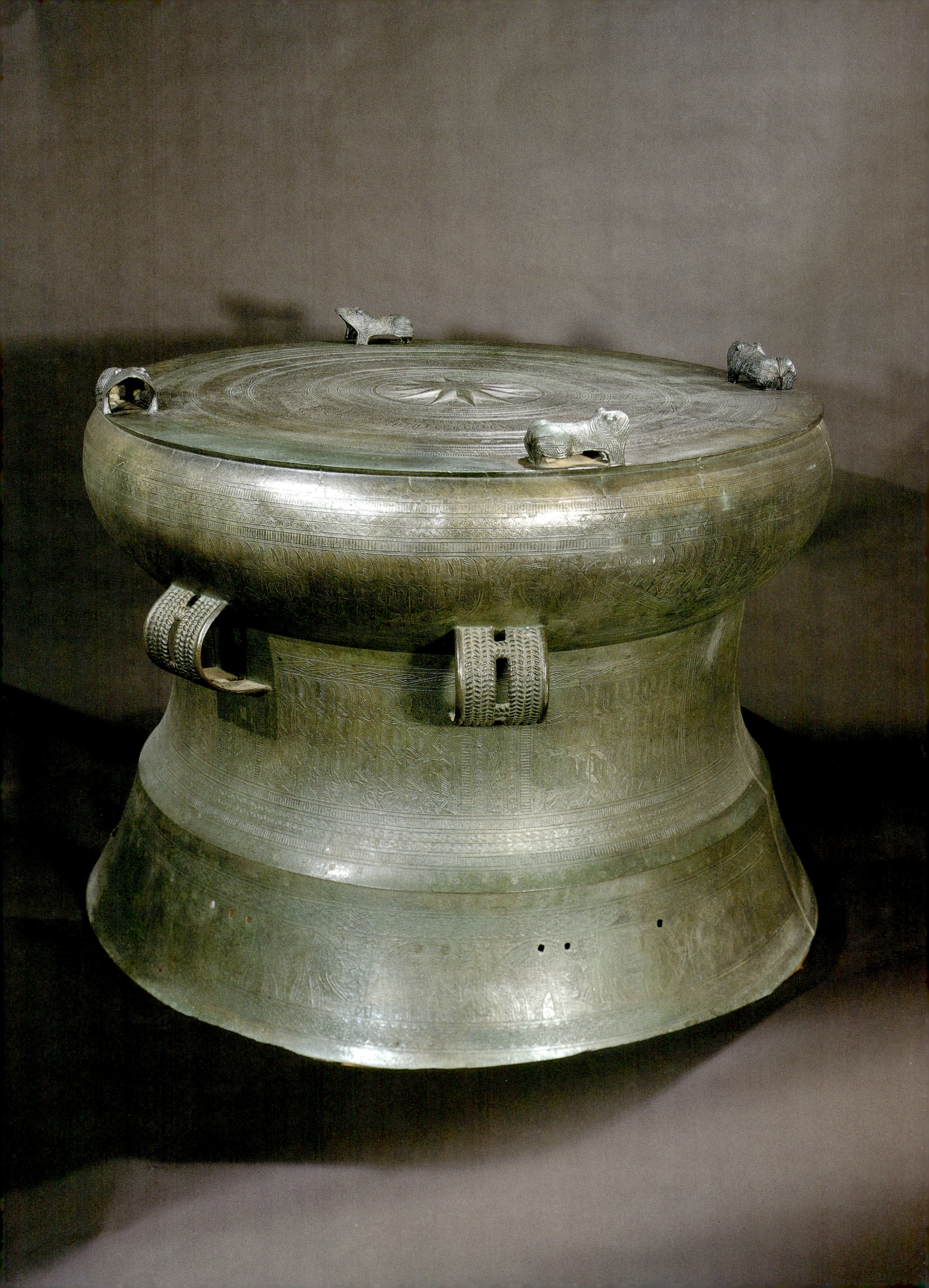

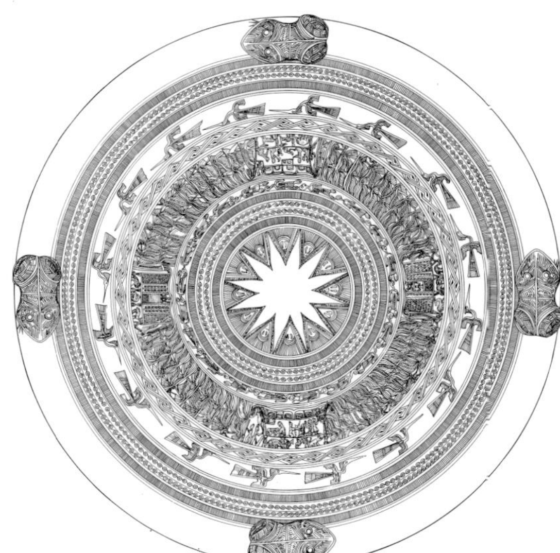

Fig. I.6 Top of Dongson drum, "Makalamau," MNI 3364. Marcia Bakry, Smithsonian Institution

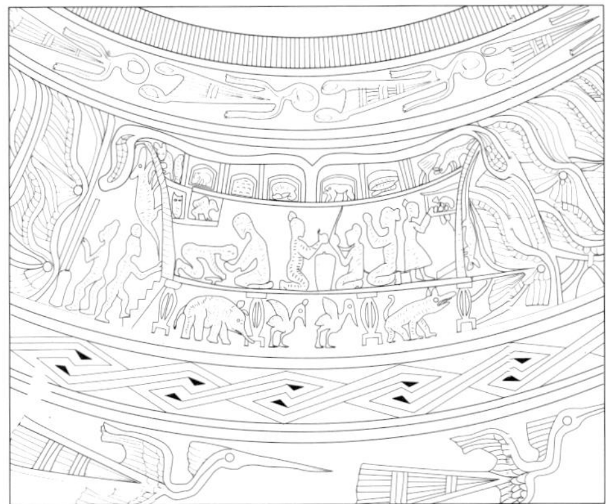

Fig. I.7 Domestic scene from top of Dongson drum, "Makalamau," MNI 3364. Marcia Bakry, Smithsonian Institution

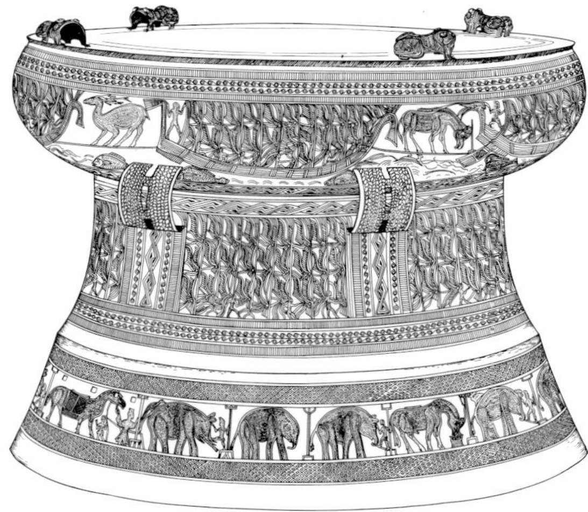

Fig. I.8 Full view of Dongson drum, "Makalamau," MNI 3364. Marcia Bakry, Smithsonian Institution

near the Bismarck archipelago (Green 1982; Spriggs 1984). Neither hypothesis has been conclusively proven (Kirch 1988a).

Bellwood notes similar designs on the stamped pottery from the Yüanshan culture of northern and eastern Taiwan, which has been dated as early as 2000 B.C., and designs found on pottery in the Philippines, Indonesia, and areas of western Oceania after 1500 B.C. (Bellwood 1985:247). Some scholars now presume that the antecedents of the Lapita pottery documented from Polynesia and Melanesia must lie somewhere in eastern Indonesia or the Philippines (Glover 1979; Solheim 1975; Bellwood 1985:252). Although new archaeological excavations are revealing more and more information, the archaeological record of eastern Indonesia remains scanty and insufficiently dated. Further excavations will need to be made in the islands of Southeast Asia and New Guinea before the four-thousand-year record of Indonesian design forms is better understood and scholars are able to determine the origins of the suggestive geometric designs seen on Indonesian artworks similar to those of the Lapita and Dongson cultures.

Dongson culture was an influential early civilization of Southeast Asia that flourished from circa 600 B.C. to A.D. 100 in the Tonkin region of Vietnam (Map 3). It is assumed to have been a stratified and semiurbanized culture based on intensive rice production using plows and buffalo traction. Improved food production presumably supported increased population in settlements controlled by an upper class, which commissioned ornamented bronzeware, such as kettledrums, for elaborate burials (Higham 1983; Bellwood 1985:275).

Bronze artifacts known from this culture have been found throughout Indonesia from Sumatra to Irian Jaya (Map 3). To date, twenty-six kettledrums and drum fragments have been found in Indonesia (Smith and Watson 1979: 514–15). Brought by Southeast Asian migrants or passed along through trade, the bronzes may have acquainted the inhabitants of the Indonesian islands with an advanced metalworking technology and style of ornamentation that can be seen on Indonesian artworks up to the present day.

Dongson metallurgy was especially advanced for its time, both for its unusual kettledrum and ax forms, which differ significantly from those of contemporary India and China, and for its use of lost-wax casting. There are two methods of lost-wax casting, one for hollow objects and the other for solid objects. To make hollow objects such as a Dongson drum, the artisan forms the object in clay (Fig. I.4). The clay sculpture is then covered with a decorated wax layer the thickness of the desired metal object. A second layer of clay is added over the wax to seal in the wax mold. Molten metal is poured into the mold. The wax melts, flows out through holes, and the metal hardens into the form of the wax sculpture. For solid pieces, the form is first carved in wax. The wax sculpture is then encased in a clay mold. Molten metal is then poured into the hardened mold replacing the wax and creating a solid metal object. Additional surface ornamentation can be added to the metal after it has hardened.

In 1937, six large kettledrums and drum fragments were located on the island of Sangeang just east of Sumbawa in the Lesser Sunda region of Indonesia. A Dutch official, deputy commissioner S. Kortleven, had them sent to what is now the National Museum of Indonesia to be added to its prehistoric collections. Three of those drums, individually named by the local community, had been placed beside graves and were revered by the Sangeang islanders, who reportedly used them in ceremonies to invoke rain for themselves and to cause fire among their enemies (van Heekeren 1958:24). The largest of these three drums (Fig. I.5, I.8), called "Makalamau," was studied in detail by Heine Geldern (1947).

Makalamau, with a diameter of 122 cm, is the third-largest drum of the type known as Heger I. Early this century, a German scholar named Heger classified all the known excavated Dongson-style drums according to size and shape (Heger 1902; Bernet Kempers 1988:30–32). The clothing and architectural styles depicted on the drum, its specific lead content, and the fact that it

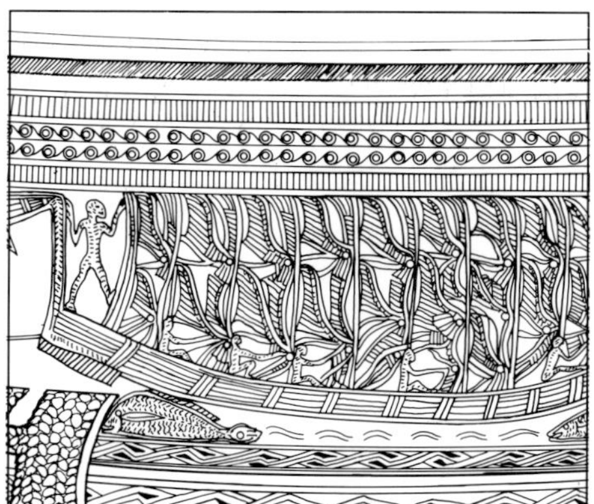

Fig. I.9 Boats and humans from upper convex zone of Dongson drum, "Makalamau," MNI 3364. Marcia Bakry, Smithsonian Institution

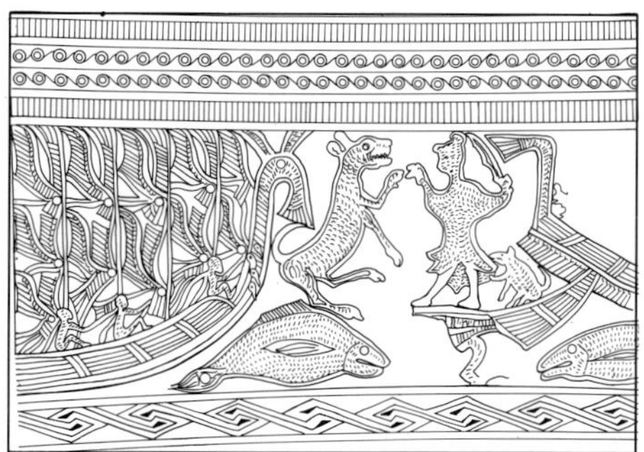

Fig. I.10 Animals and human with sword from side panal of Dongson drum, "Makalamau," MNI 3364. Marcia Bakry, Smithsonian Institution

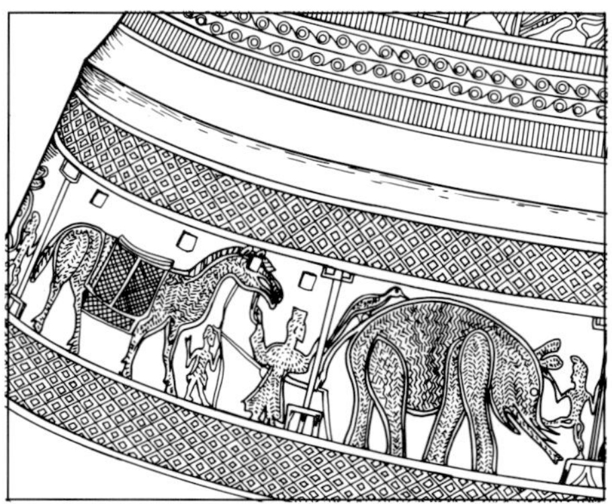

Fig. I.11 Human, horse, and elephant rider figures from bottom zone of Dongson drum, "Makalamau," MNI 3364. Marcia Bakry, Smithsonian Institution

was cast in one piece—unlike contemporary and later Pejeng-style drums of Java and Bali whose top tympanum and drum body are often cast separately—indicate that Makalamau was manufactured in Southeast Asia and subsequently transported to Indonesia. Bellwood (1985: 281) suggests that most or all of the Heger I Dongson-style kettledrums found in Peninsular Malaysia and Indonesia were produced in Vietnam prior to A.D. 100 and reached the Sunda Islands of Indonesia through trade routes during the first millennium A.D. (Map 3).

Most of Makalamau's geometric designs stand out in positive relief, whereas most of the figurative scenes are incised in negative. In the center of the tympanum (Fig. I.6) is a twelve-pointed star encircled by twelve concentric bands ornamented with either geometric or figurative designs. In the cosmology of the drum's original makers, this star represented the sun. Both sun and rain, symbolized by the thunderous sound produced when beating the tympanum, were necessary to yield fruitful crops and to sustain life in general (Bernet Kempers 1988:115). The outermost band of the tympanum is ornamented with four sculptures of frogs, placed equidistantly from each other. (Two of the original frogs are now missing, but copies were produced for the exhibition "Beyond the Java Sea: Art of Indonesia's Outer Islands").

The third band of the tympanum is most informative about the way people were living in Southeast Asia at the time the drum was manufactured. It contains four segments that depict domestic human scenes occurring in and around pile-houses with saddle-shaped roofs. Such houses are frequently depicted on Dongson drums excavated in northern Vietnam but also resemble traditional houses still constructed today in areas of Indonesia such as the Sa'dan Toraja region of Sulawesi (van Heekeren 1958:24).

In one of the four scenes (Fig. I.7), a person is ascending a ladder into the building, and another individual appears to pound rice in an hourglass-shaped mortar, a type still used in rural areas of Southeast Asia and outer-island Indonesia today. An animal with a long tail is shown climbing in front of the gable, and two chickens, a pig, and a dog are seen below the raised house. Inside the house are five kneeling figures and one standing figure who appear to be inserting or removing an object from a storage area surmounted by other storage compartments. Heine Geldern (1947:169) associated the dress and kneeling postures of the figures to decorations seen on Chinese roof tiles of the third century B.C. and Han reliefs of the second century A.D. It is also possible, however, that these scenes depict domestic life in Southeast Asia both before or after those dates. In the scene on the opposite quadrant of the tympanum, a similar version of domestic life is shown. One person appears to be playing a gong; other kneeling figures may indicate positions of homage to aristocrats.

The body of the drum is compactly ornamented with scenes of boats, wild animals, and horseback riders. The upper convex section depicts six crescent-shaped boats with bird head ornaments on the bows and sterns (Fig. I.9). Each boat carries several human figures barely discernable among the dense feathery patterns. The geometric feather patterns, similar in form to warriors' headdresses seen on other Dongson kettledrums, have been considered a stylized version of an earlier naturalistic design form (Bernet Kempers 1988:138–39). Below some boats are fish and bird figures. In the same band, there are a few human and animal scenes (Fig. I.10). A person with a raised sword fights a large mammal. Also depicted are deer, elephants, and tall wading birds. The center section of the drum is divided by geometrically adorned bands into eight separate panels. The panels include small human figures dwarfed by banners with geometric motifs. The bottom section of the drum includes twenty square sections, one now missing, which depict men beside or astride horses or elephants (Fig. I.11).

The designs and scenes depicted on the drum called Makalamau support the hypothesis that this particular bronze item was imported from Vietnam (Heine Geldern 1947; personal communication, Bellwood 1990). The trade of these Dongson drums, diverse bronze items, and the new knowledge of manu-

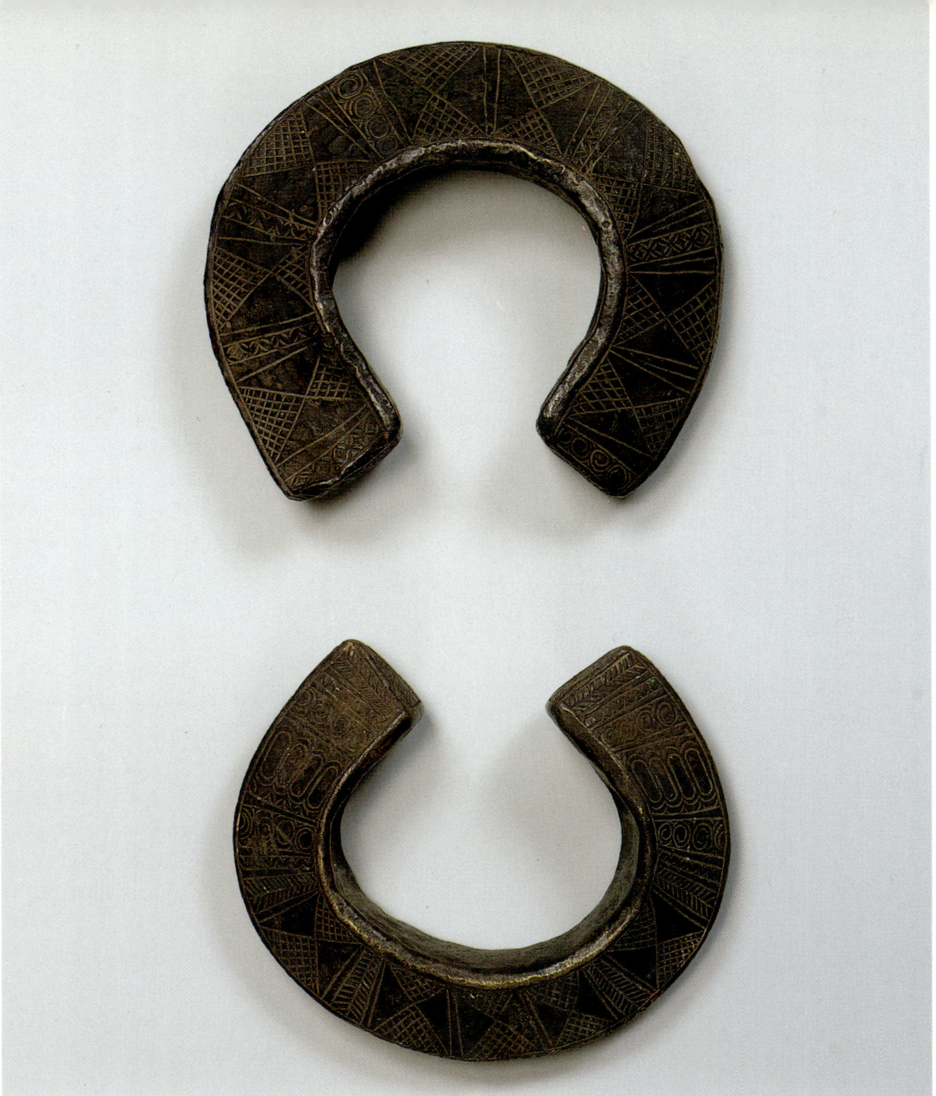

Fig. I.12 Ankle rings
West Sumba
Cast iron, 3.5 x 14
Collection of Anita E. Spertus and Robert J. Holmgren, New York, S-150, S-151

facturing techniques associated with these goods may have led to an increase in the development of local Indonesian metalworking centers, as evidenced by clay molds and large numbers of bronze axes and other vessels of innovative design excavated in areas such as Bali (Heekeren 1958; Bernet Kempers 1978; Bellwood 1985:282–89).

Cast-metal objects with geometric motifs have also been associated with Dongson technology and artistic influences. For instance, cast-metal anklets (Fig. I.12) were worn by women of high rank on Sumba to emphasize their freedom from heavy field labor. Even today such anklets are sometimes worn in wedding processions (personal communication, Joel Kuipers 1990). The cast-iron composition of these anklets suggests a more recent origin, but their designs may have been based on almost identical examples of authentic Dongson bronzeware (Goloubew 1929).

Prehistoric trade routes were responsible for distributing bronze pieces other than kettledrums throughout the Indonesian archipelago. For instance, the handle sockets of the ax head (Fig. I.13) were created with a metalworking technique unknown in Irian Jaya before the twentieth century, and so this object must have reached the area through trade. Newton (1988:12) believes the ax may have been imported to Lake Sentani via Cenderawasih Bay, as the inhabitants there had by the sixteenth century already established trade routes with, and learned metalworking from, the peoples of the northern Moluccas (Kamma and Kooijman 1973).

The ax head was acquired in 1903 along with two other copper-alloy cast objects, a second ax head and a rounded ornament, from the war trophy beams of the community house of Asé village in Lake Sentani (van der Sande 1907:225–26). Local inhabitants told van der Sande that these objects had been retrieved from the lake when their elder chief was a child. The relief design on the ax head is of particular interest because it closely resembles a face composed of spirals depicted on Lapita pottery fragments (Fig. I.3). The similarity of these

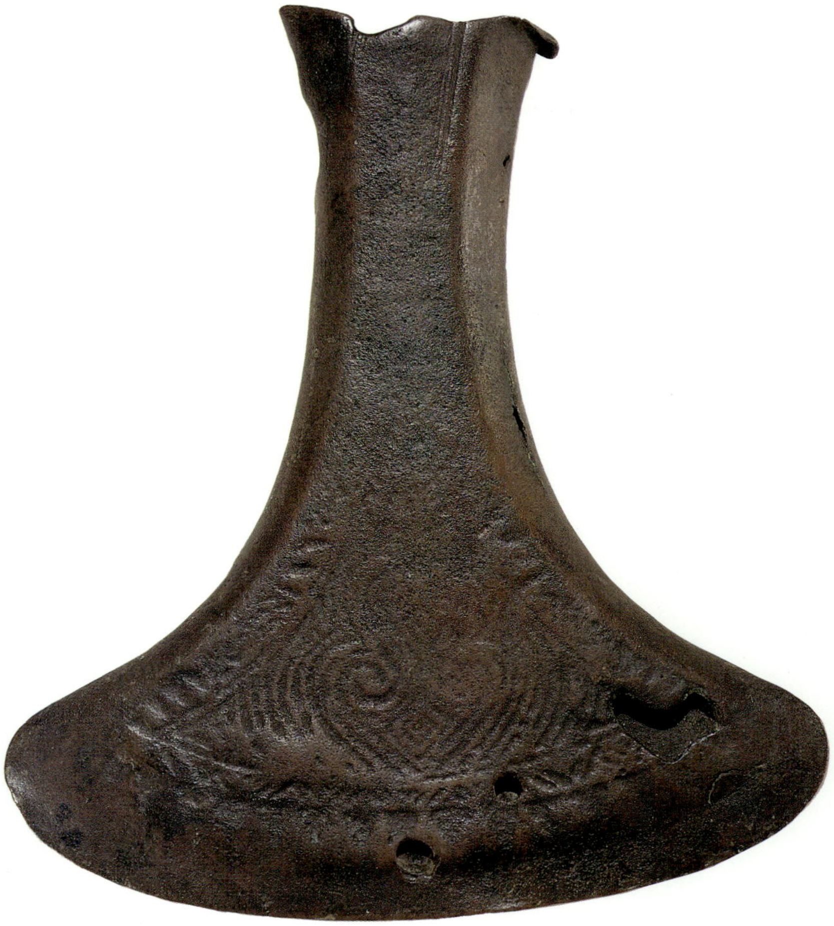

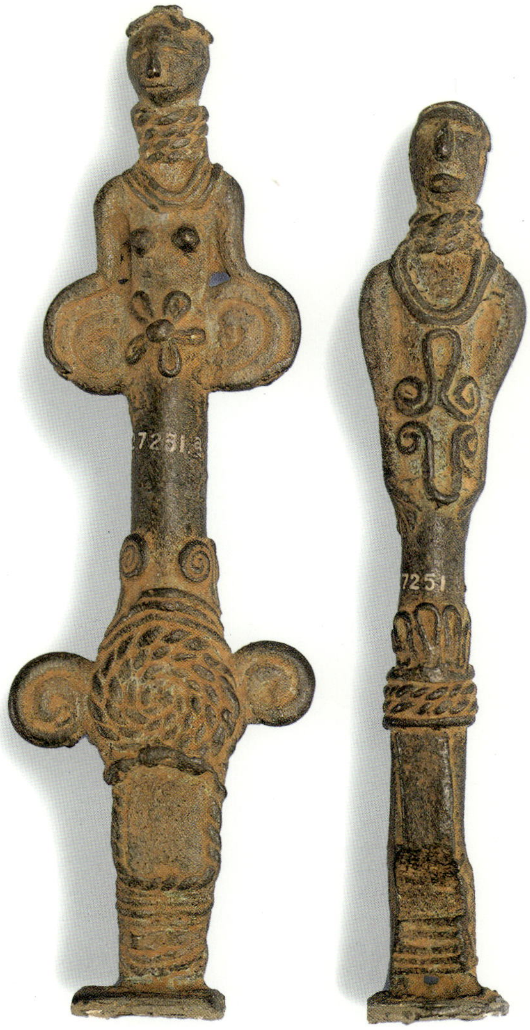

Fig. I.13 HAND AX HEAD
Bronze, 16.6 x 14.8 x 1.5
Rijksmuseum voor Volkenkunde, Leiden, 1528–445

Fig. I.14 BRONZE STATUETTES
Copper alloy, 17.7 x 5.3 x 2; 16 x 2.9 x 2.5
Museum Nasional Indonesia, Jakarta, 27251 A&B. Accessioned in 1954.

designs supports the theory of a common aesthetic among Southeast Asian artisans of the Bronze Age and prehistoric Oceanic potters.

Other bronze objects, such as the two anthropomorphic figures collected in Baumata village, Timor (Fig. I.14), may have been made in Indonesia and may represent local interpretations of Dongson-style valuables. The intricately cast figures are laden with neck ornaments, probably indicating the high rank of the individuals they depict. The five-petaled flower ornament at the genital area of the female figure suggests the pan-Southeast Asian concern with fertility, as do the spiral decorations seen on both figures, particularly the joined spirals on the front of the male figure's torso. The bases of the two figures suggest that they may have been hilts or finials on ceremonial swords or staffs.

Few contemporary scholars accept Heine Geldern's diffusionist theory promulgating the dominant influence of proto-Vietnamese Dongson bronzes on Indonesian art styles (Solheim 1975; Newton 1988:12). In particular, calling simple geometric and figurative motifs, which may well have been created without direct knowledge of bronzeware from the Tonkin region, Dongsonian has been criticized (Bernet Kempers 1988:304–7). For example, Toraja house carvings and textiles often include basic geometric and curvilinear motifs identical to the motifs identified by Heger (1902) as quintessentially Dongsonian (Fig. I.15), but no Dongson drums have ever been discovered in the Toraja region of Sulawesi. These recent criticisms of diffusionist theory are leading to new theories of an independent Indonesian origin for certain design motifs or of a common Southeast Asian artistic heritage. That a common artistic heritage existed is strongly supported by both the Lapita pottery and the Dongson bronze evidence. Design motifs may, however, have been transmitted on trade items such as textiles that disintegrated without leaving a trace of their presence.

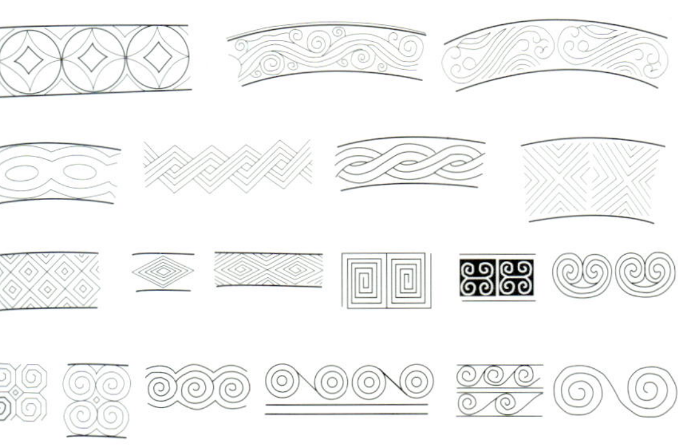

Fig. I.15 Isolated motifs from excavated Dongson drums. Heger 1902. Redrawn by Marcia Bakry, Smithsonian Institution.

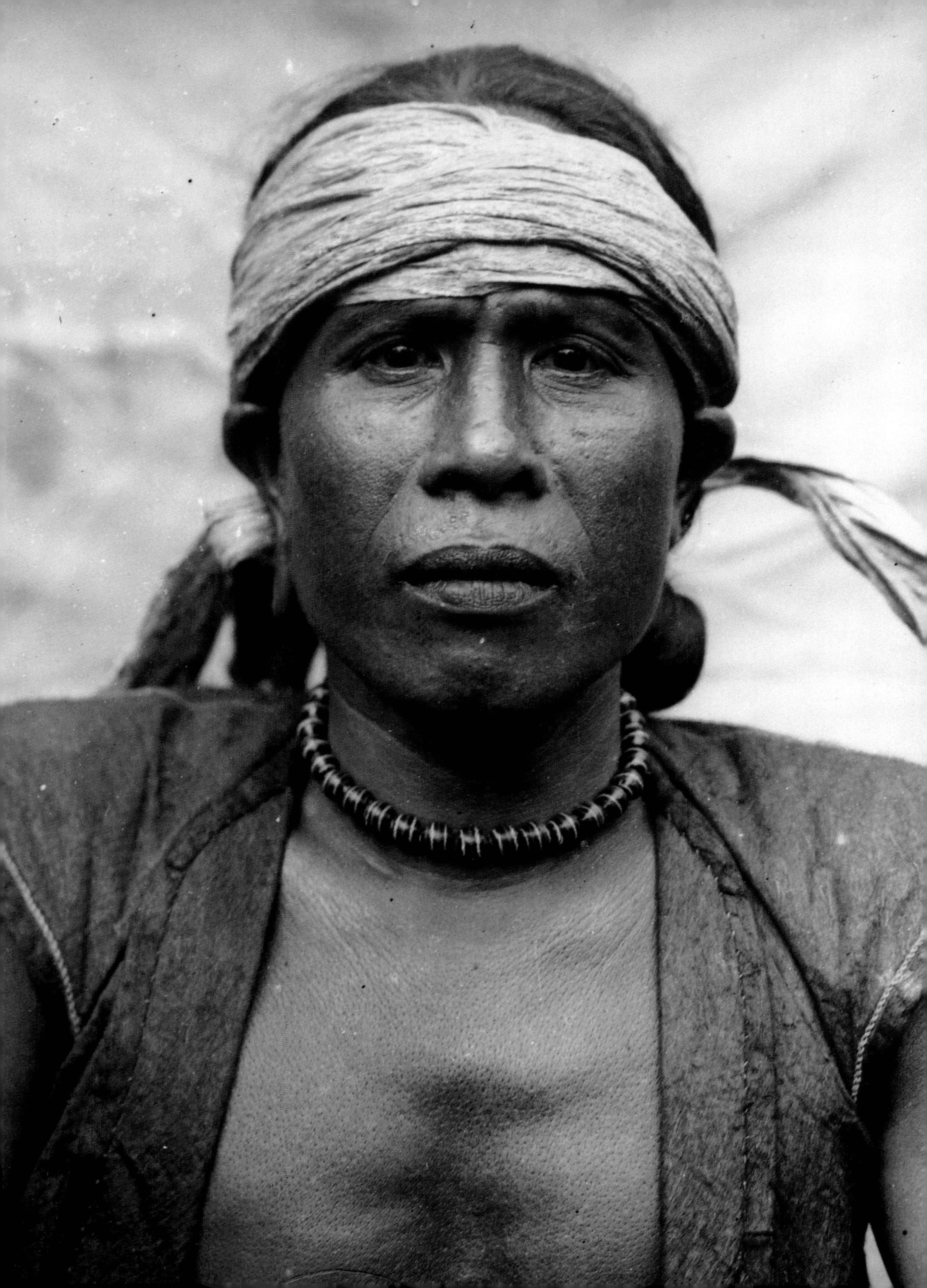

II

Nias

The island of Nias is located 112 kilometers west of Sumatra. The strait of water between Nias and Sumatra is choppy and difficult to navigate in small craft. Nevertheless, through the centuries Nias has been visited by Arab, Chinese, and Indian traders (Schröder 1917:698) and by the sixteenth century Europeans had already charted Nias on their navigational maps. The arrival of foreign cultures had an impact on many aspects of Nias life. In the seventeenth century, Nias islanders were sold into slavery by Acehnese and other Moslem traders from Sumatra, and later this trade prospered as Chinese and Dutch entrepreneurs became involved. The slave trade economically benefited some local Nias chiefs and also introduced Islam to Nias coastal ports.

Although the Dutch were not able to consolidate control of the trade in slaves and other goods from south Nias (Feldman 1977:35), Nias leaders in the north and central regions signed trade agreements with the Dutch East India Company in exchange for protection. The Dutch government therefore had greater control over the north and central regions (Sulaiman 1990:93). In this more congenial climate, both French Catholic and German Protestant missionaries began to arrive and establish local churches in Nias. Their influence and power of persuasion was so great that today the majority of the population follows Christianity. This religious conversion has had great impact on Nias art. Today, ancestor worship is discouraged by missionaries and almost no ancestor figures, *adu,* are seen publicly on Nias. Increasingly fewer people remember their use and meaning. To the missionaries, *adu* (see section below) were an embodiment of the religion they were trying to supplant, and therefore most *adu* statues were either destroyed or taken out of Nias prior to World War II.

Nias has been discussed by Western scholars in terms of three culturally and artistically distinct areas: north, central, and south (Suzuki 1958; Feldman 1977). Among these three areas, however, there are some economic and cosmological similarities. Traditional Nias economy was based on the cultivation of

Fig. II.1 Detail of Fig. II.33.

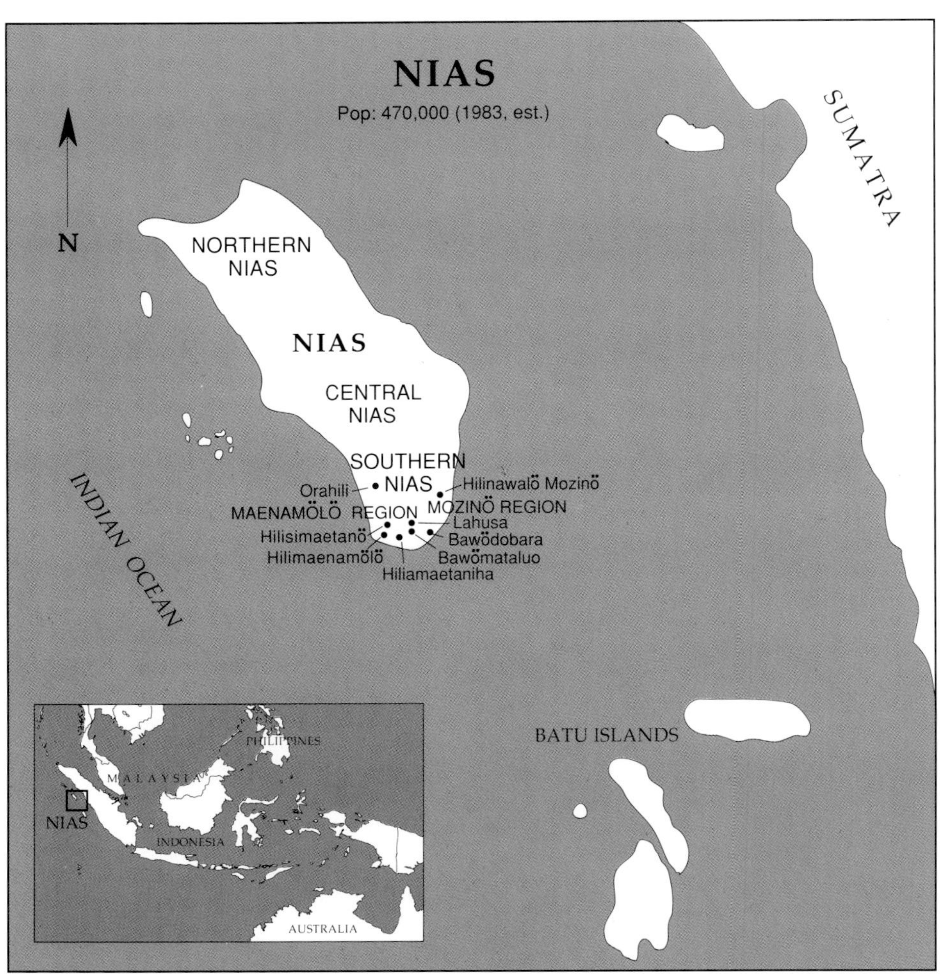

tubers, hunting, fishing, and care of livestock such as pigs and chickens. The adoption of rice as a dietary staple occurred only late in the Dutch colonial period. Although fish was an important constituent of their diet, the people of Nias never developed a seafaring tradition. Rather, most inhabitants chose to live further inland and remained farmers concerned with cultivating the land (Fig. II.3).

Social Hierarchy and the Competition for Status

The Nias traditional worldview envisioned humanity as dwelling between an upper world and a lower world, in potential contact with ancestors and spirits. Human society paralleled this tripartite cosmology. Aristocrats (nobles), considered descendants of supernatural beings, enjoyed a semisacred status (Loeb 1972[1935]:143). These nobles, actually descendants of village founders, called *si'ulu*, "those from the river source," in south Nias, and *salawa*, "the high one," in north Nias, were considered the personification of customary law (Yamamoto 1986:103). The rest of human society was subdivided into commoners, *sato*—some of whom governed with the noble rulers as part of a commoner council of elders, called *si'ila* in south Nias, and slaves, *sawuyu*, owned by nobles and required to live outside village boundaries in field huts (Suzuki 1959; Feldman 1985b:45).

Nobles and commoners each competed within their social stratum to maintain and elevate their status. To do so, they sponsored feasts marking such events in the human life cycle as births, weddings, and funerals. To commemorate these feasts, nobles commissioned artisans to carve stone sculptures for public display and use and to fabricate gold jewelry. The production of jewelry and sculpture for ceremonial display became, as a result, a highly politicized activity as nobles competed to outdo each other (Rodgers 1985:78–79; Feldman 1979, 1989). The nobleman's rank was increased through a series of feasts, each marking his entitlement to certain symbols of high status.

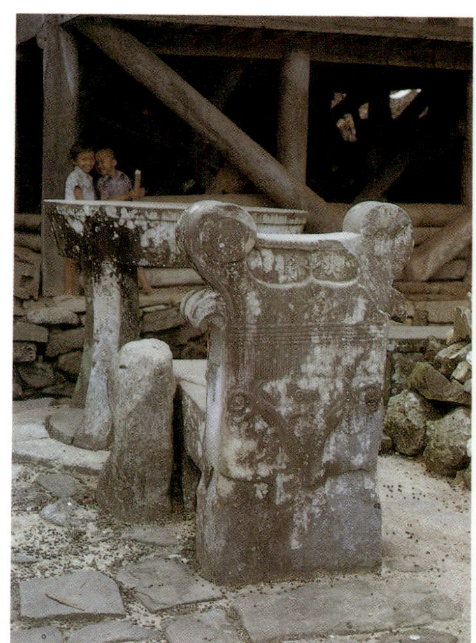

Fig. II.2 Stone sculpture, Hilisimaetanö village, south Nias, 1980. Y. Miko Yamamoto

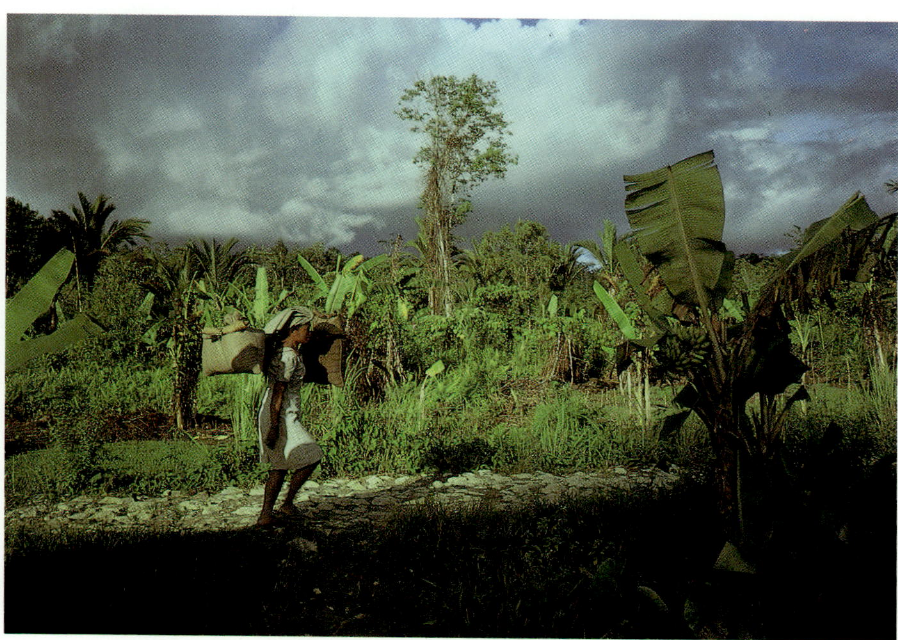

Fig. II.3 A woman carrying produce back from the field, south Nias, 1982. Y. Miko Yamamoto

Yamamoto writes that "according to Nias tradition, accumulated wealth had to be made into objects or spent in preparation for feasting. Gold objects had to be displayed and acknowledged at the pig feast" (Yamamoto 1986:201). When a feast that would entitle a noble to own gold jewelry was held, a small pig was slaughtered for a private dinner to honor the goldsmith. The goldsmith then ritually blessed and "cooled" the gold that had been melted with fire (Yamamoto 1986:202). Spiritually cooling powerful metals smelted by fire is a widespread symbolic act in outer-island Indonesia related to concepts of heat as dangerous and cold as safe.

A Nias poem translated by Steinhardt reads: ". . . I shall erect a stone for the dead, I shall erect a stone in respect of those who have died" (1937:22). It was believed that erecting vertical stone monuments and financing the accompanying feasts of merit—called *owasa* in north Nias and *tawila* in south Nias (Marshall 1976:151)—made nobles eligible to join their deified ancestors in the upper world. In central Nias, stone monuments were created in a variety of shapes (Figs. II.2, II.4) including stone seats (Fig. II.6) decorated with animal heads, called *osa-osa*. Stone platforms were carved as memorials for important chiefs. Stones for these commemorative monuments were carefully selected and dragged for many miles to their proposed village site, usually in front of the chief's house. The last known traditional funeral for a major chief, which included the erection of a stone monument, was held for Saonigeho of Bawömataluo village who died in 1914 (Schröder 1917). Reportedly it took 525 men three days to move the eight- to ten-ton stone up the hill to the village (Fig. II.5). Although goldsmithing and carving were mainly carried out by members of the aristocracy, at present many artisans are of commoner descent (Loeb 1972[1935]:136; personal communication, Yamamoto 1986, 1990.

A leading man's career of feast sponsoring could culminate in the construction of a noble house, *omu sebua*, showing that he embodied qualities of the ancestors and had mastered social and cosmic forces (Feldman 1979). When

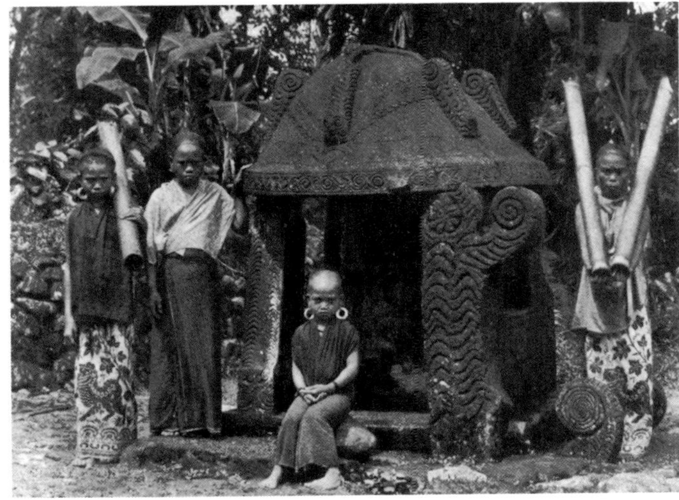

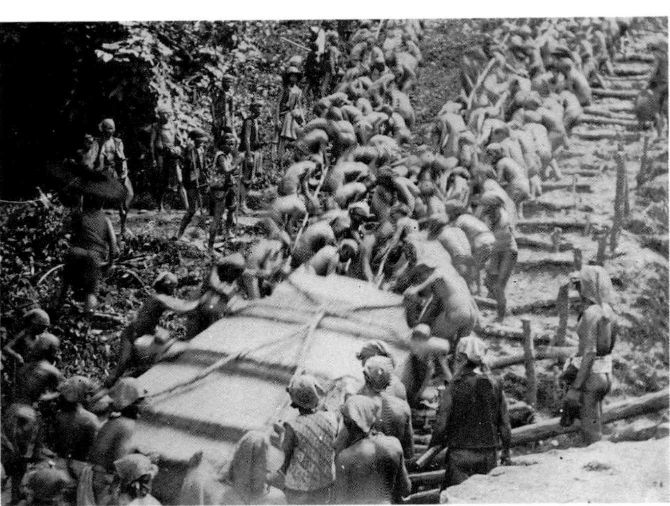

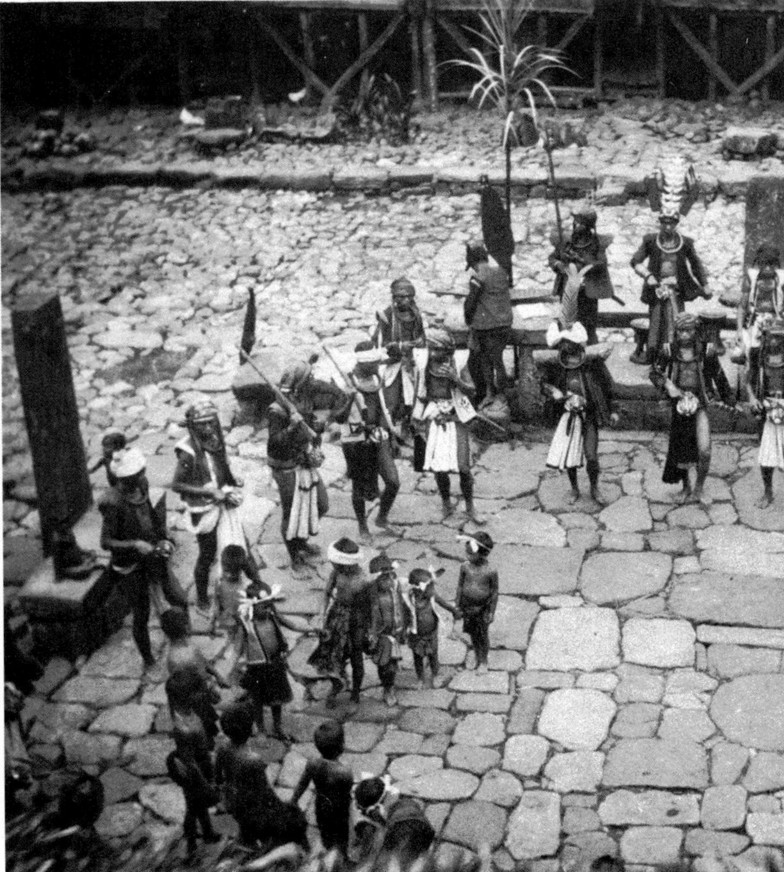

Fig. II.4 A *batu fayo,* "umbrella stone," Hilisimaetanö village, south Nias, before 1920. van Eerde 1920: 230. Courtesy Elsevier Press, Amsterdam.

Fig. II.5 Saonigeho's stone being dragged toward Bawömataluo village, south Nias, 1914. Courtesy Rijksmuseum voor Volkenkunde, Leiden.

constructing such large houses, the sponsors had to host numerous feasts for the builders. Therefore, the wealth required for this endeavor was more than that required for the production of gold jewelry. When the house was finished, the carpenter was lavished with hospitality and asked to ritually cool the house so that its inhabitants would prosper (Yamamoto 1986:232). The symbolic cooling of the house by the master carpenter was considered necessary because the construction of such a great dwelling was thought to generate heat and to provoke the jealousy of spirits.

The erection of large stone memorials (Fig. II.2), which required even more feasting to compensate the many laborers, was the most expensive enterprise of all. It was the pinnacle of success for a south Nias aristocrat. As of 1981 in south Nias, a few stones were still being erected in exchange for titles of prestige. Even some traditional-style seats, *daro daro,* were being made from concrete, which cost more in cash output but required less feasting and labor assistance than stone seats (Yamamoto 1986:240–70).

Nias art, traced through a legacy of dramatic stone and wood sculpture, architecture, gold jewelry, and traditional oration in the form of songs and poems, called *hoho* in south Nias, is inextricably linked to cosmology and social structure. According to the *hoho* legends, the four sons of the ruler of the upper world brought the first stone and wood sculptures to central Nias, thereby establishing Nias culture (Sulaiman 1990:95).

Ancestors as Intermediaries and Protectors

Freestanding wood sculptures of the human figure are most commonly seen in the form of the *adu* or ancestor spirit figures (Feldman 1977:86). These figures, used for ritual purposes, varied in style according to region and their intended religious use. For instance, when an important elder died in a Nias village, his image, *adu zatua,* "figure of an elder," was carved in wood and attached to a wall or post inside his family's house. When family members wished to contact

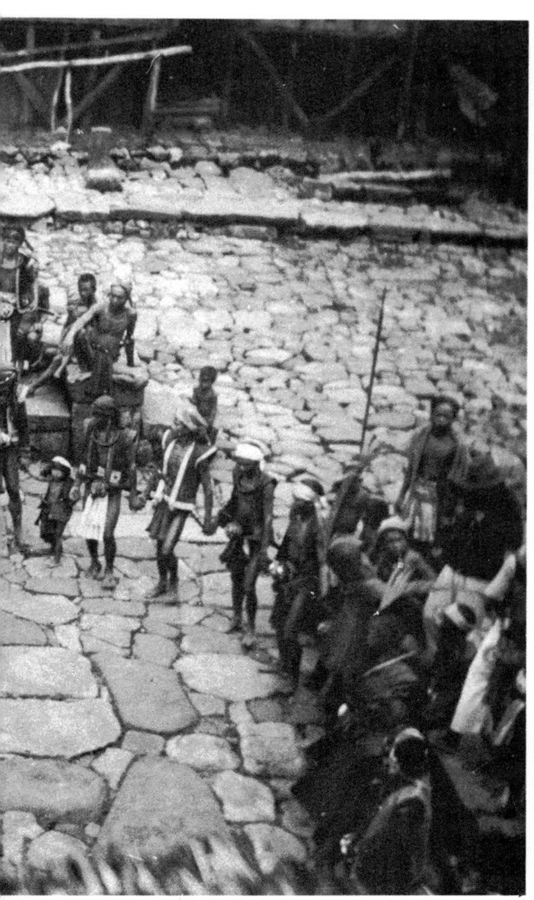

Fig. II.6 Elders sit on stone seats, south Nias, 1935. W. Blanke

him to report births and marriages or to request help, they placed food offerings on the *adu* altar. In this way, the wooden sculpture became an intermediary for communication with the spirit world, as this Nias poem reveals:

> We must make an investigation
> We must make an inquiry
> He turned to the ancestor figure
> He went to the sacrificial statue of the fathers
> Father Baloegoe Silegaitô said
> Father Baloegoe Solofo spoke:
> Say, ancestor figure of the fathers
> Say, sacrificial statue of the fathers
> We are needy on earth
> We are pitiful in this world
> We are already old
> We are already grey
> Go forth ask our Lōwālāni (the god of life and light)
> Ask our provider
> If I perhaps have sinned
> That we should be so destitute
> That we should be so needy (Steinhart 1937:163–164)

Adu ancestor figures were created to influence the fortunes of household members. Ancestors were thought to protect descendants who provided the *adu* figures with food offerings and otherwise pleased them with correct behavior. By obeying traditional ancestral rules governing social structure, marriage, land rights, ritual feasts, and headhunting, the people of Nias believed that they ensured the continued fertility of the community, land, and livestock. Most life-cycle and harvest rituals were also carried out in the presence of ancestor images (Sulaiman 1990:95).

The varieties of wood chosen for carving *adu* figures were considered sacred and representative of the upper and lower worlds (Sulaiman 1990:95). When making *adu* figures of important family ancestors, Nias carvers emphasized symbols of high social rank such as elaborate headdresses, heavy necklaces, offering cups, betel-nut pounders, earrings, and bracelets, rather than the individual's physical features. Objects, weapons, jewelry, and accessories appearing on both figurative statues and architectural reliefs were most likely owned by prominent persons in whose honor the art was created (Yamamoto 1986:305).

Each of the three cultural areas had its own carving style. In north Nias, seated positions were considered indicative of royalty and used to represent the image of a high-ranking noble, *salawa*. Such seated *adu siraha salawa*, "figures of protective spirits of high ones," were placed in individual altars attached to a freestanding post in the largest room of the house (Feldman 1985b:48). The north Nias *siraha salawa* sculptures (Fig. II.9) represent a long-deceased village or kin-group founder, a deified noble ancestor to whom the family turned for protection. The tall triangular crown, *saembu ana'a* (similar to the one worn in Fig. II.8), necklace, earring, and the cup used by descendants to offer betel-nut mixture (*afo*) to the spirit of the ancestor, are all conventional symbols used in north Nias to represent a man of high status. The north Nias carving style is identified by its distinctive style of headgear, the rounded limbs, and w-shaped position of the arms holding cups to receive offerings (Feldman 1985b:48).

Small, unpolished carvings of standing ancestor figures were created in north Nias for the ritual requirements of every commoner household. The five figures of deceased elders (Fig. II.7) were contacted by family members to announce important events and to request help in times of illness or misfortune. All five wear the basic triangular north Nias headdress but four lack an additional crown band, three lack beards, two lack necklaces, and one lacks a cup for offerings—indicating thereby several local symbols of rank. Beards, which few Nias men have, are a symbol of rank because they represent maturity, which is of a higher status than youth.

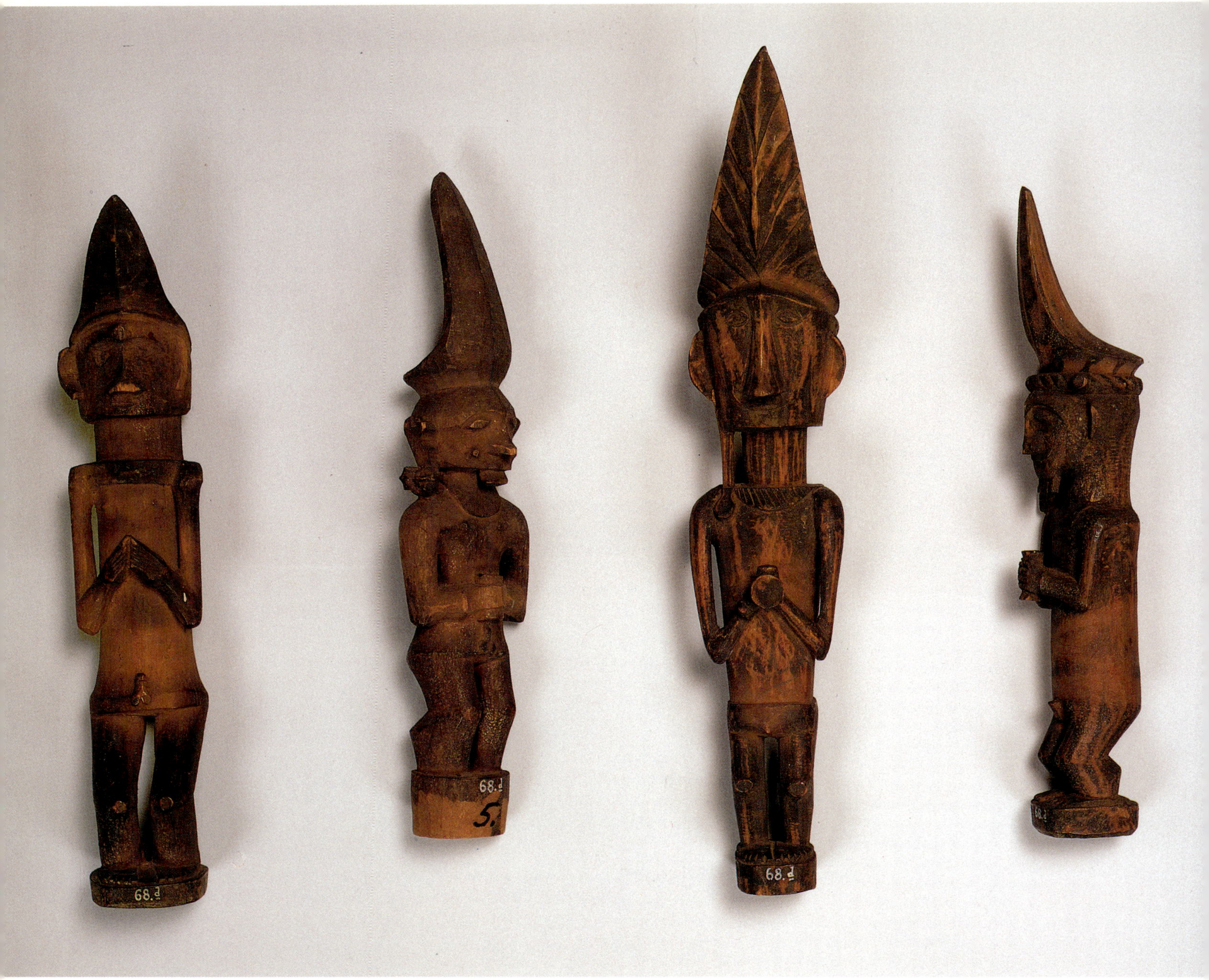

Fig. II.7 ANCESTOR FIGURE, *ADU ZATUA*
North Nias
Wood, 29.8 x 5.8 x 6.5; 28.5 x 6.5 x 5.5; 35.5 x 6.5 x 7.5; 27.7 x 5.8 x 6; 29.2 x 4.5 x 5.7
Museum Nasional Indonesia, Jakarta, 68D

Fig. II.8 Headman of Ono Geho village with triangular crown, about 1875. Courtesy Rijksmuseum voor Volkenkunde, Leiden.

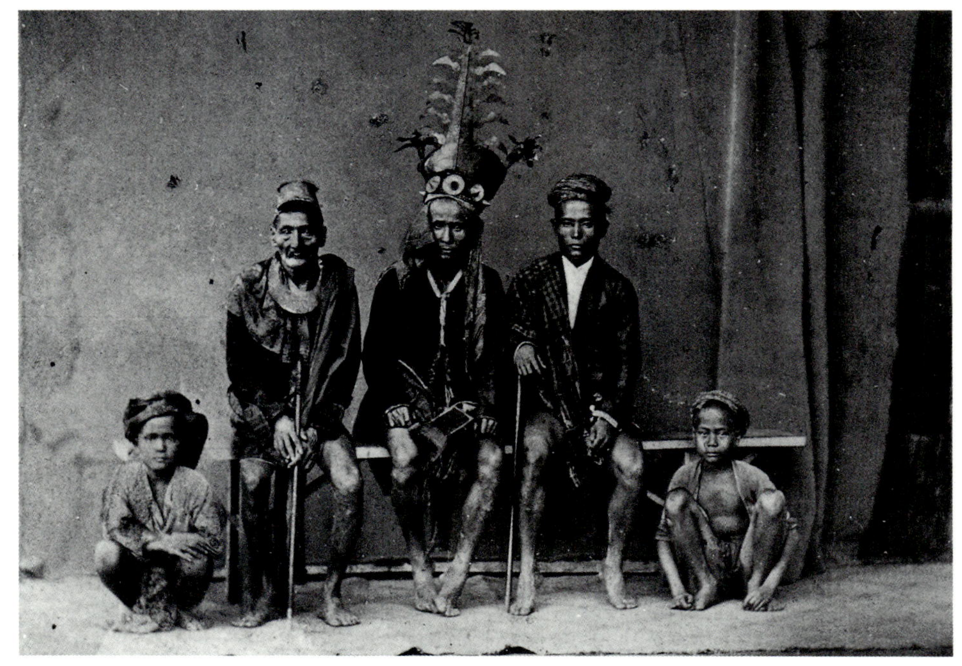

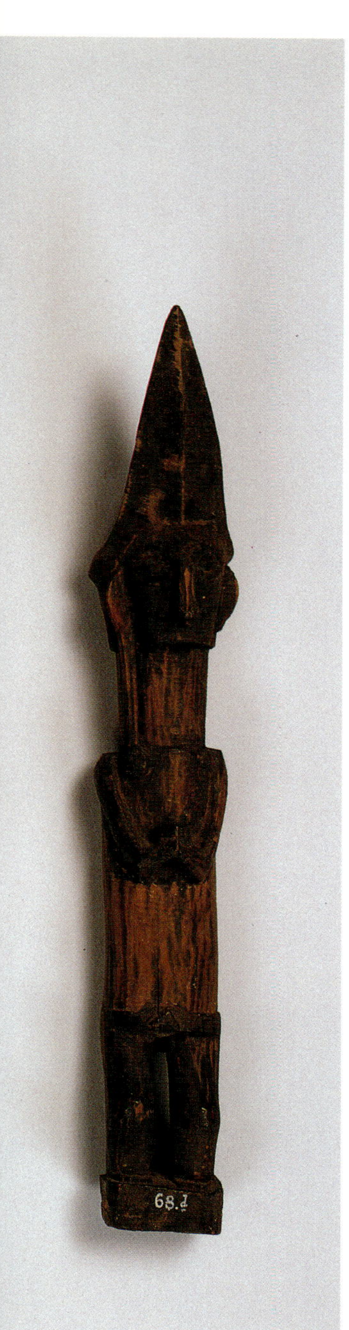

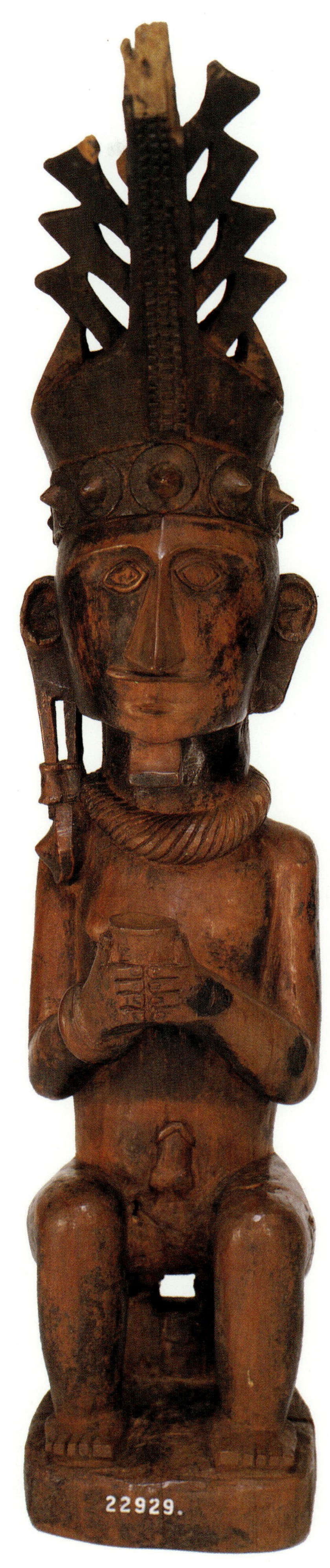

Fig. II.9 PROTECTIVE FIGURE OF NOBLE,
ADU SIRAHA SALAWA
North Nias
Wood, 61 x 13.5 x 23
Museum Nasional Indonesia, Jakarta, 22929.
Given as bequest in 1937 by J. W. van Dapperen.

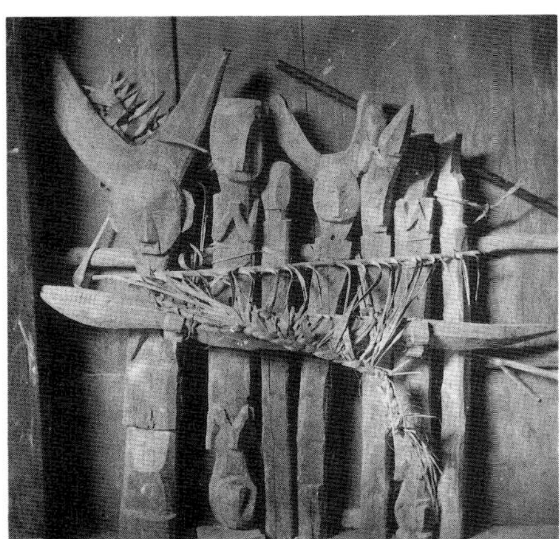

Fig. II.10 A rough two-headed *adu* and crocodile *adu* tied together on a house wall, north Nias, 1902–1905. W. L. Abbott Collection, Anthropology Archives, Smithsonian Institution.

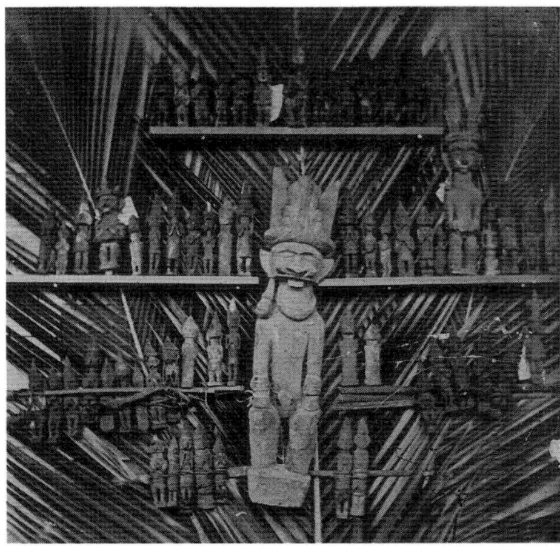

Fig. II.11 Rows of *adu* figures mounted on a wall, probably north Nias, about 1900. Courtesy Rijksmuseum voor Volkenkunde, Leiden.

OPPOSITE LEFT

Fig. II.12 ANCESTOR FIGURE, *ADU ZATUA*
Central Nias
Wood, 78.2 x 16 x 24
On loan from the Christensen Fund, Palo Alto, California.

OPPOSITE RIGHT

Fig. II.13 ANCESTOR FIGURE, *ADU SIRAHA*
Central Nias
Wood, 18.5 x 5.5 x 2.5
Museum Nasional Indonesia, Jakarta, 21449. Purchased from the estate of Dr. Bonnet in 1933.

In north Nias many small, roughly hewn, abstract ancestor figures were carved for the deaths of less-important individuals, including infants and stillborn children, or for other ritual purposes (Fig. II.10). Two-headed images were made to aid two family members who were concurrently ill or to prevent the birth of twins, considered a sign of misfortune (Feldman 1985b:52). On Nias, as in some other mainland Southeast Asian groups (Kammerer 1986), the birth of twins traditionally required the parents to perform infanticide and extensive rituals of atonement. When children were born out of wedlock, crocodile-shaped *adu* figures were carved and presented with offerings (Feldman 1985b:52–53). In Nias and many other regions of Indonesia such as Central Sulawesi, the crocodile represents an angry and punishing ancestor (Kruyt 1938).

The central Nias carving style is known for its blocky and geometric form of the face and limbs (Fig. II.12). Knees are flattened rather than rounded, noses are broad and triangular, ears are paddle-shaped, and jaws are short and square. Eyebrow ridges are prominent and often extend across the forehead to the ears. Central Nias *adu* figures, even of chiefs, do not sit but stand with flexed knees.

In central Nias, most *adu* figures are male; however, some are female or display a combination of male and female sexual characteristics to portray the concept of complementary union. Traditionally, numerous ancestor figures with both male and female features would be tied together in rows attached to, and sometimes fully covering, house walls (Figs. II.14, II.11). This large number of figures was undoubtedly accumulated over generations, as new ones were carved following successive deaths. Small sculptures honoring the ancestors of commoners were not placed in specially carved altars but were strung together for display on interior walls of the house.

Adu siraha figures with forked heads were carved to protect against illness and evil spirits, *bekhu. Bekhu* were spirits of people who had experienced an exceptionally horrible death. In central Nias the protective *siraha* often combine male and female features and are sculpted with flat limbless torsos. The enlarged breasts on the central Nias *adu* represent generosity and abundance, implying that the feast-giver who sponsored the statue's creation was as generous to his guests as a mother to her children (Hämmerle 1984:594). Different forms of *adu siraha* figures were used to ward off various illnesses (Durdik 1892). The small images carved in the headdress (Figs. II.13, II.15) may symbolize the parents or other ancestors of the main figure. The limbless torso reportedly represented the ancestor's ethereal form into which a deceased's spirit could most easily enter (Sulaiman 1990:97). *Adu siraha* were not only kept as protective statues but were also honored at major Nias ceremonies, such as feasts of merit held by nobles to raise their status, called *fondrakö. Fondrakö* were renewal ceremonies held every seven years to reaffirm customary law and cosmological balance as well as to atone for moral transgressions committed since the previous ceremony.

Adu horö, marked by tall forked headdresses, were the largest wooden figures carved in central Nias. These images were not carved to honor any particular ancestor, but rather as atonement to the ancestors in general. They were used during rituals held when a sin was thought to have been committed. Serious illness or misfortune were signs that there had been a violation of ancestral rules. When these happened an *adu horö* was placed in the front room of the family's house and presented with offerings to atone for the offence. The immense central Nias *adu horö* (Fig. II.17) is striking for the carefully incised ornamentation of the ears, chest, and headdress, as well as for the proportions of his arms and genitalia. The crown and necklace on the figure indicate that the sculpture likely was made to atone for the sin of a nobleman. During *fondrakö* ceremonies, traditional priests in north and central Nias wore forked wooden headdresses (Fig. II.16) that resemble those of *adu horö* sculptures (Feldman 1989:204).

Some roughly made, armless, standing *adu* figures (Fig. II.18) were made

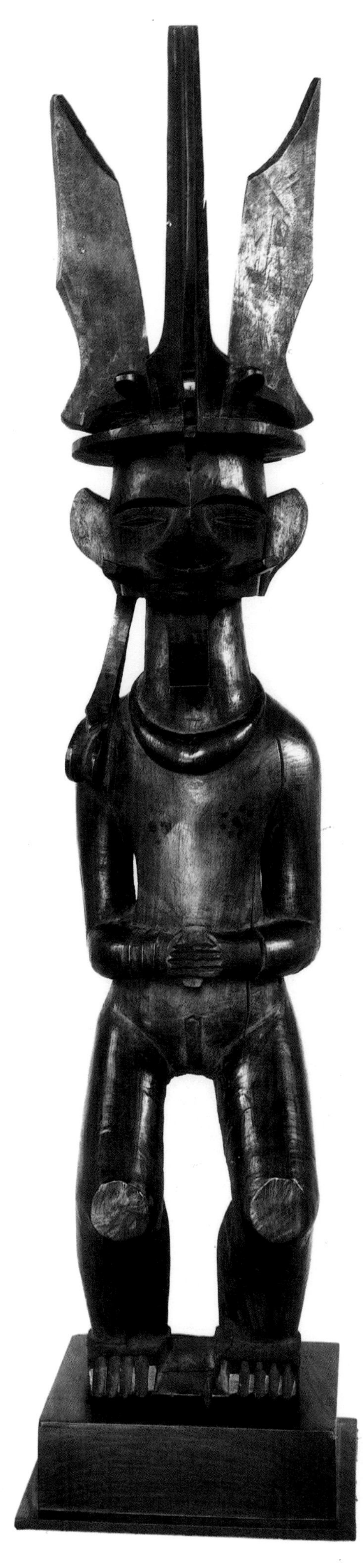

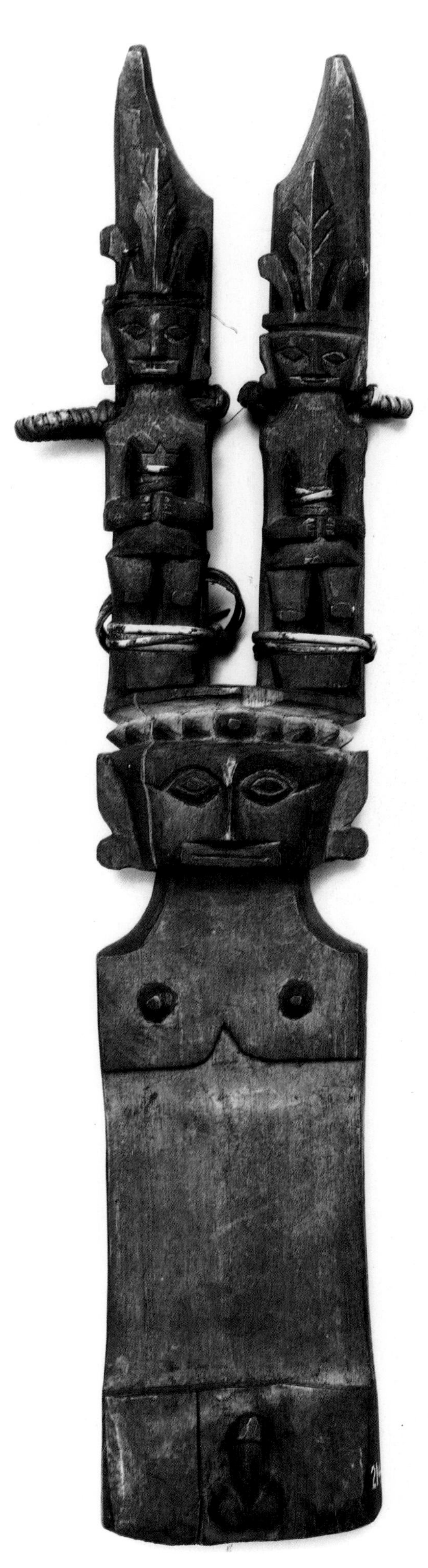

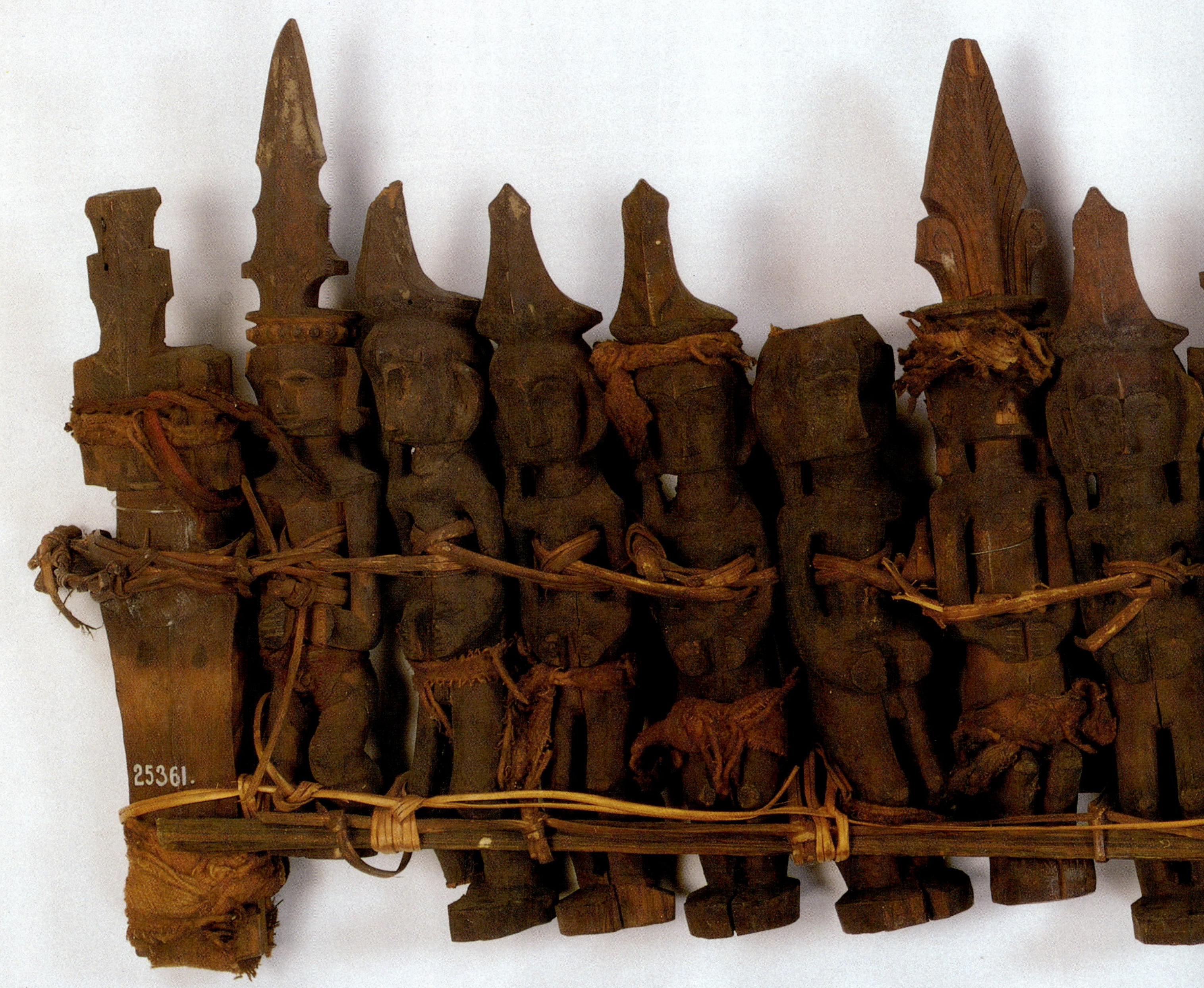

Fig. II.14 Row of ancestor figures, *adu*
Central Nias
Wood, 36 x 87.5 x 9
Museum Nasional Indonesia, Jakarta, 25361.
"Obtained through the mediation of Dr. P. Voorhoeve and a civil servant of the Dutch East India Company from an interned hostile citizen of Nias, 1941," according to the museum's catalog card.

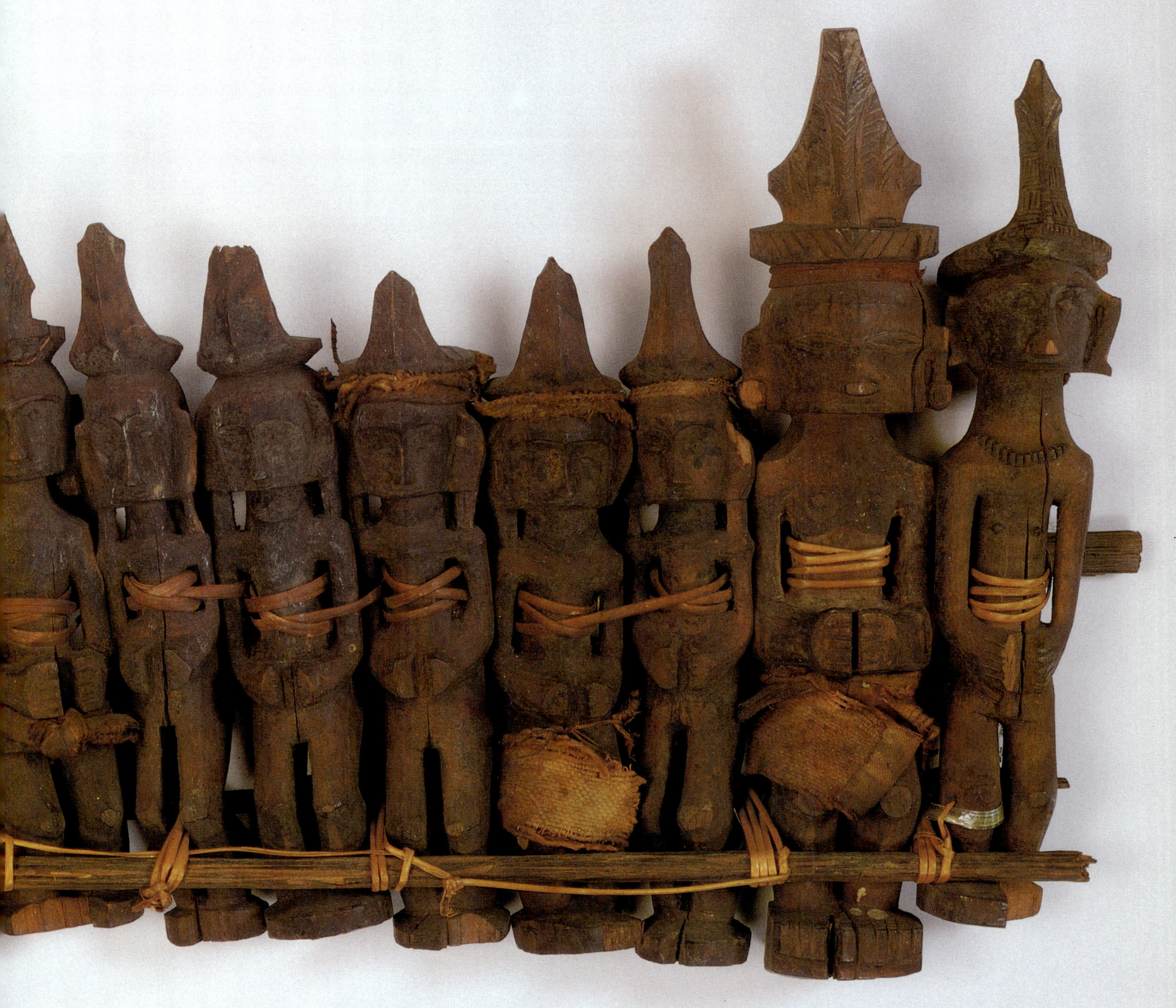

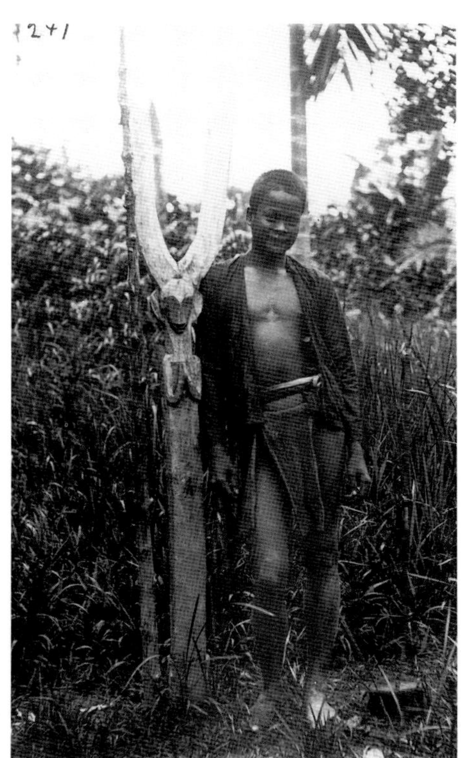

Fig. II.15 A boy with protective sculpture (*adu siraha*), 1902–1905. W. L. Abbott Collection, Anthropology Archives, Smithsonian Institution.

to request success in headhunting warfare (Fischer 1909:219) or to protect against murderous enemies (Schröder 1917:593; Feldman 1985b:58). Traditionally, trophy heads were sought for specific ritual purposes: blood revenge, the death of a chief, the ceremonial production of gold jewelry, enhancement of an oath, bridewealth payments, the cure of particularly serious illnesses, or major constructions (Loeb 1972[1935]:145). Headhunting was always considered beneficial for the victor and the presentation of enemy heads to the deities could sanctify major ceremonial events. *Lawölö* means "image of a person not yet accomplished in headhunting" (Laiya et al. 1985), and *sange'e* means "killer" or "murderer" (Thomas and Taylor Weber 1887). Thus, *adu lawölö sange'e* (Fig. II.18) refers to a would-be headhunter who has not yet accomplished his goal. The thick legs of the figure represent a warrior's strength and its enlarged chest may symbolize community fertility, the result of successful headhunting.

Although fewer *adu* were produced in south Nias than in the other regions (Sulaiman 1990), various carving styles specific to the region have been identified. The relatively naturalistic portrayal of the human form is a distinctive trait of some south Nias *adu* sculptures. Village chiefs were usually portrayed seated with an offering cup in one hand and a betel-nut pounder in the other. Fabric loincloths, usually made of imported red cloth, were wrapped around the wooden figures. Foreign merchants discovered early that Indonesians were willing to trade local products for foreign-manufactured cloth. A deep red was the preferred color, and so the traders provided it, which in later centuries was of European manufacture.

One type of carved crown on ancestor figures represents a golden comb, *sukhu ana'a*, and fernlike decorations, *wöli wöli*. Carved by the same sculptor (personal communication, Feldman 1990), the two *adu* (Figs. II.19, II.20) exemplify the naturalistic style of south Nias portraiture. The standing figure of a chief (Fig. II.19) wears both a warrior's necklace, *kalabubu*, and a golden necklace, *nifulufulu*. A seated position in south Nias portraits signified high social status. The standing figure of a warrior (Fig. II.20), which once also held a spear, was created to commemorate a feast by a nobleman of the Maenamölö region.

Adu so bawa zihönö, "image of a thousand faces" (Figs. II.27, II.28), are the largest type of ancestor figures seen in south Nias and their name refers to the relief carvings of faces that invariably appear on the forked projections, *daha*, of these armless figures (Feldman 1985b:70). These *adu* were made to alleviate misfortunes due to sins. According to early reports, the enlarged sex organs of these *adu* symbolize the fertility of crops and animals resulting from successful headhunting, traditionally a social responsibility of young males. If young men did not fulfill their duty as warriors, misfortune might befall the community. Villagers would then respond to the consequent disasters by commissioning *adu buwa zihönö* sculptures.

A particular type of cylindrical-shouldered, armless figure is known from southeastern Nias and the Batu Islands. The Batu Islands, located just south of Nias, are populated largely by Nias people and the customs of some villages are similar to those of south Nias. People in the Batu Islands are culturally varied: some migrated from north Nias, others from south and even central Nias. As immigrants who have maintained ties with their home villages, they have sought opportunities to raise their status in their home villages of Nias or in the Batu villages themselves (personal communication, Yamamoto 1990). The carved crown, earring, and golden necklace (Fig. II.29) suggest that it was made to represent a nobleman. Unlike larger figures with arms, however, these small figures grouped together in altars represented ancestors, not kin group or village founders (personal communication, Feldman 1990). The description *adu nuwu* or *hazi nuwu* translates as "image of mother's brother," an important relative for a Nias individual.

This ancestor figure (Fig. II.30), carved to commemorate a status-raising feast in the Maenamölö region (personal communication, Feldman 1990), wears

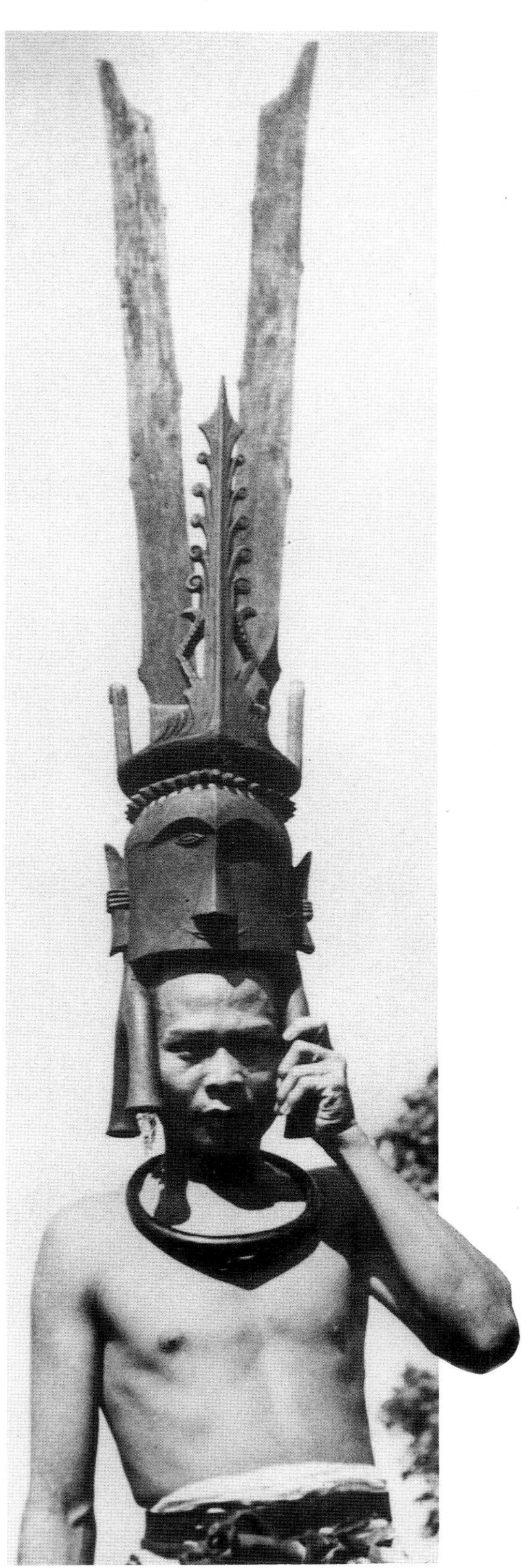

Fig. II.16 Priest wearing forked wooden headdress, central Nias, 1935. W. Blanke

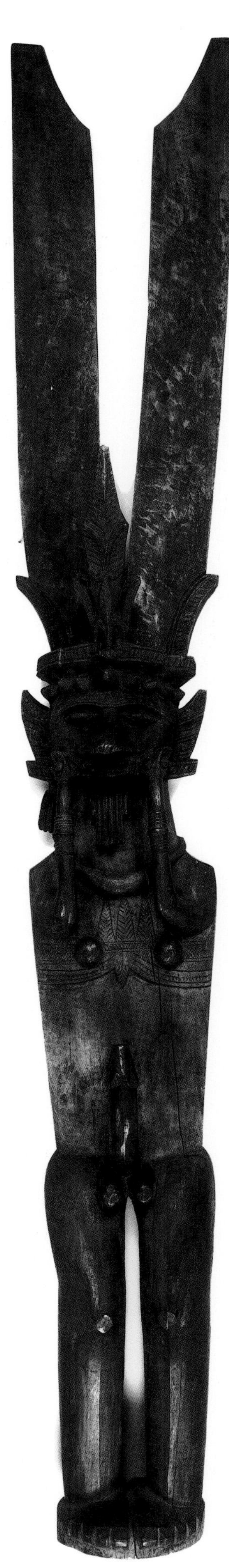

Fig. II.17 Figure for atonement, *adu horö*
Central Nias
Wood, 249 x 38.5 x 27.9
Museum Nasional Indonesia, Jakarta, 23696.
Purchased by J. Kunst in 1930.

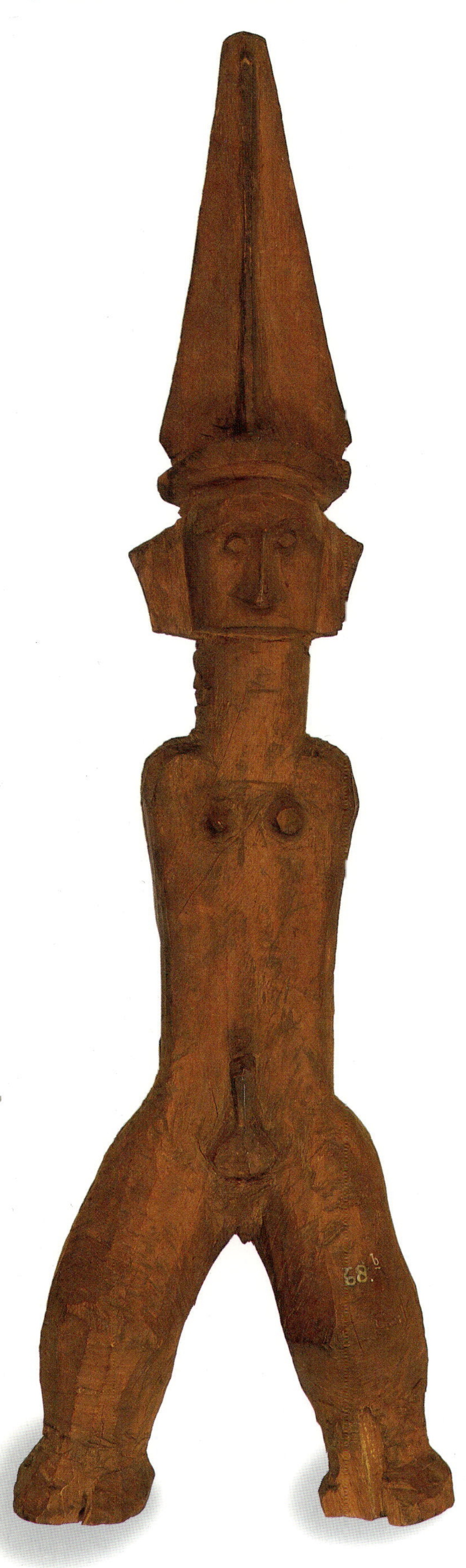

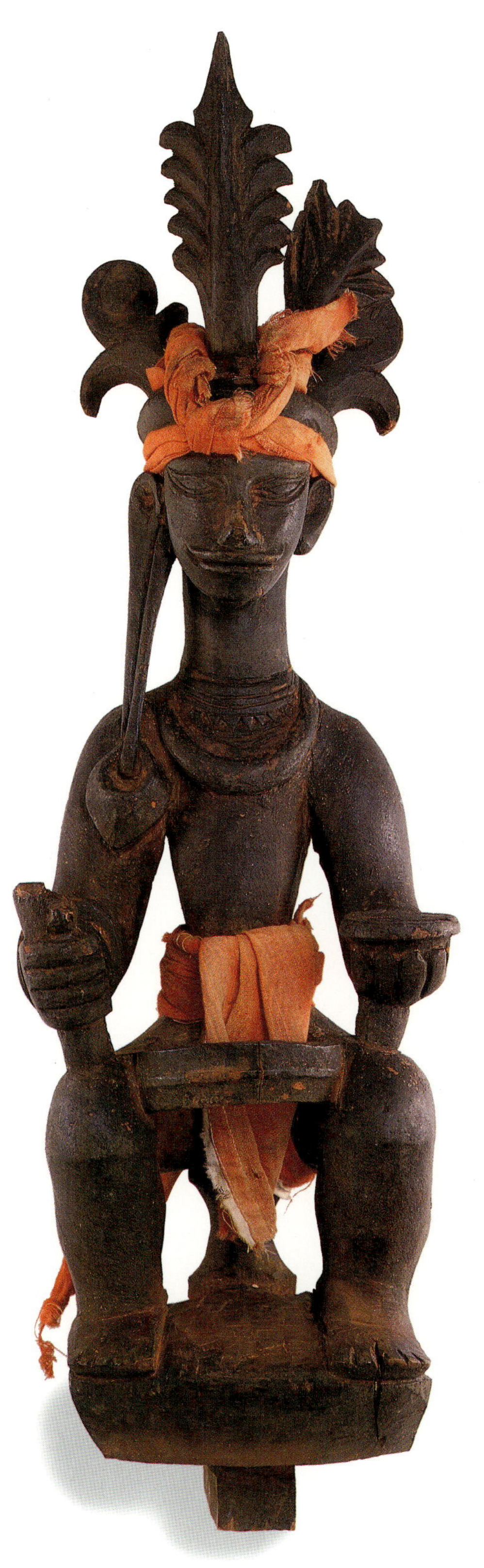

Fig. II.19 ANCESTOR FIGURE, *ADU*
South Nias
Wood, 47.1 x 14.1 x 11.2
Bernisches Historisches Museum, Switzerland, Ni 95. Collected by Caesar Feller, who traveled in Nias between 1915 and 1925.

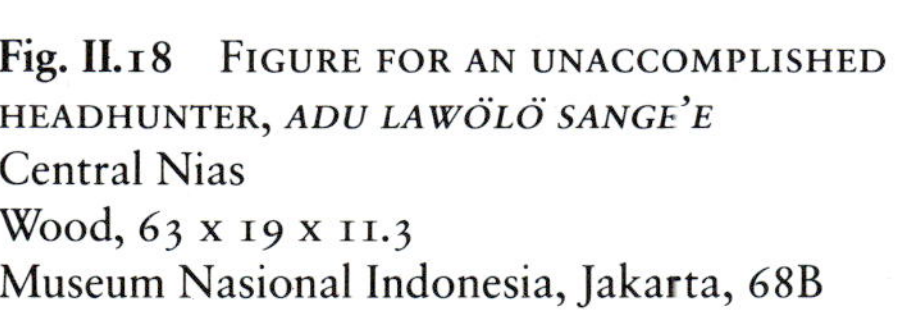

Fig. II.18 FIGURE FOR AN UNACCOMPLISHED HEADHUNTER, *ADU LAWÖLÖ SANGE'E*
Central Nias
Wood, 63 x 19 x 11.3
Museum Nasional Indonesia, Jakarta, 68B

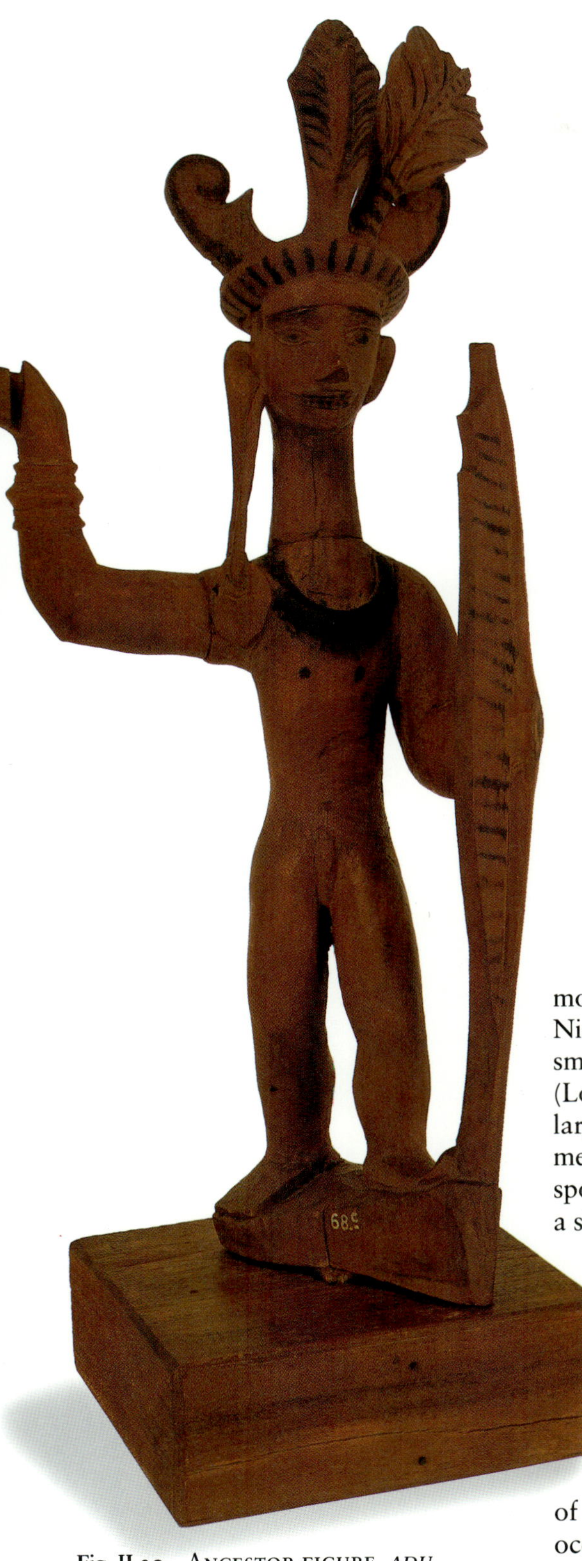

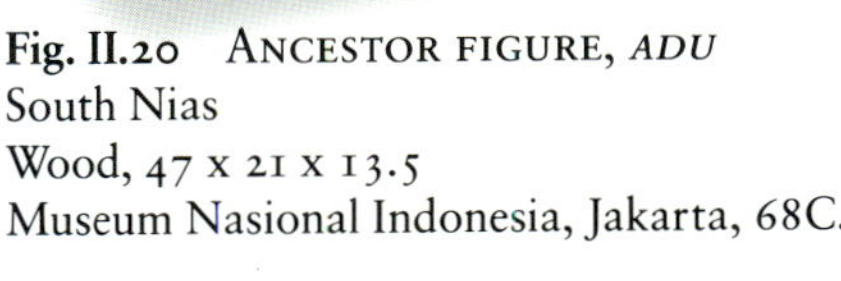

Fig. II.20 Ancestor figure, *adu*
South Nias
Wood, 47 x 21 x 13.5
Museum Nasional Indonesia, Jakarta, 68C.

TOP RIGHT

Fig. II.21 Interior wood carving, *laso so hagu*, Hilinawalö village in the Mozinö region, south Nias, 1982. Y. Miko Yamamoto

BOTTOM RIGHT

Fig. II.22 A public bath (*hele*) at Hilimaenamolo village, south Nias, 1988. Y. Miko Yamamoto

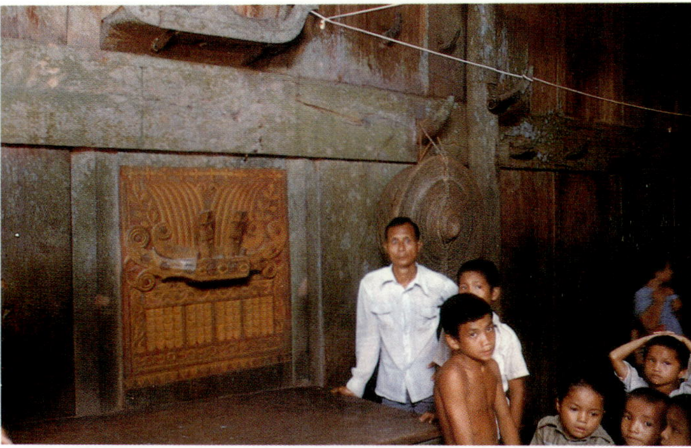

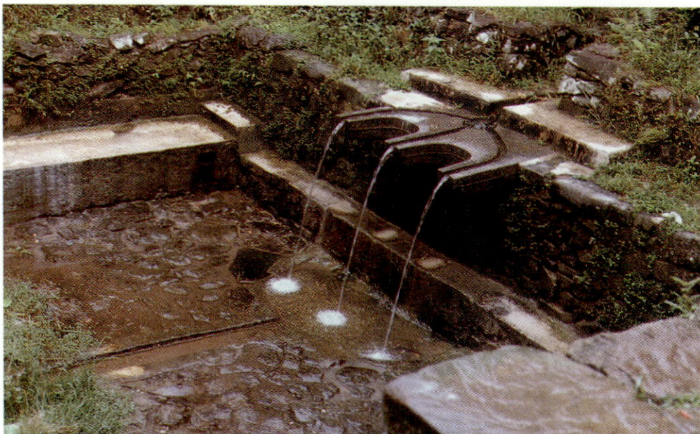

modest headgear that indicates its sponsor was not among the high nobility. In Nias, even commoners, if they were prosperous, were expected to sponsor a small series of community feasts in order to fufill their status as adult citizens (Loeb 1972[1935]:143). Nias commoners, however, were not entitled to wear large, heavy, gold ornaments or to commission commemorative stone monuments. Smaller gold ornaments, however, were permitted to commoners who sponsored the appropriate feasts. This figure's outstretched arms originally held a shield or a sword, emphasizing his role as warrior.

Adu might also be quickly carved in a rough fashion for certain religious rites. The two limbless figures (Fig. II.31) probably represent an ancestral couple of the owner. Their bodies are simple wooden shafts with some protrusions at the shoulders. Eyes, nose, mouth, and chin are barely indicated. Both figures have a small top projection, indicating a headdress. The taller, presumably male, figure has a piece of imported red cloth attached to this post, possibly a remnant of a larger headdress.

Some images represented guardians not only of particular households but of entire villages as well. An image called *be'elo banua*, "village offering," was occasionally set at various locations in the village as protection. The sites of such images became meeting houses, *bale* or *osali*, and were considered a place where founding ancestors could be contacted (Feldman 1979:137).

The stone-paved villages and complex housing construction (Fig. II.23) of precolonial south Nias demonstrate both a genius for architecture and incipient urbanization. Village baths with running water (Fig. II.22) and separate private baths for noble women were sometimes constructed (Suzuki 1958:4; 1959:34–35). The interiors of chief's houses were adorned extensively with carved and polished panels of hardwood, *hagu laso* or *laso so hagu* (Fig. II.21). Figures of plants, animals, and family heirlooms still ornament the most elaborate houses, recording the possessions of past occupants. The depiction of an early Dutch steamship in the chief's house at Bawömataluo shows the Nias

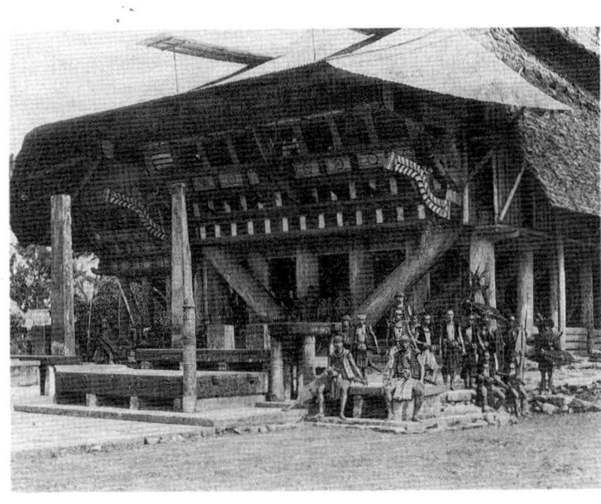

Fig. II.23 House at Bawömataluo village, south Nias, before 1920. van Eerde 1920:227. Courtesy Elsevier Press, Amsterdam.

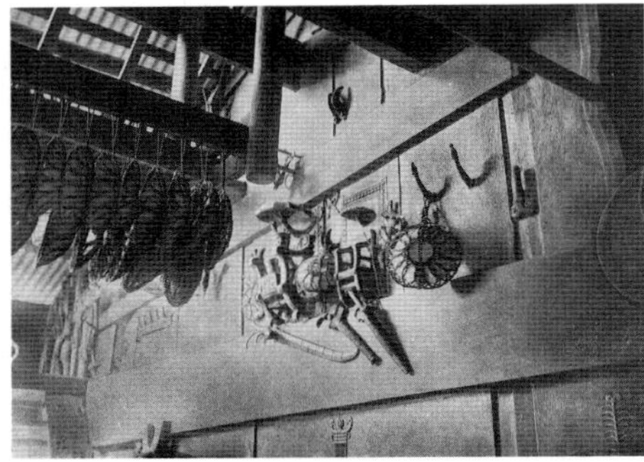

Fig. II.24 Ancestor figure (Fig. II.26) in its original altar at the chief's house in Bawömataluo village, south Nias, before 1917. Schröder 1917:fig. 228

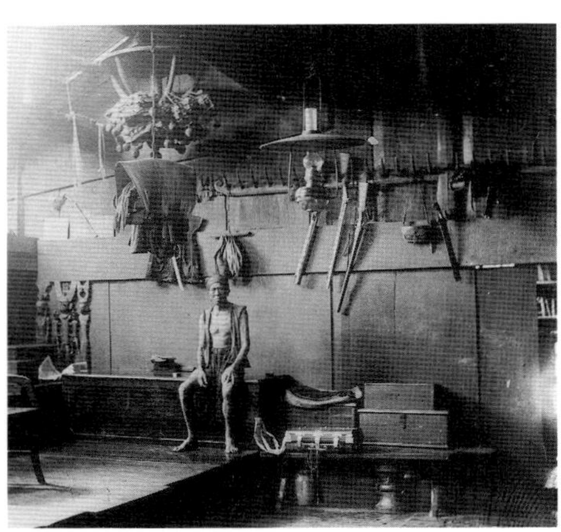

Fig. II.25 Chief Saonigeho in his house at Bawömataluo village, south Nias, before 1917. Courtesy Rijksmuseum voor Volkenkunde, Leiden.

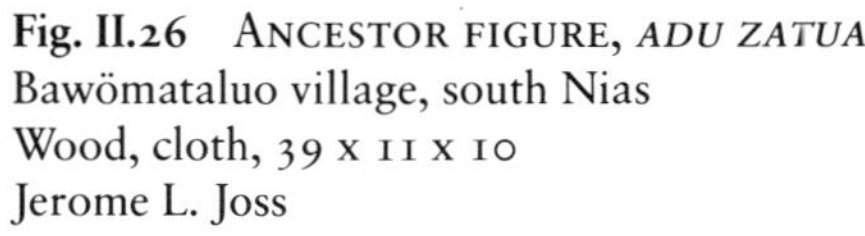

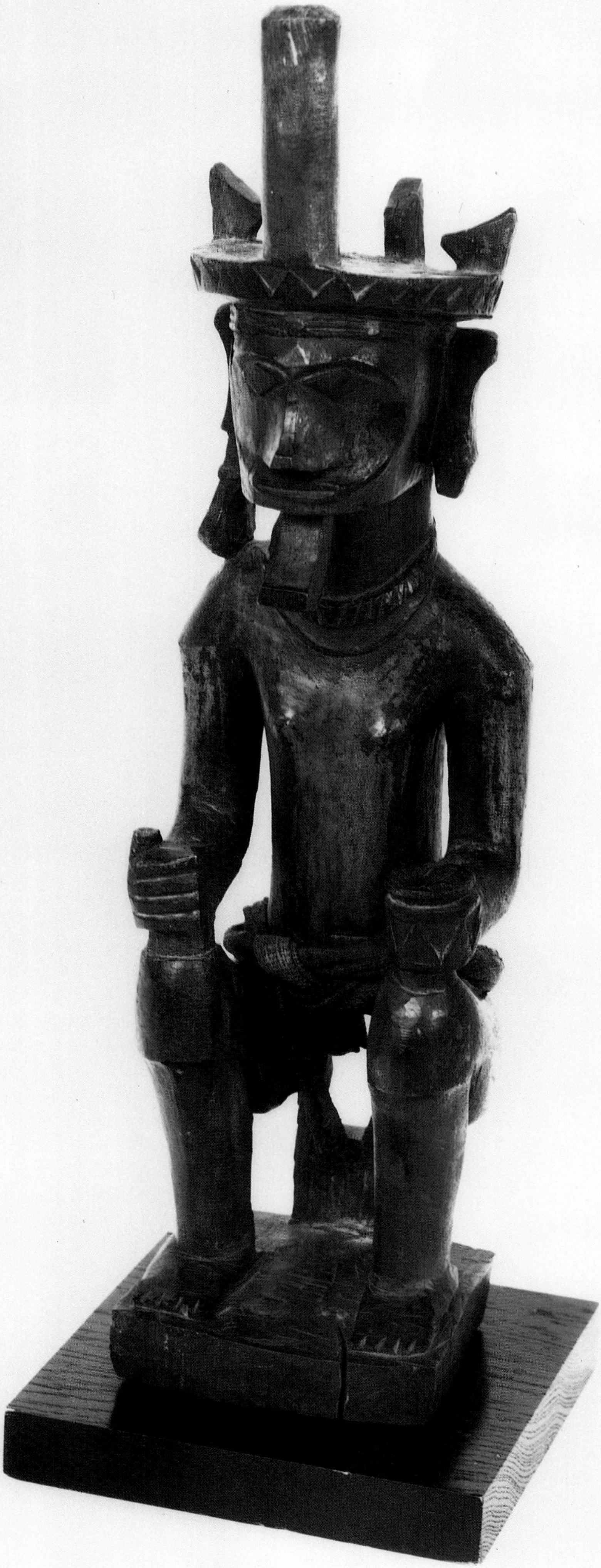

Fig. II.26 ANCESTOR FIGURE, *ADU ZATUA*
Bawömataluo village, south Nias
Wood, cloth, 39 x 11 x 10
Jerome L. Joss

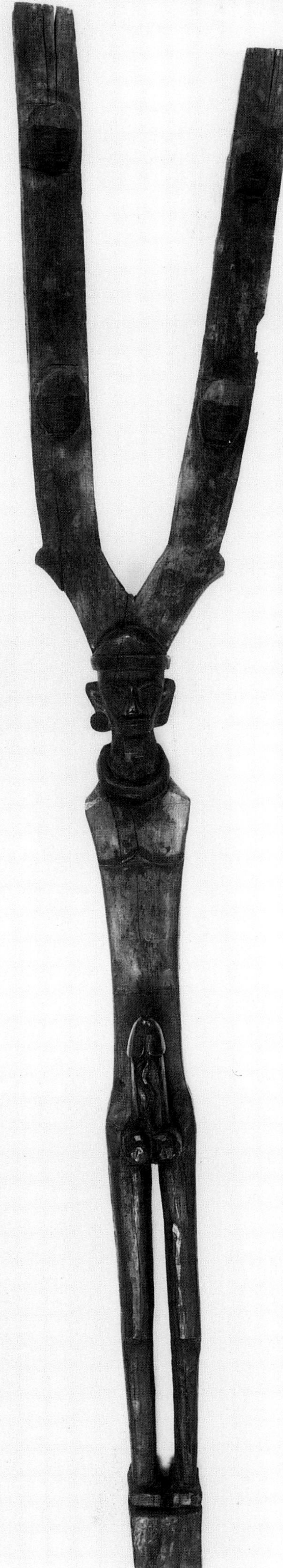

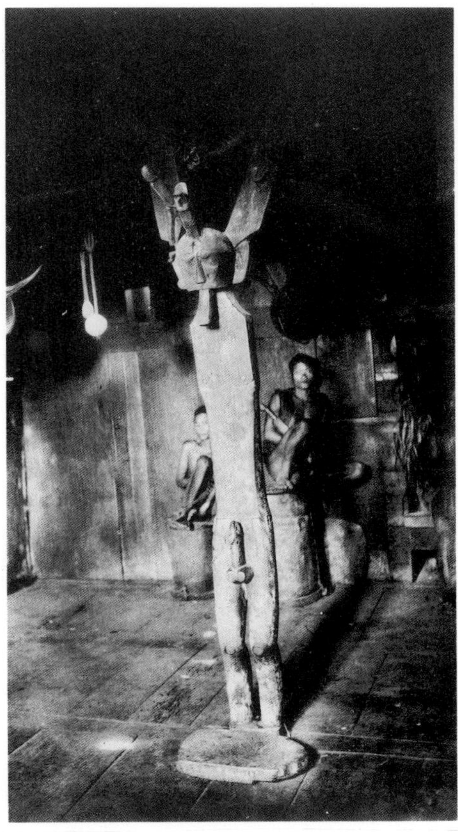

Fig. II.28 An *adu so bawa zihönö* figure in a Nias house, Bawodobara village, south Nias. Schröder 1917:fig. 10

Fig. II.27 ANCESTOR FIGURE, *ADU SO BAWA ZIHÖNÖ*
South Nias
Wood, 202 x 36.8 x 19
Museum Nasional Indonesia, Jakarta, 23695.
Purchased from J. Kunst.

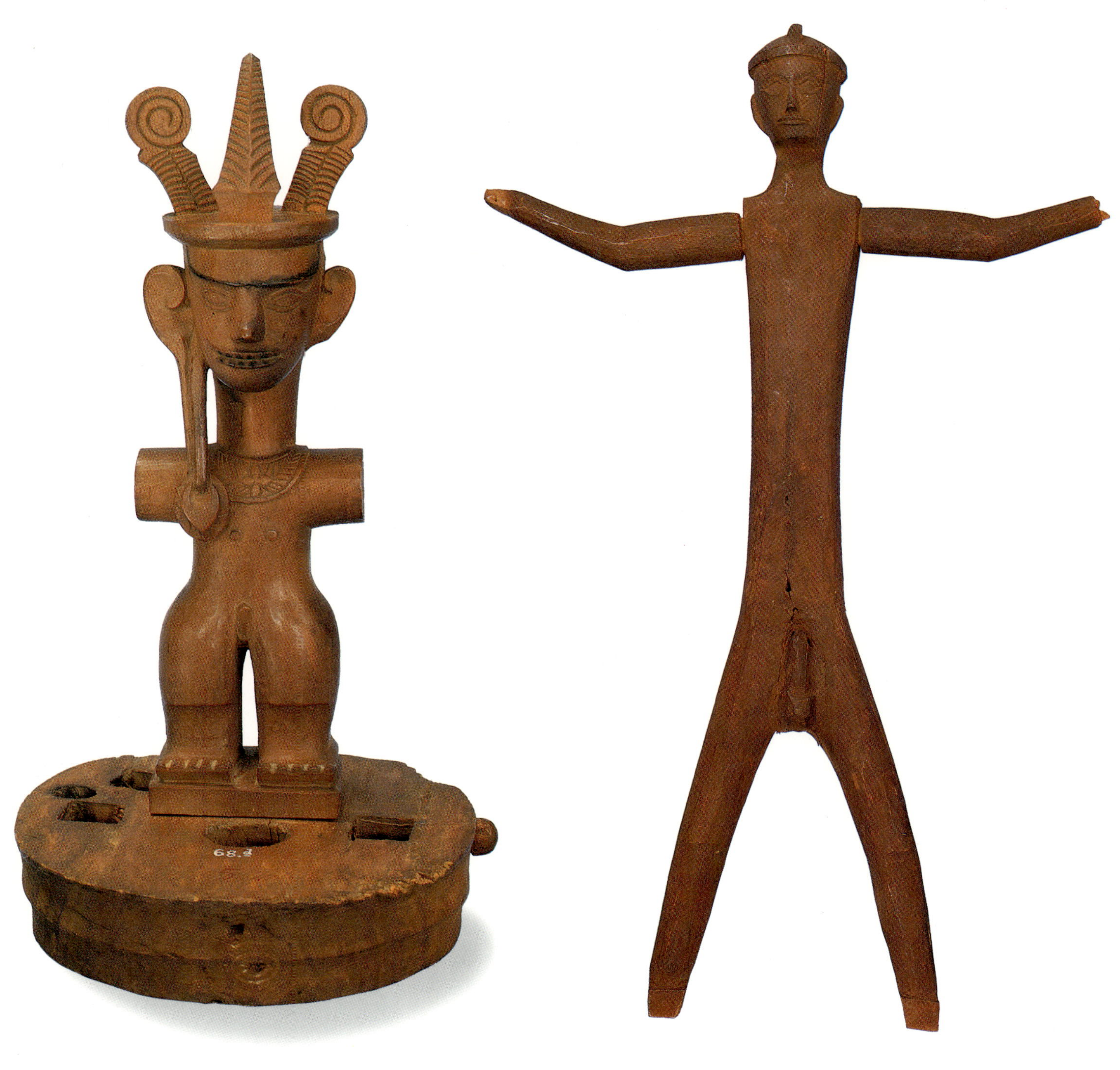

Fig. II.29 Ancestor figure of mother's brother, *adu nuwu* or *hazi nuwu*
South Nias or Batu Islands
Wood, 25 x 2 x 2
Museum Nasional Indonesia, Jakarta, 68A.

Fig. II.30 Ancestor figure, *adu*
South Nias
Wood, 56 x 36 x 7
Museum Nasional Indonesia, Jakarta, 21419.
Purchased from estate of Dr. Bonnet in 1933.

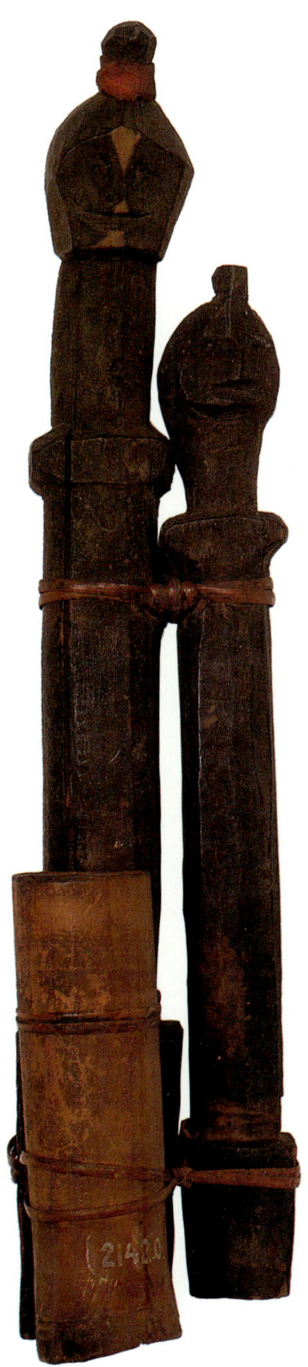

Fig. II.31 DOUBLE ANCESTOR FIGURE CONTAINER, *ADU*
South Nias or Batu Islands
Wood, bamboo, 29 x 6.3 x 6.2
Museum Nasional Indonesia, Jakarta, 21420.
Purchased from estate of Dr. Bonnet in 1933.

affinity for recording historical events through artwork. Although writing was not practiced in Nias, people nevertheless wanted to record historical events, and so they used images. This tendency developed in Nias during the colonial era (Feldman 1979:143,172; Yamamoto 1986:310–11). To this day, artwork inside the household, including family portraits, serve to convey Nias history and culture to members of the younger generation (Yamamoto 1986:313).

In the traditions of south Nias, a chief's house symbolically represented an ancestral village leader dressed in full regalia (Feldman 1979; 1985b:47, 64; 1989). The house pillars are the legs, the façade the face, and the tall roof the chief's crown. Moreover, *adu* ancestor figures were integrated into the architectural design of the chief's house, with various figures set in carved altars at prescribed locations. The position and meaning of most of the sculptures in the chief's house in Bawömataluo village have been extensively documented (Schröder 1917; Feldman 1977, 1979, 1985b). Even photographs of Saonigeho himself (Fig. II.25) indicate the arrangement of his rooms and the position of *adu* figures and other types of altars and offerings. The ancestor figure (Fig. II.26), carved for the ancestor altar of the chief's house in Bawömataluo (Fig. II.24), includes clothing depicted by carving, which would have been supplemented by the addition of cloth. The crown of the figure includes a vertical post that, according to evidence from early photographs, was probably wrapped with sacred cloth. The photographs also show that the *adu* was set into an altar sheltered by a carved umbrella, an ancient Southeast Asian sign of royalty. The figure set in the male altar represents Laowo, chief Saonigeho's father and the founder of the village of Bawömataluo (Schröder 1917:117). To the left of his altar was a second smaller altar for his female counterpart (Feldman 1985b:68).

Objects of Status and Authority

The Nias aristocracy proclaimed their authority by inheriting or commissioning the production of particular items of gold jewelry, headdresses, weapons, and other regalia. These items, as well as nobles' houses, ornaments, and clothing, all symbolized the noble's high status (Feldman 1989). Moreover, these valuables acted as a link between the nobles and the prosperous ancestors who founded the community. Elder men and ancestor figures occupied seats and raised platforms in south Nias nobles' houses, corresponding to their elevated status. Carved reliefs depicting heirloom jewelry symbolized the feast of merit necessary to obtain the right to own that jewelry and such an elaborately carved house (Feldman 1977).

Although blacksmithing is not the sole privilege of a particular family or group of families, most blacksmiths in south Nias are nobles or prominent commoners (Yamamoto 1986:141). Traditional weapons, such as bush knives and ceremonial swords (*tolögu*), are crafted by specialists. Some blacksmiths only forge the blades, but others also carve the wooden sword handles and sheaths. The iron and steel for Nias knife blades has always been imported, but today automotive springs are a common source of iron in many areas of Indonesia.

South Nias sword scabbards owned by leaders and warriors were traditionally guarded with amulet rattan balls, *ragö*, (Fig. II.37) which were decorated with a cluster of miniature *adu* ancestor figures or a collection of talismans, including animal and human teeth and stones. Tiger teeth were distinctive symbols of chiefly status and were specifically imported from Sumatra, as tigers are not native to Nias, for attaching to nobles' swords as protective charms. The creation of a charm ball was always an individual creative endeavor so that the talisman's power remained secret from all others. Men would seek their own personal charm objects, often receiving advice about their choice in dreams (Yamamoto 1986:147,155). Because nobles were considered mediators between the upper and lower worlds, some charm balls owned by nobles included figurines of hornbill birds, which possibly represent the upper world, and crocodiles, which represent the lower world (Suzuki 1959:31–32).

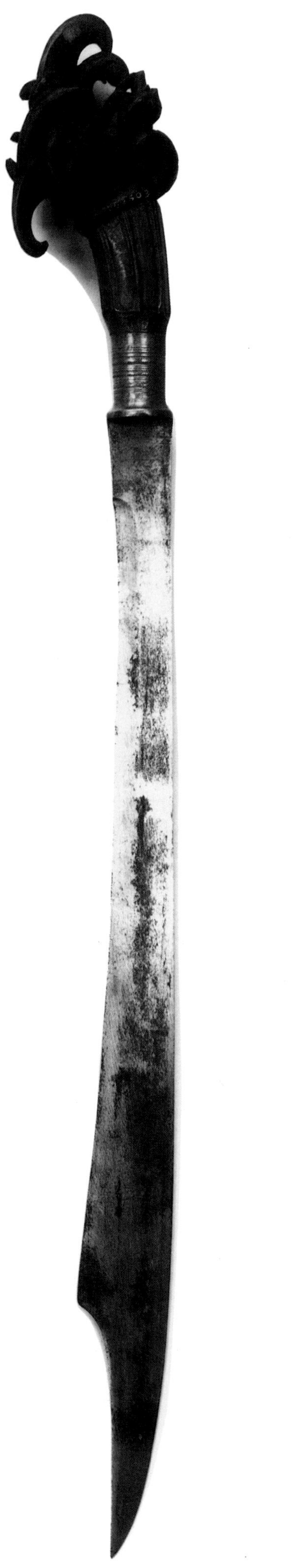

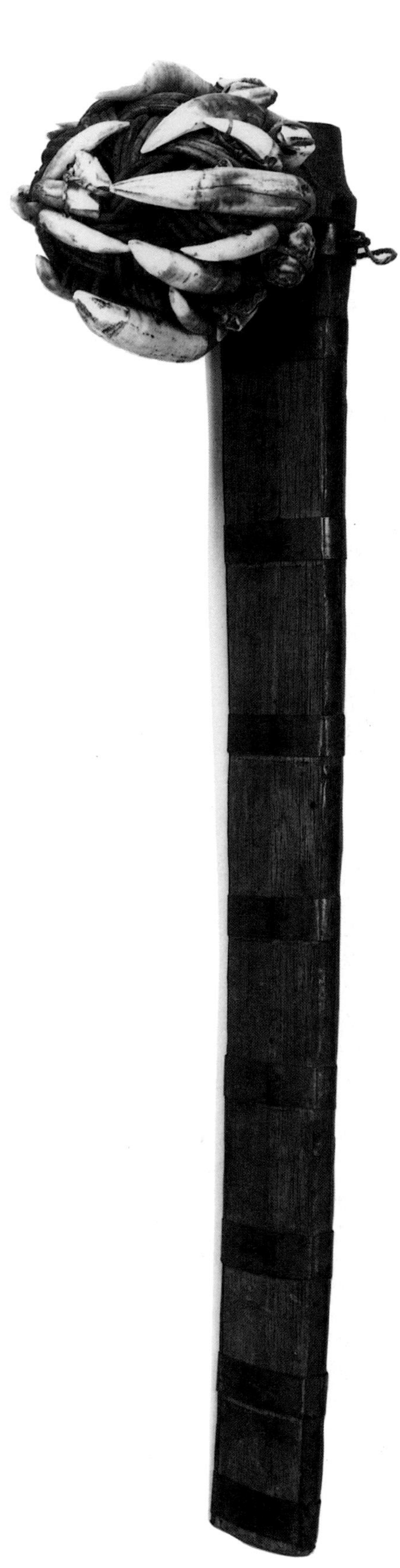

Fig. II.32 Noble's ceremonial sword and charm ball, *balatu tolögu* and *ragö*
Nias
Wood, iron, rattan, teeth, copper alloy,
67 x 10.2 x 14.2
Field Museum of Natural History, Chicago,
162503

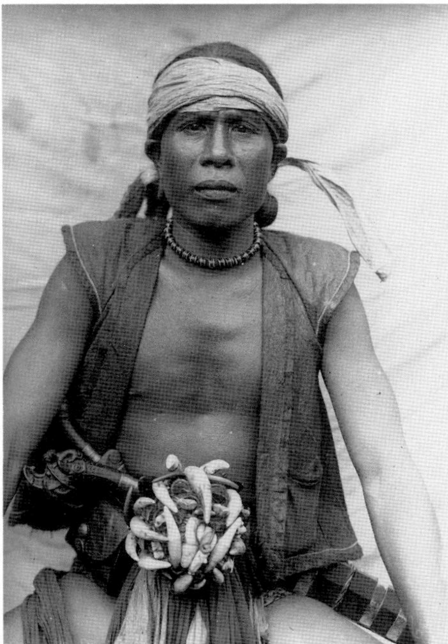

Fig. II.33 A chief of Orahili village, south Nias, wearing barkcloth jacket and sword with charm ball, 1902–1905. W. L. Abbott Collection, Anthropology Archives, Smithsonian Institution.

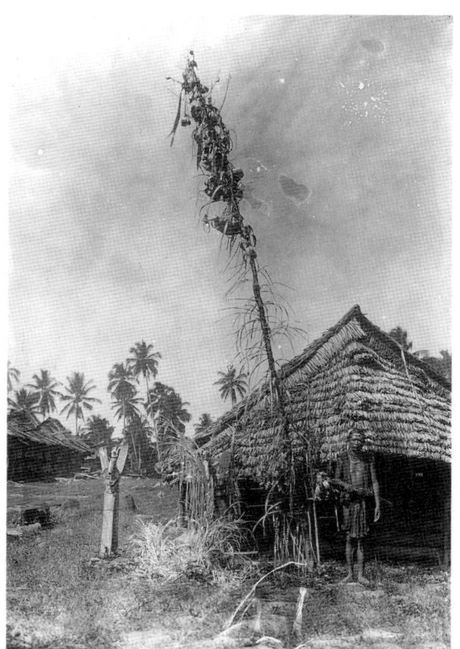

Fig. II.34 A man beside a house with a ceremonial pole and a village offering (*be'elo banua*), south Nias, 1902–1905. W. L. Abbott Collection, Anthropology Archives, Smithsonian Institution.

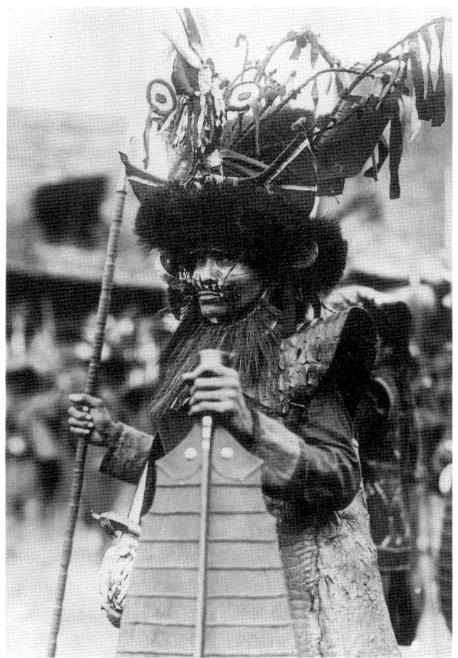

Fig. II.35 Nias warrior in full armor including metal moustache, before 1917. Courtesy Royal Tropical Institute, Tropenmuseum, The Netherlands.

Sword hilts, coffins, and house beams of noble families in south Nias and stone monuments of noble families in central Nias were characteristically decorated with a mythical protective creature called *lasara*. The *lasara* figure, sometimes said to have tiger teeth, a crocodile neck, a hornbill casque, and deer antlers, can be seen clearly on the sword hilt (Fig. II.36). The inlaid metal stripes on the scabbard represent tigers, traditional symbols of Nias village chiefs. Images of tigers, which represented the strength and intelligence of the south Nias chief, were formerly thrown ceremonially into the Gomo River as ransom to guarantee the future prosperity of the community (Feldman 1983; Hämmerle 1986). Occasionally monkey figures (seen on Fig. II.36) were carved on the forehead of the *lasara* figure. Monkeys were believed to be able to predict and warn the sword's owner of impending danger (Yamamoto 1986:152).

Swords decorated with a *lasara* figure on the hilt, *balatu nio lasara*, were formerly signs of great wealth because they could only be owned by a village chief who had taken a human head (Fig. II.33). Because swords confirm the owner's status as an adult male member of the community, to this day, the *lasara* handle is not carved for commoners—although swords with such handles may be sold to foreigners as souvenirs (Yamamoto 1986:153–43).

Like the ornamentation of sculptures, houses, and swords, colors on Nias ceremonial clothing and ornaments have specific symbolic meanings, according to early reports (Feldman 1989:205). Yellow, which indicated wealth in gold, was reserved for the highest-ranking members of society. Red signified thorough knowledge of *hada*, traditional law and custom. Blue represented victory or success, and white denoted peace and purity. Black, evincing anger and fierceness, was the warrior's color.

Nias warriors dressed almost completely in black (Fig. II.35) as a symbol of their anger and fierceness in battle. Armor jackets, formerly made of crocodile skin and later of sheet metal, were hung in the house rafters so that smoke from the hearth fire would blacken them (Feldman 1989:211). The armor jacket (Fig. II.37) is made of iron with intricately cut floral-shaped projections inlaid with mirrors. Each projection is topped with an image of a rooster. The matching helmet has both floral and deer-antler–shaped projections. Only Nias noblemen who had sponsored a long series of feasts were permitted to use motifs derived from nature (Feldman 1989:206). Floral and faunal designs undoubtedly represented the power and generative capacity of nature. The ridged segments of the carved wooden shield (Fig. II.37) may represent a crocodile (Suzuki 1959:27), an animal associated with the lower world and ancestral punishments in many areas of Indonesia.

Swords, shields, and spears were not only crucial to battle but were also an integral part of men's ceremonial attire (Feldman 1989:207). Spears with leaf-shaped blades were used only for headhunting warfare, whereas those with hooks at the neck of the blade (Fig. II.37) were used for hunting wild animals (personal communication, Yamamoto 1990). Warriors, and all men at ceremonial occasions, wore a black necklace, *kalabubu* (men wear *kalabubu* in Fig. II.6), made of polished disks of coconut shell and brass. These necklaces represented bravery in warfare, traditionally the successful capture of an enemy head (Feldman 1989:207). Metal moustaches were added to the warrior's attire for fierceness. At times, a fiber mask was worn to give the warrior the appearance of an evil spirit, *bekhu*, so that he would appear even more terrifying to the enemy (Schröder 1917).

In some areas of south Nias, youths were trained to jump over fortified walls in preparation for battle. Stone pedestals, *hombo batu* (Fig. II.38), were constructed in the village center for athletic practice. When a practicing youth could not clear the stone, a member of the commoners' village council of elders, *si'ila*, ritually purified the stone through the action of placing his foot on the stone. These jumping stones are still in place today, and young men continue to use them to demonstrate their athletic prowess, sometimes in performances held for foreign guests.

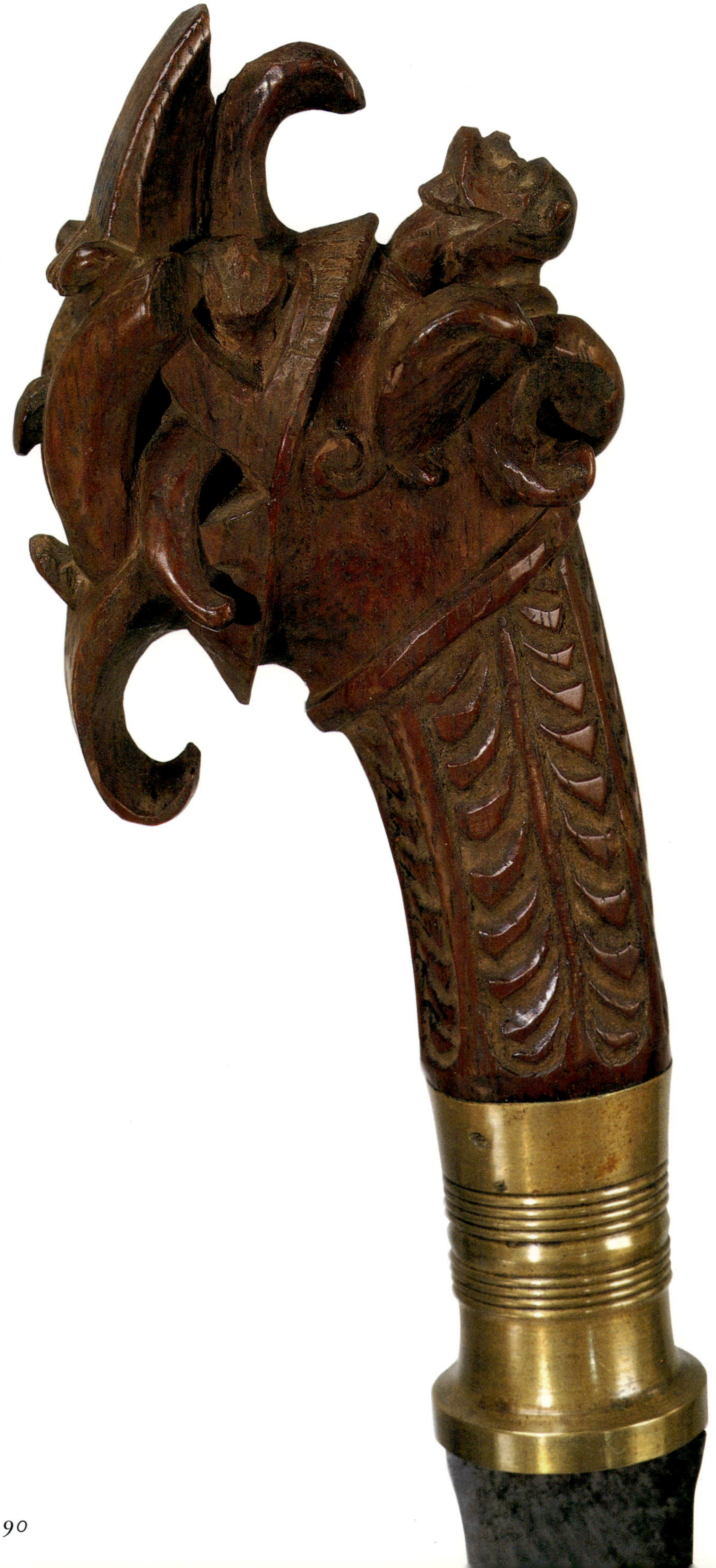

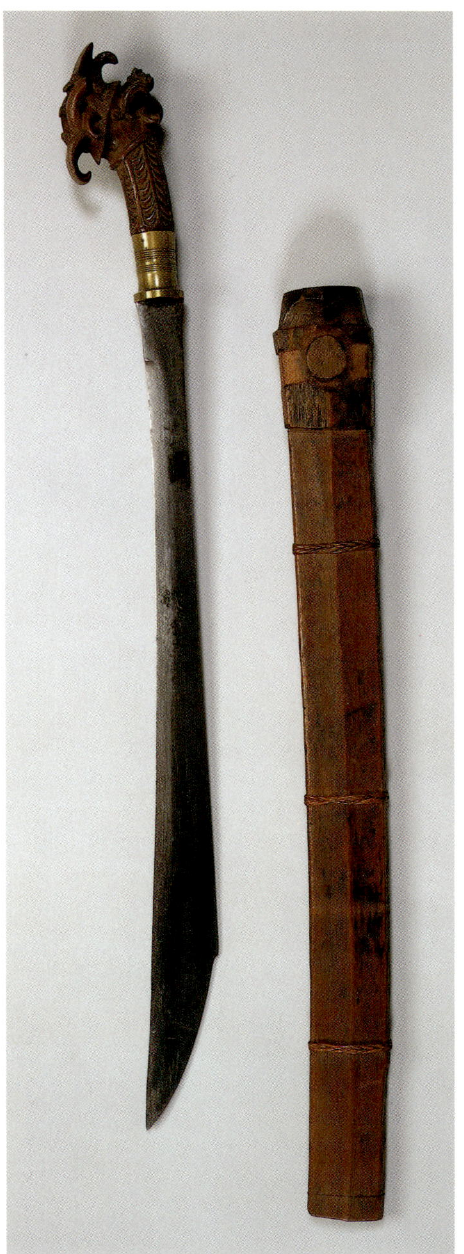

Fig. II.36 Noble's sword, *balatu tologü*
Nias
Wood, iron, brass, 71 x 6 x 6.8
Department of Anthropology, Smithsonian Institution, 237024. Collected by W. L. Abbott, circa 1905.

Opposite
Fig. II.37 Jacket (*öröba*), iron helmet (*takula tefao*), metal moustache (*bumbewe tefao*), sword (*balatu tologü*), rattan ball with amulet (*ragö*), shield (*baluse*), spear (*toho*)
South Nias
Metal jacket: 69.8 x 58 x 59.8; helmet: 43.9 x 38 x 30.5; moustache: 12.7 x 21 x 8.3; sword: 67 x 10.2 x 14.2; shield: 135.4 x 29.5 x 15.4; spear: 200.5; charmball, 10
Field Museum of Natural History, Chicago, 162484.3, 162484.1, 162484.2, 162503, 162487, Museum Nasional Indonesia, Jakarta.

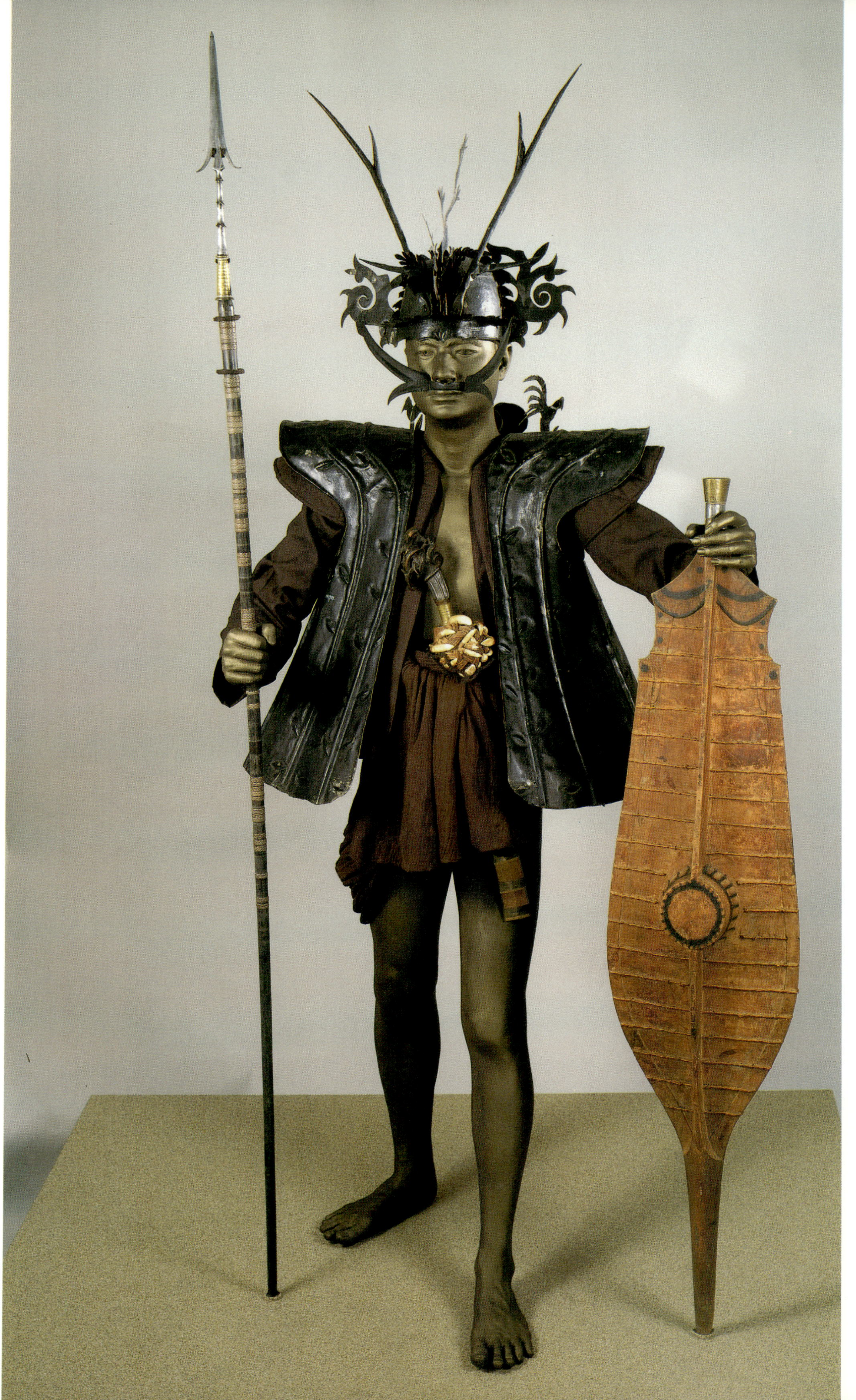

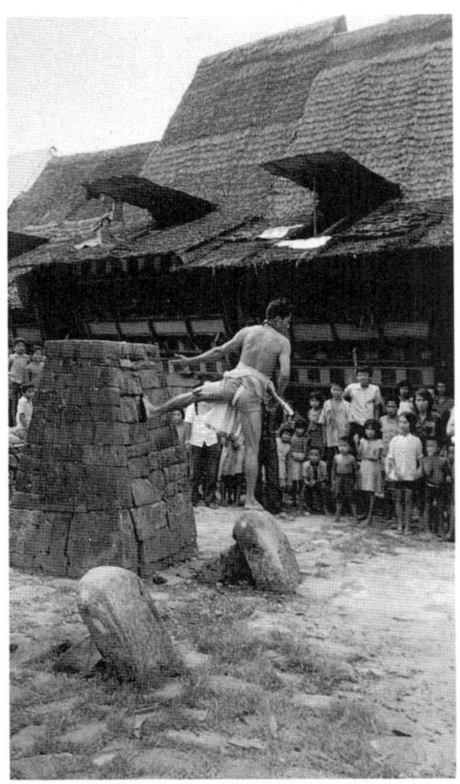

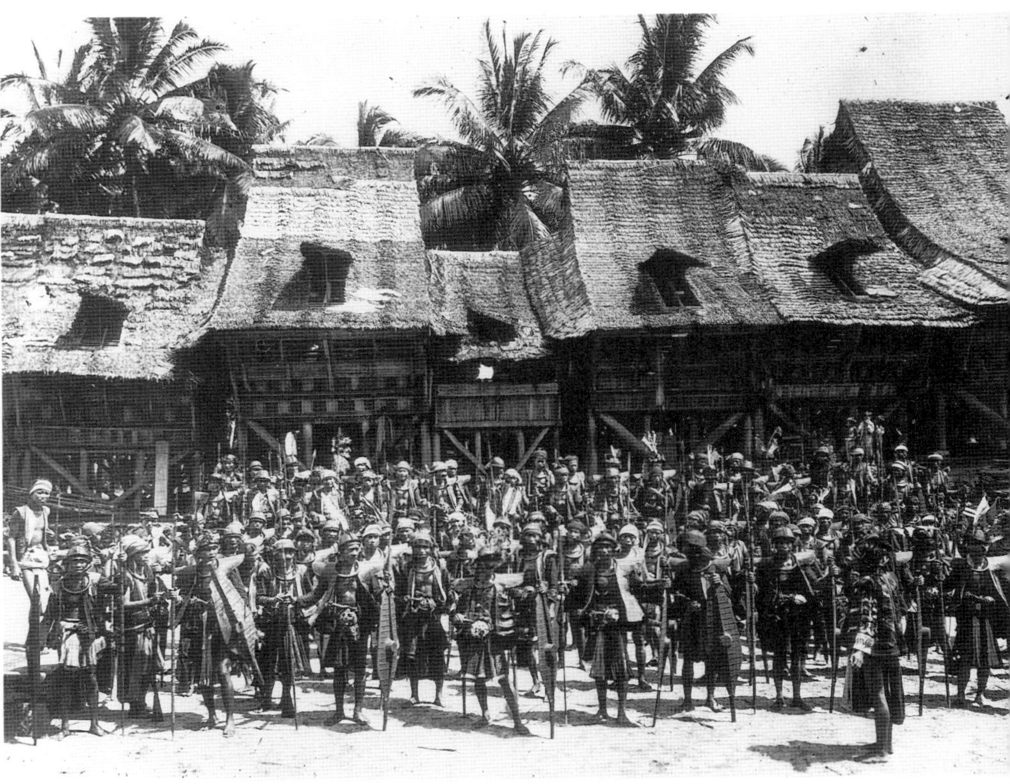

Fig. II.38 A jumping stone at Hilisimaetanö, south Nias, 1981. Y. Miko Yamamoto

Fig. II.39 A group of warriors in the square at Hiliamaetanika village, south Nias, about 1925. Courtesy Rijksmuseum voor Volkenkunde, Leiden.

In many parts of Indonesia today, respected guests are ceremonially greeted at the entrance of the village by an armed warrior who then escorts the guests to meet the headman (Fig. II.39). This practice apparently survives from a time of internecine warfare when a visitor could as easily prove to be an enemy as an ally. Warrior dances, respectively called *fatele* and *faluaya* in south and central Nias, were traditionally performed at weddings, funerals, harvest rites, feasts of merit, and for important guests (Holt 1971:8). Dances held during life-cycle events in which the dancers wore warrior costumes (Fig. II.40) were not only spectacular performance but were also intended to drive away malevolent spirits. Even now, warrior costumes are worn by male dancers at major ceremonies. Like the performances at the jumping stone, these dances are rarely seen in Nias today, except for visiting tourists who pay a large fee to the performers and village head (personal communication, Yamamoto 1990).

Women's traditional attire, which varies throughout north, central, and south Nias, tends toward symmetry, whereas men's attire tends towards asymmetry (Feldman 1989:201). On ceremonial occasions, south Nias women of high rank wore girdles of beads (Fig. II.43) or metal wire over long skirts (Figs. II.41, II.42). Yellow beads signified nobility and red beads indicated knowledge of traditional law and custom (*hada*). Certain south Nias noble women served as priestesses, *ere*, and, along with their male counterparts (also called *ere*), were able to contact the spirit who acted as intermediary between the realm of humans and the gods of the upper world. This role for women in religion has ended since the Christian and Islamic conversions and is little remembered today (Feldman 1979:130).

During graceful traditional dances (respectively called *fogaele* and *fanali moyo'* in south and central Nias) women carried adorned purses (*bola nafo*) from which they silently offered betel nut to their guests (Feldman 1989:209). Betel nut is traditionally chewed with betel palm leaves and lime as a mild stimulant at social occasions in Southeast Asia and the Pacific. On a daily basis, both

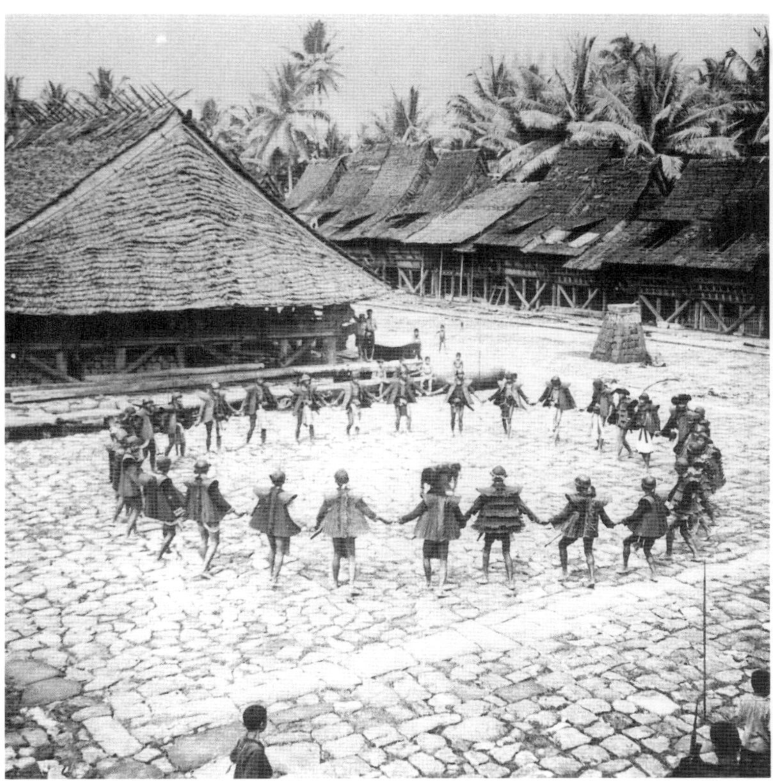

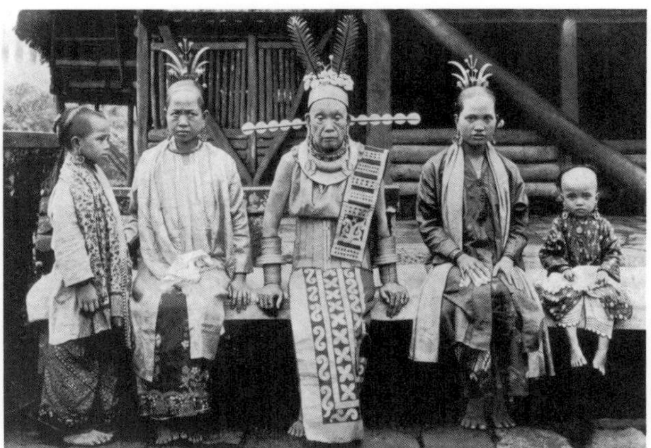

Fig. II.41 Women in ceremonial dress, Hilisimaetanö village, south Nias, before 1920. van Eerde 1920:237. Courtesy Elsevier Press, Amsterdam.

Fig. II.40 Nias warriors perform dance (*faluaya*) in village center, central Nias, 1935. W. Blanke

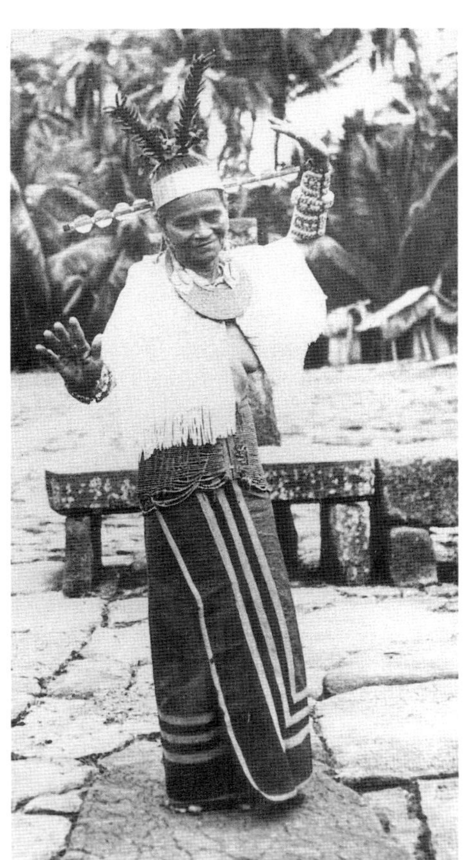

Fig. II.42 A woman dances wearing a type of *awi* girdle, Lahusa village, south Nias, 1935. W. Blanke

men and women carry betel-nut pouches, usually plaited from pandanus leaves. The craftsmanship of these betel-nut pouches is a source of pride. A would-be bridegroom must obtain a plaited *bola nafo* for his bride's family, who then uses it to offer guests betel-nut ingredients on his behalf during his marriage ceremonies (Yamamoto 1986:182). The beaded betel-nut pouch (Fig. II.44), known in south Nias as *tewaero sasa*, is a special ornamental type with a long carrying strap, and it was worn by women for dances at weddings (Modigliani 1890).

Design patterns on the costumes of the aristocracy usually symbolize prosperity and wealth (Feldman 1989:211). For example, the yellow design (on Fig. II.44) represents the golden comb, *sukhu ana'a*, worn by a south Nias woman as part of her full ceremonial attire. *Sukhu ana'a* and other such large pieces of gold jewelry could only be manufactured in conjunction with a series of feasts when a new rank was granted to a wealthy noble. In south Nias, a nobleman was required to produce jewelry items and stone monuments in a particular order. His wife's jewelry had to be commissioned before his own as a token of respect to his mother's brother whose daughter he married in the traditional alliance system (Schnitger 1939:146–49; personal communication, Yamamoto 1990).

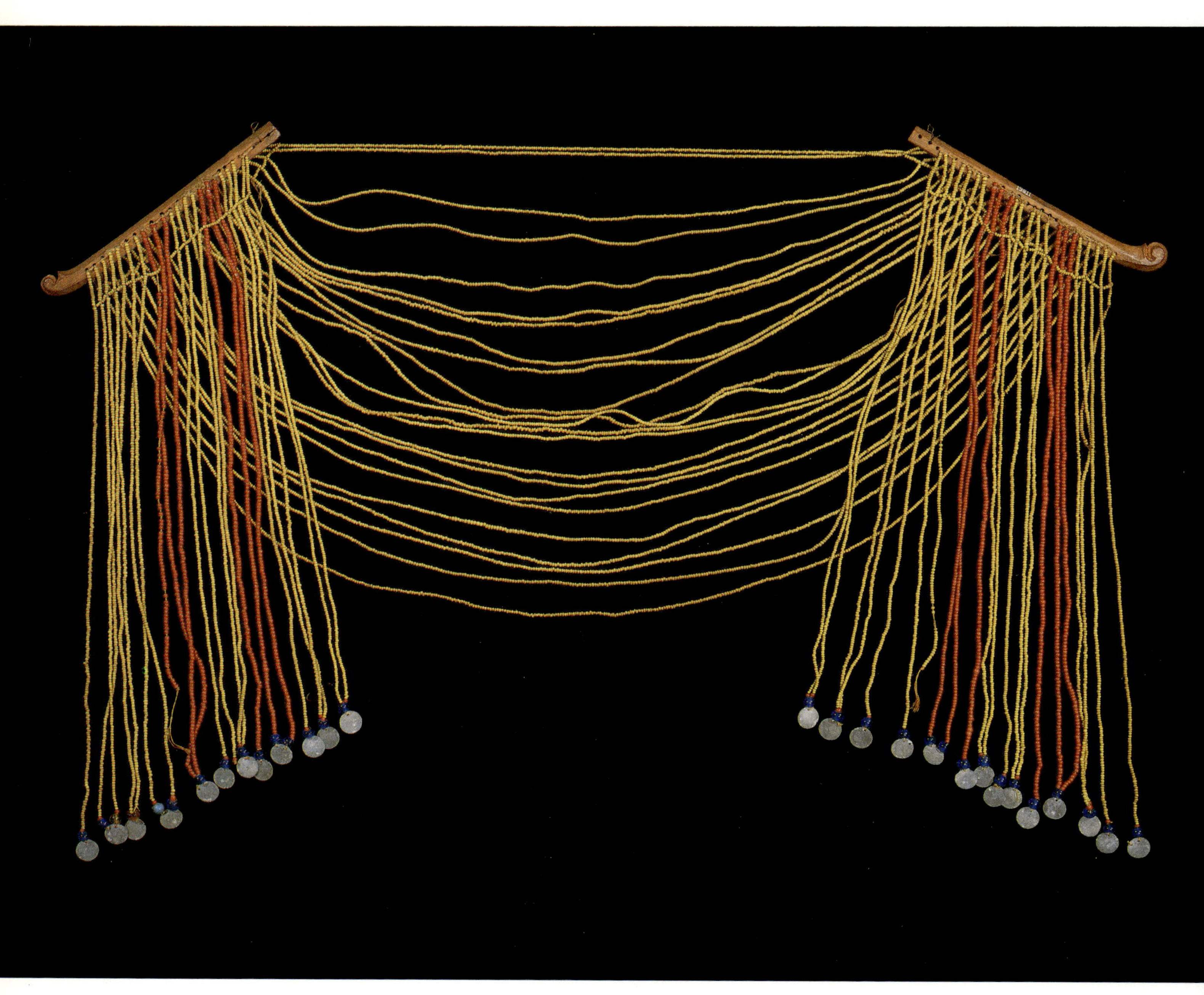

Fig. II.43 Woman's girdle, *AWI*
South Nias
Beads, wood, thread, metal disks, 50 x 42 x 2
Museum Nasional Indonesia, Jakarta, 19811.
Purchased from Dr. Bonnet in 1932.

Fig. II.44 Betel-nut pouch, *BOLA NAFO*
South Nias
Flannel, rush, glass beads, copper alloy, 28 x 22 x 5.5
Rijksmuseum voor Volkenkunde, Leiden, 115/3. Donated by C. de Grijs in 1870.

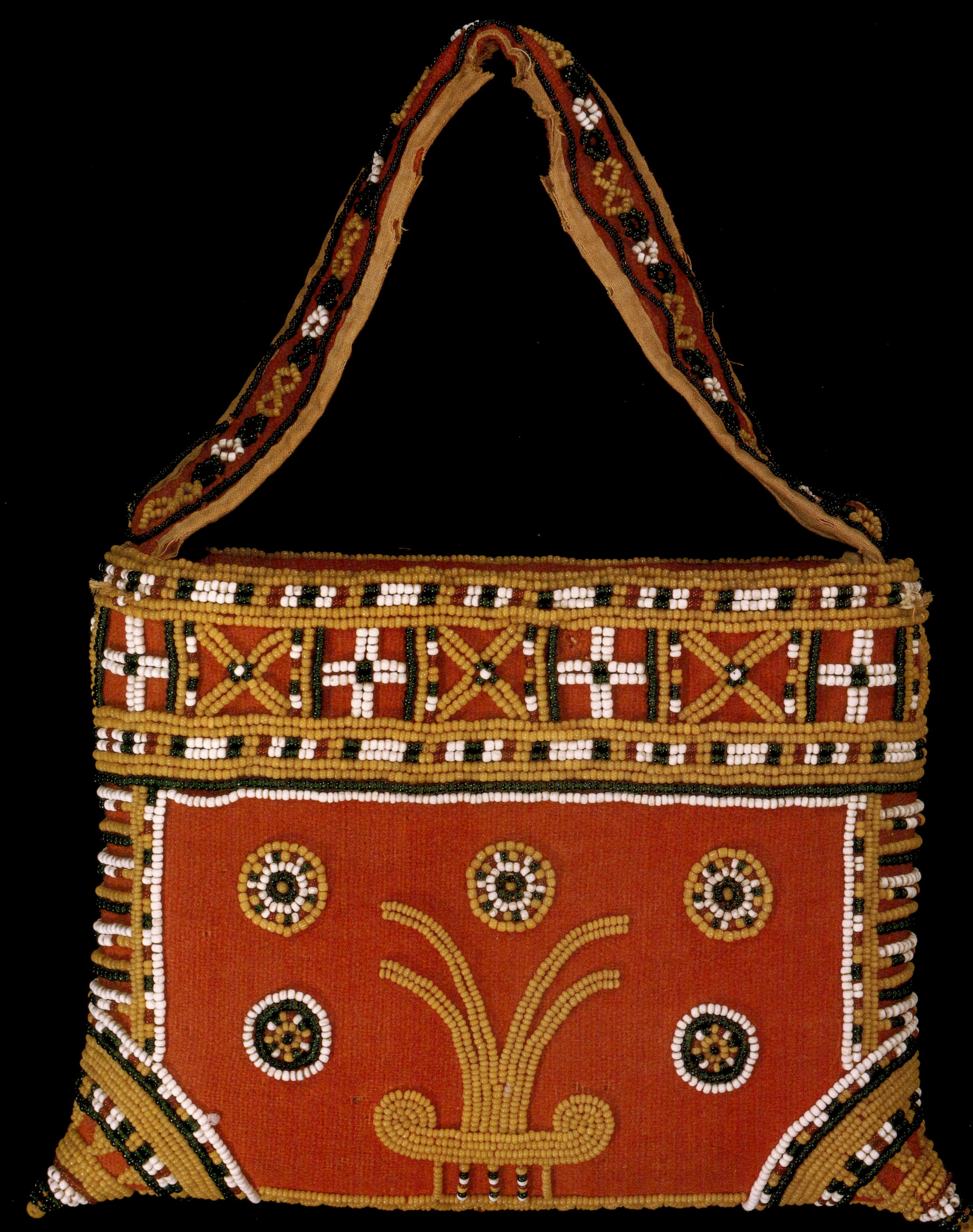

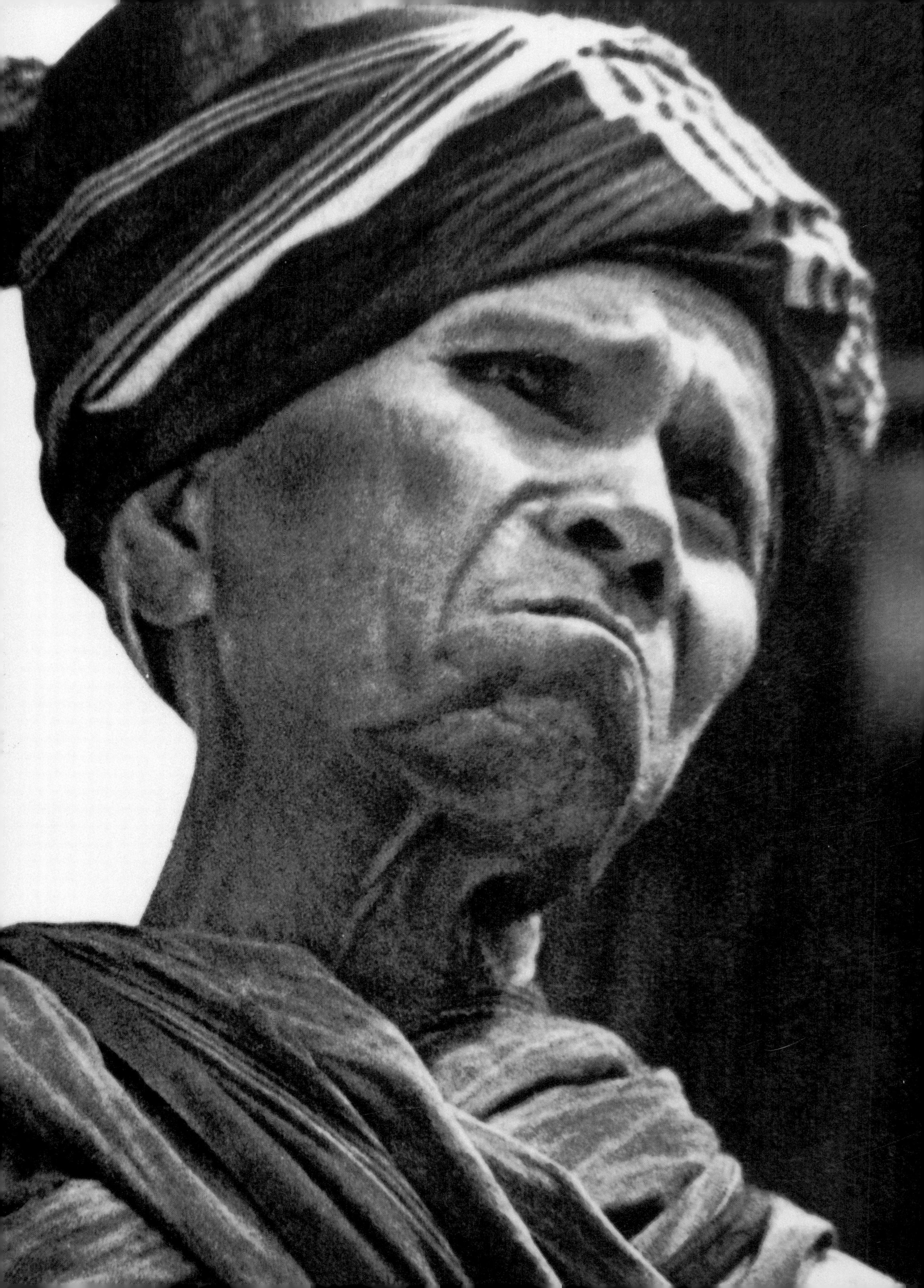

III

Batak

The Batak peoples of North Sumatra, who live in the highland regions around Lake Toba, are classified into six ethnic subgroups: Toba, Karo, Pakpak, Angkola, Mandailing, and Simalungun (Cunningham 1958:3; Rodgers 1985:93). As in many areas of outer-island Indonesia, however, Batak ethnic identity beyond the village level may be situationally defined (Bruner 1972, 1973a; Rodgers 1981:11; Kipp 1983). For example, Toba residents, when traveling to other regions of Sumatra, may call themselves simply Batak, while Karo residents in similar circumstances may stress that they are not Batak but Karo—in order to distinguish themselves from Toba people.

Batak was once a derogatory Muslim term for outsiders meaning "pig-eater," which was later taken with pride by some feisty Toba highlanders (Loeb 1972[1935]:20). Some groups such as the Toba are currently satisfied with the unifying term Batak while others such as the Karo prefer to be referred to with the name of their regional subgroup (personal communication, Rita Kipp, Susan Rodgers 1990). Still, from an outside observer's perspective, "all the Batak societies share a single core culture based on certain organizational and symbolic principles. In this sense, each Batak culture is related to the others on a theme-and-variation pattern" (Rodgers 1985:95). Specifically, all the Batak subgroups, although distinct communities, share common traditions of kinship organization, ritual customs, and subsistence strategies. They traditionally subsist upon the cultivation of rice, corn, tubers, and vegetables. Livestock such as pigs and chickens are raised for sacrifices at ritual feasts in Christian areas, while Muslim communities raise water buffalo or goats for their feasts. Today, virtually all Batak people follow one or the other of these religions.

Fig. III.1 Traditional Toba Batak priest, North Sumatra, circa 1938. Schuh 1943

Clan Heirlooms, Marriage Alliance, and Gift Exchange

The basic Batak social unit is the *marga*, or clan, a kinship group that traces its line through the male descendants of a distant male ancestor or community

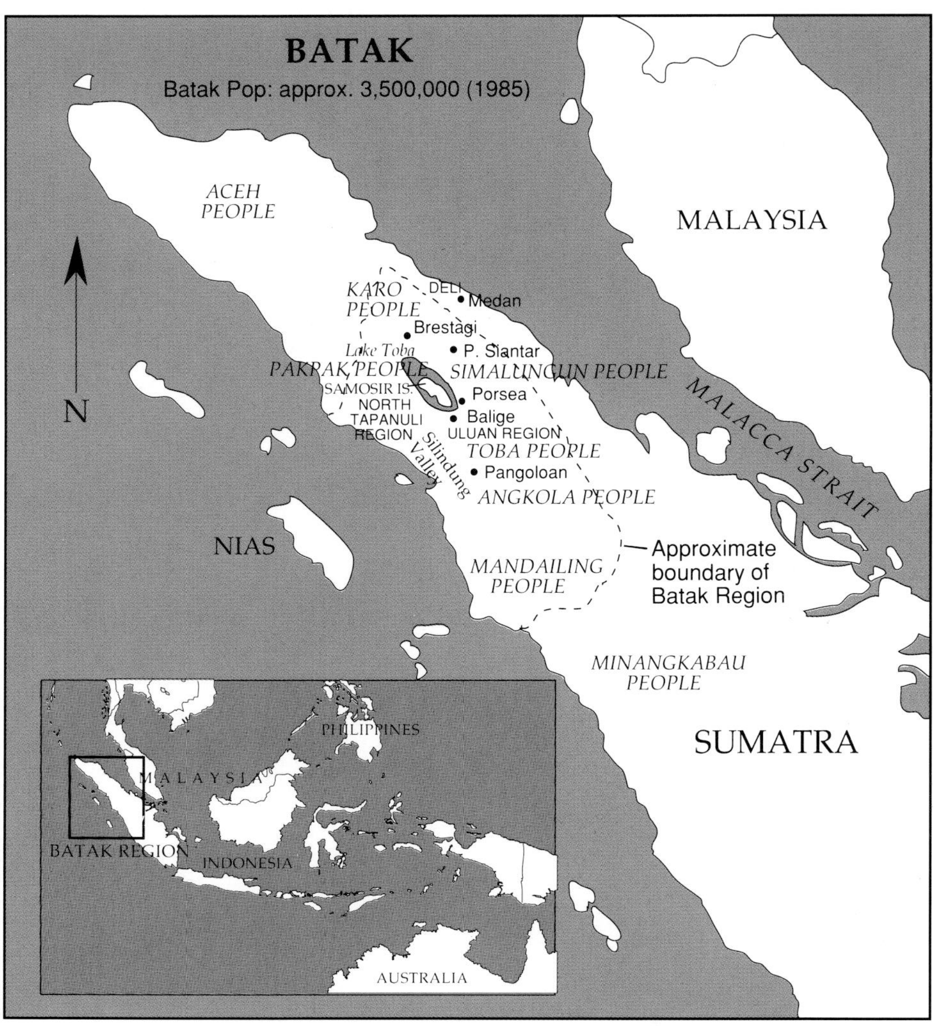

OPPOSITE
LEFT

Fig. III.2 BRACELET
Toba Batak, North Sumatra
Gilded silver and gold, 9
Royal Tropical Institute, Tropenmuseum, The Netherlands, 1772–110. Donated by G. Tillman Jr. Accessioned in 1947.

RIGHT

Fig. III.3 BRACELET
Toba Batak, North Sumatra
Copper alloy, 11.5
Royal Tropical Institute, Tropenmuseum, The Netherlands, A3261A. Accessioned before 1887.

BOTTOM

Fig. III.4 WAIST ORNAMENT
Toba Batak, North Sumatra
Gilded silver, 149
Royal Tropical Institute, Tropenmuseum, The Netherlands, A3321. Accessioned before 1887.

founder. Batak *marga* clans have a territorial basis, given that the ruling clan was the oldest *marga* of the area (Loeb 1972[1935]:42). Traditionally, Batak communities were governed through their *marga* clan leaders who made public decisions through councils held in village meetinghouses (*sopu*). In the Toba area, as the clans became too large to govern, branches of the clan or territorially based lineage segments became the governing units. Among the Karo, many clans were ritually and politically united under regional chiefs who attained the nominal status of *raja*, or king, during the Acehnese and Dutch colonial period (Rodgers 1985:98). The same patrilineal kinship and relatively egalitarian political structures were also developed among the Angkola, Pakpak, Simalungun, and Mandailing.

Many of the finest Batak artworks have been produced for clan leaders or for marital gift exchanges among lineage segments. The Batak peoples are well known for their patrilineal kinship and asymmetric system of marriage alliance, which distinguishes them from the surrounding Malay groups, whose descent structures are cognatic or matrilineal. Traditionally, a man must select his wife from a lineage (a small segment of a clan) other than the one to which he belongs. Ideally, a young man should repeat the marriage of his father by marrying a girl from his mother's clan and, in fact, from her immediate lineage. A young woman should do the same by marrying into the same lineage as that of her father's sisters. In practice, many marriages conform to this ideal only in retrospect because grooms can become appropriate—as long as the previous household alliance is not reversed (Bovill 1986). In this way, the ancestral marriage alliances are seen as persisting through the generations although they are validated or reinterpreted at each new marriage.

Ceremonial gifts and wives, which pass in the traditional direction among the many clans, circulate asymmetrically through the society. The specific gifts and counter-gifts must never be passed in the opposite direction. The Angkola Batak liken their kinship relations to the three cooking stones that support the

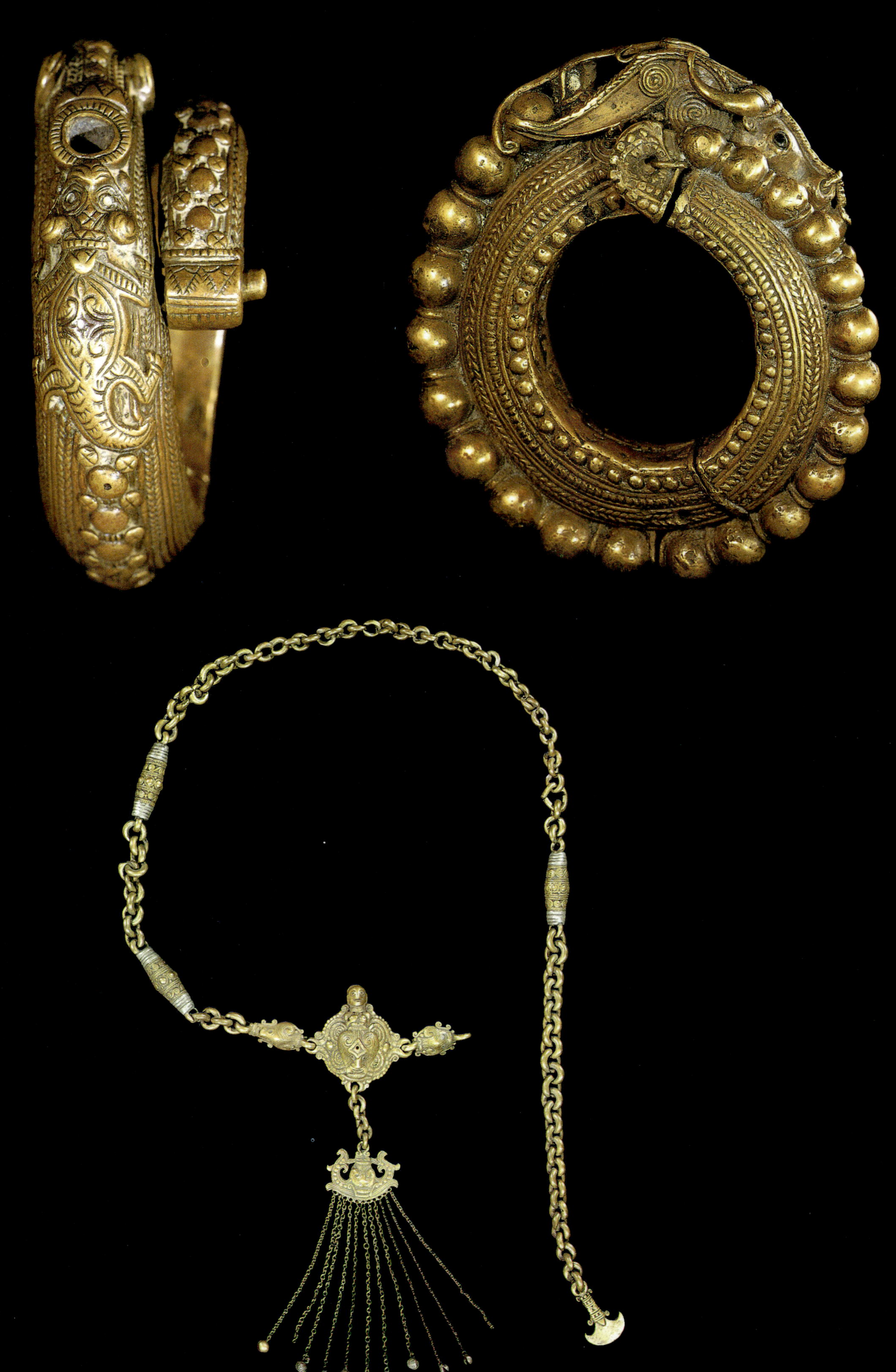

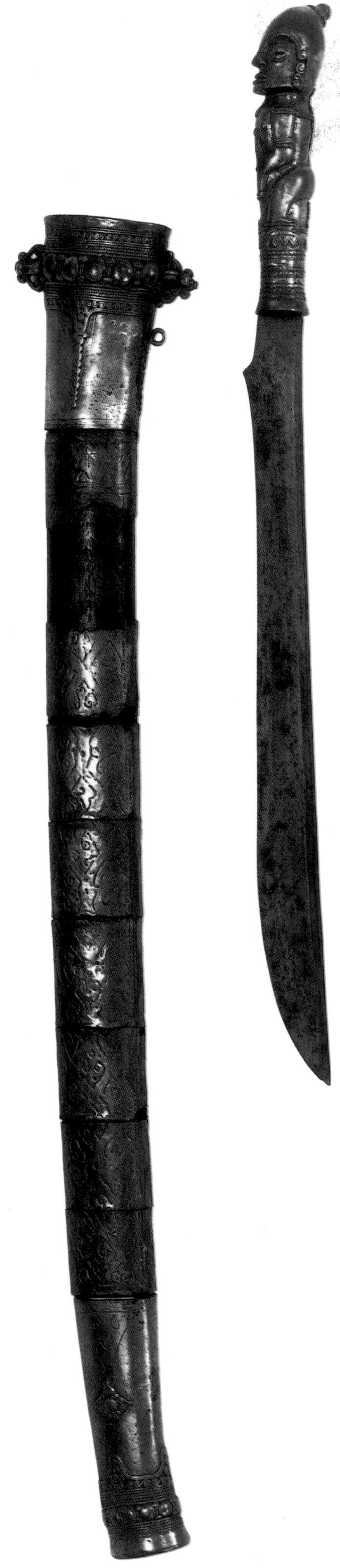

cookpot on a hearth (Rodgers 1985:95). One stone represents a man's lineage mates. The second stone represents his wife's father's lineage mates, from another clan that traditionally has given wives to his lineage ancestors. This group is seen as socially superior and the source of such spiritual blessings as health and fertility. The third stone represents the lineage to whom his own lineage will give wives and, ideally, has given for many generations. This group is seen as socially deferential, but they are also compliant providers of material goods that protect and complement the blessings of the wife-givers.

Some distinctive Batak jewelry items could be passed among individuals either through marriage-related gift exchanges or through clan inheritance. Bracelets (Figs. III.2 and III.3), signs of noble rank in the Toba region, unite images of mythical snakes (*si boganding*) symbolizing the power of the lower world, buffalo symbolizing prosperity, and protective *singa*, which were traditionally associated with the nobility. A mythological creature, the *singa* is said to support the lower world and provide protection to people. Although its name means "lion," the *singa* combines features of serpents and elephants. The animal figures, hatched ornamentation, and spiral and globe border motifs are typical of Toba metalworking. This type of bracelet was worn on the right arm by men, who inherited it as a clan heirloom or received it as a marital-alliance gift (Rodgers 1985:322–23).

Waist chains of precious metals are another type of clan heirloom, one that may have ancient roots in Hindu-Buddhist aesthetics regarding the jewelry of nobility (see illustrations of Indonesian bodhisattvas in Fontein 1990). The clasp and pendant of the Toba Batak waist chain (Fig. III.4) include the protective *singa* design, topped by a human or ancestor figure. Stylistically, this Toba waist chain closely matches the two bracelets described above. The fringe of the chain hanging at the front is terminated with tiny pellet bells, valued for their musical effects in traditional religious ceremonies throughout Southeast Asia.

Finely crafted Toba Batak swords were valued as prestige objects by local chiefs and passed on to their sons. The heirloom sword (Fig. III.5) displays a typical Toba Batak–style human figure on the hilt, one that probably represents a *marga* clan ancestor of the man who first made or commissioned the sword. The figure's head is characteristically more than a third of its total body size with prominent, square jaw and nose. Old swords become classified as sacred lineage inheritance items, only publicly displayed at such ceremonial events as the reburial of bones of a revered ancestor. Upon such occasions, lineage members who participate in the ceremony don their formal attire and bring swords, chains, and other ancestral treasures from out of their storage places (Fig. III.6).

Although somewhat less well known than the Toba Batak people, the Karo, who live in more northern regions of Sumatra, have developed a refined jewelry tradition clearly influenced by the adjacent Muslim Aceh and Malay peoples. Among the Karo, smiths traditionally had a special, and somewhat elevated, rank. Smithing skills usually passed from father to son, as it was said that smithing tools could only be inherited, never sold—or misfortune would result (Loeb 1972[1935]:26). Locally produced jewelry was worn not only to proclaim wealth but also in some circumstances to transmit spiritual power or health to the wearer (Rodgers 1985:100–101).

Traditional ornaments worn on top of a bride's or bridegroom's headdress during a Karo marriage ceremony include the *sertali*. The metal crescents on the ornament—which may represent birds or buffalo horns—resemble designs from Islamic sultanates such as the Aceh located in North Sumatra (Rodgers 1985:320). The triangular segments that rise from each separate pendant of one particular version of this headdress (*sertali rumah-rumah*) represent the roofs of Karo traditional houses (Fig. III.7; Sitepu 1980). Similar headdress ornaments also are worn by Alas bridegrooms of the southeast Aceh region (Leigh 1989: 102,127–28). Reportedly, these gilded silver ornaments (Fig. III.10), were created by Karo artisans who, however, no longer produce these pieces. Because of the scarcity of heirloom jewelry, these ornaments now are usually rented for

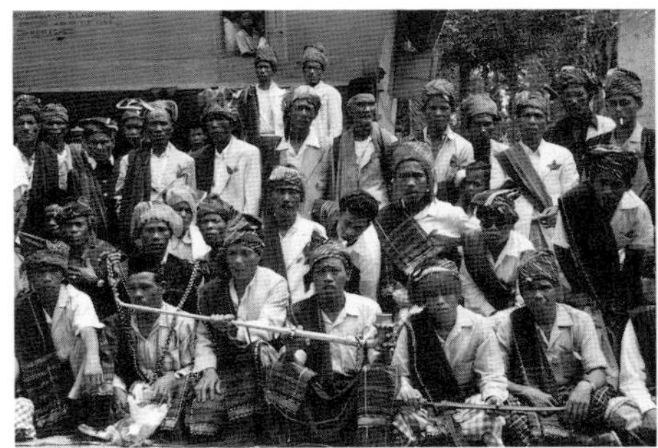

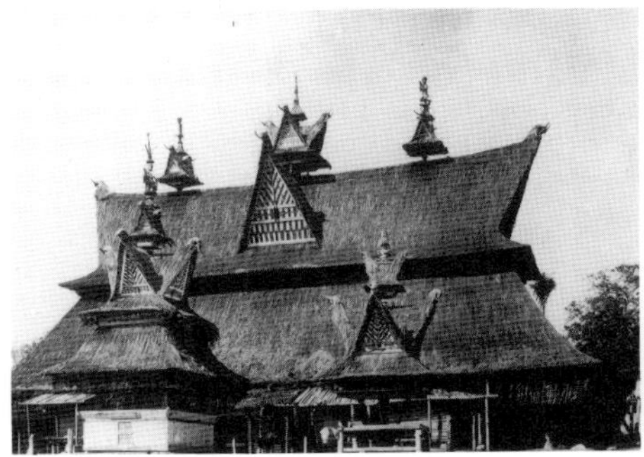

TOP
Fig. III.6 Toba Batak men of North Tapanuli hold heirlooms including a sword at a ceremony to rebury the bones of a deceased ancestor, North Sumatra, 1957. Edward M. Bruner

Fig. III.7 Traditional Karo house, North Sumatra, circa 1933. Courtesy National Archives, Washington, D.C.

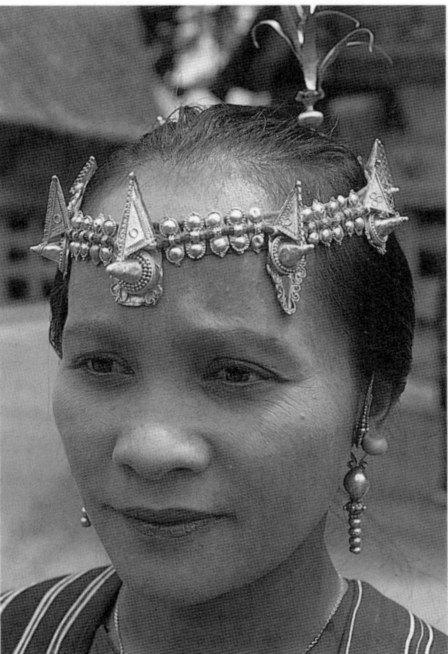

Fig. III.8 Toba Batak woman wears a ceremonial headdress (*sertali rumah-rumah*), North Sumatra, 1989. Danielle Hayes

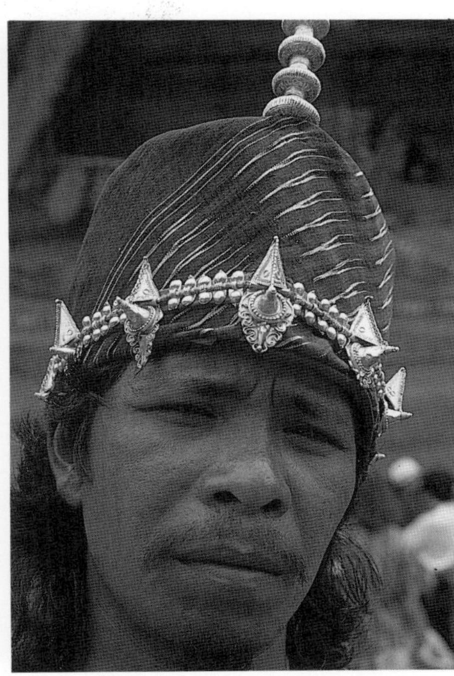

Fig. III.9 Toba Batak man wears a ceremonial headdress (*sertali rumah-rumah*), North Sumatra, 1989. Danielle Hayes

marriage ceremonies and are worn by either the groom or the bride (Figs. III.8 and III.9).

Traditionally, Batak rings were worn to indicate high rank, given in marriage exchanges, or used by traditional priests in rituals. Often heirloom rings were considered to bring luck and protection to the wearer's soul (Rodgers 1985:323). Like most delicate Karo jewelry, the metalworking techniques such as filigree and granulation used to produce this ring (Fig. III.11) show influence from Aceh or other Malay sultanates.

Traditionally, when a Karo woman married, she stopped wearing all jewelry except for one unusual type of ear ornament, the *padung* or *padung-padung* (Fig. III.12), which she continued to wear throughout her daily life (Fig. III.13; Loeb 1972[1935]:26). These heavy earrings were usually worn with one anchored forward and one back, both attached to the wearer's headscarf (Fig. III.14). The style reportedly represents the "one up and one down" pattern of married life where sometimes one partner predominates, sometimes the other (Rodgers 1985:100). *Padung* earrings are usually made of three hollow tubes of silver or alloy, with the two spirals inserted into a third connecting tube at the earlobe. These can be removed at their center joints. Some early models were of solid wire, coiled by the smith as he attached them permanently to the woman's ear (Rodgers 1985:320). The headscarf helps to support the *padung,* which can weigh more than one kilogram each. The spiral form, thought to represent vitality and the continuity of life, is an ancient motif in Southeast Asian art.

OPPOSITE
Fig. III.5 SWORD
Batak, North Sumatra
Metal, wood, sword: 63.8 x 7 x 3.5; sheath: 8 x 52
Museum Nasional Indonesia, Jakarta, 3829

Clan Houses and Monuments

As in Nias and many other regions of outer-island Indonesia, the design of Toba Batak houses carries cosmological significance. The three tiers of the Toba house parallel the three levels of the universe (Cameron 1985:80). The finest examples of traditional Toba houses are impressive structures with carved wooden façades and cornerposts. The characteristic curvilinear designs are traditionally

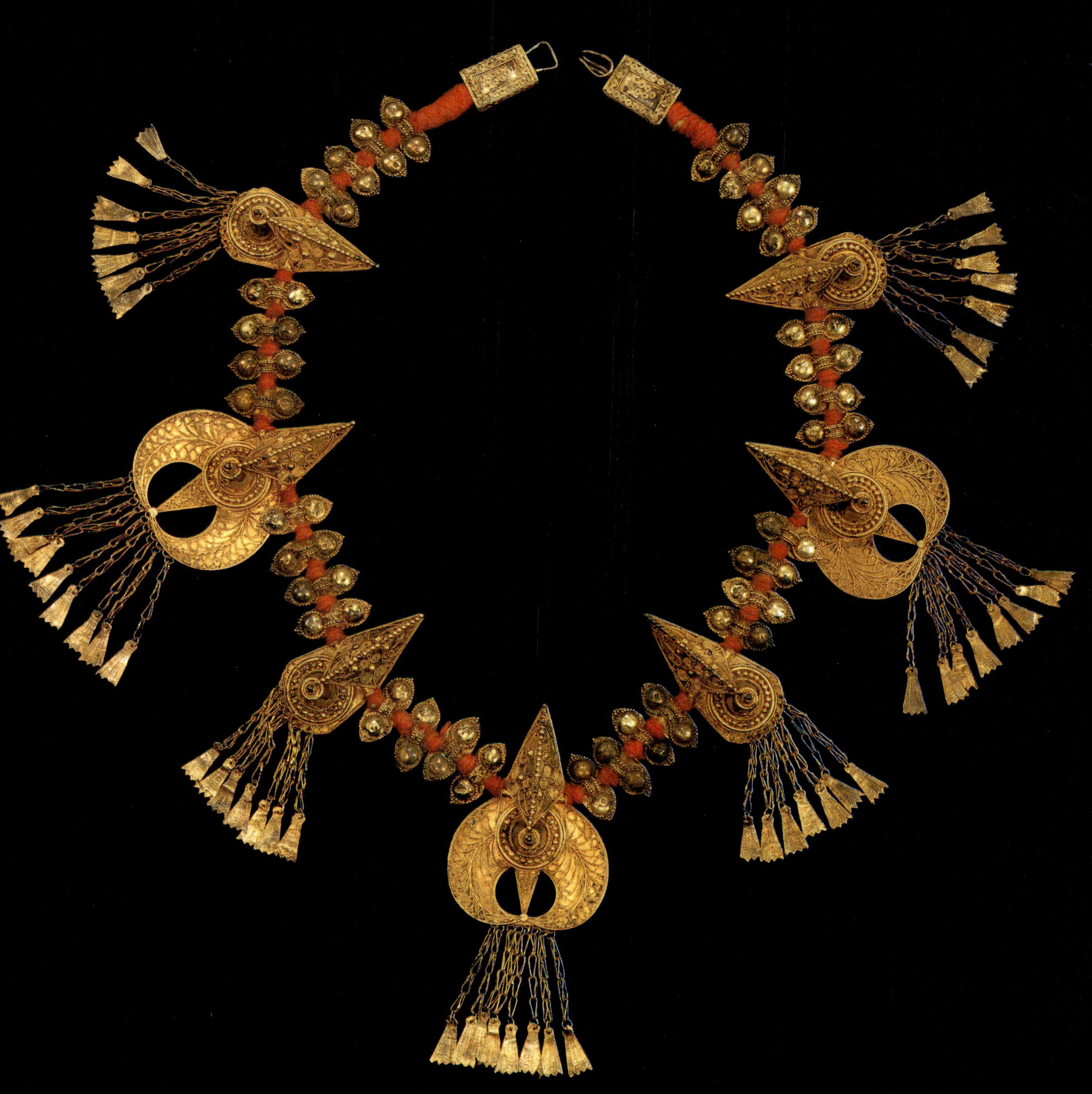

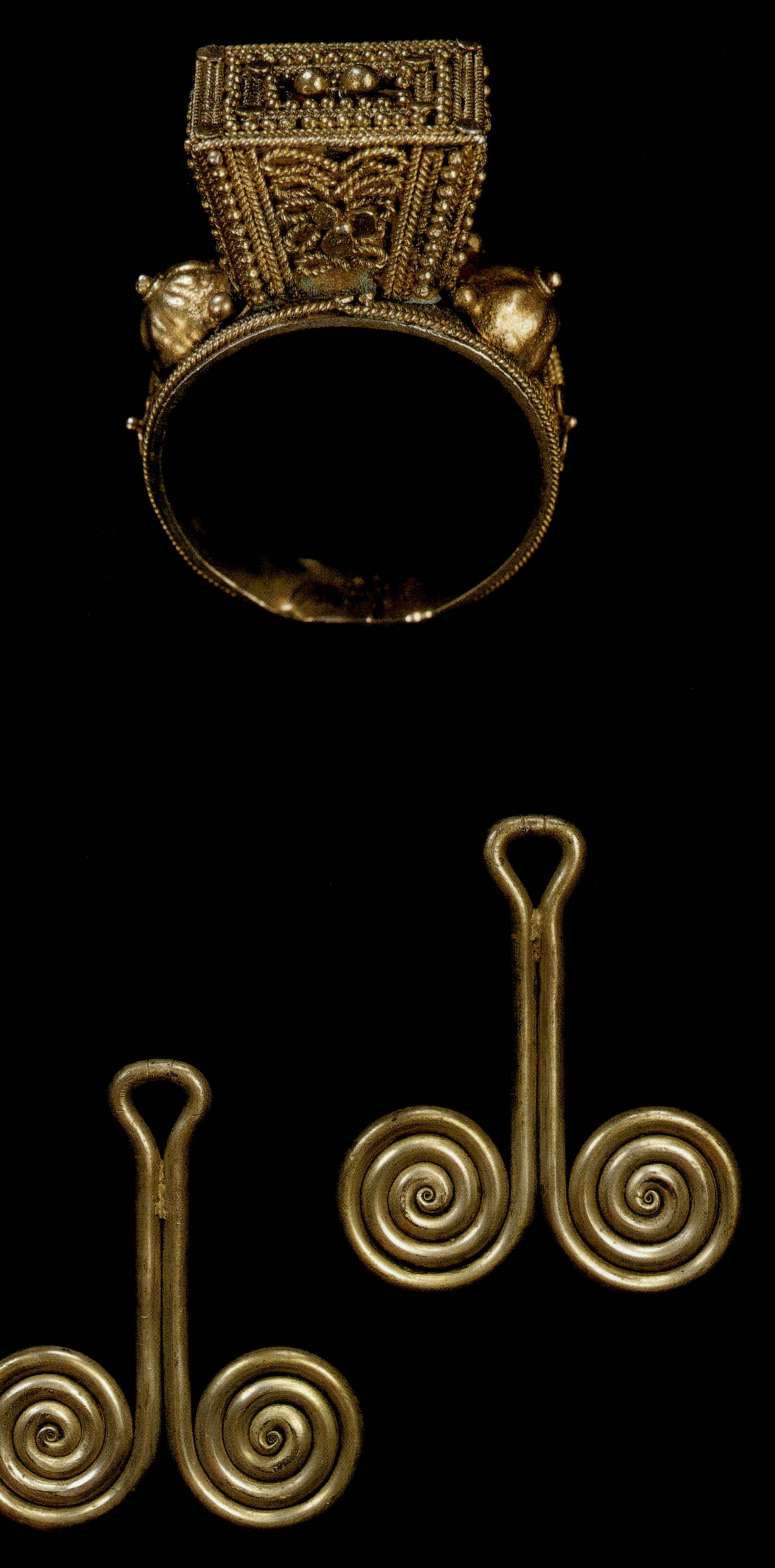

OPPOSITE

Fig. III.10 HEADDRESS ORNAMENT, *SERTALI*
Karo, North Sumatra
Gilded silver, cotton, 84 x 15 x 3.5
Museum Nasional Indonesia, Jakarta, 26677C. Purchased from Ir. J. L. Moens for 300 guilders. Accessioned in 1950.

Fig. III.11 RING
Karo, North Sumatra
Gilded silver, 1.2 x 3.2
Royal Tropical Institute, Tropenmuseum, The Netherlands, 114–19

Fig. III.12 EAR ORNAMENTS, *PADUNG-PADUNG*
Karo, North Sumatra
Silver and alloy, 14.5 x 12.4 x .5; 14.2 x 12.5 x .6
Field Museum of Natural History, Chicago, 27624. Donated by F. W. Geisler. Accessioned in 1952.

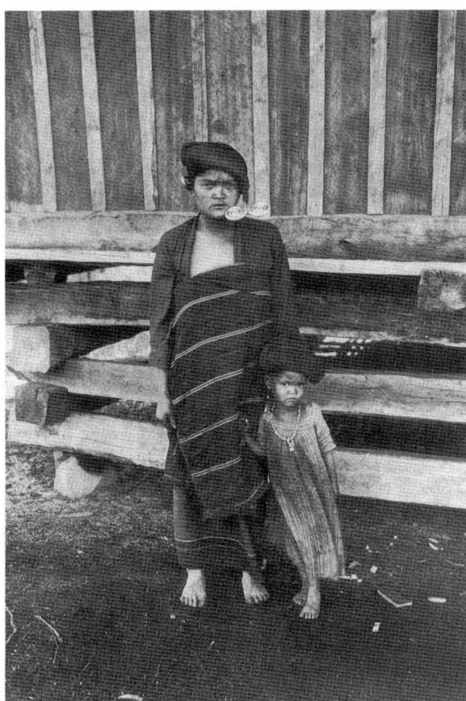

Fig. III.13 Karo woman wears *padung* earrings, North Sumatra, before 1920. van Eerde 1920:123. Courtesy Elsevier Press, Amsterdam.

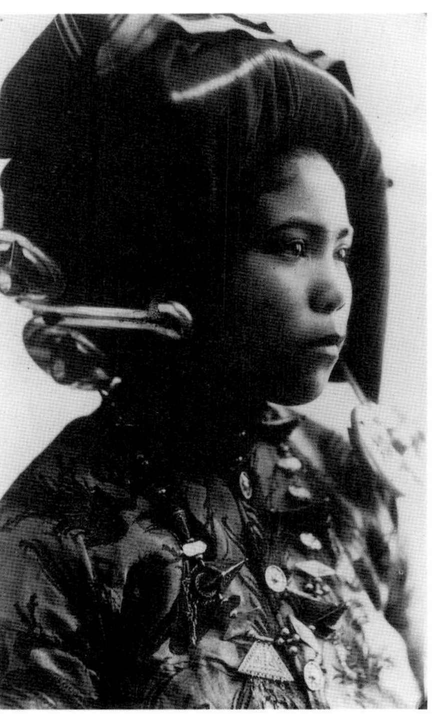

Fig. III.14 Karo woman with *padung* earring supported by headscarf, North Sumatra, 1933. Courtesy National Archives, Washington, D.C.

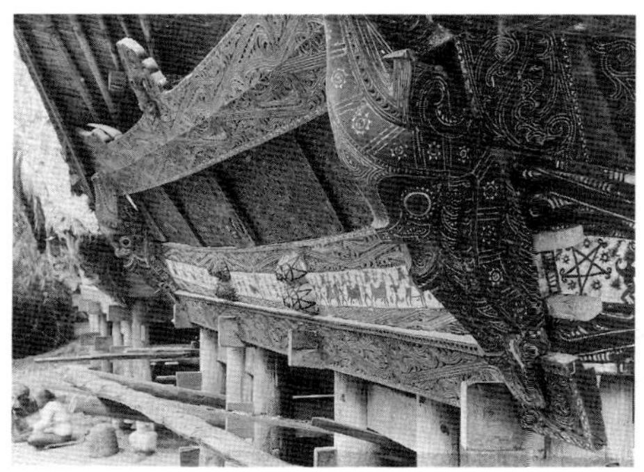

Fig. III.15 Toba Batak houses with *singa* on corner beams, North Sumatra, circa 1933. Courtesy Rijksmuseum voor Volkenkunde, Leiden.

painted in the sacred Toba colors: black, white, and red. The corner beams of important Toba clan houses were carved with images of a *singa* creature (Fig. III.15), whose image also appears widely on stone coffins (Fig. III.17), grave memorials, and heirloom jewelry (such as Figs. III.2 and III.3) traditionally commissioned by prominent members of Batak clans. Modern Toba house façades (Fig. III.16) include modified *singa* figures and other characteristic motifs in traditional colors.

Stone grave monuments of the Toba Batak have long been a medium for display of cultural imagery, although the prevailing artistic styles have changed dramatically in the last half century. Traditional monuments often depict equestrian scenes with the ancestor figures mounted on horses, elephants, or mythical creatures such as the *singa*. Formal and stately, these massive rider figures may be related to ancient Hindu images of mounted royalty. For most Asian societies, to be mounted on a horse or elephant indicated not only the privileged status gained by ownership of a valuable animal but also a physically and metaphorically elevated status.

This stone grave monument (Fig. III.18) includes the large head and prominent jaw characteristic of all Toba Batak figures. The elephant mount with its short, squared legs is diminutive in comparison to the prominent man that it carries. The elephant's trunk and tail and the man's legs all coil smoothly and evenly in the same direction. Above all else, such a monument testifies to the effort and resources of the deceased's family in commissioning such a monument—the transportation of the proper stone to the lineage grave site, compensation to a stone sculptor, and wealth to finance whatever ceremonies were needed to consecrate it.

Batak grave monuments have changed considerably since the peoples' conversion to Christianity and Islam. During and following the Padri rebellion of 1815 in Sumatra, the southern Batak areas were converted to Islam by coastal peoples fighting the Dutch. After 1860, the efforts of German missionaries

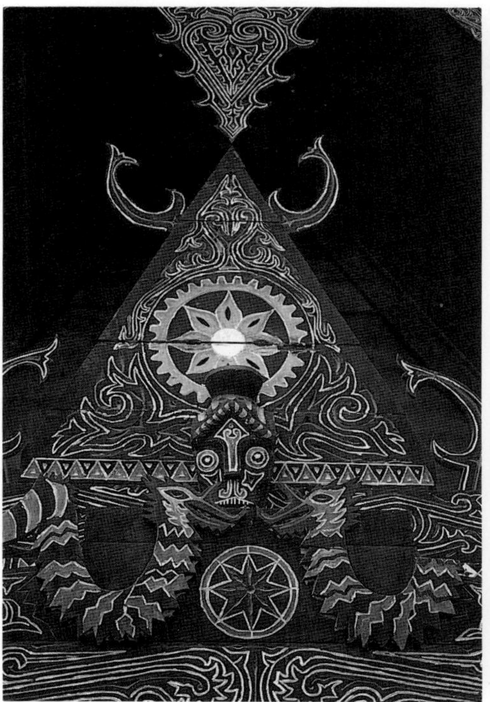

Fig. III.16 Modern Batak house façade painted with traditional motifs and colors (red, black, and white), North Sumatra, 1989. Danielle Hayes

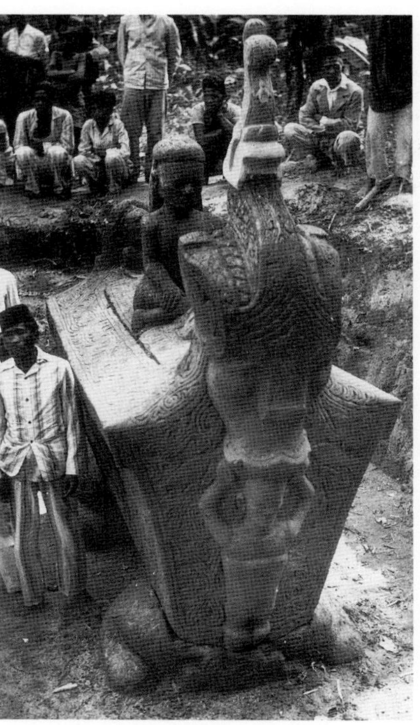

Fig. III.17 Toba Batak stone coffin with *singa* head, built circa 1840, North Sumatra. Royal Tropical Institute, Tropenmuseum, The Netherlands.

resulted in the conversion of many of the northern Batak regions to Protestant Christianity. Nowadays, grave monuments to ancestors are no longer carved in stone with *singa* figures or elephant-riding ancestors. Instead, seven- to fifteen-meter-tall concrete monuments (*tugu*) with statues of lineage founders standing at the top are erected above tombs in many rural Toba communities (Bruner 1984:71–73, 1987; Bolle 1988:32–33). Such concrete monuments (Fig. III.19) and accompanying clan rituals are often financed by Toba Batak who have migrated to urban centers such as Medan or Jakarta and who maintain their clan ties through sponsorship of *tugu* monuments and accompanying rituals in their rural homelands. According to Bruner, the urbanites who finance such monuments "give money, political power, economic support and modern knowledge. They get back memory, affiliation, generativity, and spiritual renewal" (1984:73). The traditional relations of kinship and alliance are thereby perpetuated in a modern economic and aesthetic form, in keeping with the increased monument building throughout Indonesia since the 1960s.

Marriage Alliance: Female and Male Gifts

Batak marriage-alliance rituals include prescribed gift exchanges between the bride's lineage and the groom's lineage. Gifts and counter-gifts are exchanged throughout the lifetime of the marriage. The wife's family, or "wife-givers," give gifts called *ulos*, which are traditionally textiles but can also include plots of land. The husband's family, or "wife-takers," give *piso*, which are traditionally knives or other metal objects but are more often such commodities as money, cattle, or rice. Livestock—for instance, buffalo—are a common gift from the groom's family, a kind of economic support given to balance the spiritual support represented by the *ulos* cloths. During a traditional marriage ceremony, the father of the bride wraps a gift *ulos* cloth around the newly married couple to signal their union and to envelope them with sacred protective power (Fig. III.21).

Once an *ulos* cloth was used ritually in a blessing ceremony, its power

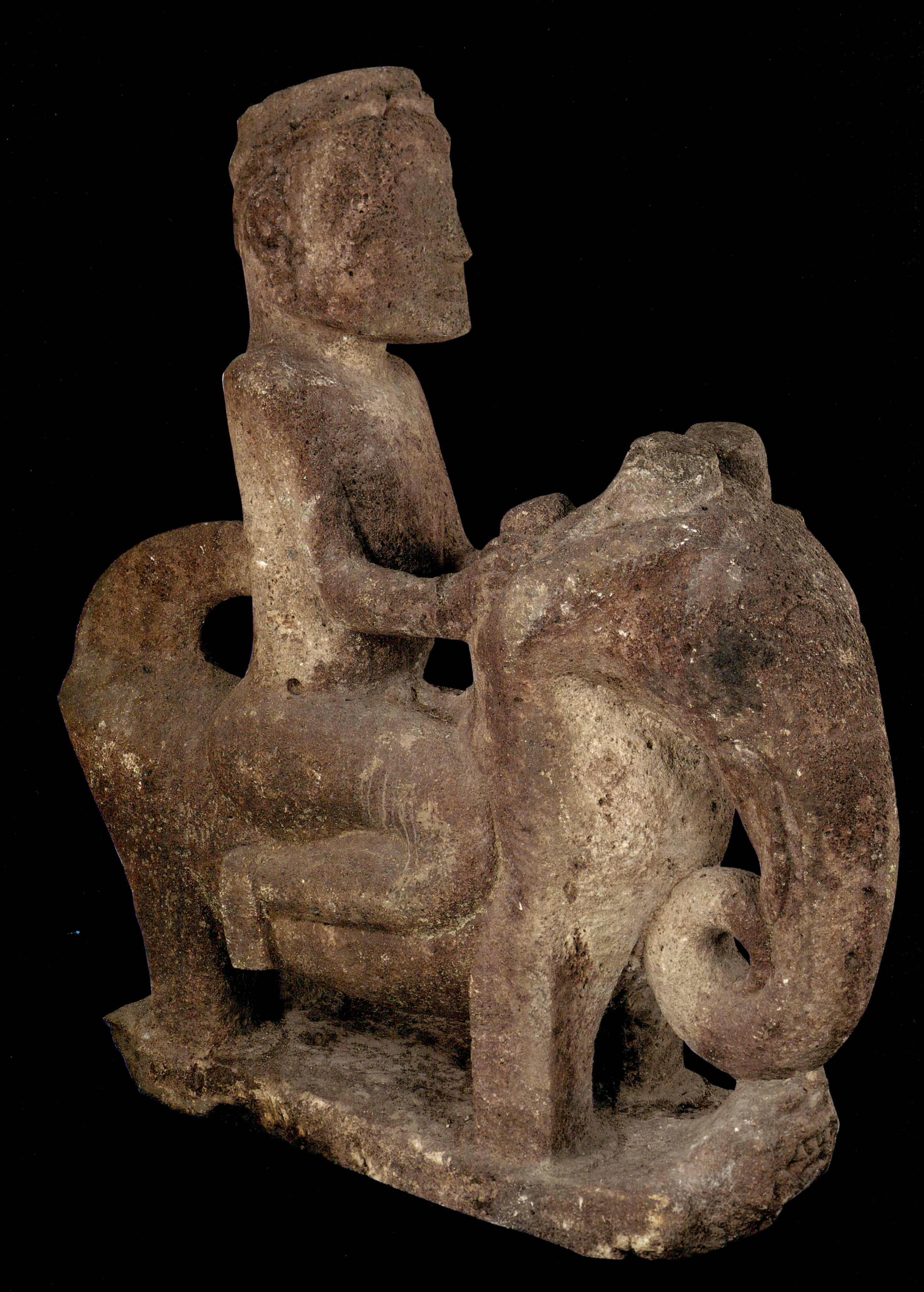

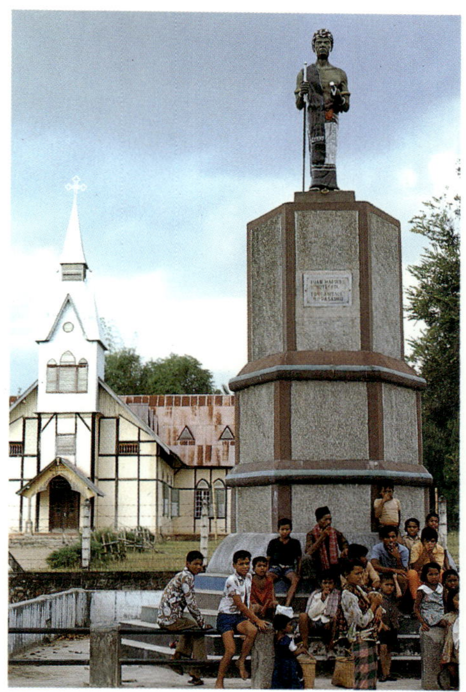

Fig. III.19 *Tugu* commemorative monument with Christian church in background, North Tapanuli, North Sumatra, 1973. Edward M. Bruner

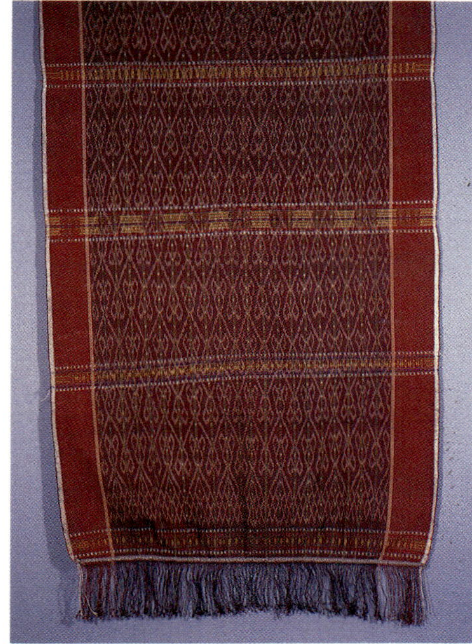

Fig. III.20 Previously unpublished type of *ulos* shoulder cloth called *bintang maratur* ("ordered stars") produced near Porsea in the Toba region, North Sumatra. Collection of Sandra Niessen. Linda Turner

OPPOSITE

Fig. III.18 GRAVE MONUMENT
Toba Batak, North Sumatra
Stone, 142.4 x 121.5 x 40.7
Barbier-Mueller Museum, Geneva, 3149.

was thereby increased for all future uses. For example, when a young Toba Batak woman was pregnant with her first child, her parents would bless (*mangupa*) her with a special cloth called *ulos ni tondi*, "cloth of her soul." This cloth, designed to protect the mother-to-be during this physically dangerous condition, could later be used to cure the mother herself or her children—with the blessing embodied in the cloth during the original ceremony (Vergouwen 1964:59). If a wife's family offered a plot of land to their son-in-law during his wife's pregnancy-blessing ceremony, the son-in-law would return a present of money accompanying it with a speech similar to this:

> You have now enriched your daughter's soul, *tondi*, with a cloth of her soul. Here now is our *piso* gift so that our souls may remain strong, *pir*. Take it, and may you keep us among your followers until your old age. (Vergouwen 1964:62)

The exchange of gifts and concomitant respect, which continue throughout the marriage, is more than a matter of etiquette. The rituals are occasions during which spiritual power is bestowed, guaranteeing fertility for the couple and their land and preventing illness and misfortune. The symbolic sexual union represented by the traded objects, as well as their exchange, heralds fertility for the marriage. Just as the rituals are spiritual events, so too are the objects that transmit blessings from the bride's family to the groom's family. The weaver of a Toba Batak *ulos* cloth traditionally was subject to behavioral restrictions that made aesthetic decisions more than a matter of casual choice (Fig. III.22). For example, if the cloth were too long or too short, the wearer would experience misfortune and death instead of long life and prosperity (Vergouwen 1964:58).

Ulos cloths are woven of cotton, which was once locally grown, and dyed with natural plant dyes. They are woven with a technique called warp *ikat*, wherein the warp threads are tied and dyed before weaving. Because Batak warp threads are so densely strung and, therefore, visually dominate the finished textiles, the cloths are termed warp-faced. *Ulos* cloths are traditionally woven on back-tension looms strung with circular, continuous warps. After weaving, the warp strings are cut and twisted, producing a fringe that is often further adorned with a twining technique (see Gittinger 1979:46–47). *Ulos* textiles are classified locally into about fifty types according to their designs, colors, and structural arrangements (Niessen 1985:12). These types are assigned relative value and are bestowed by wife-givers and used according to prescribed rules in specific ceremonial contexts (Fig. III.20). Some shoulder cloths, like the *ulos simpar* in Fig. III.24, are no longer made in the region but could be given as a ritual gift in various types of ceremonies (personal communication, Niessen 1990).

An *ulos* given by the Toba Batak bride's father to the groom's mother is called the *ragidup*, or "pattern of life," referring to the blessings that attend the marriage exchange. This cloth (Fig. III.23) has the highest status of any cloth made by the Toba Batak people; they call it the *raja*, or king, of their textiles (Niessen 1988:82). It may be worn only by persons of advanced age and high status. It is sometimes given as a protective "soul cloth" (*ulos ni tondi*) to a high-ranking bride in the seventh month of her first pregnancy. However, she must wait until she achieves grandparent status before she may wear it herself (personal communication, Niessen 1990). The *ulos ragidup* is woven in three panels, with the end of the center panel being adorned with supplementary weft patterns created with a difficult warp-extension technique (Gittinger 1979). One of these supplementary weft end sections is locally considered the male (Fig. III.23a), whereas the other is considered the female (Fig. III.23b; Niessen 1985:182–87). This union of both female and male sections, even with a gift associated with the woman's side of the family, symbolizes the complementary forces needed to produce offspring.

At funeral rituals, the wife-givers to the deceased contribute an *ulos* to adorn the coffin (Fig. III.27). For a widow of high status, an *ulos ragidup* may be given as a mourning headscarf (Niessen 1985:13). Traditionally, an *ulos ragidup*

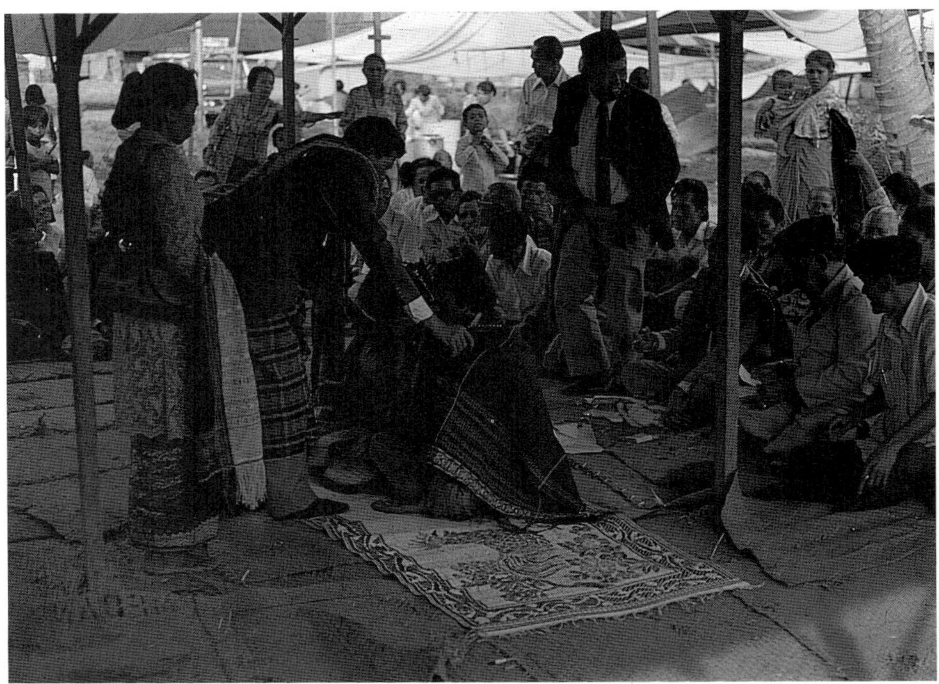

Fig. III.21 Toba Batak couple being wrapped in an *ulos* cloth at their marriage ceremony, Siantar village, North Sumatra, 1978. Kathryn Bovill

might also be worn by a paternal grandmother at the marketplace to announce the birth of a female grandchild (Niessen 1985:114). To announce the birth of a boy, an *ulos ragi hotang* cloth might be worn. The name *ragi hotang* ("rattan motif") refers to the flecks in the center panel, which resemble rattan bark. This is the highest-ranking textile that can be given to a bride and groom, whose youth makes them ineligible to wear the *ragidup* cloth. As fine traditional *ulos* become increasingly rare, elders wear their heirloom textiles primarily on ceremonial occasions (Fig. III.26).

While the *piso* marriage gifts from a husband's lineage to his wife's family are now more apt to be money or livestock than knives (Fig. III.28), some heirloom knives clearly refer to the marriage event and undoubtedly were ceremonial wedding gifts. The double handles and blades represent the man and woman united through the marriage (Fig. III.30). These male knives also include a female image on the handle, just as the female textile gifts include sections that are designated as male, like the supplementary weft end section of an *ulos ragidup* textile (Fig. III.23a). In some examples of these double knives, male and female images are represented in an abstract fashion, their identity clear only when compared with more representative versions. The nonfigurative and streamlined form of the piece (Fig. III.29) suggests influence from Aceh or other Muslim sultanates, whereas the spiral ornaments on the handles are part of an earlier regional aesthetic tradition.

Religious and Ritual Traditions

Batak traditional religion shows clear signs of Hindu influence, which may have come directly from Indian trade during the first millennium or later through contacts with Hindu-Buddhist kingdoms on coastal Sumatra or Java (see catalog chapter X; also, Fontein 1990; Jessup 1990). In varying degrees elements from this Hindu contact were incorporated within the earlier cosmology prior to Islamic and Christian influences. Early documents list the Toba region as a

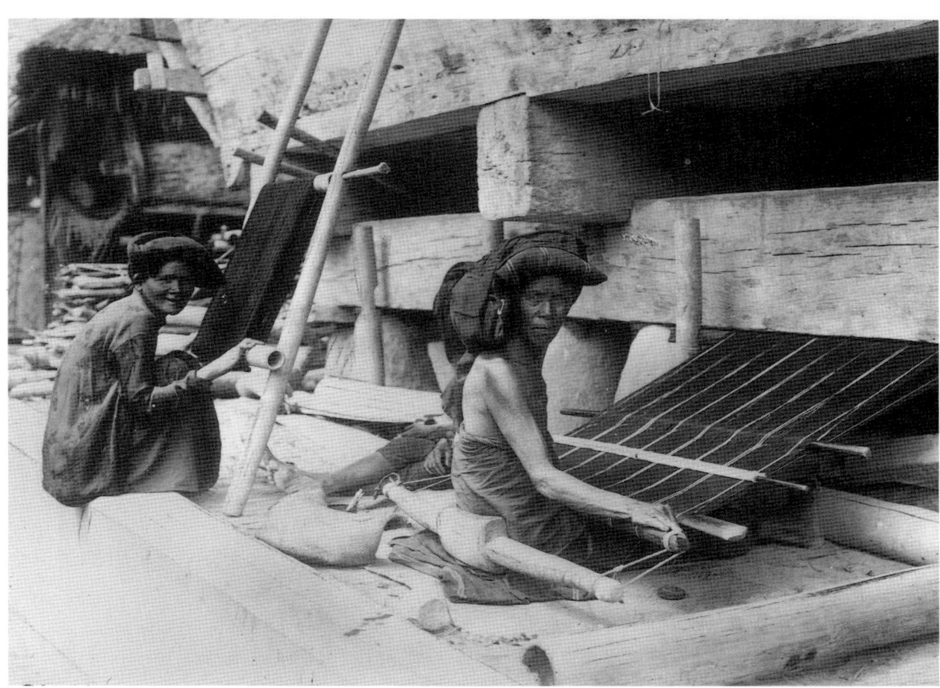

Fig. III.22 Karo Batak weaver, 1924. Courtesy Rijksmuseum voor Volkenkunde, Leiden.

tribute-paying dependency of the Hindu-Buddhist kingdom of Majapahit on Java (Loeb 1972[1935]:89). The Batak people call their traditional higher gods *debata*, a word of Sanskrit origin. Several of the Batak deity names and characteristics also have clear Indian parallels (Loeb 1972[1935]:76–78). Batak writing includes Sanskrit characters, and clan names among the Pakpak and Karo groups include Dravidian names from southern India (Loeb 1972[1935]:21). Toba Batak sacred knowledge was traditionally written in bark books (*pustaha*; Fig. III.25), made from the bark of the *alim* tree and folded accordian-style (Loeb 1972[1935]:28). The pages were treated with rice water, then glued or sewn together with other local materials. The Batak name for these books (like the Indonesian term) is derived from the Sanskrit term *pustaka*, meaning "book" or "manuscript" (Liebert 1976:231–32).

As in most of the other outer islands, traditional Batak funerary rituals were extensive and served to pacify the deceased, as well as to elevate his or her rank among the ancestors in the upper world. So honored, the deceased would then be inclined to aid their living relatives. In some areas, secondary burial was practiced; that is, the dried bones of the deceased were reburied and a larger funeral ritual was performed, once sufficient resources for the feast had been gathered.

Prior to Christian and Islamic affiliation, masked dances (Fig. III.32) were performed at funerals to appease the spirits of prominent persons. The dancers wore carved and painted wooden masks that often were adorned with woven cloth and horsehair (Fig. III.31). Four-fingered wooden hands were grasped by the dancers, extending the range of their gestures. The meaning of the dance was to inform the deceased that his descendants were prepared to provide regular offerings for him at future ceremonial feasts (Bartlett 1973).

Those who possessed no descendants to honor them were considered pitiful, and a dancing puppet, *si gale-gale* (Fig. III.33), was provided as a substitute descendant to console the newly deceased. Today, such puppets may be

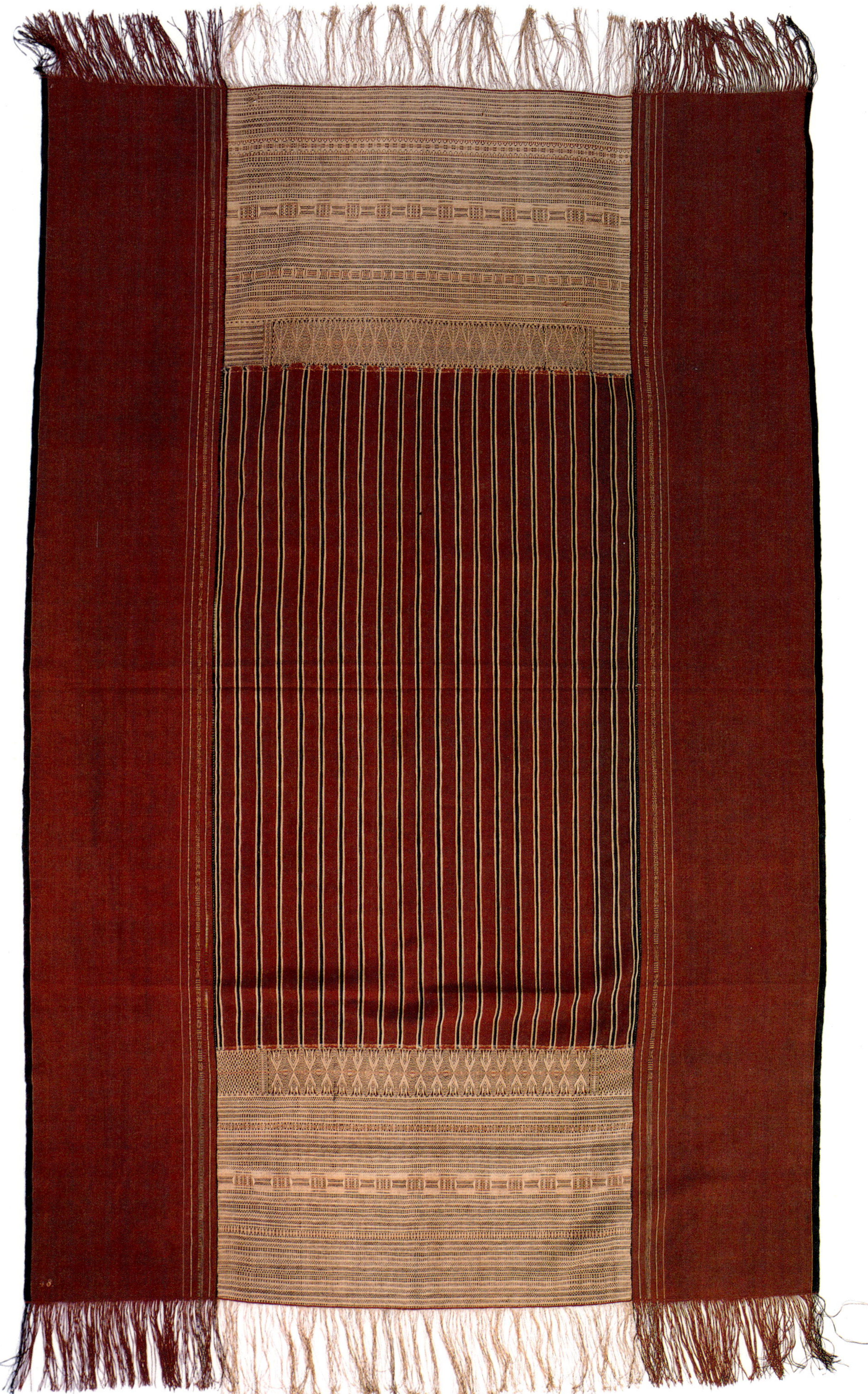

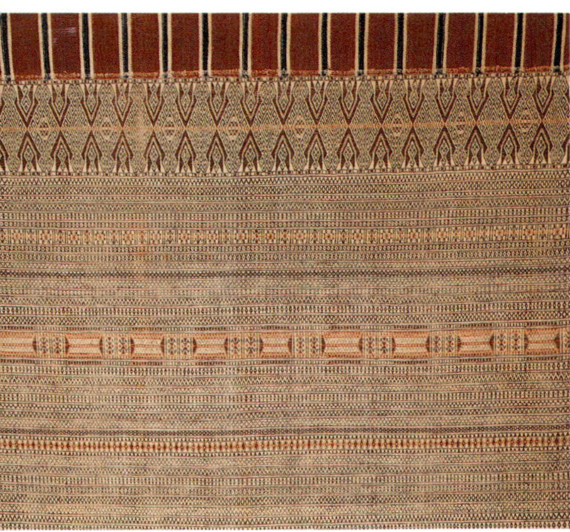

Fig. III.23a Detail of Fig. III.23 showing "male" section of textile.

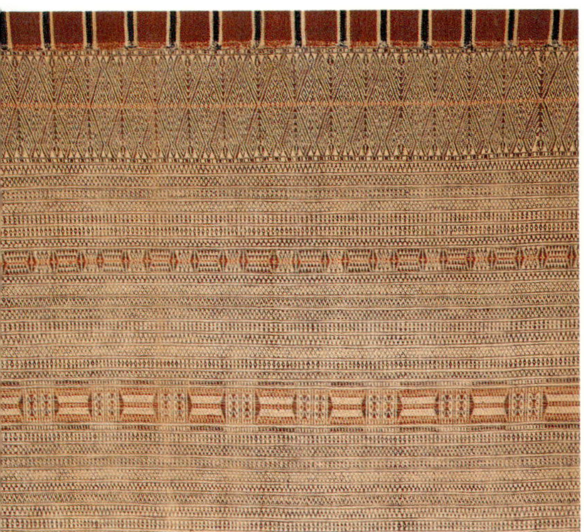

Fig. III.23b Detail of Fig. III.23 showing "female" section of textile.

OPPOSITE
Fig. III.23 CEREMONIAL CLOTH, *ULOS RAGIDUP*
Toba Batak, North Sumatra
Cotton, 203.5 x 131.5
Royal Tropical Institute, Tropenmuseum, The Netherlands, 48–30. Purchased from J. G. Jasper. Accessioned in the early 1900s.

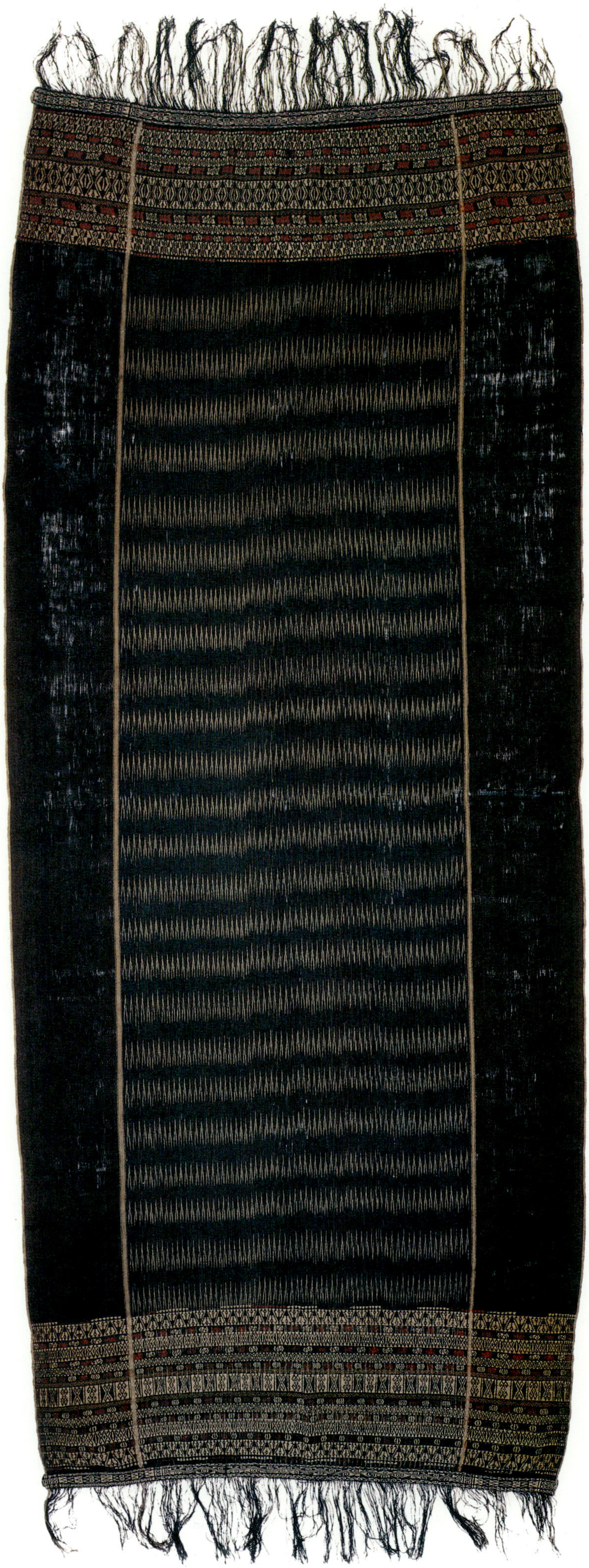

Fig. III.24 CEREMONIAL CLOTH, *ULOS SIMPAR*
Toba Batak, North Sumatra
Cotton, 206 x 85
Royal Tropical Institute, Tropenmuseum, The Netherlands, 1772–1318. Donated by G. Tillman Jr. Accessioned in 1947.

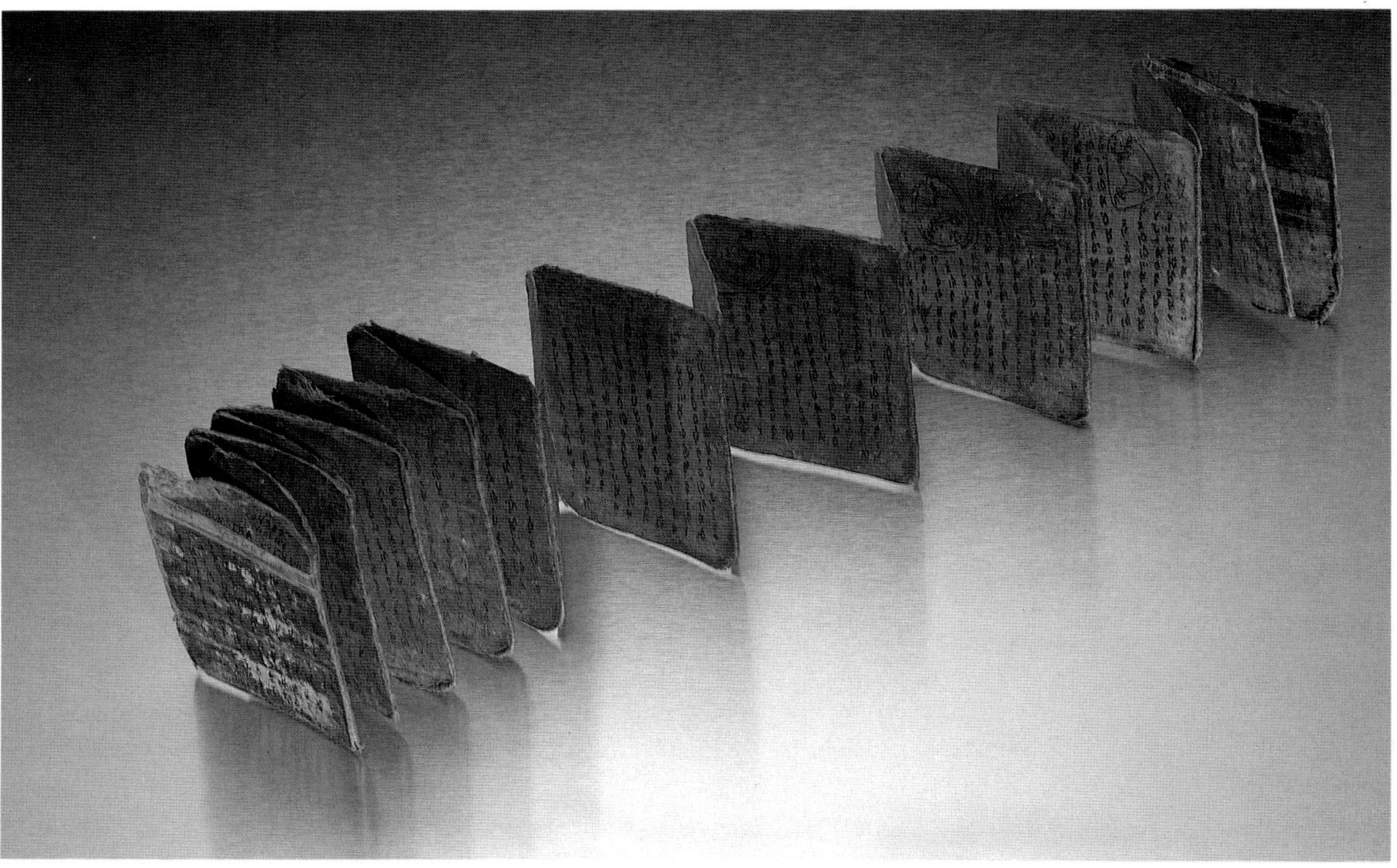

Fig. III.25 Bark book with Sanskrit-related script. Department of Anthropology, Smithsonian Institution, 334389. Donated by Rose E. Frankhauser in 1927.

displayed at Toba ceremonies celebrating their ethnic heritage, and dancing masks are more apt to be seen worn by medicine peddlers at open-air markets (Fig. III.34) than at funerals.

To ensure that the next year's harvest would be bountiful, the Toba Batak conducted an annual agricultural offering ceremony called *mangase*. The scheduling of this ceremony was decided by the chiefs or ritual specialists during an oracle sacrifice (Vergouwen 1964:76). The ceremony itself was sometimes called "the partaking of the community buffalo" (*mangan horbo bius*) because the animal to be slaughtered for the ceremony was usually a buffalo. The *mangase* feasts were intended to end any misfortunes caused by cosmic disharmony and to foretell the future of the clans. They were banned by the Dutch colonial government and Protestant missions because they led to fights among clan leaders and the method of stabbing the buffalo to death was considered cruel (Korn 1953; Tobing 1956). Although this particular ritual is no longer performed, large feasts where buffalo are quickly killed and served as the main dish are still held in the Toba region.

The *mangase* ceremony was carefully planned by selected clan leaders whose wives dressed specially for a dance where they became possessed by spirits (Fig. III.35). Among the Karo, the curer-priest was male, but the mediums who were possessed by the spirits were always women (Steedly 1989: 140). Long beaded collars, no longer made or used, were worn by the wives of Toba ritual leaders during trance dances. These beaded ornaments were made of yellow and red beads and shells and sometimes attached to a leather neck band (Korn 1953:38). This ornament (Fig. III.36) is made primarily of yellow, orange, and blue beads, cowrie shells, metal bells, and carved wood dividers all mounted on a cloth and rattan collar. Whether these fragile beaded ornaments were worn by Toba Batak women on any other occasion is not recorded.

Traditionally, most communal music and dances of the Batak were confined to ritual occasions where contact was made with ancestral spirits or de-

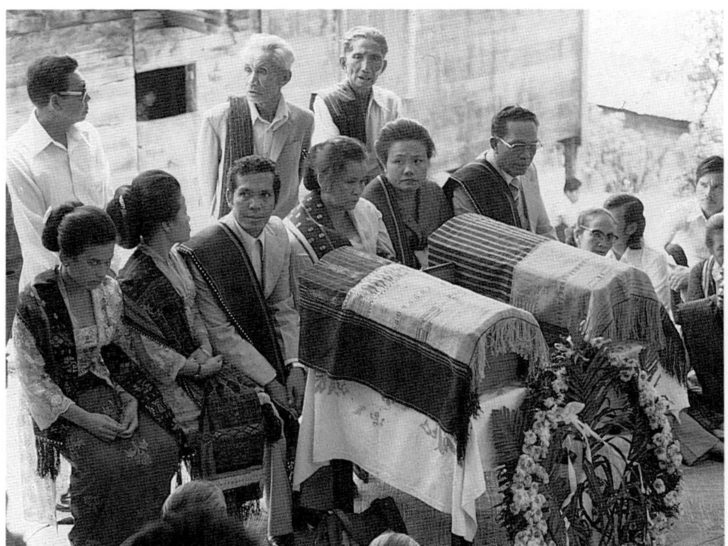

Fig. III.27 *Ulos* covering coffin at Toba Batak funeral, Medan, North Sumatra, 1980. Kathryn Bovill

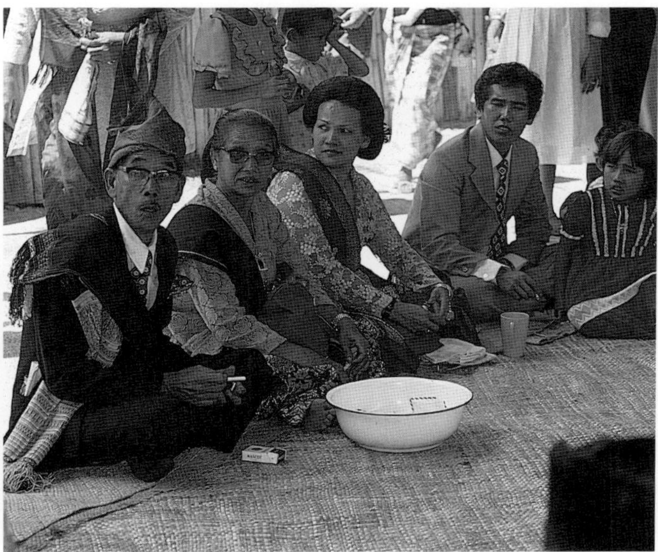

Fig. III.28 At a Toba Batak wedding, wife-takers donate envelopes of money as their *piso* gifts, near Balige village, North Tapanuli, North Sumatra, 1980. Kathryn Bovill

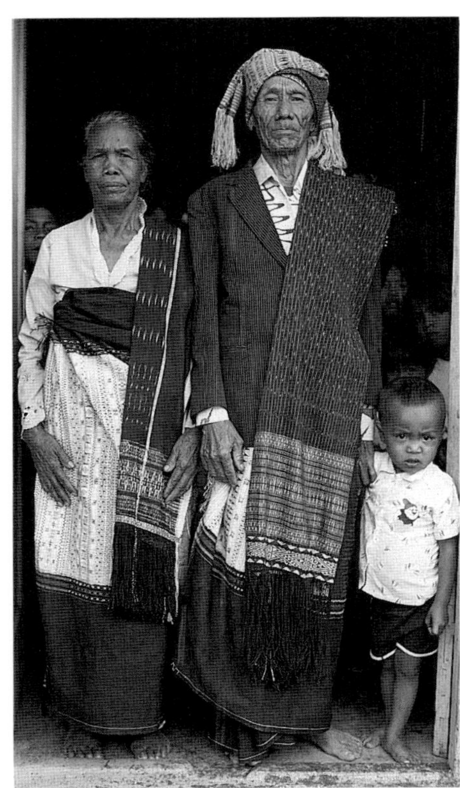

Fig. III.26 *Ragi hotang* cloth being worn as shoulder cloth by a Toba elder of the Napitupulu clan who stands with his wife, a weaving expert, near Porsea, North Sumatra, 1986. Sandra Niessen

ities. Toba musical instruments, for example, were used exclusively for religious purposes (Loeb 1972[1935]:27). Similar to the two-stringed lutes of Java, the *hasapi* instrument was part of a Toba Batak music ensemble, including gongs and drums, that was played during trance dances at traditional life-cycle rituals such as marriages or funerals. During the dance, persons would become possessed and speak for the ancestors (personal communication, Rodgers 1989). The anthropomorphic figures carved on both the front and back of this *hasapi* (Fig. III.39) may refer to these beneficial spirits.

Today *hasapi* lutes are likely to be played for mere entertainment, especially among courting teenagers, although the instrument is still sometimes played at traditional-style weddings and funerals, and even occasionally for Karo curing rituals such as *erpangir ku lau*, where people enter a trance state (Steedly 1989:144). Participants dance in trance (Fig. III.38) to call ancestor spirits who, it is hoped, will cure the woman shaman wearing a white cloth.

This instrument (Fig. III.39) is also a dynamic piece of sculpture incorporating five anthropomorphic figures and a supporting *singa* creature carved in characteristic Toba style. In profile, the noses, jawlines, and curved knees of Toba sculptures are prominent; tall coiffures made of animal hair are carefully arranged. Oversized heads with large ears wear carved hoop earrings. An angled projecting center line divides the left and right sides of the face. All of these details are carved attentively, and the entire sculpture is smoothly polished.

The Traditional Priest: Healing, Spirit Contact, and Divination

Among the Batak, the keepers of the esoteric knowledge of rituals were male priests called *datu* or *guru*, depending on the region. These ritual specialists often inherited their positions and served the local chiefs to keep the village in sacred order. Sometimes the chiefs were themselves the ritual specialists of their villages. If not, the ritual specialist was the second most powerful man of the village (Loeb 1972[1935]:82). As part of their role, they made a number of

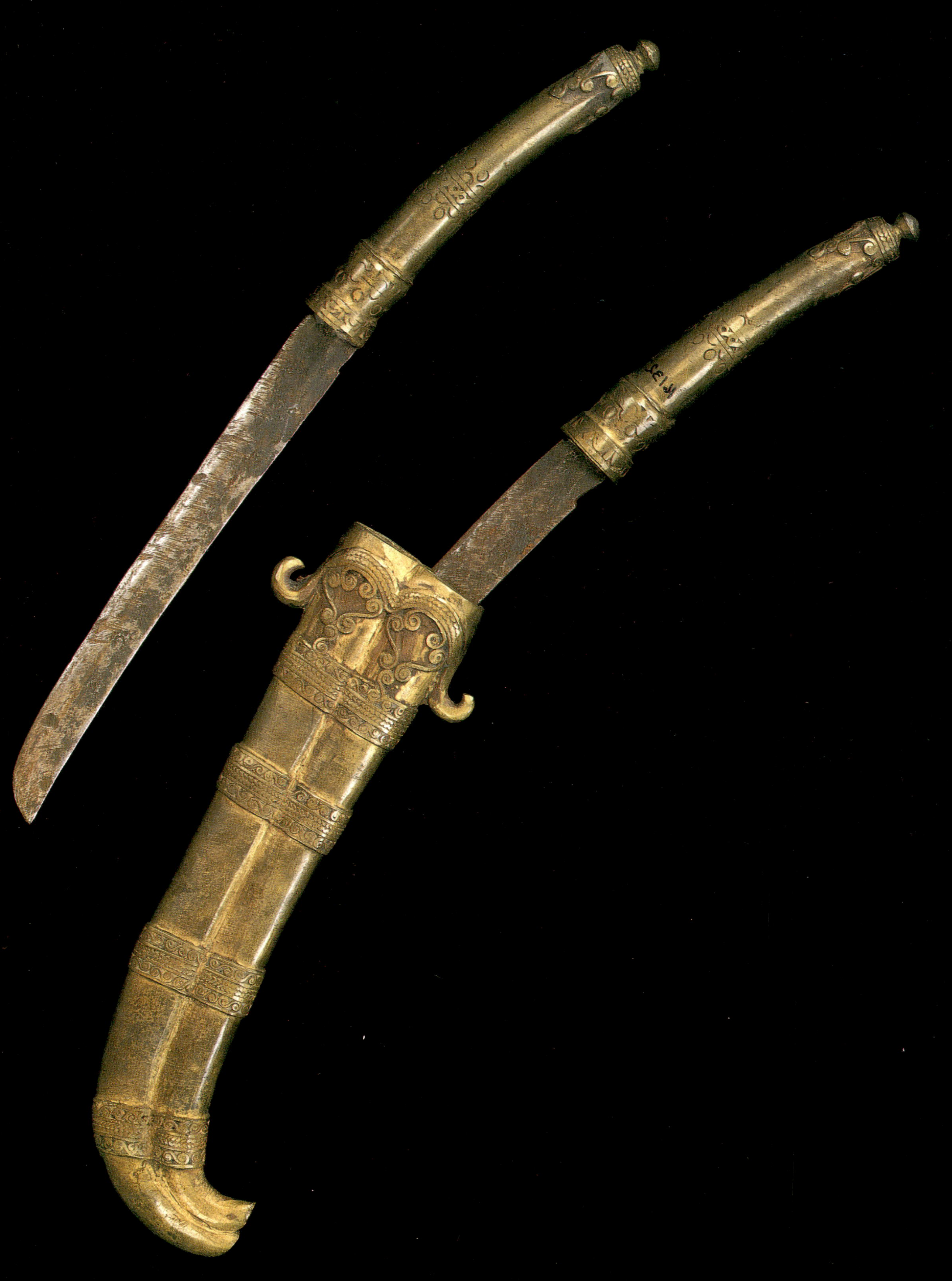

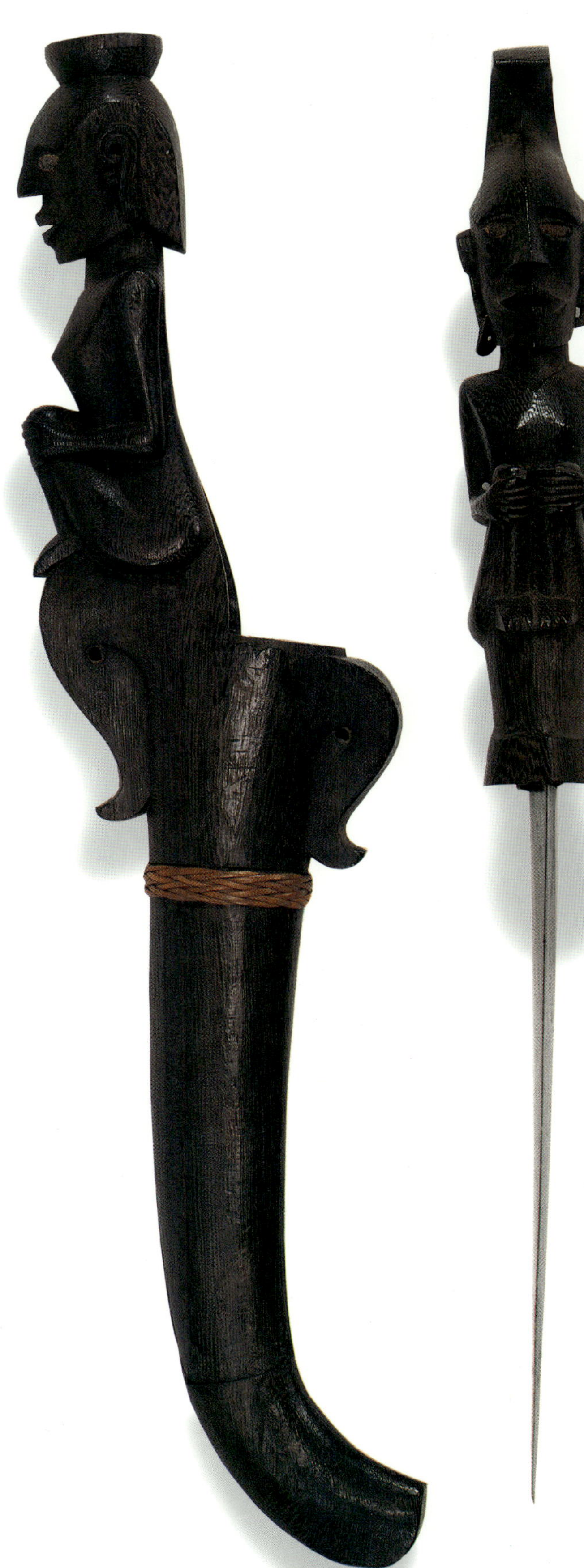

OPPOSITE
Fig. III.29 KNIFE AND SCABBARD, *PISO*
Toba Batak, Lake Toba, North Sumatra
Metal, wood, 28.5 x 6.5 x 2
Field Museum of Natural History, Chicago, 161327. Collected by F. C. Cole on the Arthur B. Jones Expedition, 1922–3.

Fig. III.30 KNIFE AND SCABBARD, *PISO*
Batak, North Sumatra
Wood, metal, rattan, 32.5 x 9.5 x 3.2
Museum Nasional Indonesia, Jakarta, 26866. Purchased for 50,000 rupiah. Accessioned in 1951.

Fig. III.31 MASK AND HANDS
Batak, Pangoloan, North Sumatra
Mask: Wood, hair, 35.5 x 31.7 x 14
Hands: Wood, 24.1 x 6 x 6.6; 24.3 x 6.3 x 4
Royal Tropical Institute, Tropenmuseum, The Netherlands, A3858. Accessioned in 1889.

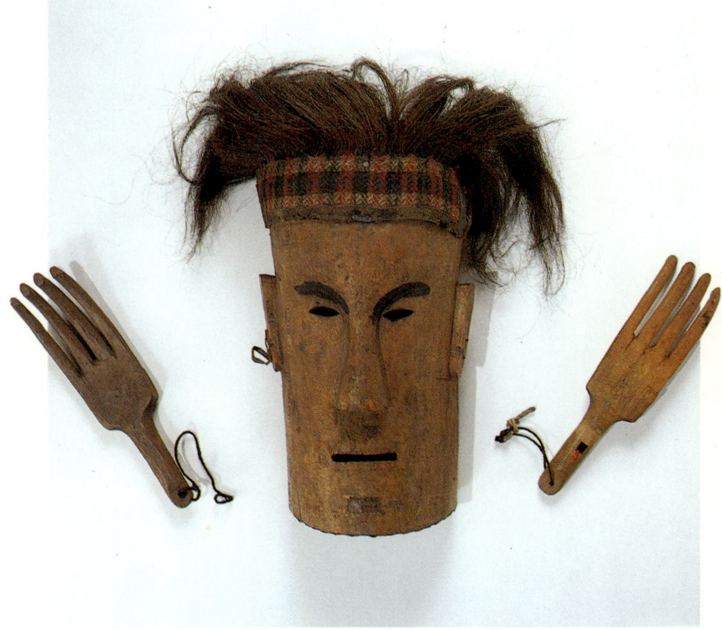

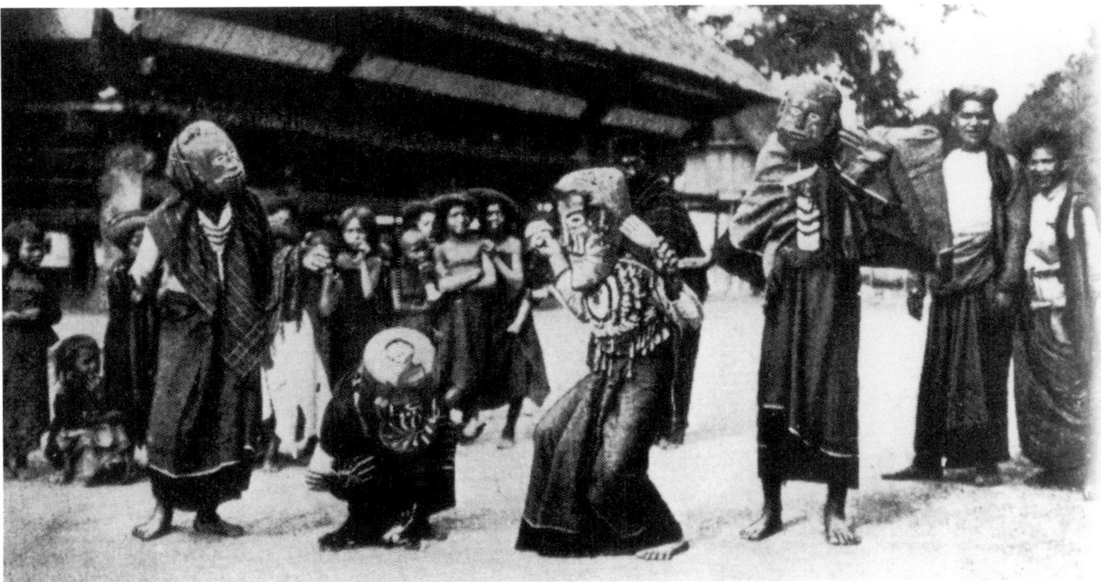

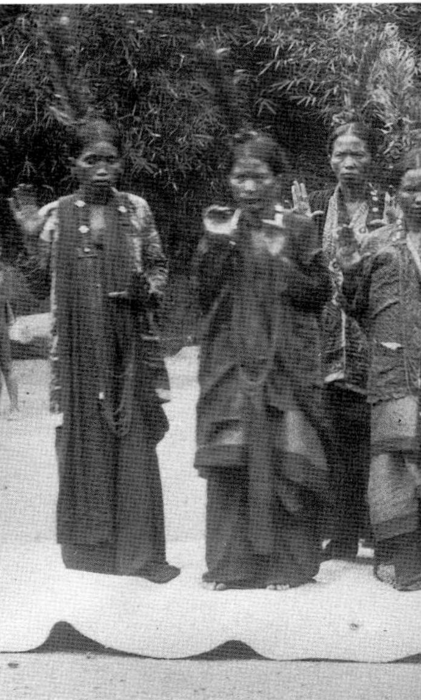

Fig. III.32 Toba Batak masked dancers at the funeral of an important man, North Sumatra, before 1935. Loeb 1972[1935]: fig. 24

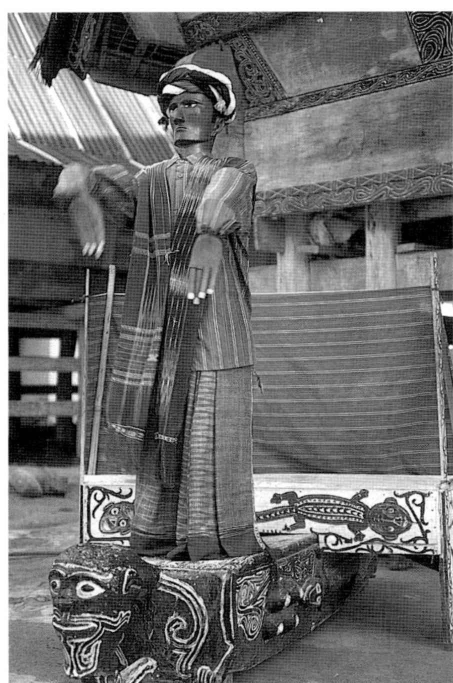

Fig. III.33 *Si gale-gale* puppet, Samosir, Lake Toba region, North Sumatra, 1989. Danielle Hayes

painstakingly carved divining tools and amulets. These objects helped them to contact spirits of the deceased, call back wandering souls of the sick, repel evil forces from the village, or divine promising days for travel, warfare, or ceremonies.

Carved and handled only by traditional priests, ornamented staffs were endowed with the power of the ancestors and were a symbol of unity with the ancestors. To activate their power, a priest "fed" the carved figures with plant or animal materials, which were sometimes carried in a small hollow inside the staff. The staff was then used to ward off misfortune or to divine the causes of disease. Reportedly, a good staff took months to carve and was very expensive because of the number of ritual animal sacrifices necessary to complete its fabrication (Loeb 1972[1935]:86). The two types of Toba Batak sacred wooden staffs differ according to the figures represented in the carvings. The *tunggal panaluan* (Fig. III.37), meaning "victory staff," was considered the "elder brother" to the *tunggal malehat*, a name perhaps derived from the Arab and Malay term *malaikat*, "angel staff" (Tichelman 1953). The *tunggal panaluan* was carved in relief from *Protium javanicum* wood, locally called *tada tada*, or "resistant" (Tichelman 1953:8). All such staffs, considered clan property, depict seven human figures, plus that of a serpent, a lizard, and a buffalo. According to one Toba Batak myth, the figures represent an incestuous pair of twins who are turned into wooden staff ornaments along with several other persons and animals who try to assist them. Guilty of having offended the spirit world with an unnatural marriage, the metamorphosis of the couple and their allies into a wooden statue is a symbolic reminder of the intractable social order. While technically a violation of the moral order, an incestuous marriage also represents, however, an ideal of clan independence and vitality, where wives from other clans would not be required (Niessen 1982). The topmost male image in Fig. III.37 wears a characteristic Toba Batak headscarf with a hairpiece spouting from the top. His illicit wife sits below him, riding on a buffalo above the other people and animals.

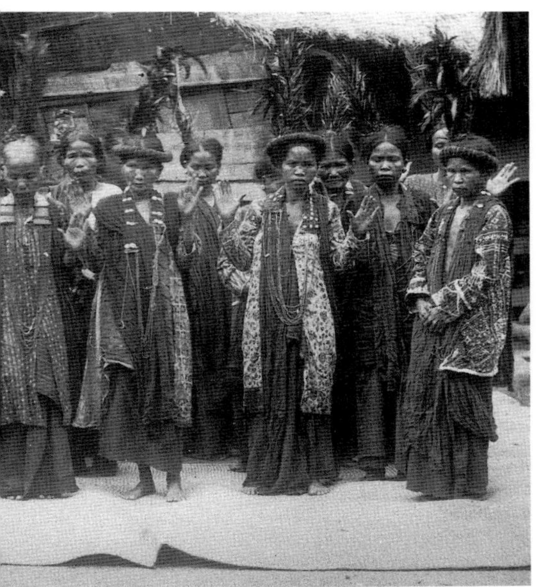

Fig. III.35 Toba Batak women wearing beaded collars during dance at annual *mangase* ritual, Sihotang, Samosir, North Sumatra, circa 1930. Courtesy Royal Tropical Institute, Tropenmuseum, The Netherlands.

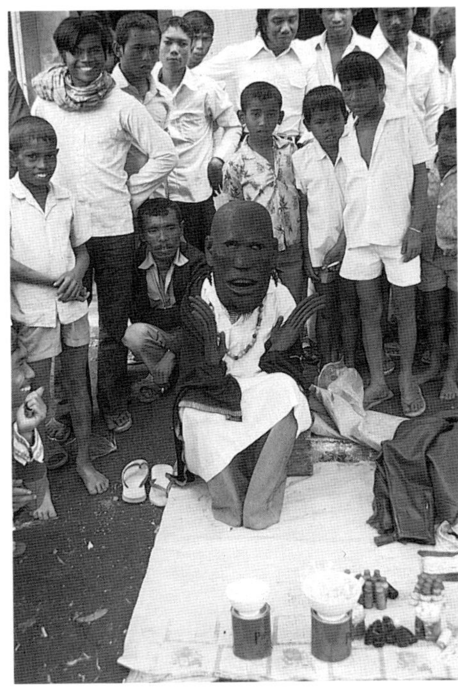

Fig. III.34 Travelling Karo medicine men wearing wooden mask and hands at open-air market, North Sumatra, 1973. Rita Smith Kipp

The traditional Toba Batak worshipper called himself a venerator of "spirits," or *begu,* the same concept with a different transliteration as the Nias term *bekhu* (Vergouwen 1964:69). Not all of this class of varied spirits were harmful to humanity, but those who died in unfortunate accidents or without offspring were thought to be dangerous because of their unhappiness about their fate. One of the ritual specialist's tasks was to give people or communities relief from assaults of bad fortune caused by vengeful *begu* disgruntled about their deaths. One technique to fight evjl spirits was the creation of a "protective fence" (*pagar*), a statue inhabited with the spirit of someone deceased (Fig. III.40). The most powerful statues contained the spirit of a sacrificed person, usually a member of an enemy village. Offerings increased the protective charm's power, but the key to the statuettes' activation was the magical words recited by the priest when petitioning the spirit of the statuettes for assistance (Vergouwen 1964:96). Some of the figures in the illustrated group carry weapons to repel misfortune. The others hold their very large hands in a palms-out position, a gesture also seen in Toba Batak dances that were performed to contact ancestor and other spirits.

Toba Batak priests (*datu*) used carved bones (Fig. III.41), bark books (Fig. III.25), and inscribed bamboo containers (Figs. III.43, III.44) as calendars (*parhalaan*), actually oracles, to predict the future and divine auspicious days for travel or rituals. These items all encoded the sacred knowledge passed down from elder to younger priest. Often the actual inscribing was done by a *datu* pupil at the behest of his mentor who dictated the characters to the apprentice (Loeb 1972[1935]:82–83). Memorizing the signs of the Batak alphabet was one of the first tasks undertaken by a youth who wished to learn the art of the priest; ritual practices and incantations were taught later. The apprenticeship process was long and costly since the man wishing to see his son become a *datu* was required to provide hospitality to the teacher, and sometimes even his entire household, for the duration of the instruction period (Loeb 1972[1935]:82). Hence the *datu* position often remained within a single lineage among the upper ranks of the community.

Predictive calendars were based on a solar calendar of twelve thirty-day months per year, with an additional month added every six years (Lubis et al. 1986:36). Days were named with Sanskrit-derived terms, and the constellation of Scorpio was considered the key ill omen for most ritual events. Although there are many similarities of characters and their meanings among the Batak groups, each calendar was said to be completely intelligible only to its maker and his students (Lubis et al. 1986:60). When community members wished to plan such important events as the opening of a new rice field, an engagement, or a marriage, they called upon the ritual specialist to check his bamboo, bone, or bark calendar to find an auspicious date according to the stars and traditional lore. The ritual specialist would also be consulted when any life-cycle ceremony was planned.

Dr. P. Voorhoeve, a specialist on Batak culture and writing, has been able to make an extensive translation of the texts ornamenting the predictive calendars of bamboo and bone (Figs. III.41, III.43, III.44). The following discussion relies on his expertise in the Toba language, with Karo information added from the linguistic work of the Reverend J. H. Neumann (Voorhoeve and Neumann 1933). The scant wear on the bamboo containers suggest that the writing was added to beautify the objects for their owners rather than to be used for actual divining ceremonies, (personal communication, Dr. P. Voorhoeve 1990). Unquestionably these calendars were valued aesthetically not only for their visual images but also for their poetry.

The writing on the bamboo calendar (Fig. III.43) describes symptoms of illness, the spirits that may cause them, and the offerings that should be made to promote a cure. A sample of this translation follows:

> If he is slanting forward, sitting in an awkward position, his name is Datu Satiya Sunggu, Datu Polnung ni Begu. An offering of a black chicken and yellow rice

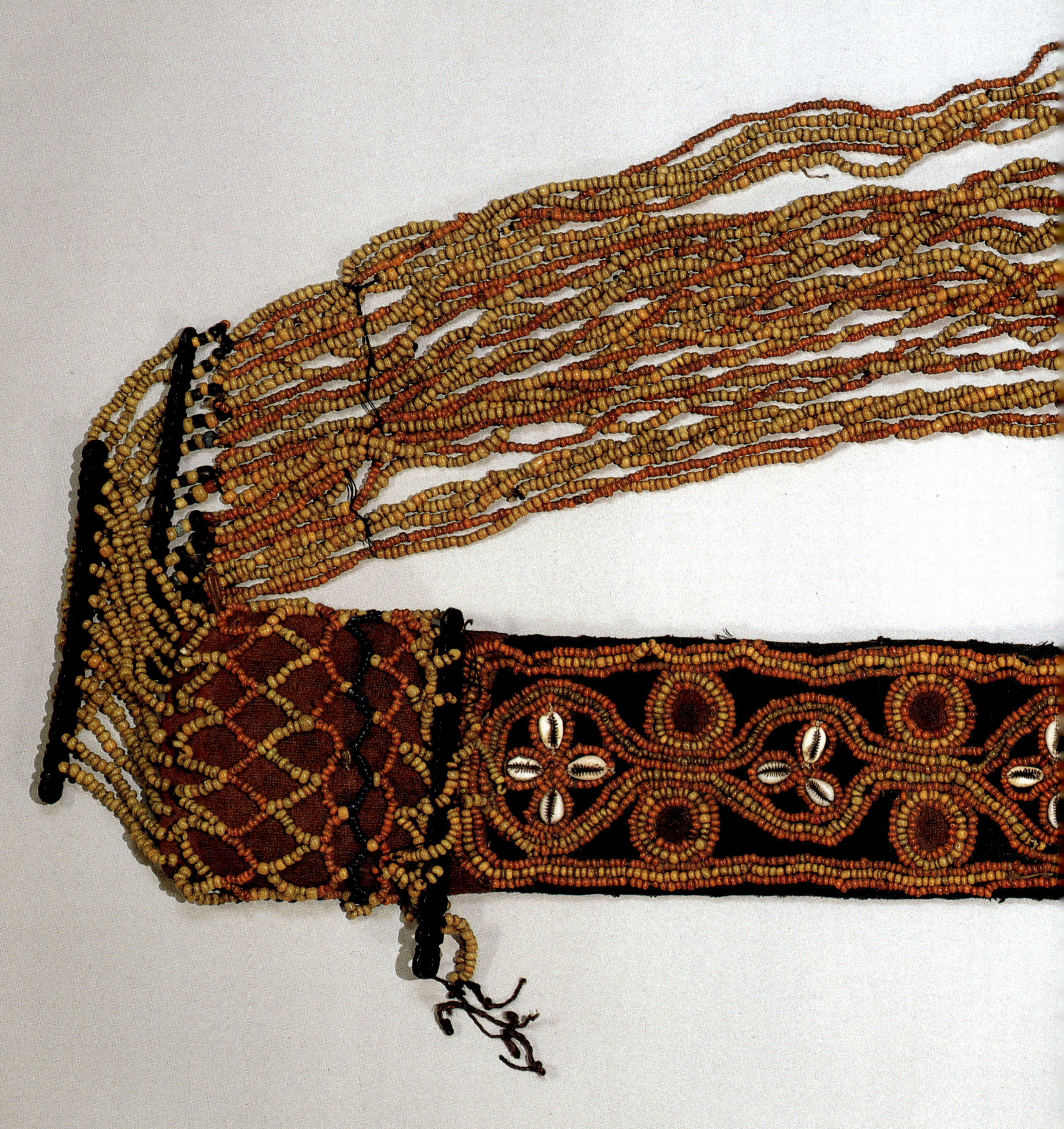

Fig. III.36 Beaded shoulder and neck ornament, *sinata godeng*
Toba Batak, North Sumatra
Beads, shells, bells, rattan, cotton, 148
Royal Tropical Institute, Tropenmuseum, The Netherlands, 137–155

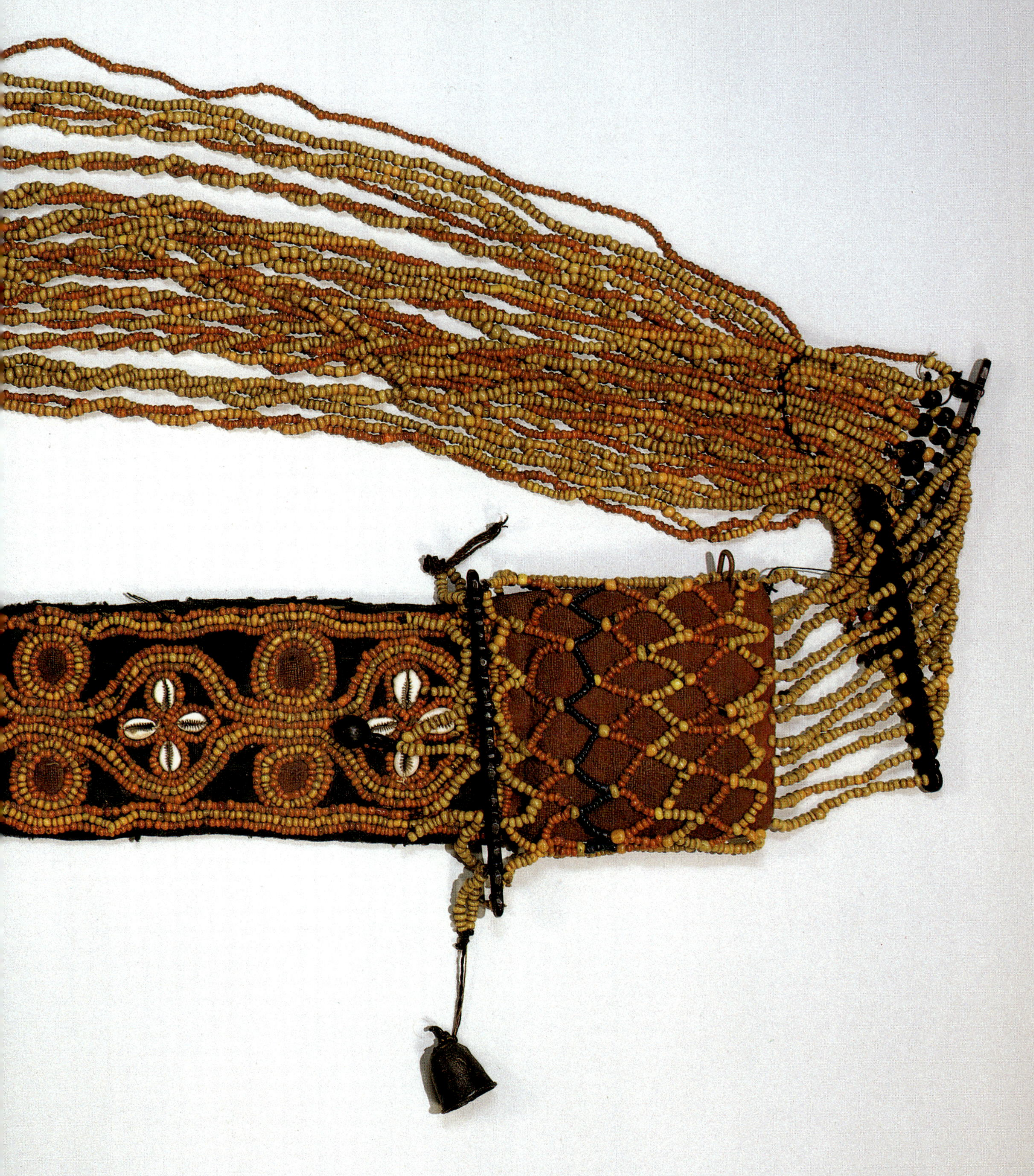

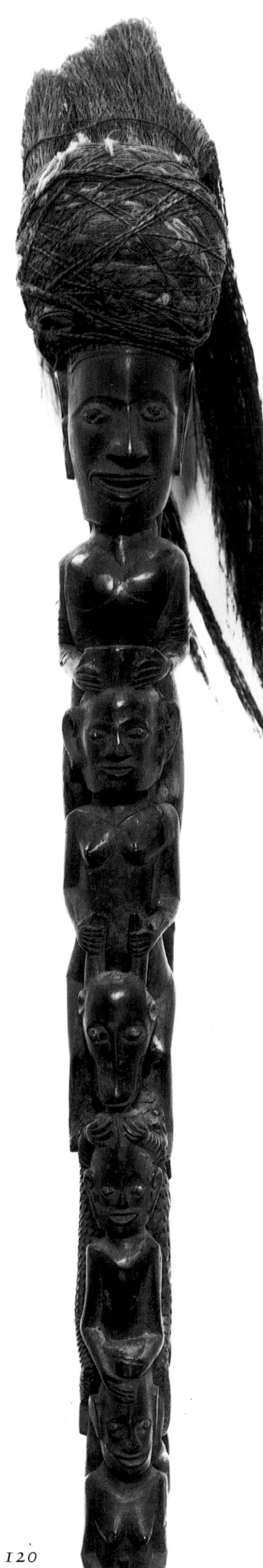

> should be given to him. If her face looks pale, her name is Si Deyang Sunting Haomasan, a mendicant ghost. An offering of roasted rice grains, rice cakes, betel, soot and oil, and a tin tobacco box should be given to her.

The writing on this bamboo container (Fig. III.44) also includes notes on protective magic, with the following references to protective statuettes, or *pagar*:

> This is *pagar salisį* [a protective statuette], to avert evil ghosts and the enemy's sorcery. This is *pagar gaguntaran*, oh sorcerer. This is *pagar panungsang*, causing the magic of evil ghosts and enemies to retire. This is a *pagar* who turns against its owner on that day [apparently the effect of the *pagar* depends on the calendar day on which it is used]. This is a *pagar* who protects and fortifies against the sorcery of men and ghosts. Hush! This is lacking on that day. This is a *pagar* who makes sorcery of men and ghosts ineffective by pointing at it. Hush! This is a *pagar* to fetch an unwilling woman on that day.

Another section lists the Sanskrit names of the twelve signs of the zodiac with their Batak translations. Beside that is a short text on omens interpreted from dreams and natural phenomena (*pormunian*). A translation of the final section follows:

> If an omen is observed in the evening, ghosts will come when people are nearly asleep, aggressive spirits who cannot be placated by reverence, spirits of the waters who cannot be placated by homage, the small dragon(s) who cannot be averted. Their influence may be made ineffective by drumsticks, leather drum straps, rice flour cakes that cannot be grasped by ghosts, clipped betel leaves, uncooked rice, a hen's egg, soot and oil in a cup. This offering should be placed in a sleeping cubicle surrounded by mats. On its completion a fowl with legs of a color which differs from that of its body should be eaten. To ensure a good result its soul should be in the rice barrel.

A possible translation of some other text on the container (Fig. III.44) reads as follows:

> Om! In the name of God, the Merciful, the Compassionate. Om! Flaming fire, blazing fire! You, grandfather are sparkling like the pupils of the eyes in this head, you are resounding as the voice of the hornbill in a *santi marea* tree, you are shrieking as monkeys on a steep slope.

Rib bone calendars (Fig. III.41) were used as amulets to bring the owner good luck. The insides of the two rib bones depict mirror image pairs of unusual anthropomorphic figures with fine hair growing from their skin. The outsides of the bones are inscribed with ritual writings. The inscription on one of the bones incites the traditional priest, "champion of the wonderous staff," to contact the spirits successfully with the aid of the wild animals depicted on the carved staff (Fig. III.37; Voorhoeve and Neumann 1933:387–389). A translation of the second bone's text, which also seems to invoke supernatural powers for the ritual specialist, reads:

> Descend, then communicate . . . one shakes, one quakes . . . anyone who still has a father and mother, who has many children, who has more than another, who grasps what is gone, who tames that which is wild, who grabs what is far, who takes what is close, who stops that which is lovely from disappearing, who is as illustrious as the spreading clouds, father of Dul Katana, mother of Beru Katalun, the large rhinoceros, as white as a young sugar palm leaf, capable of shaking a beaded necklace, which can provide green sirih, pure lime, yellow, gold, white silver, and red gold alloy. If I am ashamed, if I have been disgraced, he says, then he would make a prayer and bend in the presence of everyone. Approaching the house ladder they will become confused; they sit, and then they can no longer sit still; they lay down to sleep and they have bad dreams; their hearts pound from fright, seized by the workings of the sorcery substance.

Although the role of the traditional Batak ritual priest has virtually disappeared under the pressures of modernization and world religion (see Steedly

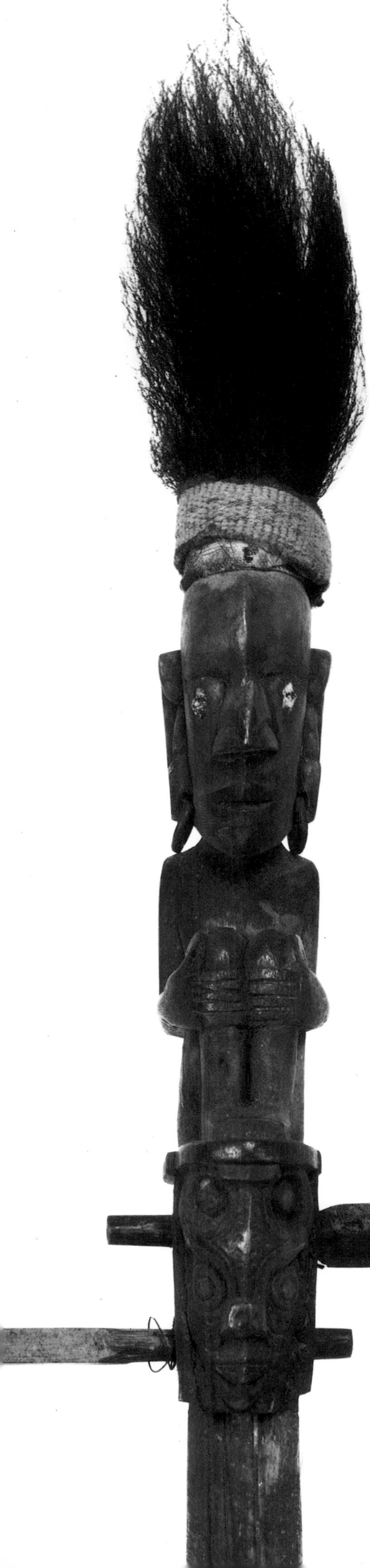

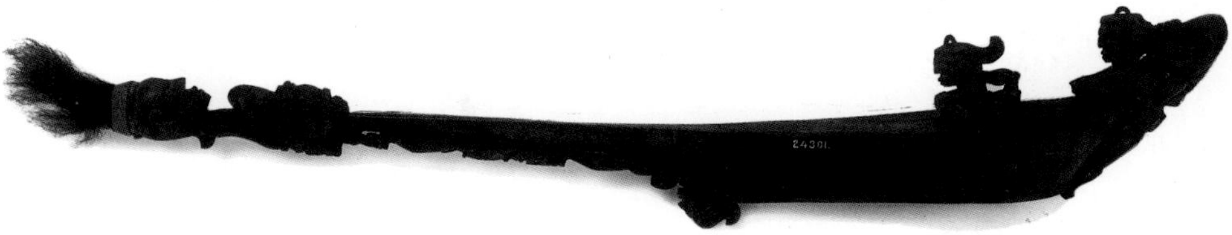

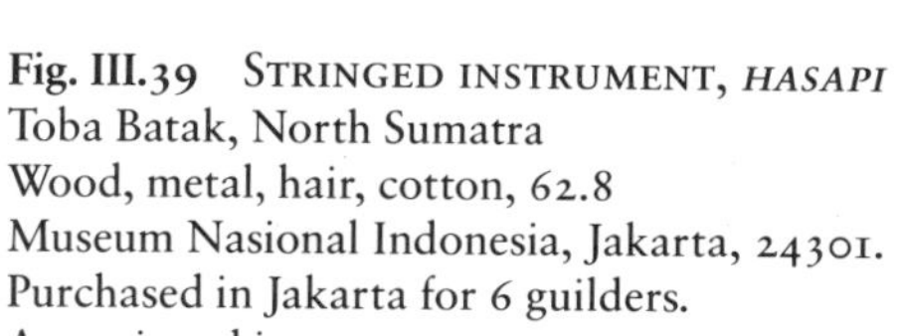

Fig. III.39 Stringed instrument, *hasapi*
Toba Batak, North Sumatra
Wood, metal, hair, cotton, 62.8
Museum Nasional Indonesia, Jakarta, 24301.
Purchased in Jakarta for 6 guilders.
Accessioned in 1941.

LEFT
Detail of Fig. III.39.

RIGHT
Fig. III.38 Karo man plays traditional lute at cleansing and curing ritual (*erpangir ku lau*), near Brestagi town, North Sumatra, 1987. Lucy A. Whalley

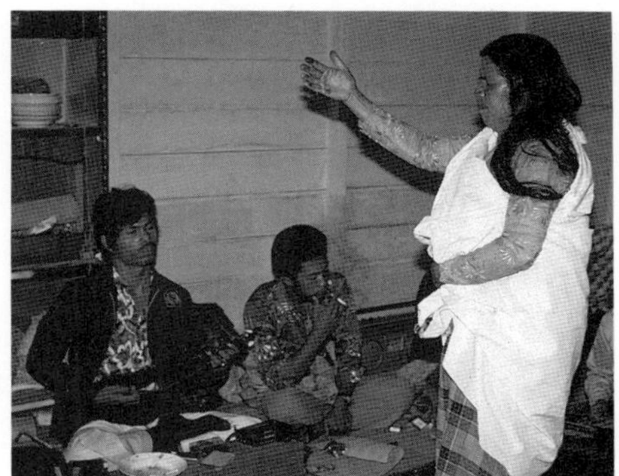

1989:146), the tools of his trade remain as impressive artworks. Decorated containers called *guri guri*, usually ceramic, stored powerful substances (*pupuk*) used in healing rituals. The delicately incised brass *guri guri* container (Fig. III.42) depicts a Toba-style human figure, probably an ancestor, riding a mythical horned animal with a cock's tail. The smaller rooster figure on the lid may represent one of the cocks sacrificed in Toba Batak healing ceremonies (Rodgers 1985:323). The body of the container is patterned with s-shaped spirals, fish scales, and four-petaled flowers in rectangular zones further ornamented with diamonds, tendrils, and flower buds. The entire composition honors the mounted figure and indicates both the ancestor's otherworldly status and the traditional priest's privileged connection to spiritual powers.

OPPOSITE
Fig. III.37 Priest's staff, *tunggal panaluan*
Toba Batak, North Sumatra
Wood, hair, 199 x 18 x 6.5
Royal Tropical Institute, Tropenmuseum, The Netherlands, 1548–1

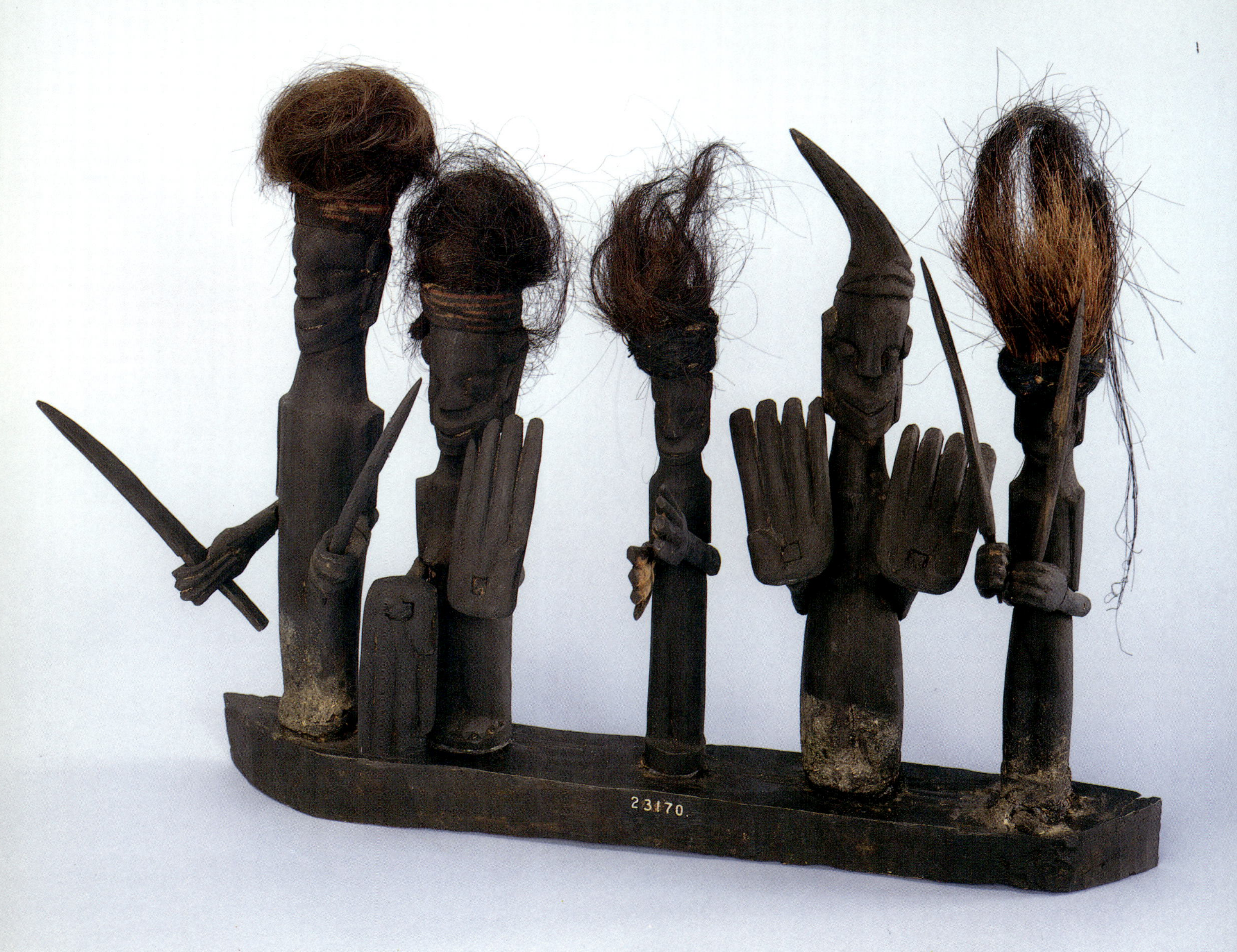

Fig. III.40 PROTECTIVE STATUETTES, *PAGAR*
Toba Batak, North Sumatra
Wood, hair, plant fiber, 25 x 33 x 12
Museum Nasional Indonesia, Jakarta, 23170.
Purchased in Simalungun area through the mediation of Dr. P. Voorhoeve. Accessioned in 1939.

OPPOSITE LEFT

Fig. III.43 CALENDAR, *PARHALAAN*
Toba Batak, North Sumatra
Bamboo, 15 x 5.1
Royal Tropical Institute, Tropenmuseum, The Netherlands, A4154. Originally donated by M. N. van der Tuuk to the Natura Artis Magistra society in the mid-1800s.

OPPOSITE RIGHT

Fig. III.44 CALENDAR, *PARHALAAN*
Toba Batak, North Sumatra
Bamboo, 10.3 x 6.4
Royal Tropical Institute, Tropenmuseum, The Netherlands, 15–544. Accessioned in 1912.

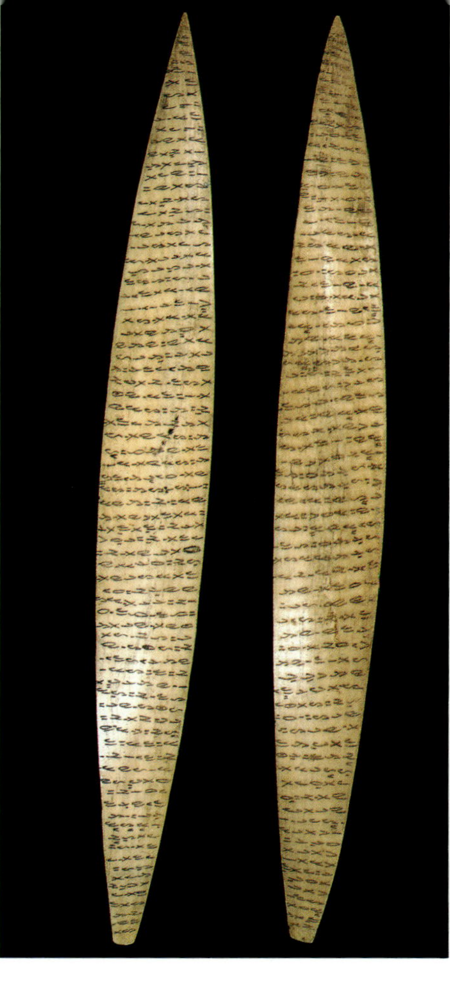

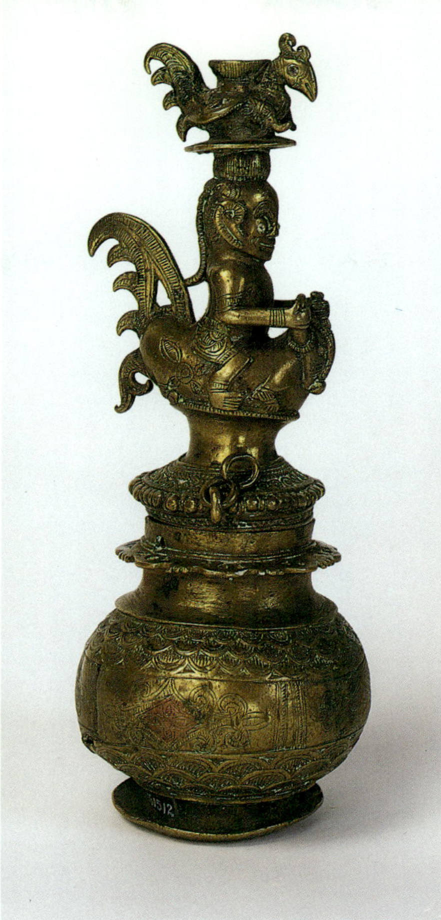

LEFT

Fig. III.41 Water buffalo rib bones
Karo, North Sumatra
Buffalo rib bone, 40.5 x 4.4; 39.5 x 4.3
Museum Nasional Indonesia, Jakarta, 20609A&B. Accessioned in 1933.

RIGHT

Fig. III.42 Brass container
Toba Batak, Lake Toba, North Sumatra
Brass, 17.5 x 6.7 x 6.7
Field Museum of Natural History, Chicago, 161512

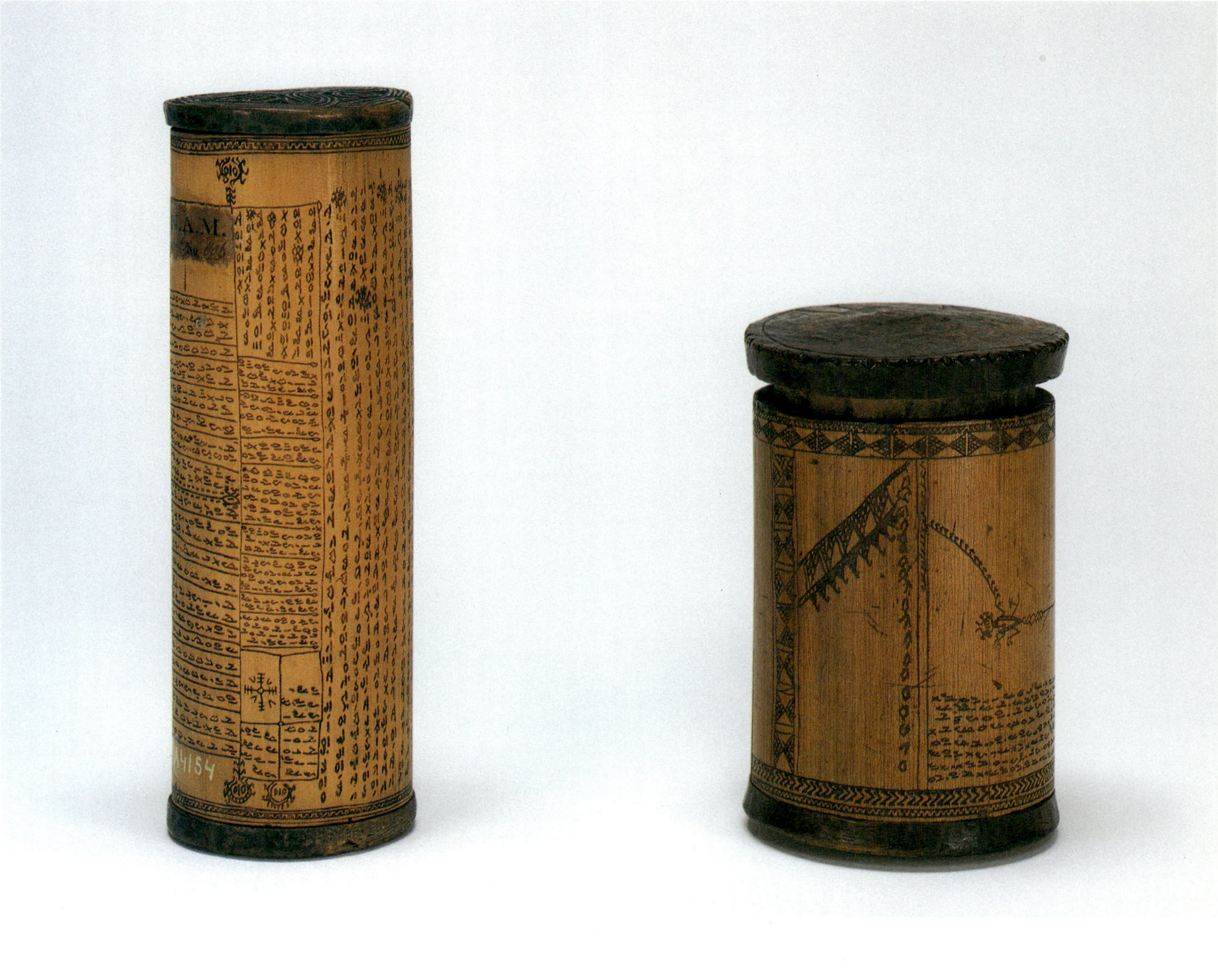

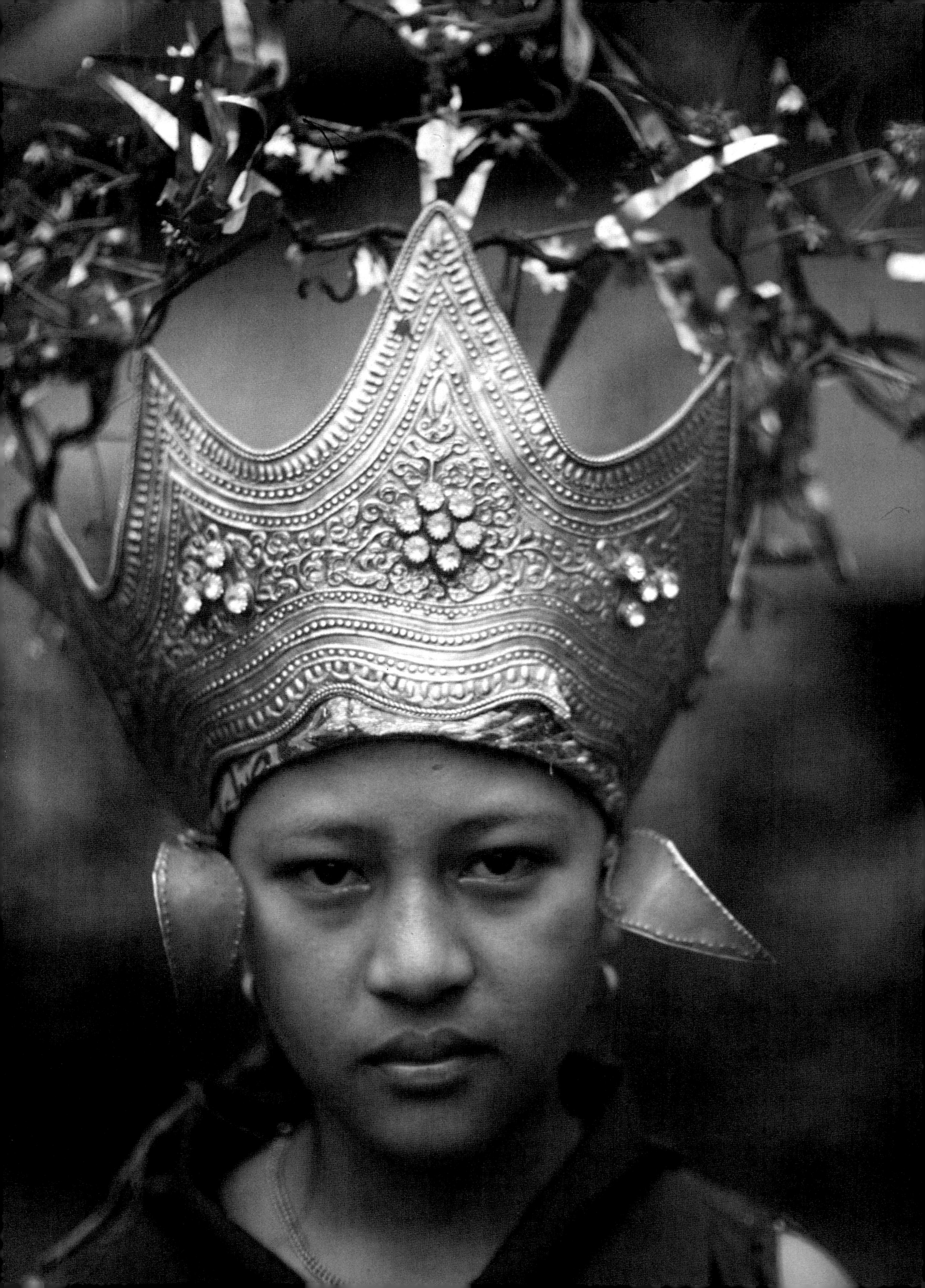

IV

Lampung

The Lampung Districts, as this region was called by the Dutch, includes about 30,000 square kilometers located along the southern tip of Sumatra. The various groups that live there are the coastal Peminggir (including the Kalianda and Telukbetung), the Pubian, and the interior-dwelling Abung. These populations are ethnically distinct from the Batak groups of North Sumatra.

The Lampung peoples grow rice and vegetables and raise animals for food. Access to the sea, particularly through the Semangka River, promoted coastal trade, and so such cash crops as pepper, cloves, coffee, tobacco, and resins have been exported for centuries (Gittinger 1972:3). The earliest European records indicate that the Lampung groups came into contact with Hindu-Buddhist people from the court centers of Palembang and Bantam (now Banten) by the fourteenth or fifteen centuries (van Dijk and de Jonge 1980:13–14; Jessup 1990; see also catalog chapter X). The Lampung coastal people became closely associated with the Javanese sultans of Bantam who bought black pepper from the Lampung area in exchange for titles of nobility and luxury goods. By the seventeenth century, Islamic traders of various Malay ethnic groups were marrying into Lampung clans, beginning a slow process of Islamic conversion. Today the coastal Lampung people are primarily Muslim agriculturalists or merchants, and most traditional artworks of textile and wood are no longer manufactured.

Some evidence of Lampung's early history is recorded in the imagery of its artworks. In rattan, wood, metal, and cloth, indigenous Lampung motifs are combined with Hindu-Buddhist mandalas, Chinese-style dragons, peacocks, and floral patterns. This mix of elements indicates a traditional society drawn into extensive contact with the Indian-influenced kingdoms of Sumatra, Java, and mainland Asia. The parallels between Lampung textile imagery and west Javanese motifs suggest their close development during the pre-Islamic period when the Srivijaya kingdom of South Sumatra was flourishing (Holmgren and Spertus 1980, 1989). Recently Gittinger (1989) has traced the resemblances of Lam-

Fig. IV.1 A young boy wears a headdress (*sigar*) for his circumcision ceremony. Lampung, Kota Agung, 1971. Mattiebelle Gittinger

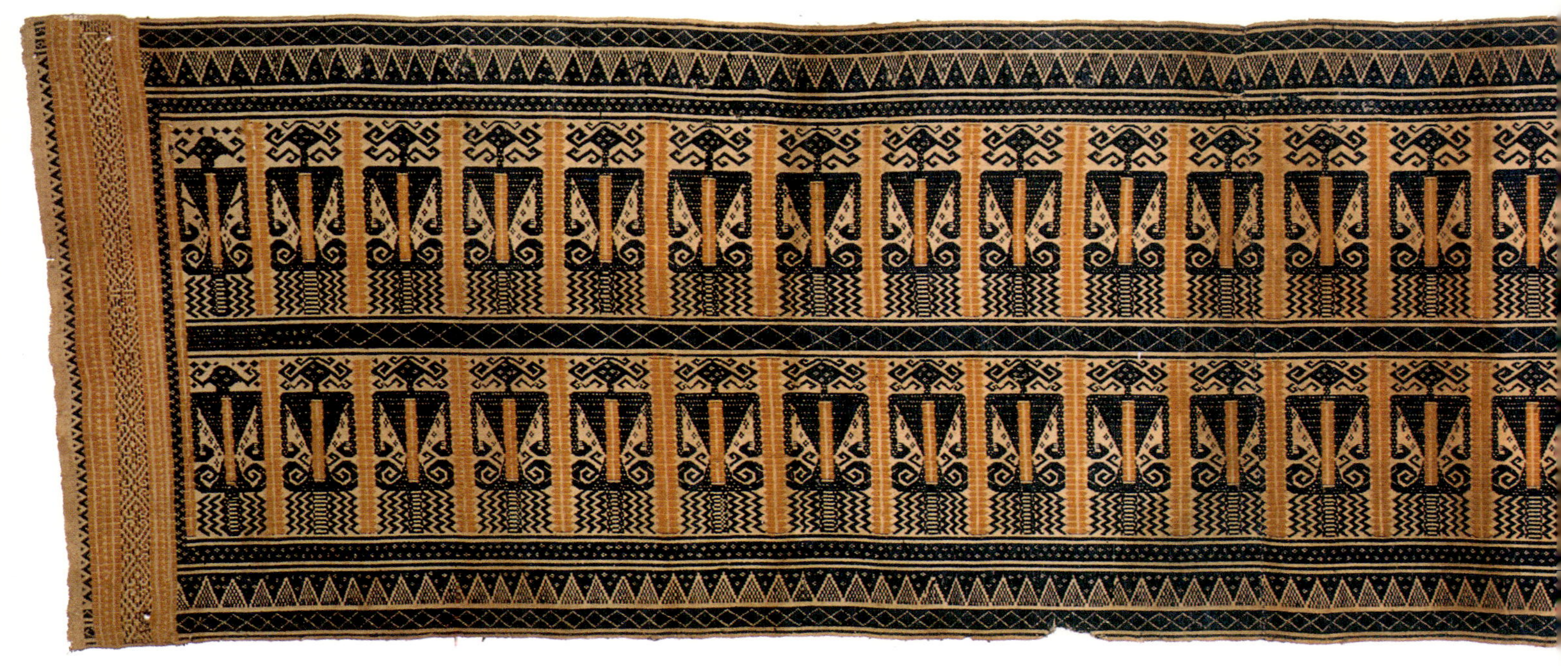

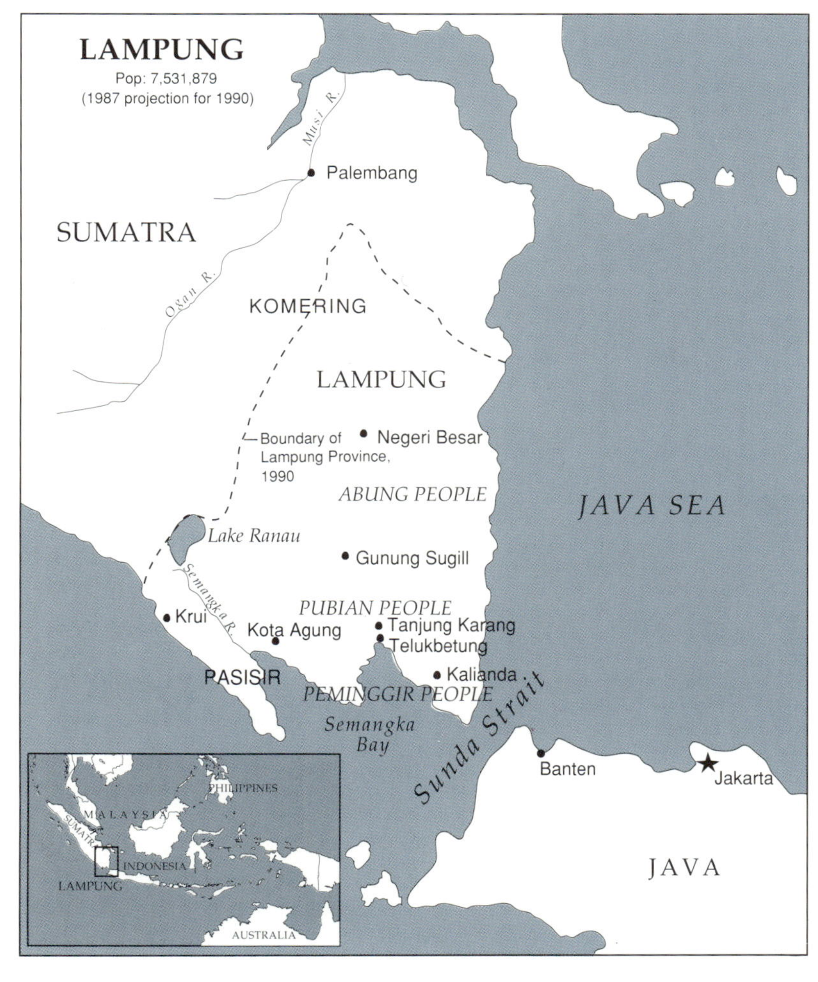

LAMPUNG
Pop: 7,531,879
(1987 projection for 1990)
Musi R.
Palembang
SUMATRA
Ogan R.
KOMERING
LAMPUNG
Boundary of Lampung Province, 1990
Negeri Besar
ABUNG PEOPLE
JAVA SEA
Lake Ranau
Gunung Sugill
Semangka R.
PUBIAN PEOPLE
Krui
Kota Agung
Tanjung Karang
Telukbetung
Kalianda
PASISIR
PEMINGGIR PEOPLE
Semangka Bay
Sunda Strait
Banten
Jakarta
PHILIPPINES
MALAYSIA
SUMATRA
INDONESIA
LAMPUNG
AUSTRALIA
JAVA

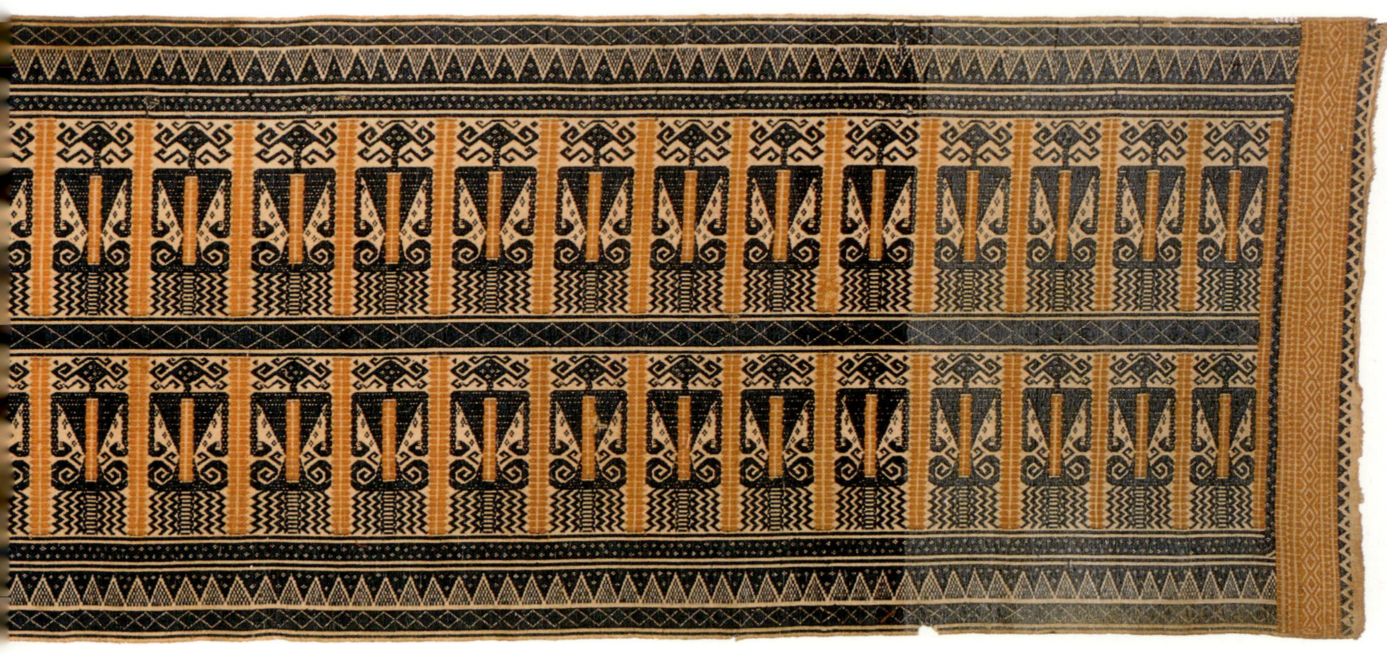

Fig. IV.2 CEREMONIAL CLOTH, *PALEPAI*
Lampung, Kelumbayan village near Kota Agung, Semangka Bay, southern Sumatra
Cotton, 63.6 x 305
Museum Nasional Indonesia, Jakarta, 20994. Accessioned in 1936.

pung designs to motifs and textile uses known from the Tai-speaking peoples of the Southeast Asian mainland. The similarities found in traditional textiles of these two regions (see also Fraser-Lu 1988 for an overview of Southeast Asian textiles) clearly supports the hypothesis that Tai, Malay, Sumatran, and perhaps Javanese kingdoms were associated closely during the second half of the first millennium A.D. The supposition that these areas were even a cultural continuum by the eighth century A.D. has also been posited by historians of the region (Smith and Watson 1979:454).

Aristocratic Competition and the Pepper Trade to Bantam

Lampung peoples are organized, like the Batak of northern Sumatra, according to patrilineal clans (*méga* or *marga*) that trace their origins to particular villages of origin. Thus the clans were both regional and genealogical entities (Hissink 1904; van der Hoop 1940:63). A clan was headed by the eldest direct male descendant of the clan's founder. Such clan chiefs, called *penyimbang*, dealt directly with the officials of the Javanese kingdom of Bantam during the sixteenth century or earlier. The first Muslim sultan of Bantam, who came to power in 1552, was Maulana Hasanuddin, and records indicate that he considered Lampung under his authority (van der Hoop 1940:63–64; Jessup 1990: 121–23). Bantam's interest in Lampung developed in the seventeenth century, during the era of the Dutch East India Company (VOC). Under the pressure of Dutch trading interests, Bantam filled its quota of pepper from Lampung resources.

Visits by Lampung chiefs to the Bantam courts were reportedly the inspiration for the Lampung seat of honor, or *pepadon*, system. According to Aeckerlin (n.d., as cited in Hissink 1904), Lampung nobles were impressed by Javanese court etiquette wherein superiors would sit on seats higher than inferiors. The right to sit on a carved seat of honor (Fig. IV.3) was granted initially to Lampung clan heads by sultans of Bantam in West Java during the sixteenth century (van der Hoop 1940:63–64). Eventually entitlement to the seat and other regalia could be purchased from the descendants of the same clan chiefs

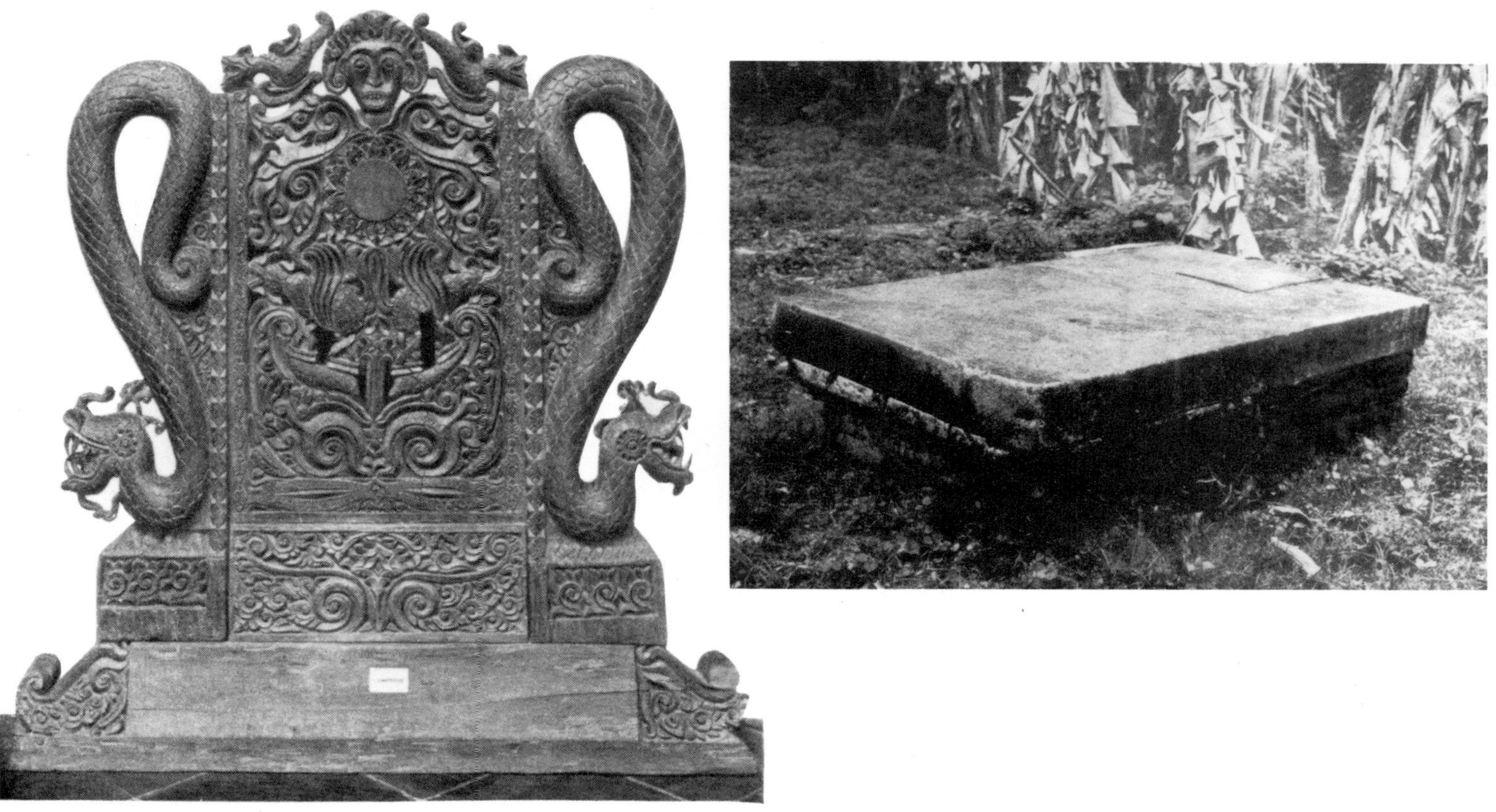

Fig. IV.3 Backrest (*sesako*) from Lampung seat of honor. Courtesy Museum Nasional Indonesia, Jakarta.

Fig. IV.4 Stone seats from the Bantam kingdom in West Java. van der Hoop 1940:fig. 9

who were originally entitled to those rights by nomination of the Bantam sultans. By sponsoring expensive feast ceremonies, including numerous buffalo sacrifices, Lampung nobles competed to acquire titles, status, and such symbols of power as carved wooden seats (*pepadon*), carved backrests for the thrones (Fig. IV.3), gates (*lawang kori*), bird-headed chariots (*rato*), and other prized possessions. The entire system of competition for titles and possession of status goods is now referred to as the *pepadon* system because the *pepadon* seat of honor was the original focus of achievement. The motifs carved on these wooden pieces, particularly the backrests and gates, are identical to floral and dragon motifs known from Javanese carving of the same period (Fontein 1990; Jessup 1990). According to Lampung informants, *pepadon* seats had guardian snakes, which could hide the seat of honor from the undeserving eye or warn the owner of danger (Jessup 1990:61).

The pepper trade brought new wealth to the Lampung region, increasing the competition between leaders of differing clans. The acquisition of luxury items became ever more expensive, and a noble's merit as warrior or statesman became less important than his ability to control wealth from imported trade goods (Schnitger 1939). The economic inflation induced by external trade pressures fed this social custom, but the *pepadon* seat of honor system also developed out of indigenous customs of status display, such as building public monuments in conjunction with the sponsorship of community feasts (van der Hoop 1940). On the neighboring island of Nias, for example, chiefs construct stone seats and posts and sponsor feasts to increase or secure their rank. This similar social system has been well documented (Loeb 1972[1935]:31; see photographs of stone monuments in catalog chapter II). The horizontal and vertical stone monuments located in a region of Lampung southeast of Lake Ranau are possible precursors of the *pepadon* seat of honor system (van der Hoop 1938, 1940:73). These, van der Hoop suggests, are evidence of indigenous monuments for Lampung clan chiefs erected prior to the colonial-era emulation of Javanese wooden thrones. He notes that Java, even Bantam itself, had an established

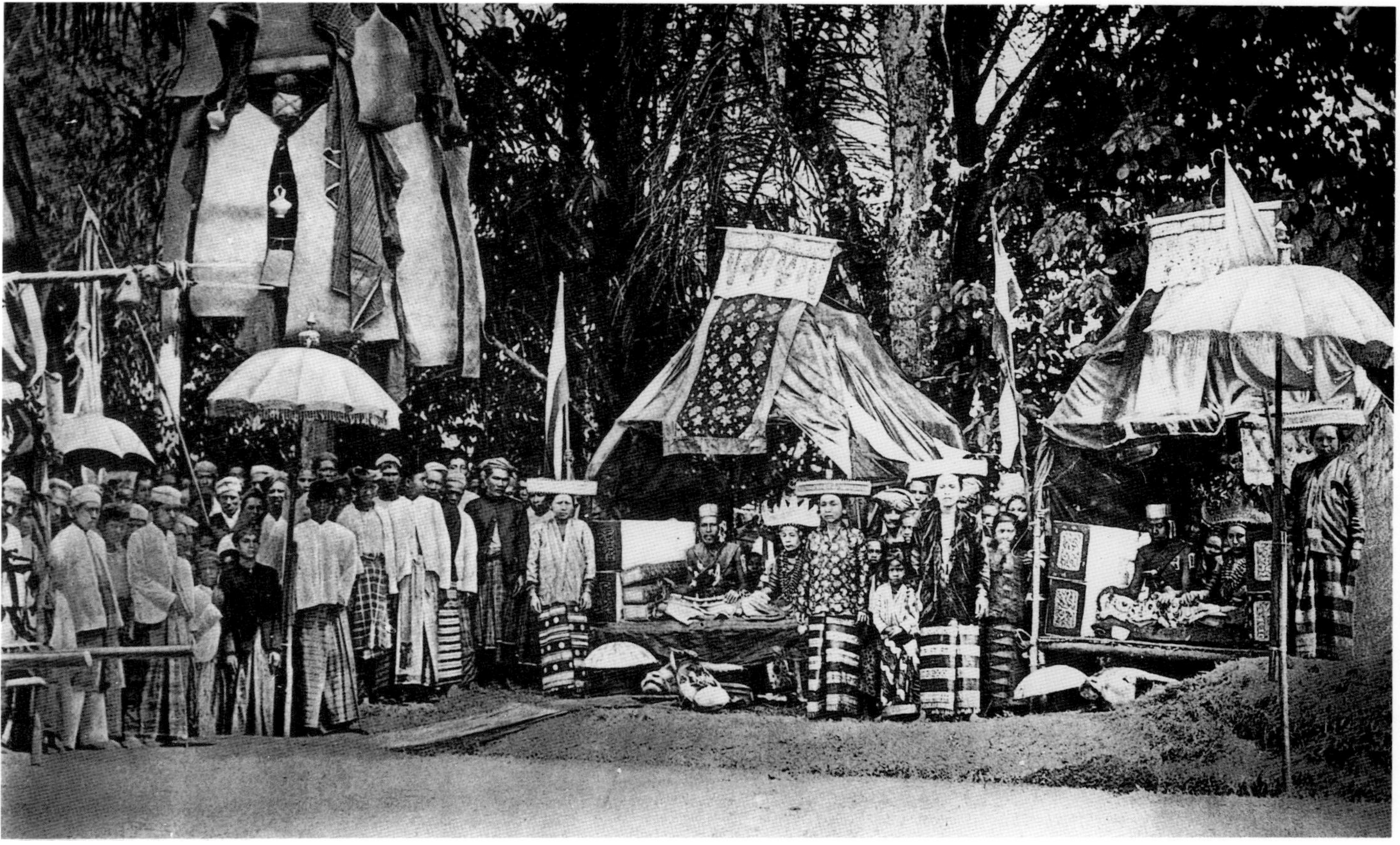

Fig. IV.5 A two-couple wedding in Lampung with heirloom textiles and mats hanging from ceremonial tree, southern Sumatra, early 1900s. Courtesy Koninklijk Instituut voor Taal-, Land- en Volkenkunde, Leiden.

history of using stone seats and tables (Fig. IV.4) prior to the production of the more elaborately carved wooden platforms and backrests (van der Hoop 1940:72).

Ship Cloths: Textiles for Rites of Passage

The Lampung region is best known for elaborate supplementary weft and embroidered textiles that were produced there prior to the twentieth century. These fine textiles have been called "ship cloths" because of the ship images, which locally symbolize passage from one stage of life to another (Gittinger 1972). The ship image expresses the coastal Lampung region's interests in foreign trade and diplomacy. The patterns on the ship cloths include depictions of traditional ceremonies that provide information on the Islamic, earlier Hindu-Buddhist, and even earlier indigenous religious history of the Lampung peoples. In the absence of extensive records on a society that has undergone considerable religious and social change in the past centuries, these textiles are now important historical documents.

Ceremonial woven cloths were used by noble families as ornamental banners and gift wrapping for all major life-cycle rituals, such as engagements, marriages (Fig. IV.5), births, circumcisions, teeth-filing (done for aesthetic reasons at puberty, see below), house building, and funerals (Gittinger 1972; van Dijk and de Jonge 1980; Holmgren and Spertus 1989). They were hung on walls or from tall poles for public display or used as a ceremonial wrapping for food or other gifts prescribed for marriage and other alliance ceremony exchanges. Ship cloths marked the status changes realized through traditional Lampung rituals. Gittinger (1972:137, 1976:219) hypothesizes that the ship motif appearing on most Lampung ceremonial textiles symbolizes a general life-cycle transition, rather than referring specifically to a "ship of the dead" taking souls to the afterworld, as was proposed by Langewis and Wagner (1964:33–34). Among these important life transitions were the ceremonies in which wealthy nobles increased their rank through the *pepadon* seat of honor system. These rituals included the display of ship cloths (van Dijk and de Jonge 1980:20–22).

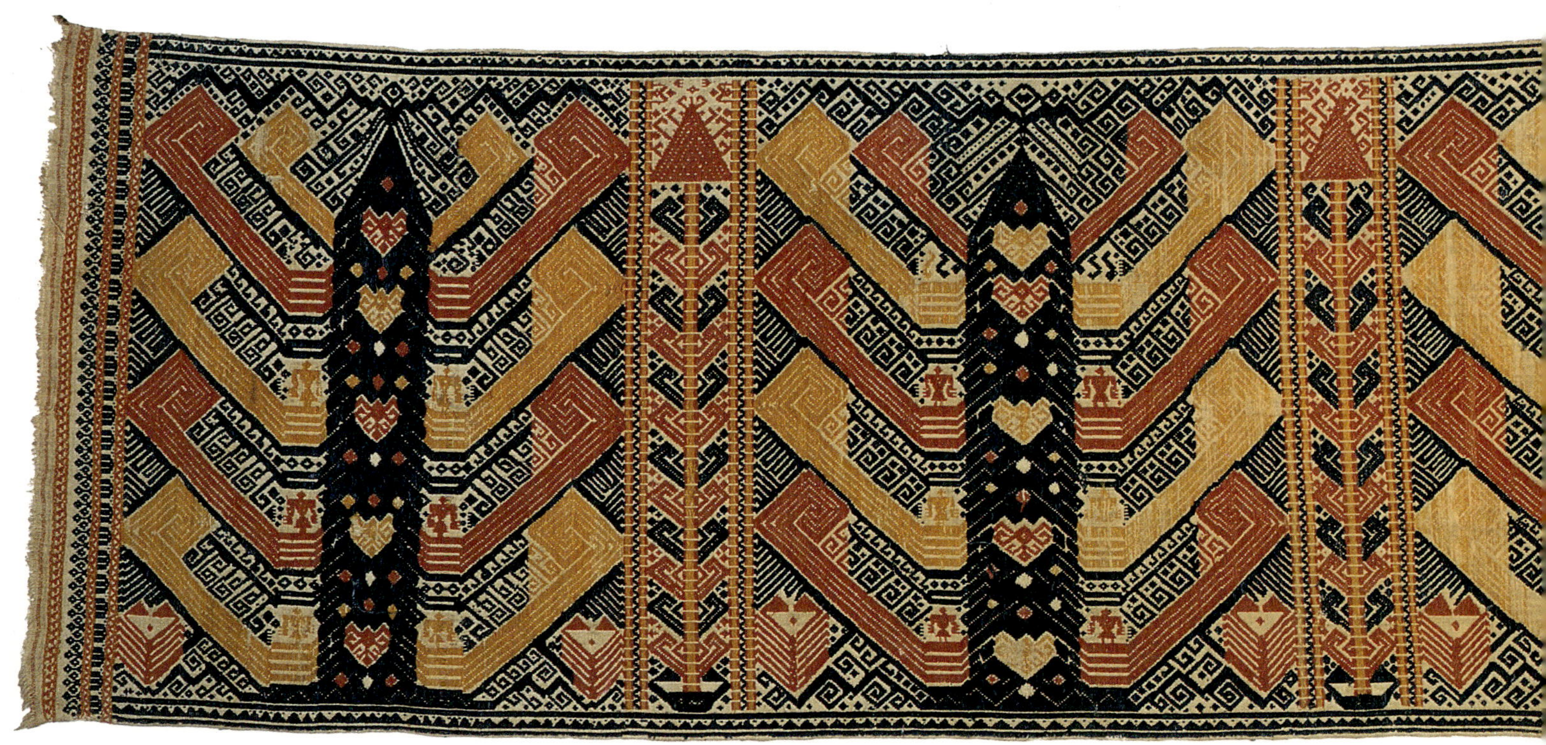

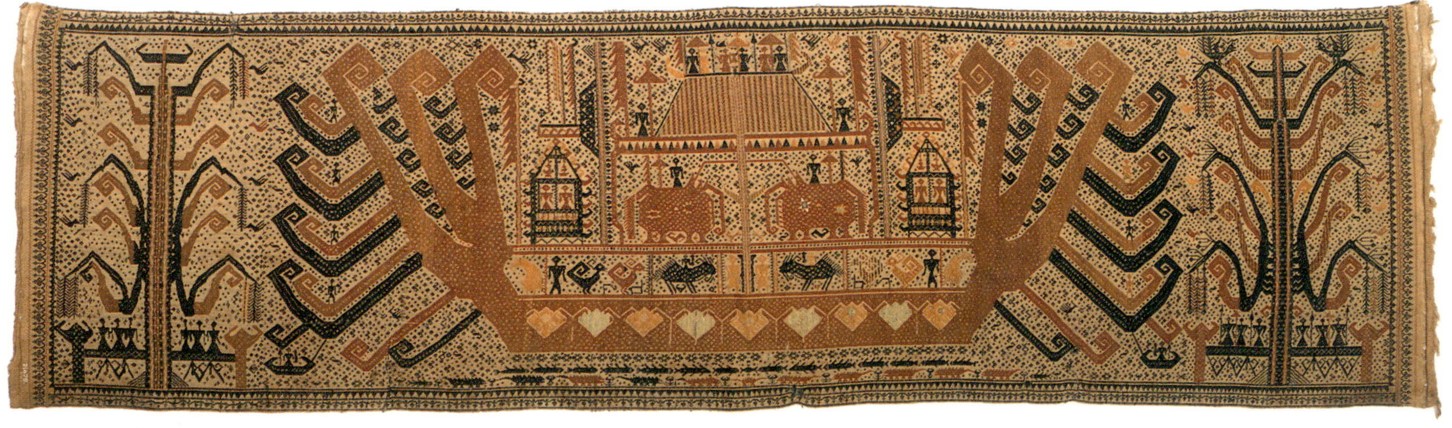

TOP

Fig. IV.6 Ceremonial cloth, *palepai*
Lampung, southern Sumatra
Cotton, 59 x 270
Museum Nasional Indonesia, Jakarta, 26562

Fig. IV.7 Ceremonial cloth, *palepai*
Lampung, Krui, southern Sumatra
Cotton, mirrored glass, 65.5 x 230
Museum Nasional Indonesia, Jakarta, 21479.
Accessioned in 1937.

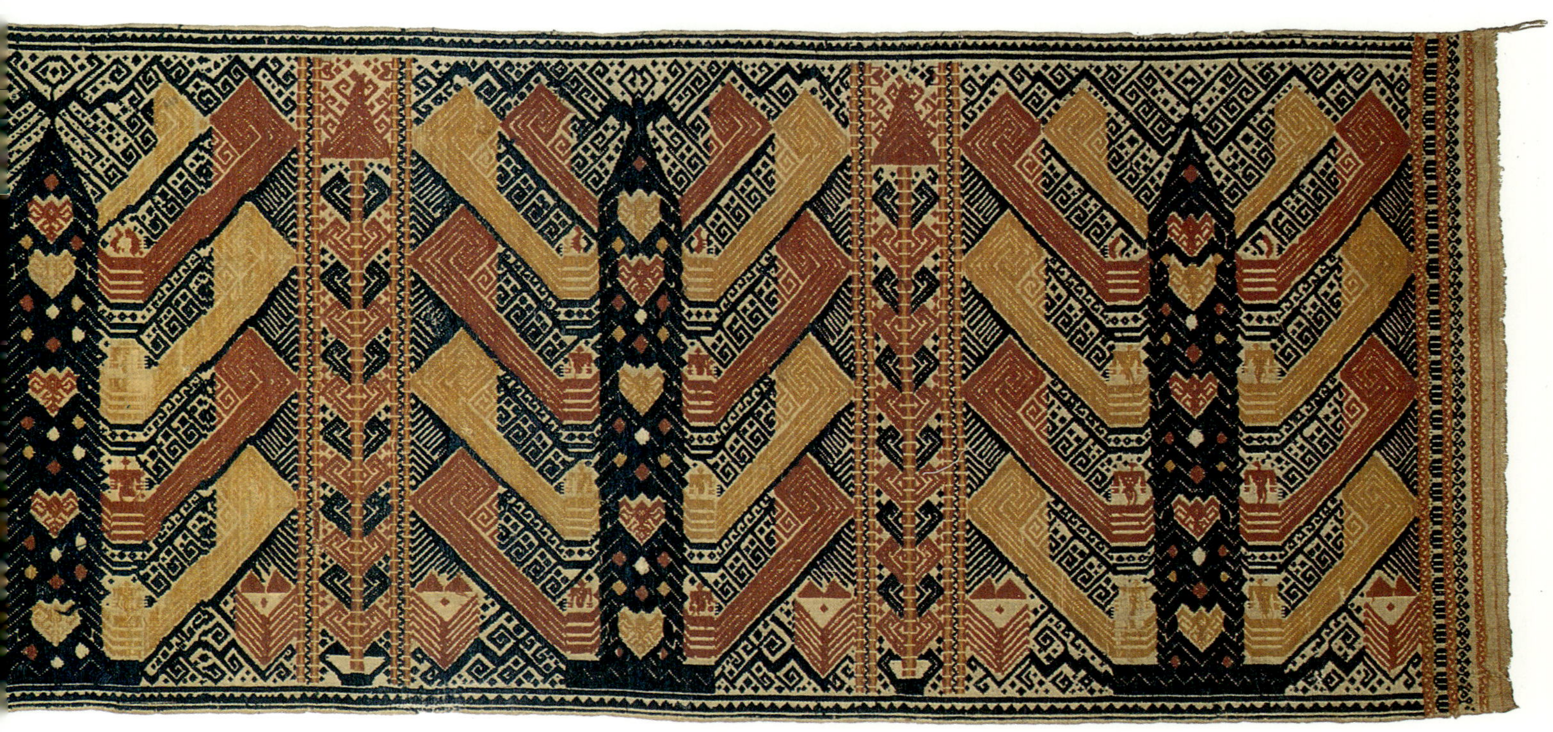

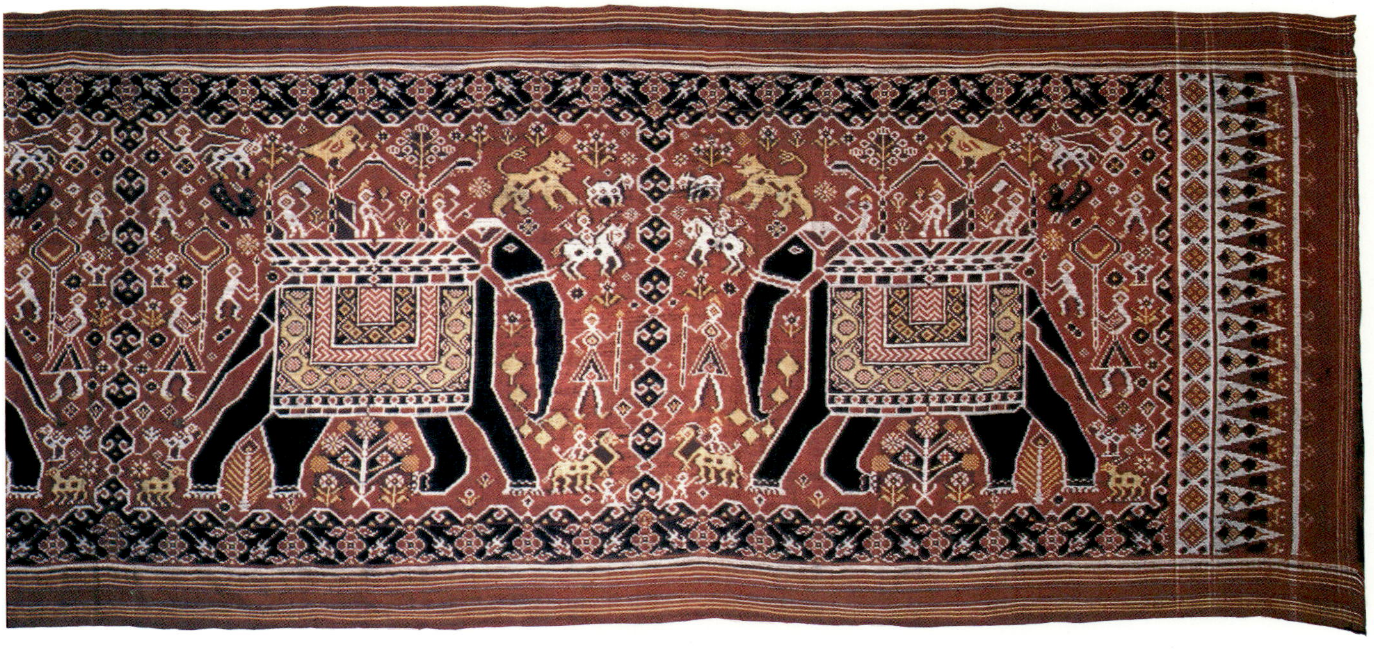

Fig. IV.8 Indian trade cloth (*patola*) depicting elephant mounts in a noble procession. Courtesy Royal Tropical Institute, Tropenmuseum, The Netherlands.

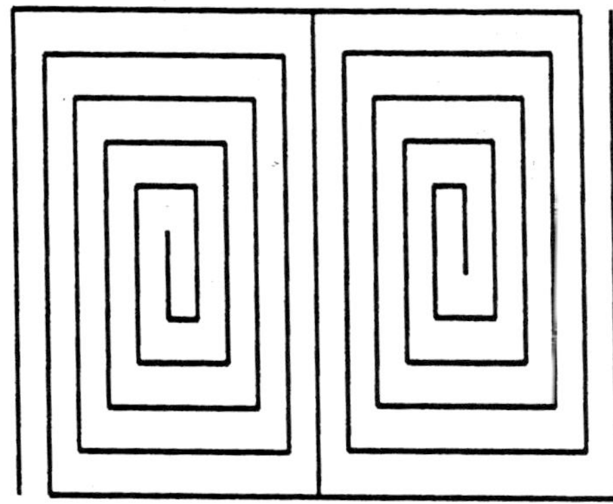

Fig. IV.9 Squared-off scroll motif. Marcia Bakry, Smithsonian Institution.

The images on ceremonial cloths provide specific information about Lampung's history of foreign trade and the local customs of its aristocracy. Honored persons are depicted in ceremonial dress, flanked by banners, servants, boatmen, trees, and animals. Some images—such as peacocks, winged beings, elephants, and floral patterns—may derive from trade objects from the Asian mainland. Ship structure, courtly regalia, and stylized human silhouettes similar to Javanese shadow puppets (*wayang kulit*) also indicate that Lampung settlements were part of the maritime Buddhist kingdom of Srivijaya (A.D. 600–1400), located near Palembang, Sumatra (Holmgren and Spertus 1980, 1989). Besides specific design features, the characteristic color palette of Lampung cloths—blues, deep reds, and ochres on a natural background—is one also preferred in the artworks of the Indian-influenced mainland (personal communication, F. K. Lehman 1990). Combined with these foreign elements are designs from Lampung's pre-Buddhist and pre-Islamic traditions, such as flattened images of humans, birds, and sea creatures.

Palepai: Ritual Cloths for the Nobility

Long ship cloths called *palepai* were owned by Lampung aristocrats, primarily on the south coast. They were reserved for the eldest males descended from the community's founder in the male line (Gittinger 1972, 1976). Usually eldest brothers of noble families (*penyimbang*) inherited the cloths, and younger brothers would borrow the pieces for their rites of passage. At aristocratic ceremonies, a *palepai* was hung on a wall behind the key participant (Gittinger 1972:45). Other such cloths were arranged in sequences to represent the relationships of other kin groups to the key participant. *Palepai* were traditionally displayed at a male noble baby's presentation to his maternal grandparents, his circumcision, and his marriage (Gittinger 1976:210). During aristocratic weddings in some Lampung regions, the bride was required to sit in state in front of hanging *palepai* cloths three times over a two-day period (Gittinger 1972:46).

Gittinger (1972:115, 1976) has classified *palepai* ship cloths into several prominent types: one features red ships and another features blue ships. Both motifs and composition differ according to these two types, and Gittinger suggests that red ship cloths include more narrative scenes than the blue ones, which include larger design configurations and appear to be more symbolic. This *palepai* textile (Fig. IV.7) depicts a ceremonial red ship framing a ritual scene such as a wedding. In the center, two honored persons ride elephants that face each other, a motif probably derived from Indian trade textiles such as the *patola* cloth (Fig. IV.8) The entire scene is set on a background of minute diamonds, crosses, and s-curves, giving the textile an animated appearance. Treelike forms on either side of the ship represent the ceremonial poles (*kayu ara*) erected for traditional Lampung weddings. The people standing beneath only one of the two trees hold spears and umbrellas of status. These might represent particular male elders among the family or that the respective families of the two mounted individuals were of different status. This *palepai* was probably used not only for weddings but also for other ceremonies marking a change of status.

One type of *palepai* (Fig. IV.6) is characterized by repeated identical ships in rectangles divided by bands featuring ceremonial poles or trees. The stylized trees and ships are composed of squared-off scrolls (Fig. IV.9), a basic motif familiar from Bronze Age drums. The ships are layered with small human forms appearing at each level, perhaps representing family generations or social ranks. The upturned scrolls that protrude from the poles probably depict buffalo horns hung on trees as trophies of ceremonial sacrifices performed at feasts (van Dijk and de Jonge 1980:40).

Not all *palepai* or long ceremonial cloths include ship motifs. Another recognized type of *palepai*, for example, is characterized by stylized human or deity figures between borders of triangles (Fig. IV.2), a pattern, called *tumpal*, that is said to invoke fertility (Langewijs and Wagner 1964:23) or protection in

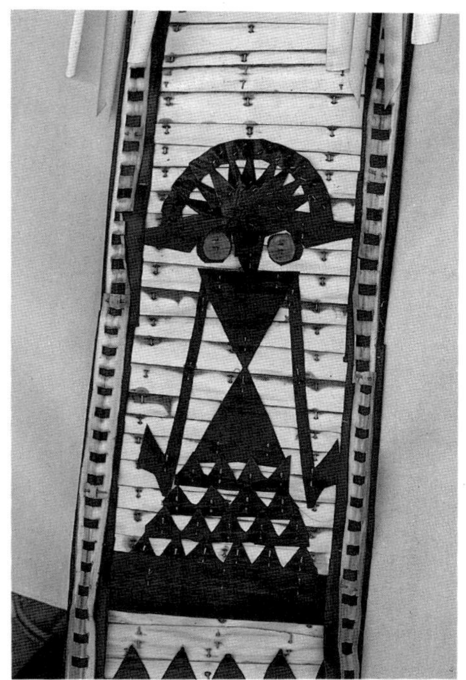

Fig. IV.10 Balinese *lamak* banner depicting rice goddess with hourglass figure. Eric Crystal

Indonesian art. The hourglass figure of the individuals patterned on the Lampung cloth is reminiscent of the Balinese rice goddess figure (Fig. IV.10) depicted on ceremonial banners called *lamak*, again suggesting historical connections between Lampung and Hindu Java (the precursor of Hindu Bali). The two rows of figures in the textile are identical except for the decoration beside their necks and the small waist ornaments, possibly representing *kris* handles, seen on the figures of the lower row. They may represent different lineages, possibly those united through marital or military alliances. It is not known whether this type of *palepai* was originally used for ritual purposes different from other design types. Some versions of this type include a central band (between the human rows) that depicts ships carrying animals and human riders (Gittinger 1976:221).

Tampan: Ritual Cloths for All

Tampan cloths are usually woven in cotton with a plain-weave background that is patterned with supplementary weft designs in cotton and/or silk threads. In the nineteenth century, these square textiles were used for ceremonial events by Lampung people of all social classes (Gittinger 1972). The cloths wrapped and accompanied bundles of food, mats, and other gifts given by the families of the betrothed during marriage negotiations. For traditional noble weddings, more than a hundred *tampan* were exchanged (Gittinger 1979). Centuries ago, *tampan* cloths may have been sewn into pillows and used as ritual cushions designating the owner's high status (Gittinger 1989:234). The varied designs on *tampan* pieces reflect regional styles and portray traditional life-cycle ceremonies about which there are few other sources of information. These designs, as well as the silk materials and weaving structure, resemble those of Thai and Chinese textiles associated with Buddhist offerings and meditation (Gittinger 1989).

Beaded *tampan* textiles are extremely rare, because of their fragility and the preciousness of their imported beads. Such hangings may have been part of the gift exchange for the marriage of Lampung aristocrats. In this lush and abstract beaded textile (Fig. IV.11), a ship carries a floral form, perhaps a mythological "tree of life" or Buddhist wishing tree. Such trees, seen frequently in art of the outer islands, are thought to symbolize fertility or Buddhist notions about the gratification of desires through community prosperity (Holmgren and Spertus 1989:76). The vivid, yellow-based color scheme and unusual composition of this Lampung beaded textile is different from the majority of Indonesian two-dimensional artworks. The center field motifs on either side of the tree are not symmetric. Most of the elemental forms in the frame do not repeat but rather merge into new forms. Holmgren and Spertus describe the compositional uniqueness of Lampung beaded textiles: "The strings of beads are disposed of in painterly fashion, densely packing areas with color and, like brushstrokes, freely shifting linear direction. . . . Beads of different hues mingle pointillistically, yielding rich textured tones" (1989:87). Both curves and straight lines are integrated in this piece in a vibrantly asymmetrical style confined within the more familiar pan-Indonesian diamond and hourglass-shaped geometric borders. Although some of the projections from the bottom of the boat form may represent oars, there is also a suggestion of animal legs that support a dragon-headed serpent. Mythical dragons or snakes (*naga*), associated with the supernatural power of rulers in Southeast Asia, were carved as figurehead ornaments on Indonesian royal boats since the seventeenth century (see catalog chapter X and Jessup 1990:61–69).

The *tampan* (Fig. IV.12) from the Kalianda region depicts a wedding on a ship, symbolizing the participation of the entire community in the marriage alliance. The bridal couple rides an elephant beneath an umbrella, which is a symbol of royalty and honored status in Hindu cultures and throughout Southeast Asia. The larger figure above the couple may be a prominent ancestor or deity. Birds and human figures, perhaps representing family members, stand at the sidelines or sit in boats beneath festive banners. Repeated sea-creature mo-

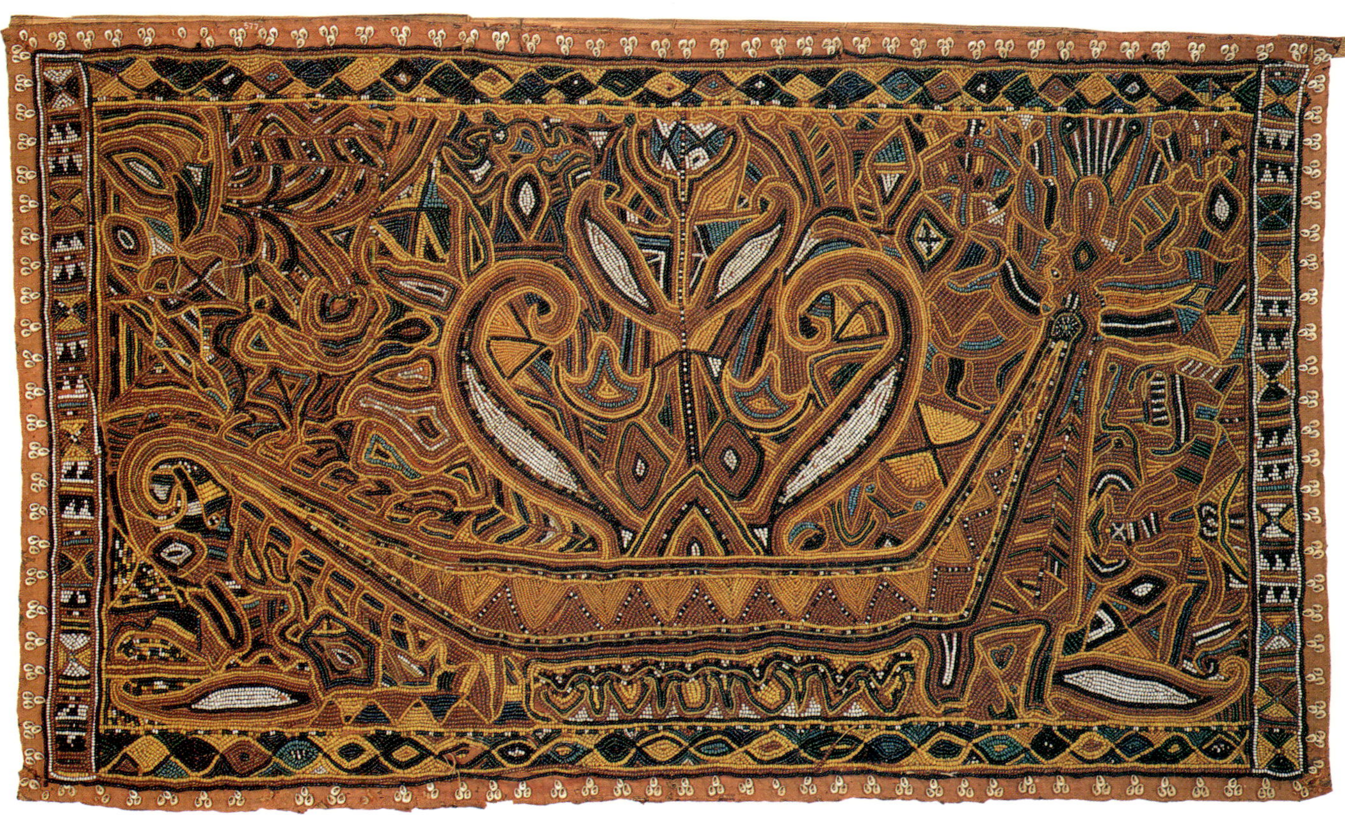

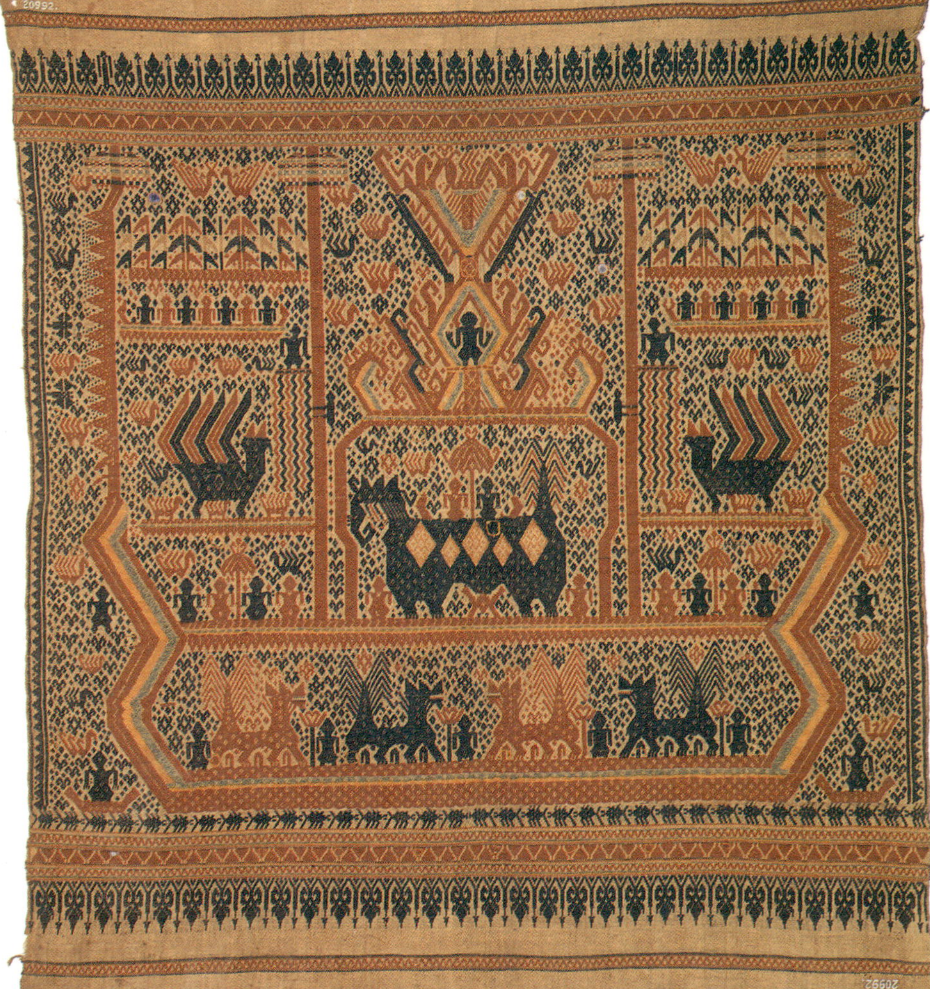

Fig. IV.11 Beaded ceremonial cloth, *tampan*
Lampung, southern Sumatra
Cloth, beads, shells, rattan, 62 x 103.5
Museum Nasional Indonesia, Jakarta, 577

Fig. IV.12 Ceremonial cloth, *tampan*
Lampung, Kalianda, southern Sumatra
Cotton, 80 x 90
Museum Nasional Indonesia, Jakarta, 20992.
Accessioned in 1936.

OPPOSITE
Fig. IV.13 Ceremonial cloth, *tampan*
Lampung, Kalianda, southern Sumatra
Cotton, 101 x 77.6
Museum Nasional Indonesia, Jakarta, 22208.
Accessioned in 1939.

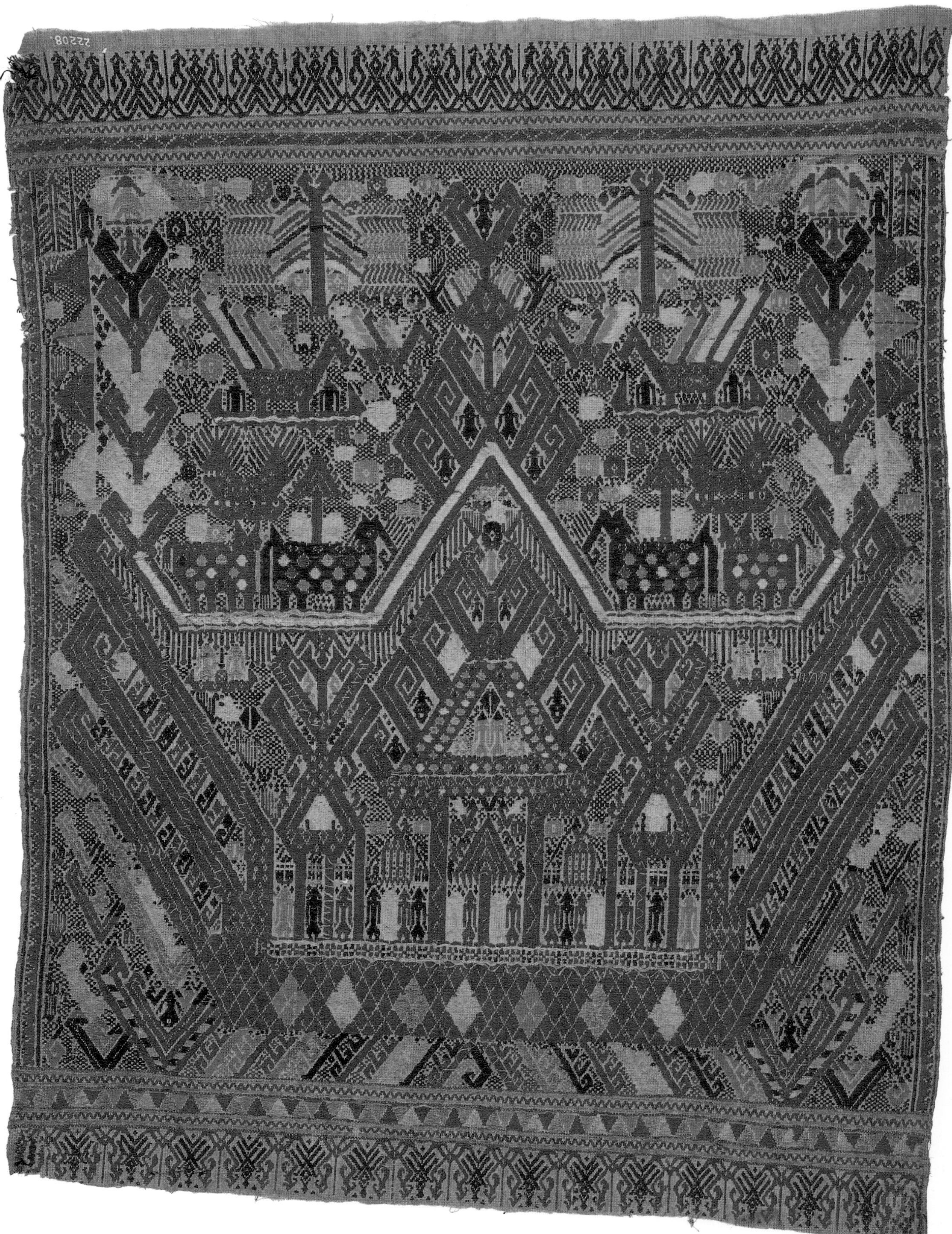

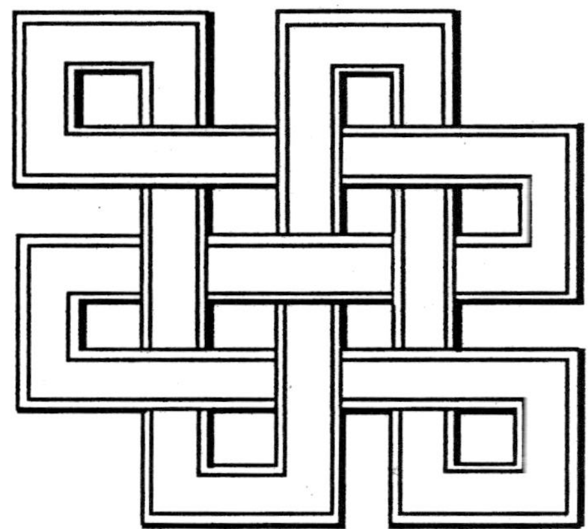

Fig. IV.14 Endless-knot motif. Marcia Bakry, Smithsonian Institution.

tifs appear to move beneath the ship toward the center point. As in the *palepai* (Fig. IV.7), the narrative scene is animated by the small diamond, cross, and other geometric motifs that dot the plain-weave background throughout. Kalianda textiles employ a varied and recognizable color palette of dark red, deep and light blue, ochre, and taupe on a beige or creamy background (Holmgren and Spertus 1989:80).

In this *tampan* (Fig. IV.13), a red ceremonial ship frames religious images—perhaps the Lampung view of the upper world (personal communication, Gittinger 1989) or an interpretation of symbols borrowed from trade items of mainland Asia. Holmgren and Spertus (1989:80–82) emphasize the similarity of these motifs to religious architectural forms and their depictions in Cambodian and northern Burmese textiles. The structures with triangular roofs seen in this *tampan* resemble traditional Lampung ancestor shrines, *rumah poyang* (Gittinger 1972:138; van Dijk and de Jonge 1980:28), as well as Southeast Asian Buddhist temple altars. Figures shown within the ancestor shrines are probably images of deceased forefathers (van Dijk and de Jonge 1980:39). The tree images at top undoubtedly represent the ceremonial poles (*kayu ara*) erected and decorated with textiles at Lampung feasts (Fig. IV.5).

An example of the *pasisir* style, made in Lampung coastal settlements, this textile (Fig. IV.15) depicts a child's birth or, more likely, a circumcision. Next to marriage, circumcision is the most important and expensive ceremony for a Lampung boy, foreshadowing his wedding ceremony (Gittinger 1972:55). Both the boy's maternal and paternal families contribute *tampan* textiles for display during the ritual and as gifts to be exchanged. In the upper levels of the ceremonial ship, a child wearing a headdress is flanked by elders and banners, signifying his high rank. A reclining woman in a lower compartment may represent the child's mother. On the same level, figures play musical instruments, gongs resembling those used by gamelan orchestras of Java. The entire ceremony takes place aboard a three-deck ship floating above a sea of lively underwater creatures. This textile, uniformly dark red on a taupe background—except for the blue-on-taupe border bands at top and bottom—portrays its narrative scene in vivid silhouette forms, which provide information on external-rudder ship construction, clothing styles, and musical ensembles known to nineteenth-century coastal Lampung people.

Another example of the *pasisir* style, this textile (Fig. IV.16) features the endless-knot motif, known from China, Tibet, India, and Persia. In China, the endless-knot motif is one of the eight Buddhist emblems of happy augury and denotes longevity (Hackmack 1973:21). This motif (Fig. IV.14) may have come to Indonesia through traded ceramics, textiles, or metalware. The red border motif of the center panel has been seen in textiles from as far away as Laos.

This cloth (Fig. IV.20) mixes Southeast Asian, Hindu-Buddhist, and Islamic motifs. A boldly geometric ship decorated with banners carries a tree of life, a symbol of unity and strength. Large bird forms perch on one leg on top of the ship's flagpoles. Spirituality and high rank are represented by the umbrella motifs, which appear above the ship's triangular center form. The Islamic emblem of a cloven sword, seen on the ship's banners, was also displayed on the flag of Bantam, the pre-colonial kingdom of western Java. This double-bladed sword image represents the "Sword of 'Ali," also known as Dhu al-Faqar (personal communication, George Atiyeh 1989).

According to an Islamic tradition, the Sword of 'Ali was given to the prophet Mohammed by the angel Gabriel. Other legends say that Mohammed won it during the Battle of Badr and then gave it to his son-in-law 'Ali, whose followers are the Shi'ite Muslims. This famous sword, enabling 'Ali to accomplish many great deeds, became a Shi'ite symbol, which is cited in verses engraved on Arab swords during the Middle Ages (personal communication, Raymond Hebert 1989).

According to Javanese history, the flag depicting the double-bladed sword was brought from Mecca to Java by Bantam ambassadors in 1638 (personal

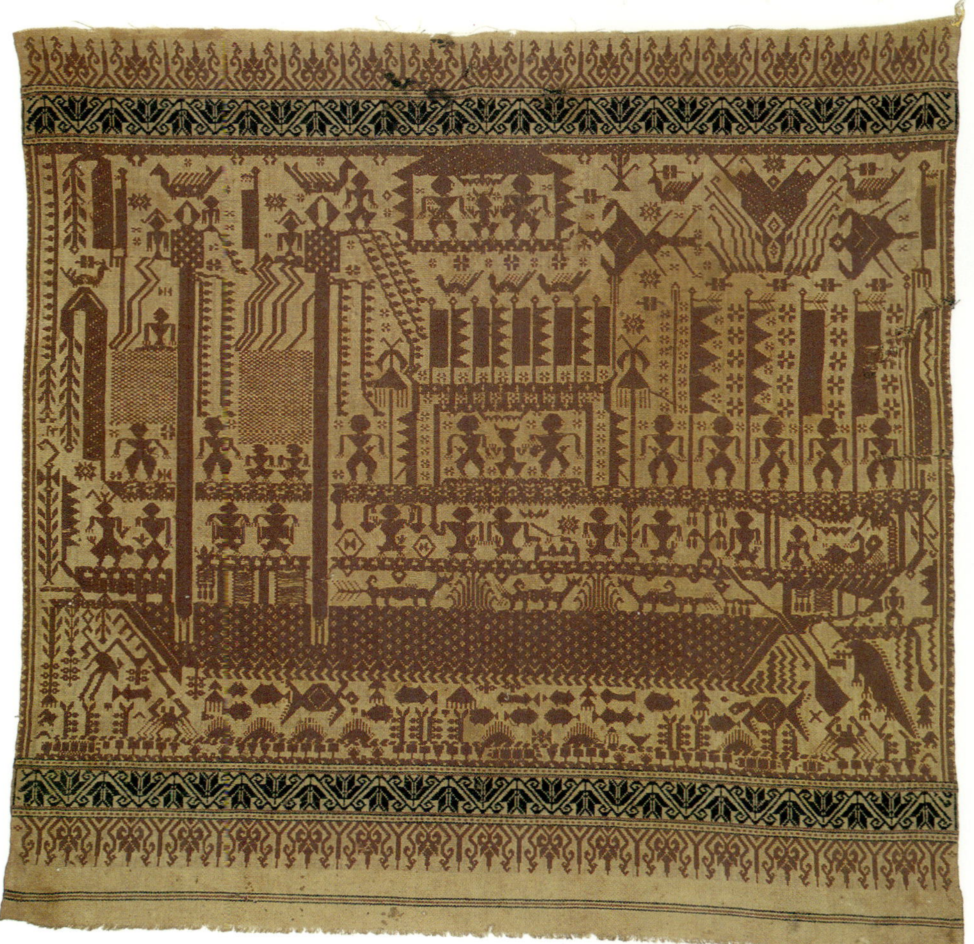

Fig. IV.15 CEREMONIAL CLOTH, *TAMPAN*
Lampung, near Lake Ranau, southern Sumatra
Cotton, 71 x 73
Museum Nasional Indonesia, Jakarta, 26357.
Accessioned circa 1950.

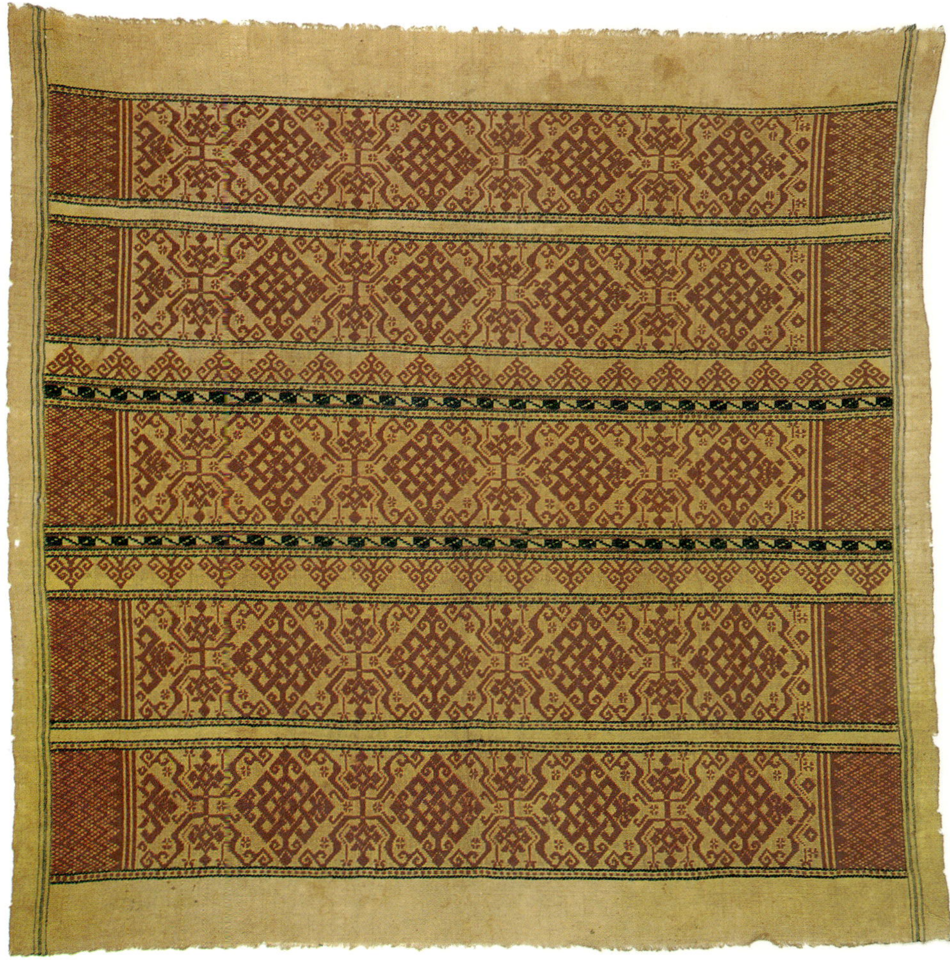

Fig. IV.16 CEREMONIAL CLOTH, *TAMPAN*
Lampung, southern Sumatra
Cotton, 74 x 74
Museum Nasional Indonesia, Jakarta, 26362.
Accessioned circa 1950.

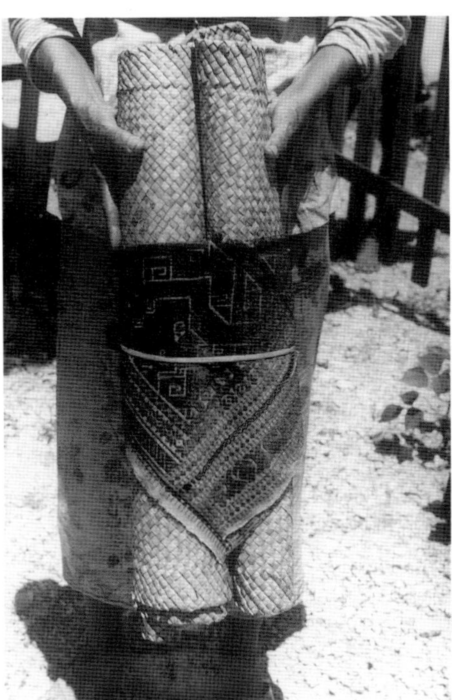

Fig. IV.17 *Tampan* cloth rolled up around sleeping mat for ceremonial presentation by woman of Krui, southern Sumatra, 1970. Mattiebelle Gittinger

communication, Halwany Michrob 1990). These ambassadors reportedly returned to Bantam with a letter from the Great Sharif of Mecca, who thereby bestowed the first title of sultan to the Bantam sovereign. The dazzling preponderance of geometric motifs in the background and the absence of figurative forms also mark this design as a creation of Lampung's present Muslim era.

A highly stylized ship (Fig. IV.19) carries two birds, probably peacocks, whose tails fill the center of the cloth. In Buddhist texts, the peacock represents a protective spiritual force. Gittinger (1989:231) convincingly argues that the numerous *tampan* textiles featuring such diamond-shaped geometric motifs strongly resemble cloths from northeast Thailand that are said to aid the meditation of Buddhist monks. These designs, meticulously copied through the generations, may date from the Hindu-Buddhist period of southern Sumatra, sometime before the seventeenth century. The sharp geometric scrolls and cross-hatching of this textile are patterned in dark blue on a taupe background with red top and bottom border bands. The composition creates a dramatic contrast between figure and ground, which almost hides the birds, ship, and human forms within the geometric whole.

Tampan Cloths used as Pillows with Sleeping Mats

Split-rattan mats, called *lampit* (Fig. IV.21), were used ceremonially during Lampung funerals, when they were placed beneath the body of the deceased (Gittinger 1972:59). Recent evidence suggests that they were used in many other ceremonial contexts, especially in conjunction with *tampan* gift exchanges. Lampung nobles, particularly, sat on such mats during life-cycle rituals. These mats were wrapped with *tampan* cloths and presented as highly valued gifts, with a gift-wrapping technique followed to the present day (Fig. IV.17). In the traditional era, some *tampan* would later have been sewn into ceremonial pillows to be used as elevating seats of privilege by nobles (Gittinger 1989:234).

The designs are burned into the split rattan, an unusual decorative technique in Indonesia. The four-directional mandala designs used on many *lampit* mats suggest an origin linked to Buddhist meditation, but the remaining ornamentation is indigenous. The dominant field of this mat (Fig. IV.21) features a central circular mandala set in a diamond frame. In the corners are four more mandala patterns, shaped as sun figures set beside crescent moons that are sprouting young plants. The two longer sides of the center field include figures of Lampung ships, which characteristically have squared-off scroll ornaments (see Figs. IV.6, IV.9) and sprout trees at their centers. The figures on the two shorter sides of the center field show modified ship designs resembling the form of traditional Lampung women's hair combs (personal communication, Mattiebelle Gittinger 1990). The remaining motifs in this area are trees, birds, stars, a figure on horseback, and a person holding a four-legged animal on a lead. The direction points and astronomical features resemble those on a navigational map. This largely geometric composition is combined with figurative scenes from Lampung daily life that are reminiscent of narrative scenes in Toraja *sarita* cloths. The border frame of the center mandala, and the entire mat, features growing plant forms and the pan-Indonesian interlocking triangle pattern known as *tumpal*.

Tapis: Embroidered Skirts for Lampung Noblewomen

Elaborate embroidery distinguishes Lampung women's skirts (*tapis*) from those of other areas in Indonesia (Fig. IV.18). Early Chinese traders probably introduced embroidery techniques to the Lampung people, who acquired imported silk and metallic gold yarns with the wealth earned from the pepper trade. Some of the embroidered designs on these skirts are similar to the ship scenes on other Lampung textiles (Fig. IV.25); others (Fig. IV.24) employ more fluid, abstract motifs (Gittinger 1979; Holmgren and Spertus 1989). The silk that is embroidered to produce the striking *tapis* band designs is not twisted into cylindrical threads but sewn in as flat strands, creating large smooth shapes set into a textured background (Holmgren and Spertus 1989:94).

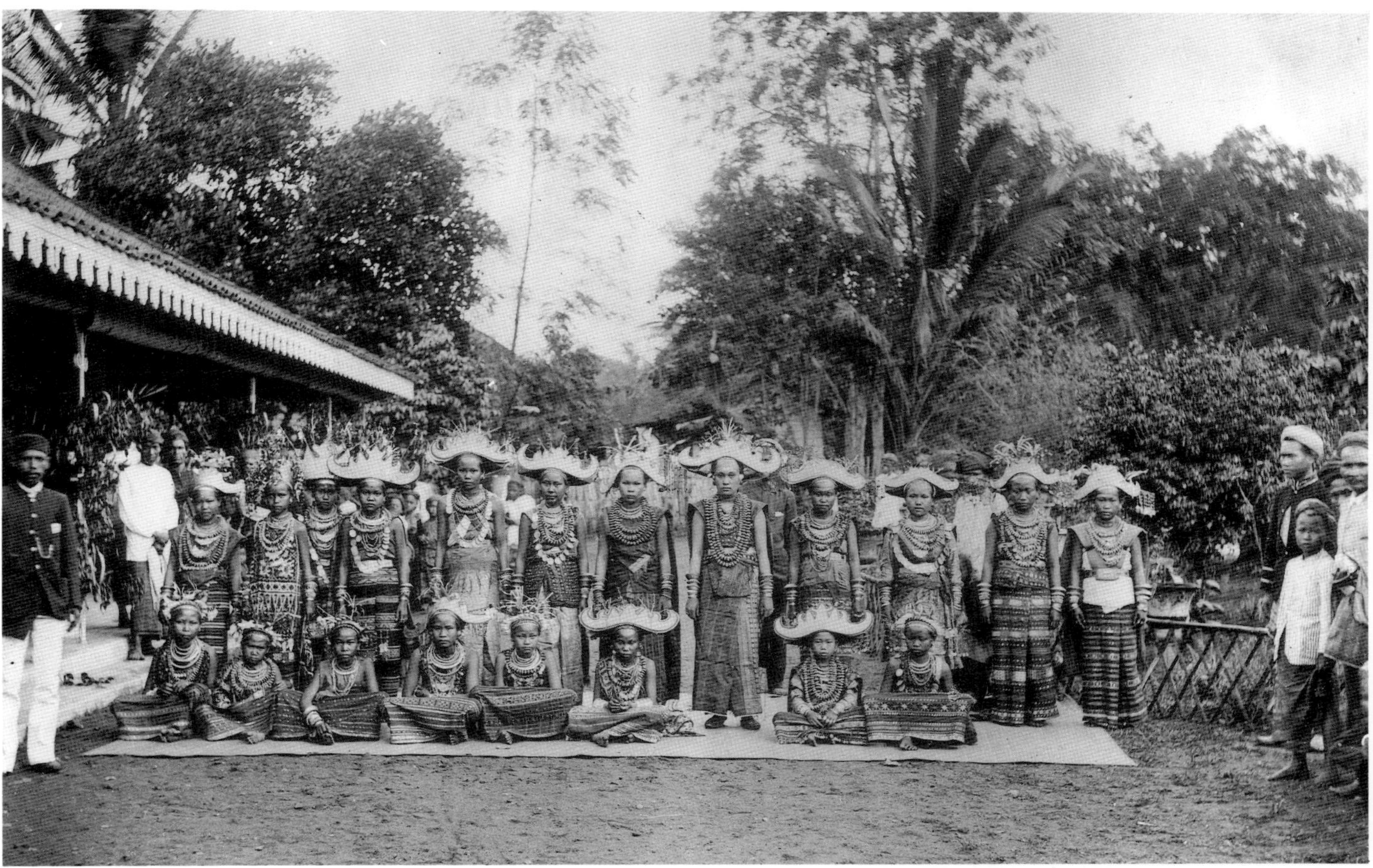

Fig. IV.18 Lampung girls wearing ceremonial *tapis* skirts, Tanjung Karang village, southern Sumatra, 1893. Rijksmuseum voor Volkenkunde, Leiden.

Two pieces of an uncompleted *tapis* skirt (Fig. IV.24) are embroidered in smoothly worked silk with human and bird figures floating within larger flat silhouettes that recall Javanese shadow puppets (*wayang kulit*). These secondary images within the principal motifs have been interpreted as representing generation and fertility (Holmgren and Spertus 1989:94). They may have symbolized local ancestral spirits, whose past existence resulted in the birth of the present community and its resources. One early ethnographic account says that these unusual fluid designs were devised by male suitors for the women they were courting (Jasper and Pirngadie 1912, vol. 2:303). In any case, these glistening embroidered silk designs contrast with the muted geometric *ikat* patterns of the background. Some other fine *ikat* background patterns have been clearly related to known patterns derived from Indian *patola* cloths (Holmgren and Spertus 1989:96–98).

These two pieces of a tube-skirt (Fig. IV.24) were never sewn together to complete the garment, although the design of the background material and most of the silk embroidery was finished. A comparison of the two skirt pieces indicates that the background was completed for one piece but not the other. The finished *tapis* skirt was to be adorned with small pieces of mirror, a technique well known from Indian textiles. When the piece was collected, the application of mirror pieces had been completed on one segment of the skirt but not on the second. In some segments of the material, only circular patterns of buttonhole stitch remain because many precious mirror fragments have been removed, possibly for use in other textiles. When the two pieces were sewn together at the selvages to form a skirt, the iconography of the embroidered bands would have run horizontally.

The embroidered bands of this *tapis* skirt (Fig. IV.25) include feathery human, ship, and tree-of-life motifs familiar from other types of Lampung textiles. One of the main bands of embroidery depicts a ship carrying human figures in tall headdresses, tree forms, what appear to be poles displaying buffalo-horn trophies, and triangular altars or shrines. The other main band of

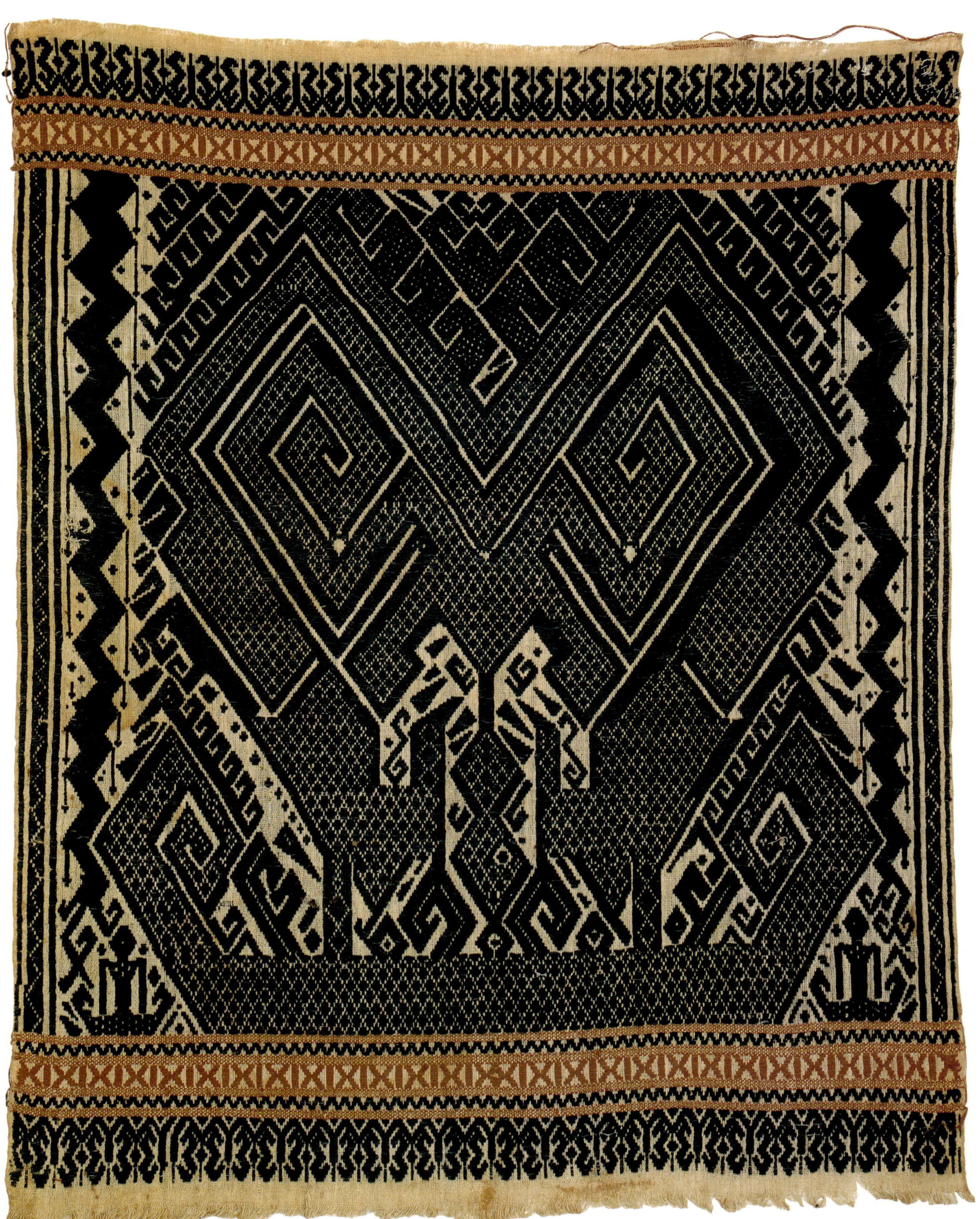

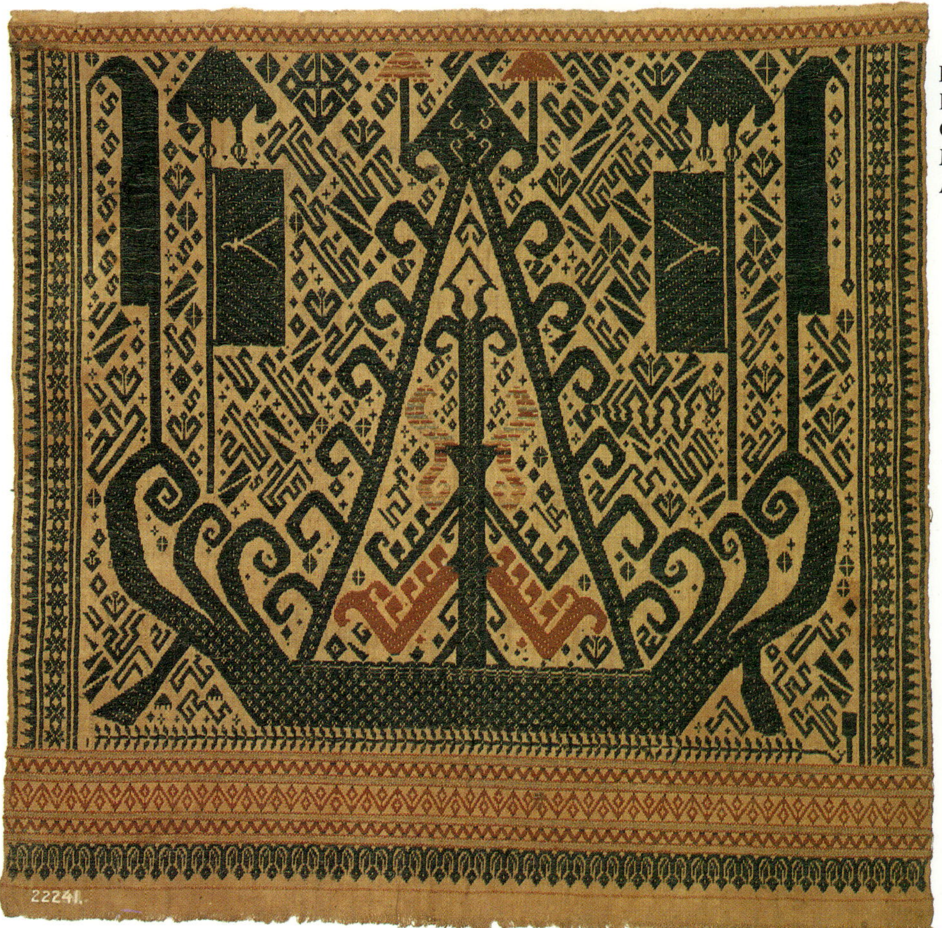

Fig. IV.20 Ceremonial cloth, *tampan*
Lampung, southern Sumatra
Cotton, 53 x 53.4
Museum Nasional Indonesia, Jakarta, 22241.
Accessioned in 1939.

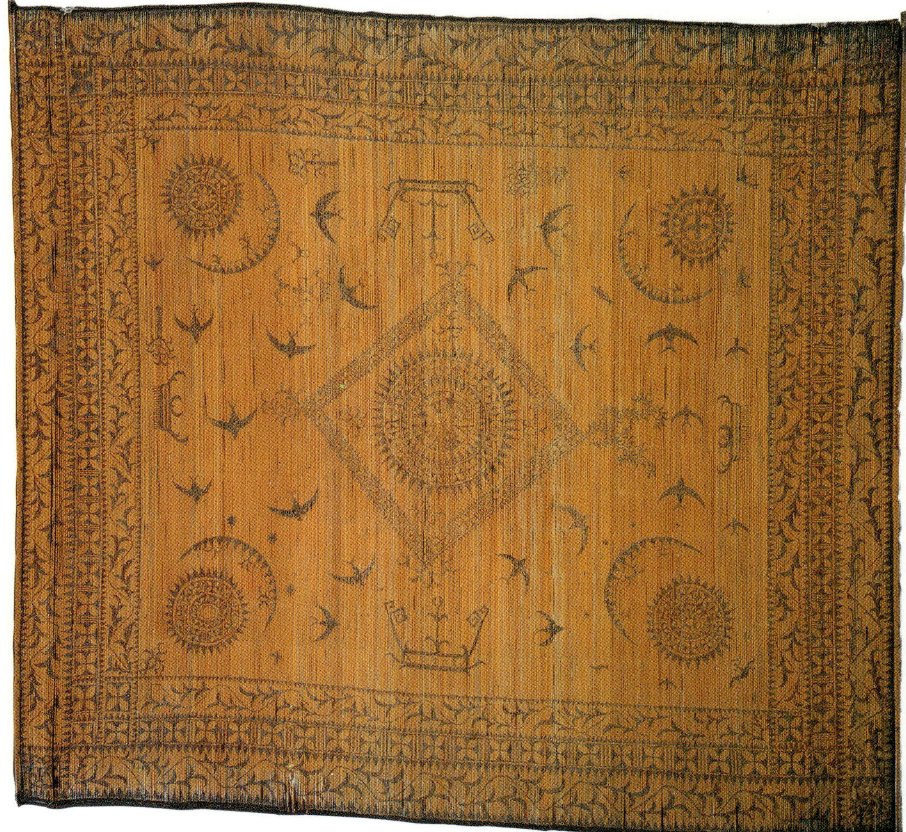

Fig. IV.21 Nobleman's rattan mat, *lampit*
Lampung, southern Sumatra
Rattan, cotton
Collection of Anita E. Spertus and Robert J. Holmgren, New York, I-492

opposite
Fig. IV.19 Ceremonial cloth, *tampan*
Lampung, Lake Ranau or Semangka Bay, southern Sumatra
Cotton, 70 x 57
Museum Nasional Indonesia, Jakarta, 26354.
Accessioned circa 1950.

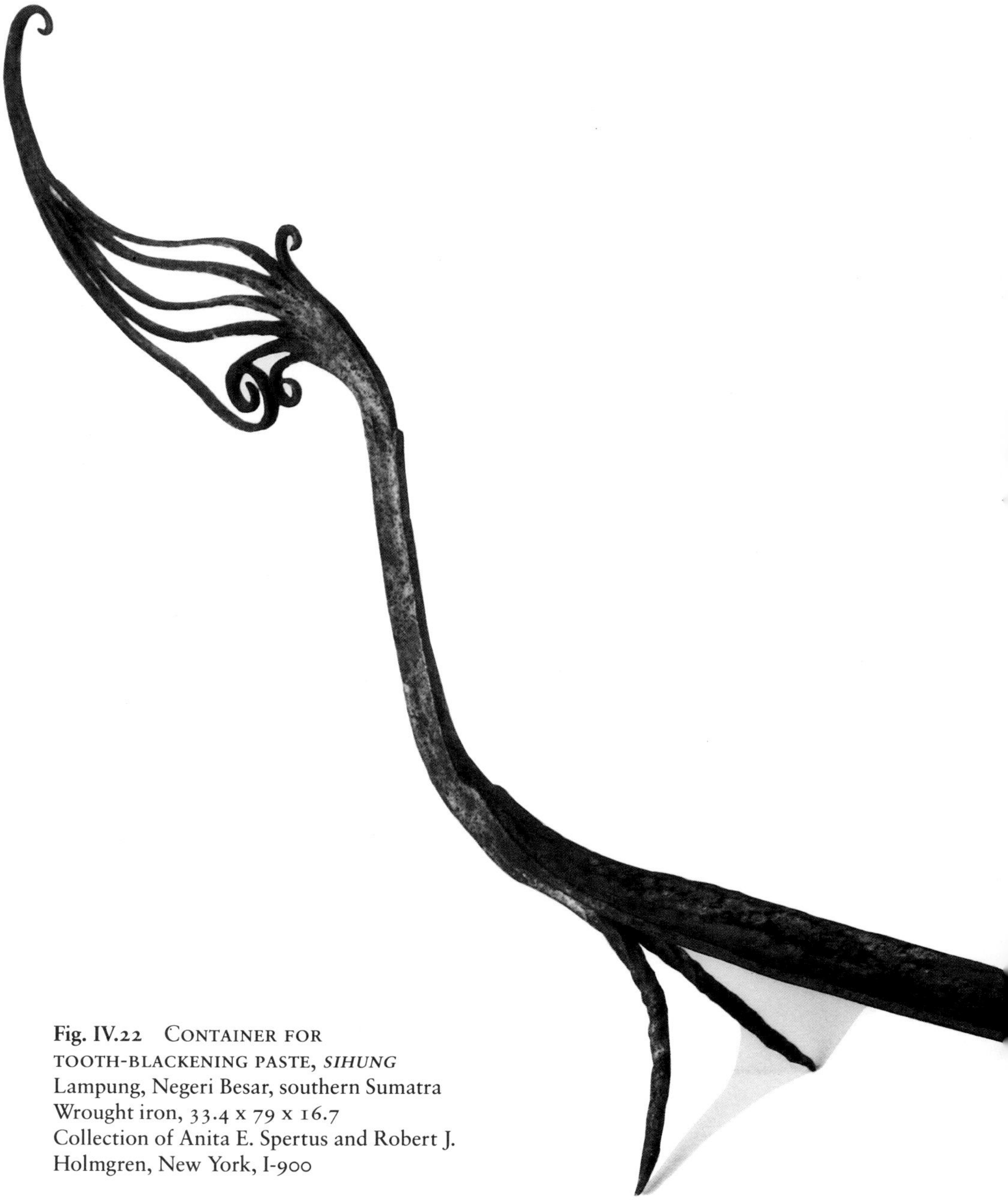

Fig. IV.22 CONTAINER FOR TOOTH-BLACKENING PASTE, *SIHUNG*
Lampung, Negeri Besar, southern Sumatra
Wrought iron, 33.4 x 79 x 16.7
Collection of Anita E. Spertus and Robert J. Holmgren, New York, I-900

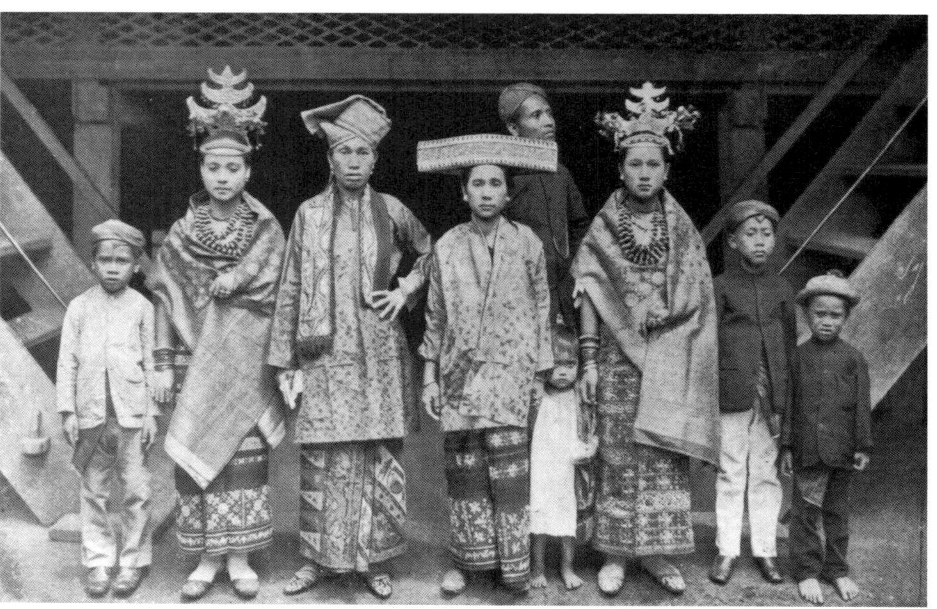

Fig. IV.23 Lampung family in formal dress, southern Sumatra, circa 1900. The woman on the right wears a *tapis* tube-skirt similar in style to the one shown in Fig. IV.25. van Eerde 1920: 183. Courtesy Elsevier Press, Amsterdam.

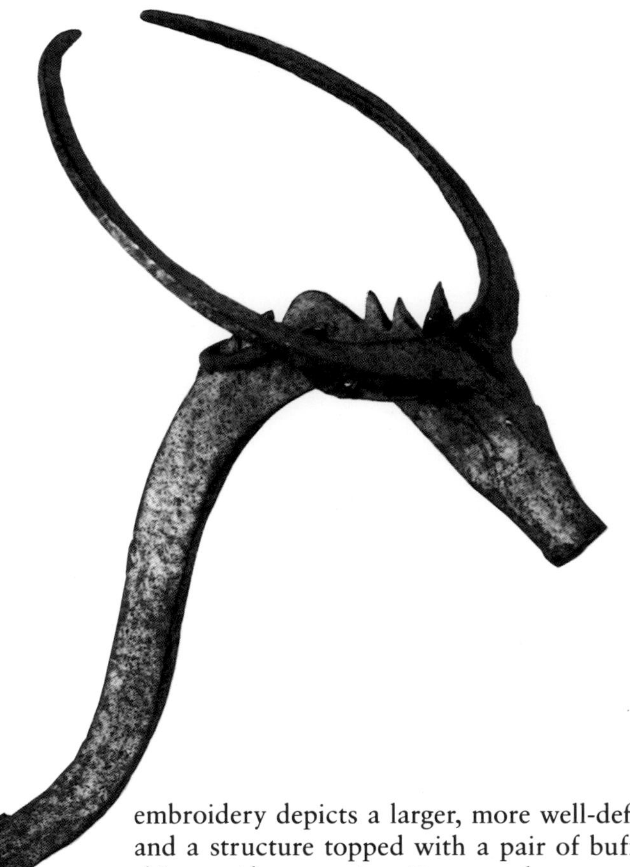

embroidery depicts a larger, more well-defined ship carrying humans, banners, and a structure topped with a pair of buffalo horns. These patterns recall the ship motifs on ancient Dongson bronze vessels (Holmgren and Spertus 1989: 98–100), but they refer more directly to traditional aristocratic Lampung life-cycle rituals, which included ceremonial trees and cloth banners (Fig. IV.5). Buffalo horns obtained from animals sacrificed for major feasts were displayed on poles or houses throughout Southeast Asia to attest to the wealth and generosity of individuals sponsoring the ceremonial feasts.

Rather than being set into a fine warp *ikat* background (as in Fig. IV.24), the embroidered panels on this *tapis* skirt (Fig. IV.25) adorn bands of heavily plain-woven red and ochre fabric accented with numerous metal and mirror chips. This vibrant background style was popular (Fig. IV.23) and is still made in some Lampung areas.

Ceremonial Tooth-Filing at Puberty

Both Lampung girls and boys traditionally had their teeth filed and blackened when they reached marriageable age (Helfrich 1889:622 as cited in van Dijk and de Jonge 1980:18). In many regions of Indonesia, this was considered a mark of beauty, which symbolically distinguished them from the white-fanged animals of the forest. Once the ceremony was concluded, the boys and girls, who were then considered available for marriage, became members of the young men's and young women's associations (*maranai* and *muli*), which were responsible for ceremonial music and dance performances at feasts (van Dijk and de Jonge 1980:18). Wrought-iron buffalo figures (Fig. IV.22) were used as ceremonial containers for the charcoal dust applied in the tooth-blackening ceremony. The delicate and fluidly curved buffalo form probably represents the animal sacrificed during the ritual event. These unusually shaped vessels (*sihung*) are one of the few known types of Lampung artworks that are not made of cloth or wood.

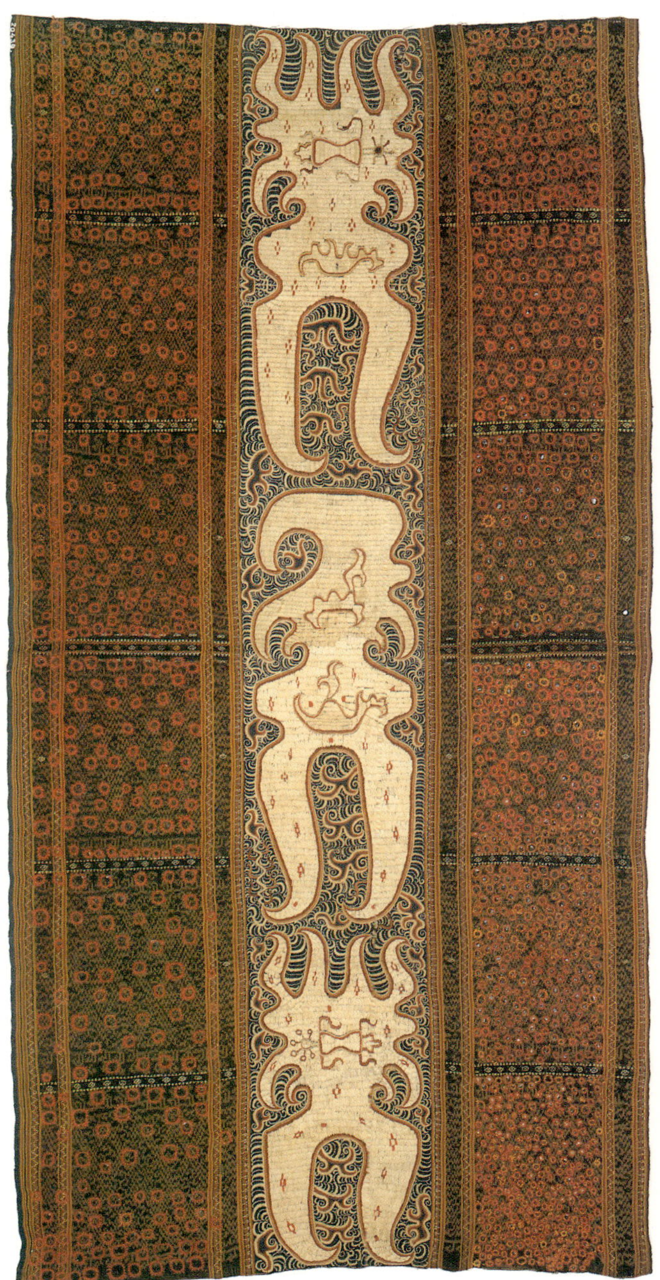

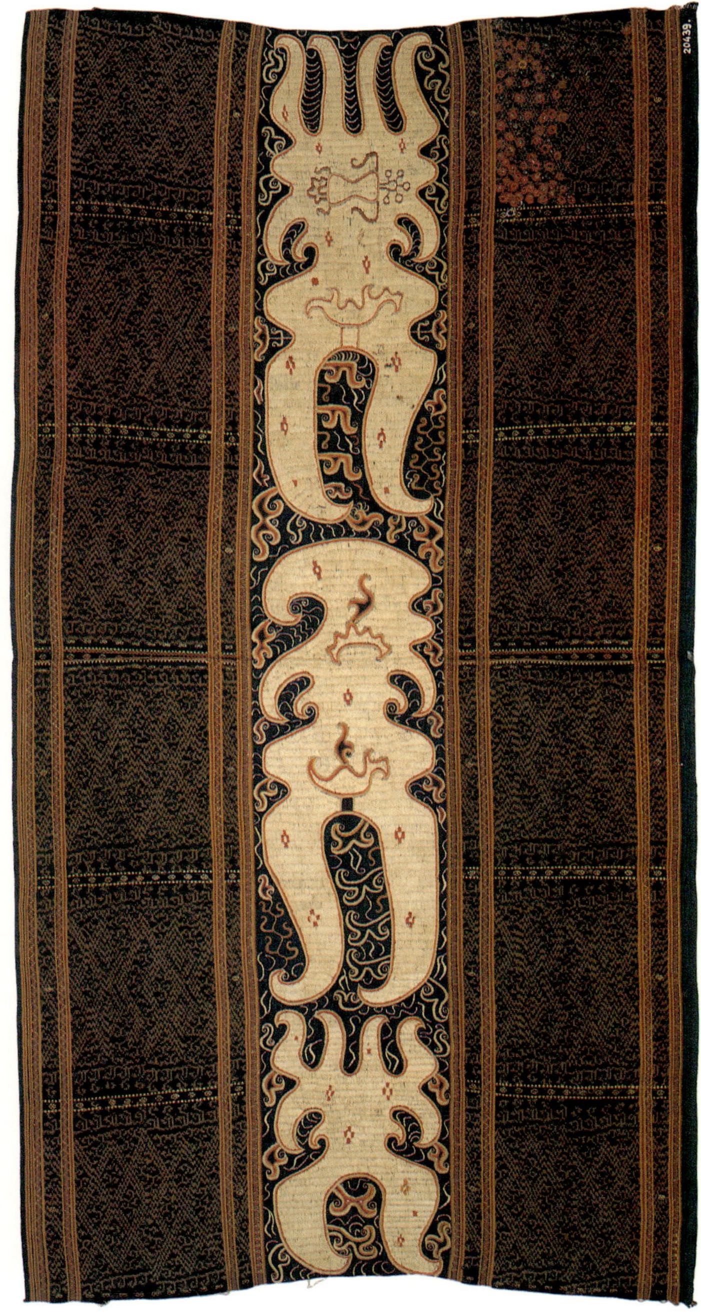

Fig. IV.24 WOMAN'S SKIRT, *TAPIS*
Lampung, Upper Ogan River, southern Sumatra
Silk, cotton, mirror pieces, 129 x 68
Museum Nasional Indonesia, Jakarta, 20439.
Accessioned in 1934.

OPPOSITE
Fig. IV.25 WOMAN'S SKIRT, *TAPIS*
Lampung, Krui, southern Sumatra
Cotton, silk, glass, copper, 107 x 65
Museum Nasional Indonesia, Jakarta, 21597.
Accessioned in 1937.

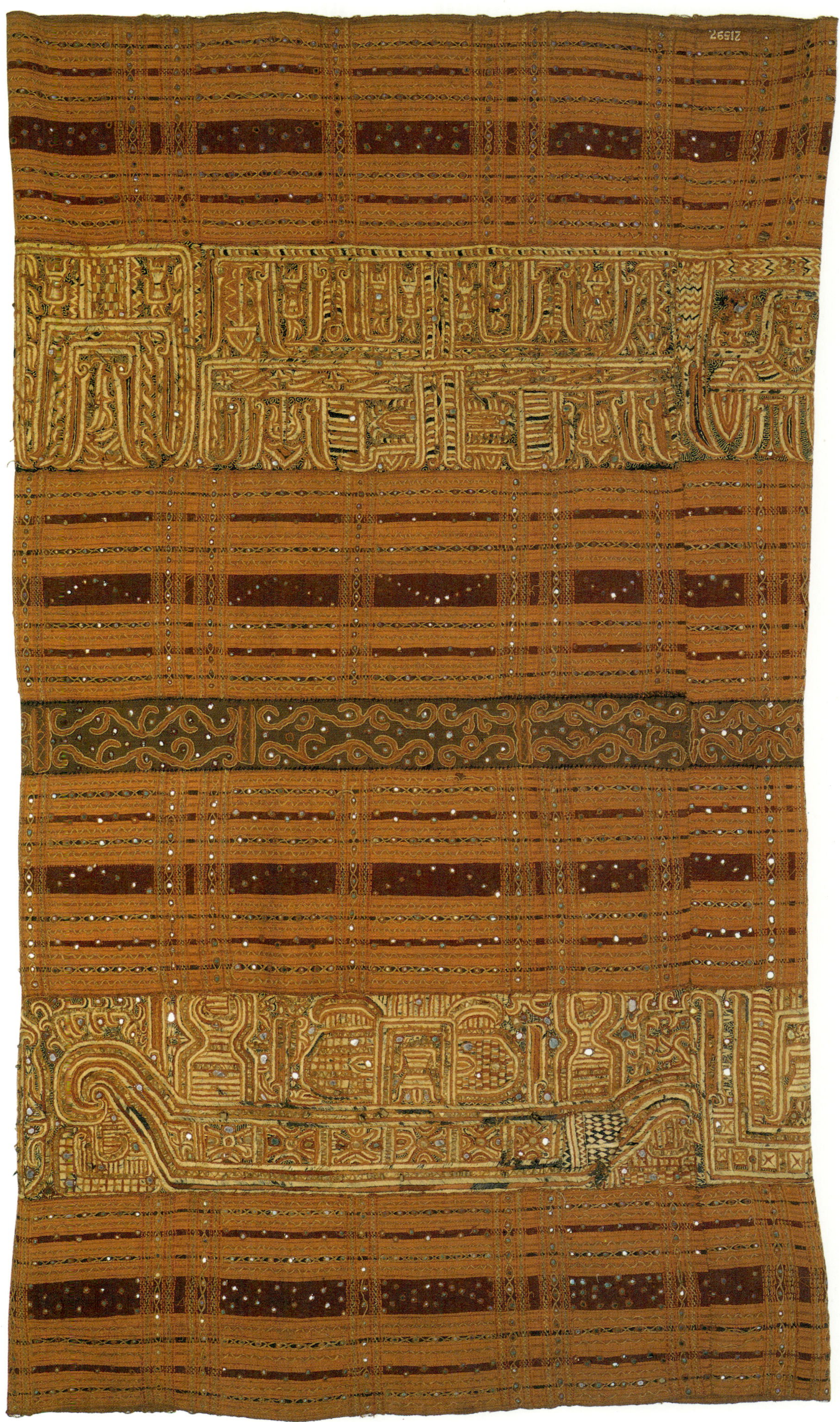

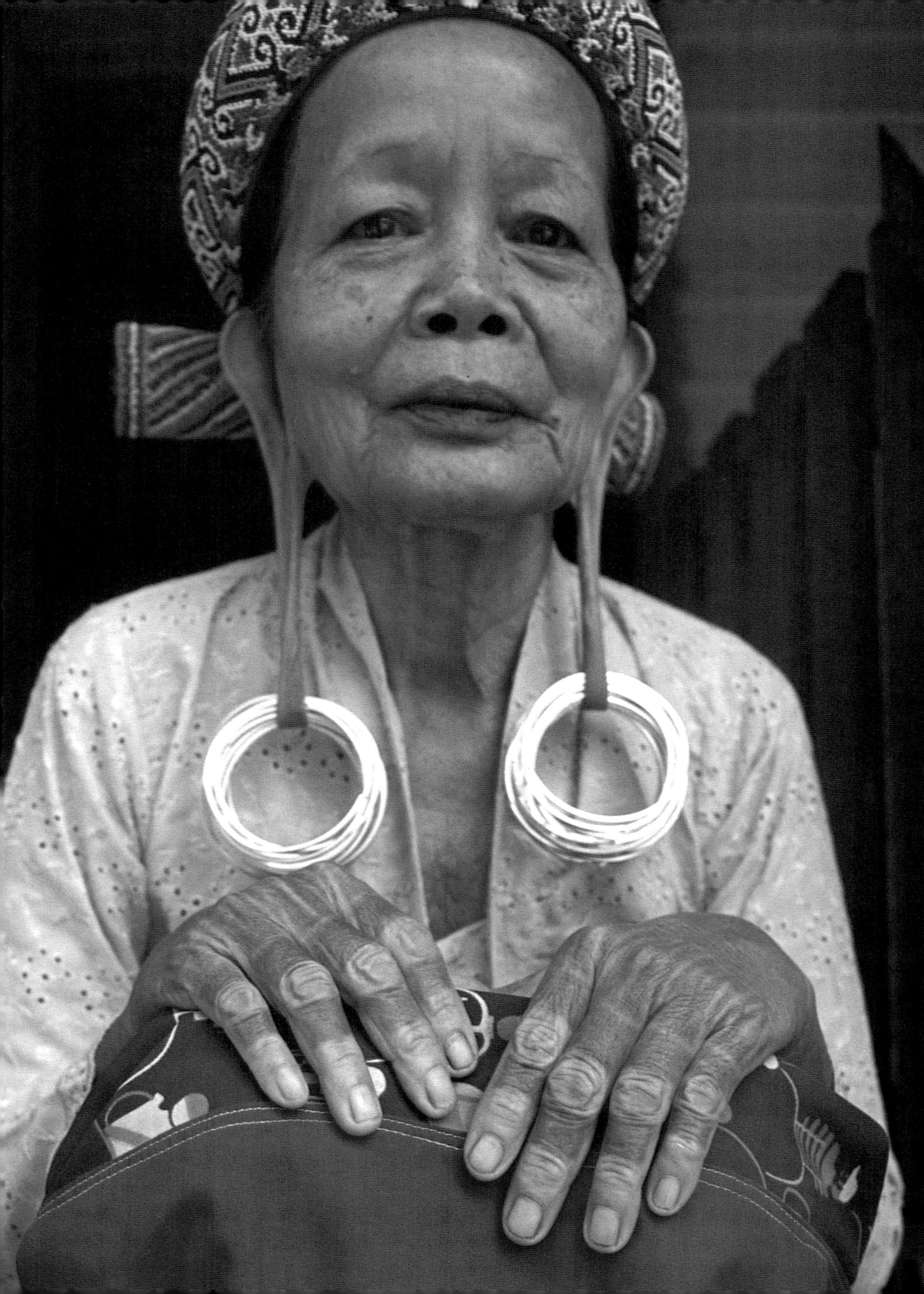

V

Dayak

Fig. V.1 Aristocratic Dayak woman in traditional dress with tattooed hands, Long Iram, 1989. Danielle Hayes

Borneo is the third-largest island in the world, after Greenland and New Guinea, and its landmass is shared among three nations: Indonesia, Malaysia, and Brunei. Brunei is a small country on the northeastern coast. The states of Sabah and Sarawak in the north and east constitute the Malaysian portion of the island. The Indonesian portion, called Kalimantan, covers the southern two-thirds of the island and is divided into the four provinces of West, Central, South, and East Kalimantan. Inland from the hot and sometimes swampy coasts are the rich forests that are home to the approximately three million people collectively classified as Dayak (Avé and King 1986:8,13). Although Borneo has been occupied for about 40,000 years, since the time when the island was connected by a land bridge to the Asian mainland, the history of the interior of the island before the nineteenth century is little known (Harrisson 1972; Jessup and Vayda 1978).

Dayak is the name given to a large number of ethnic groups of interior Borneo, each of which has its own language and separate culture. The term, which means "interior or inland person" in some Borneo languages, was originally used in a derogatory sense by Muslim coastal groups (King 1978:1). Generally denoting the agricultural peoples of Borneo, it excludes the Malay or Muslim coastal groups, who were first converted to Islam in the sixteenth century, and the interior hunter-gatherers collectively referred to as Punan or Penan. Muslims living near the coast, no matter what their ethnic origin, are often described as Malay (King 1978), even though the majority of this group consists of the descendants of Dayak people who converted to Islam, not immigrants from other Malay regions. Non-Muslim people of the interior, no matter how ethnically various, are usually lumped together as Dayak. Although Borneo specialists eschew this melding of distinct cultures, the groups called Dayak often do share similarities in material culture, cosmology, social organization, and ecological adaptation. The distribution of these groups is extremely complex, with ethnically related peoples occupying widely separated areas and peoples who are not ethnically related sometimes living side by side.

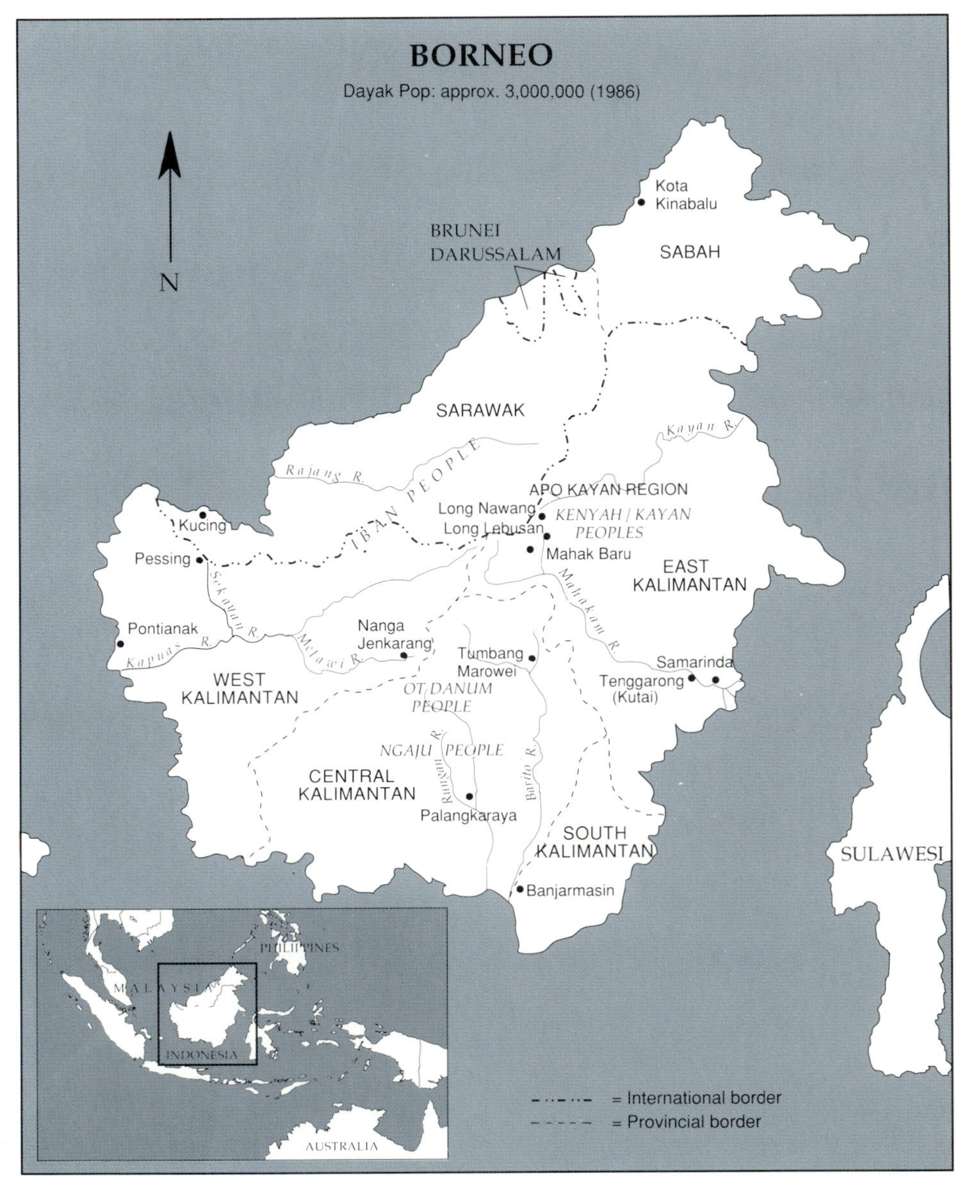

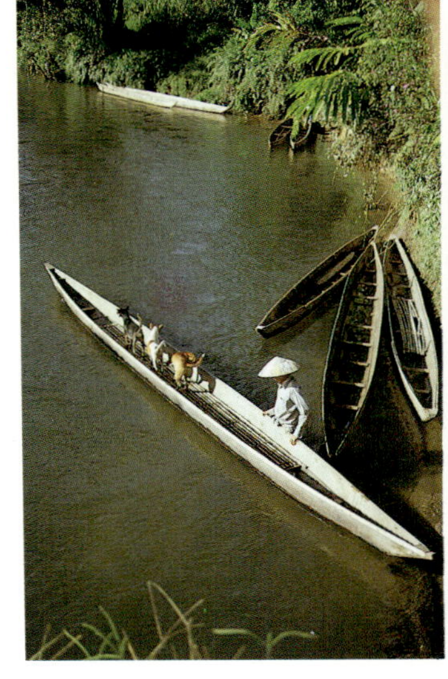

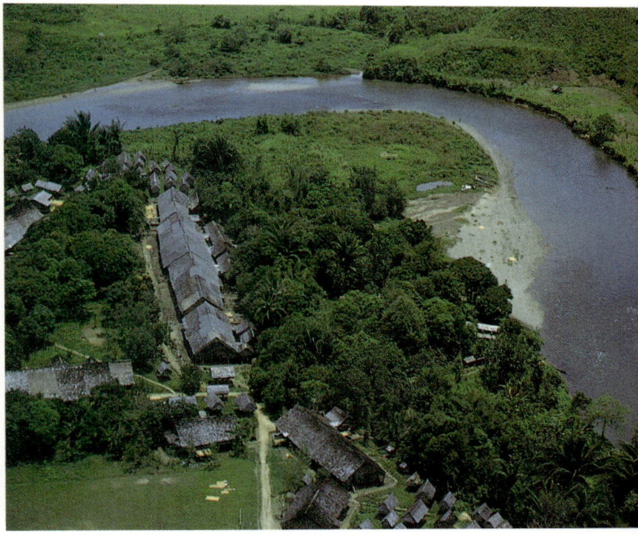

Fig. V.2 A Kenyah man, preparing to go hunting, loads his dogs into a canoe on the upper Mahakam River, East Kalimantan, 1989. Lorraine V. Aragon

Fig. V.3 Aerial view of longhouse and rice granaries at the Kenyah village of Mahak Baru on the upper Mahakam River, East Kalimantan, 1989. Maarten W. Elink Schuurman

OPPOSITE
Fig. V.4 SEAT
Ngaju, Kalimantan
Wood, 61.3 x 63 x 29
Museum Nasional Indonesia, Jakarta, 27202.
Purchased in Jakarta for 350 rupiah.
Accessioned in 1954.

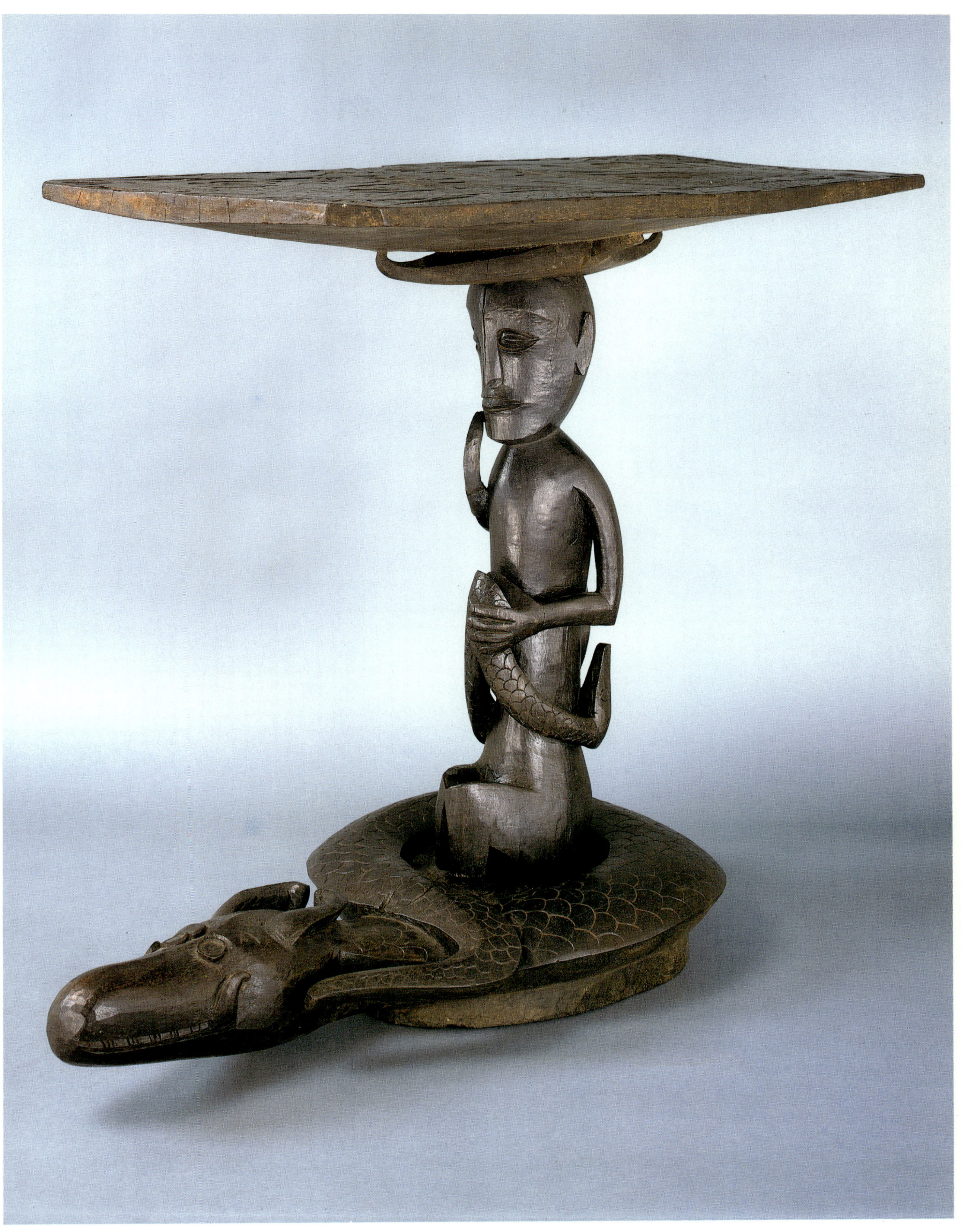

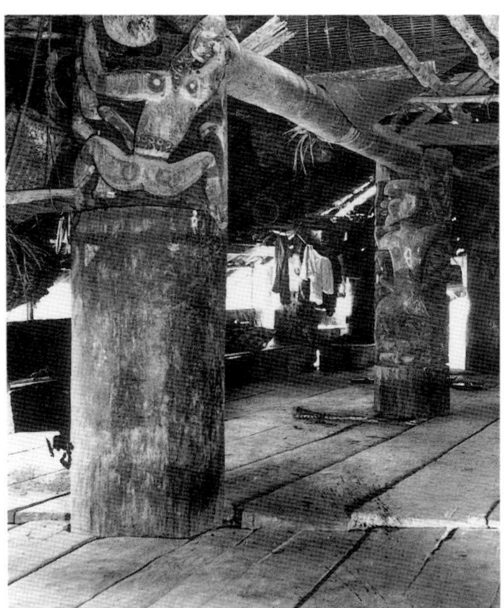

Fig. V.5 Interior of a Kenyah longhouse, Long Nawang, East Kalimantan, circa 1931–33. Courtesy Rijksmuseum voor Volkenkunde, Leiden.

Dayak villages are located primarily along Borneo's numerous rivers, which have historically formed the major transportation arteries (Fig. V.2), or in the hills nearby. The villages of most groups once consisted of one or more multiple-family dwellings known as longhouses (Fig. V.3), although in recent decades this type of housing has often been abandoned in favor of single-family houses. The characteristic Dayak longhouse is a single-story building raised high off the ground on poles. Each family unit has its own apartment, with up to two hundred families housed in the largest longhouses. The details of longhouse construction vary from one Dayak group to another, but typically a main public area consisting of an enclosed veranda runs undivided along the entire length. The Kenyah people who inhabit a highland area known as the Apo Kayan, located at the headwaters of the Kayan River in East Kalimantan, are particularly noted for their massive and highly decorated longhouses. The interior of a Kenyah longhouse at Long Nawang (Fig. V.5) was photographed by H. F. Tillema during his 1931–33 visit to the region (King 1989:10).

For centuries the Dayak have traded forest products to coastal groups to obtain Chinese ceramics, bronzes, and beads (Chin 1988). Despite this significant trade activity, Dayak settlements have remained largely isolated within their forest environments. Most groups cultivate rice and tubers in shifting or rain-fed fields.

Unlike the outer-island groups discussed in earlier chapters, most Dayak people reckon their descent through both male and female ancestors rather than through male ancestors only (Appell 1976).

Cosmology: the Layered Universe

The Ngaju people of Central Kalimantan have graphically and elegantly described their traditional cosmology, not only in their art and among themselves but also to ethnographers and visitors (see especially Schärer 1963). The Ngaju envision a cosmos consisting of a central tier, inhabited by humans, layered between an upper world and lower world. The upper world is a mountain land presided over by a god conceptualized as a hornbill, while the lower world is the watery domain of a deity represented as a dragon or water snake (Schärer 1963:12–15, plate 6). A carved Ngaju wooden seat (Fig. V.4) symbolically represents this cosmic order: humanity stands and mediates between the upper world and the lower world. At the base of the seat, the lower world is represented by a hybrid dragon having a serpent's body and the horns of a water buffalo. In parts of Borneo, water buffalo are associated with the lower world (Sellato 1989:44).

Cosmological references are included among the designs etched on a bamboo tube (Fig. V.7) collected in the early twentieth century by Ir. J. L. Moens and attributed by him to the Ot Danum people, a group closely related to the Ngaju and living primarily upstream from them in the Central Kalimantan headwaters. According to collection records, Moens was told that the tube was used as "the storage place for the highest invincible knowledge (referred to by the Indonesian term *ilmu*) that would guarantee wealth and prosperity to the owner." The maker of the tube, named Dambung Singa, was already deceased at the time it was collected. According to Moens' notes, only one remaining artist knew what "the soul place" (presumably, the upper world and lower world) looked like. As with many other outer-island groups, traditional Dayak religious knowledge was in the hands of the few, artists with inspirational knowledge regarding the spirit worlds.

The central panel of the illustration on the tube (Fig. V.6) depicts a *mihin*, or mythological fish trap, catching valuable gongs and ceramic jars associated with the animals of the lower world (personal communication, Sellato 1990). Those depicted here include crocodiles, fish, and dragons whose extremities metamorphose into ceramic jars. According to Schärer's account of Ngaju belief, the inhabitants of the lower world are represented as aquatic creatures, even though they actually possess human form where they dwell (1963:17). Only when they leave the lower world, either to help or to harm

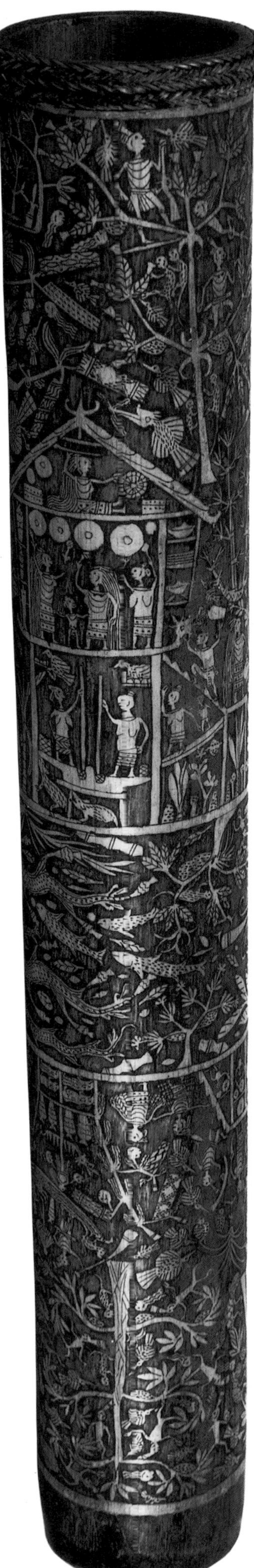

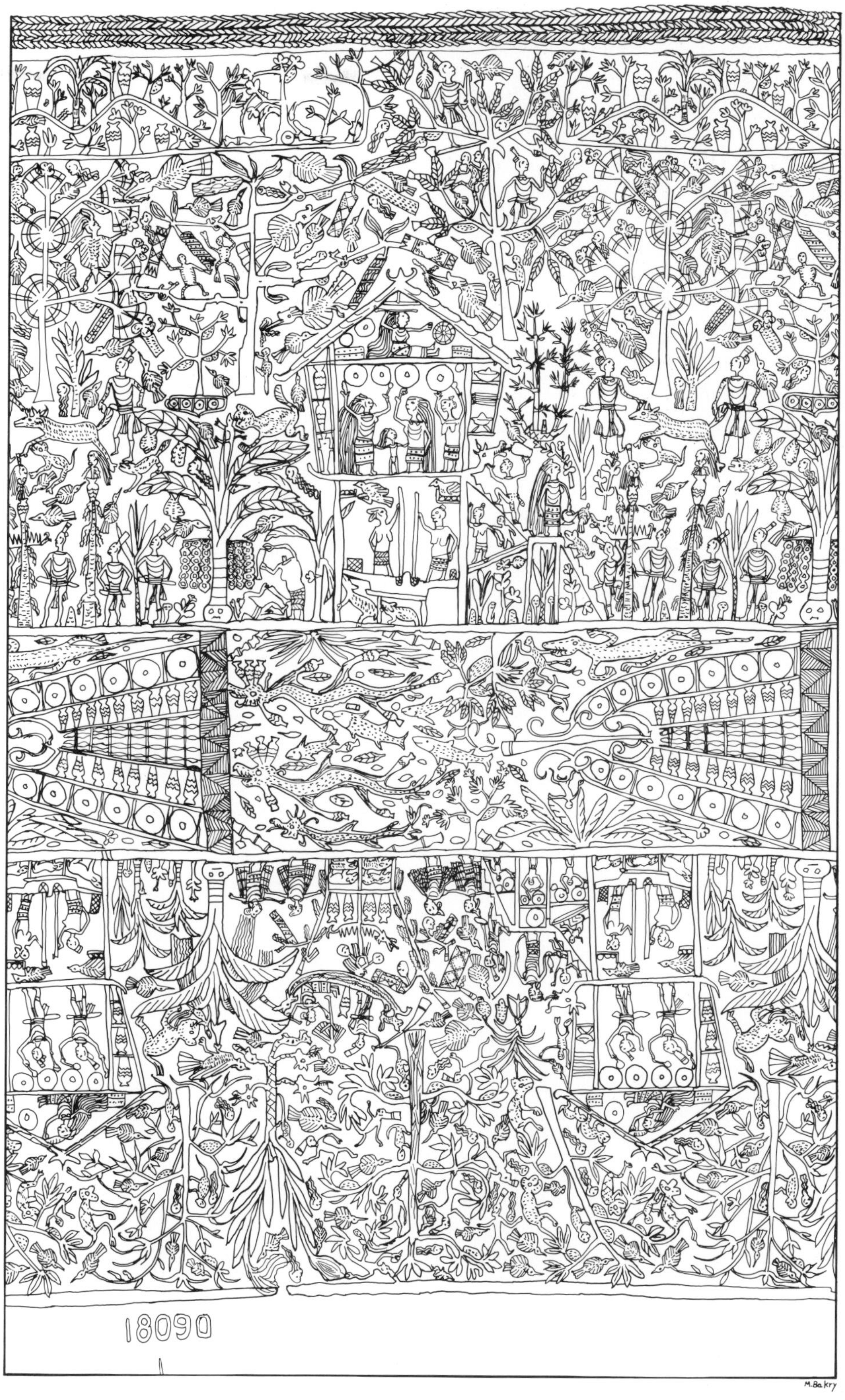

Fig. V.6 Illustration of etchings on Fig. V.7, drawn as if the cylinder were rolled out into two-dimensional form. Marcia Bakry, Smithsonian Institution.

Fig. V.7 ETCHED BAMBOO TUBE
Ot Danum or Ngaju, Rungan River, Central Kalimantan
Bamboo, resin, 39 x 6
Museum Nasional Indonesia, Jakarta, 18090.

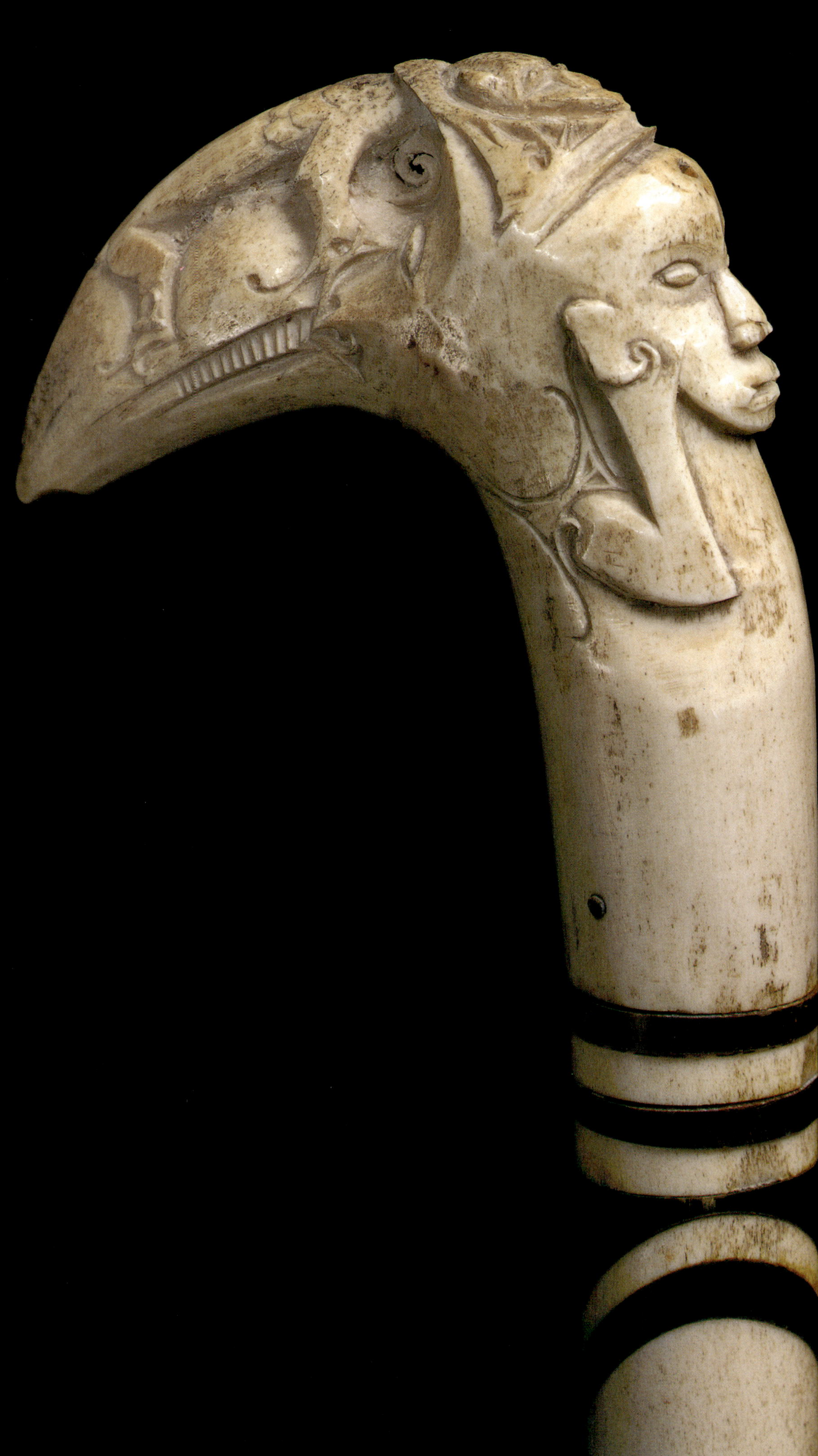

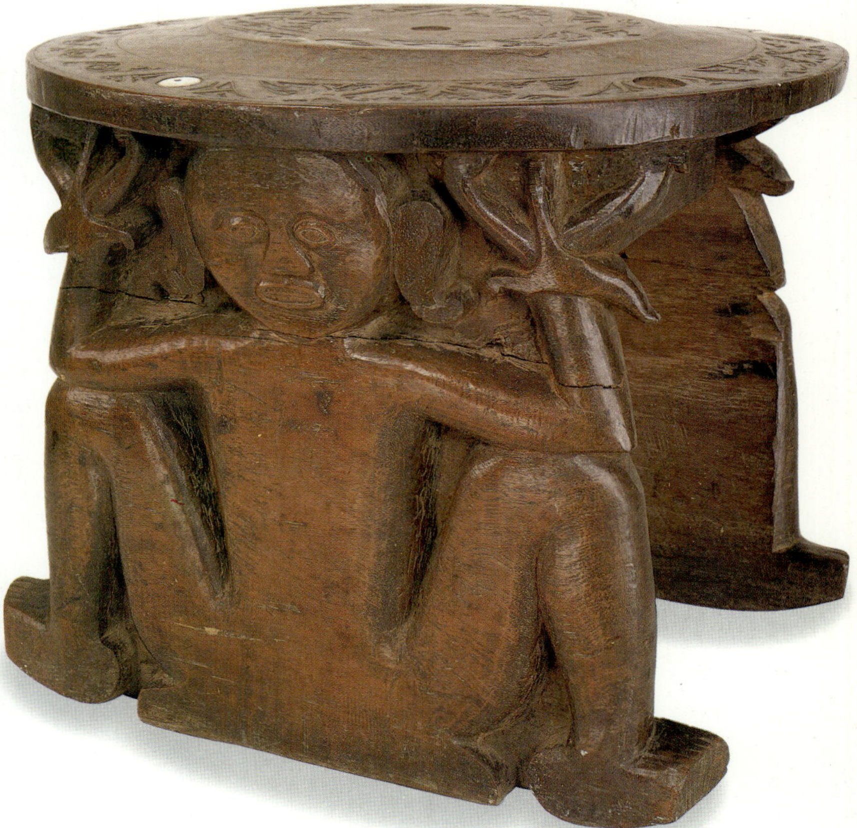

Fig. V.9 SEAT
Kayan or Kenyah, East Kalimantan
Wood, shell, 37.5 x 43.6 x 13.5
Museum Nasional Indonesia, Jakarta, 26756.
Purchased for 250 rupiah. Accessioned
in 1951.

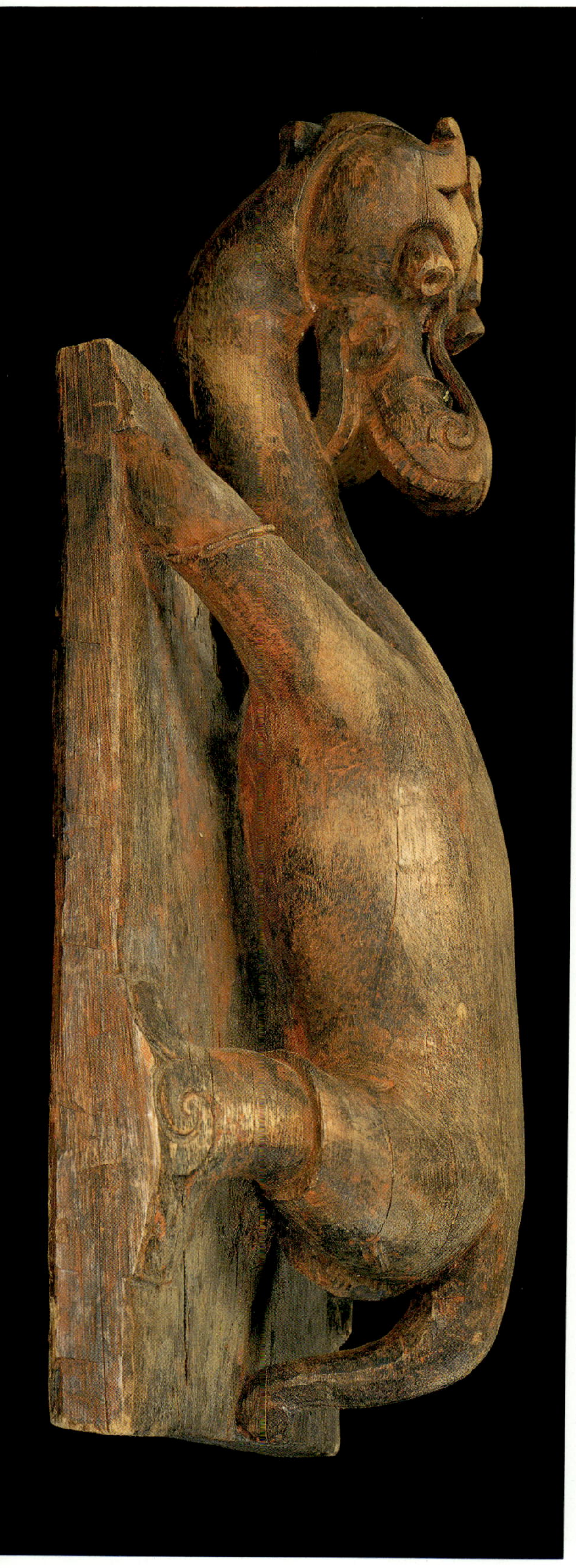

Fig. V.10 DOOR HANDLE
Kayan, Kalimantan
Wood, 57 x 31.3 x 16
Dr. and Mrs. Robert Kuhn

OPPOSITE

Fig. V.8 STAFF OR WALKING CANE
Kayan(?), East Kalimantan
Wood, horn, bone, 88.5 x 3 x 7
Department of Anthropology, Smithsonian
Institution, 301868. Given to Alfred M. Erskine
by the Sultan of Kutai. Accessioned in 1918.

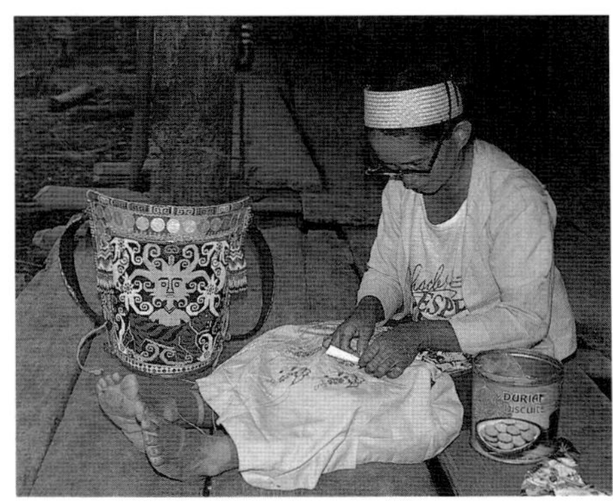

Fig. V.11 A Kenyah woman beads a decorative patch for a baby carrier, Mahak Baru, East Kalimantan, 1989. The cloth on her lap provides a work surface and the completed baby carrier serves as a model. Lorraine V. Aragon

mankind, do they appear in animal form. Because they may appear as crocodiles, these are therefore considered sacred.

On the end panels of the bamboo tube are depictions of the *tiwah* ceremony, a Central Kalimantan rite that reenacts the creation of the world, best known from Schärer's description of the Ngaju version. This rite is conducted to restore order disturbed by the death of an individual deemed to have died a "ripe death" (*pampatei masak*) by departing the world at a mature age and due to natural causes (Schärer 1963:131). Such a death—even though the best possible—still requires ceremonies of honor to bring the natural and supernatural back into harmony. The depictions include a row of priestesses beating gongs and the headless bodies of slaves, which were once sacrificed as part of the *tiwah* ritual (Schärer 1963:140).

Social Hierarchy

Among some Dayak groups, community members were once ranked in hereditary classes as aristocrats, commoners, and slaves. This was particularly the case among the Kayan and Kenyah, two closely related groups associated with the Apo Kayan region but also more widely dispersed now in East Kalimantan and parts of Sarawak. From a legal standpoint, hereditary status distinctions have, of course, been obliterated by modern Indonesian and Malaysian law, but vestiges remain, and are to some extent perpetuated, in the artistic traditions. High-ranking leaders were once privileged to own certain types of objects or to display certain motifs. For instance, aristocratic women were entitled to have a greater area of their bodies tattooed (Fig. V.1)—and with special motifs—than were women of lower status. In some cases, members of the aristocratic class were the sole artisans considered capable of manufacturing such prestige items. The staff (Fig. V.8) served as a marker of status for an aristocrat. Its bone handle is carved in the form of a hornbill head—a motif restricted to this class in Kayan and Kenyah society (Sellato 1989:46). A human face is set in the back of the bird's neck, and the wooden shaft is decorated with inlaid rings of buffalo horn.

Another example of a motif restricted to the aristocracy is the crouching human figure, symbolizing a slave supporting his master, which appears on a carved wooden seat (Fig. V.9). The antiquity of this motif in Indonesia is demonstrated by its presence on stonework from the Hindu period in Sumatra (see, e.g., Schnitger 1939:plate 6). The shell-inlaid top of the seat represents a metal gong imported from the coastal lowlands. Actual gongs were commonly used as seats for Kenyah aristocrats at community meetings (personal communication, Whittier 1989).

In the longhouses of the Kayan and Kenyah, the central quarters are reserved for the headman's family The headman's door handle is distinctively carved and his veranda is often specially painted (Fig. V.29). The door handle (Fig. V.10) takes the form of the dragon-dog (*aso'* or *asu*), a motif that is greatly admired by the Kayan and Kenyah and appears in a number of different media (Figs. V.23, V.30, V.31, V.32, V.34) *Aso'* simply means "dog" in a number of Dayak languages. When Heine Geldern (1966:195–202) investigated design parallels between Dayak art and Chinese art of the Late Chou period, he concluded, however, that the mythological *aso'* that appears in the artwork of Borneo is not really a dog but a version of Chinese dragon motifs. This motif is thought to have been adopted from decorations appearing on Chinese ceramic jars, which were highly prized trade items kept as heirlooms by wealthy Dayak families. In characteristic Kayan style, the extremities of this open-mouthed *aso'* dragon (Fig. V.10)—its nose, horns, feet, and tail—terminate in branching spirals.

Intricately designed baby carriers, or *ba'*, also reflect social rank and privilege. In some regions, these baby carriers are carved completely of wood with fiber attachments. In others, a woven rattan frame is ornamented with cloth, shells, and a carefully designed beadwork patch with standard local motifs. The decorations on the carriers are considered protective because they attract the infant's soul, which is believed to be only loosely connected to the body at birth (Whittier and Whittier 1988:55). The small glass beads required

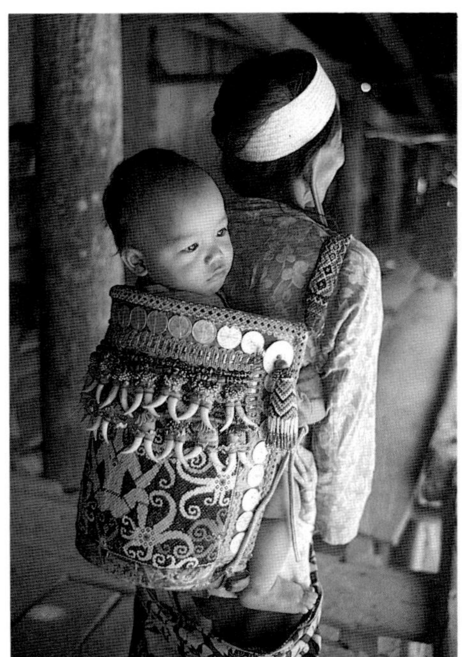

Fig. V.12 The full human figure on this baby carrier indicates that the infant is a member of a high-ranking family, Long Lebusan, East Kalimantan, 1989. Maarten W. Elink Schuurman

for the decorative patch are obtained through trade. Black, yellow, and white are the preferred colors, supplemented by flourishes of red, green, or blue (Whittier and Whittier 1988:52). Making the beadwork patch (Fig. V.11) can take as long as three months and is frequently the prerogative of the grandmother of an expected baby (Whittier and Whittier 1988:57). The designs appearing on the beadwork patches, or *aban*, accord with the baby's inherited rank. Such motifs as tigers or full human figures (Fig. V.12), as well as the attachment of imported tiger teeth to the frame, may be used only for infants of the highest rank (Whittier and Whittier 1988:52). The motif of a squatting human figure representing a slave—also seen on the wooden seat (Fig. V.9)—appears on a decorative patch from one Kenyah baby carrier (Fig. V.13). White shells were used to create the two human figures, and small colored beads were added for accents on the heads, wrists, waists, and possibly a sitting mat beneath the two figures.

Beadwork patches made for the babies of Kenyah or Kayan commoners typically feature abstract designs only. The snail shells attached to the frame, which are an essential feature of all traditional Kenyah *ba'*, are used to store the baby's umbilical cord after it falls off (Whittier and Whittier 1988:52). Other ornaments attached to the baby carrier, such as valuable heirloom beads, coins, or wild animal teeth, are donated by elder members of the baby's family, who thereby reaffirm their social ties to the infant (Whittier and Whittier 1988:57–58). These objects, and the noise they make as the carrier is used, are believed to repel evil spirits that might want to entice the baby's soul away. Kenyah baby carriers with decorative patches of small seed beads usually have one or more strings of larger heirloom beads anchored across the top above the main patch. The beaded patch (Fig. V.14) shows bands of geometric motifs including circles, triangles, spiral configurations, and designs that probably represent local pendants, which are made by joining two canine teeth of a wild animal so that they point outward. The image in the bottom figurative band may represent a boat.

Ritual Life, Shamanism, and Carving Traditions

Many of the Dayak objects that Westerners consider works of art were originally made for religious rituals. Both zoomorphic and anthropomorphic figures have been used in a great variety of Dayak ceremonies performed to invoke deities or repel destructive spirits. Rituals focus on a few common themes, including agricultural fertility, human life cycles, headhunting, and curing. An example of zoomorphic imagery can be found in the Hornbill Festival (*Gawai Kenyalang*) of the Iban people, who constitute the most populous Dayak group in Sarawak and dwell in smaller numbers on the Kalimantan side of the border as well. According to Iban belief, the rhinoceros hornbill (*Buceros rhinoceros*; Fig. V.15) is the chief of earthly birds. Its image is displayed at festivals as a sign of welcome to the principal Iban deity and god of warfare, Singalang Burong, who is himself leader of the sacred omen birds and appears to mankind in his earthly manifestation as a brahminy kite (Sandin 1977:12).

Hornbill Festivals were once organized by outstanding war leaders to honor the deity Singalang Burong and to serve as proof of the greatness of the sponsor. Only a warrior who had taken the life of an enemy was allowed to fell the tree used to make the hornbill image, or *kenyalang* (Fig. V.18). In recent decades, senior men of respected standing in the community have assumed the roles once reserved for war leaders (Sandin 1977:12). According to an Iban legend, the designs that appear on especially elaborate *kenyalang* figures are divinely inspired (Ganjing 1988:19). At the climax of the festival, the *kenyalang* figure is consecrated (see Morrison 1982:235) and placed atop a pole near the longhouse. In former times, the spirit of the *kenyalang* was thought to fly to enemy longhouses and weaken their warriors. This sculpture (Fig. V.18) is smoothly finished and gaily painted in red, green, blue, yellow, and white. The hornbill casque swirls upward into a flower-tipped spiral, and the upswept tail, wings, and scrollwork headcrest also include delicate flower forms.

Anthropomorphic, as well as zoomorphic, figures are used in rituals of the Ngaju (see Bertlin 1927; Schärer 1963; Sumnik-Dekovich 1985; Revel-

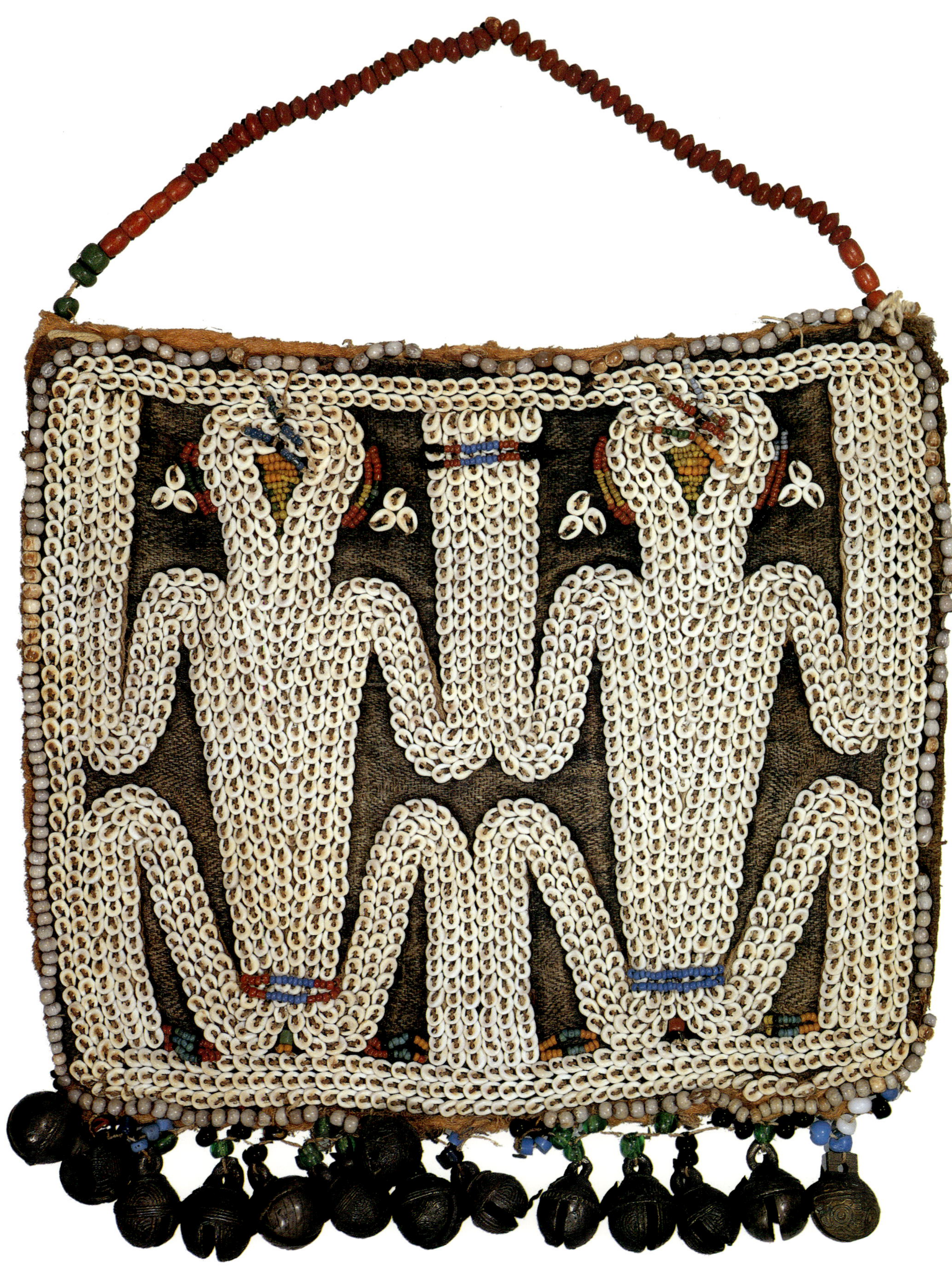

Fig. V.13 Decorative patch for baby carrier, *aban*
Kenyah, northern East Kalimantan
Cotton, shells, beads, metal bells, 50.1 x 36.2
Rijksmuseum voor Volkenkunde, Leiden, 2978-2

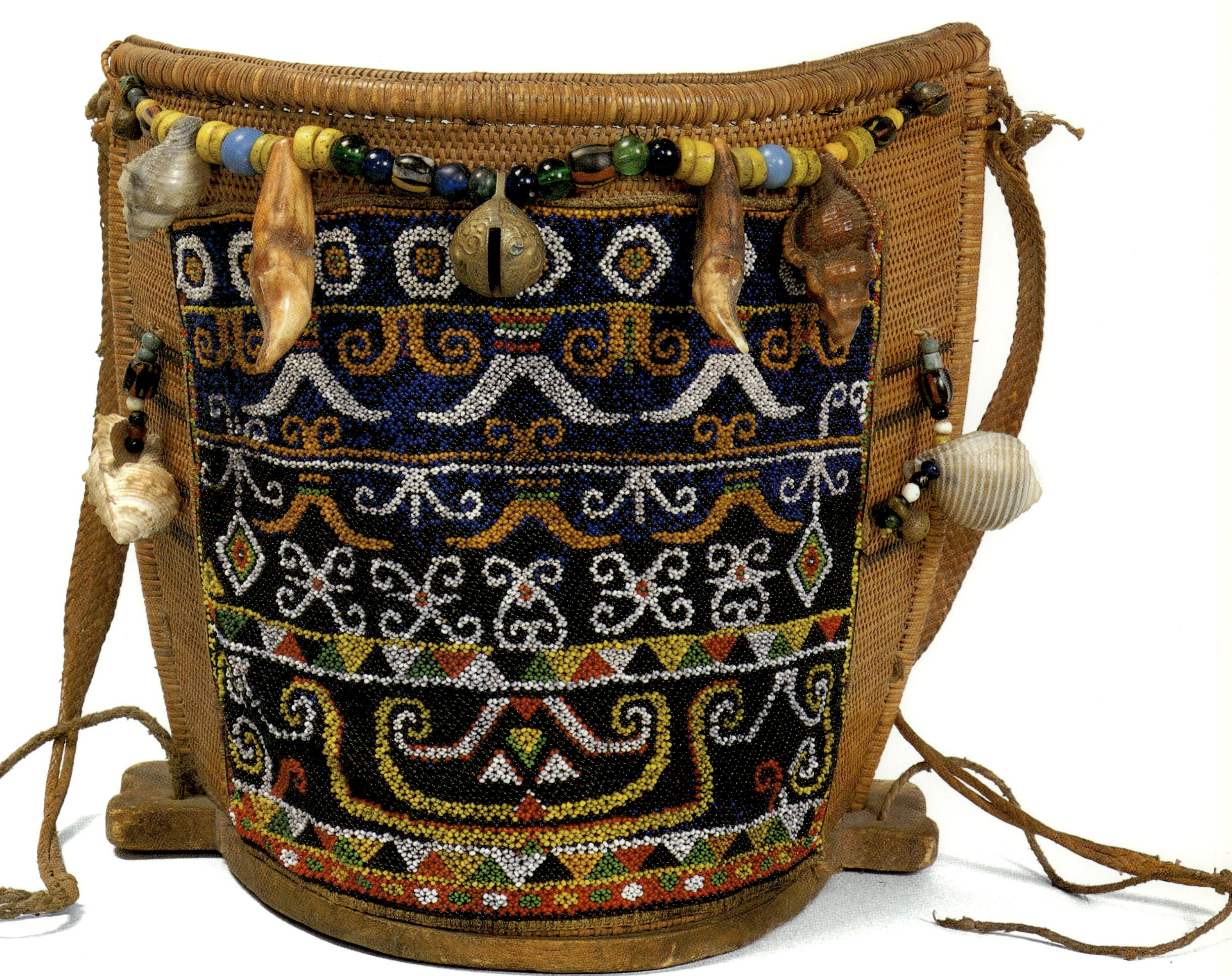

Fig. V.14 Beaded baby carrier
Kenyah or Kayan, Kalimantan
Wood, rattan, beads, bear teeth, snail shells,
28 x 31 x 18.5
Mark and Kathy Johnson, 236

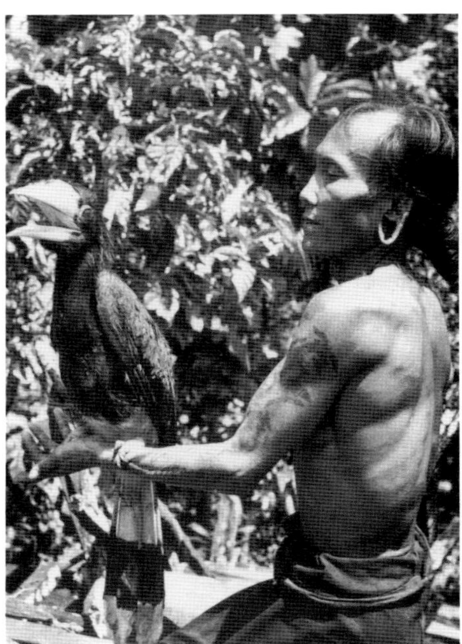

Fig. V.15 An Iban man holds a captive hornbill, reared as a pet, Sarawak, 1950s. Hedda Morrison

Macdonald 1988). The *hampatong* statues were, for example, constructed either to commemorate a deceased member of the village or to mark the taking of an enemy head in warfare (Schärer 1963:147). They were erected in separate shrine areas maintained away from the longhouse for each of these purposes.

Carving traditions involving monumental anthropomorphic figures other than Ngaju *hampatong* are less well understood, a fact complicated by the generic application of the term *hampatong*. *Hampatong* has been used by travelers and art dealers to mean any large wooden freestanding sculpted pole from a Dayak group, not just those made by the Ngaju. *Hampatong*-like figures are known from a number of widely scattered areas of Kalimantan. Carl Lumholtz, who wrote a popular account of his travels, photographed a figure in a Murung village (see Lumholtz 1921:opposite 116), at the headwaters of the Barito River, that he equated with *hampatong* in other parts of Central Kalimantan. Figures known as *temadu*, from the upper Melawi River in West Kalimantan, have also been equated with *hampatong*. A Dutch civil administrator in that region, W. C. ten Cate, wrote about these figures (1922), which are typically realistic, life-sized representations of the deceased, sometimes including such notable physical anomalies as bowlegs or missing fingers (Bertling 1927:181).

A carved pole now in the collections of the Museum Nasional Indonesia (Fig. V.17), purchased from ten Cate in 1921, is identified in the museum's records as a protective post or *hampatong/temadu*. Its complex imagery of mixed human and animal figures is, however, stylistically quite different from the *temadu* described by ten Cate. Though it is therefore a *hampatong* sculpture in the generic sense of that term, the exact identity and function of this magnificently carved pole remains unknown. The figures that intertwine up and down the central post include a man with a sun hat who sits on a tiger that holds a child in its paws. Two snakes wrap around the man and the tiger. Below them is a fanged animal face with a hanging tongue; a turtle crawls up the other side. Below the turtle is a small dog that is above an upside-down figure of a man holding a bush knife. Near this man is a woman holding a child. Beside the woman is a pig with his feet projecting from the side of the pole.

Some anthropomorphic figures, including those made by the Kenyah (Hose and McDougall 1912:plate 147; Tillema 1989:202–203), were placed near villages to scare away spirits bearing illness. Similar figures were photographed by W. L. Abbott along the upper Sekayan River in West Kalimantan, near the Sarawak border (Fig. V.16). Called *teguno* according to Abbott's field notes (National Anthropological Archives, Abbott 2/8/1), they ranged from five to eight feet in height and were erected beside the path at the entrance to nearly every village in the area. The use of such monumental anthropomorphic figures is an example of similar traditions appearing among diverse Dayak groups, but a more precise classification of the relationships that exist among the numerous different styles has yet to be made.

Carved wooden masks have been used in ritual contexts by a number of Dayak groups, including the Selako, Iban, Melanau, Kenyah, Kayan, and Modang (Heppell 1989:88). Masks, known as *hudo'* among the Kayan and Kenyah, take a variety of forms (see Revel-Macdonald 1978, 1988), including the wild boar (Fig. V.19), which was worn by dancers in agricultural rites designed to assure the fertility of the rice crop (Barbier and Newton 1988:plate 25). In such ceremonies, masked performers representing benevolent rice spirits left offerings in the fields to attract spirits who might harm the crop, then beseeched them to depart. Other performers wore frightening masks and attempted to terrify spectators, who represented the destructive spirits (Heppell 1989:89).

Hudo' masks were also worn by Kenyah shamans (*dayong*; Fig. V.20), who are ritual specialists with the power to contact spirits. Known more generally in Borneo as *balian*, they have been widely relied upon for the treatment of illness. In some parts of the island traditional religion is still practiced. Among the Melanau people of Sarawak, for example, shamans carve small anthropomorphic figures, known as *bilum*, which they use in rituals to cure the sick (see Chong 1987). Iban shamans use charms, stored in special containers

Fig. V.16 Anthropomorphic figures, Pessing village, upper Sekayan River, 1905. W. L. Abbott Collection, Anthropology Archives, Smithsonian Institution.

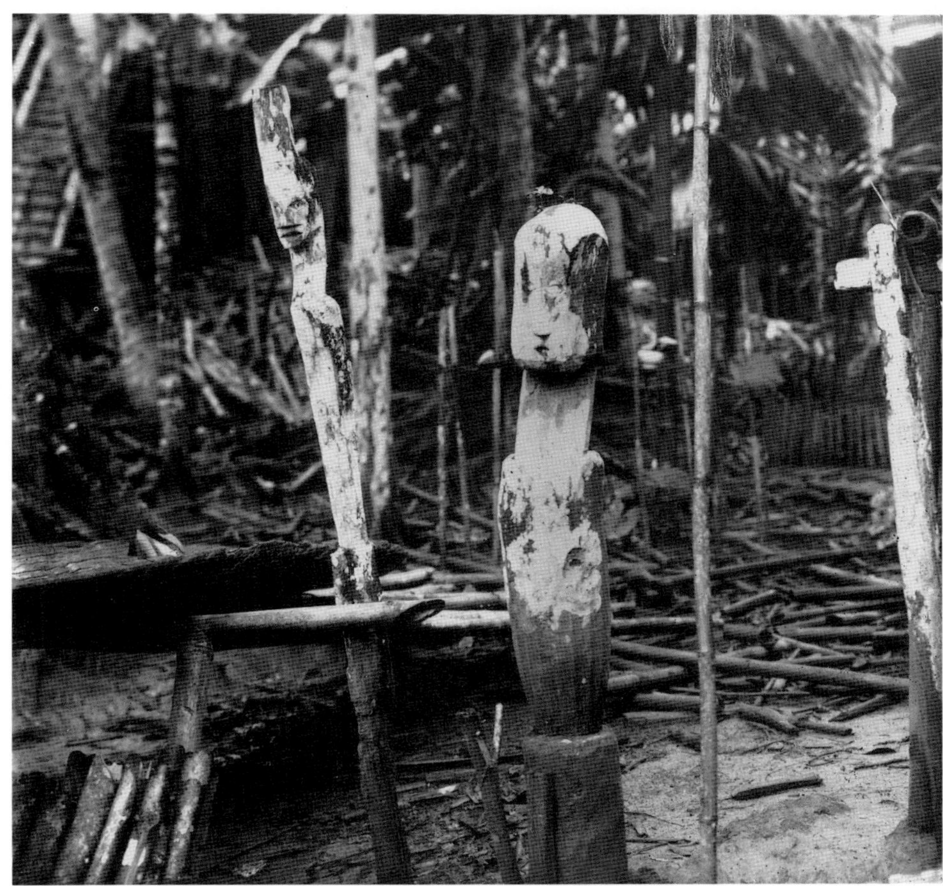

(Figs. V.23a, V.23b), to contact spirits on behalf of the patient, to identify the spiritual source of the illness, and then to restore the elements of the patient's soul to their proper balance. The container's two carved squatting figures with open toothy mouths and staring beaded eyes may have been intended to protect the shaman from the powerful forces involved in the curing ceremony. A protective item used by Ngaju and Dusun shamans is a shell tunic (Figs. V.21, V.22), worn during rituals in which the shaman battles with spiritual forces in order to cure the patient (personal communication, G. Appell 1989). The precisely polished and mounted shell discs may serve as symbolic armor as well as aesthetic decoration.

Headhunting and Weaving in Ritual Tradition

Ritual life required periodic animal sacrifices and, among some Dayak groups, human sacrifice to ensure fertility and to appease demonic spirits believed to cause illness, disease, or crop failure. Headhunting was practiced as part of warfare between enemy groups, in which the goal was the capture of slaves and the taking of heads for ritual purposes. Heads were particularly sought to end the mourning periods for a dead chief (Hose 1988 [1926]). In some areas, young men hunted heads as a prerequisite to marriage, and the successful acquisition of enemy heads was equated in ritual with the increase of community fertility (Sutlive 1989). Major rituals that followed headhunting expeditions were believed to restore balance and harmony to the cosmos, thereby promoting the prosperity of the community.

Clothing designed for warfare was specially marked with potent symbols intended to increase the warrior's success. A war jacket (Fig. V.24) from the Tebidah people of West Kalimantan, like traditional war costumes on Sulawesi, Flores, and Timor, is made from twined plant fibers probably from the leaves of the *lemba* plant (*Curculigo latifolia*), which was used in a variety of textiles and garments made on Borneo. The twining technique is an archaic technology intermediate between basket making and loom weaving (Gittinger 1979:226).

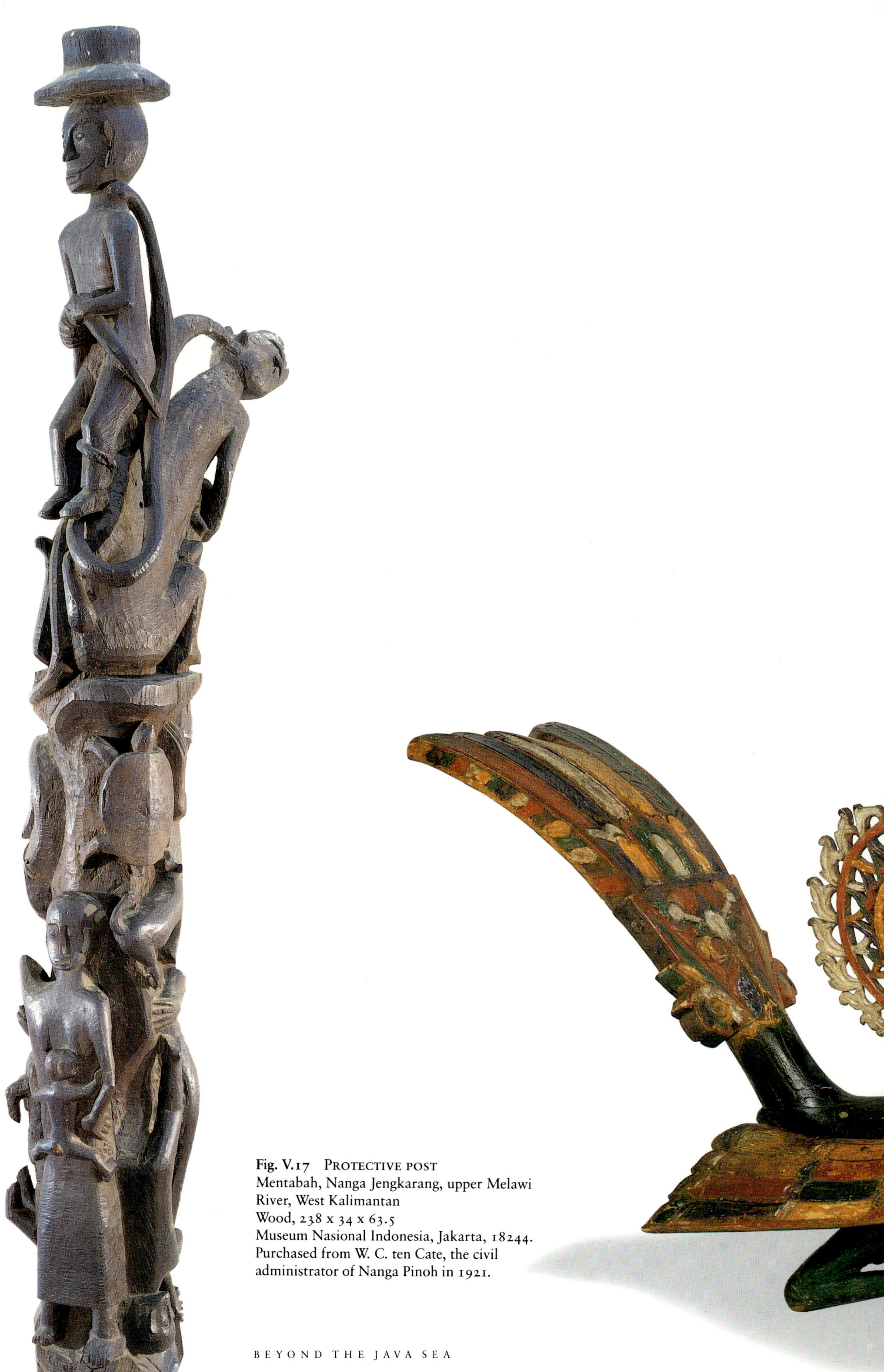

Fig. V.17 Protective post
Mentabah, Nanga Jengkarang, upper Melawi River, West Kalimantan
Wood, 238 x 34 x 63.5
Museum Nasional Indonesia, Jakarta, 18244. Purchased from W. C. ten Cate, the civil administrator of Nanga Pinoh in 1921.

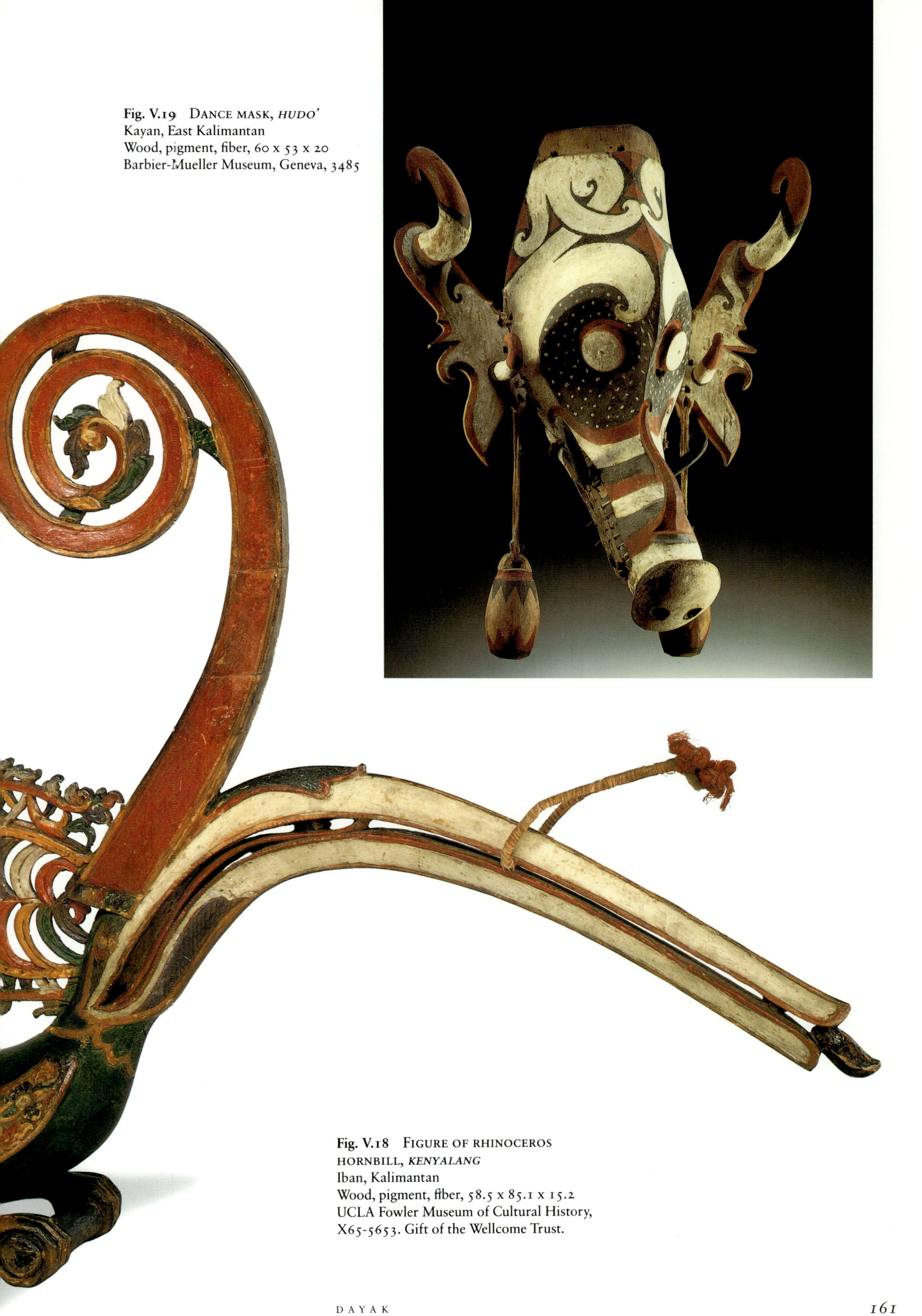

Fig. V.19 DANCE MASK, *HUDO'*
Kayan, East Kalimantan
Wood, pigment, fiber, 60 x 53 x 20
Barbier-Mueller Museum, Geneva, 3485

Fig. V.18 FIGURE OF RHINOCEROS HORNBILL, *KENYALANG*
Iban, Kalimantan
Wood, pigment, fiber, 58.5 x 85.1 x 15.2
UCLA Fowler Museum of Cultural History, X65-5653. Gift of the Wellcome Trust.

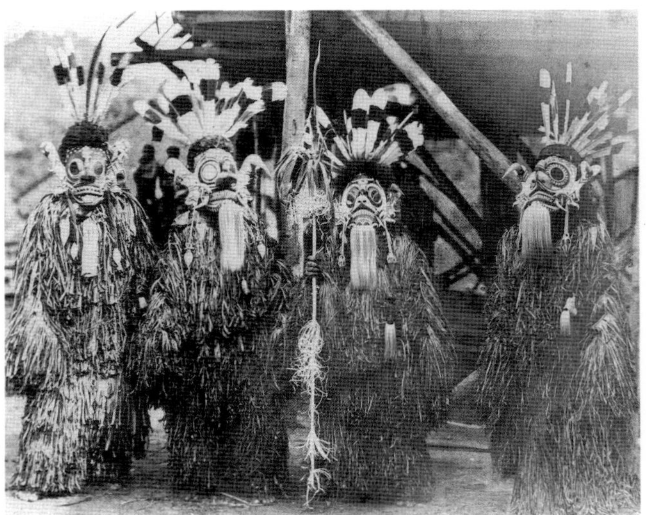

Fig. V.20 Masked Kenyah shamans, Sarawak, circa 1900. Courtesy Museum voor Volkenkunde, Rotterdam.

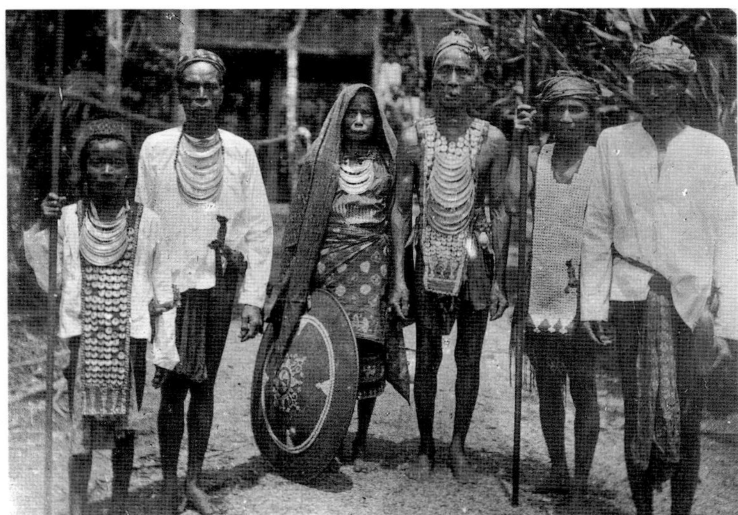

Fig. V.21 A group of Dusun people, some wearing tunics like that illustrated in Fig. V.22, Kalimantan, early 1900s. Courtesy Royal Tropical Institute, Tropenmuseum, The Netherlands.

OPPOSITE
Fig. V.22 SHAMAN'S TUNIC
Ngaju, Central Kalimantan
Cotton, opercula, shells, hair, barkcloth, 143.5 x 20
Rijksmuseum voor Volkenkunde, Leiden, 360-7443. Accessioned in 1883.

The painted checkerboard design that appears on the jacket may symbolize such dualities as black/white, death/fertility, male/female, and evil/good. This pattern is associated with warriors or guardian spirits in many areas of Indonesia (Gittinger 1979:43–44) and resembles black-and-white checkered cloths used on Bali. Also seen on this jacket are pinwheels, spirals, and triangles at the shoulders. Bands of red trade cloth run horizontally across the torso, and heart-shaped spiral forms, diamonds, and triangles are painted at the waist.

Ceremonial swords, or *mandau*, manufactured by Dayak groups are extensively ornamented, with wild animal teeth, beads, and goat hair. Hilts, often carved of deer bone, are sculptural and made to charm spirits rather than with practical intent. Even blades are adorned with inlaid copper plugs and curlicues protruding from the blunt edge of the blade. Smithing is highly developed in some Dayak groups and is readily distinguishable by the shapes of the blades from the courtly smithing traditions of Java and Bali (Jessup 1990). Similar swords are still manufactured and worn today in some areas as part of men's formal ceremonial attire. The especially fine, ornamented sword and hilt (Fig. V.25) is of Kenyah or Kayan manufacture, but it was acquired before 1918 by the Sultan of Kutai, an Islamic sultanate located on the lower reaches of the Mahakam River (see catalog chapter X).

Dayak shields may be carved and painted, traditionally using red and black natural pigments, with distinctive designs on the front and back. A design from the front of a Kenyah shield, consisting of two intertwined *aso'* dragon figures (Fig. V.30b), was believed not only to scare but also to harm the enemy during battle. The coiling, mirror-image figures are aligned back to back to create a fanged face at the center of the shield. The *aso'* spiral designs on the inside of the shield (Fig. V.30a), without the ferocious face, were intended to protect the user (Sumnik-Dekovich 1985:114). Today children play with miniature shields (Fig. V.28) decorated in a similar fashion.

Iban women received trophy heads captured by warriors in a blanketlike textile, or *pua'* (Fig. V.26). The severed enemy heads were presented ritually to

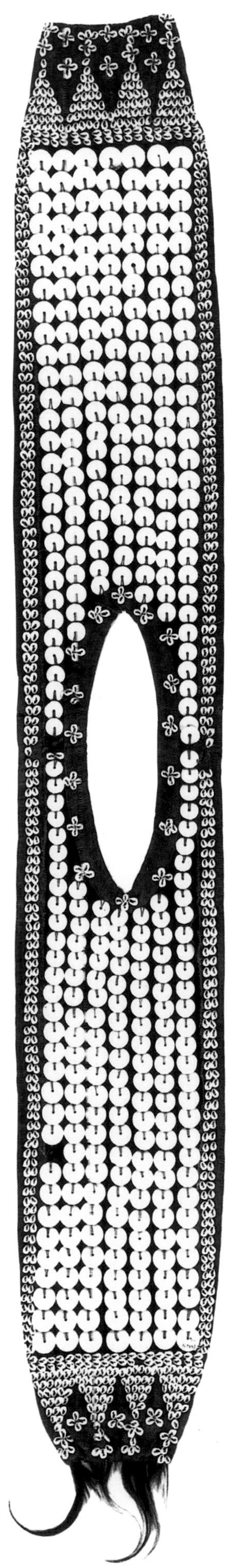

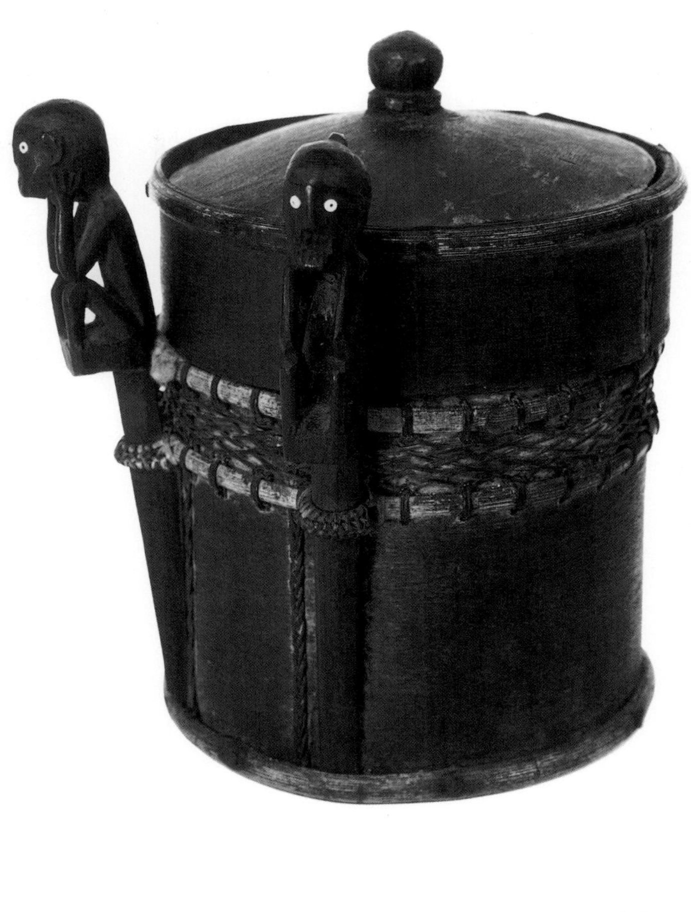

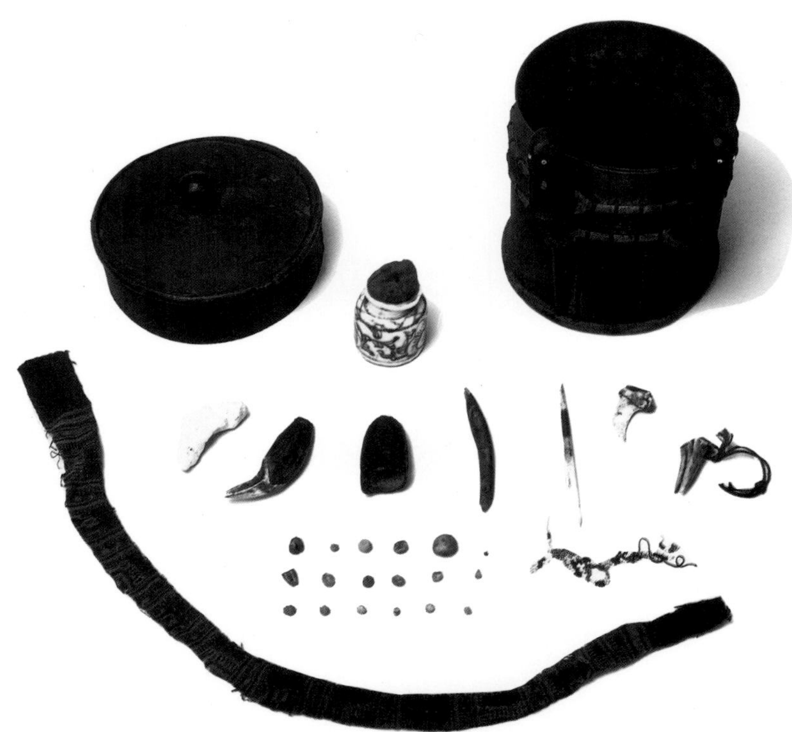

Fig. V.23a SHAMAN'S MEDICINE BOX
Iban, Sarawak or Kalimantan
Wood, bark, fiber, Chinese porcelain, leopard and bear teeth, porcupine quill, beads,
19 x 13.5
Dr. and Mrs. Robert Kuhn

Fig. V.23b Contents of shaman's medicine box, Fig. V.23a.

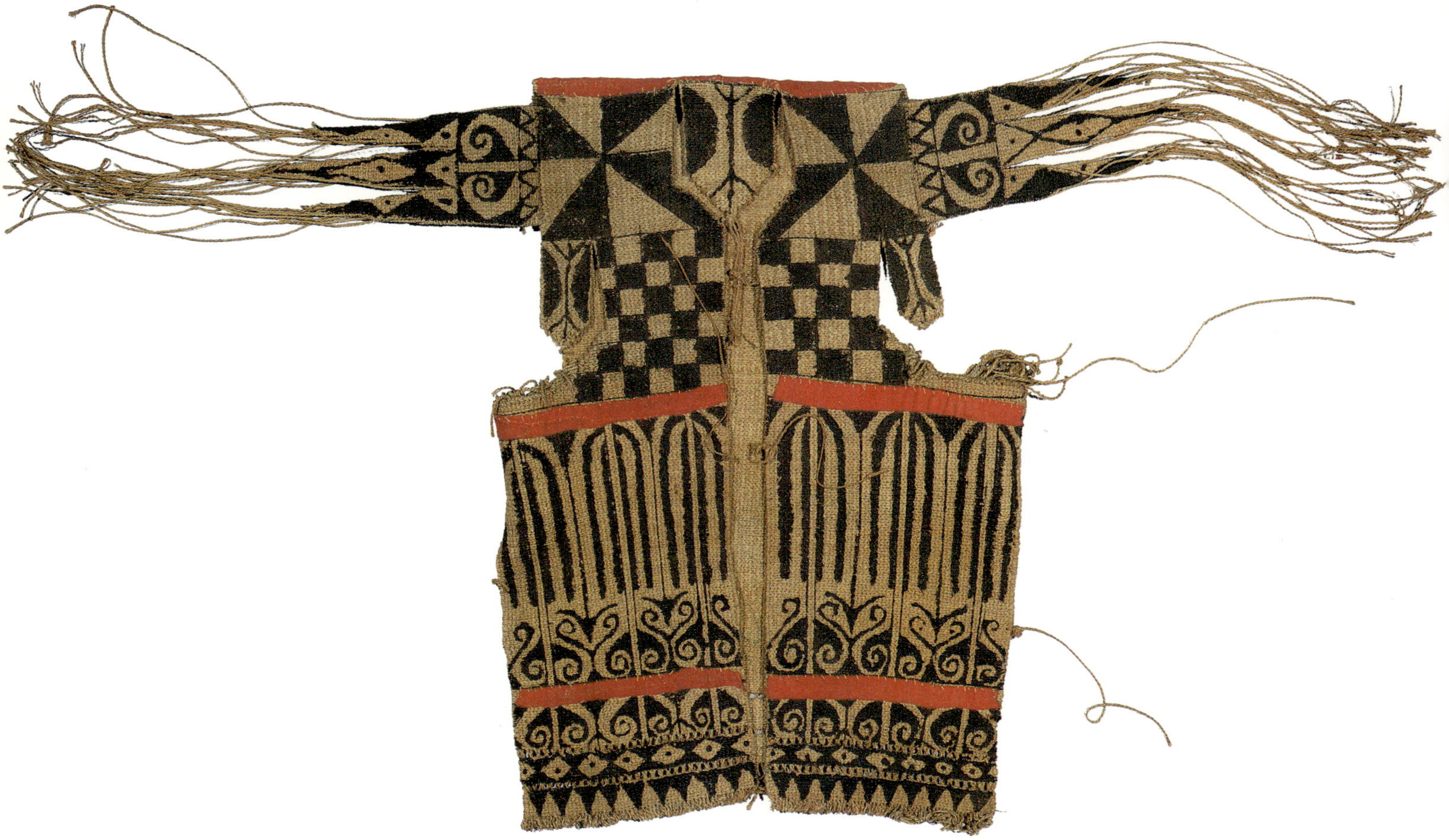

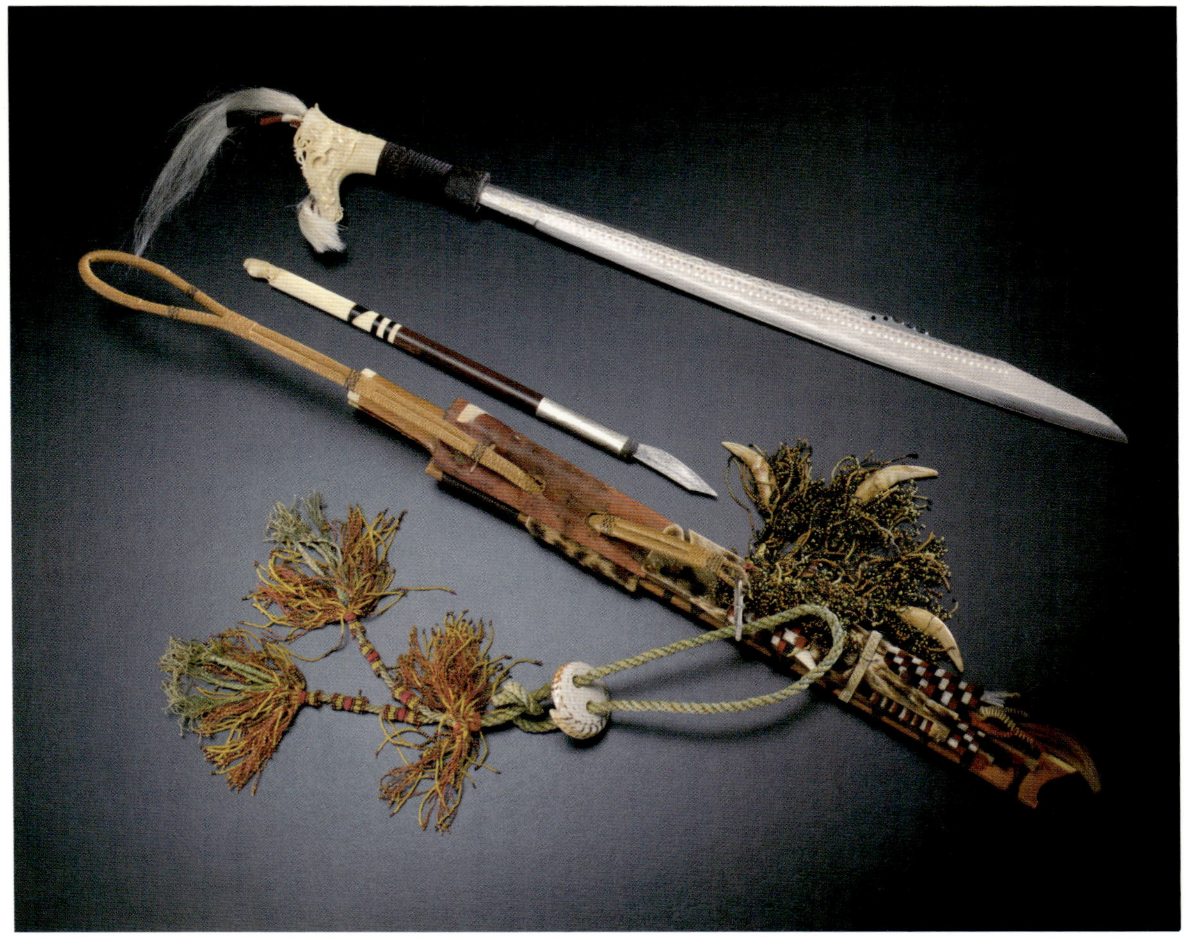

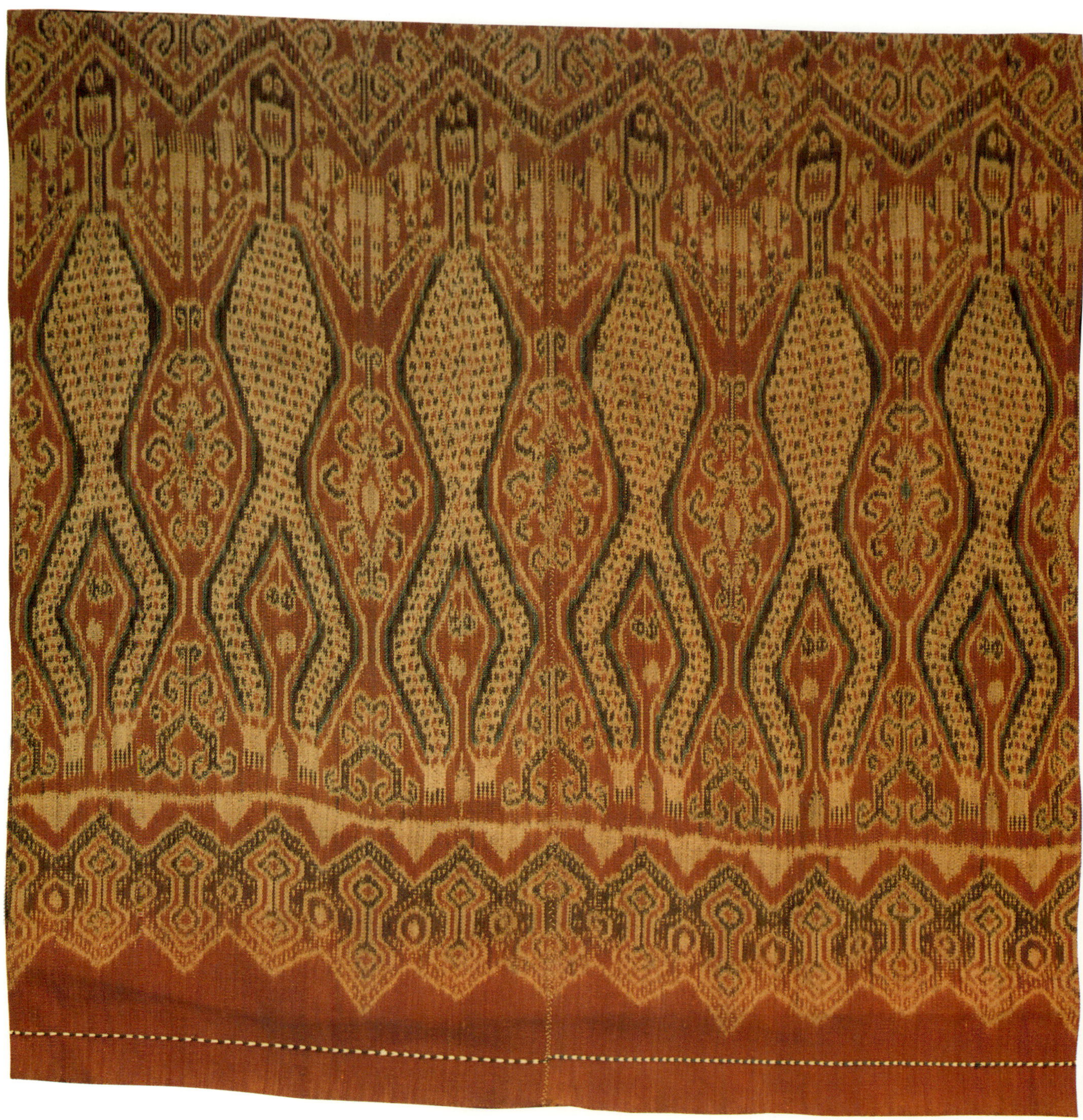

OPPOSITE TOP

Fig. V.24 WARRIOR'S JACKET
Tebidah, West Kalimantan
Twined plant fiber, 55 x 107
Royal Tropical Institute, Tropenmuseum, The Netherlands, H1687. Accessioned in 1900.

OPPOSITE BOTTOM

Fig. V.25 CEREMONIAL SWORD, *MANDAU*
Kenyah or Kayan, Kalimantan
Metal, wood, fur, beads, teeth, shell, silk, plant fiber, 78.7
Department of Anthropology, Smithsonian Institution, 301833. Given to Alfred M. Erskine by the Sultan of Kutai. Accessioned in 1918.

Fig. V.26 CEREMONIAL TEXTILE, *PUA'*
Iban, northern Kalimantan
Cotton, 247 x 108.3
Loaned by the University Museum, University of Pennsylvania, 603a.

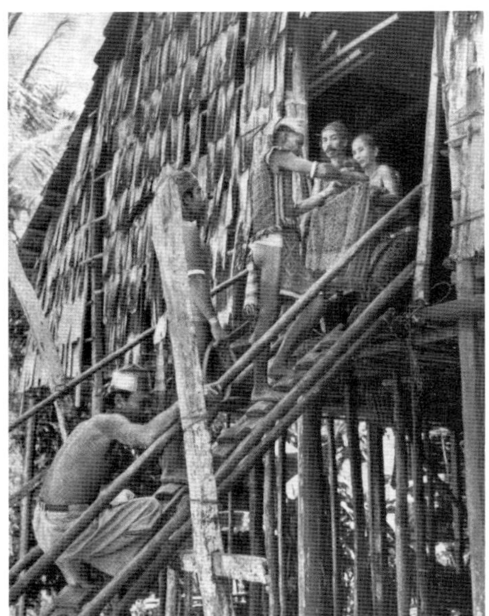

Fig. V.27 Trophy head received in a *pua'* cloth at a Mualang longhouse, Sarawak, before 1955. Courtesy Koninklijk Instituut voor Taal-, Land- en Volkenkunde, Leiden.

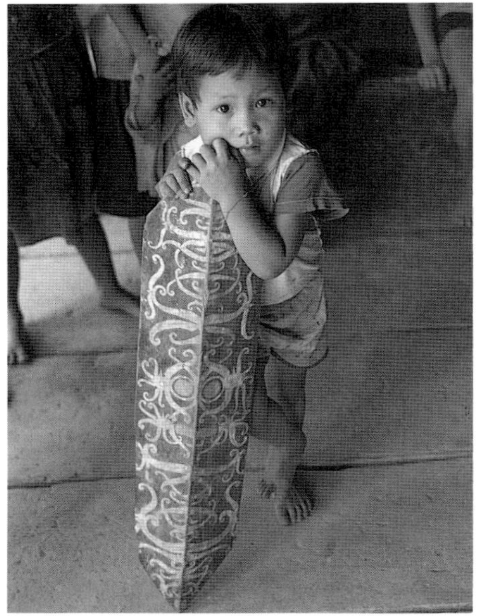

Fig. V.28 Kenyah boy plays with a miniature shield, Long Lebusan, East Kalimantan, 1989. Maarten Elink Schuurman

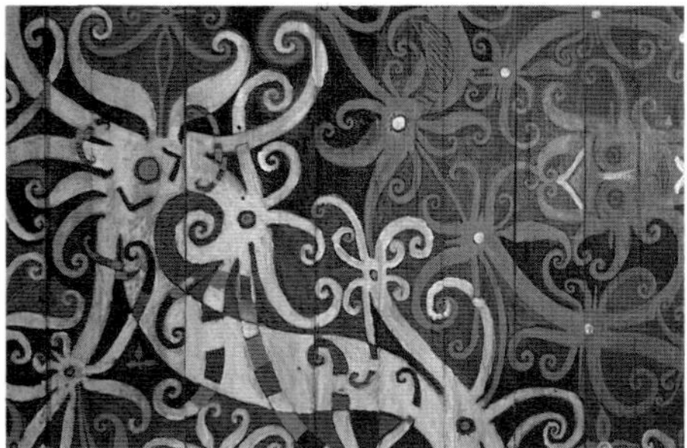

Fig. V.29 Designs painted by a Kenyah aristocrat as interior decoration, Long Lebusan, East Kalimantan, 1989. Maarten W. Elink Schuurman

the senior women of the community at the top of the longhouse steps (Fig. V.27). Headhunters seeking physical protection and guidance in warfare would sleep beneath *pua'* to elicit guidance from deities in their dreams (Freeman 1979). Headhunting was largely ended in all Dayak regions during the nineteenth century (Vayda 1976, Jessup and Vayda 1989:9), but *pua'* continue to be woven and used in a variety of ritual contexts, retaining their association with certain traditional cosmological ideas.

Pua' are patterned by the warp *ikat* technique (see Ong 1988:19–24), a complex and time-consuming process of resist dyeing that requires great mastery. Ritual knowledge and actions, including the sacrifice of a pig or chicken, are required as well. The multistage dyeing process is called "women's war" (*kayau indu'*) by the Iban, because weaving ceremonial textiles and headhunting are perilous and parallel ventures (Drake 1988:32). Experienced weavers gained prestige and enhanced status just as warfare success ranked the community's men (Freeman 1970; Drake 1988).

Much of the religious knowledge of the Iban is attributed to communication with spirits through dreams (Freeman 1979), and new *pua'* designs are first revealed to weavers in their sleep. Weaving certain designs is considered risky because it brings the weaver into dangerous contact with the spirit world. Charms, often in the form of small stones, are kept by weavers to assist them through the dangers of their art (Vogelsanger 1980:116). Novice weavers confine themselves to more simple, abstract designs and may be assisted by their elder relatives in tying *ikat* sections that might be too potent for them (Vogelsanger 1980:117). Complicated patterns with humanlike figures representing ancestors and spirits are attempted only by older, more experienced weavers. Designs that are copied are considered less dangerous than those that are newly created on the basis of dreams. Well-executed, innovative designs are believed to be pleasing to the deities and to attract their beneficence to rituals where they are displayed (Freeman, as cited in Vogelsanger 1980:118).

In addition to headhunting rituals, *pua'* have been used in many other ritual situations. They are displayed or used at agricultural rites, births, children's naming ceremonies, and funerals, where the cloth was said to act symbolically as the roof for the boat carrying the deceased downriver to the afterworld (Vogelsanger 1980:119). This *pua'* cloth (Fig. V.26) shows a mature weaver's design featuring a row of large anthropomorphic spirit figures with smaller human figures on either side of their heads. By their feet are even more abstract anthropomorphic figures designed from floral forms. The large, frontally posed figures have gaping mouths and speckled bodies. The lozenge-shaped motif between their waists appear to be insect or crustacean designs.

Cosmology and Dayak Design

In the artwork of many Dayak groups, images of humans, animals, and plants merge into one unit, expressing the proliferation of life and the integration of living beings in the cosmos. The designs characteristic of the Kenyah and Kayan groups are based primarily on a spiral motif that seemingly grows to cover the entire ornamented surface (Fig. V.29). Compared to the design systems found in other parts of Indonesia, which tend to favor the repetition of small-scale geometric patterns, Kenyah and Kayan designs are markedly more expansive and integrative and less confined by symmetry (Heine Geldern 1971:52).

Dragon imagery, associated with the lower world, has been a particularly fruitful source of inspiration in Dayak design. Best known is the *aso'* motif, which figures prominently in many such designs and can be seen on Kenyah and Kayan jewelry, clothing, tattoos, toys, baby carriers, architecture, weapons, coffins, and other household objects. Its coils are often transformed into other living forms. Considered to be protective and also associated with fertility, the *aso'* recalls the *lasara* of Nias and the *singa* of the Batak. Two fanciful carved figures, painted in black, white, and red (Figs. V.31, V.34), represent varied manifestations of the *aso'* dragon. The use to which these figures were put remains unclear, but the symbolic importance of the *aso'* motif suggests that

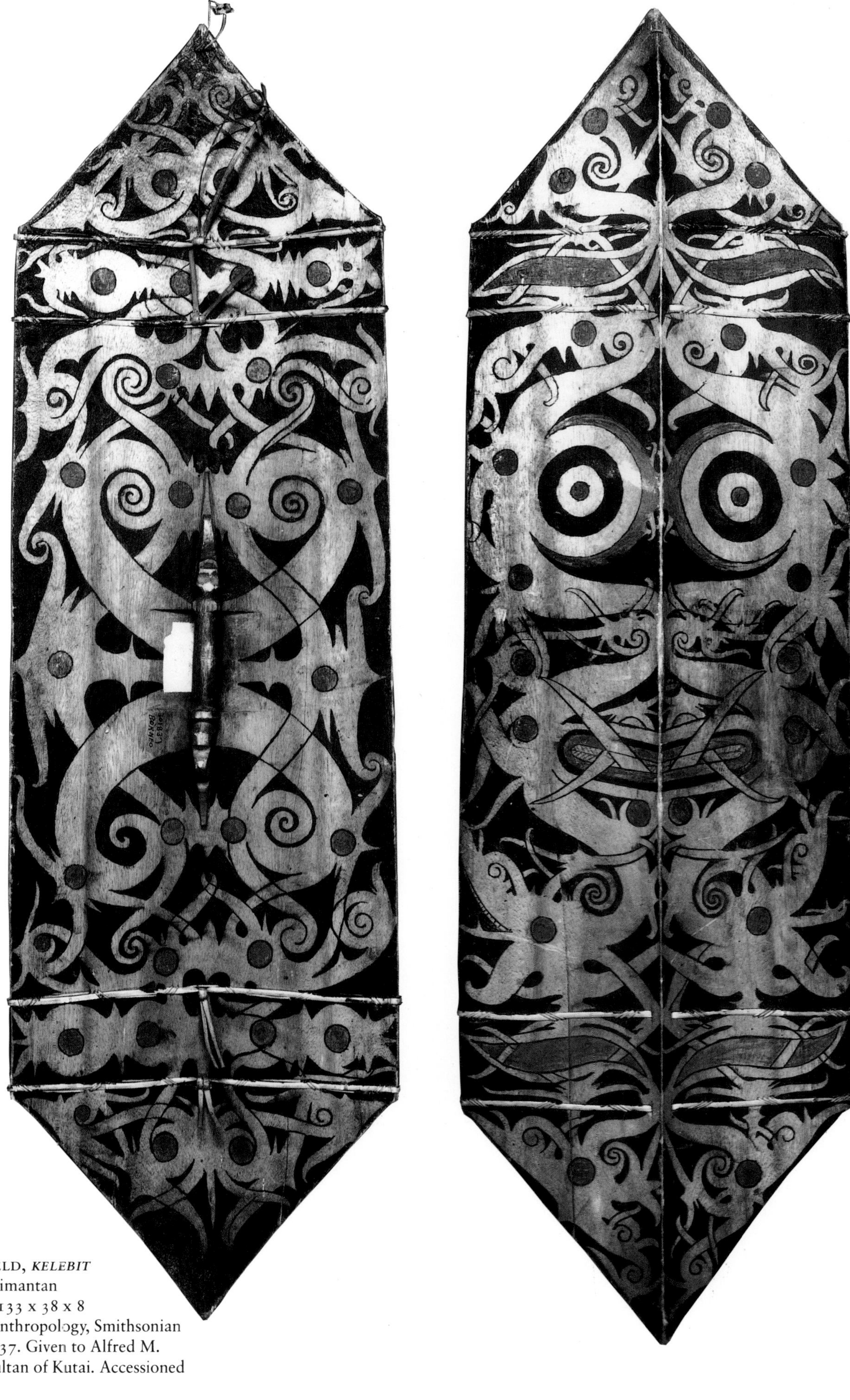

Fig. V.30a SHIELD, *KELEBIT*
Kenyah, East Kalimantan
Wood, pigment, 133 x 38 x 8
Department of Anthropology, Smithsonian Institution, 301837. Given to Alfred M. Erskine by the Sultan of Kutai. Accessioned in 1918.

Fig. V.30b Outside of shield, Fig. V.30a.

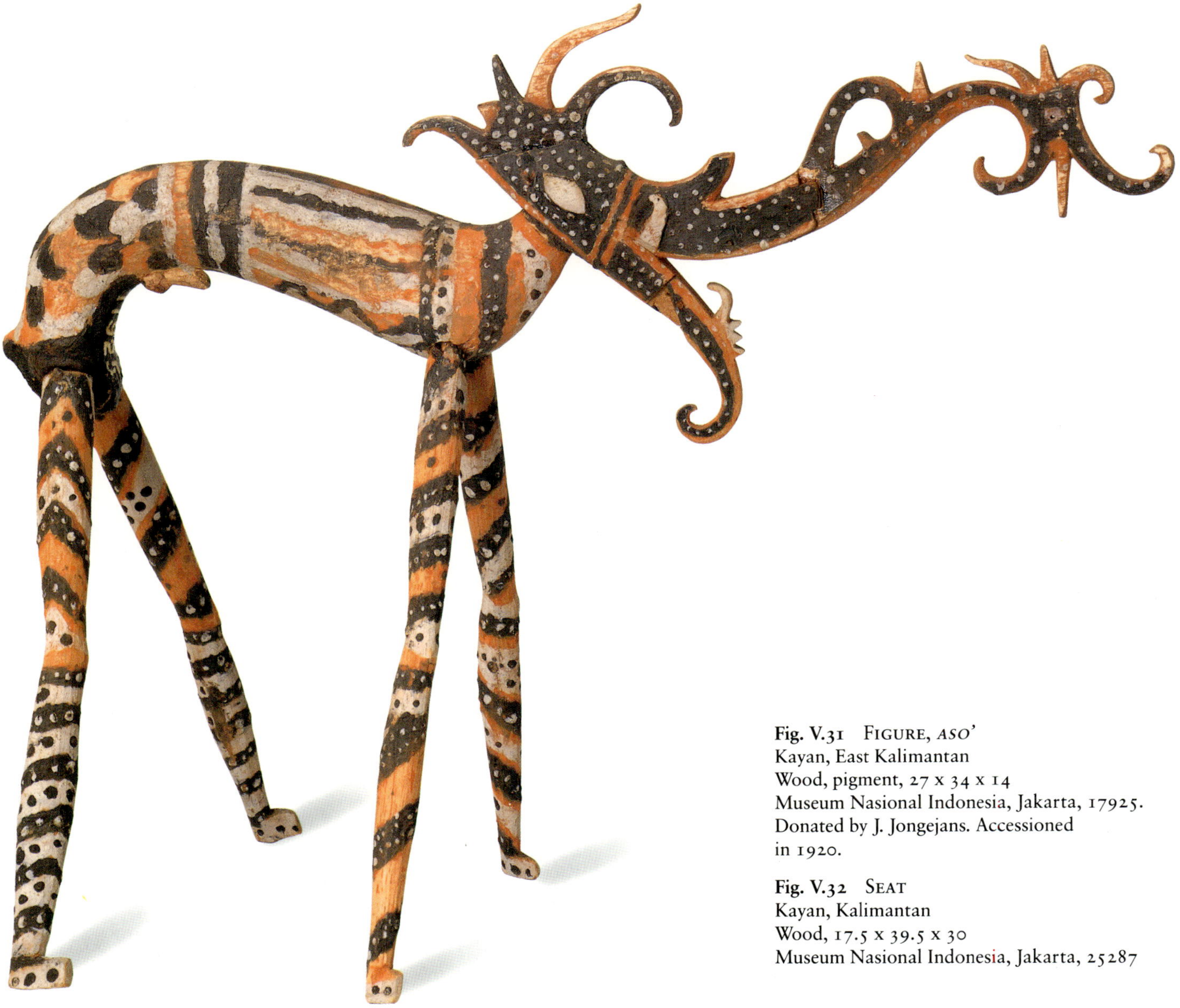

Fig. V.31 FIGURE, *ASO'*
Kayan, East Kalimantan
Wood, pigment, 27 x 34 x 14
Museum Nasional Indonesia, Jakarta, 17925.
Donated by J. Jongejans. Accessioned in 1920.

Fig. V.32 SEAT
Kayan, Kalimantan
Wood, 17.5 x 39.5 x 30
Museum Nasional Indonesia, Jakarta, 25287

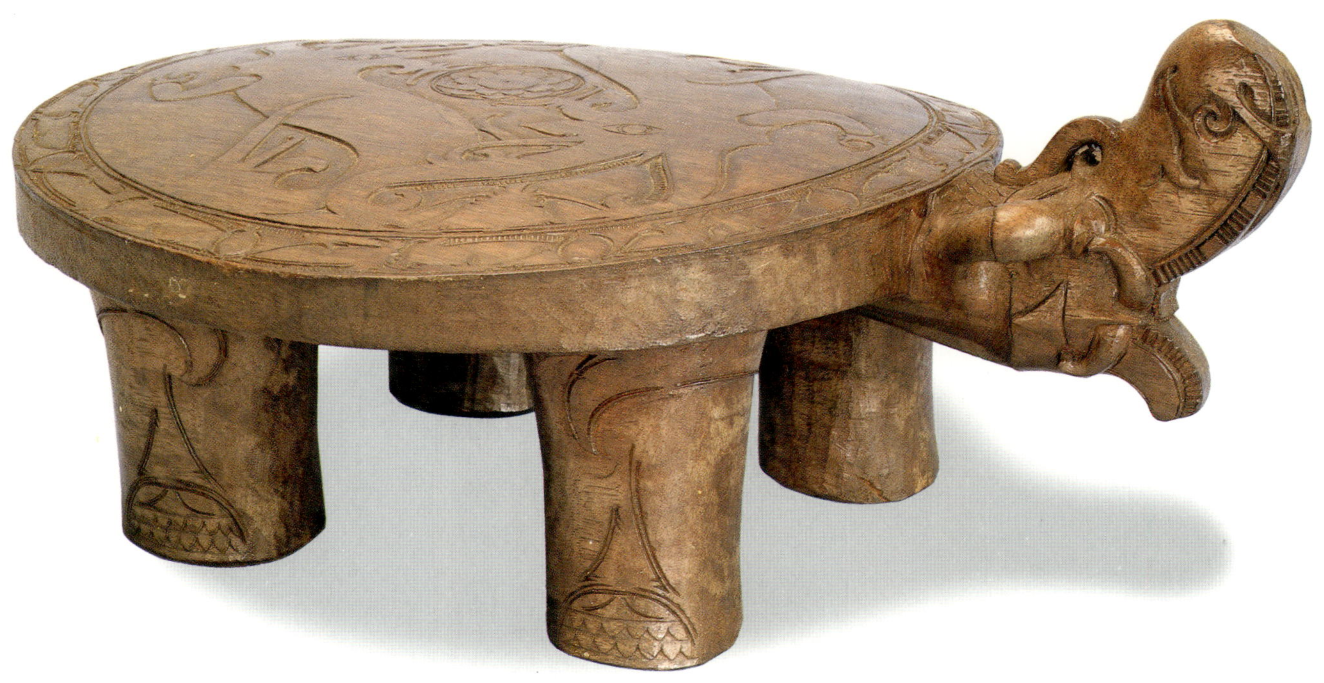

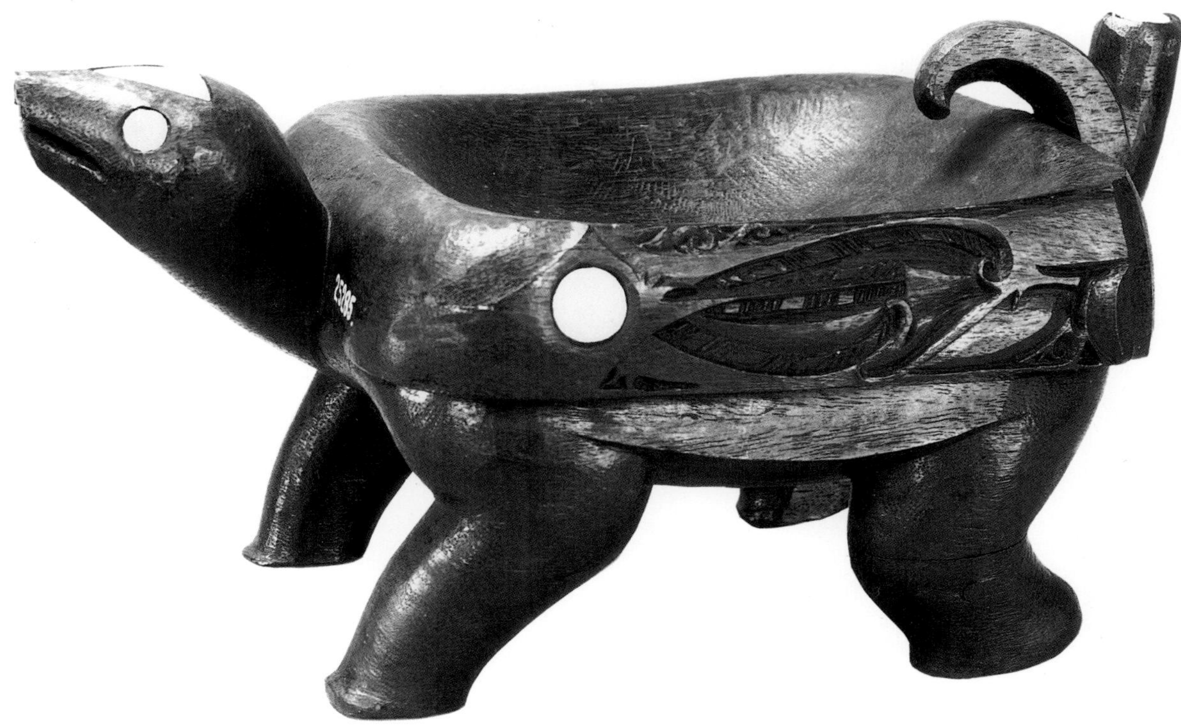

Fig. V.33 Dish or Mortar
Dayak, Middle Mahakam River,
East Kalimantan
Wood, shell, 12 x 25.5 x 13.5
Museum Nasional Indonesia, Jakarta, 25285

they were probably more than simple toys. The *aso'* sculpture (Fig. V.31) is a long-legged creature painted with polka dots, stripes, and scales on his loins. The rider of the dragon-headed chariot (Fig. V.34) wears a carved headdress and red loincloth, and he may have a quid of tobacco or betel nut in his mouth.

The wooden seat (Fig. V.32) appears to confirm Heine Geldern's hypothesis that the *aso'* motif was adopted from Chinese trade ceramics. The form of the seat itself is an animal with one type of characteristic rounded *aso'* head. The two *aso'* figures carved on the flat top closely resemble the encircling dragon designs known from Chinese Ming and Ching period ceramics (compare with Fig. 8). In the center of this seat is a lotus motif, probably also copied from imported Chinese ceramics. Although the seat's original ownership is not documented, it may have belonged to a family in possession of a ceramic piece with a similar circling dragon design. Chinese ceramics, particularly large jars used for water storage or even urn burial in some areas, remain highly prized heirlooms among many Dayak groups.

The animal form of the shell-inlaid dish or mortar (Fig. V.33) is another form of dragon imagery (personal communication, B. Sellato 1990). This innocuous creature perches on his haunches as if ready to jump. In addition to their use in rituals, animal figures decorate many Dayak utilitarian objects. Some, such as the small sculptures attached to bamboo quivers (Figs. V.36, V.37), may have been talismans. Such quivers were used by Dayak hunters to hold blowgun darts (Fig. V.35). The darts needed to be carefully protected because they were often treated with plant-derived poisons to effect the kill. A great deal of care went into the manufacture of quivers, which often feature intricately designed plaiting of rattan and other fibers, in addition to finely carved animal figures. Such adorned utilitarian pieces exemplify the spiritual concern and aesthetic skill that Dayak artisans in many areas of Borneo apply to the material resources at hand.

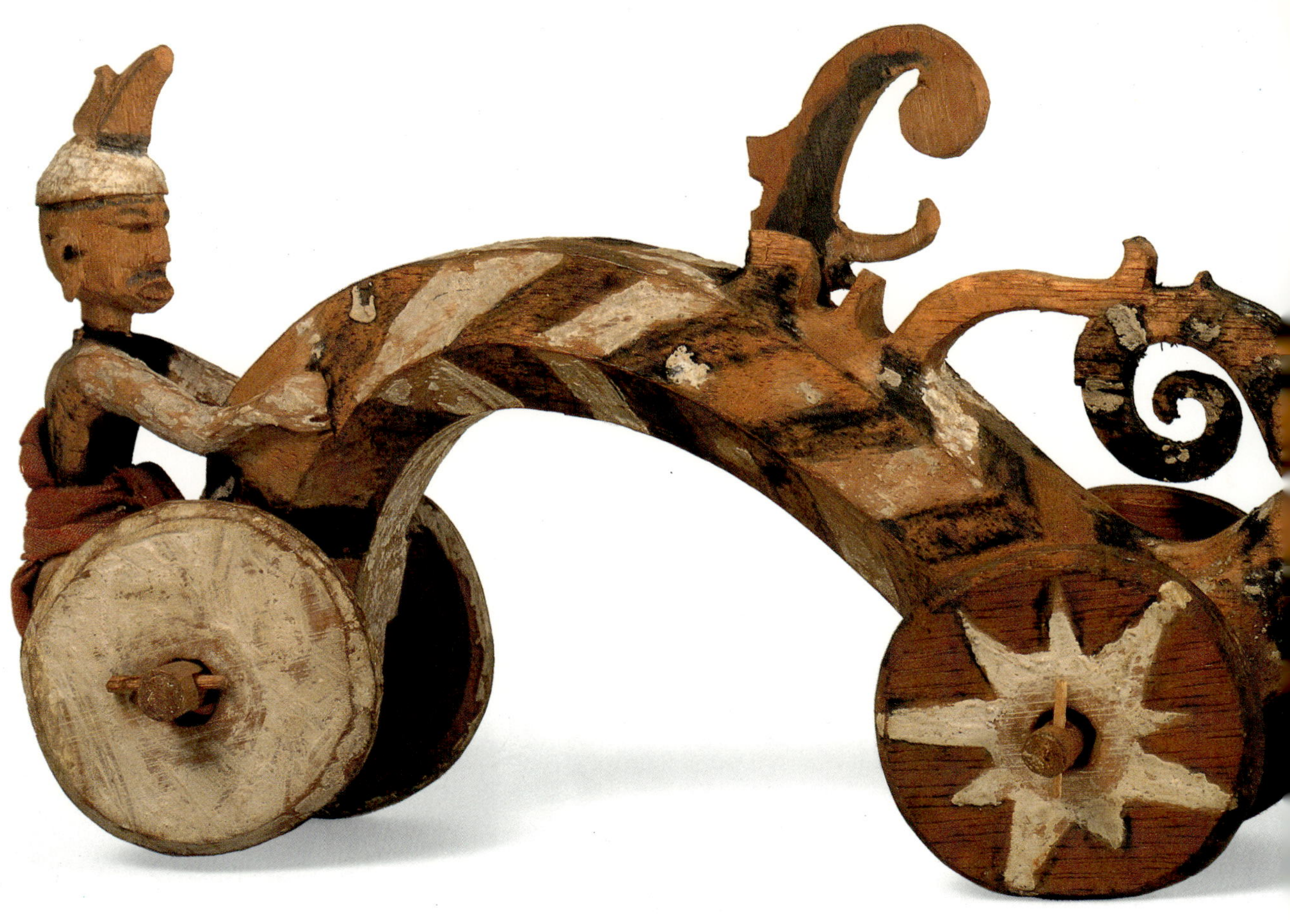

Fig. V.34 MODEL CHARIOT
Kenyah or Kayan, East Kalimantan
Wood, paint, cloth, 12.6 x 34.5 x 7.5
Museum Nasional Indonesia, Jakarta, 17929.
Donated by J. Jonejans. Accessioned in 1920.

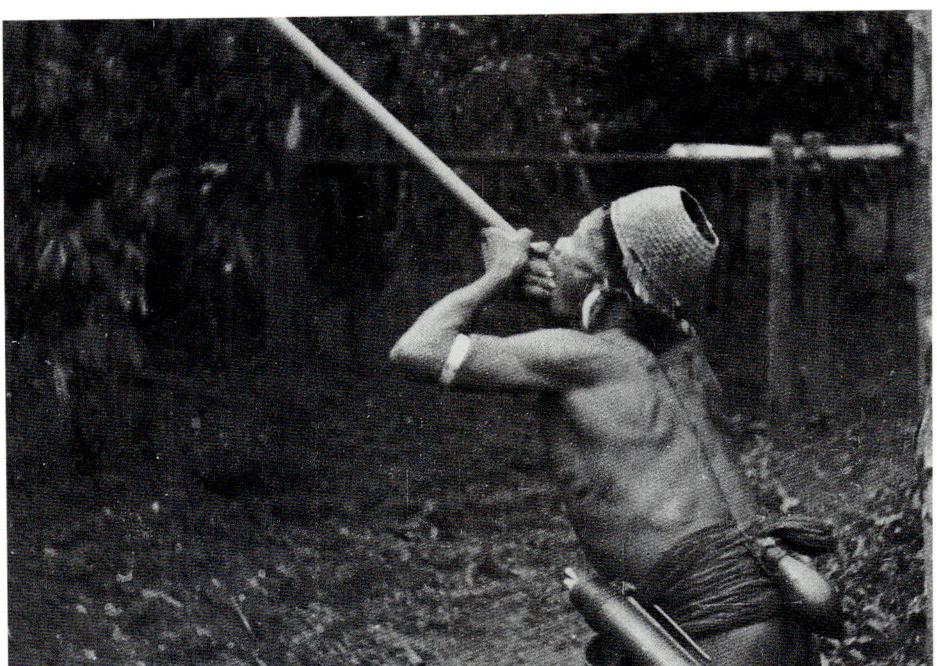

Fig. V.35 A Punan blowgun hunter wears a quiver for his darts similar to those illustrated in Figs. V.36 and V.37, East Kalimantan, early 1930s. Courtesy Rijksmuseum voor Volkenkunde, Leiden.

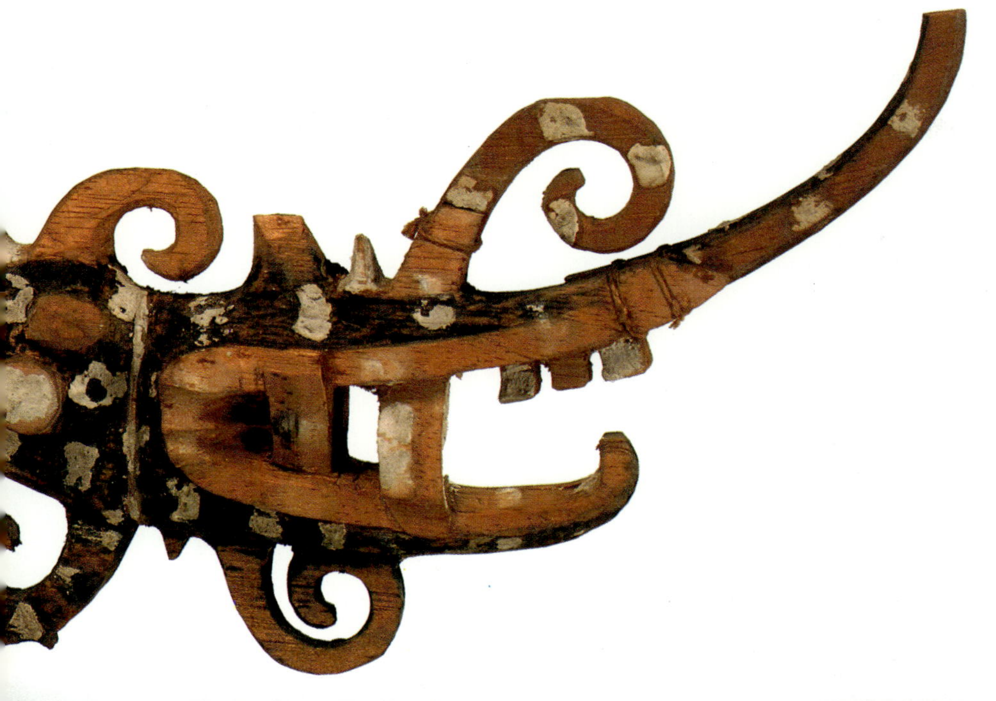

BOTTOM LEFT

Fig. V.36 QUIVER
Kayan, East Kalimantan
Bamboo, plant fiber, shell, wood,
36.5 x 10.6 x 7
Museum Nasional Indonesia, Jakarta, 2467A

Fig. V.37 QUIVER
Central Kalimantan
Bamboo, plant fibers, wood, 42.1 x 10 x 6.1
Museum Nasional Indonesia, Jakarta, 24055

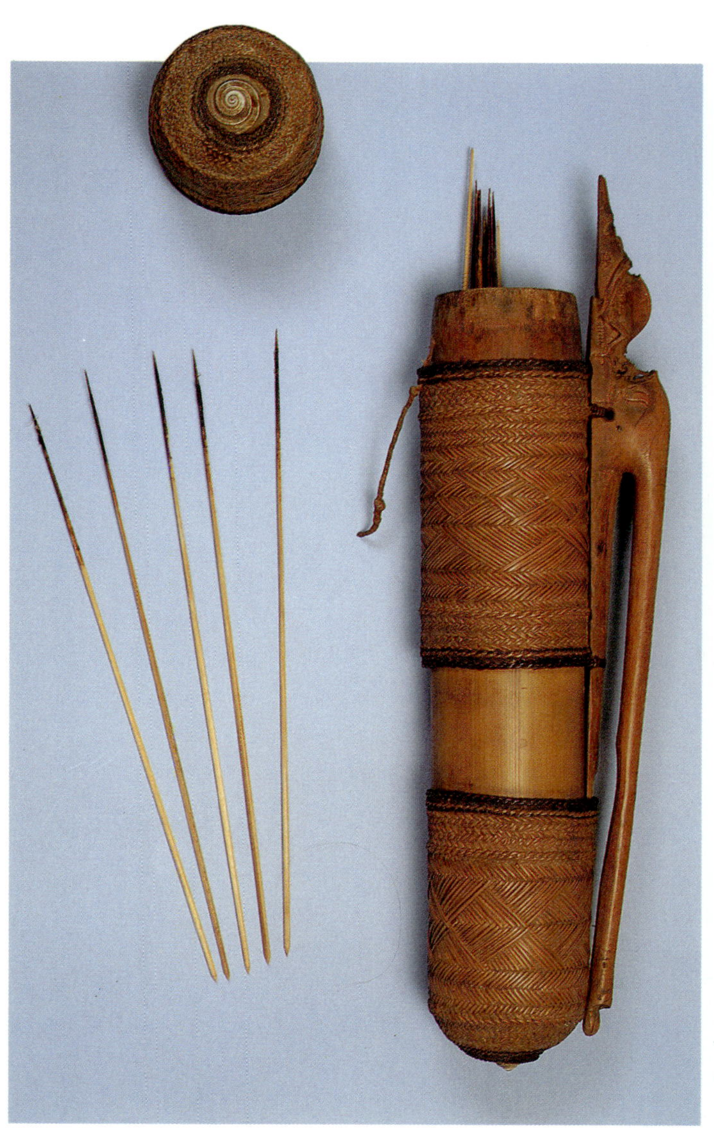

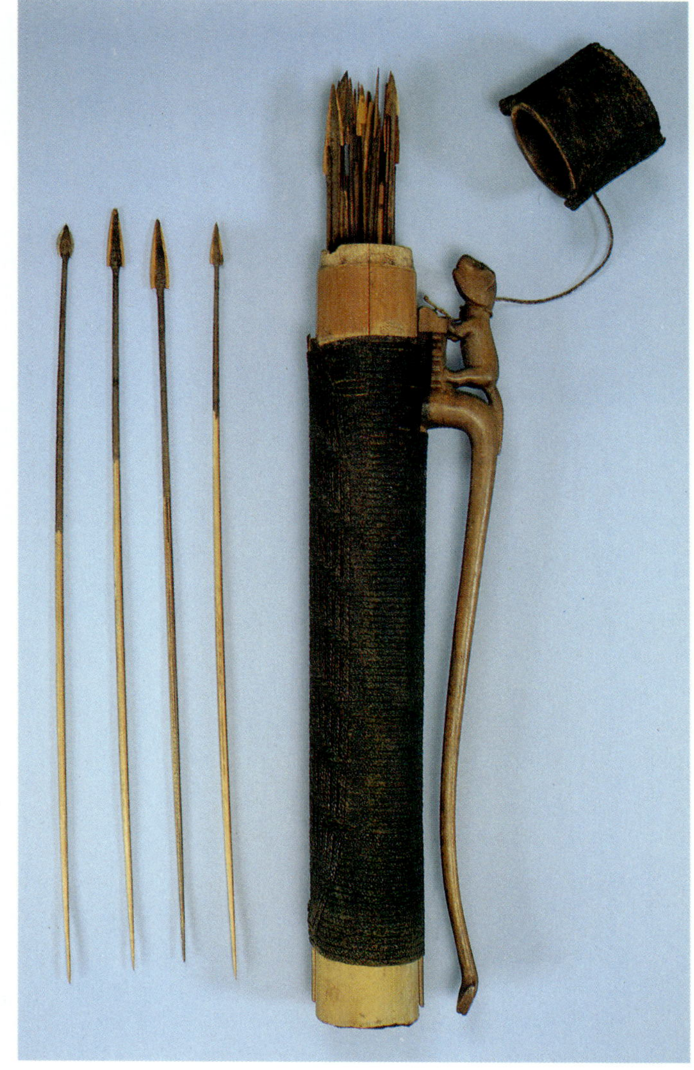

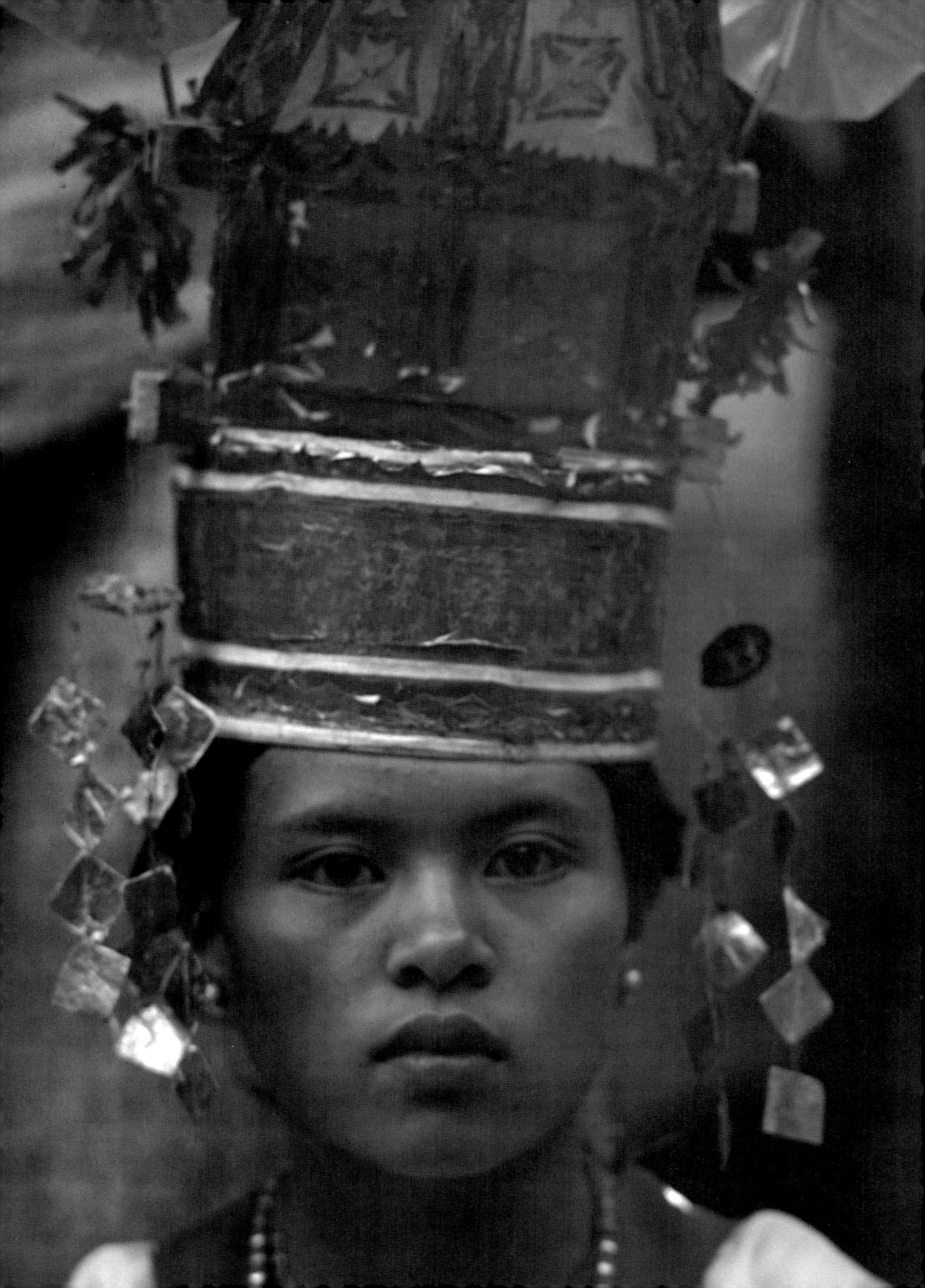

VI

Sulawesi

by Lorraine V. Aragon

The island of Sulawesi, known as Celebes during the Dutch colonial period, has an unusual pinwheel shape matched with a rough mountainous topography (Fig. VI.2). The island's difficult interior terrain partially isolated many of its highland populations both from outsiders and each other until the twentieth century. By contrast, the coastal Makassar and Bugis kingdoms of South Sulawesi rose to prominence even in the precolonial period through vast local and long-distance trade networks established prior to the region's Islamization.

With the exception of the coastal Minahassa people who live at the northern tip of the island, the present population of Sulawesi is largely comprised of South Sulawesi groups such as Bugis, Makassar, and Mandar, living on the coasts, and many, often geographically isolated peoples living in the interior highlands. The traditional artworks of most of these latter groups were collected and documented by early European explorers. The ritual and artistic traditions of the Sa'dan Toraja of South Sulawesi have continued most actively to the present day, undergoing commercial development because of recent tourist interest (Fig. VI.1).

The term "Toraja," like the labels "Batak" and "Dayak," was a name invented by outsiders to categorize the relatively unknown peoples of the interior. Scholars reconstruct the origin of the term "Toraja" from the Luwu Buginese phrase *to ri aja*, meaning "those people in the highlands to the West" (Nooy-Palm 1975a:54). Early Dutch missionaries such as A. C. Kruyt elevated the term to general use among missionary and Dutch colonial personnel. Reportedly Kruyt found the term more dignified than the term "Alfur," (reportedly from *halefuru*, Ternate language for "wilderness, forest"), connoting "heathen," which had been used heretofore by European explorers to label the non-Islamic, non-Hindu peoples living on the eastern outer islands (Pakan 1977:22). Kruyt and other interested Europeans applied the term *Toraja* to all highland Sulawesi groups, distinguishing them from each other only with adjectives such as West, East, and South.

Fig. VI.1 A woman dancer at funeral ceremony wearing golden headdress symbolizing abundant rice plumes, Sangallangi, Sa'dan Toraja, South Sulawesi, 1985. Eric Crystal

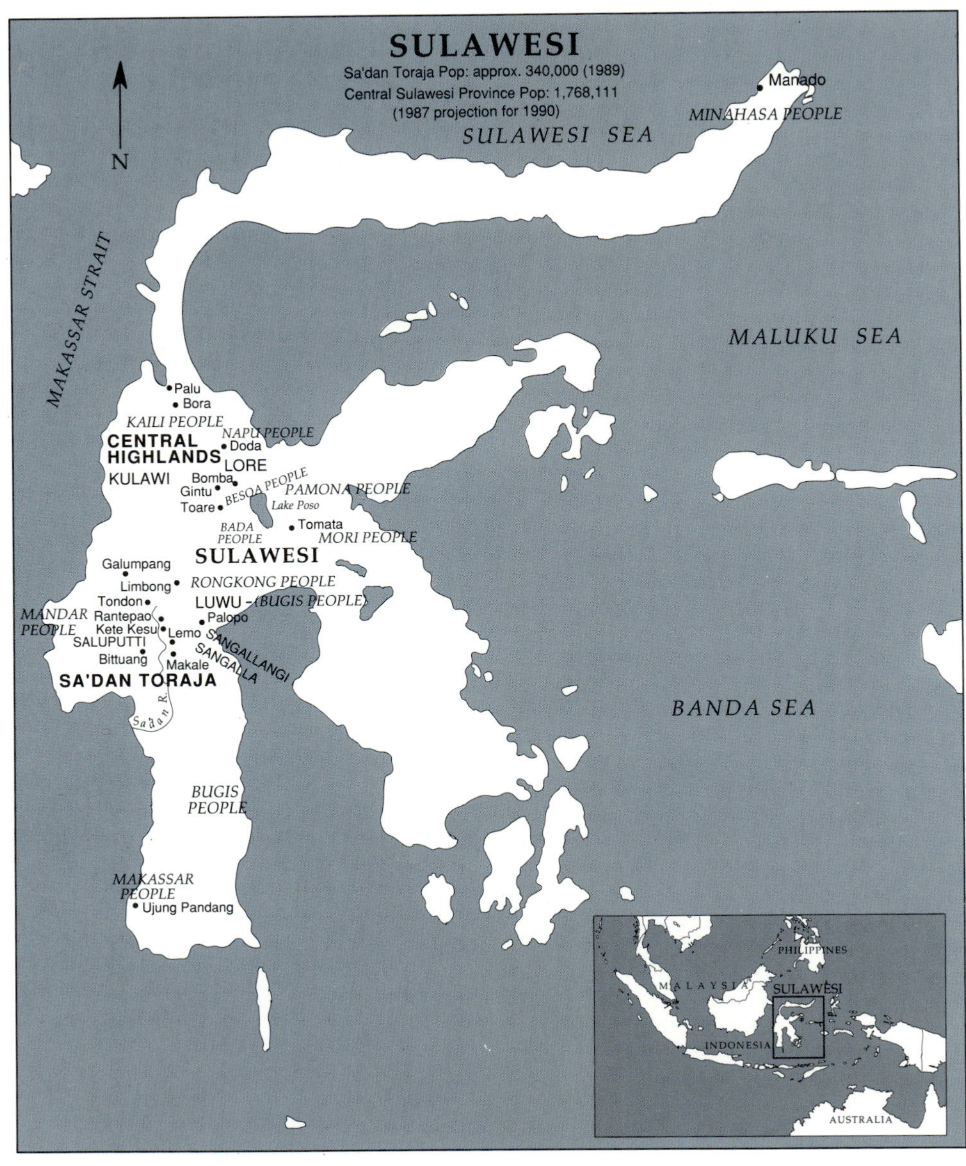

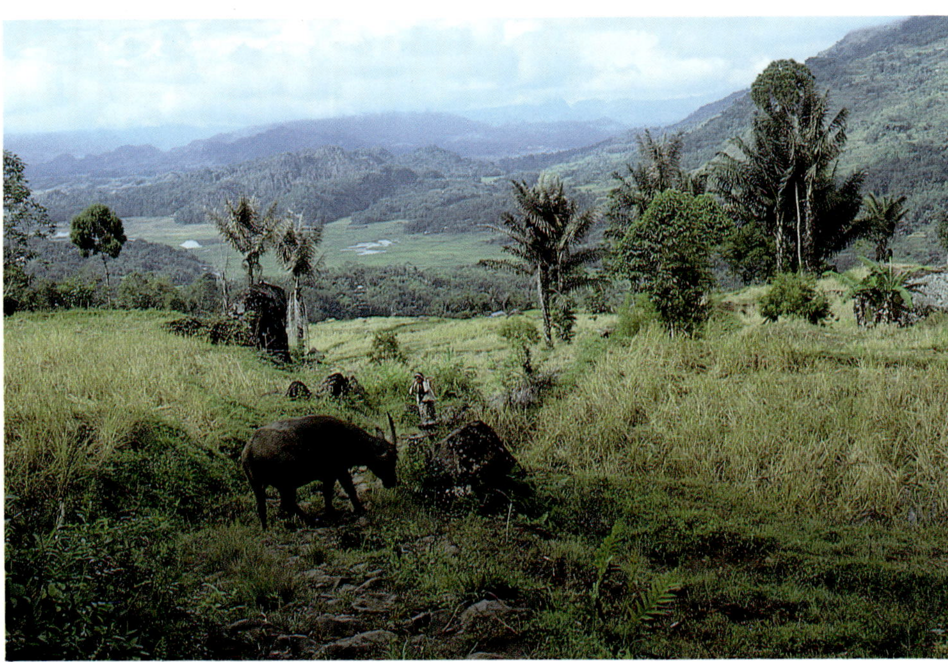

Fig. VI.2 Highland landscape, Mount Sesean, north of Rantepao, Sa'dan Toraja, South Sulawesi, 1984. Lorraine V. Aragon

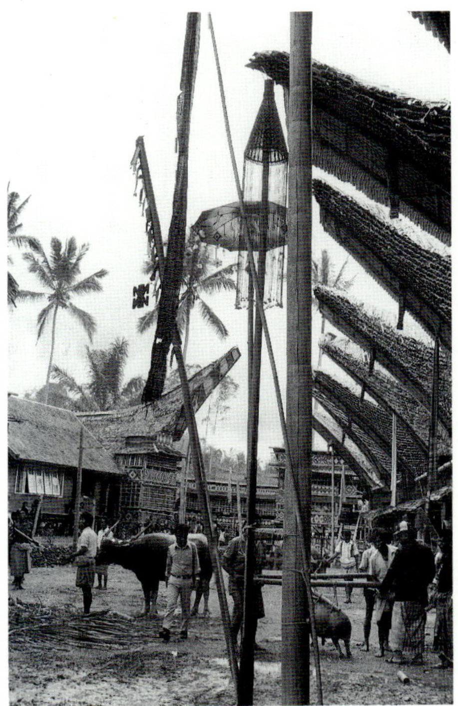

Fig. VI.3 At a funeral, a rite of the west, such regalia items as *sarita* textiles and *kandaure* beadwork ornaments hang from ceremonial poles in front of traditional houses, Sa'dan Toraja, South Sulawesi. C. H. M. Nooy-Palm, Royal Tropical Institute, Tropenmuseum, The Netherlands.

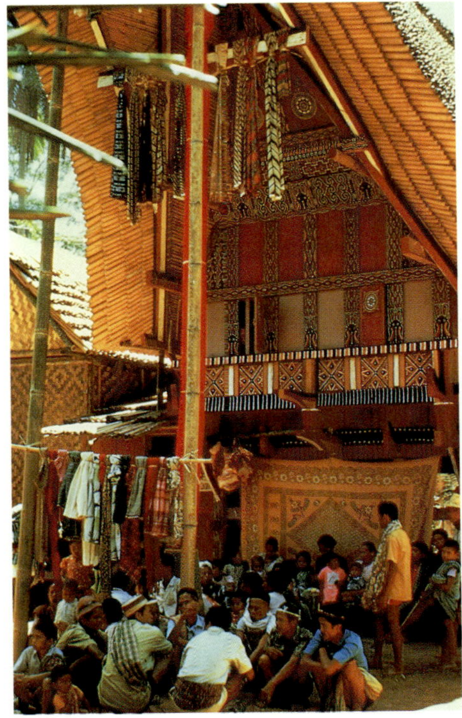

Fig. VI.4 At a house-consecration ceremony, a rite of the east, family heirloom textiles are displayed before the community, Saluputti, Sa'dan Toraja, South Sulawesi, 1971. Eric Crystal

When concerns of nationalism and ethnic identity developed during the 1930s, the large and relatively united South (or Sa'dan Valley) Toraja group came to identify themselves as Toraja, emphasizing the morpheme *raja*, which means "king" or "ruler" in Indonesian (Nooy-Palm 1975a:54; Bigalke 1981:13–16). By contrast, the more fragmented interior groups to the north and east began to evolve separate ethnic identities, eschewing the Toraja label that they see as referring instead to the rather different South Sulawesi people. The indigenous traditions and artwork of the Sa'dan Toraja of South Sulawesi are explored below, followed by those of some Central Sulawesi highland groups.

Traditions of the Sa'dan Toraja

The Sa'dan Toraja people call their traditional religion "the ways of the ancestors," *aluk to dolo*. While the majority of the Toraja population is now Christian (estimated at 80 percent by 1983 government statistics), the traditional cosmology has sufficient support that led it to be registered officially with the Indonesian government in 1969 as a religion (*agama*) related to Hinduism (Nooy-Palm 1979:107; Volkman 1990:93). The Toraja themselves classify their rituals into two discrete types: the rituals of the east (*aluk rampe matallo*) and the rituals of the west (*aluk rampe matampu'*). Both concern ancestors, but the types of ancestors differ. Funeral ceremonies (Fig. VI.3) are rites of the west, and they move souls of the newly dead from the village to a Land of the Dead (*puya*), said to be located on earth somewhere southwest of the Toraja homeland. After some time and many expensive rituals have been performed, souls of high-ranking nobles may themselves become a kind of deity (*deata*) and pass on to the upper world with the major gods (Nooy-Palm 1986:3). These deified ancestors are venerated periodically with rites of the east that concern fertility and prosperity and are connected with agricultural and life-cycle transitions (Coville 1988). Rites of the east include rituals celebrating wealth and accomplishment, such as house consecrations (Fig. VI.4).

The two sets of rituals, although complementary and equally necessary to the well-being of the community, are carefully segregated (Nooy-Palm 1986:4). For example, in most areas, no funeral ceremonies are held when the rice is still growing, and mourning family members should not eat rice at funeral feasts.

The Toraja House of Origin

> Hail to this house, with its front shaped like the faces of the gods,
> where the supreme feast is to take place,
> abundant be the blessing upon this façade,
> formed like the countenance of the lords,
> where the foremost adat performances are to be carried out.
>
> (van der Veen 1965:18)

The focus of Toraja ritual life is the kindred house, or *tongkonan*. This elaborately carved structure, usually occupied by leading members of the aristocracy, is a key indicator of family status and the center of several major rituals. More than just a physical building, the *tongkonan* is a symbol of family identity and tradition, representing all descendants of a founding ancestor (Nooy-Palm 1979; Crystal 1989). The designs carved on each *tongkonan* have particular local meanings signifying the status of the occupants (Kis-Jovak et al. 1988; Waterson 1990). Toraja individuals make claims of affiliation through either male or female genealogical lines to particular *tongkonan* houses and validate those claims through contributions to ceremonial feasts sponsored by the household. Descendants of the nobility can make greater claims to more prestigious houses than can descendants of commoners or traditional slaves who have few ties and are not able to afford the contribution of pigs that guarantees an honored reception at community feasts. Lower-status people traditionally lived in smaller, less elaborate houses and often participated in feasts mainly in service capacities, for which they were compensated with foodstuffs. Although *tongkonan* houses traditionally were identified closely with noble families, tourists, who have visited the Toraja area in increasing numbers in recent years, identified this architectural style with Toraja people in general, as a unique ethnic marker distinguishing them from other ethnic groups (Adams 1988).

Toraja Motifs: Shared Traditions for Ornamenting Cloth and Wood

In Toraja artwork, standardized geometric designs have local names and meanings. Traditionally these patterns were carved or painted on a range of objects from coffins, houses, and granaries to textiles and miniature bamboo containers. Throughout Southeast Asia, bamboo or other containers for lime powder (which is chewed with betel nut) are usually intricately decorated. Bamboo of many varieties is abundant in the interior of Sulawesi, and it is a favored medium for two-dimensional designs. The bamboo lime container (Fig. VI.6) illustrates a compositional style characteristic of highland Sulawesi artisans: geometric motifs are repeated in bands and boxes alternated in a symmetrical arrangement around the bamboo surface.

Some basic Toraja design elements are identical to motifs seen throughout Southeast Asia, including on Bronze Age kettledrums (Waterson 1988:44–45). Others are renditions of Hindu motifs, which likely derive from Indian textiles that came to the Toraja through trade. Whatever their origins, in this context the carved motifs refer to plants, animals, and other elements of the Toraja environment. Certain designs, such as those depicting heirloom valuables, refer to the status of the owners of an ornamented house or may commemorate an elaborate funeral once sponsored by the owners.

The Toraja decorate their houses and rice barn façades (Figs. VI.7, VI.8) with carved motifs important to the owning families. Buffalo heads refer to prosperity and ceremonial sacrifices. Gold knives, or *kris* (called *gayang* in the Toraja language), represent heirlooms and wealth of high-status people. Circular motifs (*pa'barre allo*) symbolize the powerful sun. Riders on horseback depict nobles touring their lands. The square cross motifs (*pa'doti langi'*) in the center of the lower band, depict plans of Hindu-Buddhist temples and probably derive from Indian trade textiles, but to the Toraja this motif represents wealth or, for some present Christians, an expression of their faith. Other motifs to be found on the granary façade (Fig. VI.8) represent cock's feathers, water buffalo horns, betel leaves, ficus or fig leaves, crabs, and storage baskets for heirlooms (see Crystal 1985:196–97). Most of the carved motifs on Toraja houses and granaries suggest fertility and prosperity, concepts that are closely related, if not identical, from the local viewpoint. The rice granary is considered an extension of the ancestral house that faces it, and major agricultural ceremonies are located at or between these two structures (Crystal 1985:194).

Toraja Funerals

The funerals of Toraja nobles, sponsored by heads of particular *tongkonan* houses, are festive and expensive rituals that proclaim a family's high social status. According to traditional Toraja religion, deceased nobles who are honored with extensive rituals and animal sacrifices will join the local deities and bring prosperity to the living community. When major funeral rituals are held, the deceased's kin arrive from near and far and deliver such gifts as water buffalo or pigs (Fig. VI.9), which either repay old family debts or begin new ones. Such debts and repayments are carefully recorded at each event.

Toraja burial customs, now considered a distinctive mark of Toraja ethnic identity, have apparently changed radically since the seventeenth century when the area was invaded by Buginese warriors from the south (van der Veen 1924:364; Nooy-Palm 1979:259). Prior to that time, family bones and heirloom treasures were stored in elaborately carved wooden coffins (Fig. VI.12) set at the base of limestone cliffs. When faced with plunder of their grave goods during warfare, the Toraja began to place less-ornamented coffins in high cliff-face vaults, reserving more intricate carving for the tomb doors and portrait statues of the deceased, called *tau tau*.

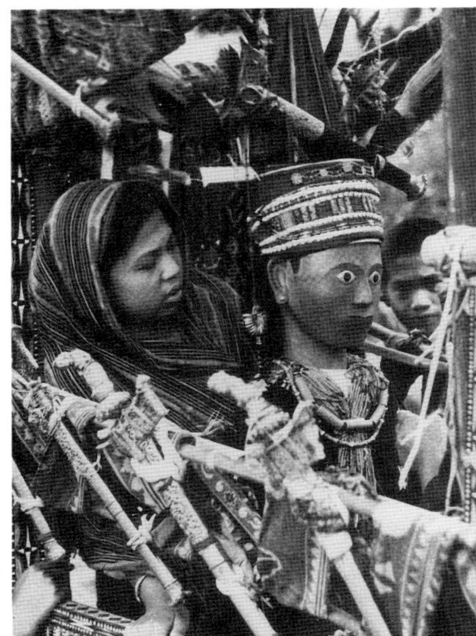

Fig. VI.5 *Tau tau* sculpture and other family heirlooms such as ceremonial knives (*gayang*) being carried during funeral procession, Sa'dan Toraja region, South Sulawesi, before 1949. Wilcox 1949: opposite p. 49. Courtesy Collins Publishers, London, England.

The Toraja never depict their higher deities in human form, which is only used to portray the living or recently deceased (Nooy-Palm 1979:131). Wooden ancestor figures, called *tau tau*, usually are commissioned only for very high-status persons whose families can finance funeral feasts lasting five or seven days, including the sacrifice of dozens of water buffalo. At traditional funeral rituals, the statue is consecrated with prayers and pig blood to become "the soul that is seen" (*bombo dikita*). The *tau tau*, meaning "little person" or "like a person," is then carried near the corpse in ritual processions over a period of days (Nooy-Palm 1979:261).

Although styles of *tau tau* carving vary by region and artisan, all *tau tau* statues are carved of jackfruit wood by community specialists. Traditionally, the role of *tau tau* carver is passed from fathers to sons among certain aristocratic families (Koubi 1979:164), although today the occupation appears more open to any youth interested in this potentially limited career. It takes four to six weeks to complete a single *tau tau* figure, and the carver normally receives one water buffalo or a cash equivalent. During the manufacture of the figure, the carver slept near or under the house where the corpse lay in state. After the carving was finished, it was set beside the deceased and ritually offered food, just as the deceased was (Nooy-Palm 1979:262). Today, however, carvers usually produce the *tau tau* in their own homes or workshops, modelling their likenesses of the deceased upon photographs instead of the corpse itself. *Tau tau* sculptures are often explained by contemporary Toraja Christians less as receptacles for souls of the deceased and more as portraits, akin to the personal photographs that also are displayed on funeral biers (Fig. VI.10).

Most *tau tau* figures have detachable arms and heads to facilitate their insertion into the cliff vaults. These carved portrait sculptures are relatively naturalistic, including eyes of bone, appropriate coiffures (formerly of pineapple fiber, but now usually painted), and genitalia. Clothing appropriate to the status of the deceased is added separately and renewed periodically, often before the burial of another high-status person (Fig. VI.11). During several days of rituals the *tau tau* is moved alongside the corpse of the deceased, then the corpse is buried in a chamber carved high in a rocky cliff, and the *tau tau* is placed in a carved balcony fronting the burial chamber where it is visible from below. The *tau tau* watches over the living and reminds them to observe the ancestral customs and moral codes.

Toraja ethnic identity, social organization, and traditional rituals and artwork are undergoing rapid change because of increased tourism and modern economic, religious, and political pressures, especially the interest of the international "primitive art" market in the *tau tau* ancestor figures (Crystal 1977; Volkman 1985, 1990; Adams 1984, 1988; Coville 1989). Valued according to Western aesthetics for their life-sized naturalistic portraiture, finely carved surfaces, and aged-wood patinas, many of the *tau tau* statues placed decades ago in grave-site balconies have found their way into the collections of museums and private art dealers (cf. Ellis 1980; Crystal in press). Many Toraja people assert that thefts of these figures from grave sites represent the abduction of their ancestors, and some say that recent crop failures and other misfortunes are the result of these crimes (Volkman 1986:21). The Indonesian government has become increasingly concerned with this removal of cultural property, and some museums refuse on ethical grounds to display consecrated *tau tau*. In certain Toraja grave sites, *tau tau* balconies emptied by vandalism have been filled with replacement *tau tau* commissioned by local government offices concerned with tourism, while remaining old *tau tau* statues have been hidden by families concerned to protect their ancestors (Figs. 19, 20, 21).

The elaborate warrior's costume of the Sa'dan Toraja may not have been suitable for forest travel or combat, but it was worn in rituals before and after fighting (Nooy-Palm 1986:315). In recent years, these costumes have been worn for the ceremonial greeting of foreign guests and at the burial of important men. At funerals of noblemen, they may adorn effigy figures and be worn by "warrior

Fig. VI.6 Bamboo container
Sa'dan Toraja, South Sulawesi
Wood, pigment, 12.8 x 4
Thomas Murray

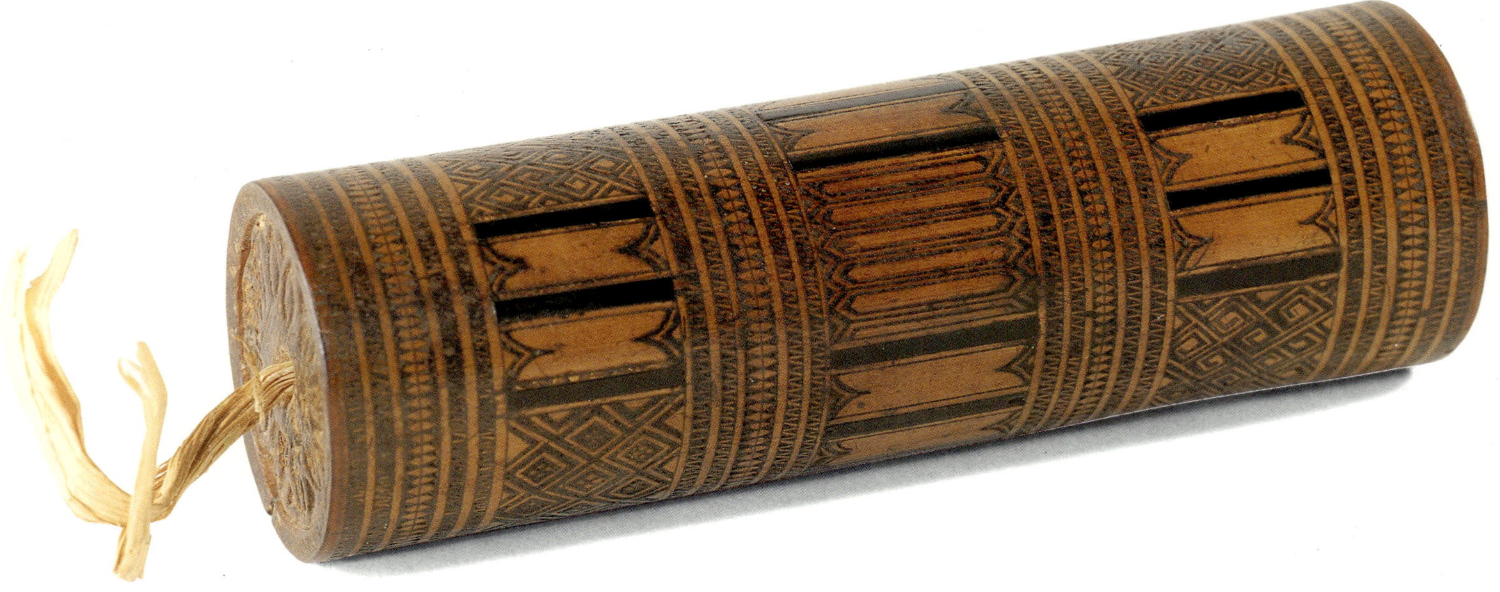

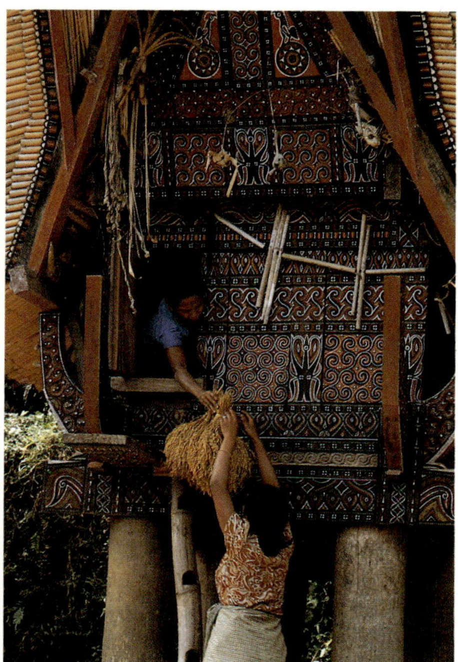

Fig. VI.7 A woman removes rice sheaths from granary, Makale, Sa'dan Toraja, South Sulawesi, 1968. Eric Crystal

OPPOSITE
Fig. VI.8 Rice granary façade
Sa'dan Toraja, Tondon village, South Sulawesi
Wood, pigment, 191.5 x 209.5 x 13
UCLA Fowler Museum of Cultural History, MCH X85–855. Gift of Dr. and Mrs. Robert Kuhn.

dancers" (*to ma'randing*) who perform at certain funerals (Fig. VI.17).

The jacket (Fig. VI.14) is finely executed with a twining technique that is prevalent in warriors' costumes throughout the outer islands (Gittinger 1979). At least some of these jackets are made from ramie (*Boehmeria nivea*) fibers (Nooy-Palm 1986:313). The jacket is ornamented with the smoothed tops of conus shells, a design that resembles that of warrior jackets and vests made by Ngaju Dayak people (Fig. V.22). Imported red cloth seals and adorns the selvages. The matching helmet (Fig. VI.14) is also decorated with conus-shell disks attached with decorative coconut-shell washers and metal buffalo horns.

Sacred Textiles and Other Heirlooms from the Ancestors

Hail to this house, with its front shaped like the faces of the gods,
where the supreme feast is to take place,
abundant be the blessing upon this façade,
formed like the countenances of the lords,
where the foremost *adat* performances are to be carried out.
Hail to this old long narrow blue woven cloth [*sarita*],
with the design of men fording a river,
abundant be the blessing upon this old short wide fabric [*maa'*],
with the pattern of swimming men.
Hail to this gold *kris* of great size,
abundant be the blessing upon the piece of beadwork
[*kandaure*], with the cords hanging low.

(van der Veen 1965:19–20)

During Toraja rituals, ancient textiles (including *maa'* and *sarita*; Fig. VI.15) and beadwork ornaments (*kandaure*; Figs. VI.18, VI.19) are worn by members of the sponsoring family or set out in public view to decorate their ceremonial structures (Fig. VI.3). Ownership of such cloths reaffirms a kin group's high social position. The most ancient cloths—some are centuries old, imported from India (Gwatkin 1986)—are owned collectively by members of

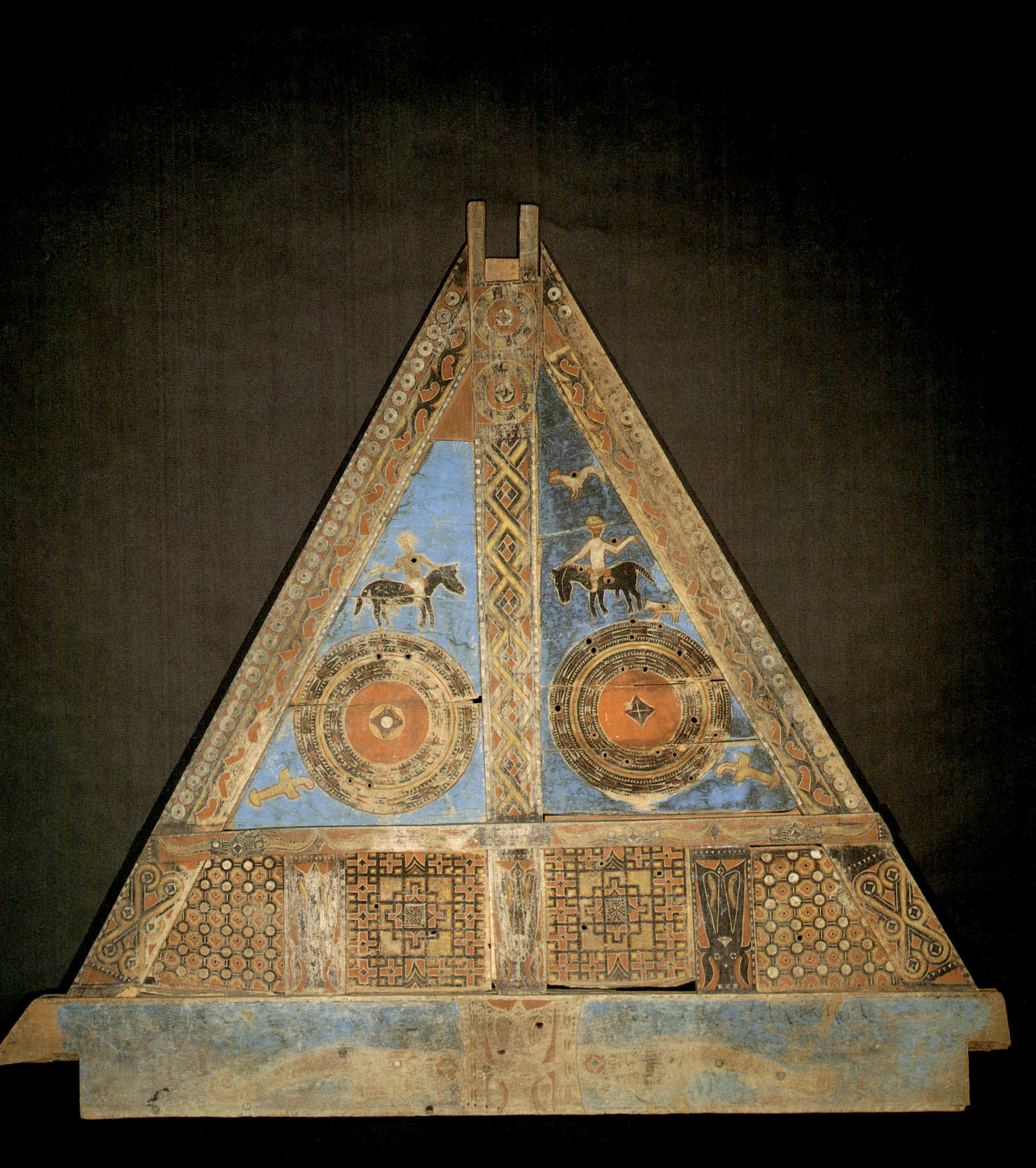

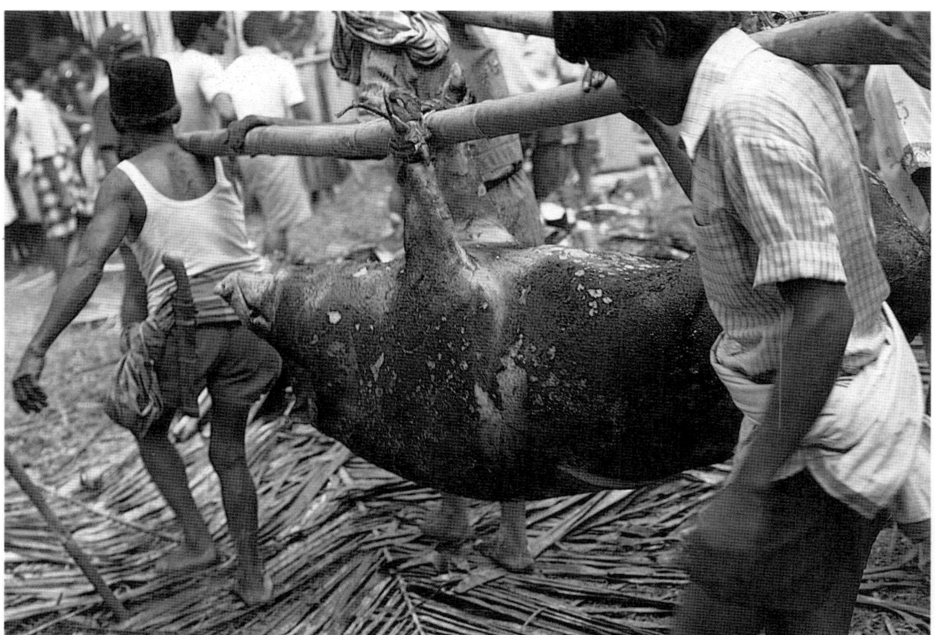

Fig. VI.9 Pigs, contributed for sacrifice at a funeral, are carried to the ritual site, Sangallangi, Sa'dan Toraja, South Sulawesi, 1985. Eric Crystal

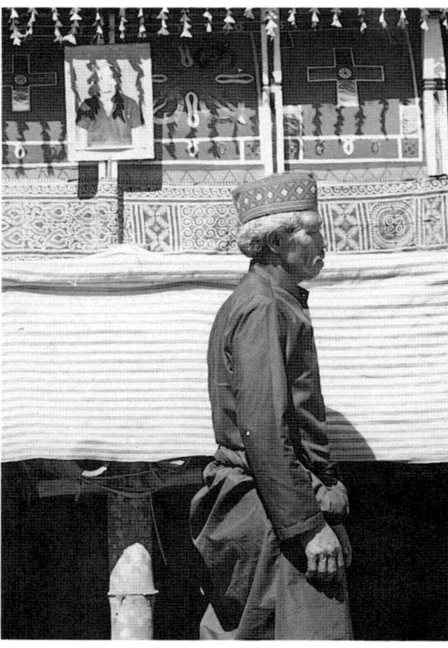

Fig. VI.10 The primary sponsor of a funeral passes by the funeral bier, which is adorned with a photo of the deceased and a *sarita* cloth, near Rantepao, Sa'dan Toraja, South Sulawesi, 1984. Lorraine V. Aragon

traditional Toraja kindred houses (*tongkonan*). The various cloths, whose origins are attributed to the sacred powers of ancestors, are displayed at funerals, as well as at such life-affirming rites as post-harvest and house-building ceremonies.

Sarita (Fig. VI.15) are one distinctive type of heirloom cloth owned by Sa'dan Toraja family groups. They are recognized by their extremely long (up to at least 598 cm) and narrow shape (Nooy-Palm 1989:166). Decorative patterning is applied with a resist process similar to that used in making the batik of Java (van Nouhuys 1925; Gittinger 1979). Like all sacred Toraja cloths, *sarita* are stored inside containers kept in the rear chamber of the ancestral house. This area of the house is associated symbolically with the family's ancestors, who are said to live in a land to the southwest. Indeed, *sarita*, like other types of sacred Toraja textiles, often are said to have been made by the ancestors or to have come into the ancestors' possession by miraculous means. Recent research by Nooy-Palm indicates that some *sarita* were painted by hand in the Sa'dan Toraja villages of Pangala', Riu, and La'bo', although others were blockprinted and factory dyed in The Netherlands and exported to Indonesia between 1880 and 1930 (Nooy-Palm 1989:171). Van Nouhuys (1925) hypothesized that a hand-painted Toraja-made *sarita* cloth must have been the model for Dutch versions, whereas van der Veen (cited in Nooy-Palm 1989:180, note 13) thought that the Dutch cloths must have been the inspiration for Toraja versions. The most recent evidence indicates that van Nouhuys's theory was correct (Nooy-Palm 1989:171).

Imported factory-manufactured *sarita* cloths can easily be differentiated from the handmade Toraja examples because of gaps in the color where different patterns overlap and at the outside edges, which were sewn onto reels for dyeing. The cloth (Fig. VI.15), an extremely long *sarita* made from hand-spun and handwoven cotton, is an example of indigenous Toraja workmanship. The red dye used to print and paint the textile was obtained from the East Indian mulberry (*Morinda citrifolia*). The circular figures were applied with stamps,

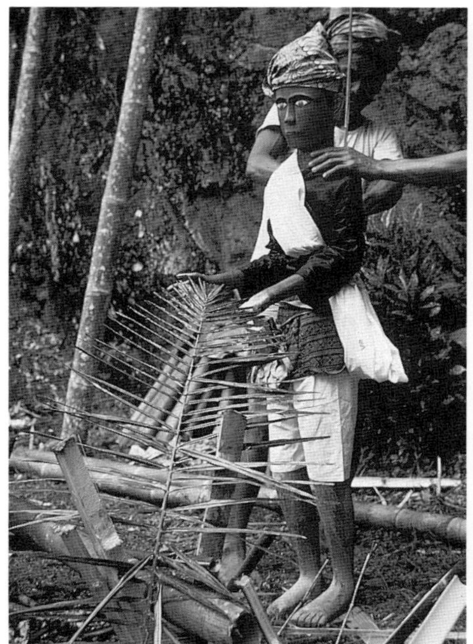

Fig. VI.11 *Tau tau* figure with new clothes is returned to a cliffside balcony during a renewal ceremony, Rante Lemo, Sa'dan Toraja, South Sulawesi, 1971. Eric Crystal

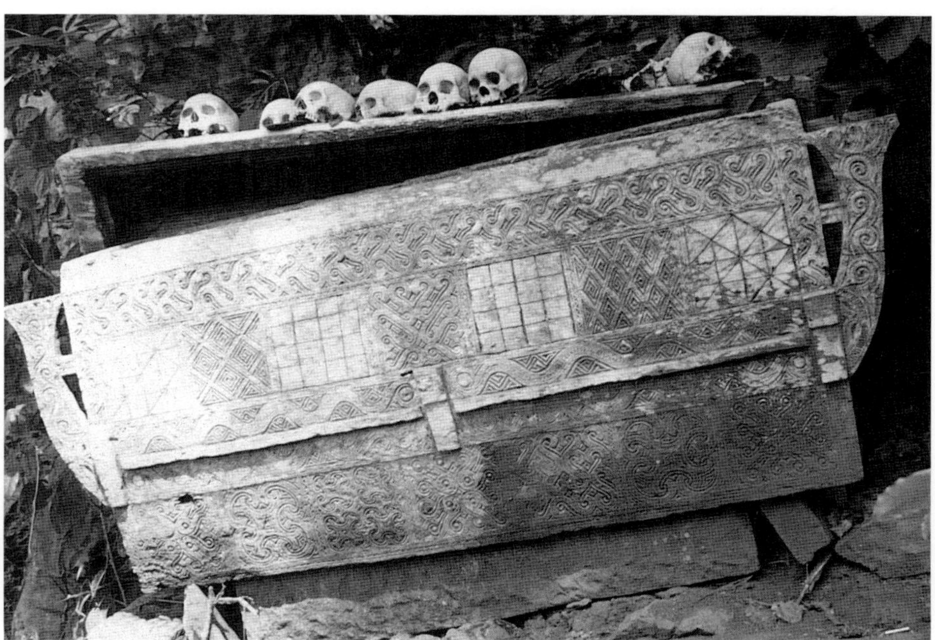

Fig. VI.12 Elaborately carved traditional coffin at Kete Kesu', Sa'dan Toraja, South Sulawesi, 1984. Lorraine V. Aragon

probably made from bamboo tubes, while the other figures were painted freehand (Nooy-Palm 1989:173). Both traditional Toraja motifs and Indian-influenced designs can be seen on this *sarita* cloth. The characteristically Toraja freehand designs include narrative scenes of men plowing fields with the aid of buffaloes, women pounding rice beside their houses, a hunter with his dog and spear, ducks or chicken foraging, a rider on horseback, and a warrior with his spear and shield.

The Indian motifs are probably not derived from direct historical contact with India. Rather they were most likely introduced through the seventeenth- and eighteenth-century trade of textiles by the Dutch East India Company to the Toraja region and South Sulawesi coastal traders such as the Bugis, Mandar, and Makassar peoples (Waterson 1988; Nooy-Palm 1989:46–47). Among the Indian-influenced designs found on this *sarita* is a motif called "bindings of a lidded basket" (*pa'kapu' baka*), referring to the storage containers used for sacred textiles and other family heirlooms. This pattern also occurs in Bali and the Toba Batak region where it signifies what in Sanskrit is called a "power point" (*bindú*). While the Balinese and Batak say the outer coils represent *naga* serpents, the Toraja only associate this design with their local baskets, saying that the motif symbolizes prosperity or the wealth stored in the *baka* baskets (Nooy-Palm 1979:239; Waterson 1988:47–48).

The cross-shaped motifs, often represented as concentric or encased within circles, derive from imported Indian silks that schematically depict the foundation structures of Hindu-Buddhist temples (Crystal 1979). In Hindu doctrine, the symmetrical cross design represents the four cardinal points arranged around a central fifth point. According to Toraja lore, however, the design represents the "spots (stars) of heaven" (*doti langi'*) or the spotted buffalo (*pa'doti siluang*), a Toraja symbol of wealth (Crystal 1979; Waterson 1988:45–46). The repeated geometric designs on the *sarita* cloth are named by the Toraja after plants, animals, and objects in their environment (Kadang 1960). The concentric circle

Fig. VI.13 ARMOR, *BABU'*
Sa'dan Toraja, Bittuang, South Sulawesi
Rattan, cotton, shell, cuscus skin, barkcloth, 69 x 40
Royal Tropical Institute, Tropenmuseum, The Netherlands, 46–9. Donated by H. Wolvekamp in 1917.

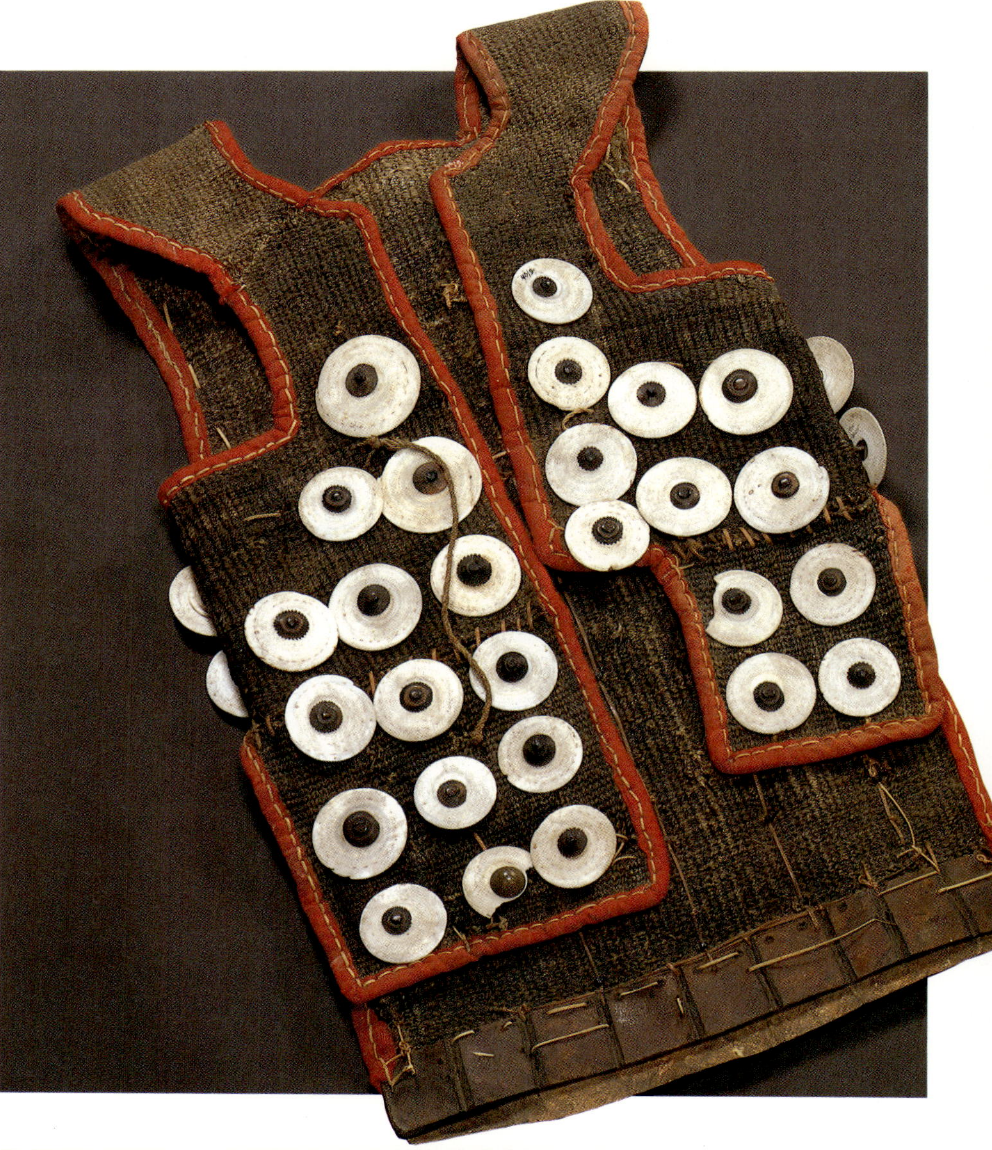

Fig. VI.14 HELMET, *SALULUNG*
Sa'dan Toraja, South Sulawesi
Rattan, shell, cuscus fur, brass, buffalo horns and leather, wood, horse hair, chicken feathers, 17 x 62 x 34
Royal Tropical Institute, Tropenmuseum, The Netherlands, 46–40. Donated by H. Wolvekamp in 1917.

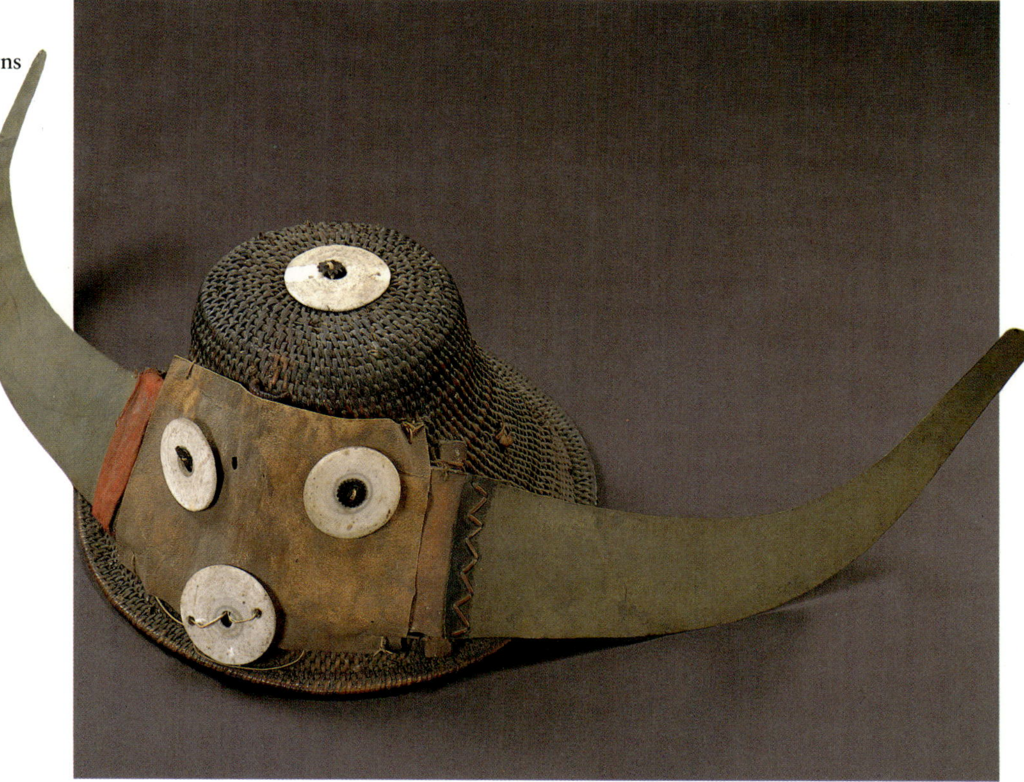

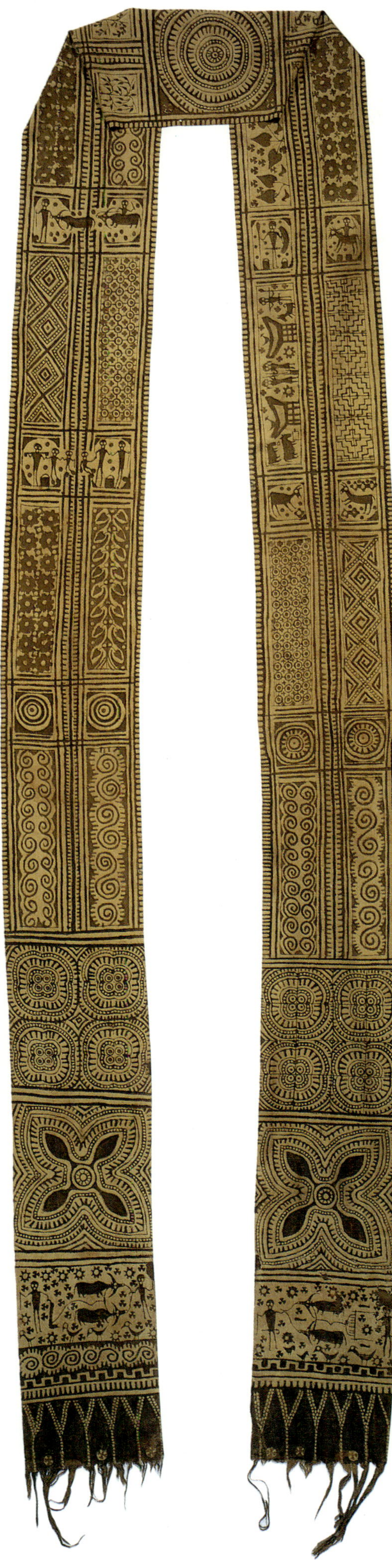

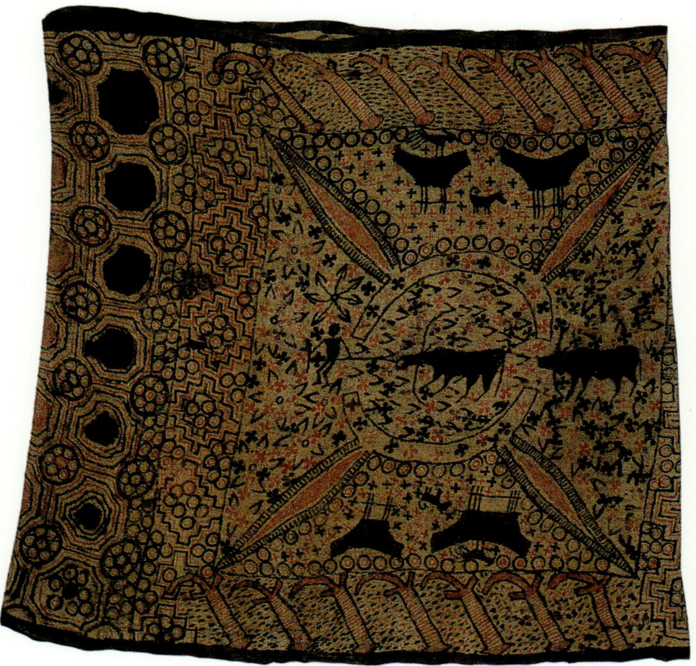

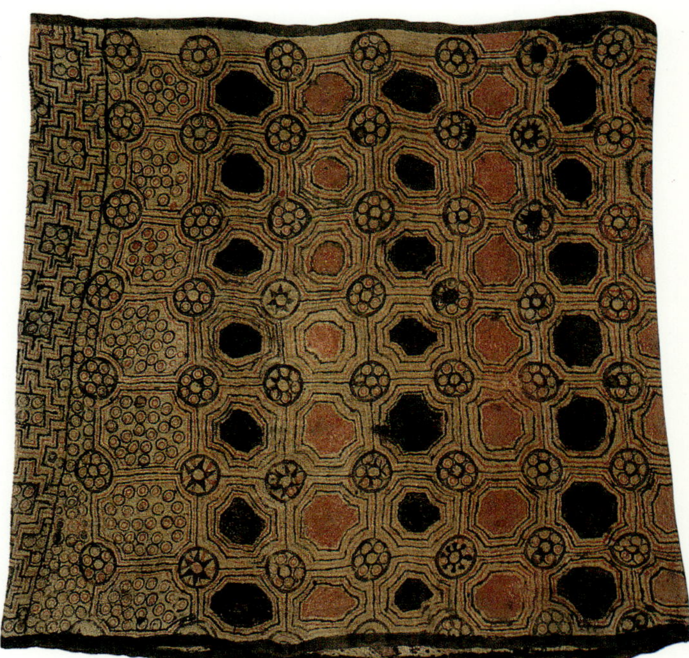

Fig. VI.16a Woman's ceremonial skirt, *sarong deata*
Sa'dan Toraja, South Sulawesi
Cotton, 56.5 x 124.5
Collection of John and Anne Summerfield

Fig. VI.16b Another view of Fig. VI.16a.

Fig. VI.15 Ceremonial cloth, *sarita*
Sa'dan Toraja, South Sulawesi
Cotton, natural dye, 598 x 27.5
Collection of John and Anne Summerfield

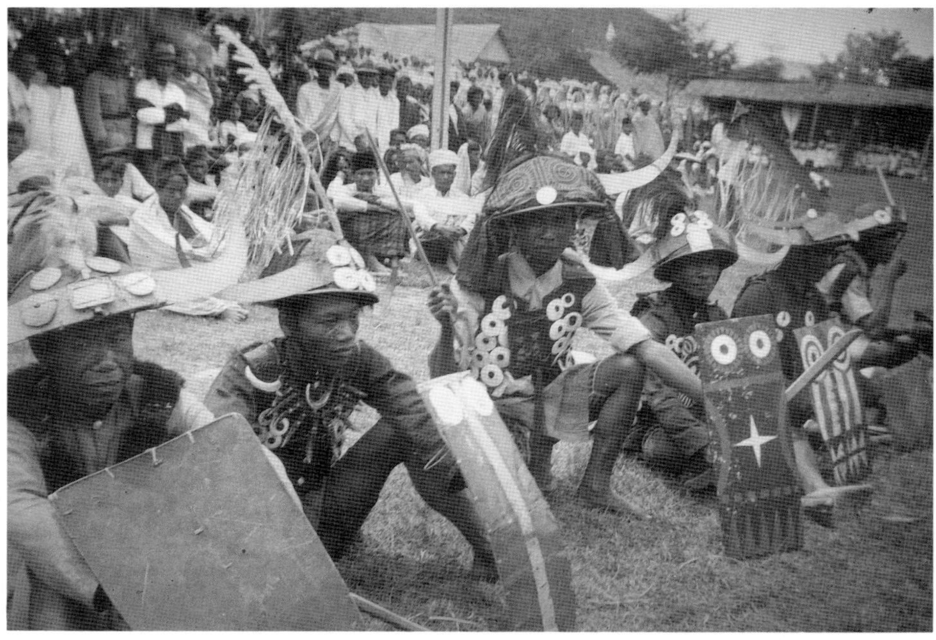

Fig. VI.17 Men wear warrior costumes at the funeral of a noble in 1937, Sa'dan Toraja, South Sulawesi. C. H. M. Nooy-Palm, Royal Tropical Institute, Tropenmuseum, The Netherlands.

OPPOSITE
LEFT
Fig. VI.18 BEADED ORNAMENT, *KANDAURE*
Sa'dan Toraja, South Sulawesi
Beads, rattan, metal, 156 x 37
Royal Tropical Institute, Tropenmuseum, The Netherlands, 2198-2. Donated by A. W. A. Michaelsen in 1952.
MIDDLE
Fig. VI. 19 BEADED ORNAMENT, *KANDAURE*
Sa'dan Toraja, South Sulawesi
Beads, rattan, metal, 157 x 41
Royal Tropical Institute, Tropenmuseum, The Netherlands, 2198-1. Donated by A. W. A. Michaelsen in 1952.
RIGHT
Fig. VI.20 MOURNING HOOD, *POTE*
Sa'dan Toraja, Palopo, South Sulawesi
Cotton, beads, 142 x 78.5
Royal Tropical Institute, Tropenmuseum, The Netherlands, 1641-1. Donated by L. J. J. Caron Bussum in 1944.

patterns (*pa'barre allo*) are sunbursts, symbols of high rank and spiritual power. The diamond-shaped hook motifs (*pa'sekong kandaure*) are named after the beaded ornaments worn or displayed at great feasts.

Sarita cloths are worn or displayed at rituals of the East as well as rituals of the West, in both cases symbolizing the host family's ties to their ancestors. These extremely long textiles are used during rituals of the west to adorn the structures housing or carrying the corpse (Fig. VI.10). *Tau tau* effigies often are given a headdress fashioned from a family-owned *sarita* cloth (Nooy-Palm 1989: 167). In rituals of the east like the post-harvest feast (*merok*), *sarita* serve as banners connecting a ceremonial sandalwood tree to the family house (Nooy-Palm 1989:166). During house consecrations, *sarita* and other sacred heirlooms are hung on the outside of the house for ceremonial display. During the *bua'* ceremony, another ritual of the east that can engage several villages, the hosts construct a symbol of fertility from eight lengths of bamboo entwined by a single *sarita* cloth (Nooy-Palm 1989:166). *Sarita* cloths also were traded northward into Central Sulawesi where they were displayed ceremonially as banners or worn as layered skirts for women (Fig. VI.41, far right) and waistbands for men (Fig. VI.22).

A remarkable specimen of weaving technology, the tube-skirt (Fig. VI.16a, b) appears to be a seamless cylinder, the continuous warp ends having been filled by needled-in weft threads. The design motifs used on this skirt are characteristically Sa'dan Torajan, including saddle-shaped houses, dogs, chickens, and a man leading buffalo through a central corral. The ceremonial knives (*gayang*), set in two bands bordering the scene, depict valued heirlooms belonging to noble houses. The concentric crosses, set in the other two bands framing the scene, symbolize prosperity. These Hindu-Buddhist architectural motifs are also seen on the *sarita* cloth (Fig. VI.15) and granary façade (Fig. VI.8) illustrated here. The corral scene includes blade or leaf forms oriented to the four

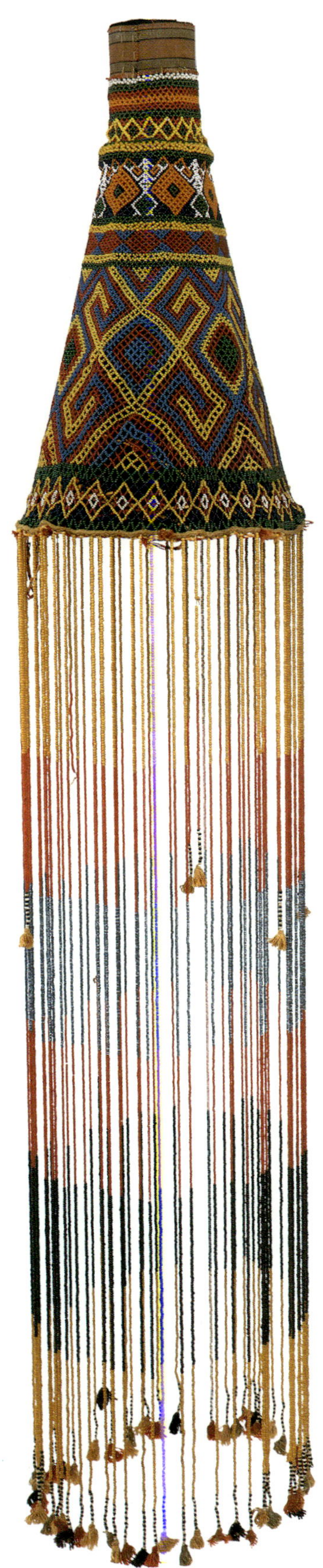

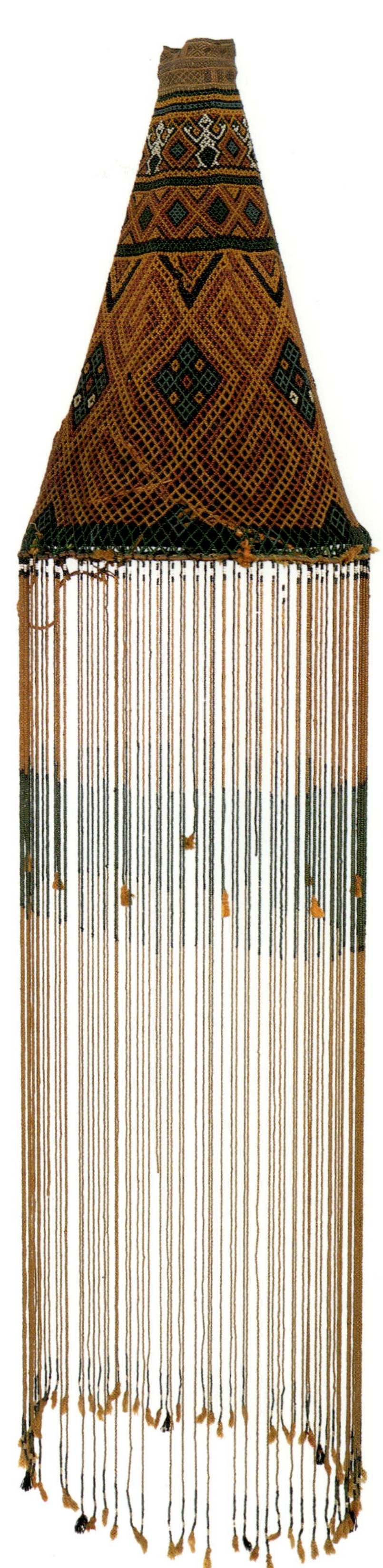

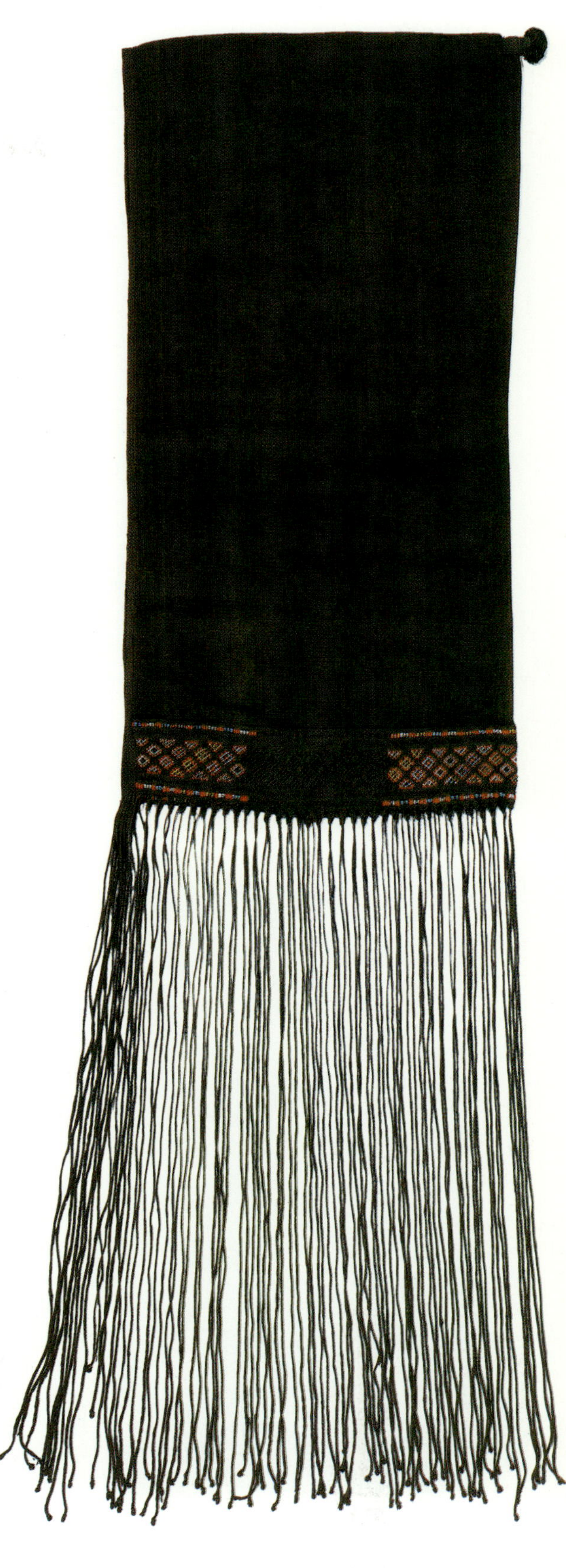

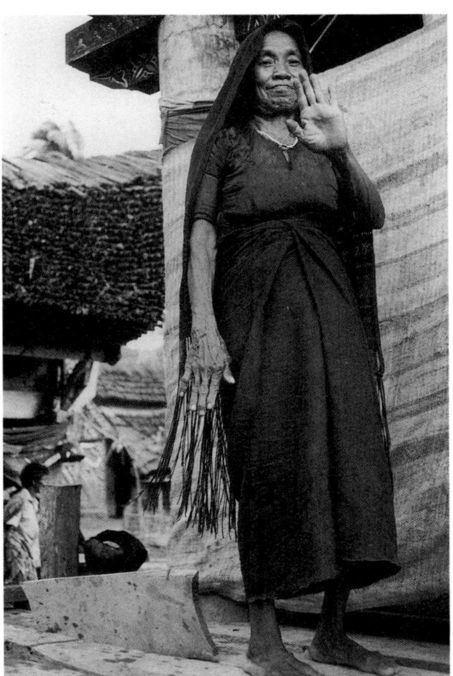

Fig. VI.21 A female relative of a deceased noble wears a black mourning hood (*pote*), indicating that she is observing mourning taboos, Sangalla' area, Sa'dan Toraja, South Sulawesi, before 1975. C. H. M. Nooy-Palm, Royal Tropical Institute, Tropenmuseum, The Netherlands.

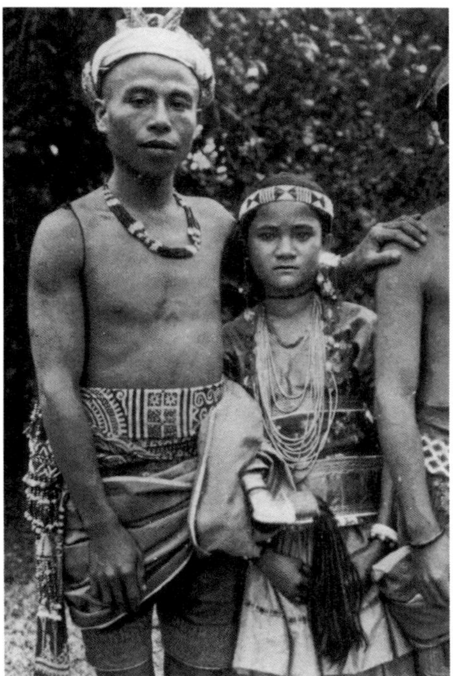

Fig. VI.22 The male dancer in this line is wearing a *sarita* as a waistband, Kulawi, Central Sulawesi, before 1938. Kruyt 1938:plate 42

cardinal points, and the background of the scene is completely filled with small crosses, flowers, circles and v-shaped forms. The busy pattern of unrelated geometric figures in the background scene (which is seen also on traditional Lampung textiles) expresses an aesthetic that recalls the pan-Indonesian enjoyment of crowded places and bustling cooperative activities, usually characterized by the Indonesian term *ramai-ramai*, meaning "crowded, bustling."

This rare type of seamless skirt (only four specimens are known to the collectors) was reportedly worn by women for a dance during which they became possessed by a divine spirit of a deified ancestor. Toraja informants call this type of skirt *sarong deata*, "tube-skirt of the deified ancestors," (personal communication, Anne Summerfield 1989) although *sarong* is the Indonesian (not Torajan) word for tube-skirt.

Black is the color of Sa'dan Toraja mourning attire. Long black hoods, called *pote*, traditionally are worn by close female relatives of the deceased as a sign that they are observing mourning taboos until all funeral rites are completed (Fig. VI.21; Nooy-Palm 1986:288). Men in mourning wear a braided headband, also called *pote*, to signify their observance of these same taboos. To commiserate with the dead, close relatives eat only cold foods, such as boiled tubers and pickled meats, and do not eat rice at all.

Pote (Fig. VI.20) are finely woven from black cotton with a tassel at the point of the hood and beaded bands alternating with card-woven bands at the border of a long fringe. Card or tablet weaving is an ancient technique (dated to 4000 B.C. in Egypt), in which the shed opening of the warp is created not by heddles, but by square tablets, often of bone or shell, that each have four warp threads passing through holes in the corners (Bolland 1970). Patterned bands are created by coloring the warp threads running through each tablet and subsequently rotating the cards during the weaving process. In South and Central Sulawesi, card-woven bands, some up to twelve feet long with complex floral or even figurative patterns, were always woven by women (Bolland 1970: 185–86). To adorn this mourning hood (Fig. VI.20), brown, red, yellow, white, blue, and green trade beads were knotted into a crosshatched diamond pattern. Such finely woven beaded mourning hoods are no longer produced or worn in the Toraja region (Nooy-Palm 1986:288).

Kandaure (Figs. VI.18, VI.19) are cone-shaped beadwork ornaments with a long beaded fringe that the Sa'dan Toraja produce and use for ceremonial display at both mortuary and life-affirming ceremonies. Beaded ornaments are hung from bamboo poles and structures near the coffin, and they decorate the site of buffalo sacrifices held in honor of the deceased (Fig. VI.3; Nooy-Palm 1986:188, 214). These beaded ornaments and other displayed heirlooms are moved ceremonially from site to site along with the deceased's body throughout the many days of funeral rituals. Relatives who officially greet the funeral guests also wear beadwork ornaments hanging down their backs with the long fringe plaited in front, as do lead funeral dancers (Nooy-Palm 1986:210, 234). These ornaments are worn with the fringe knotted in front and hanging down the backs of female dancers at the *gellu'* dance performed at the *maro* rice ritual, a ceremony of the east.

Unlike most woven textiles, Toraja beadwork ornaments are always made by men (Fig. VI.24). The beads are strung on thread (Fig. VI.23) over a split bamboo form, like an umbrella frame, to create an even, funnel shape (Nooy-Palm 1975b:34–36). Traditionally, the narrow end, ornamented with a row of human figures, was attached to a locally manufactured, card-woven cloth band. Such bands are no longer woven, and antique *kandaure* ornaments with old imported glass beads, such as the two illustrated here, are kept as valuable heirlooms and are only displayed on important ritual occasions. The main body of the beaded funnel is ornamented with a pattern of squared-off scrolls known as the *sekǫng* motif. The *sekong* motif, suggesting a body center with four appendages, has been interpreted as anthropomorphic in all its Indonesian variations (Jager Gerlings 1952; Holmgren and Spertus 1989). Old and sacred

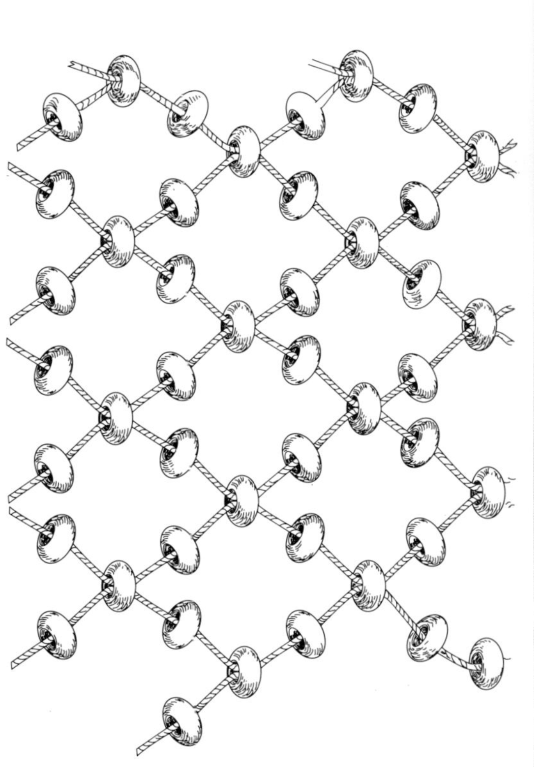

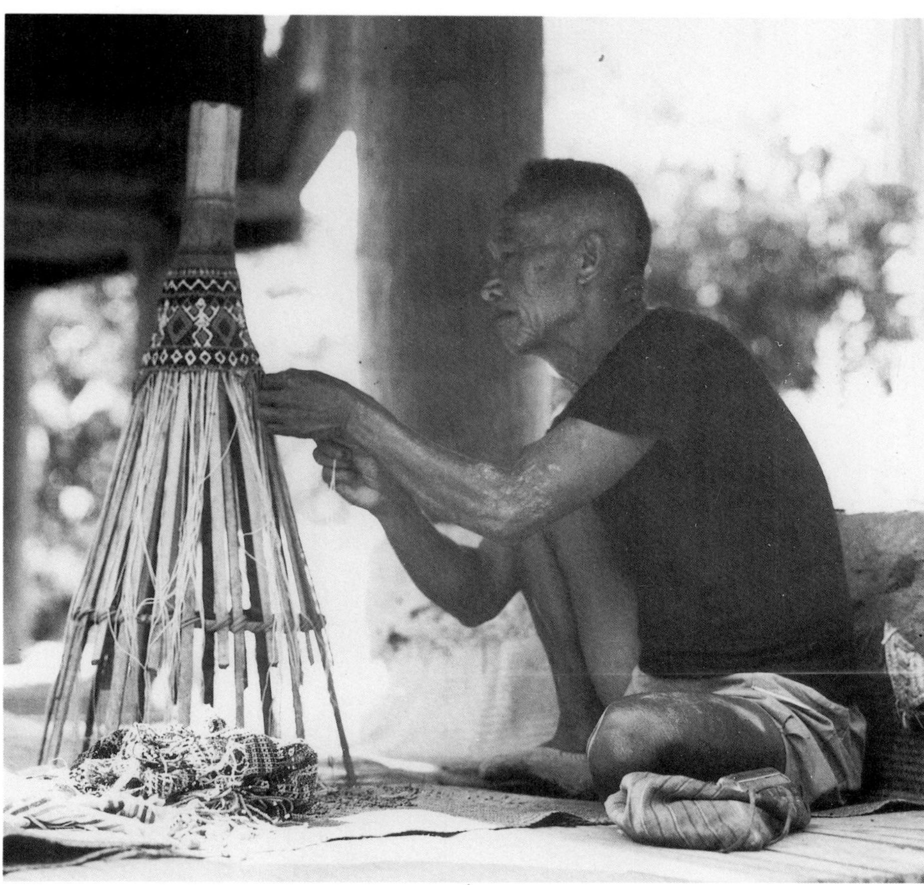

Fig. VI.23 Sa'dan Toraja beadwork technique used for *kandaure* ornaments. Nooy-Palm 1975:35. Redrawn by Marcia Bakry, Smithsonian Institution.

Fig. VI.24 A man makes a beaded *kandaure*, Sa'dan Toraja region, South Sulawesi, before 1975. C. H. M. Nooy-Palm, Royal Tropical Institute, Tropenmuseum, The Netherlands.

kandaure made from imported beads often were given personal names or titles and considered as aids in preventing such misfortunes as too much rainfall (Nooy-Palm 1979:255). These beadwork valuables belong to particular ancestral houses and may be loaned out to other houses for particular ceremonies. The families of these houses will later give a comparable favor in return. As a ritual object, the beaded *kandaure* ornaments represent abundance, like a cornucopia (Nooy-Palm 1969:189). In ritual speech, they are metaphors for a flourishing cognatic descent group (van der Veen 1929:409; Nooy-Palm 1969:189, 1979:256).

Some sacred textiles displayed at the funerals of Sa'dan Toraja nobility were traded from India or other parts of Indonesia by South Sulawesi or European traders. Certain very long *ikat* cloths, produced on a back-tension loom, were objects of trade from Rongkong or Galumpang, more northern areas of South Sulawesi inhabited by different ethnic groups (van Nouhuys 1921; Bezemer n.d.:29; Langewijs and Wagner 1964). *Pori lonjong* (Fig. VI.27) and *sekomandi* textiles were among the largest and most valuable *ikat* cloths produced until the turn of the century in the Rongkong and Galumpang regions of South Sulawesi and traded south to Sa'dan Toraja people, who displayed them at major rites such as funerals for the nobility (Nooy-Palm 1975:75–76; Holmgren and Spertus 1989:60–61).) They also were traded north into regions of Central Sulawesi, where they were hung as sacred banners for major feasts. Although rarely used for clothing, the large *ikat* cloths woven in the northern regions of South Sulawesi were used locally to pay fines and make peace between rival aristocrats (Jager Gerlings 1952:96–97). Such large, painstakingly made *ikat* cloths are no longer produced in the Rongkong region, which was subject to unsettled political conditions in the past century.

Pori lonjong textiles are characterized by black, red, blue, and tan cotton threads colored with natural dyes. According to van Nouhuys (1921:239), *pori* means "to wrap," referring to the threads wrapped on the warp before dyeing.

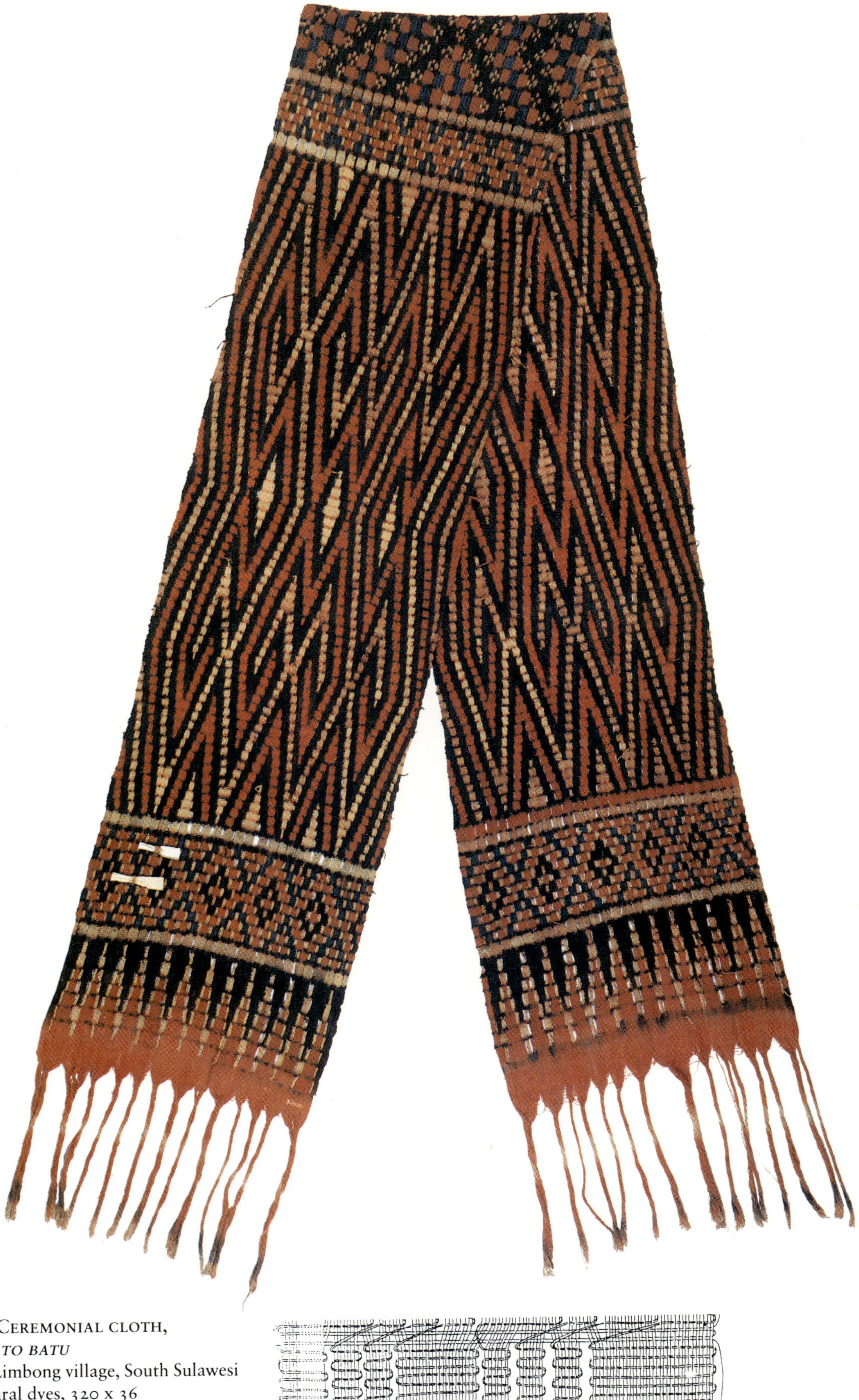

Fig. VI.25 Ceremonial cloth,
MBESA TALI TO BATU
Rongkong, Limbong village, South Sulawesi
Cotton, natural dyes, 320 x 36
Royal Tropical Institute, Tropenmuseum,
The Netherlands, 1752-8. Donated by
J. Langewis in 1947.

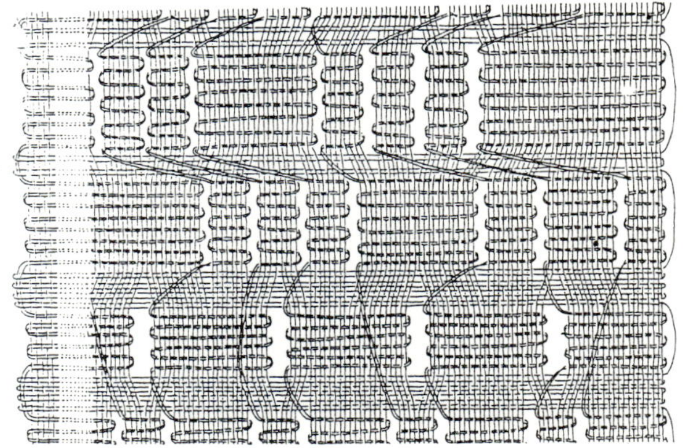

Fig. VI.26 Pattern of slit-weaving technique used for *mbesa tali to batu* cloth. Jager Gerlings 1952:41

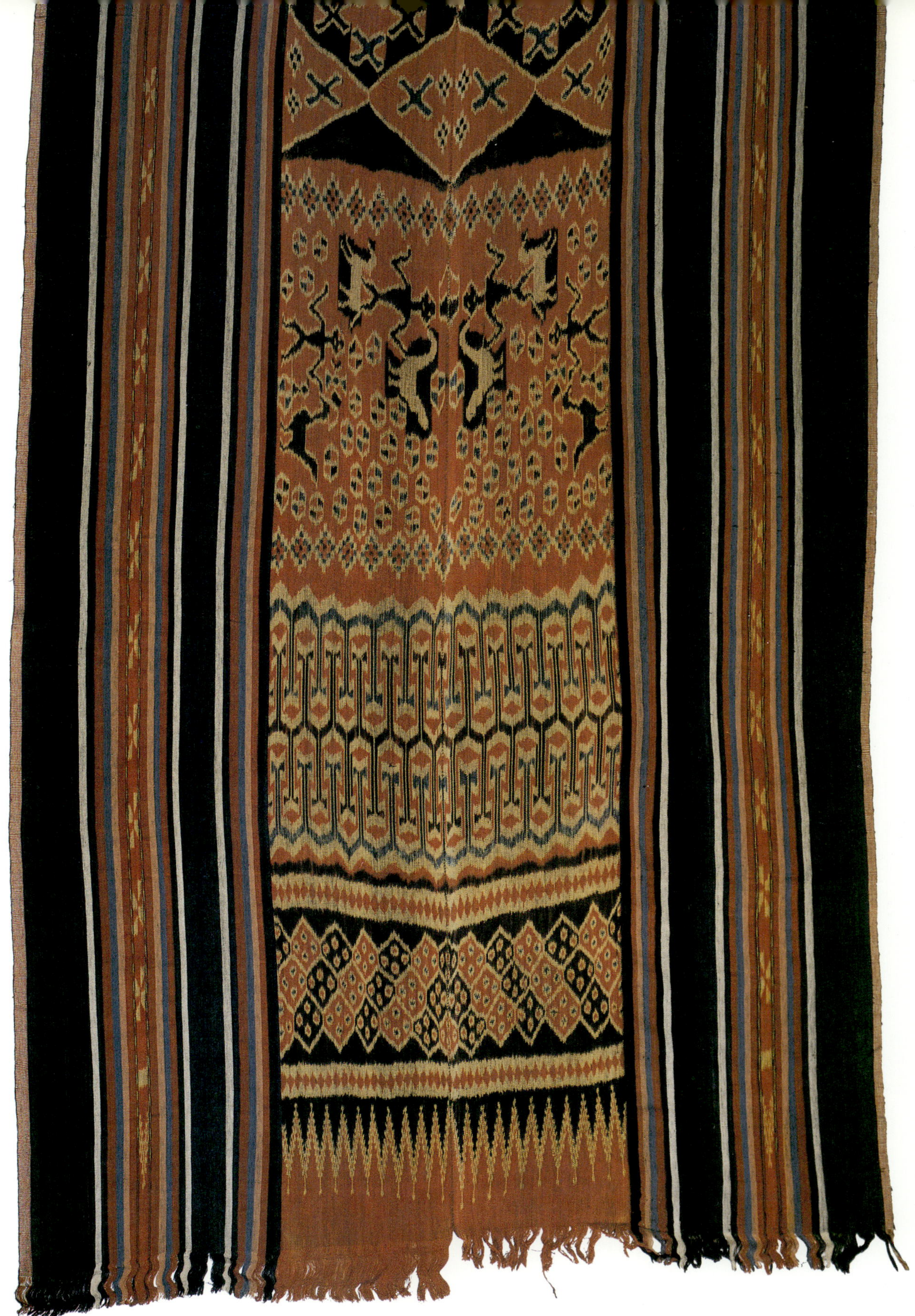

Fig. VI.27 CEREMONIAL FUNERAL CLOTH,
PORI LONJONG
Rongkong, South Sulawesi
Cotton, 440 x 154
Rijksmuseum voor Volkerkunde, Leiden,
2078-7. Purchased by P. Enserinck.
Accessioned in 1925.

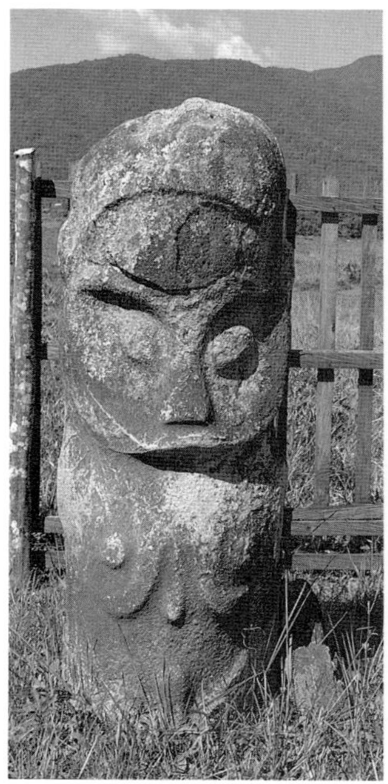

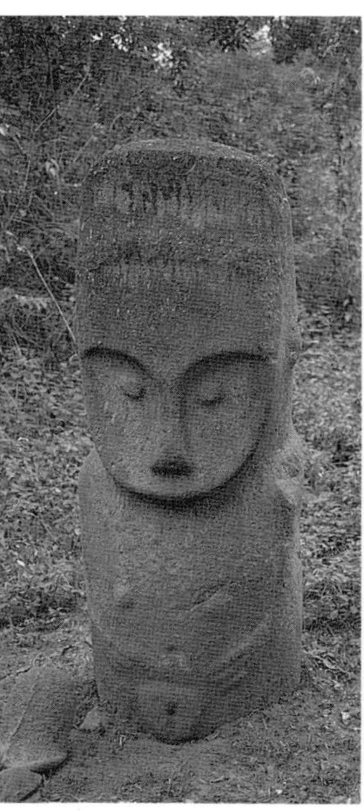

Fig. VI.28 A male stone statue called "War Leader" (*Tadulako*), near Doda village, Besoa, Central Sulawesi, 1987. Lorraine V. Aragon

Fig. VI.29 A female stone statue called "Golden Anklets" (*Langke Bulawa*), near Bomba village, Bada', Central Sulawesi, 1987. Lorraine V. Aragon

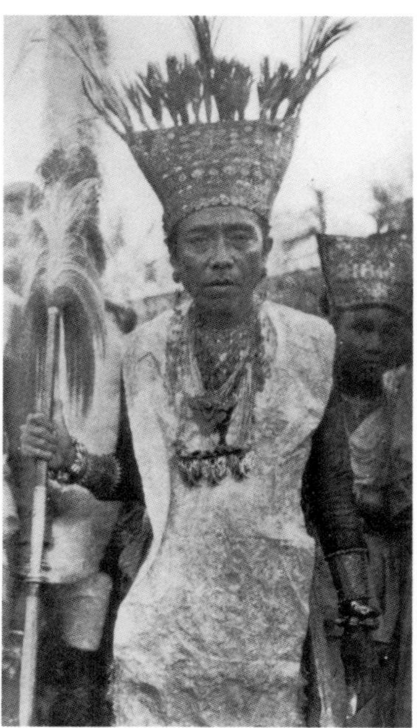

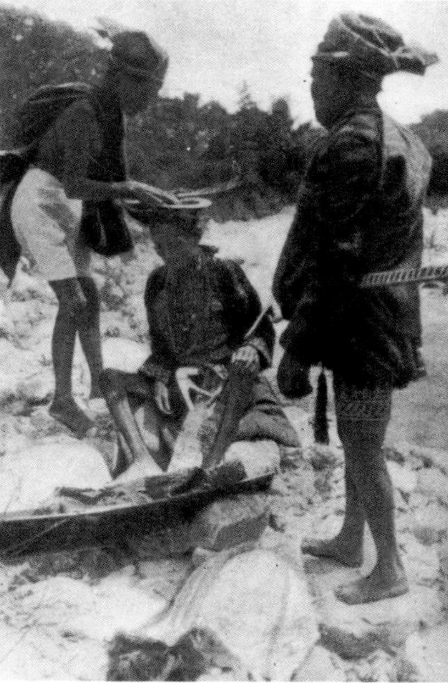

Fig. VI.32 The head transvestite shaman of Bora village wearing *taijanja* as pendants, Central Sulawesi, before 1938. Kruyt 1938: plate 16

Fig. VI.33 Kŭlawi shaman attaches a spiral ornament to the head of a village leader as part of a healing ritual, Central Sulawesi, 1917–20. Kaudern 1944:324

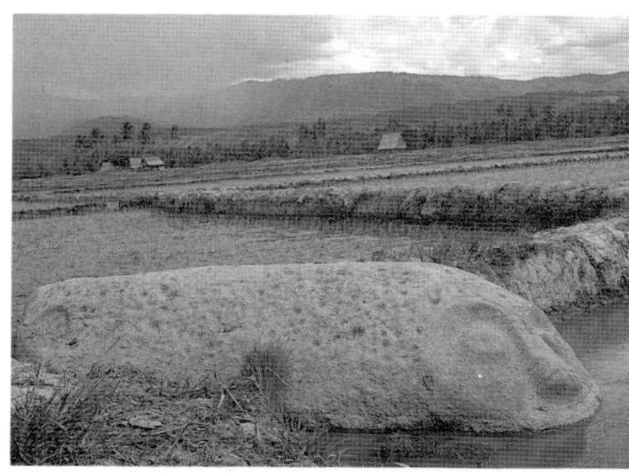

Fig. VI.30 A stone statue thought to represent a buffalo, near Badangkaya village, Bada', Central Sulawesi, 1987. Lorraine V. Aragon

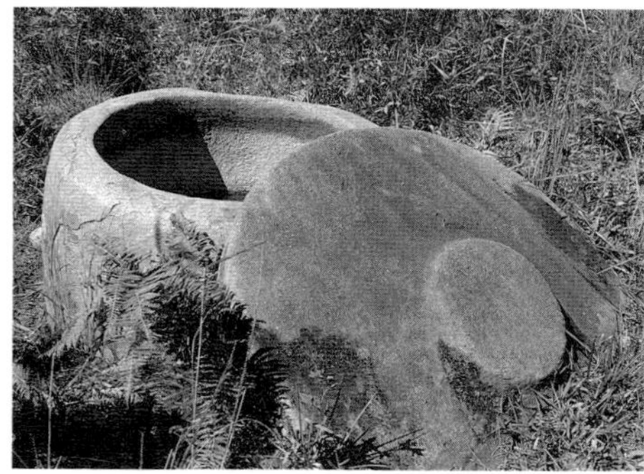

Fig. VI.31 A lidded stone vat (*kalamba*), near Doda village, Besoa, Central Sulawesi, 1987. Lorraine V. Aragon

Alternating stripes and geometric *ikat* patterns form outer borders along the length. The central zone is patterned in mirror-image *ikat* bands with a unique center zone, similar to those used on *hinggi* mantles in east Sumba. This configuration is created by tying the top and bottom warp threads through a frame on which they are already strung (van Nouhuys 1921:241). This striking example (Fig. VI.27) includes two bands of figurative images portraying humans, horses, and cocks set within a background of lozenges and diamonds.

Another type of Rongkong cloth, called *mbesa tali to batu*, displays a rare slit-weaving and post-weaving tie-dyeing technique unique to interior Sulawesi. This particular specimen (Fig. VI.25) was collected newly made from the Rongkong village of Limbong by Jaap and Laurens Langewijs in the late 1920s or early 1930s (Jager Gerlings 1952:40–43). Since the textile still had a few dye-resistant plant fibers tied to it, the collectors were able to see clearly that, contrary to most Indonesian *ikat* techniques, this cloth was tied and dyed after the weaving process was completed. The cloth was woven like a tapestry, with weft threads worked back and forth over a few warps. Narrow slits remained where the wefts did not interlock. Because the supplementary weft yarns are inserted with a bamboo needle, this technique is called "sewn weaving" (*tannunan dasi*). The resulting weave is most unusual because the main warp threads sit loosely at the back of the cloth behind the supplementary weft sections (Fig. VI.26). After the cloth was woven, ties were passed through the slits, binding off specific areas. The ties resisted penetration from the dye, and so those areas of the cloth remained the color of the natural threads once the ties were cut off. This tying and dyeing process was repeated for different colors. The resulting patterns in blue, black, red, and beige are triangles, diamonds, and a central motif related to the anthropomorphic *sekong* pattern.

Mbesa tali to batu cloths reportedly were used at Rongkong mortuary rituals (Jager Gerlings 1952:40). The long narrow cloth was worn as a headdress at funerals by the closest living relative of the deceased. The term *mbesa* in Rongkong and Central Sulawesi, like the term *maa'* in the Sa'dan Toraja region, refers to a varied assortment of sacred ceremonial cloths of either local or foreign production. *Tali* means "band" or "string," including headband or scarf, *to* means "person" or "people," and *batu* means "stone," and thus the textile's name is literally "ceremonial headscarf of a stone person." Holmgren and Spertus (1989:56) suggest that the name might relate to the stone megaliths of Central Sulawesi (located in the Lore Valley over 80 kilometers away through dense mountain forests), but it is more likely that the name refers to the behavior of the mourning relative who attends the corpse in a silent and immobile state. Holmgren and Spertus (1989:56) also use the term *pewo* for this type of cloth, a word meaning men's loincloth in most Central Sulawesi languages. Although there is no evidence that *mbesa tali to batu* cloths were used as ceremonial loincloths, their long and narrow shape make this suggestion feasible. In the Tanimbar archipelago of the Moluccas, for example, ceremonial textiles once designed as loincloths have in recent times more often been used as head or chest cloths.

Since Holmgren and Spertus have collected *mbesa tali to batu* from areas far north of Rongkong, they have hypothesized that a historical weaving center existed in the Palu district of Central Sulawesi (Holmgern and Spertus 1989:68). However, the well-documented development of barkcloth production and the absence of evidence concerning weaving technology in highland Central Sulawesi suggest that their collection results are probably an artifact of internal Sulawesi trade—which was vast—rather than the discovery of a heretofore unknown center of weaving development.

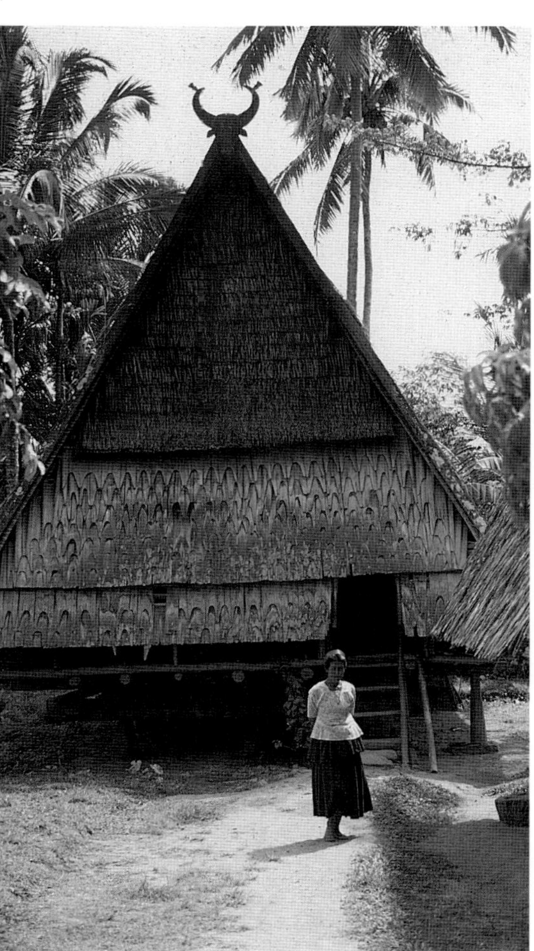

Fig. VI.34 A Bada' woman in front of the last traditional house in Gintu village, Central Sulawesi, 1987. Lorraine V. Aragon

Fig. VI.35 Pamona funeral effigy head (*pemia*) adcrned with a copper-alloy spiral ornament, Lake Poso, Central Sulawesi, before 1913. Kaudern 1944:73. Redrawn by Marcia Bakry, Smithsonian Institution.

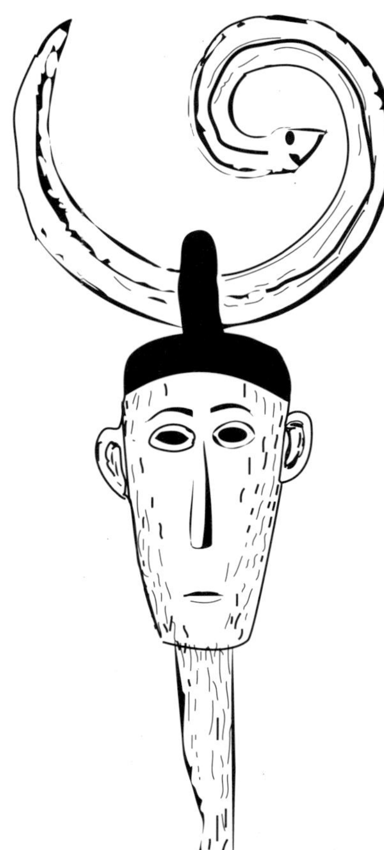

Central Sulawesi: Funeral Monuments of Remote Ancestors

The indigenous groups of Central Sulawesi are less well known and more ethnically diverse than the peoples of the Toraja region of South Sulawesi. Although described as West or East Toraja in the literature of the colonial period (Adriani and Kruyt 1912; Kruyt 1938), they now call themselves by local regional names such as Kaili, Kulawi, Bada', and Pamona. Many of the region's artistic traditions, known from precolonial artifacts in stone, metal, barkcloth, and wood, are no longer practiced. Even the traditional highland house form, characterized by a dramatically steep roof, is infrequently seen (Fig. VI.34). The region's precolonial rituals and painted barkcloth attire (Figs. VI.42, VI.43) have long given way to Christian or Muslim affiliation and modern dress (Aragon 1990). Recent writings claiming that the "Palu Toraja" believe that their ancestors were deer or crocodiles (Holmgren and Spertus 1989:60) are based on statements in reports by early Dutch missionaries (Adriani and Kruyt 1912, vol. 1; Kruyt 1938) that recorded local myths of ancestors who intervene in the lives of their descendants through appearances as powerful wild animals.

Megalithic human and animal statues (Figs. VI.28–30) and large vats (Fig. VI.31) were reported by the first European explorers to the Lore Valley (Sarasin and Sarasin 1905; Kruyt 1938, vol. 1; Kaudern 1938). The present inhabitants of these valleys have little idea of the origin or meaning of the carved statues and vats, but they have given them personal names and associate them with their own ancestors, who may or may not have been the sculptors. The gender of anthropomorphic sculptures, which range from one to four and a half meters tall, is clearly depicted, and some details are carved in the headdresses of many pieces. All of their faces are characterized by prominent brow lines connected to nose forms that extend nearly to the chin line. When seen in profile, most faces are virtually flat and details of the torso are also in low relief. Indonesian excavations have shown that the lidded vats (*kalamba*) found clustered near the statues in certain valleys were used as burial chambers for corpses and grave goods (Team Prasurvey 1973:44). The stone statues may have been memorial monuments to their creator's most prominent ancestors, but they may also represent dieties.

Fig. VI.36 HUMAN STATUETTES, *TAU TAU* or *ANANOI*
Kulawi region, Central Sulawesi
Copper alloy, 6.7 x 3.5 x 1.5; 6.5 x 3.5 x 2
Department of Anthropology, Smithsonian Institution, 301403, 304202. Collected by H. C. Raven. Accessioned in 1917.

Fig. VI.37 BUFFALO STATUETTES
Central Sulawesi
Copper alloy, 2.75 x 5 x 4
Department of Anthropology, Smithsonian Institution, 301402A&B. Collected by H. C. Raven. Accessioned in 1917.

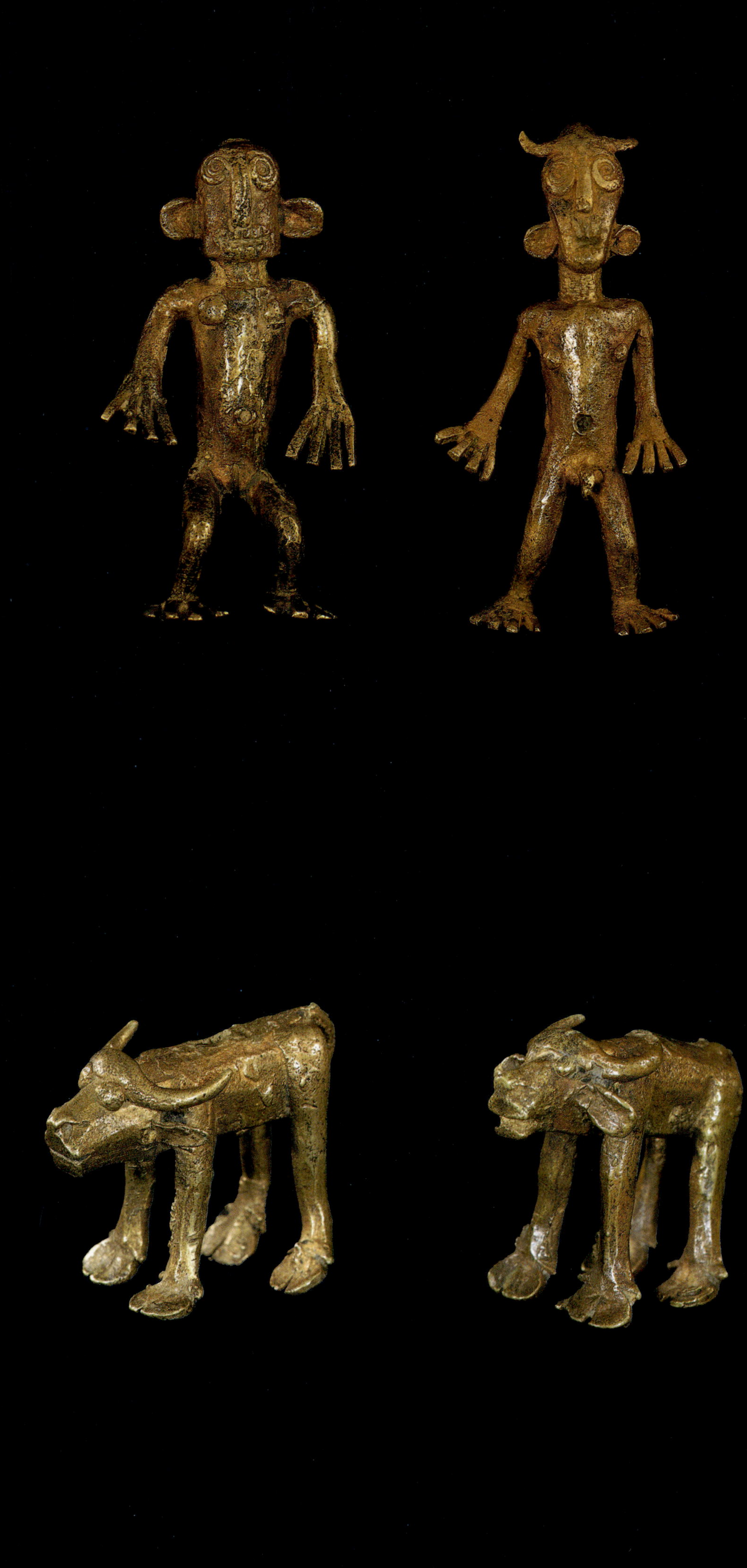

OPPOSITE
TOP

Fig. VI.38 ORNAMENTS, *TAIJANJA*
Central Sulawesi
Copper alloy, A, B, C: 6 x 5 x 1.5; center: 6 x 4.4 x 2.5; D (lower right): 4.5 x 4. x 0.75
Department of Anthropology, Smithsonian Institution, 304201 A, B, C, D; Collection of Anita E. Spertus and Robert J. Holmgren, New York.

BOTTOM

Fig. VI.39 MAN'S HEAD ORNAMENT, *SANGKORI*
Bada', Central Sulawesi
Copper alloy, 24
Collection of Anita E. Spertus and Robert J. Holmgren, New York, C-150

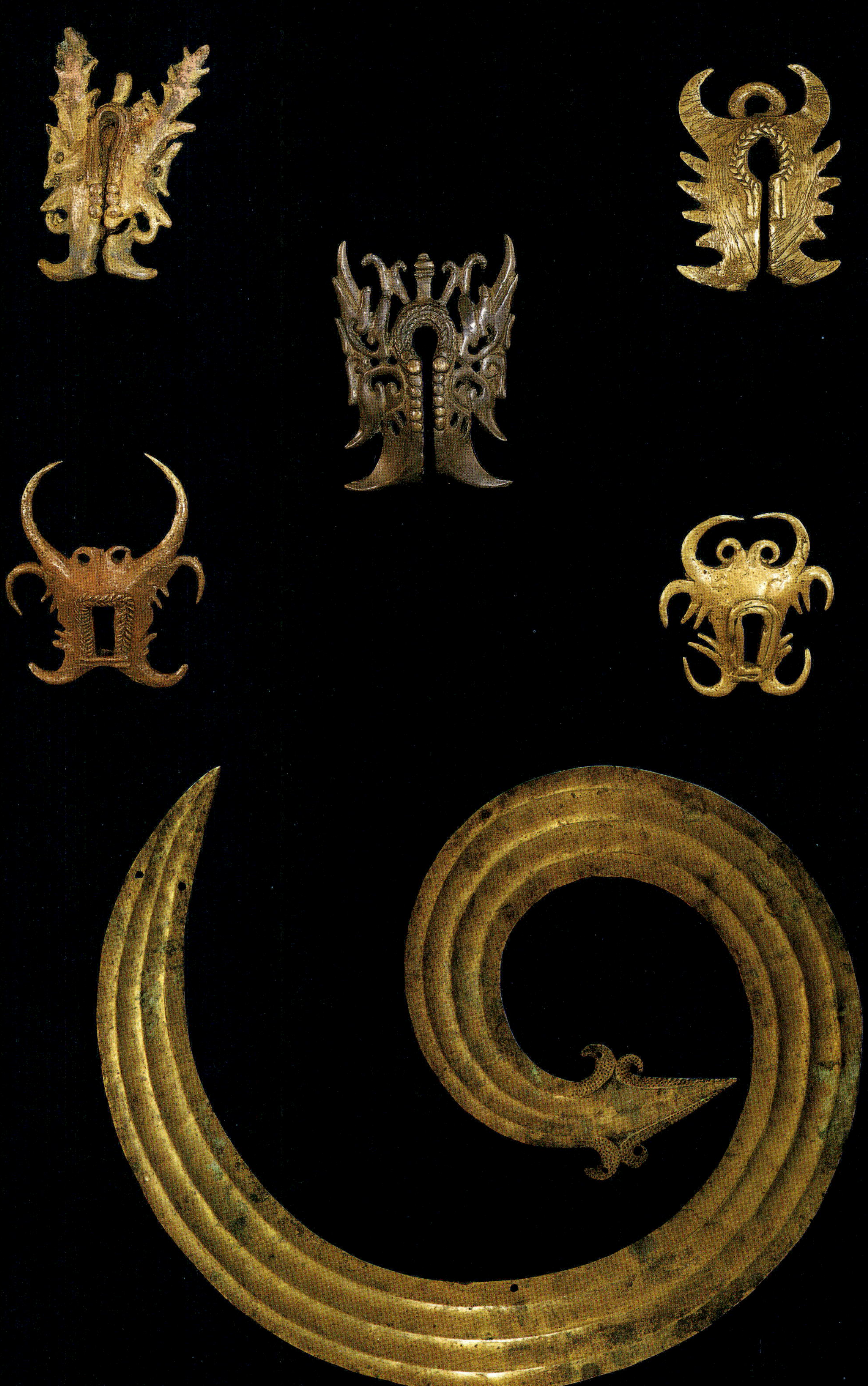

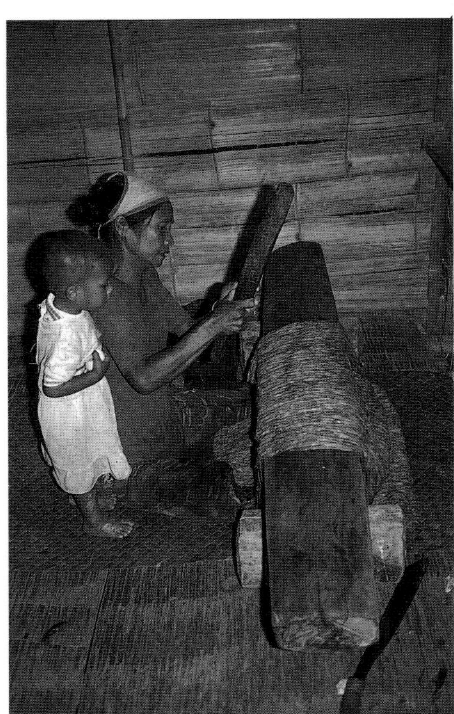

Fig. VI.40 Tina Due' beating barkcloth from ficus bark strips, southern Kulawi district, Central Sulawesi, 1988. Lorraine V. Aragon

Metalwork in Central Sulawesi: The Lost Art of Lost-Wax Casting

A range of unusual cast-metal ornaments and statuettes were once manufactured in Central Sulawesi. Cast by the lost-wax method—a technique no longer known in the region, they are products of a culture that predates the twentieth century. The metalworking technology of lost-wax casting was known since the Bronze Age and by classical civilizations of the Asian mainland. In lost-wax metal casting, a figure is sculpted in wax and encased in a clay mold. When molten metal is poured into the mold, the wax melts and runs out of a hole, and the metal takes the form of the mold. How this technique was introduced to Central Sulawesi is no longer known, but the earliest European reports tell that locals themselves said these artisanry skills were disappearing at the turn of this century (Kaudern 1944:308).

When the Dutch colonial government began actively to rule Central Sulawesi in 1905, copper-alloy ornaments (Figs. VI.35–39) were used as warfare talismans, ornaments for funerary statues, health-promoting amulets, noble regalia, and marriage-alliance gifts. In the Kulawi region of Central Sulawesi, for example, human and buffalo statuettes were brought to the home of a newly married couple to promote the fertility of the couple and their livestock (Kleiwig de Zwaan 1923:2–3; Kaudern 1944:312). If a woman failed to become pregnant after several months of marriage, she might carry human images as fertility charms in her betel-nut bag. These human statuettes are distinctive for their spiral eyes, enlarged ears, prominent navels, shortened legs, four-fingered hands, and four-toed feet. The male figure has horns, or more likely, wears a buffalo-horn headdress. The mouths of both figures are incised vertically, as if to represent teeth, and the form of these incisions match the treatment of the fingers, toes, and female genitalia. The buffalo figures also display unusual proportions, and their stylized forms include expressive heads, cloven hoofs, and long, straight legs, minimizing the animal's torso.

Ornaments called *taijanja* (Fig. VI.38) were used by Central Sulawesi peoples as ceremonial regalia and as wedding gifts from the groom's family to the bride's. The hollowed center of the ornament, said to represent female sexual organs, is a motif occurring in jewelry throughout Indonesia (Rodgers 1985:49). It bears a distinct resemblance to a type of earring worn by Toba Batak in North Sumatra (Kaudern 1944:319; Rodgers 1985:276), the *bela* earring of central Flores (Rodgers 1985:326–27), the *mamuli* ornament of Sumba (Fig. VII.29), and the *loran* earring of Tanimbar archipelago in the Moluccas (Figs. VIII.28, VIII.27). Many of these ornaments, which were originally earrings worn in stretched earlobes, were later worn as pendants around the neck or on headdresses. A visually similar motif has been identified by Holmgren and Spertus on a nineteenth-century embroidered Lampung shoulder cloth (1989:102–03). Given the historical ties of Lampung and Batak to mainland Asia, the parallel designs lend credence to Kaudern's thesis that this basic jewelry form may have had a common origin with earlier types of jewelry made on the Asian mainland (Kaudern 1944:319).

The surface ornamentation of *taijanja* vary greatly from streamlined abstractions to intricate reliefwork suggesting floral or faunal elements. On his travels earlier this century, Kaudern was told by a village headman that the top hooks represent buffalo horns and that the side hooks represent crab pincers (Kaudern 1944:318). Similar interpretations may be elicited today from southern Kulawi peoples, who no longer own such heirlooms but remember that their grandparents had such pieces. Local residents also agree that the *taijanja*'s shape suggests female sex organs, and some mention that the minute balls around the center opening represent human "eggs." The central opening of many *taijanja* are decorated with motifs identical to the rice plume and cotton balls still seen today on the Indonesian Republic's national emblem.

Rodgers (1985:134) illustrates the use of *taijanja* as pendants fastened to the headdress of a nobleman's cap. Hissink (1912) enumerates these ornaments in his list of valuables necessary for bridewealth in the Palu Valley. According to

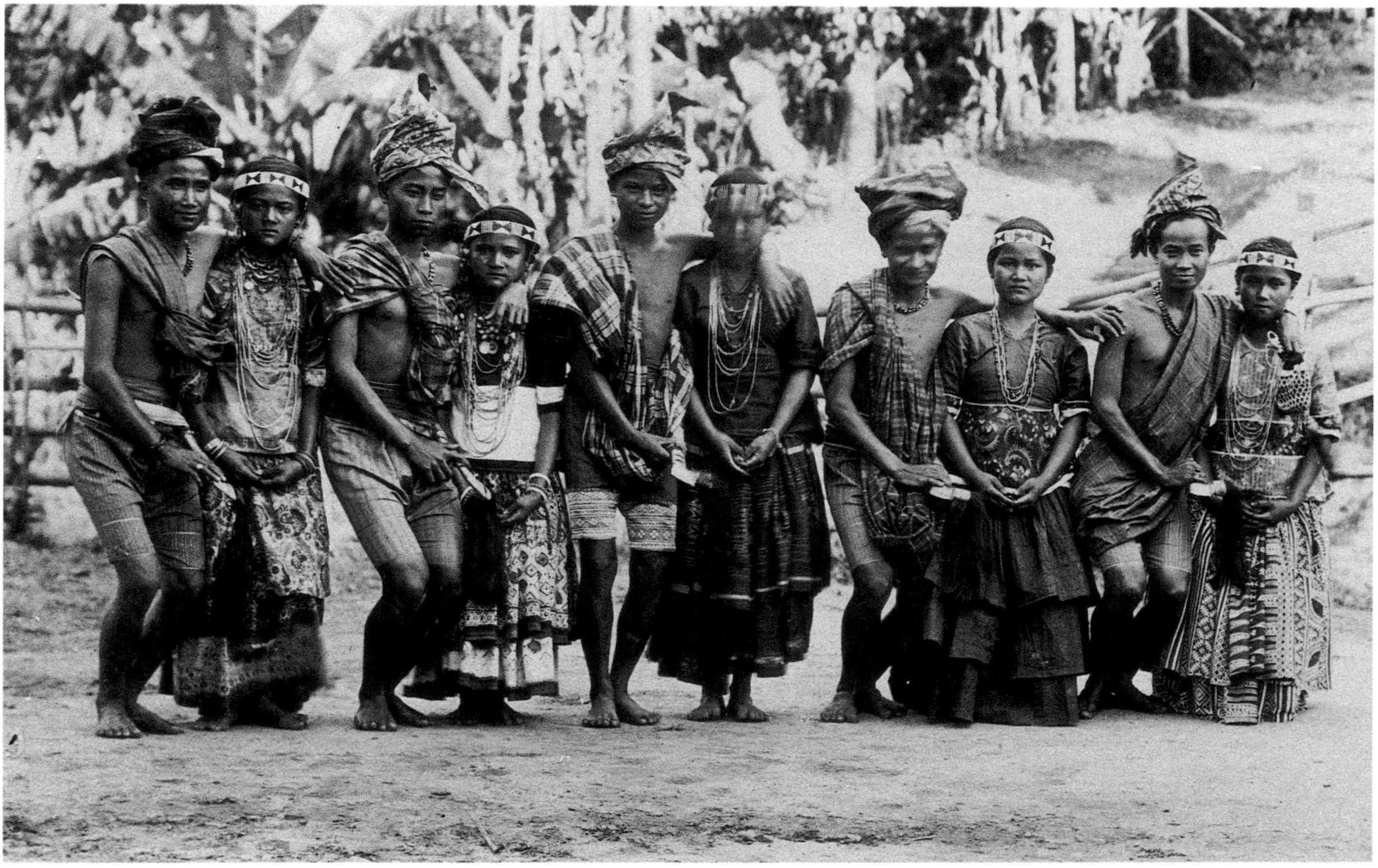

Fig. VI.41 Highland Central Sulawesi dancers wearing barkcloth and other ceremonial attire including *sarita* cloth, Kulawi, Central Sulawesi, early 1900s. Courtesy Royal Tropical Institute, Tropenmuseum, The Netherlands.

scholars from the Palu Museum in Central Sulawesi, *taijanja* ornaments were used by Kaili commoners as gifts from the groom's family to the bride's family at the commencement of marriage negotiations (Masyhuda 1982–3). The copper-alloy human and buffalo statuettes were reportedly used by aristocrats for the same purposes. *Taijanja* ornaments also were said to be worn on headdresses by adolescent Kaili girls during their teeth-filing puberty rites (*mokesa*). Local reports in the Kulawi region claim that, in the recent past, *taijanja* were given to children to wear as protective amulets. Early twentieth-century photographs show that *taijanja* were worn as neck pendants by Sigi Kaili transvestite shamans during public ceremonies (Fig. VI.32). These various ceremonial uses for *taijanja* ornaments are now largely obsolete because of local participation in world religion.

In the early twentieth century, spiral ornaments cast from copper alloy were collected throughout Central and parts of North and Southeast Sulawesi (Kaudern 1944:322). These flat, longitudinally ridged ornaments often include a head at the inner end of the coil, suggesting a snake, eel, or serpent. The ornamentation varies from plain coils with only one ridge and three small holes (serving as the figure's eyes and point of attachment for a headdress) to more elaborately ridged coils with well-defined faces and geometric body ornamentation. The metallic composition and color of the ornaments also vary, ranging from very light golden to dark bronze copper alloys. Their circumstances and places of production are not well-documented, but Adriani and Kruyt (1912, vol. 2: 227; Adriani 1928:685) write that the Lake Poso or Pamona peoples acquired their spiral ornaments from the Mori people, then known as the most skilled metalworkers of Central Sulawesi.

According to all early witnesses (Sarasin and Sarasin 1905, Hissink 1912, Grubauer 1913, Kaudern 1944), the spiral ornament was worn on the head exclusively by men. Three major uses of the spiral ornament are known from early European reports and the current recollections of elders—during healing

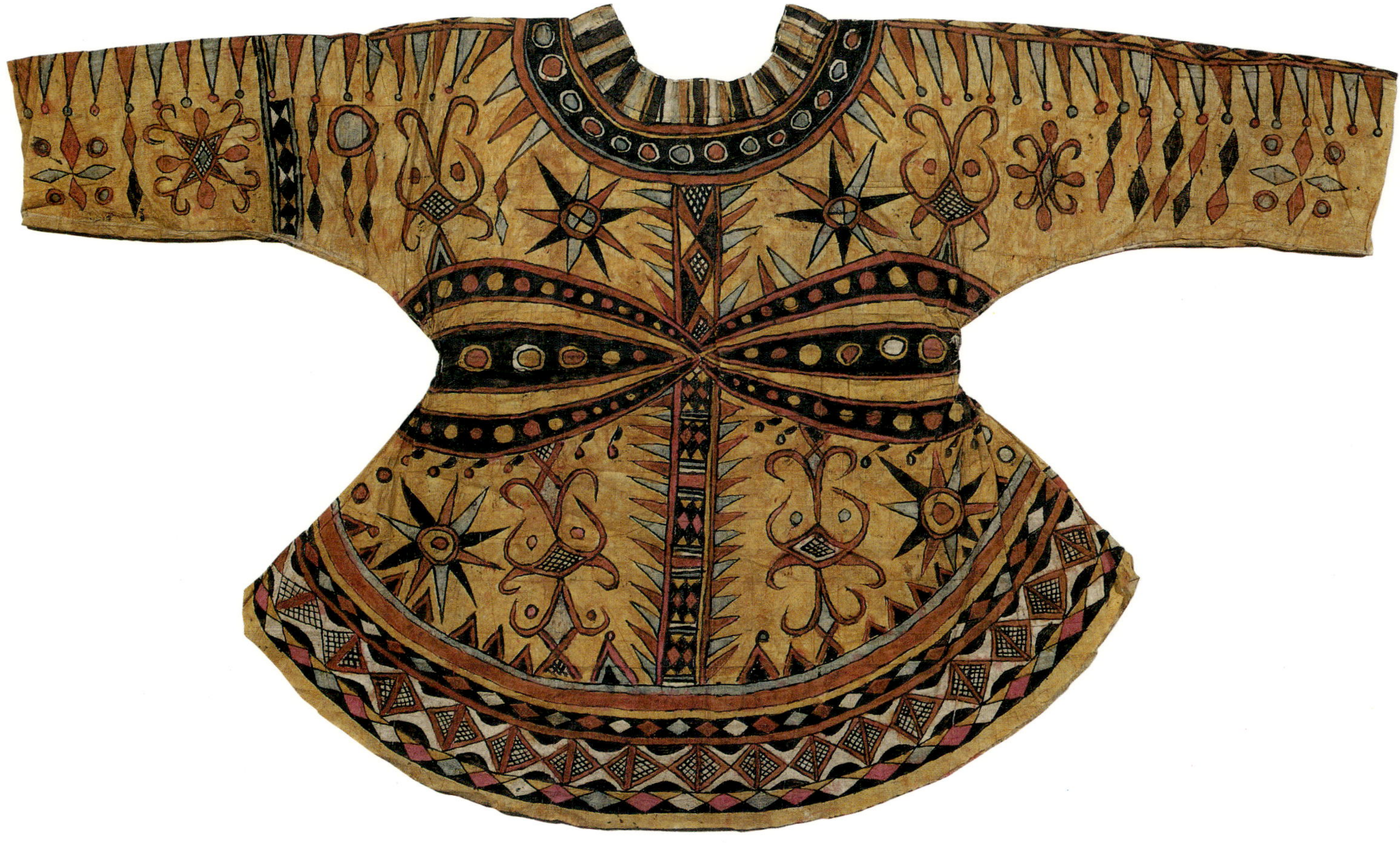

Fig. VI.42 Woman's blouse, *lembe*
Bada', Toare village, Central Sulawesi
Barkcloth, 59 x 99
Department of Anthropology, Smithsonian Institution, 304102. Collected by H. C. Raven. Accessioned in 1918.

OPPOSITE
Fig. VI.43 Man's headscarf, *siga*
Bada', Toare village, Central Sulawesi
Barkcloth, 126 x 109
Department of Anthropology, Smithsonian Institution, 304107. Collected by H. C. Raven. Accessioned in 1918.

rituals, during warrior expeditions, and during mortuary rituals. The first was in shaman ceremonies for the healing of sickness or other cosmological imbalance. At a healing ceremony for an aged Kulawi aristocrat, the bronze spiral was attached to the top of his head horizontally (Fig. VI.33; Kaudern 1940, 1944: 324). Other reports (Sarasin and Sarasin 1905, vol. 2:70; Hissink 1912:87–89) state that the spirals were worn by traditional shamans (*tobalia*) during ceremonies to cure the sick or to end droughts. The spiral was usually worn vertically, with the coil's tail pointing upwards above the wearer's head. The spiral ornament was also worn as a protective head ornament by warriors on expedition. Adriani and Kruyt (1912, vol. 2:225) describe this use among the Pamona, and it is still recounted by elders of the Kulawi. In the Pamona and Mori regions, the spiral ornament was attached to the headdress of an effigy used in mortuary rituals (Fig. VI.35). Pamona and Mori peoples traditionally practiced secondary burial, reburying bones, cleaned of their decomposed flesh, with ceremonies including the carving of a wooden effigy head of the deceased (*pemia*). The carved wooden effigy head was attached to a bundle of cleaned bones of the deceased (Adriani and Kruyt 1912). These effigy heads were made for both males and females. The female ones were distinguished by earrings and female tattoo patterns, and the male ones included a projection post at the top of the head for fastening a copper-alloy spiral ornament (Kaudern 1944:76–80). Only male effigy heads were adorned with spiral ornaments, which were probably signs of their warrior status. Kaudern (1944:327) reports seeing a shrinelike installation in the village of Sampalowo, east of Tomata, which featured a carved effigy head sporting a spiral ornament and set on top of a life-sized doll. Since most interior Central Sulawesi peoples are now Protestant Christians, they practice the funeral rituals introduced by European missionaries earlier this century. Kaudern's report indicates, however, that in some parts of Central Sulawesi the population formerly honored effigies of the dead, which may have been similar to the *tau tau* statues (Figs. VI.5, VI.11) made by the Sa'dan Toraja of South Sulawesi.

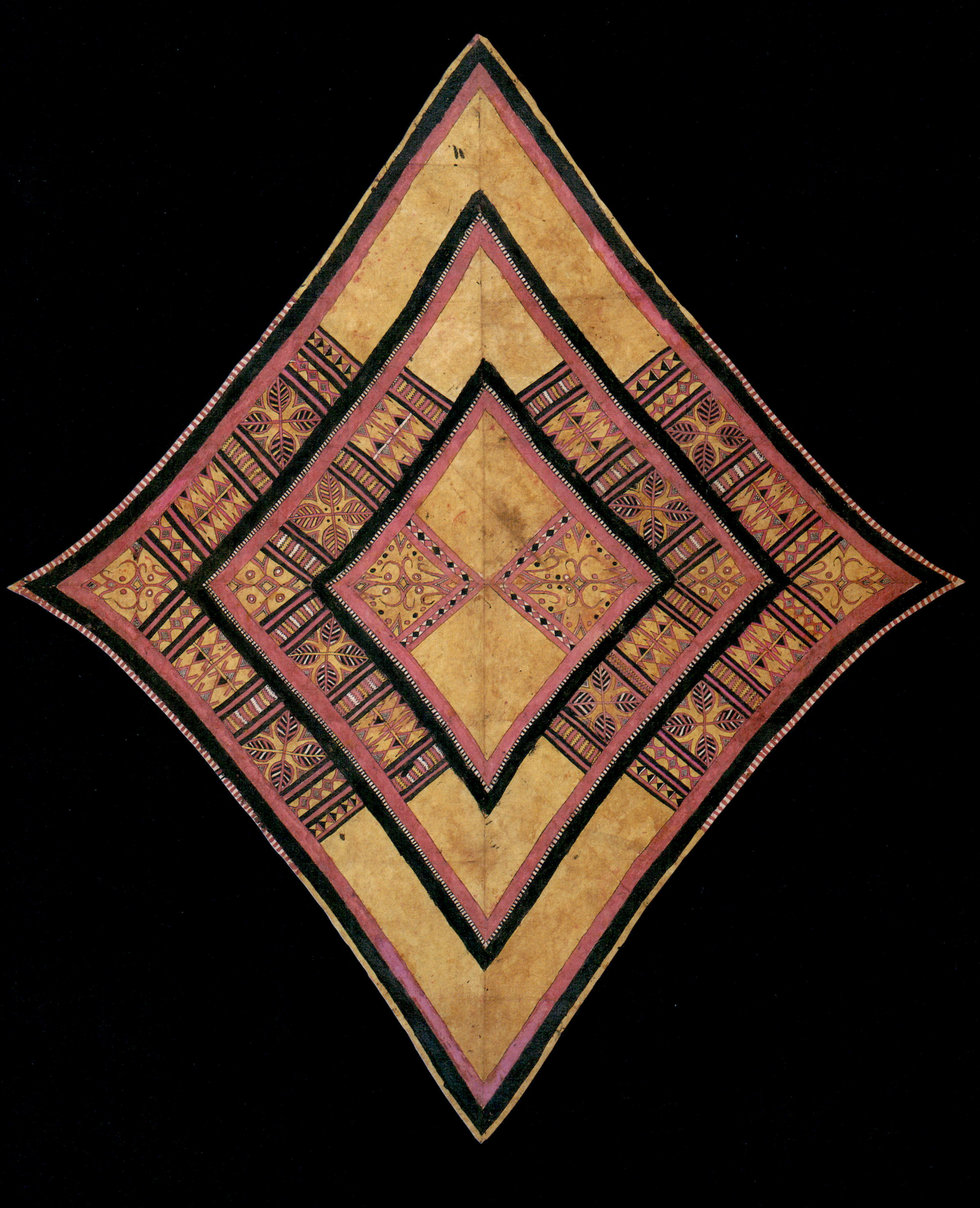

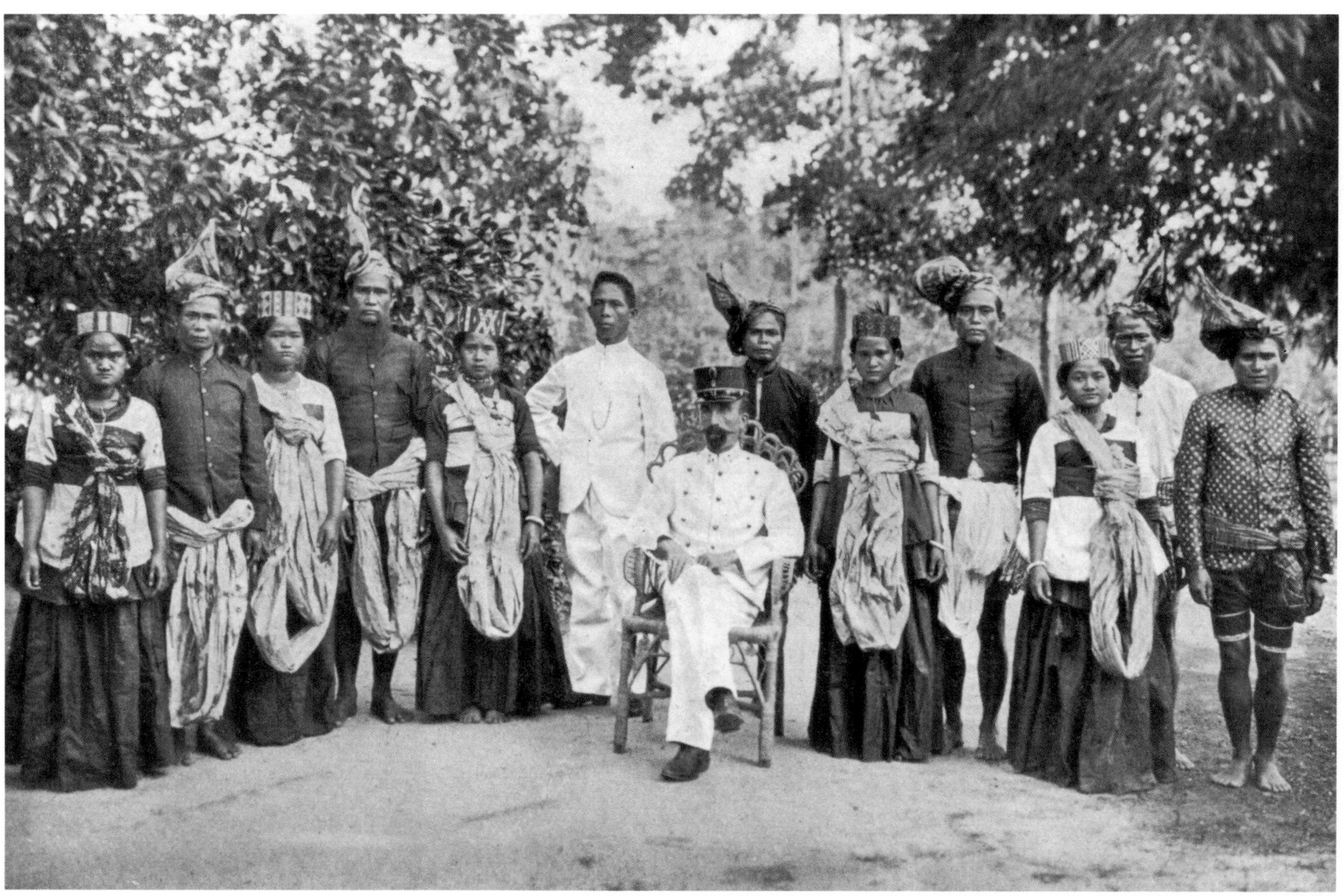

Fig. VI.44 Men wearing barkcloth headscarves and women in festive dress stand beside a seated European official, Central Sulawesi, before 1921. van Eerde 1921:3. Courtesy Elsevier Press, Amsterdam.

Kaudern (1944:327–329) notes that certain peoples of northeastern Central Sulawesi made a spiral ornament also called *sualang*, but it was fashioned from curved tusks of the wild pig deer (*babirusa*), not from metal. The Minahasa people of North Sulawesi used the same term for their brass spiral ornaments. The design of these ornaments may have been inspired by the tusks of these rare wild pigs that exist only on Sulawesi. This pale gold spiral ornament (Fig. VI.39) has three spine ridges and is embellished with small dots and protruding coils at the head end of the eellike form.

Barkcloth: Indigenous Fabric and Painted Canvas

The Spanish friar Domingo Navarrete, who first traveled to Central Sulawesi in the seventeenth century, reported that barkcloth manufacture was a highly developed technology in the region (Cummins 1962). By the start of the twentieth century, woven cloth was introduced through trade, gradually replacing both plain and painted barkcloth attire for a variety of practical, social, and religious reasons (Aragon 1990). The vibrantly painted barkcloth of the Poso Lake, Lore Valley (Bada', Besoa, and Napu), and Kulawi regions is now only a distant memory to the grandchildren of its makers. However, unpainted barkcloth is still produced in some highland regions, and styles of women's traditional barkcloth clothing are now reproduced in woven cloth for some ceremonial occasions.

The process of making barkcloth and the terminology used to describe it in Central Sulawesi is very similar to that of Polynesia (Kennedy 1934; Kooijman 1972). The bark of certain trees is peeled, cooked, fermented, and then pounded with wooden and stone mallets (Fig. VI.40) to produce a felted cloth that can be dyed, painted, or further ornamented. The process of producing barkcloth, prior to painting or any other coloring technique, takes from two to nine days, depending on the species of tree bark used. Manufacture was, and still is, carried out almost entirely by women.

In highland Central Sulawesi, plain barkcloth skirts, blouses, loincloths, and headscarfs were traditionally worn as everyday dress. Elaborately painted barkcloth clothes and accessories were reserved for agricultural and life-cycle feasts. Ornamented barkcloth clothing was produced specially for such traditional ceremonies as weddings, funerals, and harvest rituals. Thin barkcloth blouses were made from the bark of the paper mulberry tree and painted with colors obtained from forest plants. By 1916, when this blouse (Fig. VI.42) was collected, some aniline dyes were being used to paint white barkcloth clothing (Hough 1932:6), but certain shades of red, yellow, black, purple, and green were still produced from local plants and minerals (Adriani and Kruyt 1905:19).

The primary motifs on this blouse (Fig. VI.42), as well as on many other painted barkcloth samples, are said to be configurations of buffalo horns, symbols connoting wealth and feasts throughout much of Sulawesi. In other areas of eastern Indonesia, the same designs represent frigate birds (Hough 1932; Kooijman 1963). Tichelman (1940a, 1940b) called this pattern the "headhunting motif" (*snel-motief*) because of its significance for warriors on the island of Ceram in the Moluccas, and because it appears on the headscarves of Central Sulawesi warriors who had successfully captured heads (Fig. VI.43). Since this design and related ones appear on a wide range of painted barkcloth apparel, however, it is unlikely that they always refer to headhunting. Hough's argument that the pattern is a stylized rendition of buffalo designs also found on carved house hooks is far more convincing.

Certain aspects of Central Sulawesi blouse design—including the cut, use of embroidery or appliqué techniques, and the ornamentation with chips of reflective material such as mica—bear a distinct resemblance to clothing produced in the Gujarat region of India (cf. Nicholson 1988). Although traditional women's clothing of Central Sulawesi may be of independant origin, the appearance of similar features in widely separated areas is striking. Given the evidence of prehistoric Indian textile exports to Sulawesi (Gwatkin 1986; Nooy-Palm 1989), the possibility that some early blouses from India entered the region cannot be discounted entirely.

The patterning of this headscarf (Fig. VI.43) is characteristic of traditional Central Sulawesi compositions. Motifs are primarily geometric with some four-petaled flowers and a composite design representing buffalo horns. Individual motifs are placed in boxes separated by bands running in alternating patterns. These rows of motifs are arranged concentrically around bands within the diamond shape of the headcloth. The owner would have folded the diamond in two along the unpatterned diagonal before tying the headscarf ceremonially (as seen in Fig. VI.44).

In the area near Lake Poso, the designs on a man's headscarf reportedly were related to his prowess in headhunting. Six headhunting experiences allowed a man to have a very colorful headscarf, and seven or more gave him the right to wear human and sword images (Adriani and Kruyt 1905:18). Headhunting was invoked to end mourning taboos incurred by the death of a regional leader or provoked by an enemy raid. The paintings on men's barkcloth headscarves signified changes in their social rank, one use of Central Sulawesi barkcloth clothing in marking status transitions, which parallels that of woven textiles in other areas of Indonesia.

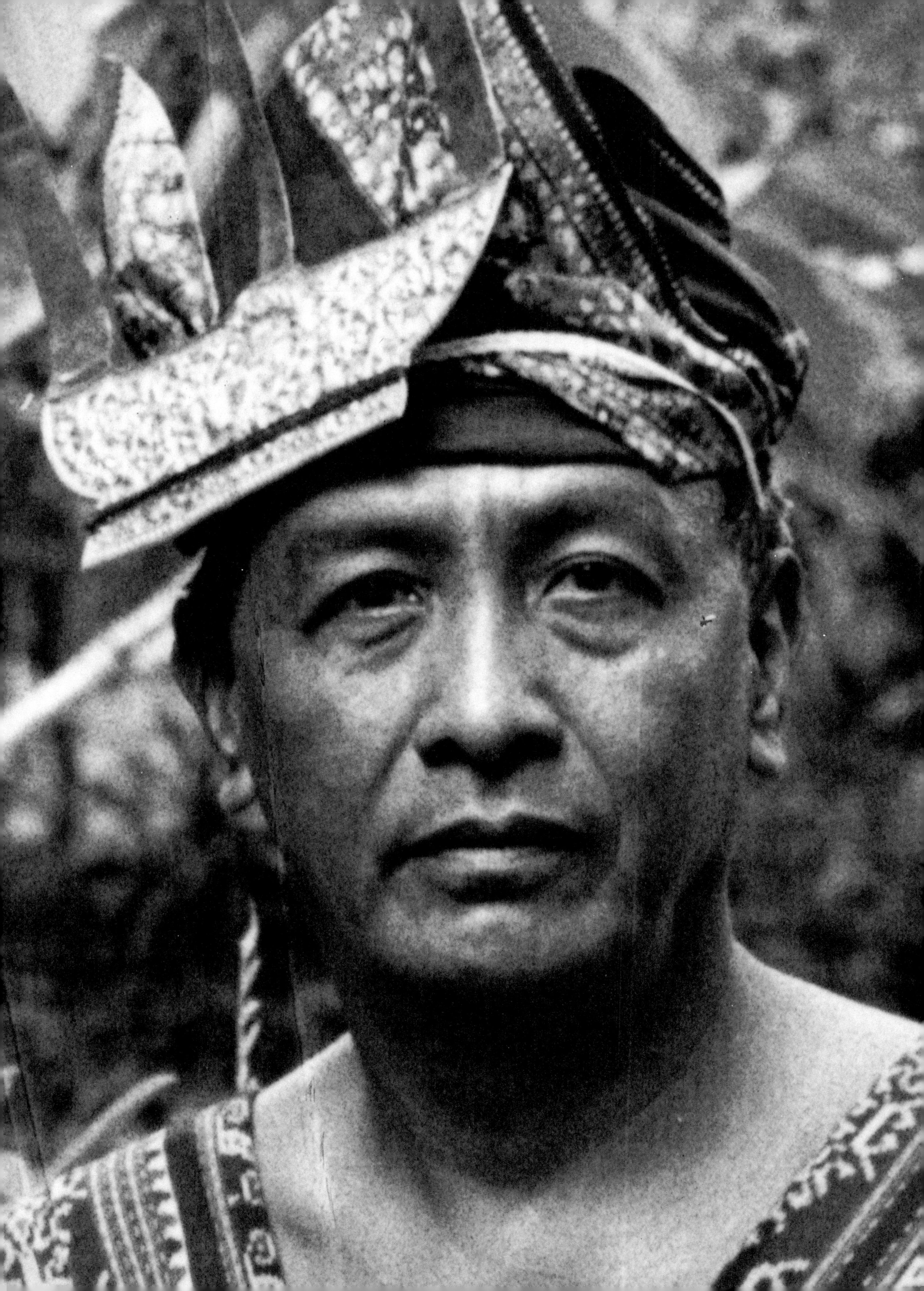

VII

Lesser Sunda Islands

The Lesser Sunda Islands are the chain of relatively small islands that extend eastward from Java. The ecology of these eastern Indonesian islands is markedly different from that of Java. For the most part, the islands lack fertile volcanic soil and have a much drier climate (Fox 1977). Hence subsistence is more diverse and oriented to such crops as millet, corn, and local palms rather than to rice alone. A wide range of weaving and metalworking techniques is known from the Lesser Sunda Islands, which by the sixteenth century received Indian cloths, including the *ikat* silks known as *patola*, and European coins from an active coastal trade that exported horses, slaves, and forest products such as sandalwood and beeswax.

Ethnic Variation in Art Forms

Isolated from each other by interisland seas and mountainous terrain, Lesser Sunda societies developed diverse and distinctive regional designs in their textiles and other art forms. Although different ethnic groups in neighboring regions often actively traded their valuables (Rodgers 1985:200), local creations of the same types of objects often show unmistakable regional identities. In certain regions, these distinctive styles are particularly evident in such ceremonial items as textiles and carved spoons (Figs. VII.7 and VII.8) that were used to serve food at feasts. For example, carved ceremonial spoons of the Tetum people of Timor vary from those of the neighboring Atoni people in the more rounded motifs and in the axis and length of the carved handles. Both styles are characteristic of openwork carving traditions resembling those in the Moluccas and Cenderawasih Bay (Irian Jaya), yet demonstrate an intricate carving technique like that developed in coastal court societies (see catalog chapter X). The handle of the Atoni spoon (Fig. VII.7) is finely carved and divided into four registers depicting long-legged, long-billed birds. The second register from the bowl of the spoon is unique, with two large birds set in mirror image on left and right. S-spiral bands separate the figurative boxes. The design of the Tetum

Fig. VII.1 A former hereditary ruler of Seba, Savu (detail of Fig. VII.35).

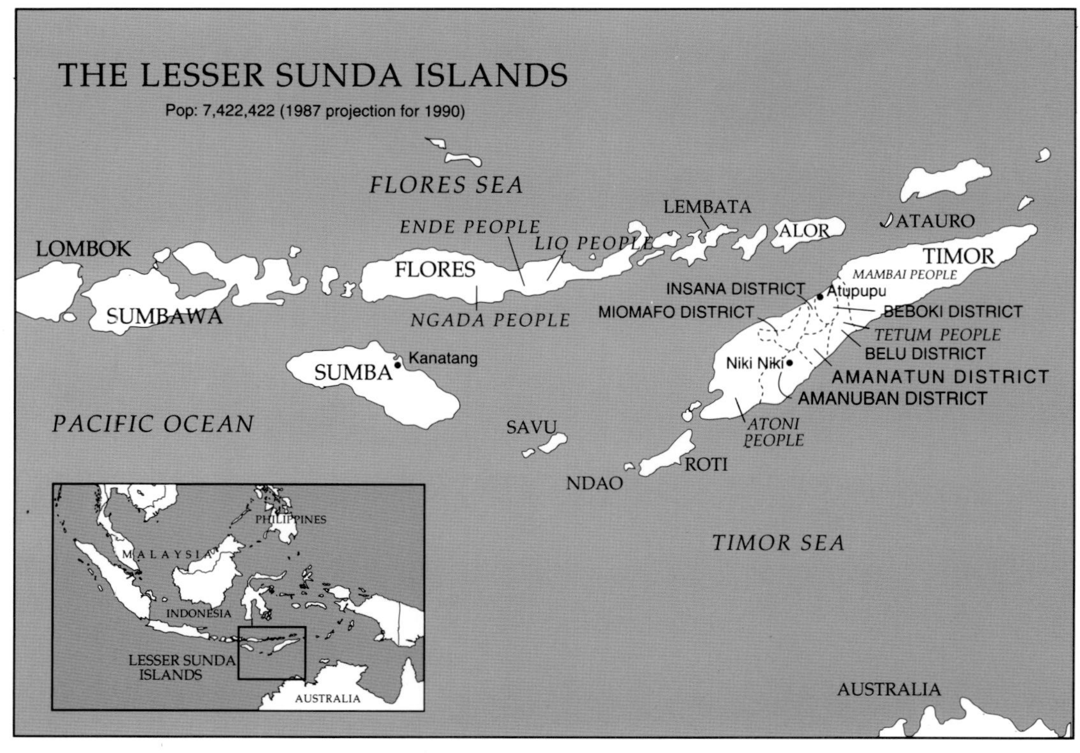

spoon (Fig. VII.8) is more geometric, but a bird form surrounded with geometric borders is suggested in the central band.

Such variations in the material culture of neighboring peoples reflect a complex distribution of ethnic groups and fluid interactions, including trade and intermarriage. An example may be found in the textiles made by Ende and Lio weavers on Flores (Hamilton 1989). Even though these two closely related groups make women's sarongs in a number of styles (Fig. VII.2), the general characteristics of Ende and Lio styles can be distinguished. Ende fabric designs typically have a very formal structure, often with small motifs arranged in a grid (Fig. VII.4). The background is nearly black, created by over-dyeing the dark blue produced by indigo with red produced by morinda, and two plain black bands appear near the ends of the sarong. Lio styles show more variation in color and motif and are less gridlike in structure (Fig. VII.5). In addition to their unique patterns, Ende or Lio have long shared some styles of sarongs. Others have more recently been popularized across the ethno-linguistic boundary. One group of Lio villages, historically oriented toward the nearby port of Ende rather than toward more distant Lio areas, produces more Ende patterns than Lio (Fig. VII.6; Hamilton 1989:43). Today the many Lio weavers who have settled in the town of Ende, the modern capital of the region, continue, however, to make the Lio-style patterns of their natal villages (Fig. VII.5).

Dual Cosmology: A Balance of Contrasts and Obligations

According to traditional beliefs held by people in the Lesser Sunda Islands, the world is balanced between such contrasting elements as male and female, older and younger, living and dead, light and dark (van Wouden 1968[1935]; Barnes 1974; Forth 1981). Such polarities are expressed in daily life through exchanges between family members and in obligations toward ancestors or people of high rank. Contrasts and parallelism feature prominently in Lesser Sunda art forms, from ritual speech to textile design and house architecture (Fox 1971; Kuipers

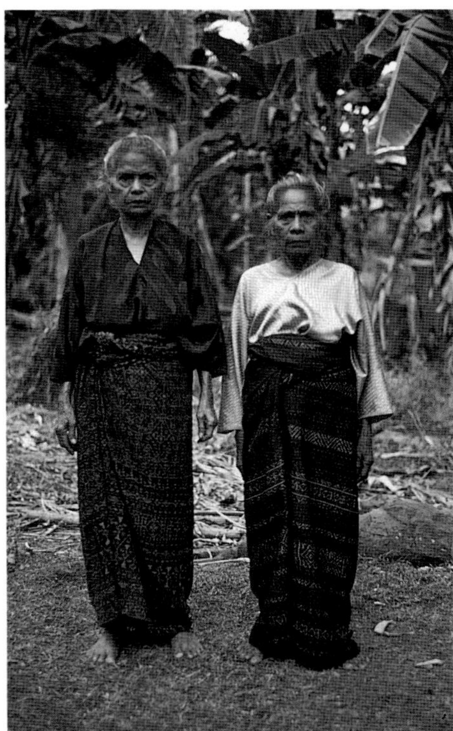

Fig. VII.2 The sarongs worn by these Lio women represent two of the many styles made in a single village: *lawo luka semba* (left) and *lawo nepa mite* (right), Flores, 1988. Roy Hamilton

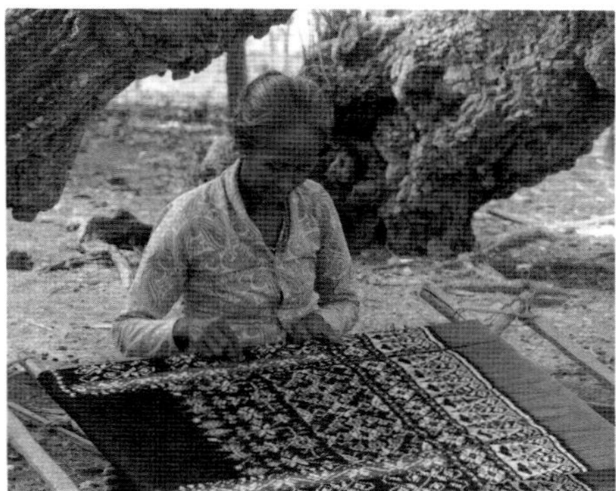

Fig. VII.3 Aristocratic weaver working on a warp *ikat* textile bearing *patola* designs that can be worn only by the nobility, Termanu, Roti, after 1970. James J. Fox

1988; Hoskins 1988; Schulte Nordholt 1971). The concern with the balancing of these polarities is stated succinctly in the following poem from the Mambai people of Timor:

> When white is not enough
> Increase it with black;
> When black is not sufficient
> Augment it with white.
> (Traube 1986:11)

The Mambai classify their traditional agricultural and fertility rituals as white, and their mortuary rituals as black (Traube 1980:298–99). The two domains of life and death are symbiotic: the living help their deceased relatives to obtain a good place in the afterlife through rituals, and the ancestors bestow prosperity on the living.

Artwork of Lesser Sundas embodies these concepts about ensuring harmony through the balancing of dual forces. In Lesser Sundas sculpture, for example, two-headed figures commonly represent a male-and-female deity or an ancestral couple. The two-headed post carved by Tetum people of the Belu region (Figs. VIII.9,VII.10) was used as an altar for offerings. At ceremonial events, the carved post would be dressed with locally woven cloths, as if it were a living person (Fig. VII.11); Vroklage 1952–53, fig. 242; Hicks 1988:141). Food gifts would be placed on the post to feed the ancestors; in exchange, the ancestors were expected to make men and women fertile, enabling their descendants to reproduce (Hicks 1988:143). These offering posts, characterized by square or rounded faces in square frames and limbless cylindrical torsos, were made of either stone or wood. The wooden posts have largely deteriorated, but the stone posts that remain have masklike faces and are adorned with bands of spirals, diamonds, and animal figures on their torsos.

The Ngada of Flores traditionally carved matched pairs of male and female figures from single beams of wood and set them before houses to ward off misfortune. The statues, which represented ancestral couples with jurisdiction in the region, were rounded and smoothly finished (Fig. VII.15) and installed in front of a shrine built for offerings to ancestors. Such statues, considered pagan idols, were removed or destroyed by early missionaries and are no longer made by the contemporary Christian population.

The Flores ancestor statues (Fig. VII.15) share aesthetic conventions with comparable figures in other outer-island regions. Their eyebrow line continues down to outline a long nose almost reaching the chin, a composition seen also on the stone sculptures of Central Sulawesi. One hand crosses their chests, the other approaches their genitals—arm positions also seen on Tanjung Dayak ancestor figures of Kalimantan. The Flores statues stand in a frozen, bent-knee position that is reminiscent of north Nias ancestor figures (*adu*). Their relatively unmodelled torsos are elongated in comparison to their short legs. Vibrant blue eyes of inlaid glass trade beads, stare piercingly at the living—possibly serving as a reminder to observe the ancestral customs and rituals.

Displaying male and female symbols in combination at household doors and village gates is common throughout the Timor highlands (personal communication, Clark E. Cunningham 1989). Belu house doors often symbolically depict women's breasts along with the buffalo-horn motif of warriors' headdresses to invoke both household protection and the combined male and female elements that result in community fertility (Fig. VII.14). In some Belu areas, one house entrance is said to be male and the other is female. In the Tetum language, both entrances are called "the steps that lead to the source of life" (Hicks 1988:147). The geometric, often spiral, designs ornamenting Belu doors are labyrinthine and can cover much of the door's front surface.

Timor highland houses (Fig. VII.12) are also divided into male and female, right and left, higher- and lower-ranked domains. A house represents the ordering of local cosmology: physically higher spaces represent socially and spiri-

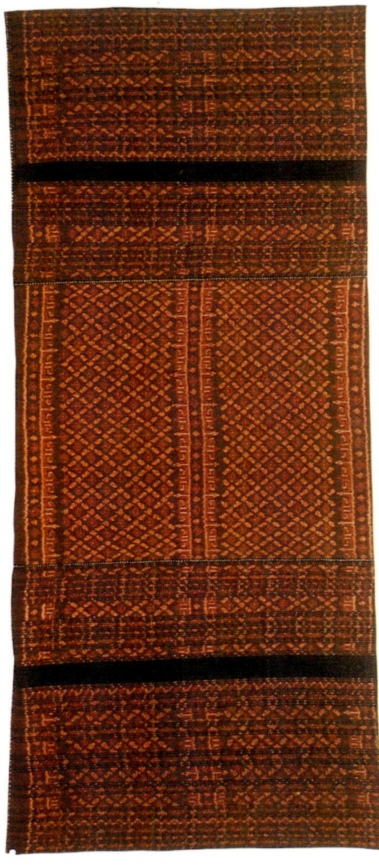
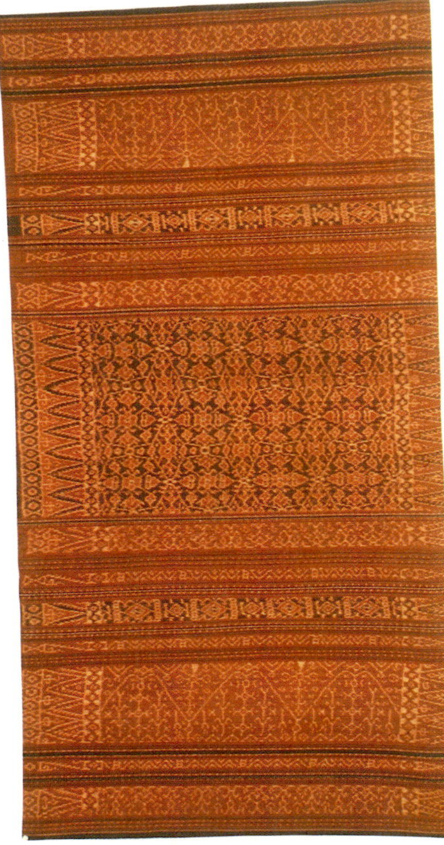
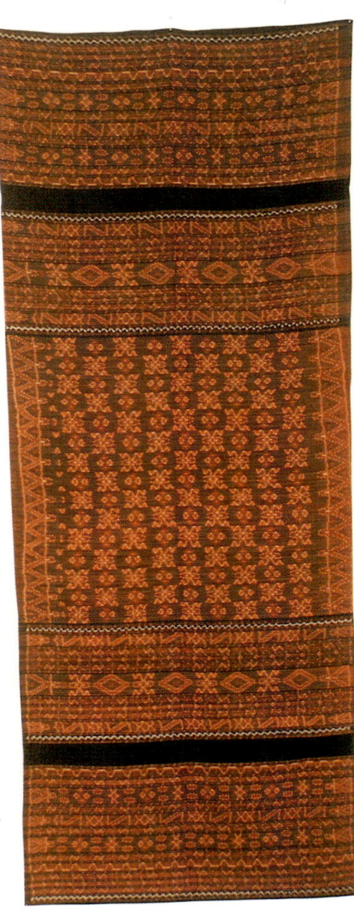

TOP
LEFT

Fig. VII.4 The local name for this Ende woman's sarong, *zawo zombo so*, refers to the borders that divide the center panel vertically into two sections, Flores. Courtesy UCLA Fowler Museum for Cultural History, X88-1258.

MIDDLE

Fig. VII.5 *Lawo sinde*, a Lio woman's sarong style, made circa 1980 by a Lio weaver living in the town of Ende, Flores. Courtesy UCLA Fowler Museum for Cultural History, X88-1272.

RIGHT

Fig. VII.6 *Lawo pea* is the Lio name for this sarong. Although it was made in a Lio village, its structure and the plain black bands identify it as an Ende style, Flores. Courtesy UCLA Fowler Museum of Cultural History, X88-1262.

tually elevated domains, and a loft storage space is usually reserved for ancestral heirlooms and ritual relics. The Atoni people of Timor link male activities with the right of the house and female activities with the left (Fig. VII.13; Cunningham 1964:53).

Other forms of sculpture in the Lesser Sundas, while not depicting ancestors or deities directly in anthropomorphic form, still refer indirectly to the relationship of humans to ancestral traditions. One example is the stylized dragon figures traditionally carved on the island of Alor. According to the collector's information, these two effigies (Figs. VII.21, VII.22), were called "mouse-catchers" (*pragden*) and were set in grain fields at planting time to prevent damage from mice. Mice are a pest that represent in many eastern Indonesian regions the wrath of ancestors toward their descendants because of violations of ethical and ritual laws. Such figures emphasize the harmony between the living and the dead that is necessary for both crop and human fertility.

The missionary-ethnographer Ernst Vatter wrote about the Alor dragon sculptures more generally as protective figures serving both communities and individuals (Vatter 1932:233–37). These figures were placed in the ritual houses located in Alor village centers beside the ceremonial dancing ground. The figures were ritually fed offerings of rice and chicken so that they would protect the lineage community and ensure fertility. Men also could carve their own personal dragon figures to protect themselves and promote good fortune. Such figures had a close association with their creator—for example, the sculpture could never be sold without bringing misfortune to its guardian owner (Vatter 1932:250–51).

In some areas of Alor, the dragon-snake is portrayed naturalistically in sculpture, but in the central and eastern regions its design is abstract (Figs. VII.21, VII.22). The dragon's depiction on a great variety of different objects and its range of stylistic interpretations (see Vatter 1934) suggest that it

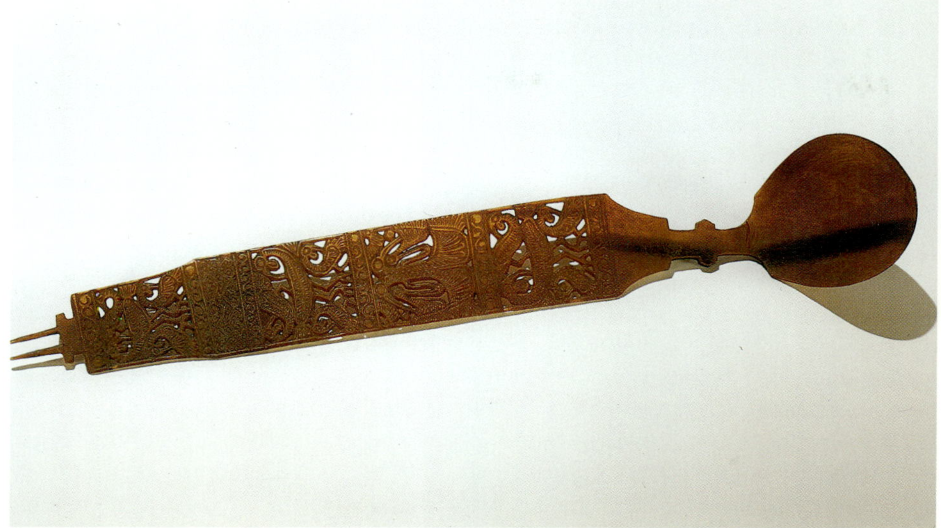

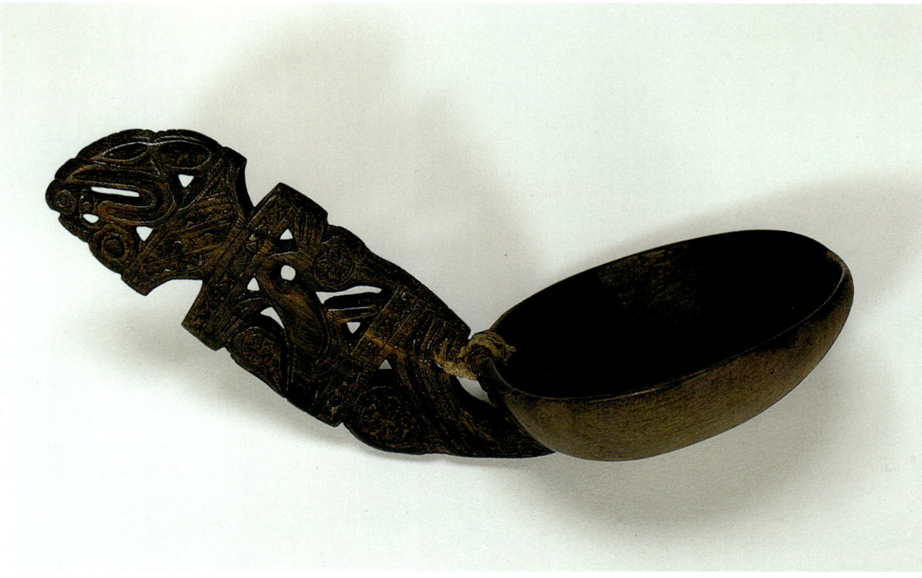

Fig. VII.7 Ceremonial serving spoon
Atoni, West Timor
Buffalo horn, 29 x 4.5 x 5.4
Royal Tropical Institute, Tropenmuseum, The Netherlands, 1772–2159. Donated by G. Tillman, Jr. in 1947.

Fig. VII.8 Ceremonial serving spoon
Tetum, Belu region, Timor
Buffalo horn, 6.5 x 5.5 x 11.5
Rijksmuseum voor Volkenkunde, Leiden, 16-195. Donated by S. Muller in 1861.

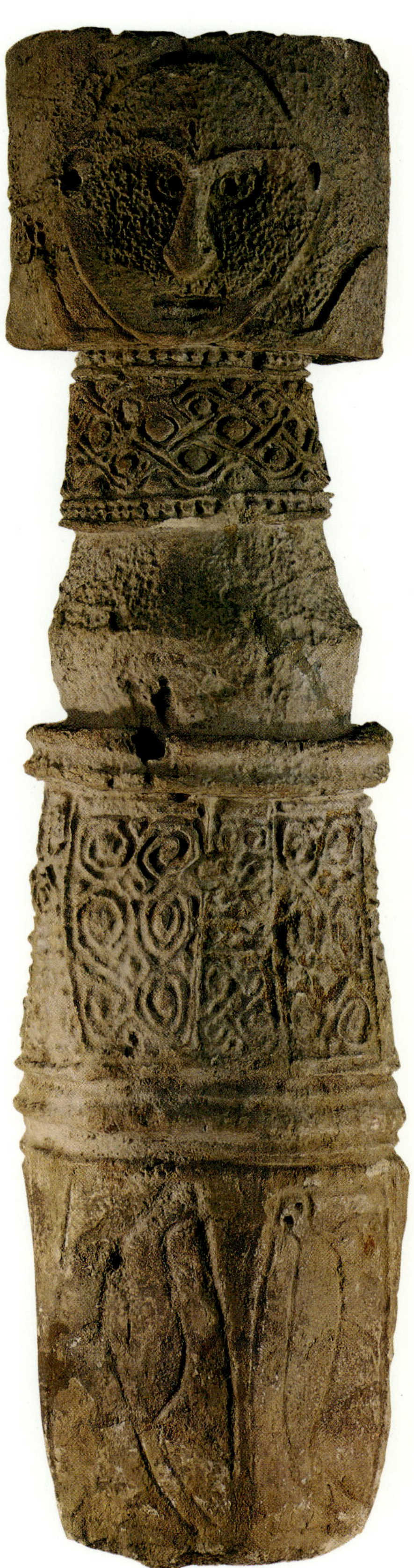

Fig. VII.9 Figurative post, *aitos*
Belu region, Timor
Stone, 93
Jerome L. Joss

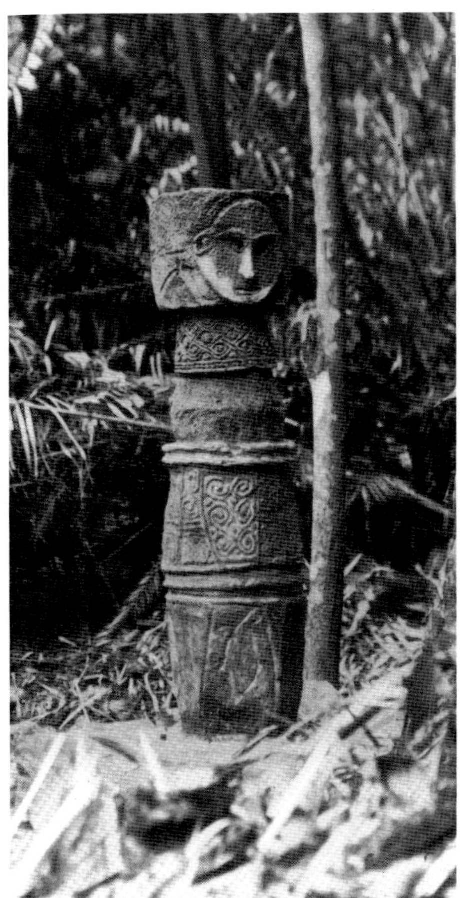

Fig. VII.10 The Tetum male-and-female offering post in Fig. VII.9 as it looked in its original site in Timor, before 1952. Vroklage 1952–53:fig. 233

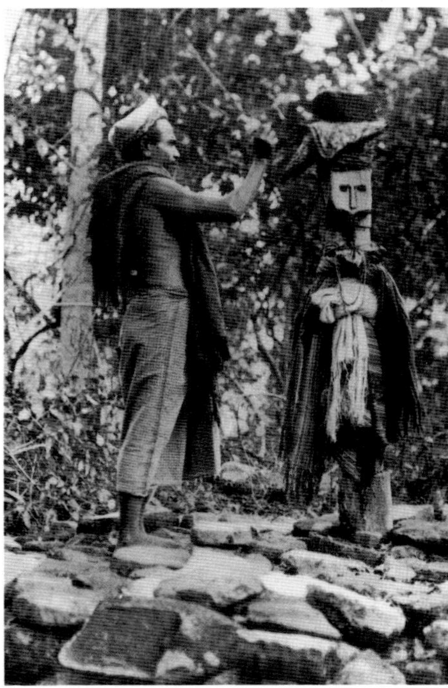

Fig. VII.11 A Tetum man tends the offerings placed on the head of a wooden offering post dressed with heirloom cloths, before 1952. Vroklage 1952–53:fig. 242

was an Alor version of the protective Batak *singa* and Kenyah *aso'* figures (personal communication, Ruth Barnes 1990; see Figs. III.15, V.31). The fanciful openwork carving style of these Alor sculptures is part of a sculptural tradition emphasizing scroll forms that continues eastward into the Moluccas and Cenderawasih Bay (see Figs. IX.22, IX.32, VIII.15–16).

The complementarity of elder and younger in the family is depicted in a sculpture from Atauro (Fig. VII.19), a small and little-known island north of Timor. Although it is not uncommon for rural Indonesian women to nurse their infants publicly within their home community, the image of a nursing mother is rare in Indonesian sculpture. Despite the extraordinary concern and love for infants found throughout the area, outer-island artists far more frequently focus their efforts on images evoking fertility through the combination of male and female elements, rather than on the results of childbirth per se. Squared-off body parts such as feet and hands are typical of the rough-hewn Atauro figures. Such sculptures are not usually found in colonial-era museum collections since the island was not actively occupied by the Dutch. Atauro figures were usually, if not always, carved in matching ancestor pairs, and these pairs were bound together with rope before being sold to private collectors in the 1970s (Moss 1986:12–13). The rope wrapped around the female figure (Fig. VII.19) may have originally tied it to a male counterpart. The mother figure has been dressed in imported cloth and a separate strip of fabric is tied on as a baby carrier.

Social organization in the Lesser Sundas was based on the interdependence of the high and low social ranks. In East Sumba, society was divided between persons who had a standing in one of the patrilineal clans (*kabihu*) and slaves (*ata*) who had been captured in war or sold into bondage because of violations of traditional law (*adat*) (Adams 1969:18–23). The distinctive and less populous group among the freemen was the noble class (*maramba*), who traced their lineage to early village founders.

Lesser Sunda arts also embody such culturally defined concepts as the privilege and power of the aristocratic class. On the island of Roti, for example, patterns of *ikat* cloth distinguish nobles from commoners. High-ranking Roti weavers (Fig. VII.3) pattern the warp *ikat* threads of their cloths to incorporate Indian *patola*-derived patterns that are the prerogative of the aristocrats of precolonial Termanu (personal communication, James Fox 1990).

In East Sumba, one traditional privilege of the leading nobles was the right to erect carved stone tombs and funerary monuments (Figs. VII.18, VII.20), called *penji*, which means "flag" or "flagpole." The shape of the *penji* is not only phallic but also reminiscent of an unfurling fern spiral, a frequent image of generation in Southeast Asia. The relief carving on the surfaces of these vertical stone sculptures is largely symbolic. Chiselled images of heirloom jewelry or aspects of clan history signify the importance and wealth of a deceased noble. The turtle, which is seen on the *penji* in Fig. VII.20, indicates that the deceased was of aristocratic descent. Turtles, considered one of the oldest animals in the sea, are associated with seniority, wisdom, and diplomacy (Hoskins 1988:120). Sumbanese myths describe female ancestors who were kidnapped by crocodile husbands and whose families received golden valuables as marriage gifts in return (Hoskins 1988:131–32). Hence, fish and other sea creatures carved on the *penji* funeral monuments refer to mythical sources of ancestral power. Imported wealth objects, such as the gongs seen on this *penji*, are also often depicted on these stone monuments.

For a very wealthy and prominent Sumba noble's funeral, enormous stones were, and in some regions still are, dragged by hundreds of men for miles to the grave site (Fig. VII.16). At the ensuing feasts, nobles traditionally slaughtered hundreds of buffalo and interred up to a hundred textiles with the corpse (Fig. VII.17). Slaves in East Sumba often played key roles in their masters' ceremonies, being dressed in the finest clothes and playing ceremonial roles as substitutes for their owners (Adams 1980:216). The most valuable clan heirlooms depicted on *penji* were worn not by their noble owners but by the nobles'

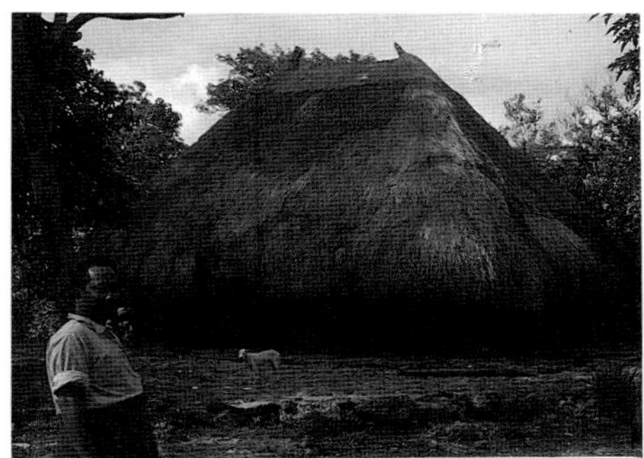

Fig. VII.12 Atoni house, West Timor, 1960. Clark E. Cunningham

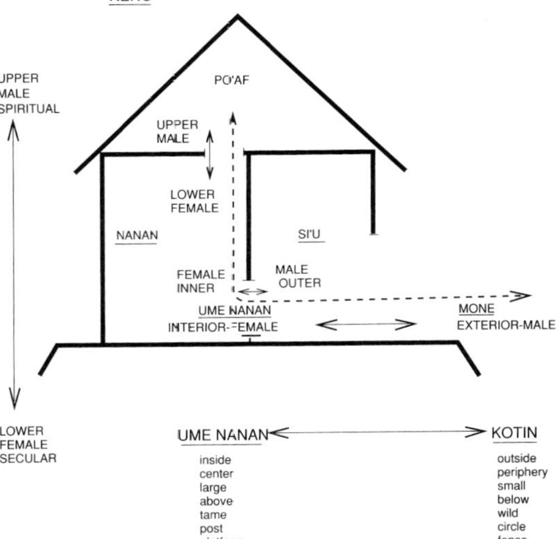

Fig. VII.13 Symbolic divisions of a traditional Atoni house. Cunningham 1964:57. Redrawn by Marcia Bakry, Smithsonian Institution.

slaves, who incurred the risks of wearing such dangerously hot and sacred jewelry for the benefit of their masters (Hoskins 1988:134; see also catalog chapter II).

Many individual elements in Lesser Sunda rituals and artworks refer to a contrasting thematic partner. For example, textiles, which are female goods, are used to fashion Atoni Timor warrior costumes (Fig. VII.23), which were inextricably linked to the male domain of headhunting. Beautifully woven warrior costumes that incorporate colorful elements of slit tapestry (Fig. VII.28) were worn by the warrior at ceremonies after the capture of an enemy head. In some regions, such as Belu, women wore headhunting costumes in ceremonies after the birth of their first child, symbolizing the similar risks of the two ordeals (Gittinger 1979:33). The male and female domains of valuables often incorporate or refer to each other to express the union of complementary elements.

The finely woven headdress (Fig. VII.28) was traditionally worn with the fringe hanging down beside the warrior's face (Fig. VII.26). The body of the textile is patterned with zigzag bands dividing repeated *sekong* motifs, a design composed of four spirals sprouting from a center resembling human limbs. The fringe motifs include s-spirals, hourglass shapes, and outlines of four-limbed beings. The rhythmic alternation of natural-dye colors—red, ochre, and two shades of blue on a taupe background—set the patterns in vivid relief and dramatize the figure-ground relationships within each row of motifs.

Among the Atoni of Timor, the roles of ruling political and ritual leaders were symbolically classified as male or female. The cooperation of these two executive leaders was seen as complementary and necessary for prosperity. The traditional headhunting warrior (Fig. VII.24), as representative of the secular community leader of each Atoni domain or princedom, was a symbolic male counterpart to a sacred ritual leader who, although a man, was considered female (Schulte Nordholt 1971; Cunningham 1965).

Foremost among male goods owned by patrilineal clans in the Lesser Sundas were the warrior's weapons, chiefly swords (Figs. VII.25, VII.27). Sword blades often were obtained from European swords, and many bear the stamp of the Dutch East India Company (*VOC*, for Verenigde Oost-Indische Compagnie) or Portuguese inscriptions. Sheath decorations including geometric carvings are of Timorese design, often sporting a large silver crescent moon and protruding silver buffalo horns (Fig. VII.25). According to Schulte Nordholt (1971:340–42), the waxing moon symbol represented growth and the buffalo horns symbolized power and strength. These elaborate and unwieldy sheaths, traditionally adorned with the hair of a sacrificed animal, emphasize the dramatic importance of weapons and war costumes for impressing allies and for terrorizing enemies.

The Male Gifts of Metal

Similar to the practices of the Batak of Sumatra, Lesser Sunda marriage practices include the exchange of female textiles for male metals or ivory (Adams 1969; Barnes 1974:282–83; Forth 1981; Hicks 1976:83; Rodgers 1985). As Hoskins writes about Sumba, "the transfer of valuables at marriage organizes a widespread system of affinal ties which form the backbone of the Sumbanese political and religious organization" (Hoskins 1988:131). In certain areas of East Sumba, only the payment of bridewealth incorporates a wife and offspring into a husband's clan. The standard gifts brought by wife-takers, or the groom's family, to the wife-givers, or the bride's family, make up the bridewealth. Marriages can, if necessary, take place without the bridewealth payment, but then the wife and children remain allied to the wife's natal clan (Forth 1981:368). Important gifts given by the husband's family are gold pendants (*mamuli*) and chains (Fig. VII.30).

Goldsmithing in Sumba was formerly dominated by immigrants from the nearby islands of Ndao and Savu or by resident Chinese, although recently many Sumbanese themselves have entered the trade (Fox 1977:29; Rodgers 1985:

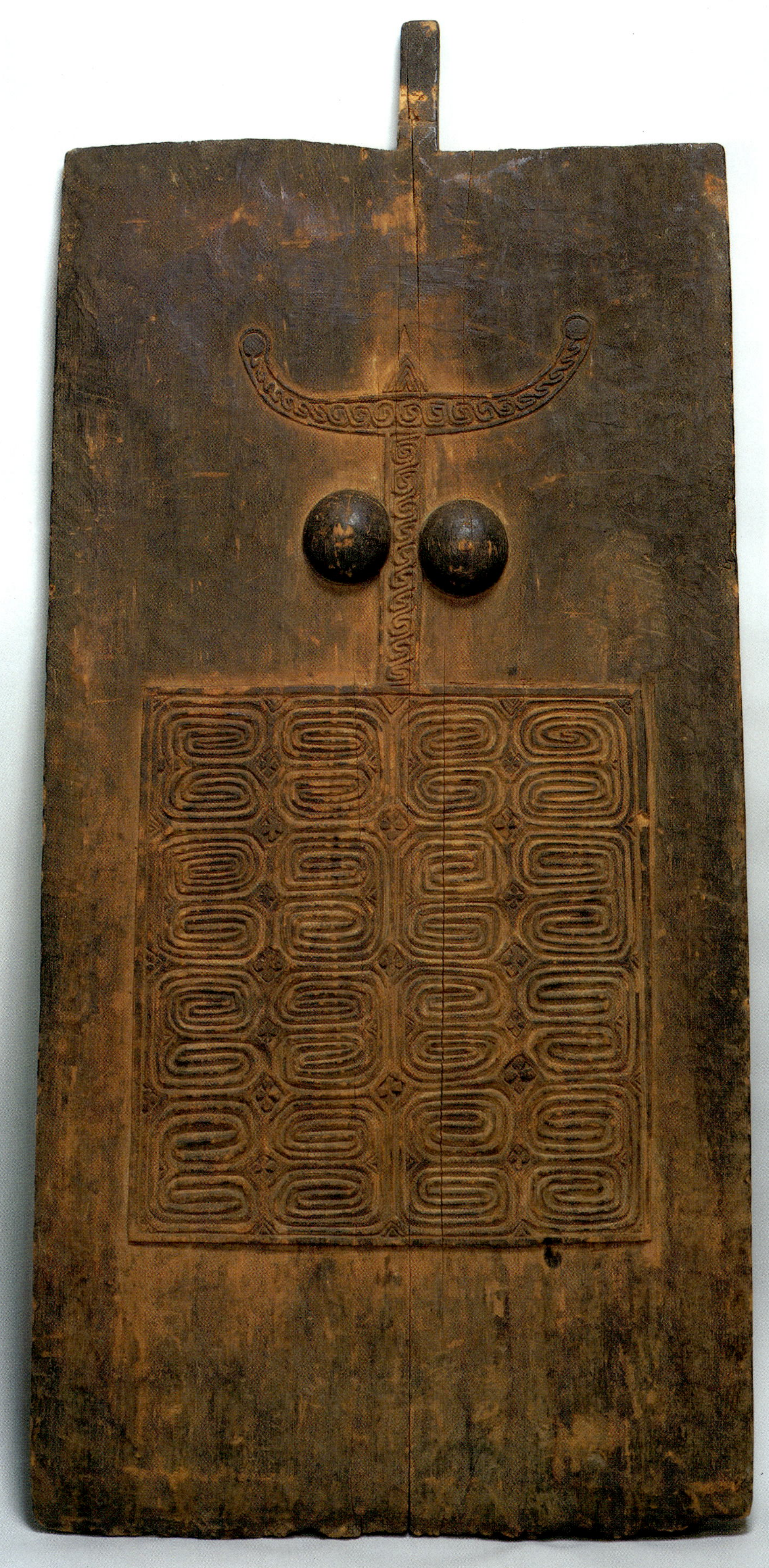

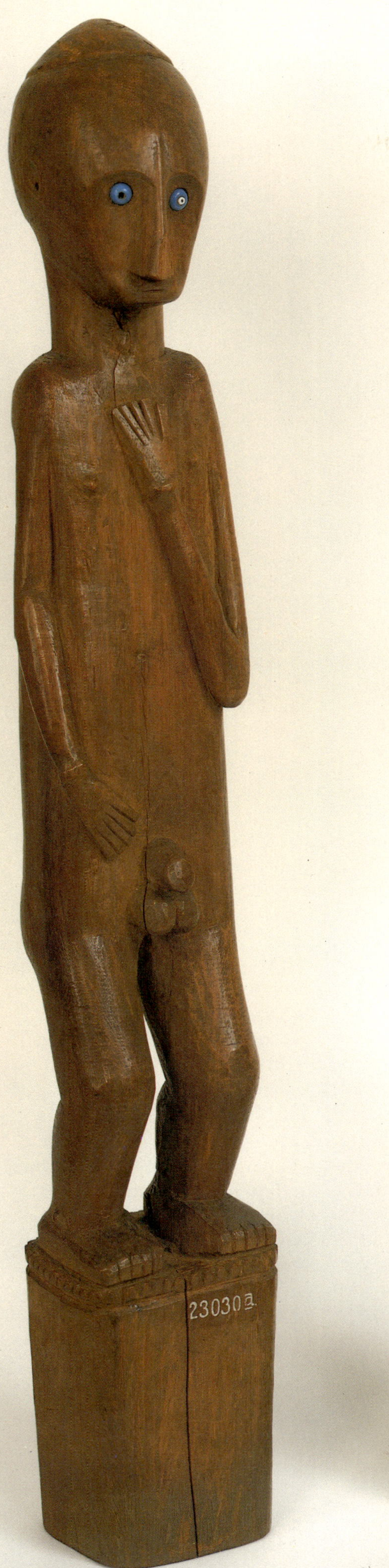

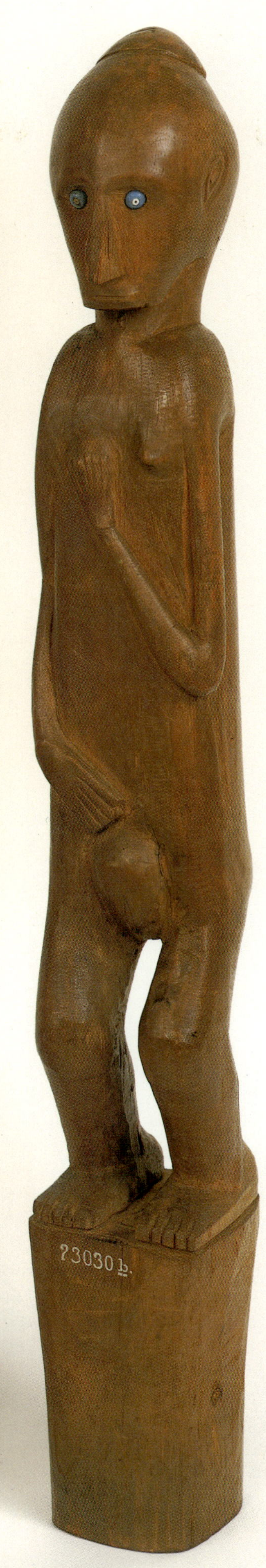

OPPOSITE
Fig. VII.14 DOOR, *ODA MATAN*
Tetum, Belu region, Timor
Wood, 140.8 x 64.7 x 11.2
Rijksmuseum voor Volkenkunde, Leiden, 2380-267. Donated by B. A. G. Vroklage in 1939.

Fig. VII.15 MALE AND FEMALE FIGURES, *ANA DEO*
Ngada, Flores
Wood, glass beads, 59 x 7.5 x 8; 59.9 x 9.5 x 9.3
Museum Nasional Indonesia, Jakarta, 23030a. Donated by J. A. van Staveren in 1938.

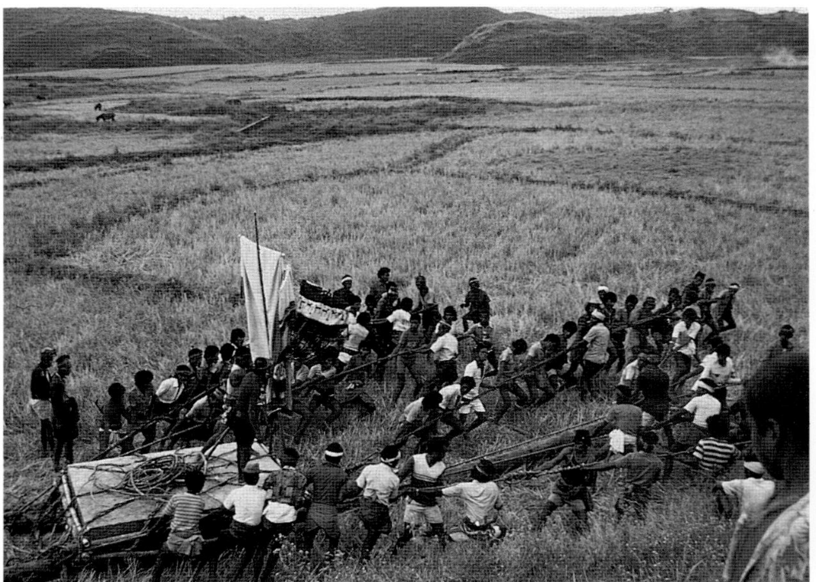

Fig. VII.16 Men dragging the top piece of a tombstone, carried on a wooden sledge, from a quarry to their village. Two men's mantles, donated by the family of the sponsor's wife, are raised as banners above the stone, while the man beside them sings traditional stone-dragging songs, Anakalang, West Sumba, 1986/87. Webb Keane

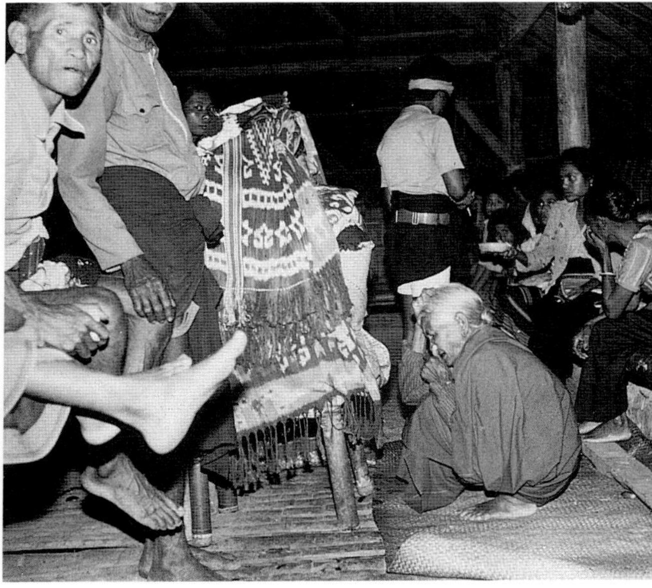

Fig. VII.17 Mourners at a wake keep watch and sing keening songs over the body of a deceased relative. During the weeks prior to burial, numerous textiles are donated in honor of the deceased; some are interred but most are redistributed to surviving family members, Anakalang, West Sumba, 1987. Webb Keane

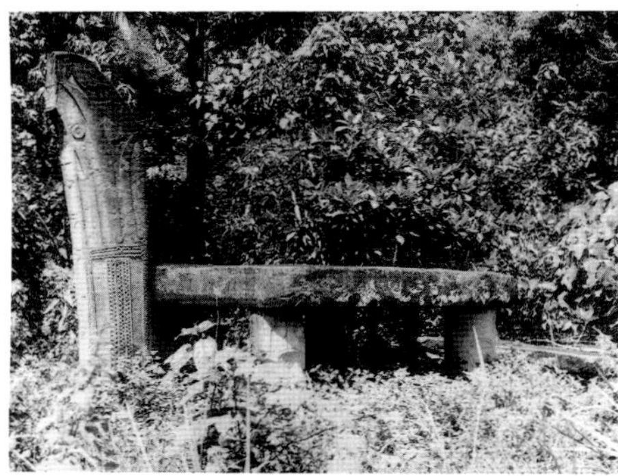

Fig. VII.18 Commemorative monument (*penji*) with stone tomb, Weijelo, East Sumba, 1976. Gabriel Barbier-Mueller

167). Gold and other precious metals were accumulated on the island after the seventeenth century when the Dutch colonial authorities traded coins to local nobles in exchange for the small horses bred by the Sumbanese. Noble families traditionally keep sacred caches of clan valuables called "possessions of the ancestors" (*tanggu marapu*), which include ancient textiles, weapons, ceramics, looms, and gold ornaments (see Rodgers 1985 for a discussion of the full range of Sumba jewelry).

Among the most beautifully crafted and symbolic of these clan heirlooms are ear pendants (Fig. VII.29). These, like other precious clan valuables, are stored in the dark loft of a clan house and are associated with the clan's founding ancestors (Forth 1981; Rodgers 1985; Geirnaert 1989b:459). The oldest *mamuli* heirlooms, which are used periodically in ceremonies contacting clan ancestors, are almost never traded in marriage-alliance exchanges. *Mamuli* that have been more recently traded into the house can be worn and then given away again in marital exchanges. According to early Dutch reports (Rouffaer 1911), battles were at one time waged over ownership of particularly valuable *mamuli*, which signified clan leadership and hereditary rights. The portrayal of the most sacred *mamuli* ornaments on stone grave monuments (Fig. VII.31) was intended to indicate their privileged, and ideally, continuing ownership. Keane writes, "the tomb is particularly suitable as the most permanent sign of a stable value. It is death which removes a person, as a corporeal and individual presence, from the risks of exchange, and constitutes a first step to becoming an ancestor and a *marapu* [ancestor spirit], elevated like a clan valuable beyond circumstance and change" (Keane 1988:11).

Sumbanese say the *mamuli* shape represents the female sexual organs (Hoskins 1988:125; Forth 1981:360). Holmgren and Spertus have documented this identification as it appears in the iconography of Sumba textiles by illustrating a *mamuli* shape located in the anatomically correct place on a female figure (Holmgren and Spertus 1989:31–32). Nevertheless, there are both male and

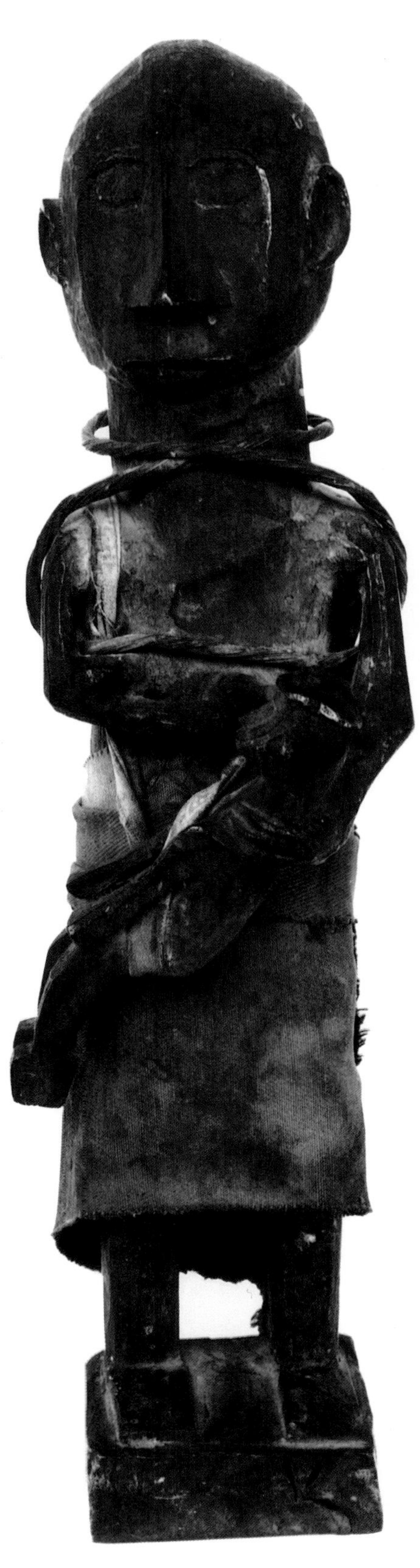

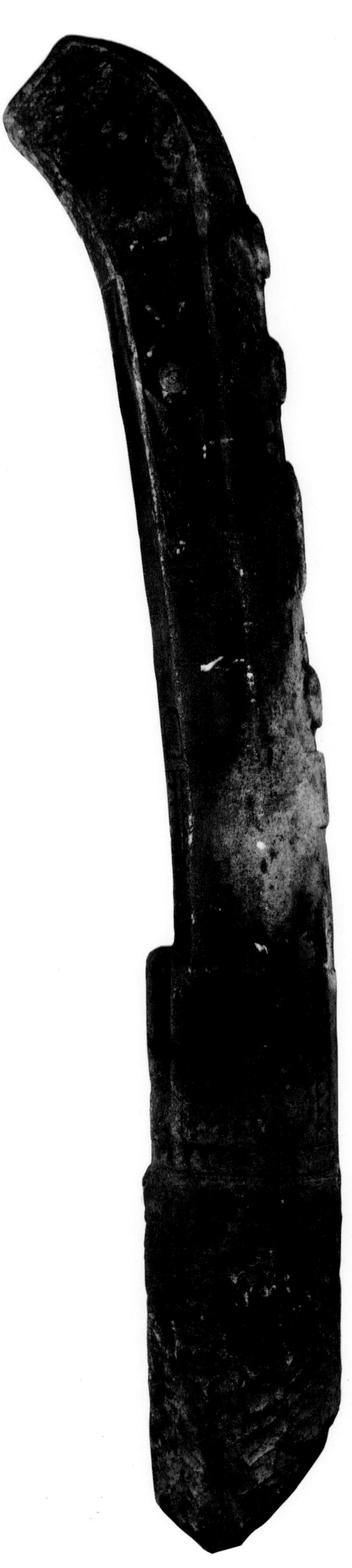

Fig. VII.19 FEMALE FIGURE WITH CHILD
Atauro
Wood, 27 x 7.5 x 9
Dr. and Mrs. Robert Kuhn

Fig. VII.20 FUNERARY HEADSTONE, *PENJI*
East Sumba
Stone, 259.1 x 53.8 x 30.5
Barbier-Mueller Museum, Geneva, 3686C

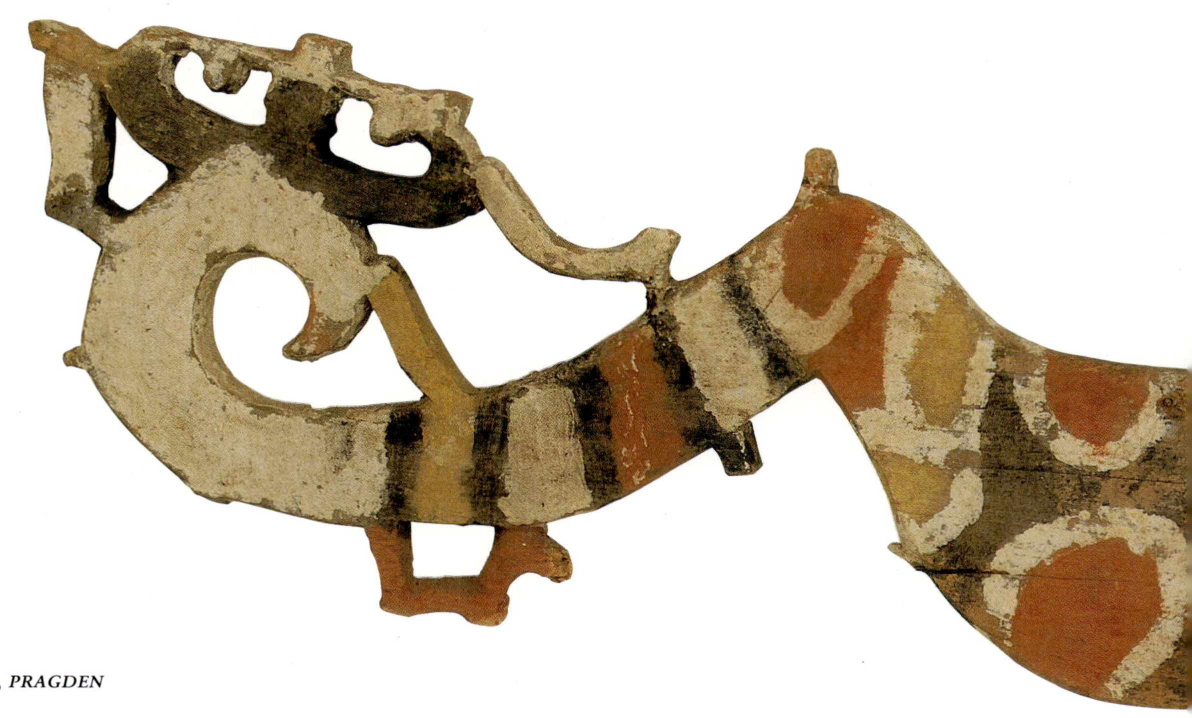

Fig. VII.21 Dragon effigy, *pragden*
Alor
Wood, pigment, 88 x 34.5 x 72
Museum Nasional Indonesia, Jakarta, 18890

Fig. VII.22 Dragon effigy, *pragden*
Alor
Wood, pigment, 35.5 x 106.5 x 7.5
Museum Nasional Indonesia, Jakarta, 18899.
Donated by A. A. van Dalen in 1924.

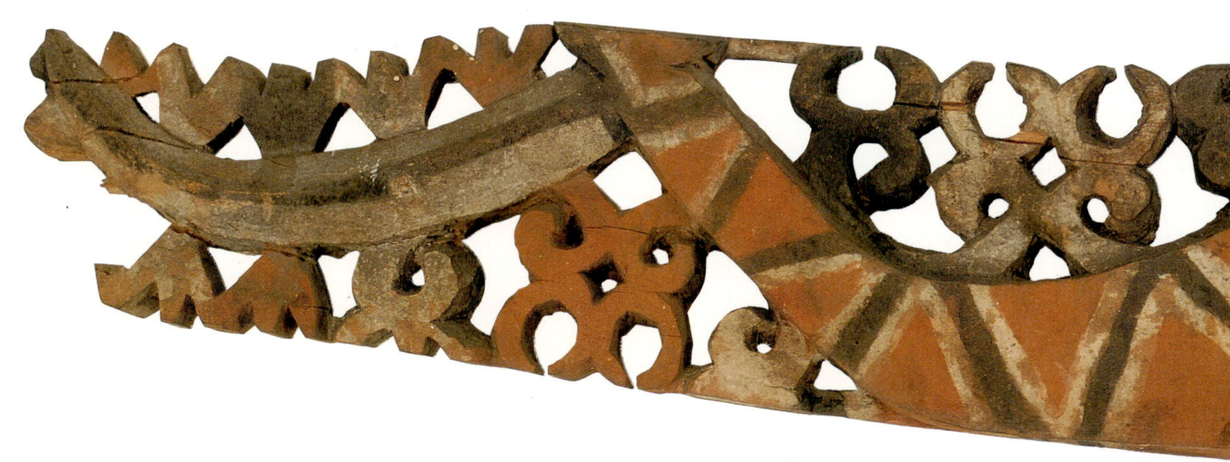

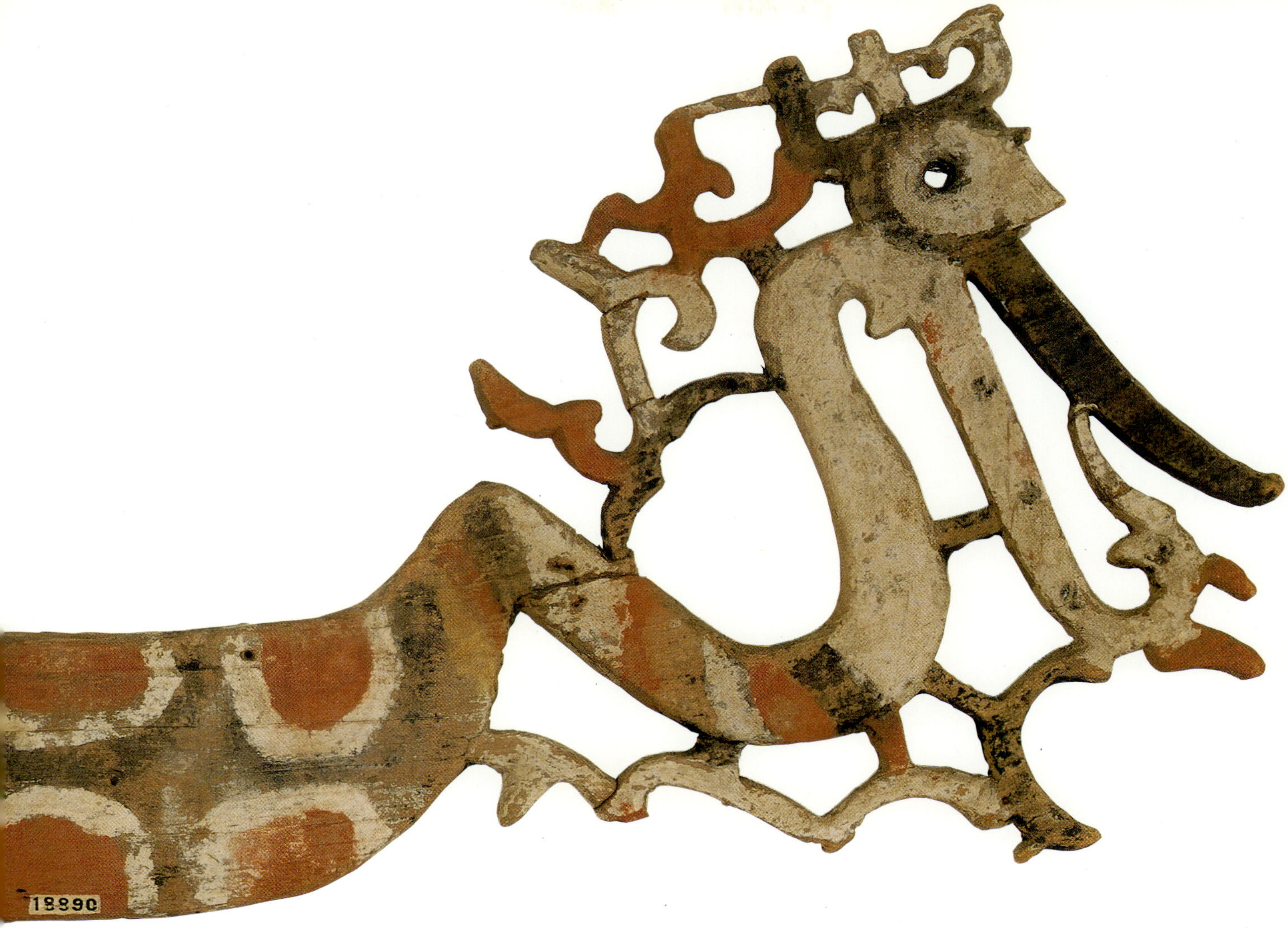

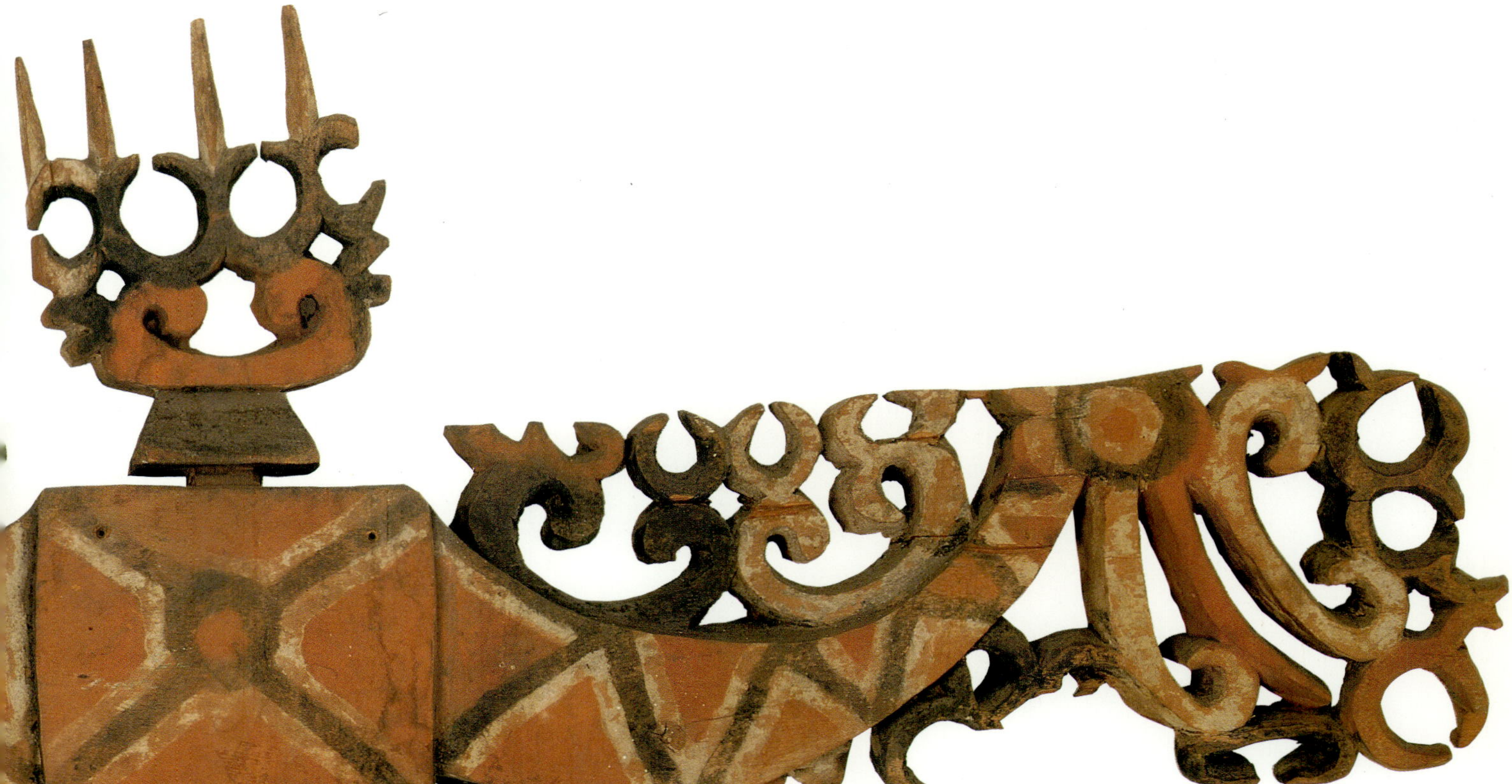

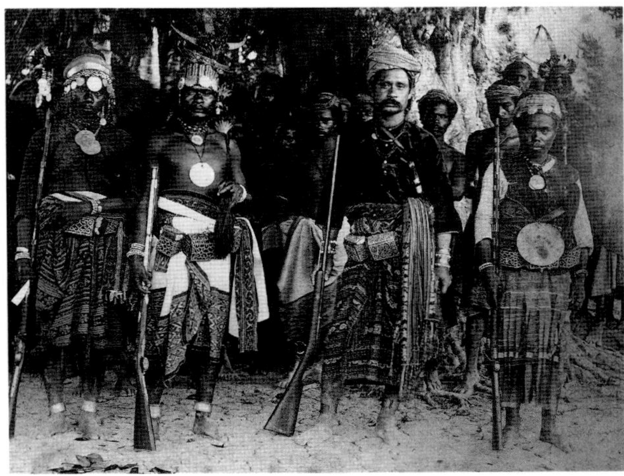

Fig. VII.23 Atoni men wearing warrior costumes, Amarasi region, West Timor, circa 1890. Courtesy Museum voor Volkenkunde, Rotterdam.

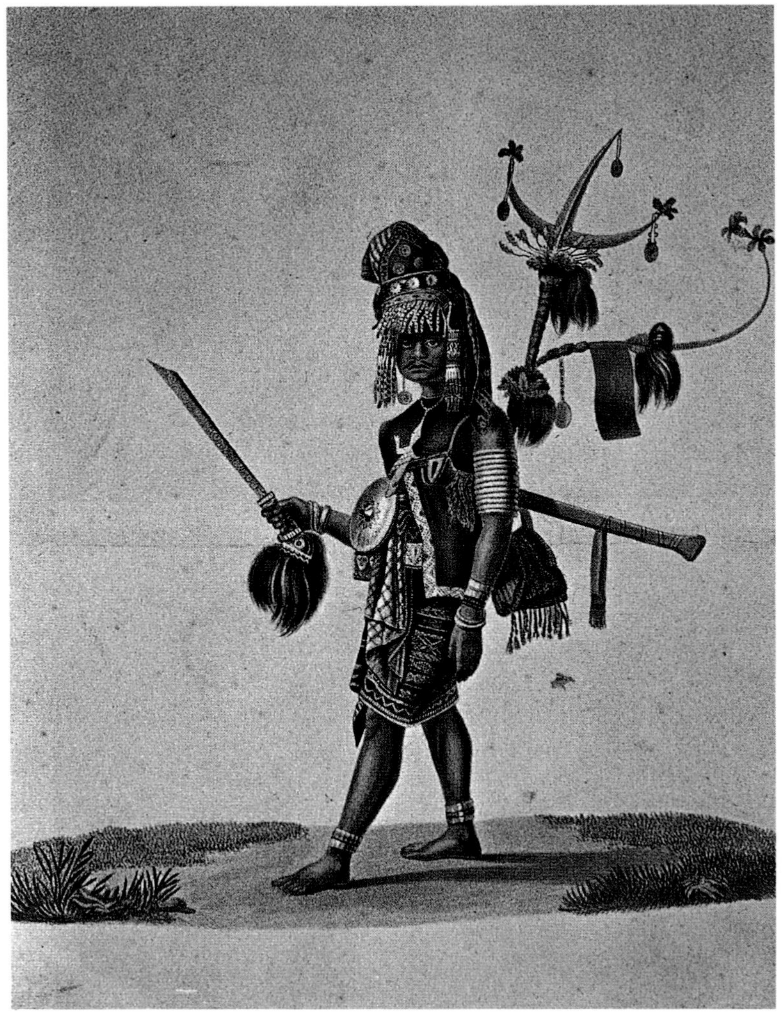

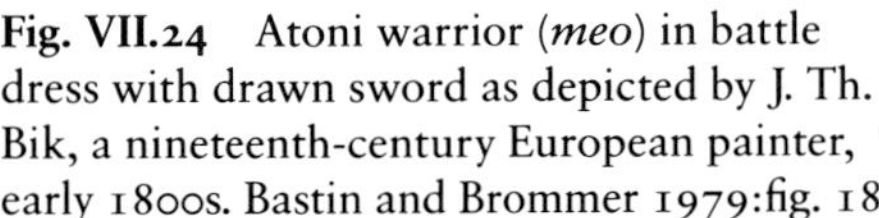

Fig. VII.24 Atoni warrior (*meo*) in battle dress with drawn sword as depicted by J. Th. Bik, a nineteenth-century European painter, early 1800s. Bastin and Brommer 1979:fig. 18

female *mamuli*. Those ornamented with metal-braid spirals and beads or with decorated bases, or "feet" (*ledu*), are considered male; those that are plain and without feet are considered female (Geirnaert 1989b:459). The bases are often decorated with bird figures, especially cockatoos (Fig. VII.29). According to Adams (1969:142), in East Sumba only members of the nobility owned *mamuli* with very elaborate figures at their base. The finely wrought figurative decorations are warriors in battle dress with accompanying slaves and "skull trees" (ceremonial stands for headhunting trophies and buffalo horns) set beside forked stakes, traditional Southeast Asian monuments commemorating sacrificial feasts. Hoskins points out that the human and animal figures adorning the *mamuli* bases are always male, "representations of the wealth and power of the men who give *mamuli* to acquire wives" (Hoskins 1988:125). In this way, *mamuli* refer to both male and female forces, which are joined through the exchange of gifts that result in the union of marriage.

On Sumba, prospective grooms present *mamuli* to the bride's family during marriage negotiations. They are one of the standard gifts brought by the wife-takers, the others being buffalo, horses, dogs, weapons, and other gold ornaments. The wife-givers give counter-gifts of pigs, cloth, rice, ivory bracelets, and sometimes gongs (Geirnaert 1989b:456). The following passage describes the *mamuli*'s symbolic significance as an irreplaceable marriage gift:

> In the context of marriage prestations, in daily life, and in myth, a *mamuli* appears to be a substitute for the body of the bride. It is a replacement for her capacity for giving life from the moment *mawo* and *dewa* [soul elements] are joined together, until death, when putrefaction sets them apart once more. The *mamuli* embroidered on the plaited betel and areca nut bags, worn by married women of childbearing age, refer to this idea. At weddings, the *mamuli* is a countergift for the fertility that is given away by the house. The flow of *mamuli* between houses characterizes marriage exchanges.
>
> (Geirnaert 1989b:460, bracketed words added)

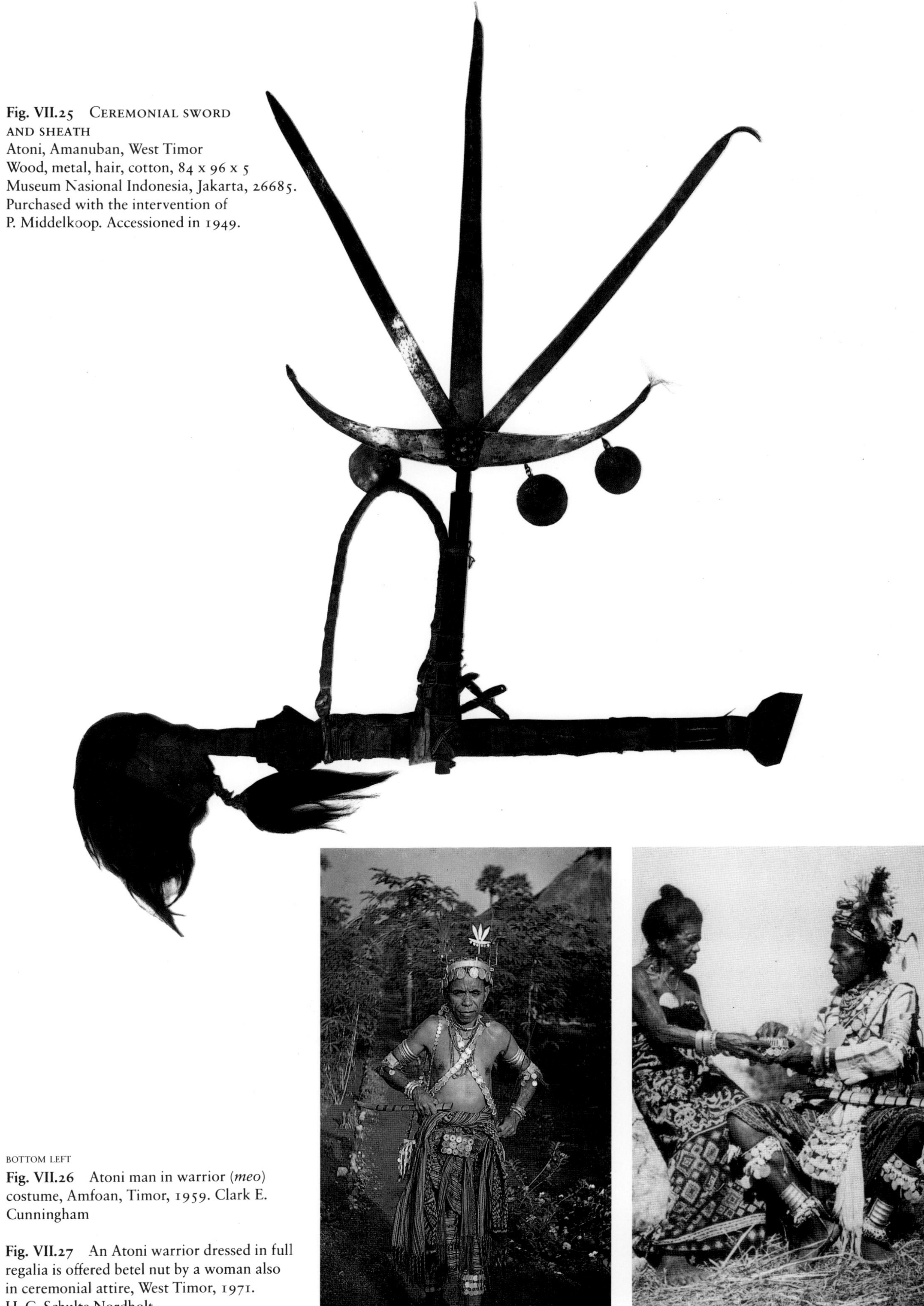

Fig. VII.25 Ceremonial sword and sheath
Atoni, Amanuban, West Timor
Wood, metal, hair, cotton, 84 x 96 x 5
Museum Nasional Indonesia, Jakarta, 26685.
Purchased with the intervention of P. Middelkoop. Accessioned in 1949.

BOTTOM LEFT

Fig. VII.26 Atoni man in warrior (*meo*) costume, Amfoan, Timor, 1959. Clark E. Cunningham

Fig. VII.27 An Atoni warrior dressed in full regalia is offered betel nut by a woman also in ceremonial attire, West Timor, 1971. H. G. Schulte Nordholt

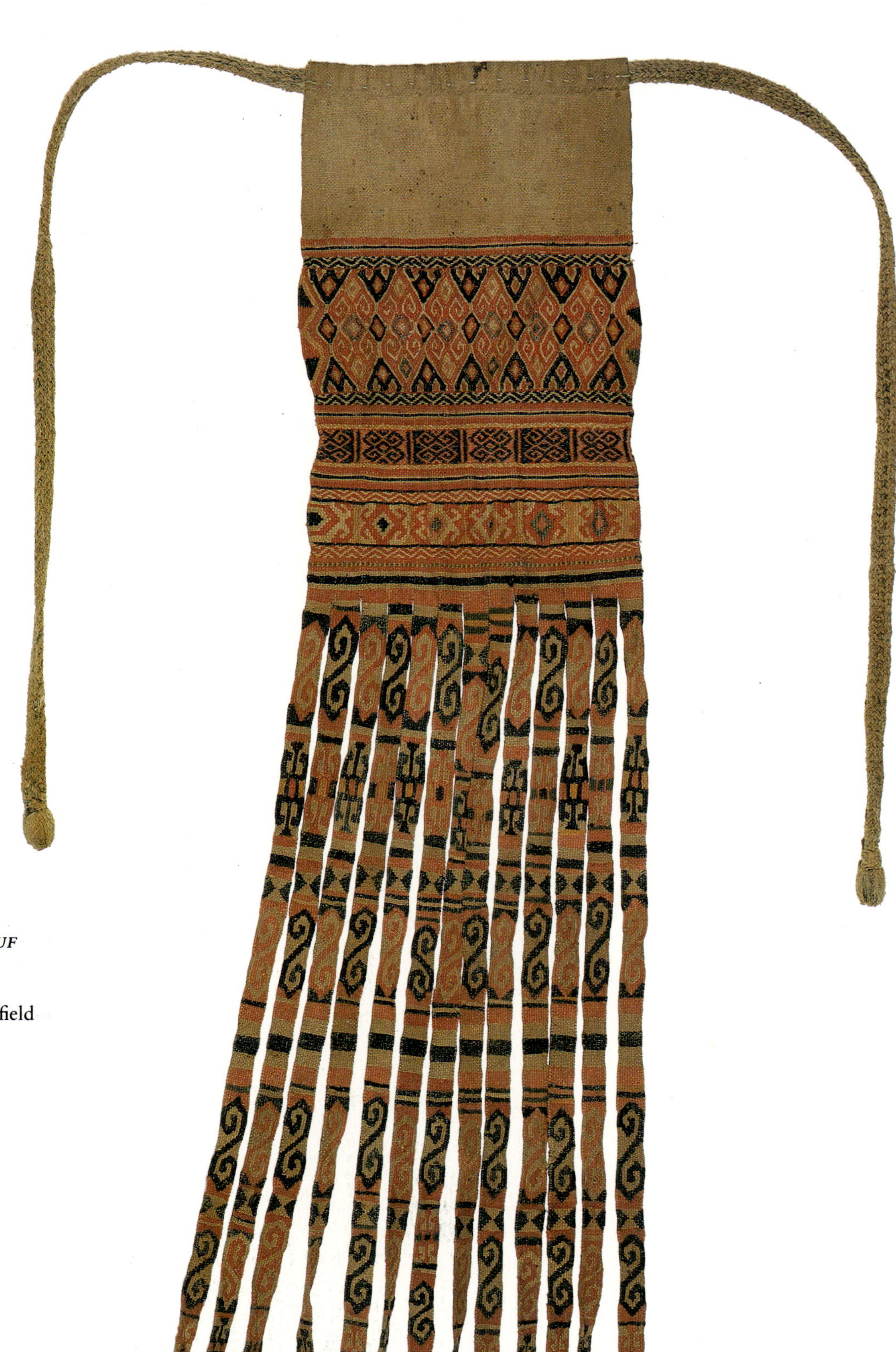

Fig. VII.28 Headdress of a headhunter's costume, *pilu saluf*
Atoni, West Timor
Cotton, 59 x 98
Collection of John and Anne Summerfield

OPPOSITE
Fig. VII.29 Ear ornaments, *mamuli*
Sumba
Gold, 8 x 6.5 x 1.6; 7 x 6 x 1.4; 10 x 9.3 x 2; 10 x 10.2 x 2.2
Collection of Anita E. Spertus and Robert J. Holmgren, New York (left top and bottom)
Metropolitan Museum of Art, New York (right top and bottom)

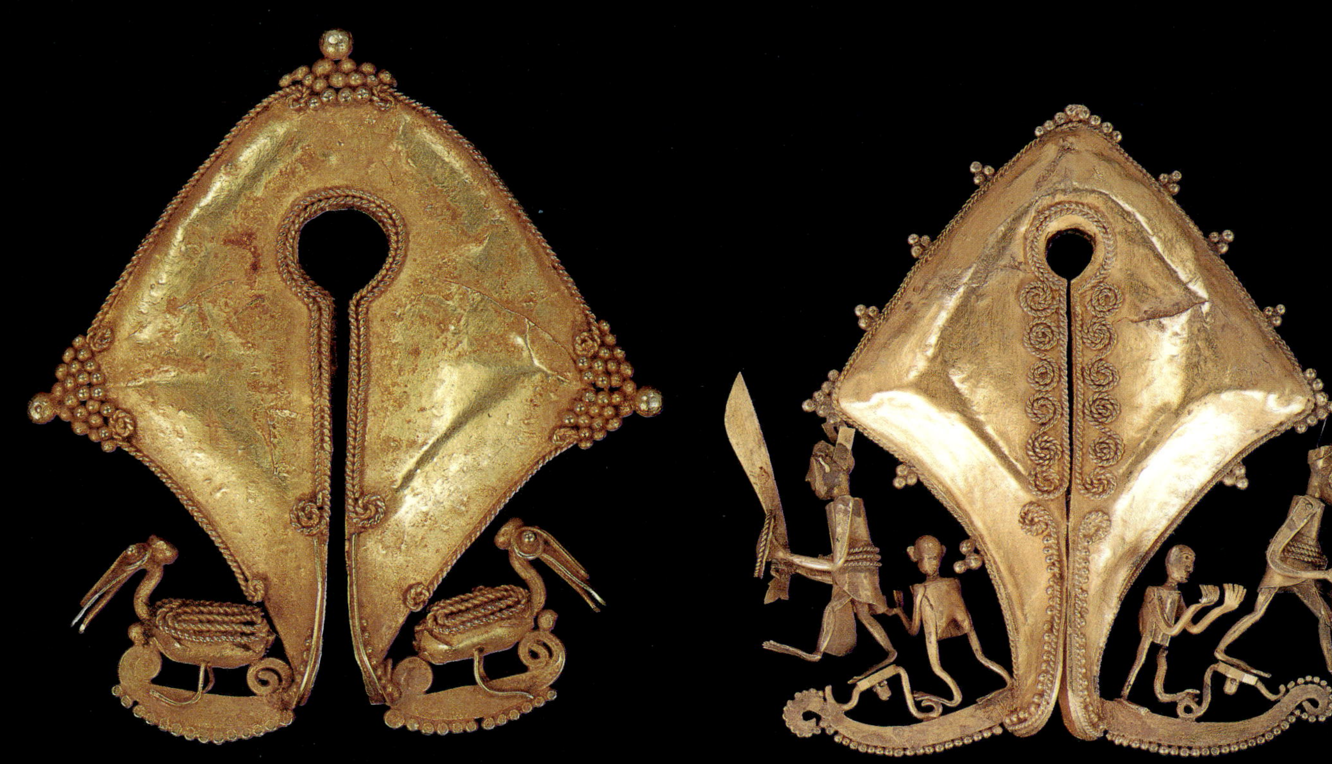

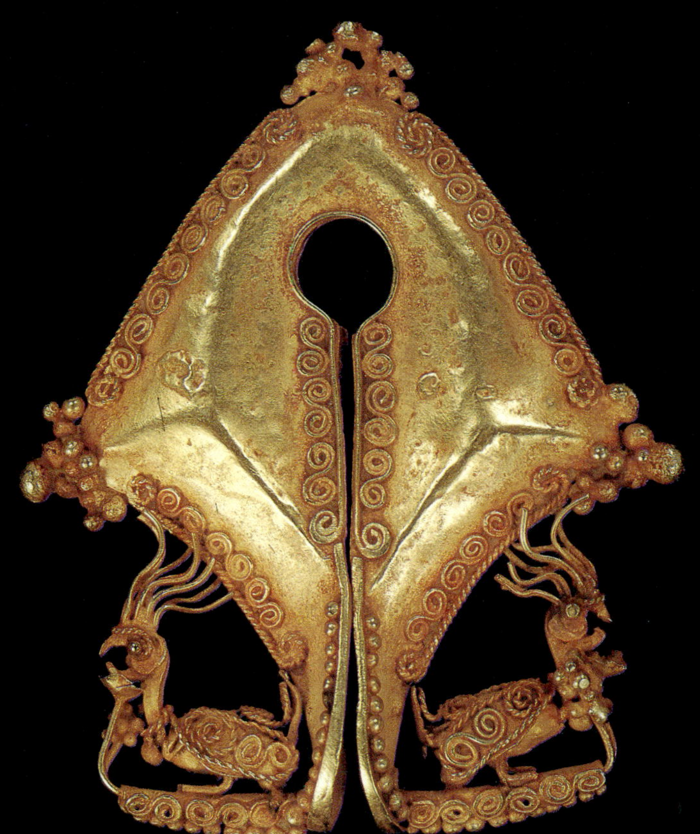

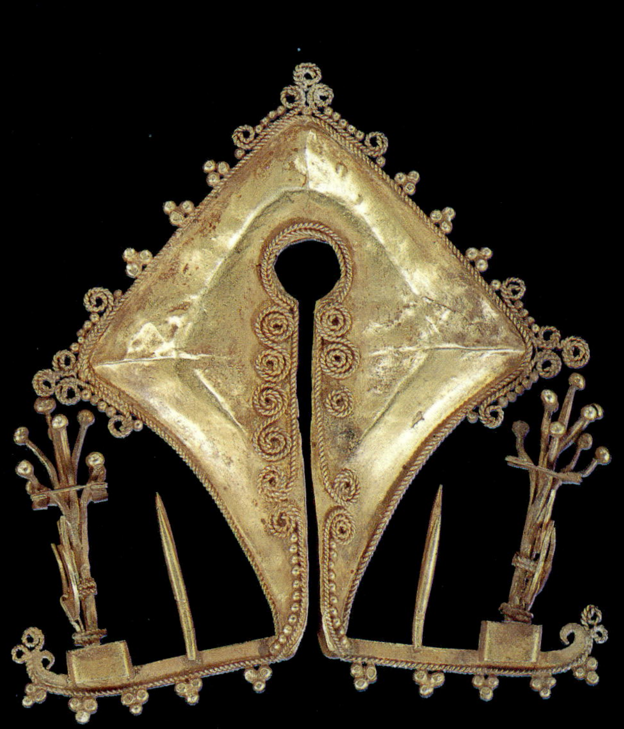

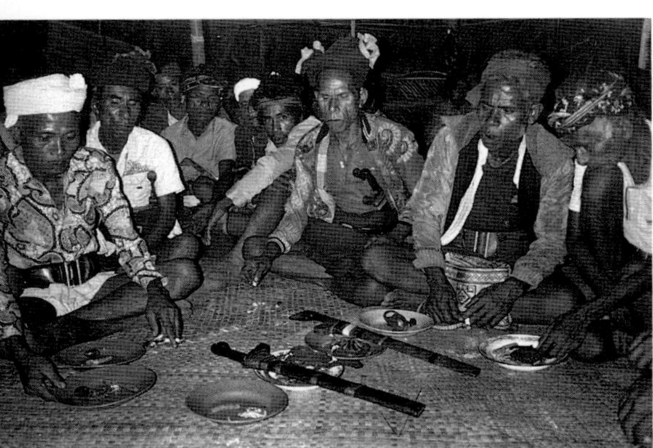

Fig. VII.30 Elders of bride's family have just received dishes of marriage-alliance gifts from groom's family. The plates represent horses or buffalo that will be given and, in addition to betel-nut refreshment, they contain *mamuli* ornaments, spun-copper chains, and machetes, Anakalang, West Sumba, 1987. Webb Keane

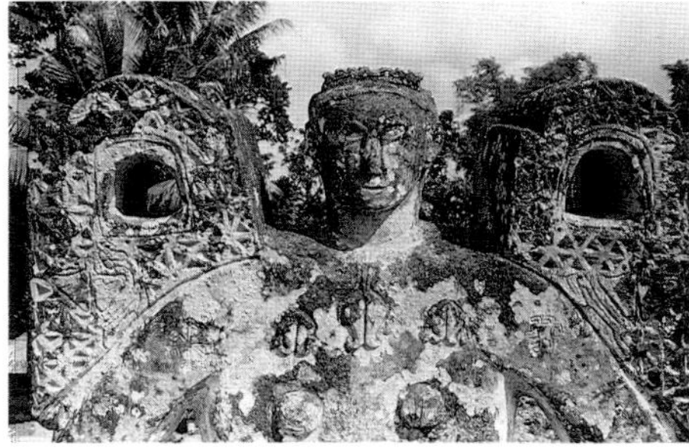

Fig. VII.31 The most rare and prestigious stone monument is a carved vertical stone set at the head of a tomb. This "horn of a tomb" or "flag" (*penji*) is decorated with a female figure wearing *mamuli* ornaments, West Sumba, 1987. Webb Keane

Like *mamuli*, the looped pendants from Flores called *taka* are inherited from parents or received as bridewealth (Rodgers 1985:329). *Taka* ornaments can be worn by women or men around the neck or on headbands. Before wearing them in ceremonies, a person asks permission to borrow them from the ancestors by sacrificing a small animal. This simple but elegant design (Fig. VII.37) is frequently used on Lesser Sunda breast ornaments of various sizes; on Flores it is said to represent an ax head. The distinctive form of *taka* pendants are carved as design ornaments on the walls of traditional houses in the area of the Ngada people (see Rodgers 1985:329, fig. 117) just as *mamuli* appear as motifs on Sumbanese stone monuments and textiles.

Aristocrats on the island of Savu traditionally wore royal chains of office (Fig. VII.35; Fox 1977:121). The extremely fine quality of manufacture of many of the oldest gold chains indicates a knowledge of metalworking probably derived from Javanese or other Southeast Asian courts (personal communication, James Fox 1990). This knowledge was acquired by smiths from the island of Ndao, an area with few natural resources and food supplies. Ndao goldsmiths developed a highly successful subsistence strategy of producing and trading jewelry throughout the Lesser Sundas for food and other necessities. The products of goldsmiths from Ndao, Roti, and Savu include delicately wrought chains (Fig. VII.38), which were used not only for heirlooms of nobility but also in marriage exchanges. Early Dutch reports list gold chains as important male goods given to the bride's family during Sumba wedding ceremonies (de Roo van Alderwelt 1890). East Sumbanese identify long jewelry chains as a male counterpart to the female *mamuli* (see Fig. VII.30; Onvlee 1949:453; Forth 1981:360), again illustrating their invariable assignment of male and female identities to materials, objects, shapes, and motifs.

Prior to the nineteenth century, on the island of Alor, hourglass-shaped bronze drums called *moko* (Fig. VII.32) were traded as part of marriage-alliance and other gift exchanges (Fig. VII.33). How these drums first came to be imported to Alor is unknown, but some of the earliest ones were produced during the Bronze Age, perhaps associated with the Dongson culture of Vietnam (Bernet Kempers 1988:365). By 1900 newly made facsimiles in brass were imported to Alor from Java and traded as currency for agricultural produce. The introduction by outside entrepreneurs of thousands of newly made *moko* drums created havoc in the local monetary system during a time when the colonial government was trying to establish a stable currency. In 1914 the Dutch colonial government introduced silver and copper coins. They simultaneously forbad the use of *moko* as currency, but, in order to draw as many drums as possible out of circulation, tax payments could be paid with *moko* drums. As a result, at least 1,660 drums were acquired by Dutch officials, who had them flattened and sold as scrap metal. The government did allow drums remaining on Alor to be used in marriage-alliance gift exchanges (Du Bois 1944).

Even at the time when Alor was flooded with both Bronze Age and newly made *moko* drums, the Alor people classified them according to age, decor, and individual *moko* trade histories (Bernet Kempers 1988:367–70). Some designs were favored over others and a drum owned in the past by a prominent person was considered more valuable than one that was not. Alor people were apparently well aware that the newer brass drums were manufactured at Gresik in Java or imported by Makassar traders. Besides being valuables exchanged at weddings and other ceremonial occasions, *moko* drums were used in Alor as musical instruments. They were played at important events by striking their top surface with the palm of the hand, much like the indigenous hourglass-shaped wooden drums are played throughout the Lesser Sundas, the Moluccas, and New Guinea (Fig. VII.34). The oldest *moko* drums were venerated as the sacred abode of ancestral spirits and hence rarely traded in marriage exchanges (Du Bois 1944).

Moko ornamentation, especially in the newer models such as the one in Fig. VII.32, tends to be more floral and Chinese- or Indian-influenced than that

Fig. VII.32 DRUM, *MOKO*
Brass, 39 x 24.5
Museum Nasional Indonesia, Jakarta, 27256.
Manufactured in East Java and purchased in Jakarta for 350 rupiah in 1954.

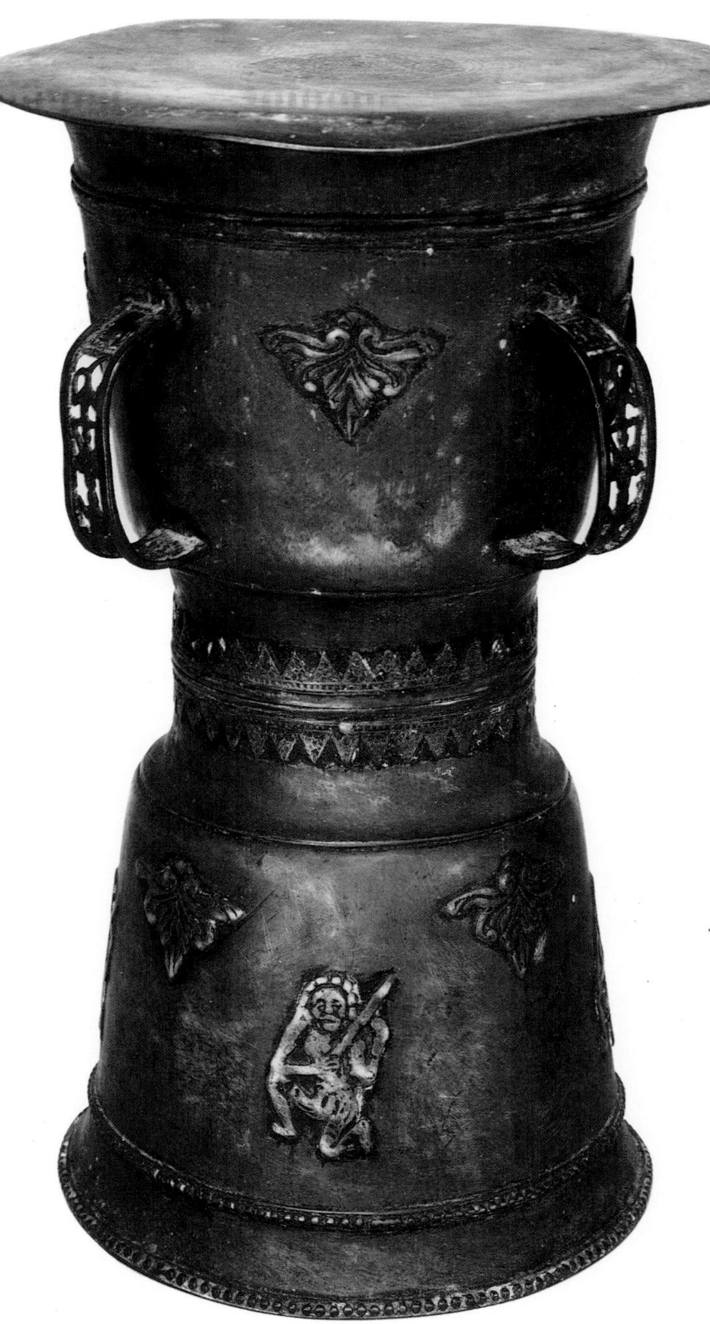

Fig. VII.33 *Moko* drums and gongs on display at a funeral feast. They are placed around the traditional village altar in order of their local value, Alor, before 1944.
Du Bois 1944: following p. 32–33. Copyright © 1944 by the University of Minnesota, 1972 Cora Du Bois.

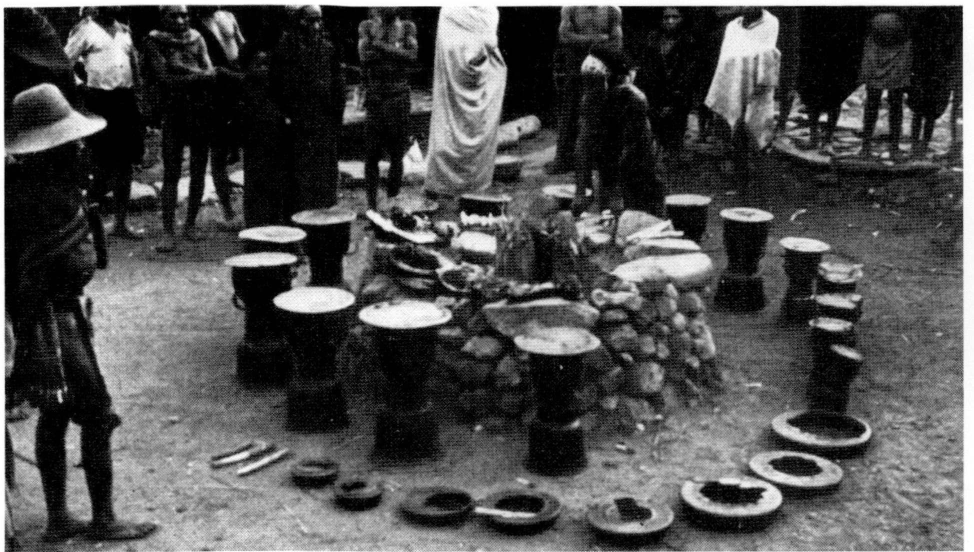

Fig. VII.34 Tetum women of Timor play drums during a traditional dance, Belu region, Timor. Vroklage 1952–53:fig. 311

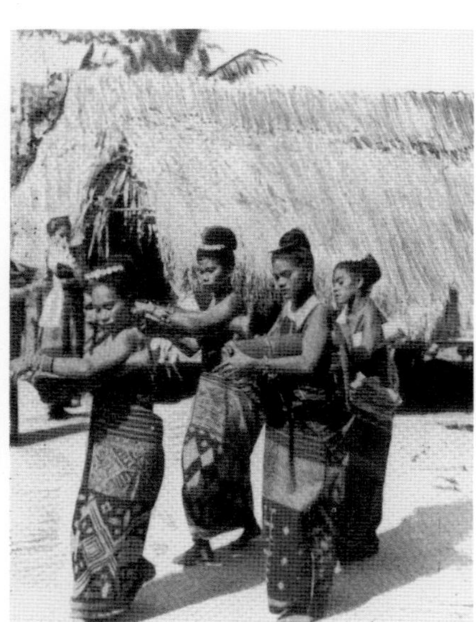

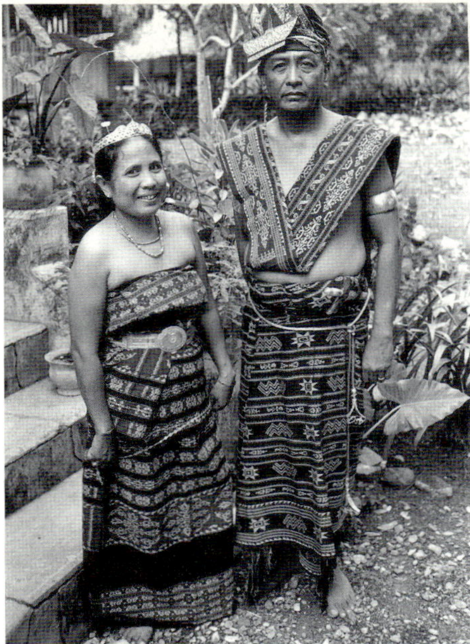

Fig. VII.35 The former hereditary ruler of Sèba, D. D. Bireludji, wearing an heirloom gold chain and standing with his wife who also wears the ceremonial dress of their region on Savu, before 1977. James J. Fox

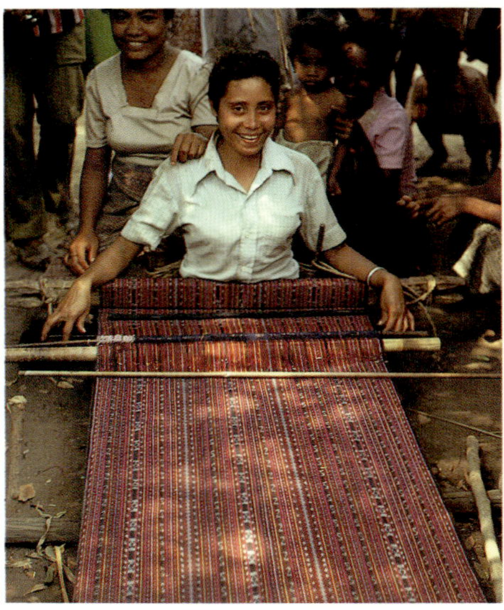

Fig. VII.36 A Lamaholot woman weaving an almost-completed woman's cloth. Textiles from this region do not include center panels that have Indian-derived *patola* motifs, Solor, 1982. Ruth Barnes

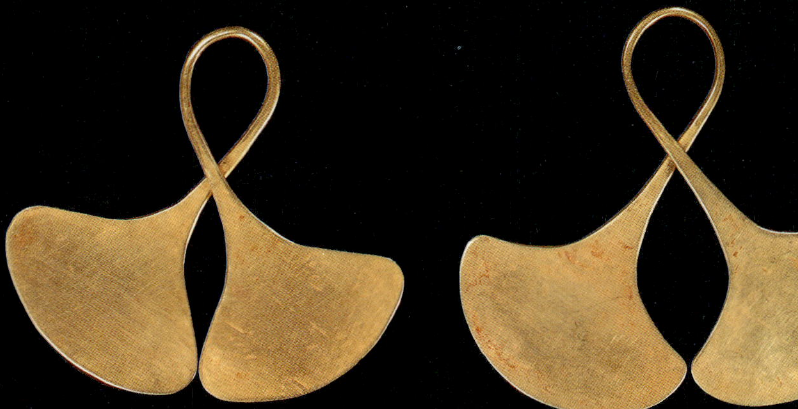

TOP RIGHT

Fig. VII.37 GOLD ORNAMENTS, *TAKA*
Ngada, Flores
Gold, 7.8 x 8.4; 7.1 x 7.5
Collection of Anita E. Spertus and Robert J. Holmgren, New York

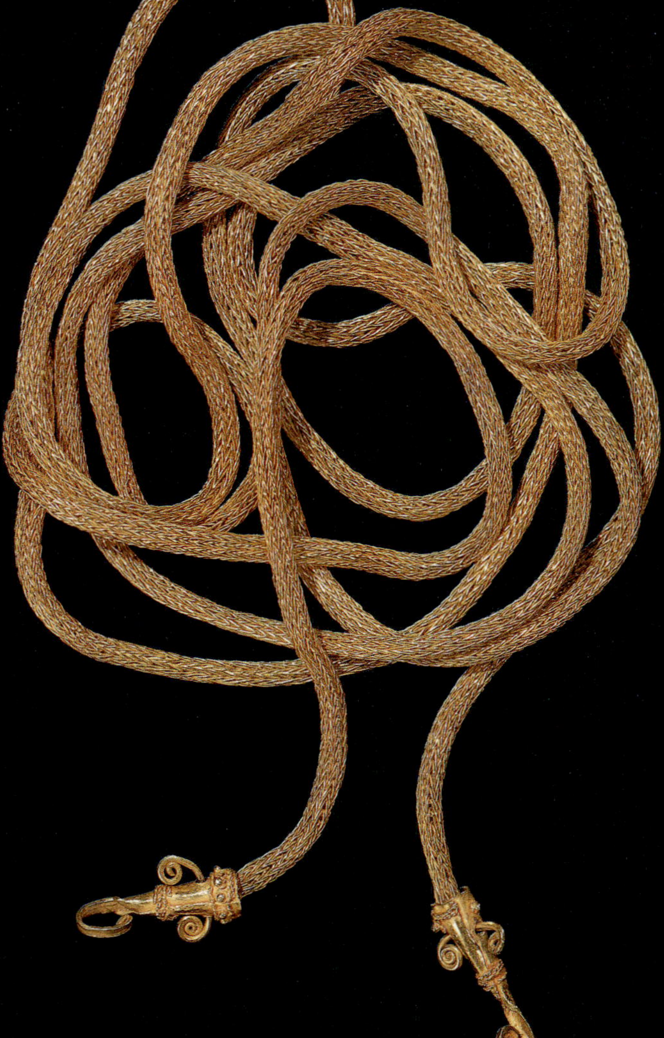

BOTTOM RIGHT

Fig. VII.38 CHAIN
Savu
Gold, 236
Royal Tropical Institute, Tropenmuseum, The Netherlands, 789-18. Purchased from K. Heynen in 1932.

OPPOSITE

Fig. VII.39 MAN'S CLOTH, *HINGGI KOMBU*
East Sumba
Cotton, 240 x 139.5
Royal Tropical Institute, Tropenmuseum, The Netherlands, 1772–1116. Donated by G. Tillman, Jr., in 1947.

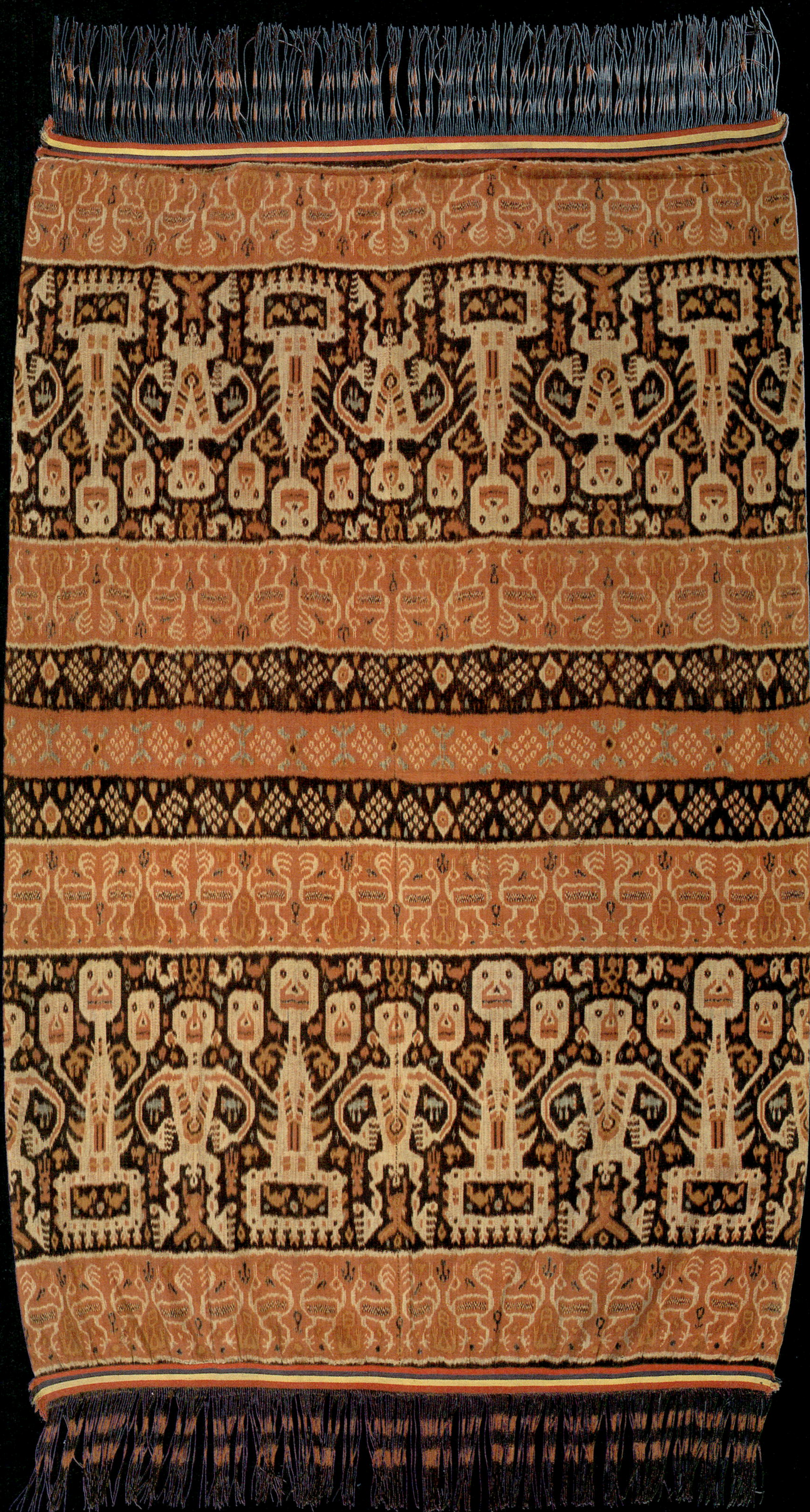

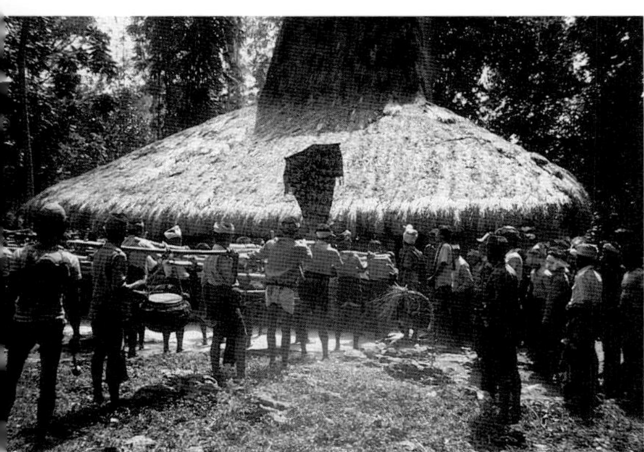

Fig. VII.40 A procession from the bride's family arrives in the village of the groom to negotiate what horses, buffalo, and metal objects (male goods) will be given in return for pigs and textiles (female goods). A man's mantle is carried as a banner at the head of the procession, representing the wife's party, West Sumba, 1987. Webb Keane

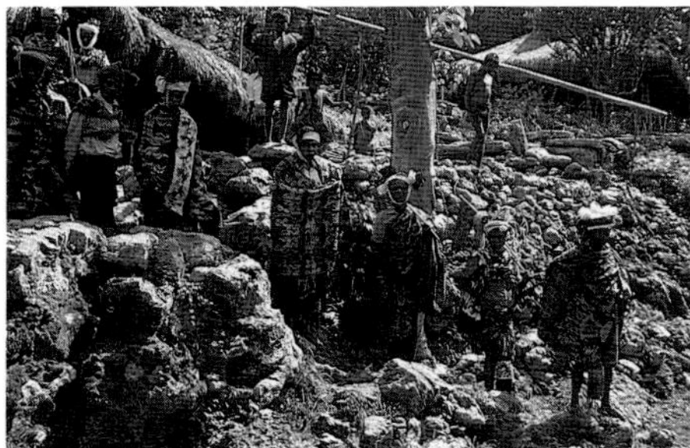

Fig. VII.41 At a ritual procession of traditional priests, many men are draped in fine men's cloths, West Sumba, 1987. Webb Keane

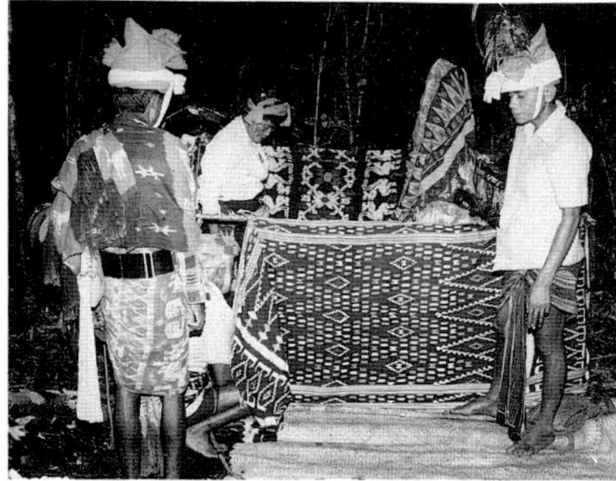

Fig. VII.42 Men's mantles are hung by traditional priests as ritual shields to mark off an area where there are dangerously "hot" spirit offerings, West Sumba, 1987. Webb Keane

of the Dongson kettledrums, which were manufactured many centuries earlier (see catalog chapter I). A "swastika" design (from the Sanskrit *svastika,*) is stamped and cut into the handles, and a design of concentric circles and floral patterns is embossed on the top. The swastika in Indic tradition is an auspicious and mystical symbol that in some areas is intended to remind humans that a self-contained, supreme reality is not within the grasp of human control (Liebert 1976:291).

The Female Gift of Textiles

Female goods exchanged in Indonesia usually include locally woven textiles, and the Lesser Sundas are no exception. Whether designed to be worn by women or men, cloth is given by the bride's family to the groom's family at ceremonial occasions throughout the course of every marriage (Fig. VII.40). Nevertheless, in Sumba at least, the imagery that is prominent on the gift textiles refers to the male goods and forces that are exchanged for the cloth. These include depictions of gold *mamuli* ornaments, livestock, and sea creatures that symbolize the mythical power of the founding ancestors (Hoskins 1988:129).

In most areas of the Lesser Sundas, full ceremonial dress for men included a mantle over the shoulders and another cloth around the waist (Fig. VII.41). Traditionally, such cloths would be buried with their owners. Sumbanese noblemen would be wrapped in dozens of woven mantles (Fig. VII.39) and other valuables, creating an extravagant burial mound to attest to the deceased's importance (Adams 1969:65). In addition to their use as ceremonial garb, men's mantles were, and still are in some areas, also used as sacred boundary markers to mark the taboo space for spirit offerings (Fig. VII.42).

The multicolored men's mantle (*hinggi kombu*; Fig. VII.39) is patterned with warp *ikat*, then dyed with indigo and morinda (locally called *kombu*). Afterwards, uncolored portions are painted with a tan stain (Adams 1969:88). The patterns on this textile include male human figures, probably ancestral warriors, standing beside skull trees. In precolonial Sumba after successful warfare, a skull tree was created from a barkless tree trunk and adorned with captured heads. This post was set before the clan leader's house, which served as a village temple (Adams 1969:13). Although headhunting is no longer practiced on Sumba, the skull-tree motif is prominent among the traditional male design patterns still created by East Sumbanese weavers to adorn female cloths (Fig. VII.43). The male figures are depicted in a characteristic East Sumbanese X-ray fashion: ribs and stomach cavities are depicted, as are areas of greater muscle tissue concentration. The background around the men and skull trees is filled with animal figures including birds and mantis shrimp. The four bands bordering the two bands featuring humans include rows of confronting roosters with the upper halves of human torsos set between them. The cock motif is recognizable by the bird's comb, high tail, and three front toes and one rear toe (Adams 1969:139). Chickens are a common animal used for traditional sacrifices, augury, and entertainment (in cockfights) throughout Indonesia, as well as being important to the local economy.

Locally dyed Timor men's cloths could be worn as sarongs (Fig. VII.44) or mantles, displayed as ceremonial hangings at feasts, used as funeral shrouds, or made into ceremonial horse blankets. In the warp *ikat* mantle (Fig. VII.46), subtle, predominantly red shades in repeated, small-motif patterns create a cloth whose appearance varies greatly according to the distance from which it is viewed. The lengthwise bands of geometric motifs, interspersed with narrow solid stripes, resemble certain textile styles woven in the Southeast Moluccas (see Figs. VIII.34, VIII.36).

Timorese warp *ikat* textiles vary considerably according to region, marking the wearer's local political identity. Beside the cloths designed with geometric patterns are ones with pictoral representations more comparable to the *hinggi* mantles woven in East Sumba. On the textile (Fig. VII.47), the design of human figures, whose extremities change into birds, may represent a traditional

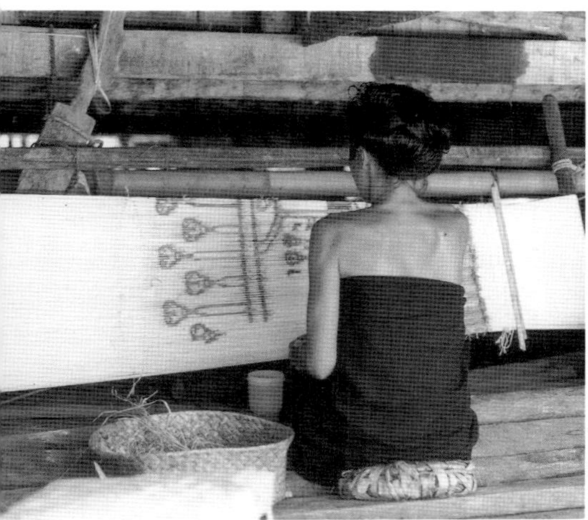

Fig. VII.43 East Sumbanese weaver tying skull-tree pattern into warp threads of a man's mantle, 1978. Laurence A. G. Moss

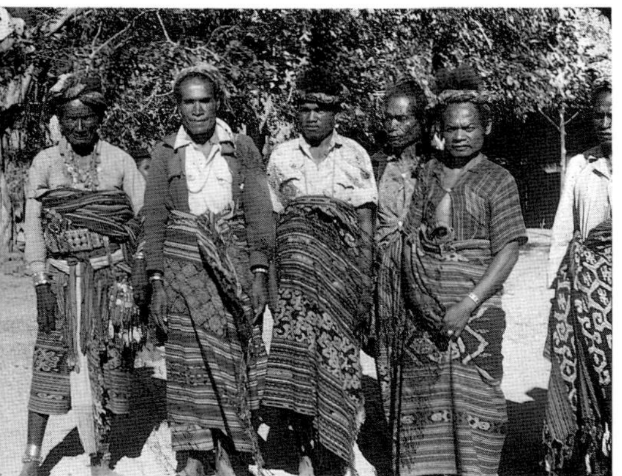

Fig. VII.44 A group of ceremonially dressed male elders from the Amanuban region visit a neighboring area to attend a funeral, West Timor, 1961. Clark E. Cunningham

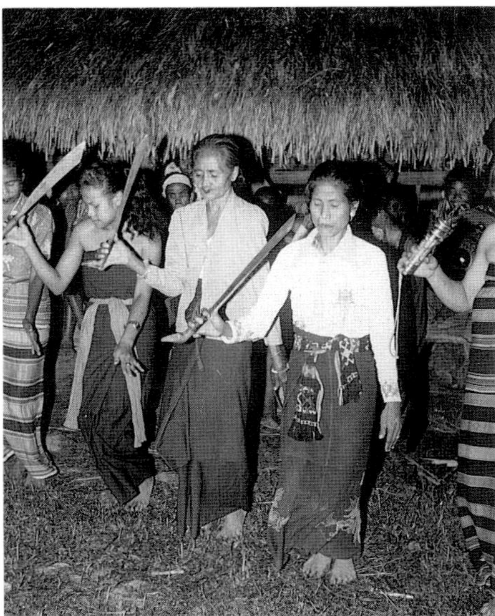

Fig. VII.45 Dancing a traditional dance (*negu*) performed with machetes, women wear black tube-skirts (*lau*). The tube-skirt on the right is embroidered, Anakalang, West Sumba, 1987. Webb Keane

Atoni belief that deceased persons are transformed into birds after funeral rites are completed (Gittinger 1979:76). The complex iconography, patterned with mirror-image duplication at the center line like Sumba *hinggi* mantles, includes triple-headed figures sprouting within and beside the primary figures. The use of only indigo dye on a natural cotton background creates a bold positive-and-negative design not seen on the multicolored textiles.

Beaded and embroidered skirts with fringed tufting were also important gifts in Sumbanese wedding exchanges. Such a garment, usually with a black background, would be worn by a bride as she walked in procession to the house of her husband's family or by a noble woman at funerals and other major ceremonies (Fig. VII.45; personal communication, Joel Kuipers 1989). The beads and shells attached to *lau hada* skirts (Fig. VII.49) were precious because they were all imported (Adams 1969:85); hence, the skirts were traditionally identified with the nobility (Forth 1981; Holmgren and Spertus 1989:30). The imagery on *lau hada* skirts often includes a large single male or female figure shown with animal or plant forms, evoking fertility according to Holmgren and Spertus (1989:28–31). This skirt (Fig. VII.49) has a geometric pattern composed of four human forms, possibly two male and two female, joined at the genital area. This motif may also suggest homage to ancestors and community fertility. The bottom hem is bordered with a colorful geometric band of hourglass-shaped figures. The bottom half of the textile is extremely heavy because of the combined weight of the shells and antique glass beads. When worn, the unadorned top portion of the tube is folded down and belted (Fig. VII.45) to create a long dress or skirt of the desired length.

Another type of woven woman's skirt, called *lau pahudu*, is visually dominated by bands of figures created by means of supplementary weft technique, where additional yarns are added into the weft between the foundation yarns. Recent *lau pahudu* include light figures on dark backgrounds, but the example included here (Fig. VII.48) is an older type, with dark geometric and outlined figurative patterns set into a lighter background (Holmgren and Spertus 1989:38–39). Such patterns predate the larger and more rounded figurative forms that became popular during nineteenth- and twentieth-century foreign trade. The one-eyed, three-fingered, and three-toed figures on the skirt band are unusual in modern Sumba textiles. The motif set between each larger human figure, patterned from squared-off scrolls, may also have been considered anthropomorphic. Supplementary weft bands for Sumba skirts were often woven separately—according to inherited pattern guides—and later sewn onto the foundation material. The background fabric of the skirt was daubed with brown dye after weaving (Adams 1969:82).

Lesser Sunda textiles often display Indian design influences, attesting to centuries of foreign commerce that delivered such Indian trade textiles as *patola* cloths to the region in exchange for natural resources. The weavers of the Lamalera region of Lembata, a small island located east of Flores, are particularly well known for incorporating Indian *patola* designs into local textiles. In Lamalera villages, certain *patola* patterns came to be associated with particular family lineages, who assigned them local meanings and wove them on the center panel of their ceremonial cloths (Barnes 1989b:136). Although less finely woven than some Lembata skirts, the cloth (Fig. VII.50) is striking for its heart-shaped leaf images in the center panel, a motif most certainly derived from imported Indian *patola* textiles (see illustrations in Bühler 1979). This heart-shaped motif is no longer common in its original village, but it was undoubtedly produced by a woman whose lineage owned a similarly patterned cloth. The figurative designs in the two main outer panels of the cloth represent a boat (*jo* or *jon*) and a manta ray (*moku*). These two designs are in general use throughout southern Lembata. The Indian-derived motifs, seen only on the center panels of Lamalera cloths, indicate their aristocratic foreign heritage (allegedly tied to Sulawesi) and seafaring trade history. Neighboring Lamaholot groups weave cloths with identical techniques but without such center panels or

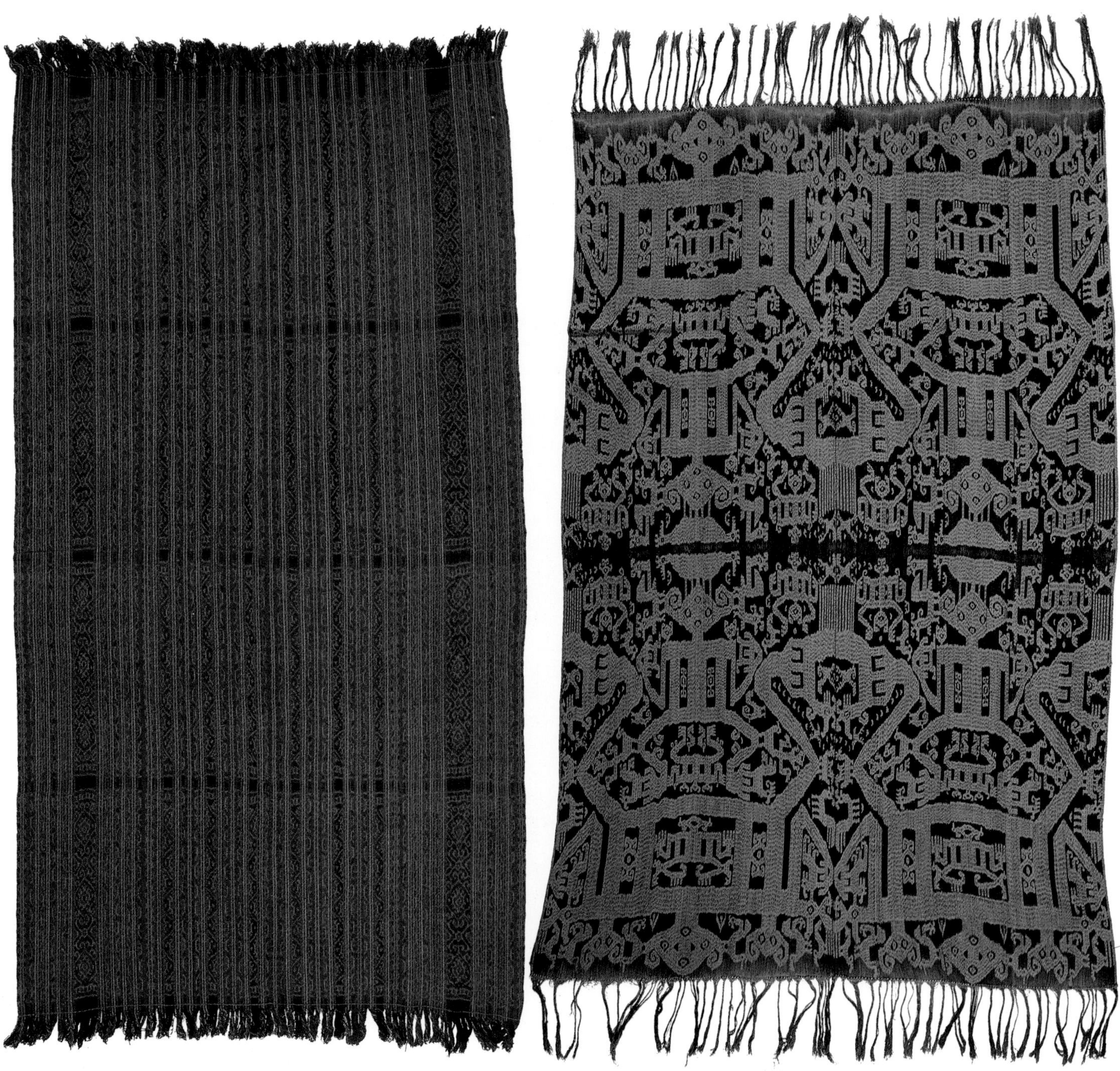

Fig. VII.46 MAN'S CLOTH
Beboki, West Timor
Cotton, 229 x 118
Rijksmuseum voor Volkenkunde, Leiden, 2380–241. Purchased from B. A. G. Vroklage. Accessioned in 1939.

Fig. VII.47 MAN'S CLOTH
Atoni, Niki Niki village, Amanuban, West Timor
Cotton, 233 x 131
Royal Tropical Institute, Tropenmuseum, The Netherlands, 2071-14. Purchased from E. B. G. Beckering in 1951.

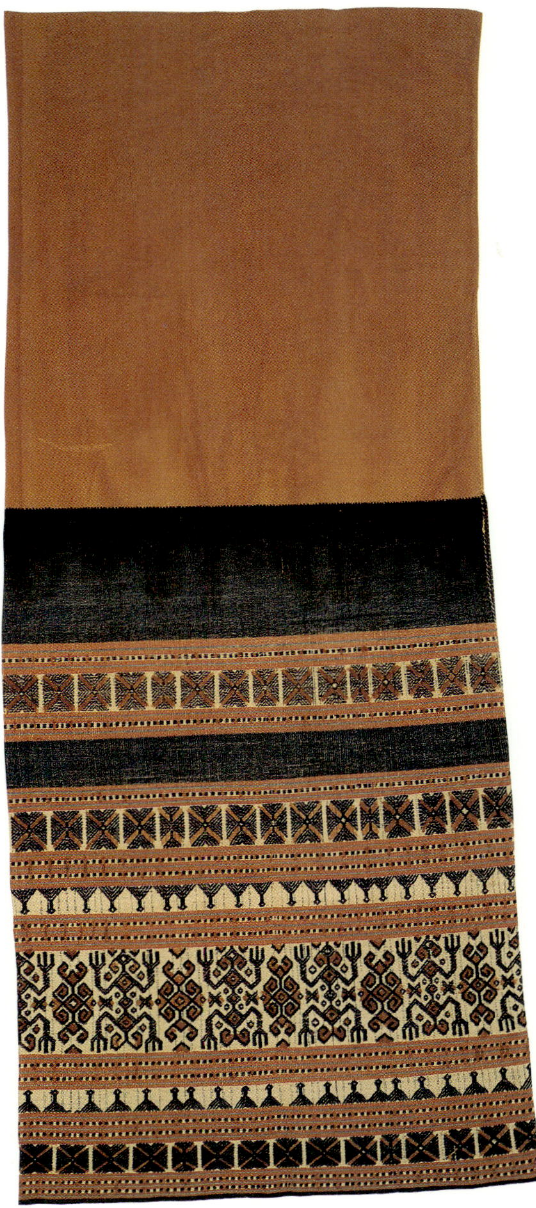

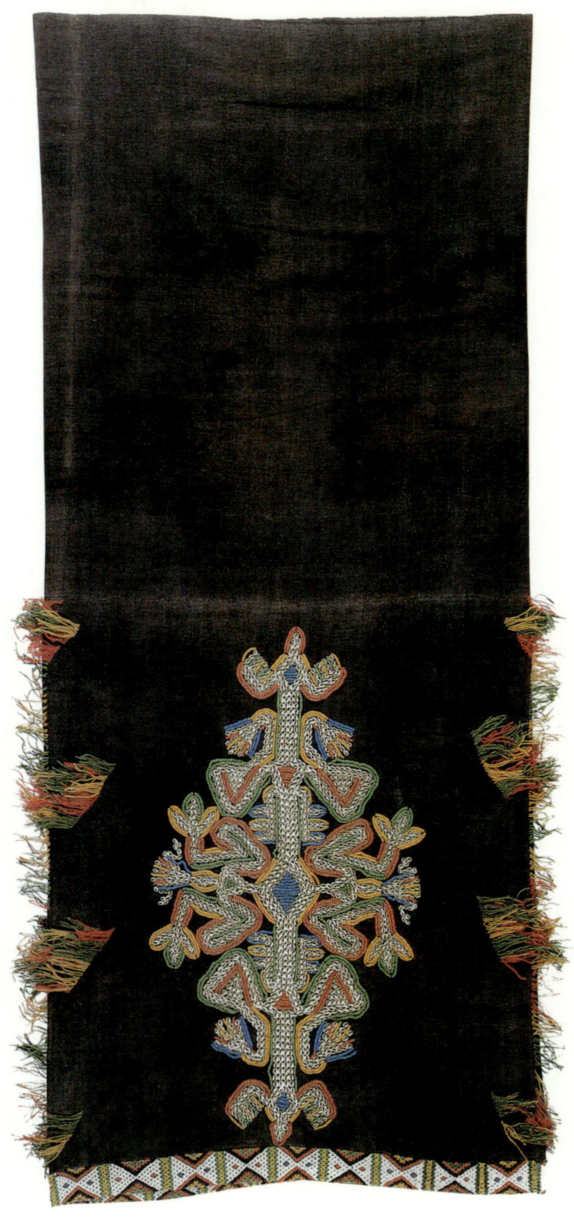

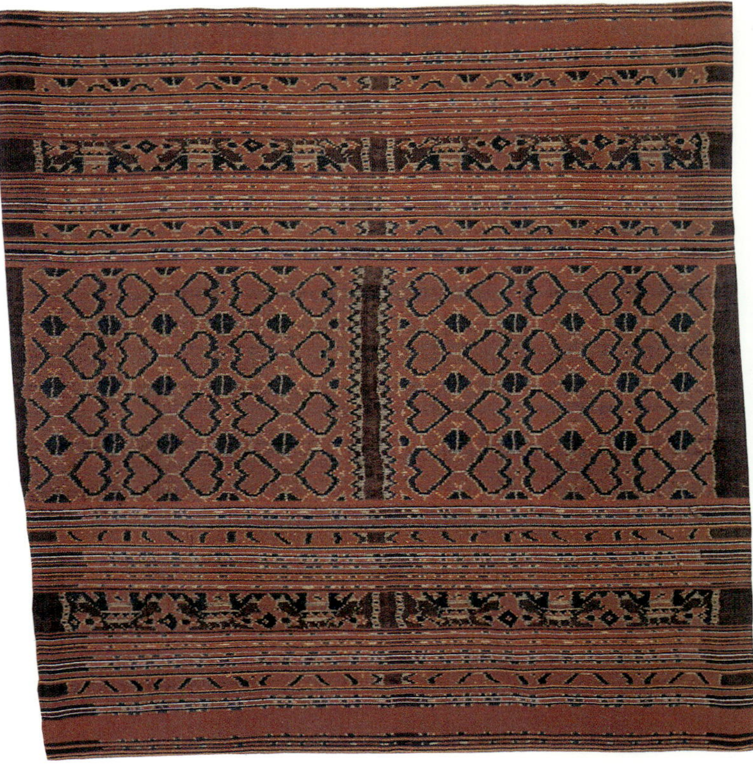

TOP LEFT

Fig. VII.48 WOMAN'S SKIRT, *LAU PAHUDU*
Kanatang village, East Sumba
Cotton, 131 x 58
Collection of Anita E. Spertus and Robert J. Holmgren, New York

Fig. VII.49 WOMAN'S BEADED SKIRT, *LAU HADA*
East Sumba
Cotton, glass beads, nassa shells, 149 x 64
Rijksmuseum voor Volkenkunde, Leiden, 370-3767

Fig. VII.50 WOMAN'S CLOTH, *KEWATEK NAI TELO*
Lamalera region, Lembata
Cotton, 141 x 140.4
Royal Tropical Institute, Tropenmuseum, The Netherlands, 1772-1179. Donated by G. Tillman, Jr., in 1947.

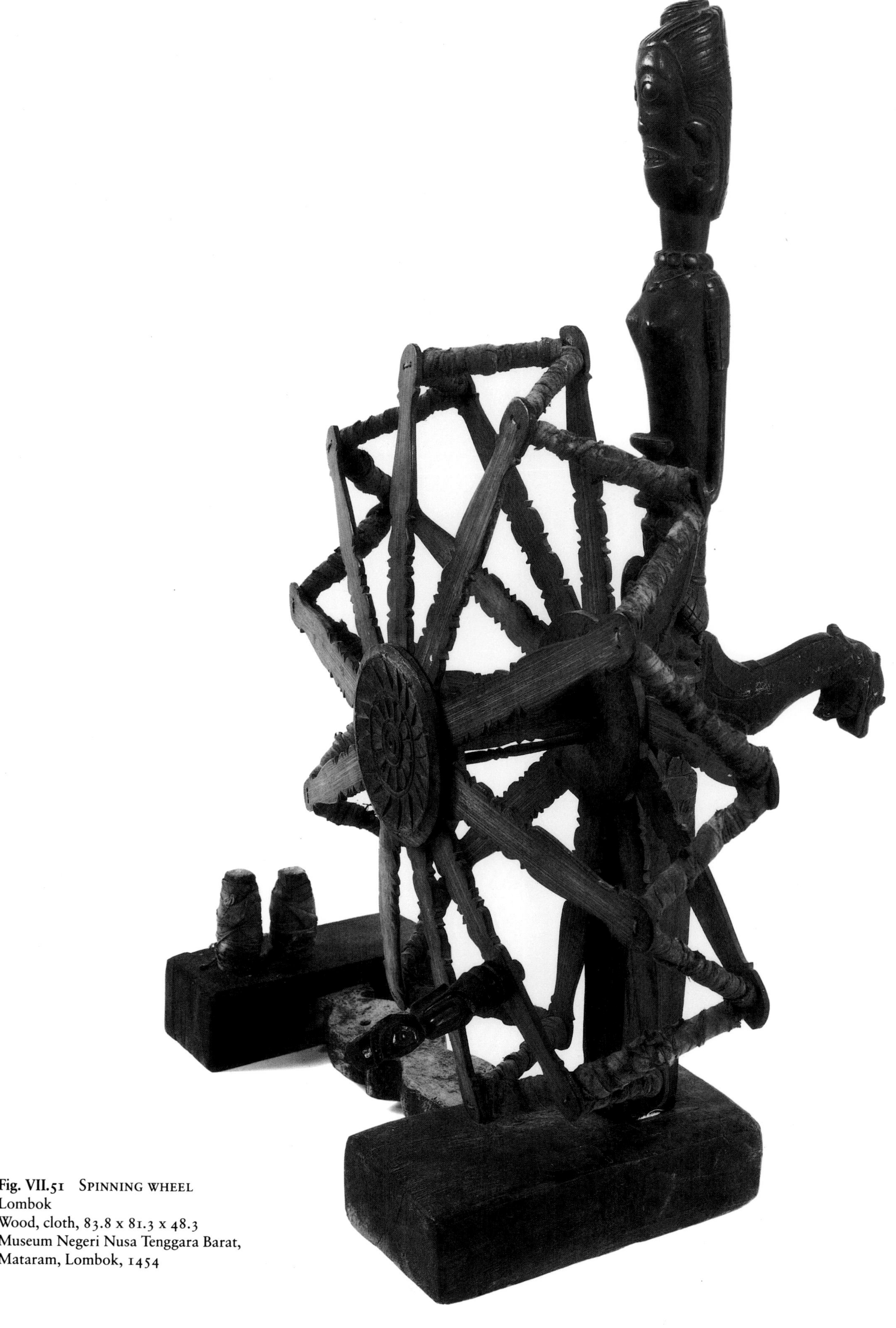

Fig. VII.51 SPINNING WHEEL
Lombok
Wood, cloth, 83.8 x 81.3 x 48.3
Museum Negeri Nusa Tenggara Barat, Mataram, Lombok, 1454

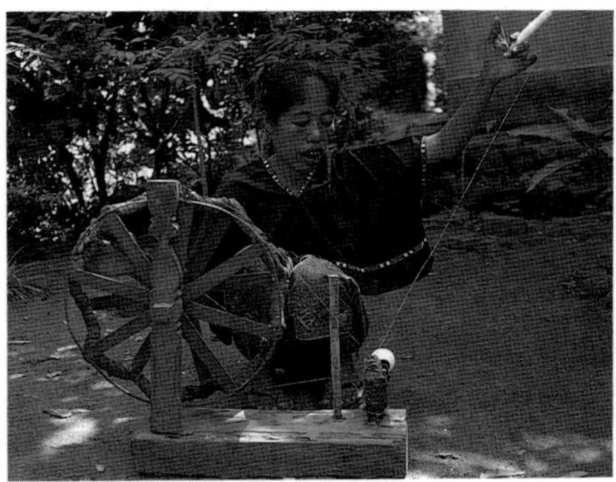

Fig. VII.52 Woman spinning wool fiber with traditional spinning wheel, Sukaraja, Lombok, 1990. Hermine Dreyfuss

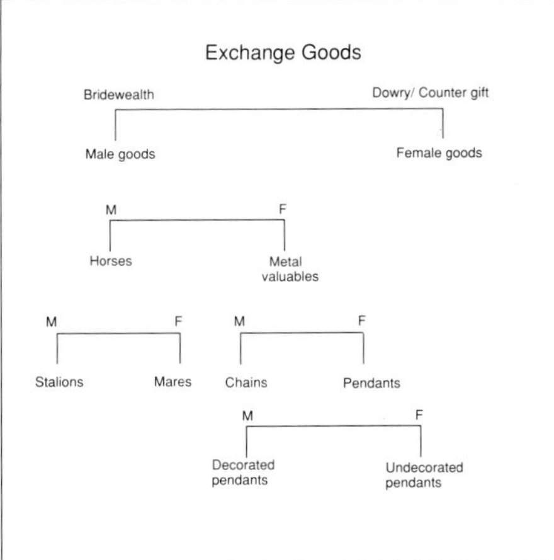

Fig.VII.53 A classification of valuables exchanged in marriage alliances as they are locally defined as male and female. Fox 1989:46. Redrawn by Marcia Bakry, Smithsonian Institution.

patola motifs (Fig. VII.36; Barnes in press a). The textile (Fig. VII.50) is locally called *kewatek nai telo*, a "woman's cloth of three parts," because it includes one central and two side bands. This kind of cloth is an essential gift presented by a woman's lineage both during and after marriage. The textiles are given with five bracelets, which evoke a counter-gift of an elephant tusk from the groom's lineage (Barnes 1989a:52).

Spinning wheels found in Lombok share a form well known from India, suggesting the antiquity of Lombok trading networks. The ornately carved spinning wheel (Fig. VII.51) shows distinct foreign influence, probably from the neighboring island of Bali, which has been Hindu since about the fifteenth century. Balinese influence is particularly felt on the western half of Lombok, which was settled by Balinese migrants since the 1700s (van der Kraan 1980). The spinning wheel's center is carved with a floral figure with radiating spikes. The teeth-baring grimace, carefully incised hair, and clothing of the wheel's main figure derive from a distinctively different carving tradition than that of indigenous ancestor figures produced on most islands of the Lesser Sundas. The skilled carving delineates a plaid skirt and patterned jacket as well as jewelry and an elegant, wrapped hairstyle. A second and stylistically dissimilar carved figure, which serves as the small handle to rotate the spinning wheel (Fig. VII.52), wears a headdress and perhaps a long robe. A dragonhead figure protrudes from the back of the wheel's base, serving as the bolt head for the wheel's axle. The main female figure on the spinning wheel, who holds a cup to receive offerings in her hands, may represent a deity or an ancestor who introduced weaving technology or who protected weavers. In the neighboring island of Sumba, thread spinning was a skill that traditionally had to be mastered by all girls before marriage. Indeed, on Sumba at least, spinning was a metaphor for the primary female role of creating offspring by fusing components of the human soul within the womb (Geirnaert 1989:71).

Such cosmological concepts of gender often surround Indonesian weaving tools and technology, which are a focus of female identity as well as activity. The classifying and unifying of contrasting natural and social elements is apparent throughout Lesser Sunda artwork, as is most clearly demonstrated through the objects of Sumbanese marital-alliance gift exchange. Marital gifts are categorized as male metals and female textiles. Within the male metals are male chains and female *mamuli* pendants. Within the female textiles are male *hinggi* cloths and female *lau* skirts. Within the female *mamuli* pendants are male ones with ornamented bases and female ones with plain bases. Within the male *hinggi* cloths are male sea creature designs and female *mamuli* designs. The contrasting classifications continue, as ongoing aesthetic interpretations are made about differences (Fig. VII.53). As with the ancient Chinese concept of yin and yang the things of this world are thought to exist within a unified yet always contrasting universe (Fox 1989:46).

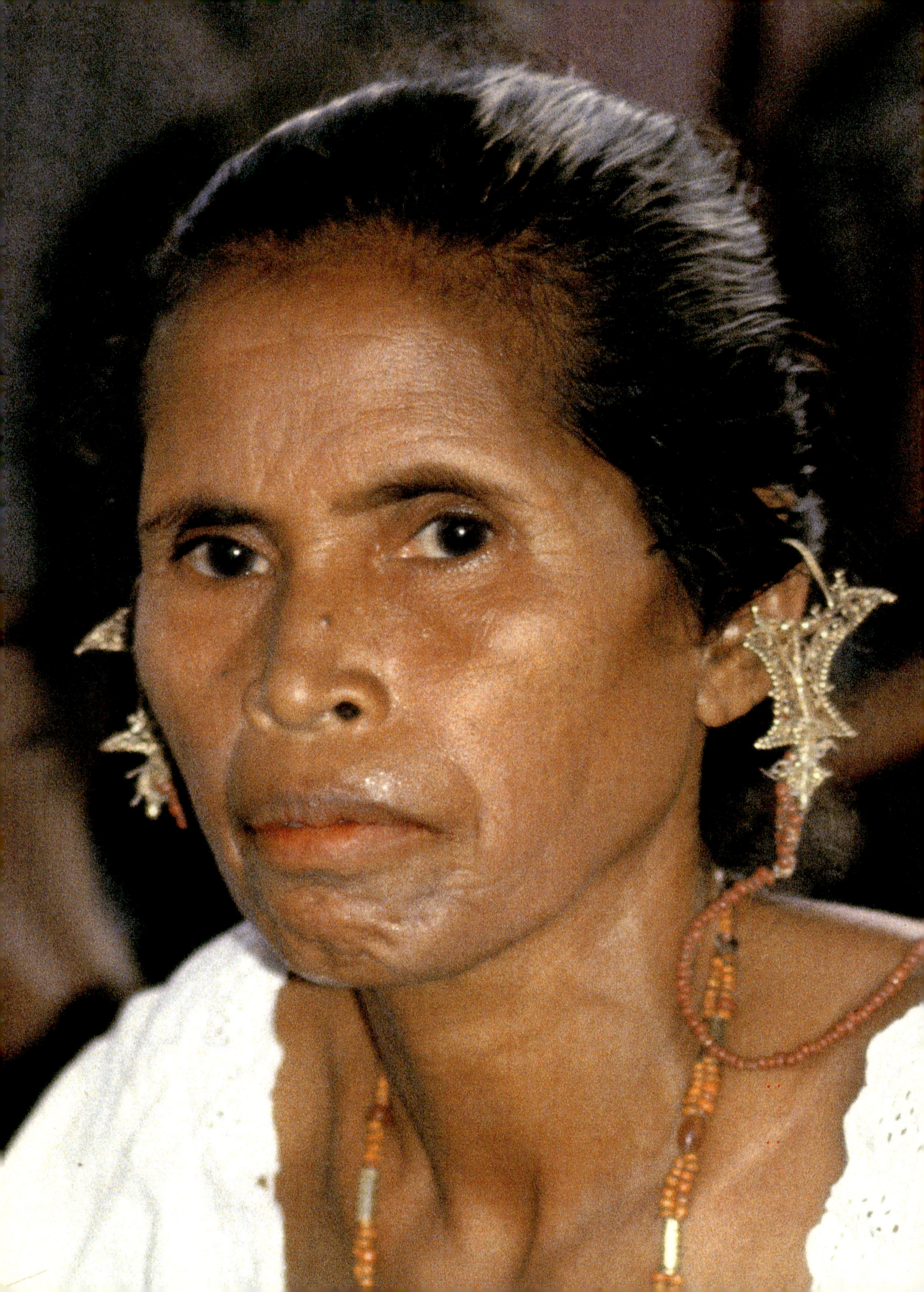

VIII

Southeast Moluccas

Once known as the spice islands, the northern Moluccas played an important role in the spice trade to Europe from the 1500s to the 1800s. The Southeast Moluccas, by contrast, were posed on the southern peripheries of the spice-trading Islamic sultanates of Tidore and Ternate (see catalog chapter X) and the Dutch-controlled missionary centers that developed in the capital of Ambon during the colonial period beginning in the seventeenth century. For centuries prior to European contact, however, the area was visited by other Asians in search of precious spices. Through centuries of foreign trade and interisland migration, the people of the Southeast Moluccas acquired imported jewelry and precious materials—gold, ivory, and cloth. During the colonial period, southeastern islands—for instance, Tanimbar—were connected in exchange networks with peoples from the other Moluccan Islands, with Bugis and Makassar traders from South Sulawesi, and with Dutch, Portuguese, and English traders, whose ships competed in the region (McKinnon 1983:87–88).

Locally woven textiles and heirloom jewelry were, and still are, exchanged at Tanimbar life-cycle rituals among kin groups identified with particular ancestral houses (McKinnon 1983). They continue to be ceremonially exchanged between villages, often on differing islands that maintain friendship and defense alliances. Such interisland alliance networks, which allow for the exchange of seasonal subsistence goods as well as heirloom valuables and wives, are also known from the Leti (Renes 1977) and Kai archipelagoes (Barraud 1979). In addition to exploiting marine resources, Southeast Moluccan people subsist upon a variety of plant foods that are cultivated in their seasonally dry environment. These include yams, maize, rice, millet, mung beans, taro, coconut, and sago. Today people in most areas of the Southeast Moluccas are Christian, but their traditional social organization is generally still maintained.

Although many Southeast Moluccan regions have patrilineal descent systems and maintain asymmetrical marriage alliances like those in many areas of the Lesser Sundas and among the Batak of Sumatra, their social organization

Fig. VIII.1 A woman wears female earrings (*kmene*) connected by a string of beads, Tanimbar, 1979. Susan M. McKinnon

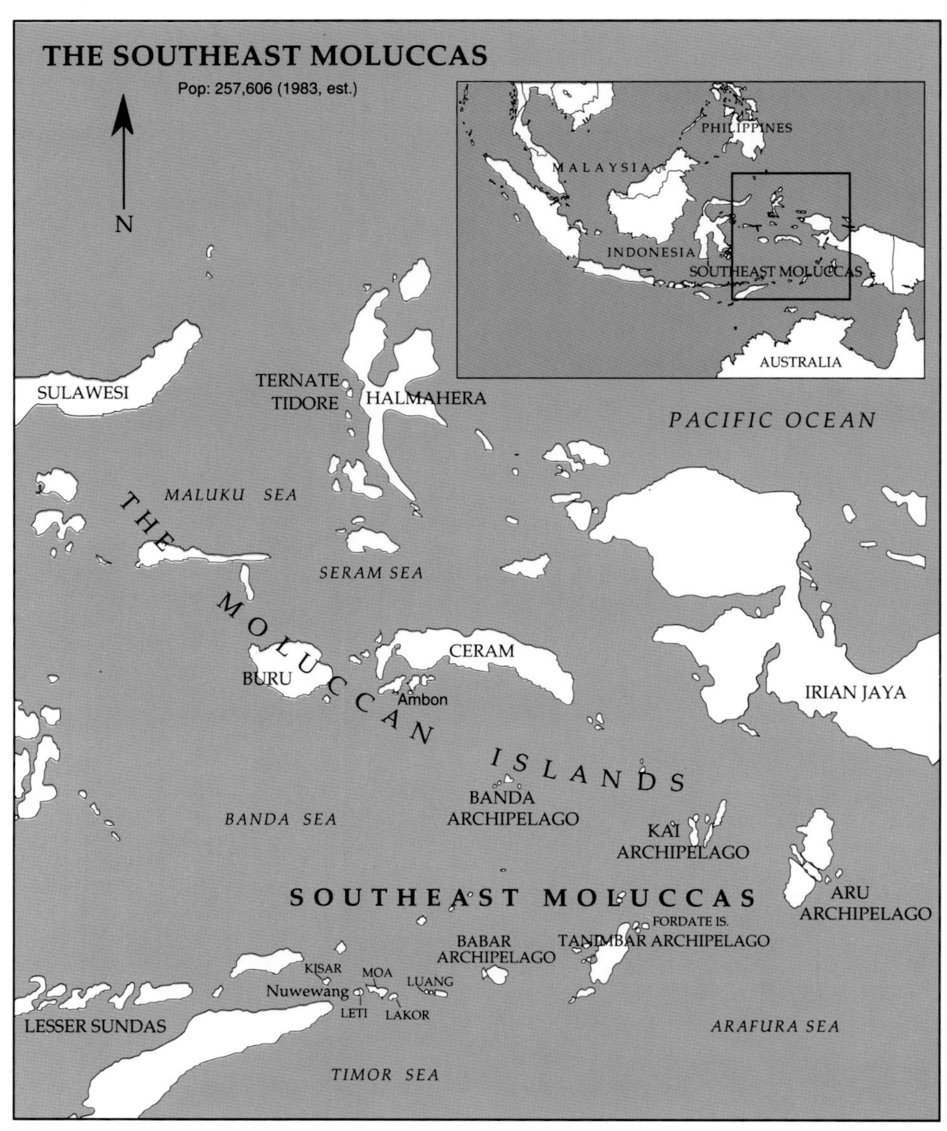
THE SOUTHEAST MOLUCCAS
Pop: 257,606 (1983, est.)
N
PHILIPPINES
MALAYSIA
INDONESIA
SOUTHEAST MOLUCCAS
AUSTRALIA
SULAWESI
TERNATE
TIDORE
HALMAHERA
PACIFIC OCEAN
MALUKU SEA
SERAM SEA
THE MOLUCCAN ISLANDS
CERAM
BURU
Ambon
IRIAN JAYA
BANDA ARCHIPELAGO
BANDA SEA
KAI ARCHIPELAGO
ARU ARCHIPELAGO
SOUTHEAST MOLUCCAS
FORDATE IS.
BABAR ARCHIPELAGO
TANIMBAR ARCHIPELAGO
KISAR
MOA
LUANG
Nuwewang
LETI
LAKOR
LESSER SUNDAS
ARAFURA SEA
TIMOR SEA

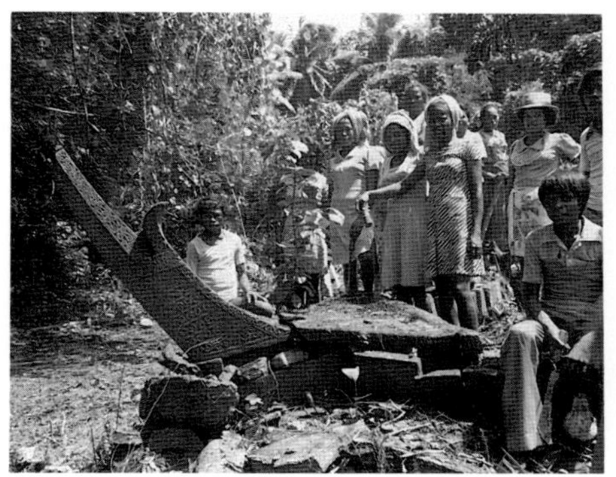

Fig. VIII.2 A stone boat altar, now overgrown by plants at an abandoned village site, Tanimbar, 1980 (see Drabbe 1940:fig. 19). Susan M. McKinnon

varies considerably from island to island. For example, groom's families in Luang, Leti, and parts of Babar present no bridewealth gifts to the wife's family. And, the people of Kisar and Babar have matrilineal endogamous (in-marrying) descent groups and other cultural features that are distinctly different from the more eastern Tanimbar societies (personal communication, de Jonge 1990). The marriage patterns among the social ranks also vary more than was previously realized: idealized norms are most strictly followed by members of the upper class (McKinnon in press). The discussion of artworks that follows will include pieces from various islands of the region, but much of the social information is drawn from research on the people of Tanimbar.

Boats in Religious Ritual: Symbols of Spiritual Power

Certain major deities in traditional Southeast Moluccan cosmology have combined male and female aspects. Worship on Tanimbar was, prior to Christianization, directed to a male-and-female deity called *Ubila'a*, which means "Supreme Grandparent/Grandchild." This name evoked the continuity of the life force from the ancestors to future descendants.

Southeast Moluccan cosmology was also distinctive for its graphic conceptualization of boats as unified communities whose success depended upon the differentiation of roles and status. Tanimbar villages were centered on stone altars, sometimes in the shape of a boat, but always symbolizing the community as a boat with ritual officials forming its crew (McKinnon 1988). At the stone boat altar, villagers held community discussions, danced, and made offerings to *Ubila'a* and their ancestors. Most of these stone altar sites are no longer used for ceremonial gatherings because many villages have moved to new locations (Fig. VIII.2). In Tanimbar ritual songs, the name of the stone boat is used as a metaphor for the village, which traces its origin to distant islands, often to the southwest (McKinnon 1988:158–60). Boats themselves were not only a means of transportation but also objects of great ritual and metaphoric significance throughout the Southeast Moluccas (Barraud 1979; van Dijk and de Jonge 1990:12). Boats long enough to carry thirty passengers were constructed and adorned with intricately carved prow boards (*kora*) to make journeys for inter-village alliance ceremonies, warfare, or trade (Geurtjens 1910, 1921). The prow boards of such boats feature graceful open scrollwork and carving of single and double spirals that is a hallmark of Moluccan sculpture (Figs. VIII.3, VIII.5).

The depiction of birds on prow boards in many areas of Southeast Asia reportedly symbolizes ancestor spirits as well as wishes for a speedy journey. In Tanimbar, the rooster represents a nobleman dressed in full regalia, displaying his finery to an opponent (McKinnon 1988:157–58). Before important journeys to visit villages on other islands were made, magical substances were applied to the prow board to make it "hot" and deadly to any enemy the boat encountered. In many regions of Indonesia hot and cold are metaphors for danger/masculinity and safety/femininity. The prow board (Fig. VIII.5) depicts a large cock pecking at the ground with spirals emerging from his back, symbolizing wings. Smaller spirals grow from the back of his tail toward the top of the sail-shaped prow ornament. A miniature version of the entire composition is repeated at the back of the board. A small fish swims in front of the large cock's feet, and another figure, now lost, was once behind his feet. Below the figures is a row of rolling spirals, perhaps representing the waves of the sea.

The carved prow board (Fig. VIII.3) features a mammal, possibly a dog, at its base. The creature's tail and head (or ear) begin a chain of s-spirals that wind their way to the top point of the board, becoming smaller as they approach the narrow apex. The front of the board is ornamented with a row of shells attached with bark fiber rope.

Although boats with beautifully crafted prow boards are no longer made in Tanimbar, village-alliance ceremonies—to which villagers had traveled in such boats—are still held intermittently. Before the boats leave, villagers on board dance (Fig. VIII.4). One goal of these expeditions is to renew traditional

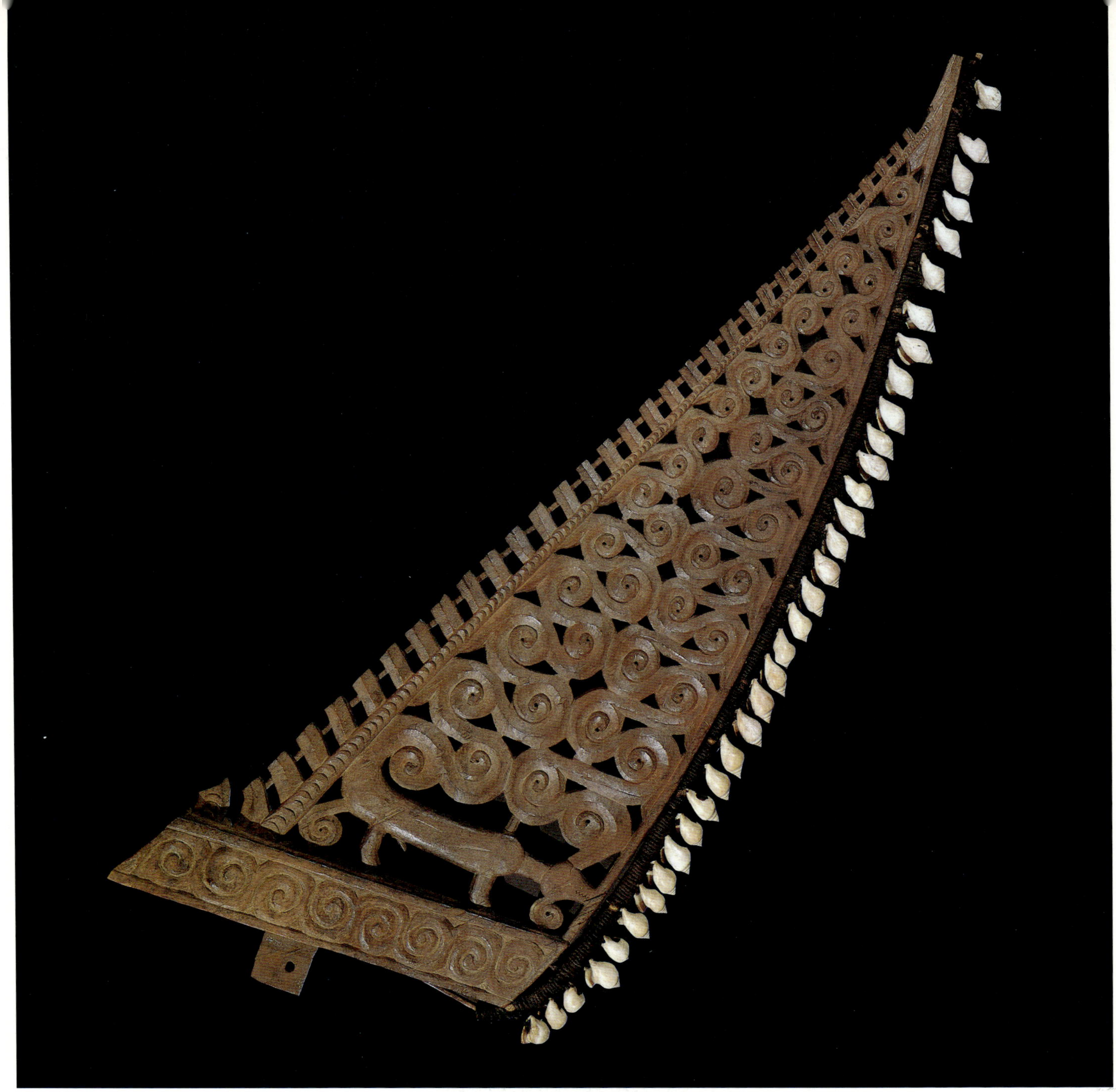

Fig. VIII.3 BOAT PROW BOARD, *KORA*
Tanimbar, Southeast Moluccas
Wood, shell, sugar palm bark fiber rope, 110 x 49
Museum Nasional Indonesia, Jakarta, 14305. Gift from the Director of the Training School for Native Teachers in Ambon in 1910.

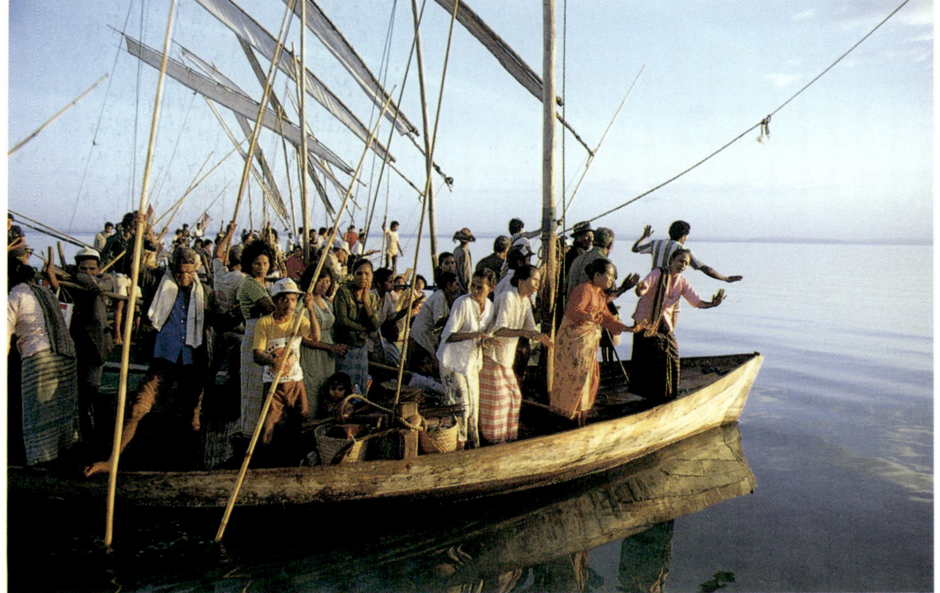

Fig. VIII.4 Sera villagers dancing on board their boats, departing for a ceremony to renew a village alliance, Tanimbar, 1980. Susan M. McKinnon

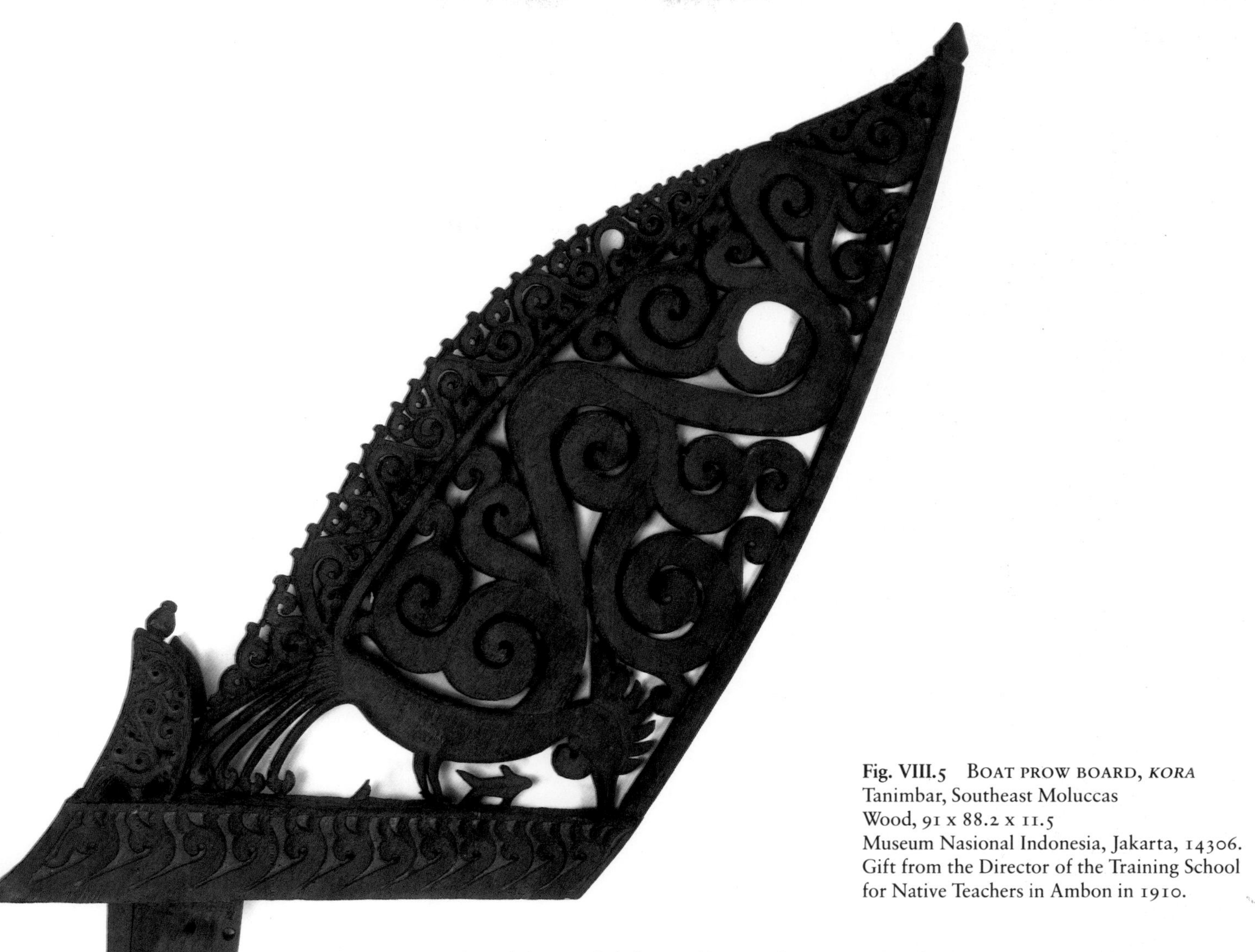

Fig. VIII.5 BOAT PROW BOARD, *KORA*
Tanimbar, Southeast Moluccas
Wood, 91 x 88.2 x 11.5
Museum Nasional Indonesia, Jakarta, 14306.
Gift from the Director of the Training School for Native Teachers in Ambon in 1910.

friendship and defense alliances between island villages, which are conceived of as elder and younger brothers. During village-alliance ceremonies, the visitors dance in boat formation in the village center of the hosts (see Fig. VIII.10). Women with outstretched arms are said to dance like the frigate birds that hover above a ship, and the accompanying drummers are said to be the boat's sail (McKinnon 1988:163–65). The accompanying songs describe the swiftness of their boat, and its beauty is compared to that of a brilliant rooster.

In many areas of the Southeast Moluccas, a large standing wooden drum, accompanied by smaller hourglass-shaped drums, is played at village dances. In Babar, large drums standing on legs (Fig. VIII.9) are used to beat the rhythm of traditional dances at new year's feasts, which invoke human and crop fertility for the upcoming year (de Jonge 1989; van Dijk and de Jonge 1990). This drum (Fig. VIII.11) has a modified human form, with the head of the drum representing the head of a person. The pedestal of the drum is a fully sculpted human torso with hands supporting what would be the chin of the blank-faced drumhead. The body's knees-up, seated position with arms resting on the knees is characteristic of Southeast Moluccan ancestor figures (Figs. VIII.6, VIII.7). Similar drums, always made from the hardwood of a sugar palm, have been acquired from Moa and Leti (personal communication, Jean Pierret 1990).

Village Altars and Sculptures: Homage to Supreme Deities and Ancestors

Traditional Leti religion paid homage to a male sun god (*Upuleru*) and a female earth goddess (*Upunusa*). Their sexual union, celebrated at an annual festival, was thought to produce rain needed for the yearly planting of maize. For periodic fertility rituals, newly carved altars were erected in the middle of the village. Village altars on Leti were carved of a special hardwood and erected on piles of stones in the village centers (Fig. VIII.8). Figures, carved at the top of the altars, were usually poised in a squatting or seated position and carry bowls for collecting ritual offerings to the deities. The ancestor figures on these altars sat high

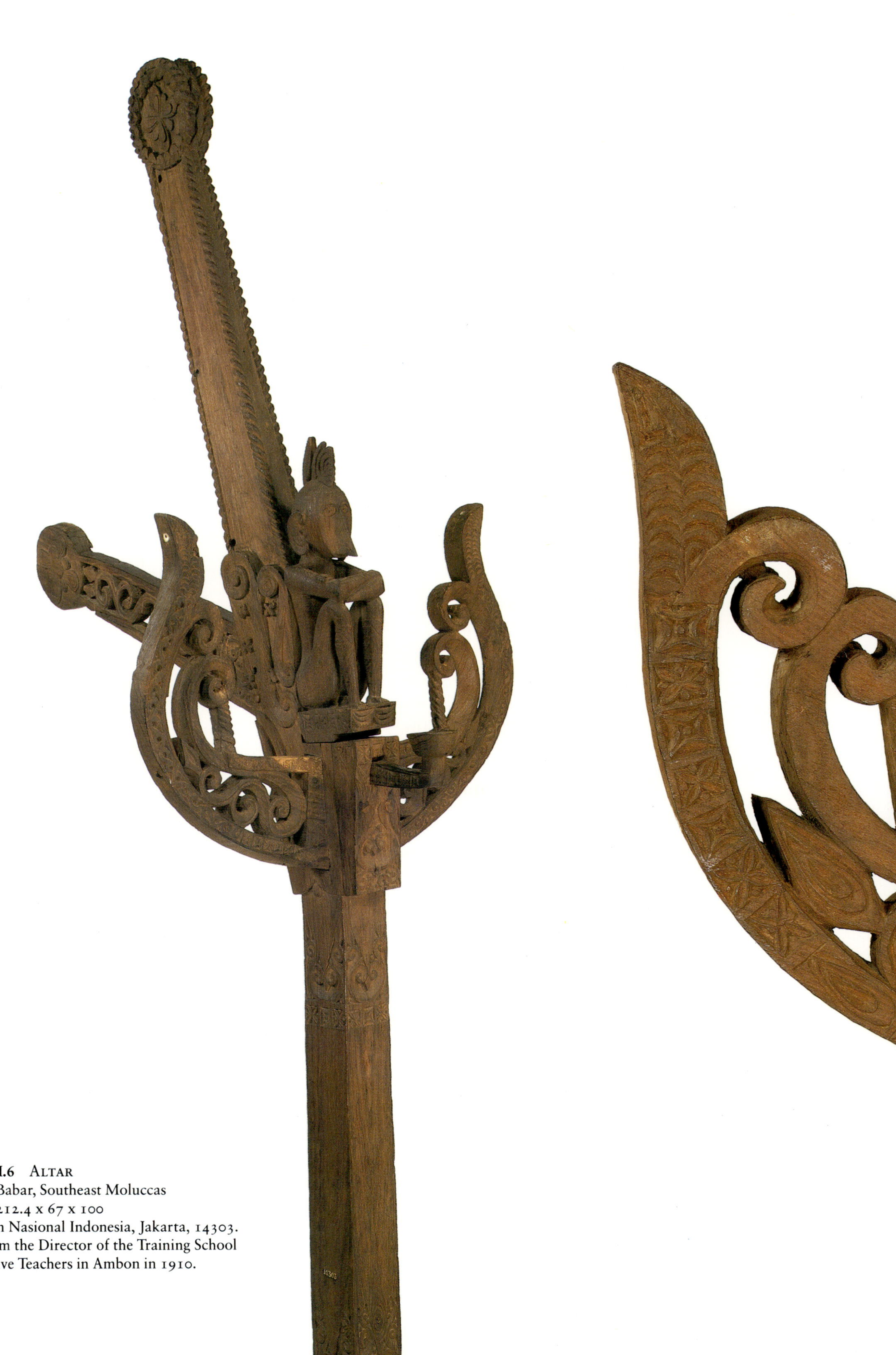

Fig. VIII.6 ALTAR
Leti or Babar, Southeast Moluccas
Wood, 212.4 x 67 x 100
Museum Nasional Indonesia, Jakarta, 14303.
Gift from the Director of the Training School for Native Teachers in Ambon in 1910.

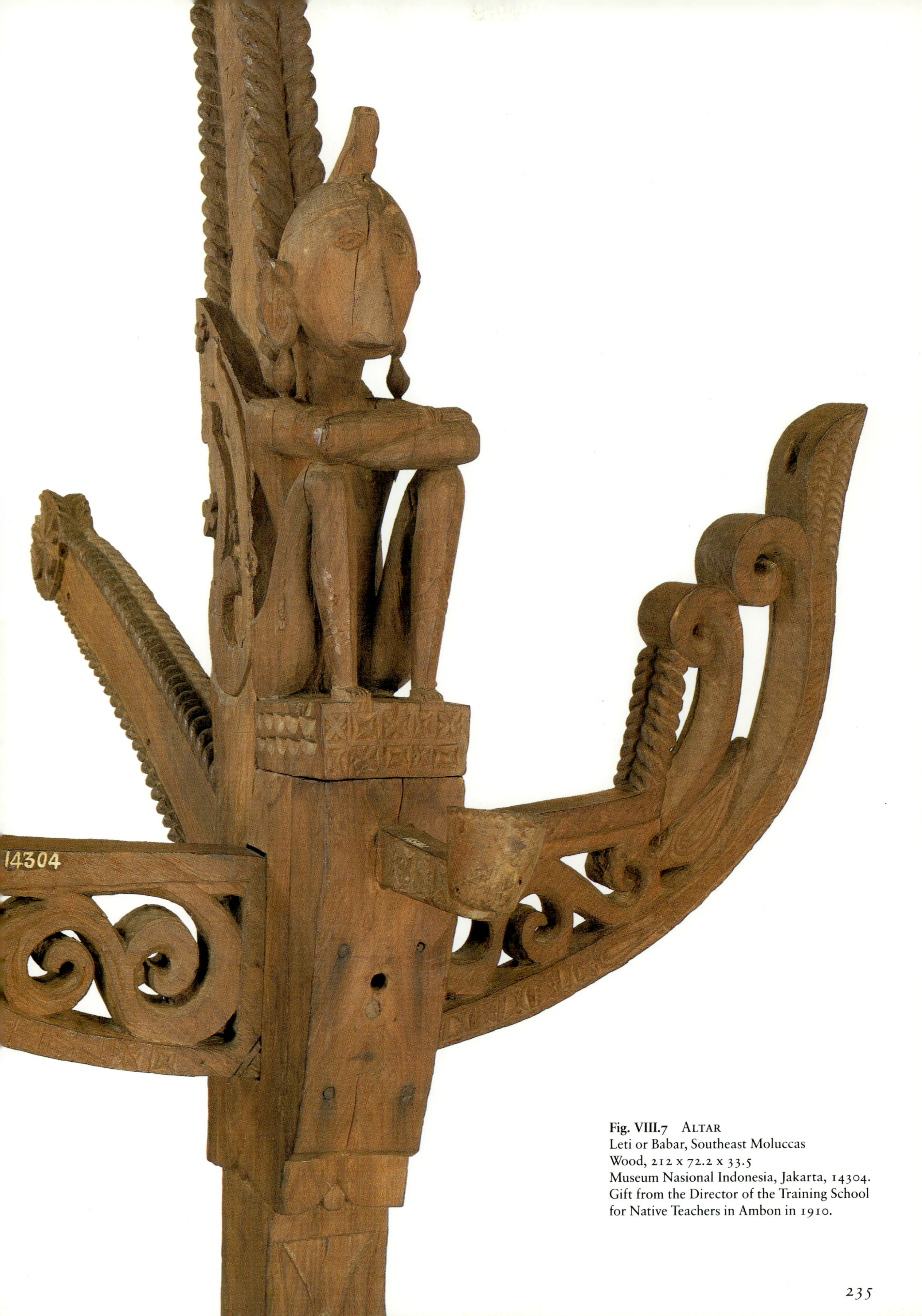

Fig. VIII.7 ALTAR
Leti or Babar, Southeast Moluccas
Wood, 212 x 72.2 x 33.5
Museum Nasional Indonesia, Jakarta, 14304.
Gift from the Director of the Training School for Native Teachers in Ambon in 1910.

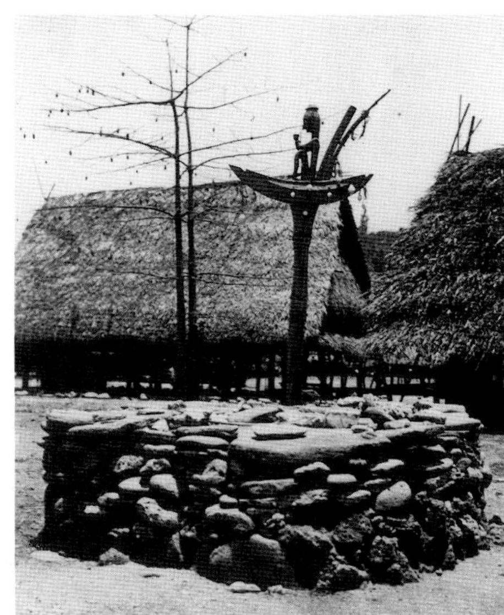

Fig. VIII.8 A village altar in place above a platform of stones, near Emroin, Babar, before 1913. Courtesy Rautenstrauch-Joest-Museum, Cologne.

above the worshipping villagers, who would squat upon the stone platform at the sculpture's base.

On Luang, such wooden village altars (*aitiehra*) appear to represent a first ancestor or village founder (van Dijk and de Jonge 1990:10). A corresponding female ancestor image, along with another male image probably representing her brother, were kept in a separate building for sacrifices. Traditional Luang great feasts were held only every several years and honored the ancestors represented by these carved figures. They also celebrated the wife-taking and wife-giving descent groups, whose union of hot and cool forces created fertility in both the village and the fields.

The form of two very similar altars (Figs. VIII.6, VIII.7) indicates that they were carved in either Babar or Leti because they display several characteristic aspects of Southeast Moluccan iconography. The ancestors sit on a platform above a crescent of openwork scrolls, which undoubtedly represents a boat, a metaphor for the community. Both figures are male although the gender is not especially emphasized. The ancestors' faces are dominated by extraordinarily large noses, set just below the downward-angled eyes, which reach almost to the chin. The eyes were probably inlaid with shell. Ornaments indicating high status are carved on the figures and include a pair of dangling earrings, a headdress with a horizontal band, a comblike extension on the top, and a pair of decorative leg bands below the knees. The ancestors' backs rest against carved posts that rise high above the figures and that terminate in rounded flower forms. Similarly shaped posts extend from the backs of the altars, carved with open scrollwork like that of the crescent boat forms. The woodwork around the ancestors and their offering cups is extensively carved with spiral forms and four-petaled flowers. The theme of generation and fertility is probably implied. At the base of the tall altar posts are globes that have been painstakingly carved within the confines of the square vertical columns as if to suggest that the ancestors rise above some celestial or universal body.

From about 1820, the Protestant church established missions across the Leti islands from the regional capital of Ambon. During subsequent years, many ancestor figures and altars were burned, and so those stored in museum and private collections are almost the only ones that remain (personal communication, Jean Pierret 1990).

On Leti, busts of important ancestors were sometimes mounted on three-post altars set into a base of stones. Three busts were mounted on these triple altars, one atop each support post, with the largest figure set in the center (personal communication, Jacques Pierret 1990). Perhaps the central figure represented an apical ancestor figure and the two side figures were more recent progenitors. The bust (Fig. VIII.12) was a finial of such an altar post. In addition to the characteristic long nose, the figure has a small but clearly incised mouth, intact shell eyes, and a tall sprouting headdress. According to collection records, a banner of imported red cloth was originally attached to this wooden bust, but it was missing by the time of an inventory in 1950.

Public sculptures in the Southeast Moluccas also included figures of such mythic heroes as Atuf (Fig. VIII.14) in Tanimbar, who created the present universe by spearing the sun to pieces (McKinnon 1988:158–59). Atuf had a hermaphroditic sister, Inkelu, who may be represented in this ancestor figure (Fig. VIII.13). The sculpture's graceful outstretched arms resemble the gestures of women performing a traditional dance that is said to imitate flying frigate birds (Fig. VIII.10). The carved armbands on the figure would, in Tanimbar, indicate that the wearer is female (personal communication, McKinnon 1990); however, the sexual organs of this figure are clearly male, suggesting a mixed-gender identity. The union of genders, featured in numerous outer-island artworks such as the ancestor figures of Nias and carved doors of the Tetum people of Timor, generally refers to the potency of sexual creation.

Collection records do not specify the island of origin of this sculpture (Fig. VIII.13), but it could derive from the Babar islands, where men as well as women wear carved-shell armbands, and so the sculpture would represent a deified male ancestor or village founder (personal communication, de Jonge 1990). The puzzling figure, its wood structure revealed by weathering, is characterized by an elongated torso and relatively short legs beginning below a waistband ornamented with s-spirals. The face has worn, small features; the comb extension of the headdress and some neck decoration have also been eroded.

Ancestor Altars in the Household

Although Southeast Moluccan village altars and other public sculptures were dedicated to supreme male and female deities, mythic heroes, and village founders, beautifully carved household altars were dedicated to ancestor figures. In Tanimbar, house altars (*tavu*), carved in the form of human beings with outstretched arms, stood in the center of family dwellings. These *tavu* altars (Figs. VIII.15, VIII.16), which no longer exist in Tanimbar, were associated with the ancestors of particular houses. A bench was placed before the altar for the head of the house, who sat there during such ritual occasions as marriage negotiations to represent the family's interest. Above these altars were shelves (*kalulun tavu*), on which were placed the skulls and neckbones of revered ancestors, a ceramic plate for offerings, small ancestor figurines, and other heirloom valuables (Drabbe 1940:36; Geurtjens 1941:19–20).

According to McKinnon, the term *tavu* is related to a Tanimbar word for the "beginning, starting point, base, or root of something," because the ancestors are considered the root of the present family household. The *tavu* "represents the ancestor as a human figure abstracted into the structure of the house itself: that is, as a founding figure transformed into an enduring social entity" (McKinnon 1987:11). Male, female, or ambiguous sexual characteristics are exhibited in different *tavu* altars, perhaps to represent either specific ancestors or the abstract concept of ancestral parentage.

The ancestor in this *tavu* altar (Fig. VIII.16) is clearly male, and he wears a waistband, plumed headdress, and heirloom earrings. Sprouting spirals fill the bell-shaped background around his body and below the ground upon which his feet rest. The ancestor's body has a rather smooth surface. His arms, seemingly terminating in wing feathers, are practically unmodelled, and his legs are turned outward with the heels touching each other.

Some of the carvings on *tavu* altars depict heirloom treasures owned collectively by the house, jewelry such as gold breastplates and earrings that were never given away in marriage exchanges (McKinnon 1987:10). The ancestor on this *tavu* (Fig. VIII.16) wears a pair of male earrings, called *loran* (Figs. VIII.27, VIII.28). Animal carvings, also seen on many *tavu* altars, refer to the names and origin stories of the family owning the house. The *tavu* from Tanimbar (Fig. VIII.15) includes depictions of two fish wearing earrings at the top, and a man's gold breast pendant at the center of the intricately carved altar board. Although this *tavu* altar represents an ancestor, it is carved in a very abstract scrollwork style.

Ancestor Figurines

Small ancestor figures, called *walut* in a Tanimbar language, were stored with such heirloom valuables as ancestors' skulls and offering dishes on the shelf above the *tavu* altar (Fig. VIII.17). Ancestor figures were sometimes taken from the house and used by men to invoke ancestors' aid in such dangerous work as smelting metal, boat building, and hunting. Seated in a customary cross-legged sitting position, these female ancestor figures (Figs. VIII.18, VIII.19) hold containers for betel nut. Typical Leti-style carving, an elongated tapering torso, prominent triangular nose, and inlaid shell eyes characterize this ancestor (Fig. VIII.19) who wears earrings and her hair in a coiled topknot. The Tanimbar sculpture (Fig. VIII.18) wears additional jewelry: anklets, bracelets, and a long string of beads with a pendant. She sits soberly above a platform decorated with four-petaled flowers.

Fig. VIII.11 Drum
Babar or Leti, Southeast Moluccas
Wood, plant fiber, goat skin, 82.3 x 35
Museum Nasional Indonesia, Jakarta, 14302.
Gift from the Director of the Training School for Native Teachers in Ambon in 1910.

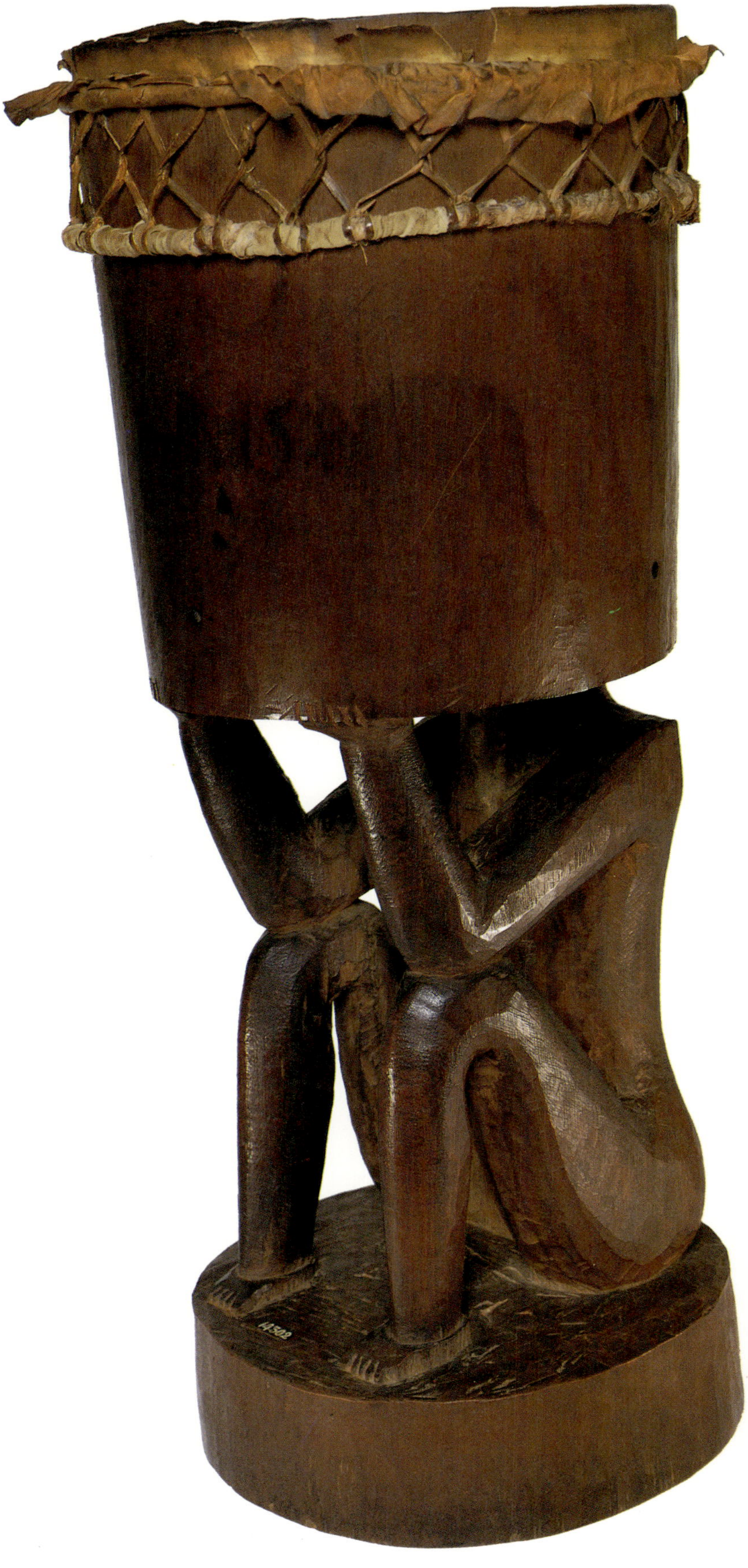

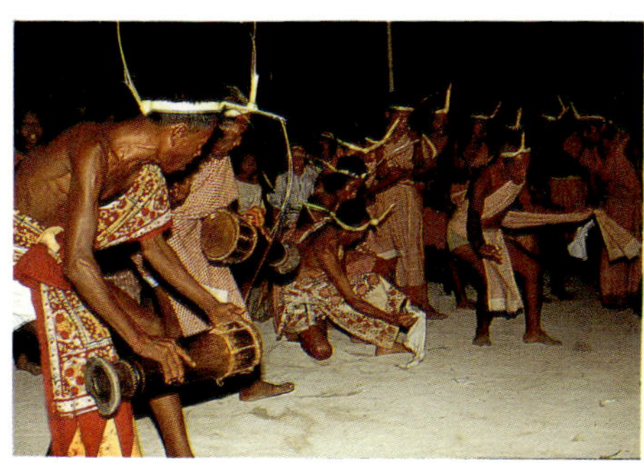

Fig. VIII.9 Men dancing with ceremonial drums, Luang. Nico de Jonge

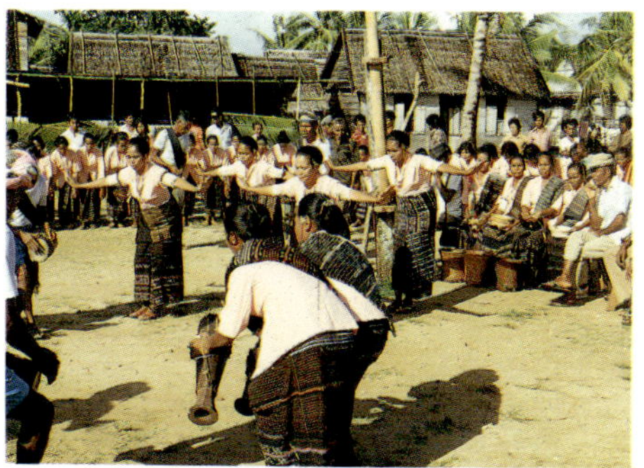

Fig. VIII.10 Women perform a ceremonial dance, their arms like the wings of flying frigate birds, Latdalam village, Tanimbar, 1980. Susan M. McKinnon

Fig. VIII.13 ANCESTOR FIGURE
Tanimbar or Babar, Southeast Moluccas
Wood, 140 x 64.4 x 11
Museum Nasional Indonesia, Jakarta, 18058

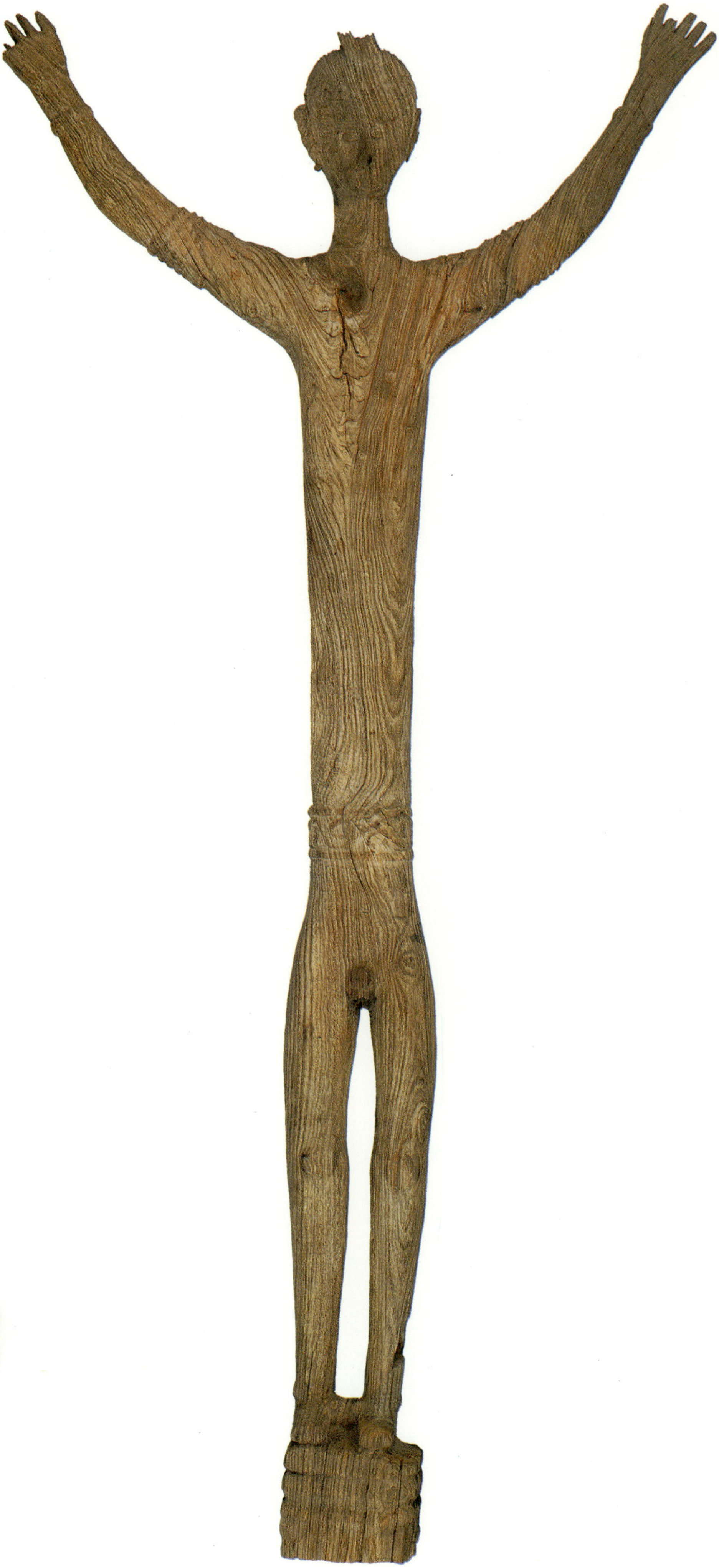

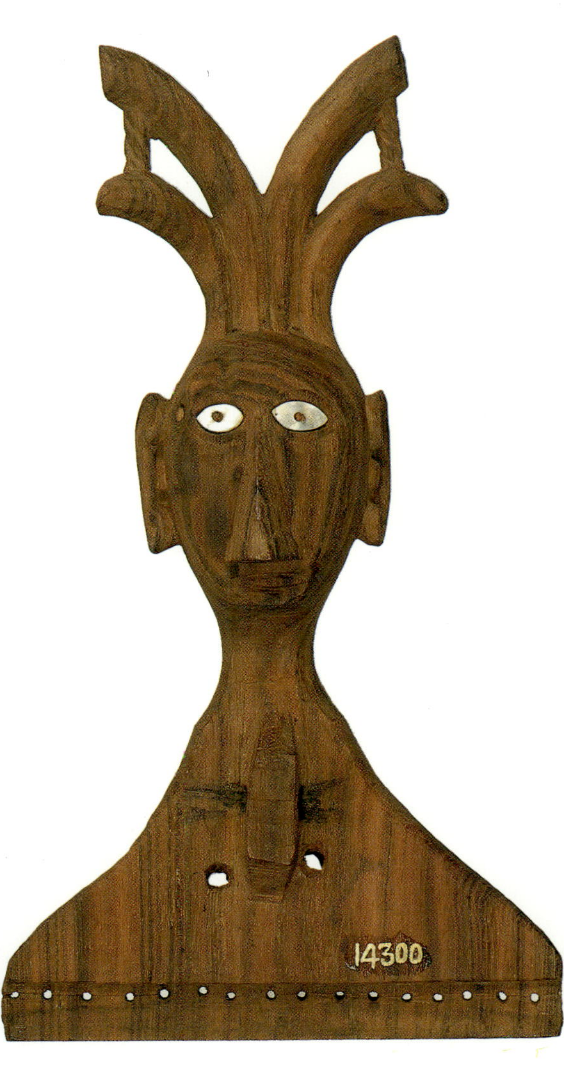

Fig. VIII.12 ANCESTOR FIGURE
Leti, Southeast Moluccas
Wood, shell, 30 x 16 x 7
Museum Nasional Indonesia, Jakarta, 14300.
Collected before 1910.

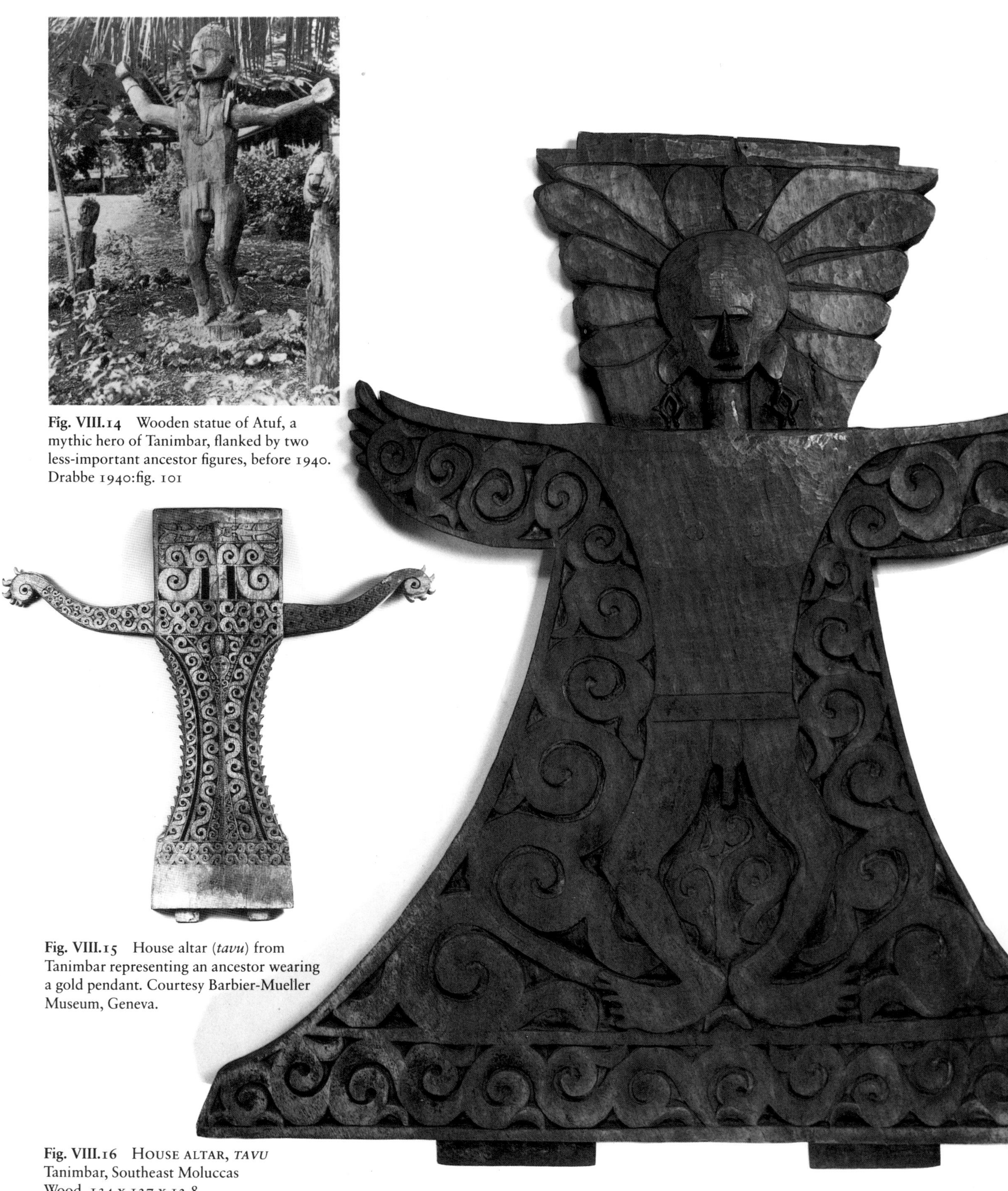

Fig. VIII.14 Wooden statue of Atuf, a mythic hero of Tanimbar, flanked by two less-important ancestor figures, before 1940. Drabbe 1940:fig. 101

Fig. VIII.15 House altar (*tavu*) from Tanimbar representing an ancestor wearing a gold pendant. Courtesy Barbier-Mueller Museum, Geneva.

Fig. VIII.16 HOUSE ALTAR, *TAVU*
Tanimbar, Southeast Moluccas
Wood, 134 x 127 x 12.8
Rijksmuseum voor Volkenkunde, Leiden, 2235/1

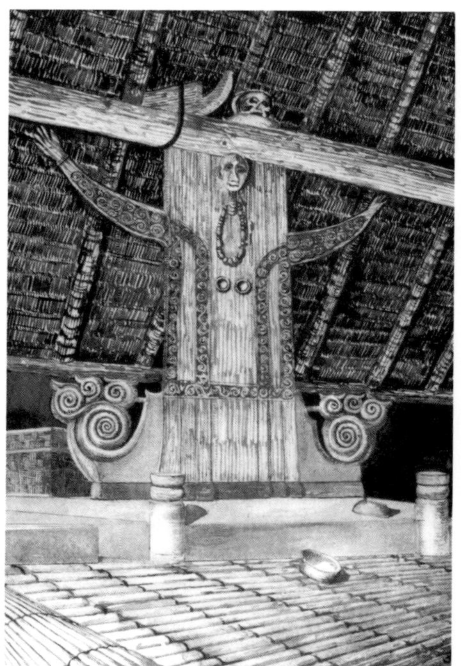

Fig. VIII.17 An early twentieth-century artist's rendition of a Tanimbar *tavu* altar with heirloom valuables set on a shelf above the altar. Drabbe 1940:front plate

Southeast Moluccan ancestor figurines depict revered individuals, as the heirloom jewelry and other items included in the statues reveal. The male ancestor (Fig. VIII.20) is poised in a traditional sitting position and has been honored by the inclusion of a chair, which, as an imported object, was a symbol of high status. Although his nose, earrings, and headdress have been damaged and his inlaid shell eyes lost, his inlaid shell teeth, each individually carved, remain. The individual (Fig. VIII.21) is portrayed sitting in a Western chair with his feet hanging down in the Western manner and wearing a distinctively European hat as signs of his prominence.

Some Southeast Moluccan ancestor figurines (Figs. VIII.20, VIII.21) are sculpted abstractly as in the case of Nias ancestor figures (*adu*). They have streamlined, limbless bodies without the spiral ornamentation characteristic of much regional carving. Their eyes and mouths are barely more than dents, and their human form is indicated only by the modelling of their rounded heads, necks, and waists. The smaller statuette (Fig. VIII.26), carved of ox bone and petite enough to be easily portable, was probably carried as an amulet in the owner's betel-nut bag.

Other Wood Carvings

In Leti and Lakor, carved planks (Fig. VIII.31) are also kept as charms in the household (personal communication, Hans Rijoly 1989). The roosters and trees carved in the top register and the fish and frog in waves in the lower sections recall the cosmic divisions between the upper world and the lower world and between land and water. The original use of these carved planks is not known. This carving (Figs. VIII.30a, b) depicts a cock, a popular Leti image, on one side and only geometric forms on the other side. The dominant motif on both sides is a fully rounded spiral set in undulating patterns bordered by bands of diamonds and triangles.

The Gender of Objects and Activities

The prominence of gender in classifying activities and objects has been noted often by scholars of Indonesia, particularly of eastern Indonesia (van Wouden 1968[1935]; Fischer 1938; van der Kroef 1954). In Tanimbar, virtually all objects, activities, and social groups are considered to have a gender (Drabbe 1923; McKinnon 1989). Traditional male valuables, such as breast pendants, solid earrings, swords, and elephant tusks, are given by a husband's family to that of the wife during and following marriage ceremonies. Female valuables, given by a wife's family include textiles, beads, openwork earrings, and shell armbands. Highly valued heirlooms are owned and exchanged by aristocratic houses, and lesser valuables are exchanged by commoners. Male objects tend to be solid and heavy, associated with death, heat, and hunting. Female objects tend to be light and integrating—textiles, for example, that intertwine warp and weft threads. These female objects are associated with birth, coolness, and gardening (McKinnon 1989).

In Tanimbar, gold breast pendants (Fig. VIII.29), whether worn by men or women, are considered male valuables and are given by the husband's kin group. Important pieces of gold jewelry are considered to have supernatural origins or powers and may be kept as heirloom valuables in particular family houses (McKinnon in press). Little goldsmithing was done in the southeastern Moluccan region except for some specialized manufacture of earrings and rings, particularly in Luang. Hence, many of the heirloom ornaments were probably traded from other Indonesian regions, such as the Lesser Sunda Islands, where they are also found (see Fig. VII.23). Because the gold pendants were obtained in the distant past by ancestors, they are granted sacred or otherworldly status. According to de Jonge (personal communication, 1989), round gold pendants are often used in the islands of Leti, Moa, Lakor, and Luang to pay fines for traditional law (*adat*) offenses, such as a man's having had sexual relations with a woman of a higher social rank. Such gold disk pendants, which could be

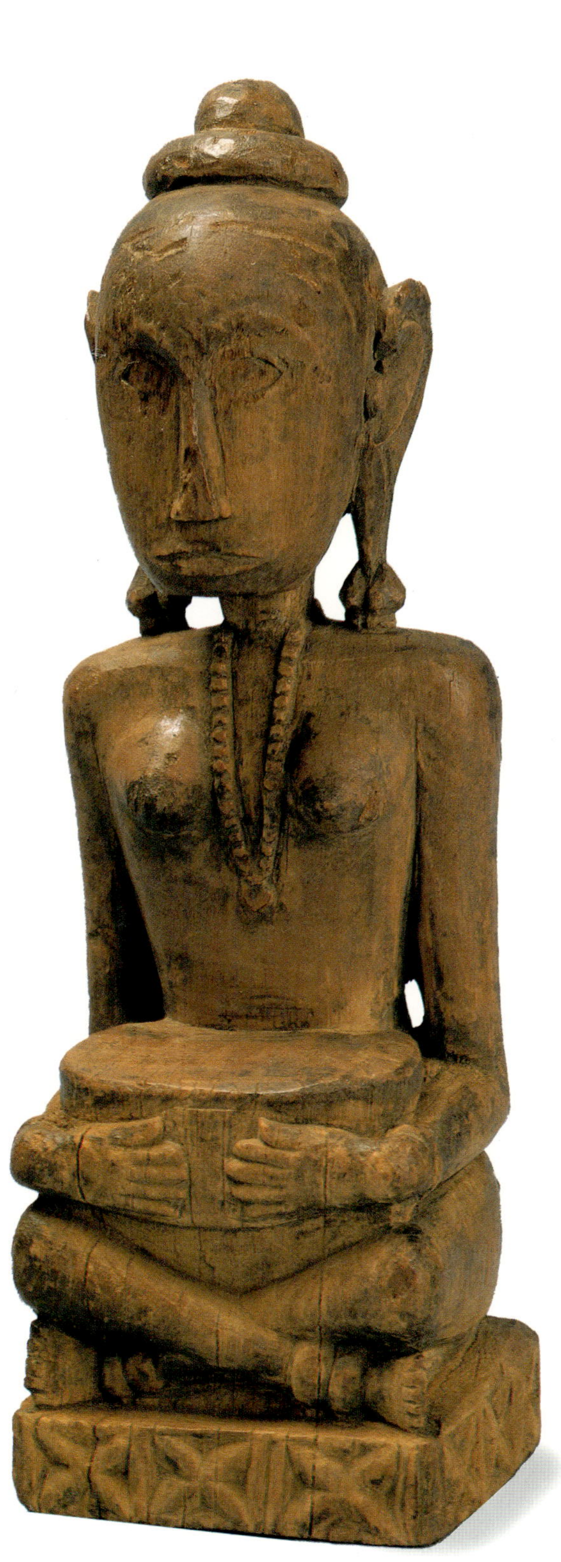

Fig. VIII.18 Female ancestor figure
Tanimbar, Southeast Moluccas
Wood, 18.5 x 6 x 5
Museum Nasional Indonesia, Jakarta, 6799

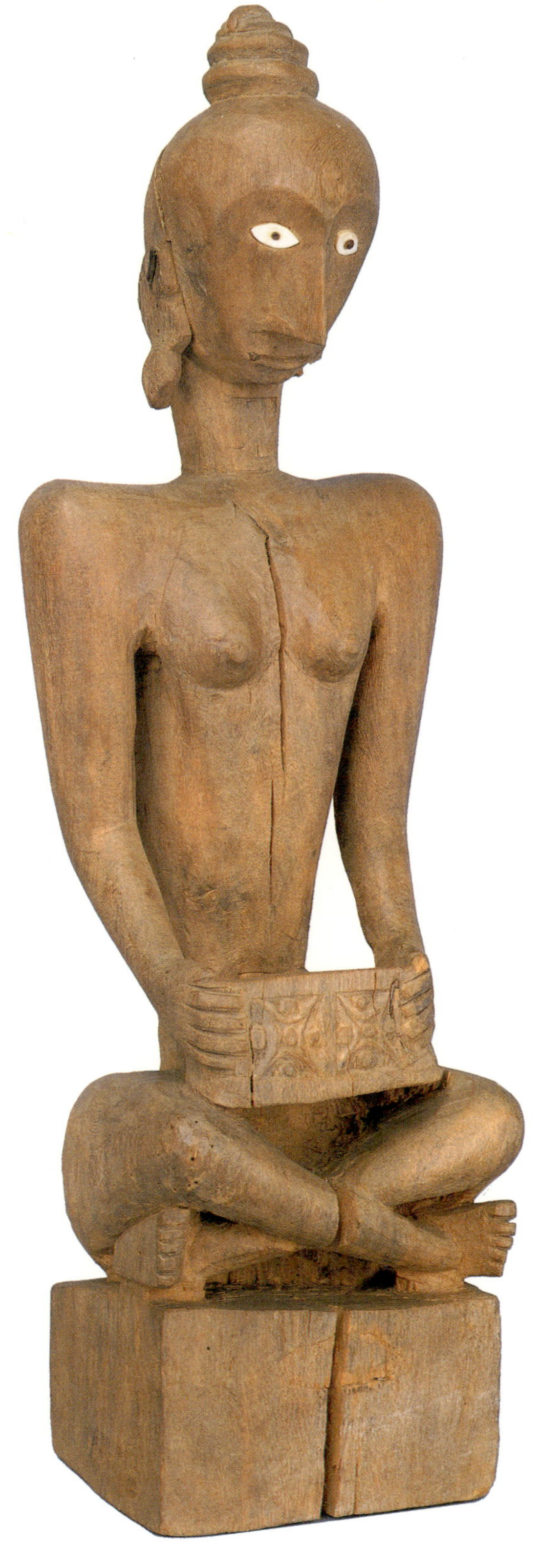

Fig. VIII.19 Ancestor figure
Leti, Southeast Moluccas
Wood, shell, 41.2 x 13.2 x 9.5
Museum Nasional Indonesia, Jakarta, 14295.
Accessioned in 1910.

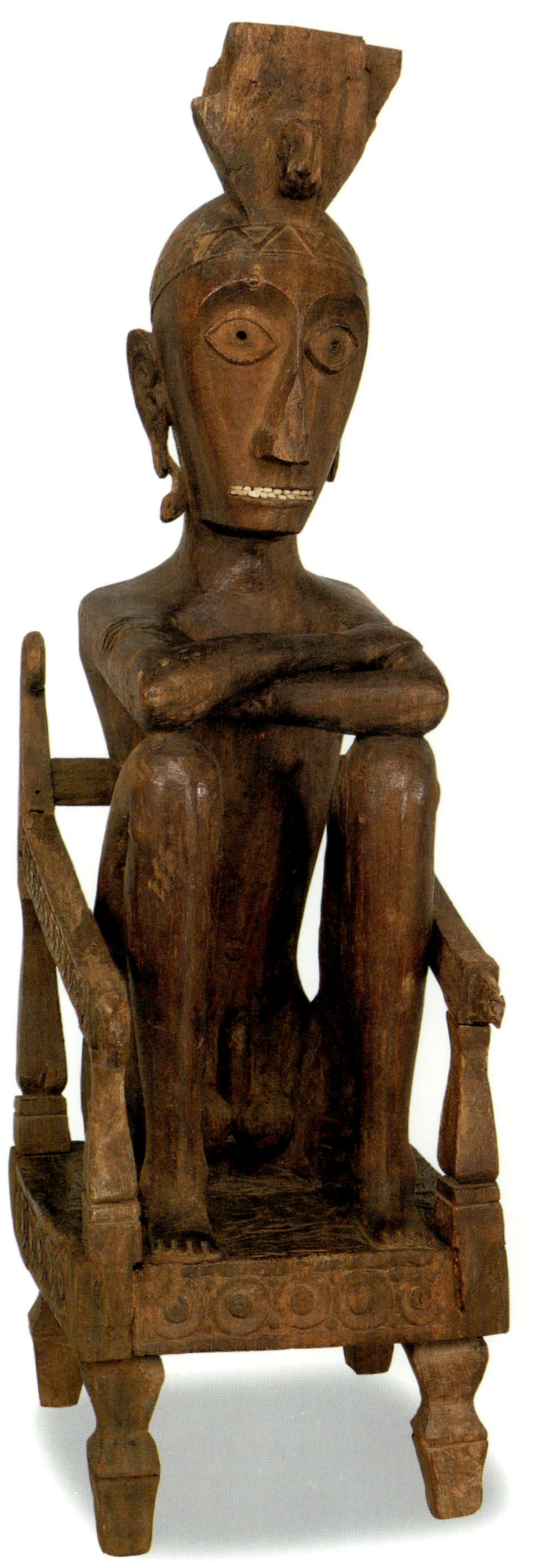

Fig. VIII.20 ANCESTOR FIGURE
Lakor, Southeast Moluccas
Wood, shell, 45.5 x 12.2 x 20.2
Museum Negeri Siwa Lima, Ambon, 297

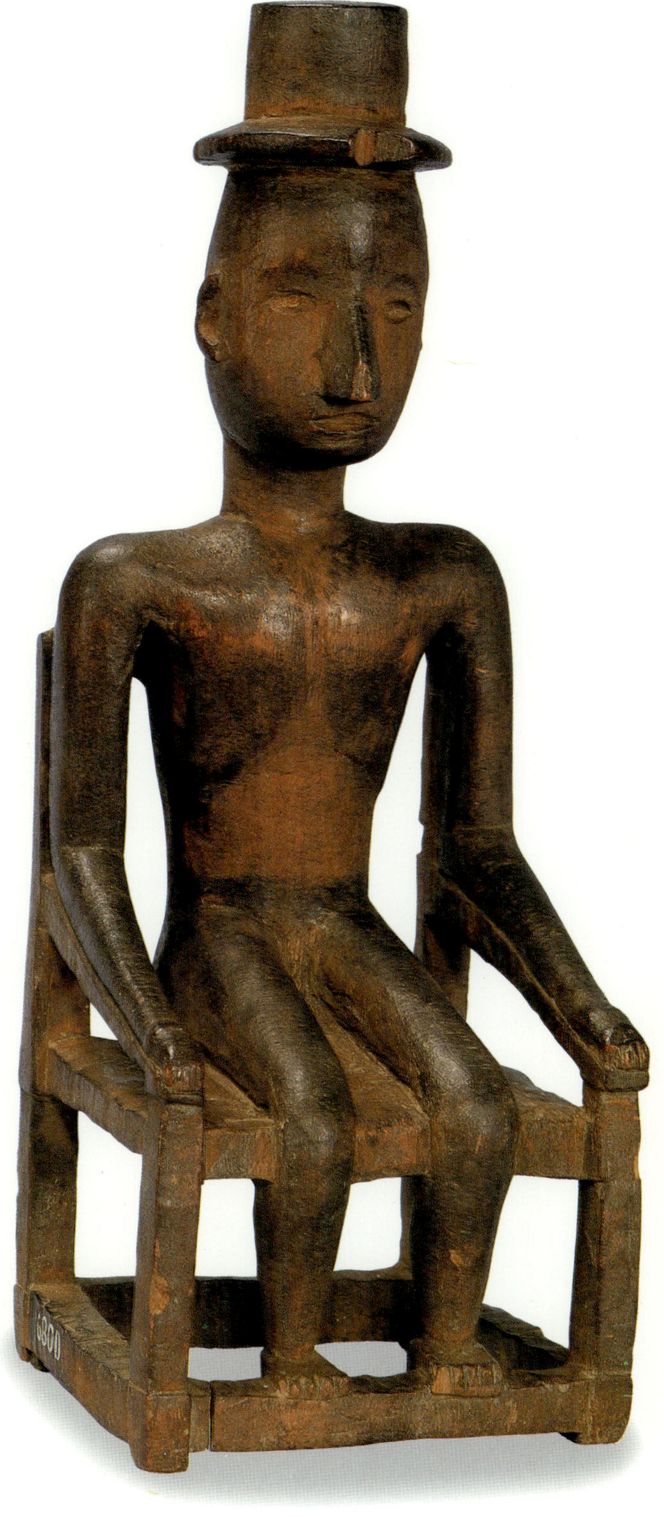

Fig. VIII.21 FIGURE
Southeast Moluccas
Wood, 19 x 7 x 6.6
Museum Nasional Indonesia, Jakarta, 6800

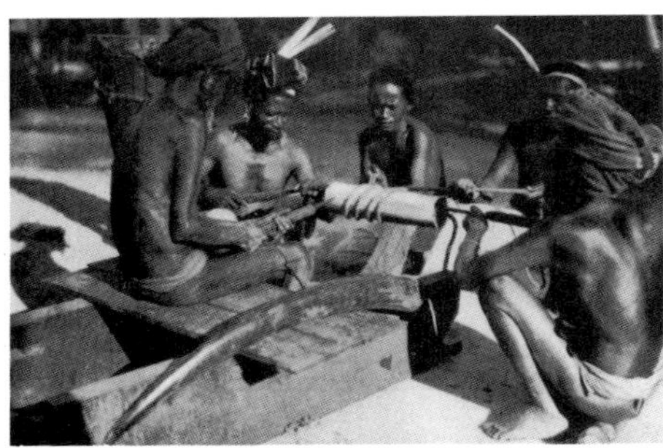

Fig. VIII.22 A group of men cut an elephant tusk to make jewelry, Tanimbar, before 1940. Drabbe 1940:fig. 43

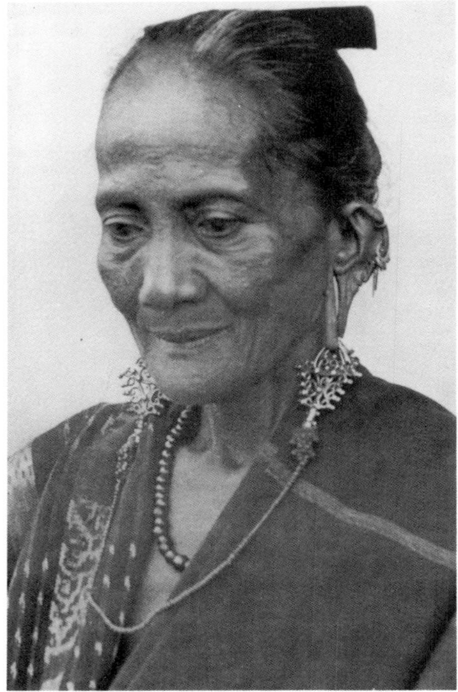

Fig. VIII.23 An elder woman wears female earrings (*kmene*) that are connected by a string of beads, also considered a female valuable, Tanimbar, before 1940. Drabbe 1940:fig. 45

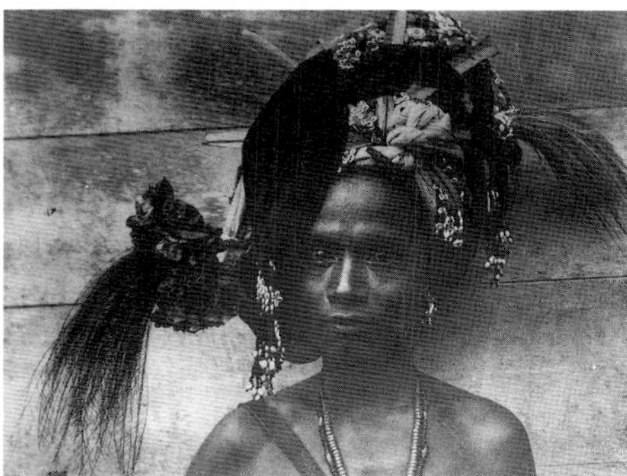

Fig. VIII.24 A youth wears ceremonial attire including a male earring (*loran*) similar to that in Fig. VIII.28, Tanimbar, early 1900s. Courtesy Royal Tropical Institute, Tropenmuseum, The Netherlands.

owned by members of lower social ranks, were less privileged valuables than ornate gold headdresses, which were traditionally reserved for ownership by the highest social class. The breast pendant (Fig. VIII.29) is a flat disk of beaten gold with two protruding eyes outlined with a fine metal braid. The fiber cord at the top served as a carrying handle or an attachment loop to hang the pendant on a neckband.

Elephant tusks are another male item, which the Tanimbar people reportedly obtained in trade with the Dutch during the seventeenth century. The cutting of elephant tusks into male armband rings was considered a dangerous male activity and was always accompanied by ritual music and dance (Drabbe 1940). Elephant tusks also were carved (Fig. VIII.22) to produce combs for personal adornment. An ornamental comb from Tanimbar (see illustration in Rodgers 1985:223) also made of elephant tusk depicts two dragons among delicately carved ivory scrolls set within concentric trapezoid wood frames. According to collection records, this comb was probably worn by women as a hair ornament.

Solid-cast earrings, usually made of gold or silver, are a male valuable despite their slit pear-shaped form, which signifies the female anatomy in other eastern Indonesian regions (see, for example, the *taijanja* ornaments of Central Sulawesi and the *mamuli* ornaments of Sumba). Because of its solidity this type of Tanimbar earring (Figs. VIII.27, VIII.28) is considered male, in contrast to open filigree or granulated-style earrings, which are classified as female (Fig. VIII.23). Male earrings and breast pendants are kept as heirloom valuables and worn on ceremonial occasions (Fig. VIII.24). Every aristocratic Tanimbar house tries to maintain possession of at least one valuable of high status as a sign of its prominence and social power (McKinnon 1987:10). *Loran* earrings, at least some of which are locally manufactured by Luang smiths, are one of the more common male valuables that are given by a young man's family when they begin marriage negotiations on his behalf.

Some types of gold and silver ear pendants are still produced in the Babar region of the Southeast Moluccas (personal communication, de Jonge 1989). The unusual earring (Fig. VIII.27) is made from the tooth of a sea cow, or manatee. These large aquatic mammals, which can be three to four meters long, are prized in the coastal Moluccas not only for their ivorylike teeth but also for their ample meat.

All locally made Tanimbar textiles, whether worn by women or men, are considered female goods (McKinnon 1989:33). Although no longer produced, men's loincloths (Fig. VIII.35) were traditionally woven in Tanimbar or imported from Babar and Luang (Drabbe 1940:21). Such loincloths are distinctive for the shells and bands of red trade cloth that were sewn onto a long, narrow plain-weave strip of locally woven cloth. Factory-manufactured red cloth from Europe was highly valued for men's loincloths, perhaps because it was identified with the male domain of sea trade. Since loincloths are no longer woven in Tanimbar, the remaining examples are prized as heirloom possessions and not traded in alliance exchanges (McKinnon 1989:33). Loincloths are still sometimes worn on ritual occasions but usually are wrapped around the chest instead of being worn draped at the hips in the traditional manner.

Tanimbar loincloths are decorated only at the ends, which are the only areas visible from the front when they are worn as originally intended. The long body of the cloth is a plain-weave strip dyed blue-black with indigo. The ends, or front flaps, have by contrast alternating bands of shell-ornamented red trade cloth and bands of black-and-white geometric motifs patterned with supplementary weft. The geometric motifs have a black-and-white figure-ground composition. The warp ends are woven as open slits and twisted into fringe terminated with seeds.

On other islands of the Moluccas, the composition and meanings of patterns in woven textiles is less well documented. De Jonge reports that, in Luang, especially long, three-panelled skirts with particular motifs were worn

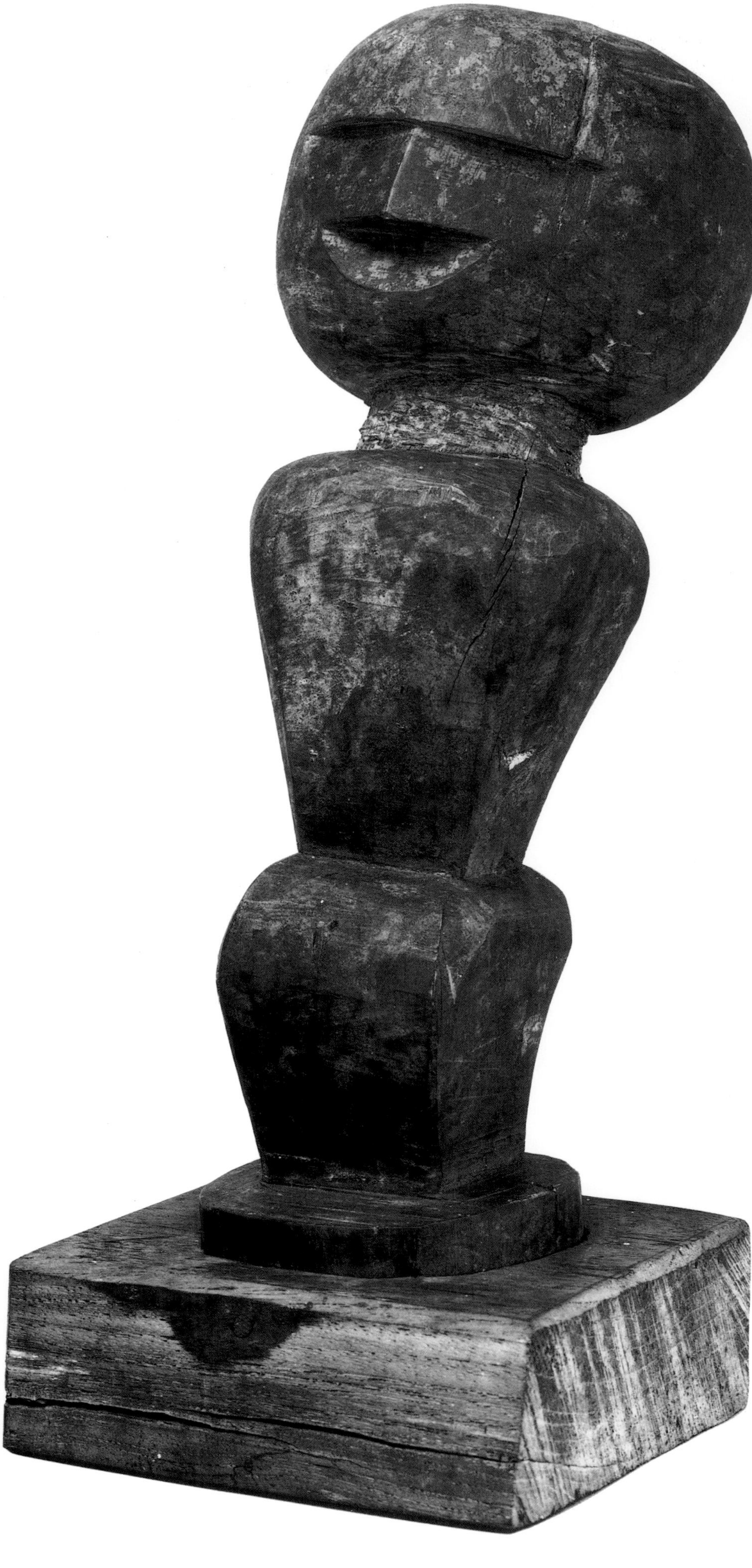

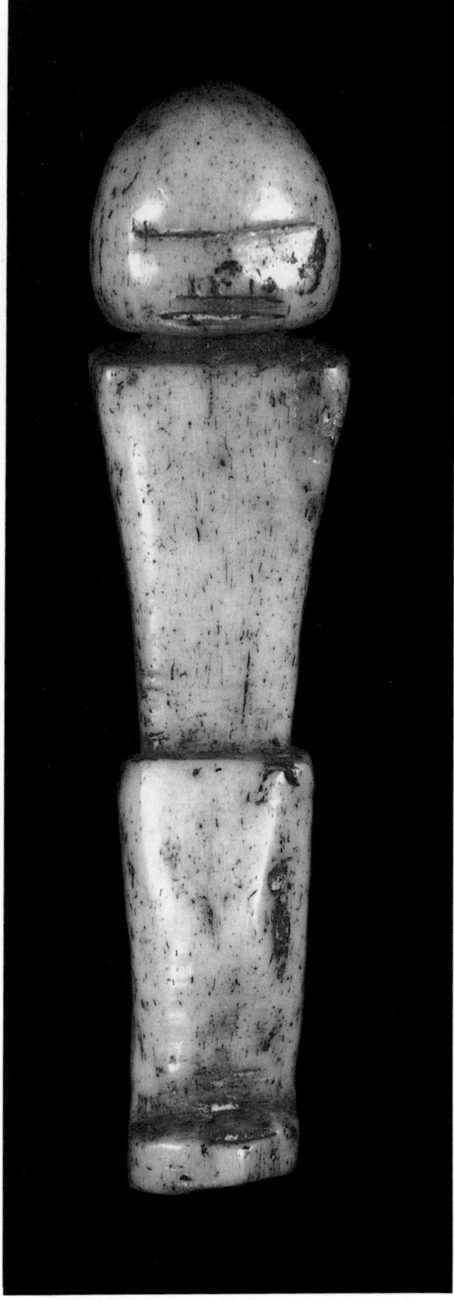

Fig. VIII.26 Ancestor figurine, *walut*
Tanimbar, Southeast Moluccas
Ox bone, 6.3 x 1.5 x 1.4
Royal Tropical Institute, Tropenmuseum, The Netherlands, 234-57. Donated by Jos. v. d. Kolk in 1924.

Fig. VIII.25 Ancestor figure
Babar or Tanimbar, Southeast Moluccas
Wood, pigment, 38 x 15.5 x 18.5
Museum Nasional Indonesia, Jakarta, 6771

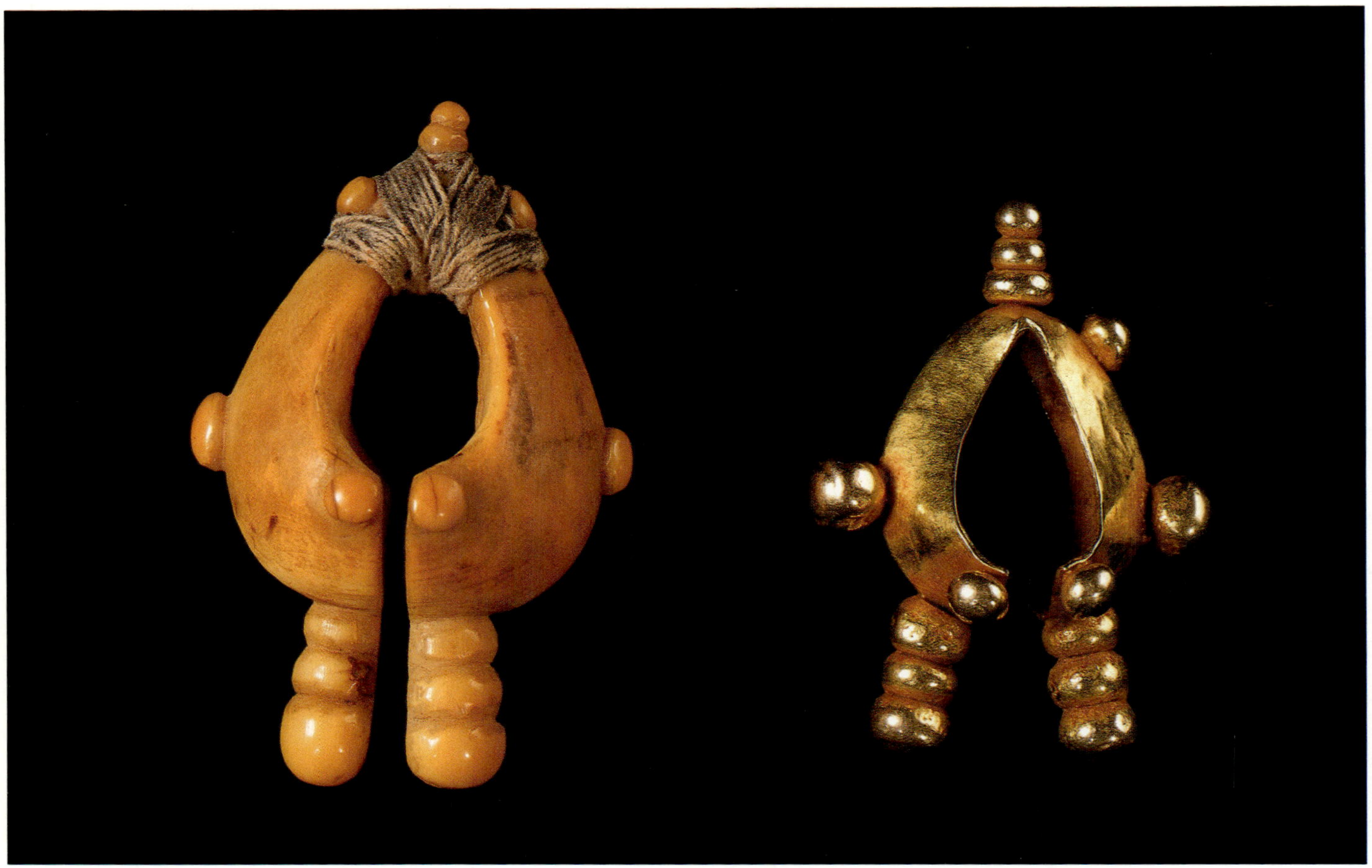

Fig. VIII.27 Ear ornament, *loran*
Tanimbar, Southeast Moluccas
Sea cow tooth, 5.9 x 3.6 x 2.8
Royal Tropical Institute, Tropenmuseum, The Netherlands. 1468/158. Accessioned in 1941.

Fig. VIII.28 Ear ornament, *loran*
Tanimbar, Southeast Moluccas
Gold, 4.5 x 3.2 x 2.4
Thomas Murray

opposite
Fig. VIII.29 Gold breast pendant, *karse*
Moa, Southeast Moluccas
Gold, fiber, 6.3 x 1.5 x 1.4
On loan from the Christensen Fund, Palo Alto, California.

traditionally by only the women of the highest social class. Shorter, black sarongs with only a single central panel were worn by women of the lowest social class. Aristocratic descent groups owned the right to weave particular patterns for their women's skirts and men's loincloths, and violations of these rules were supposedly punishable by fines (see Barnes 1989c for a parallel case on Lembata in the Lesser Sundas). In Luang today, *sarong* cloths are still woven for trading purposes although most people wear Western-style clothes (personal communication, de Jonge 1990).

Painstakingly woven warp *ikat* cloths were made for Kisar men to wear around their waists or to drape over their shoulders as a mantle. Long-armed, frontally poised human figures, cocks, and triangular-shaped trees, which decorate the two outer and a pair of intermediary bands (Fig. VIII.36), are characteristic designs of one type of Kisar textile (see also Gittinger 1979:194). This cloth was created by sewing the two halves of a single longer woven panel side by side to create a mirror-image opposition. The patterns in the cloth appear on the naturally colored, undyed warp threads that have been tied by the *ikat* process. The background areas of the warp threads are dyed with indigo and natural red. Between the four blue figurative panels are three larger red geometric panels filled with growing spiral forms bounded with hexagonal frames. Between these major panels are rows of red, blue, and natural stripes including thin blue *ikat* stripes with small crescent forms.

Textiles for women are still woven in Tanimbar, where they play an important role in the gift exchanges made throughout the lifetime of a marriage. Representing the "composite and binding qualities characteristic of females" (McKinnon 1989:35), textiles are key female objects, although they incorporate male as well as female design motifs. The most valued type of woman's tube-skirt is the oldest known style, the "antique sarong," or *bakan mnanat* in the Fordatan language. These elegant but relatively plain cloths include a large black

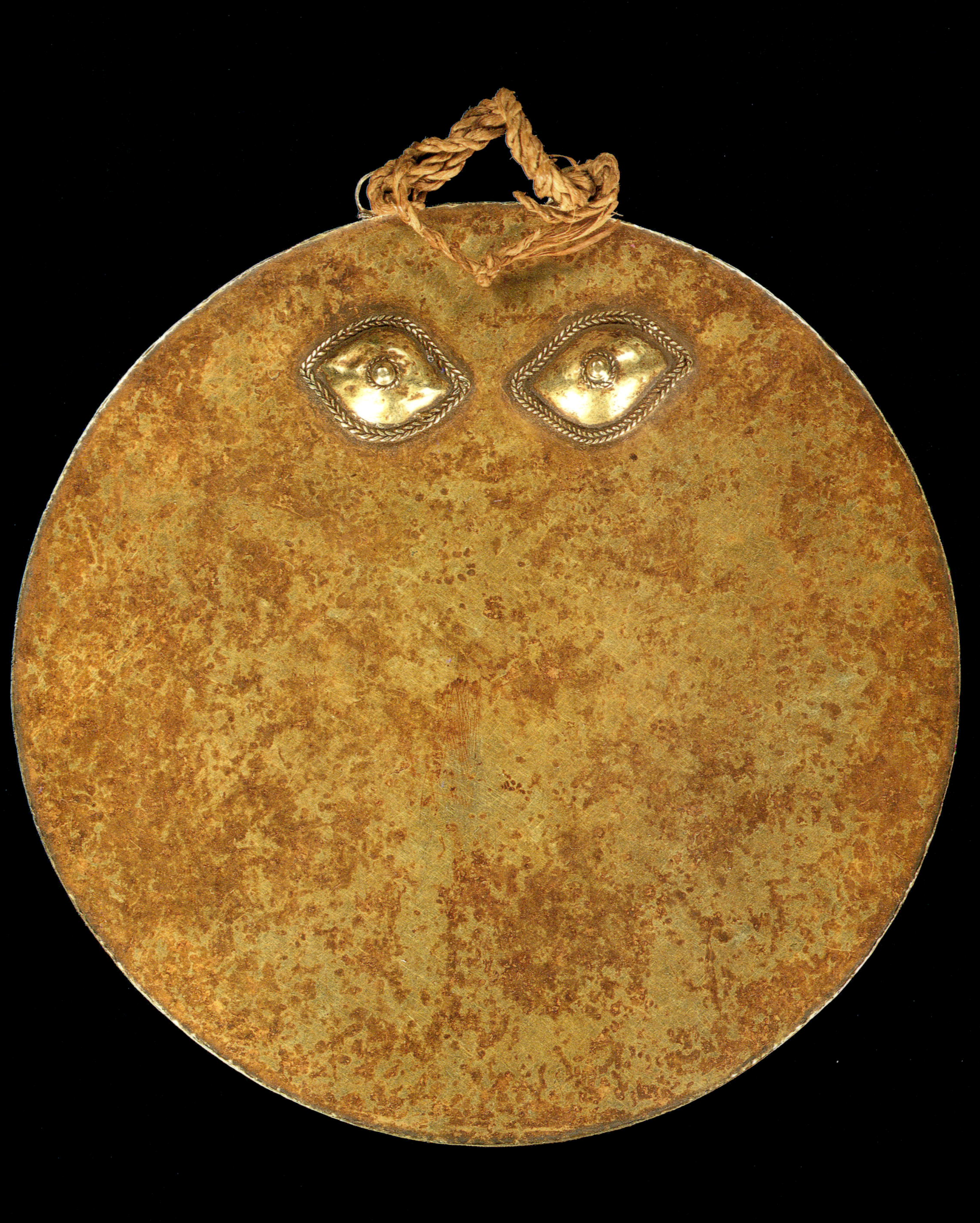

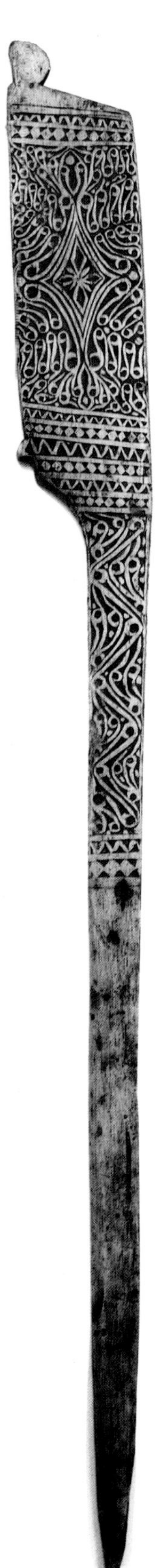

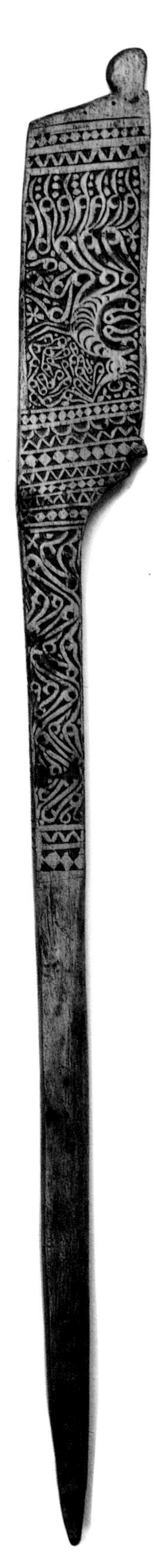

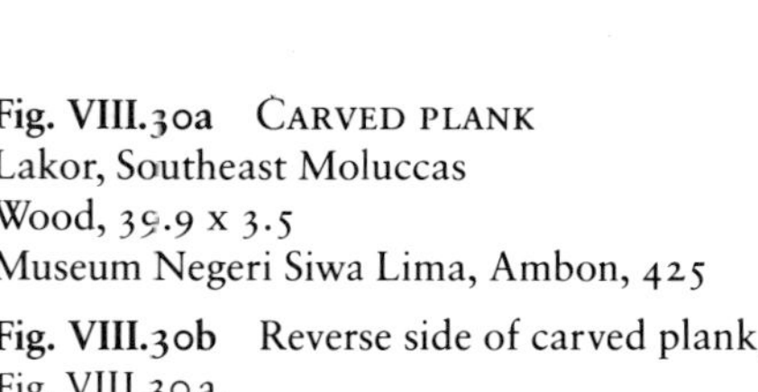

Fig. VIII.30a Carved plank
Lakor, Southeast Moluccas
Wood, 39.9 x 3.5
Museum Negeri Siwa Lima, Ambon, 425

Fig. VIII.30b Reverse side of carved plank, Fig. VIII.30a.

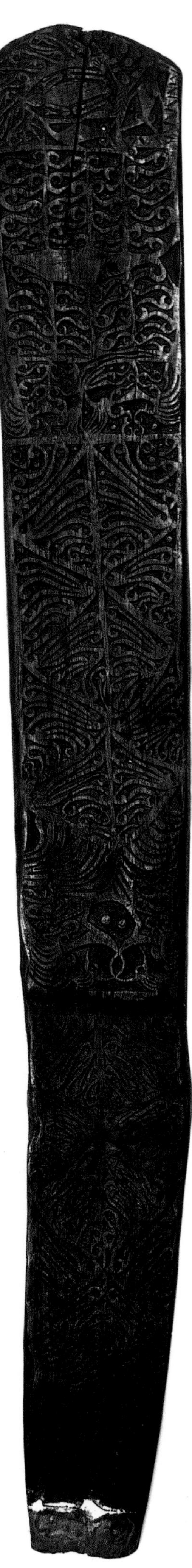

RIGHT
Fig. VIII.31 Carved plank
Nuwewang, Leti, Southeast Moluccas
Wood, 68.8 x 8.7 x 1.7
Museum Negeri Siwa Lima, Ambon, 426

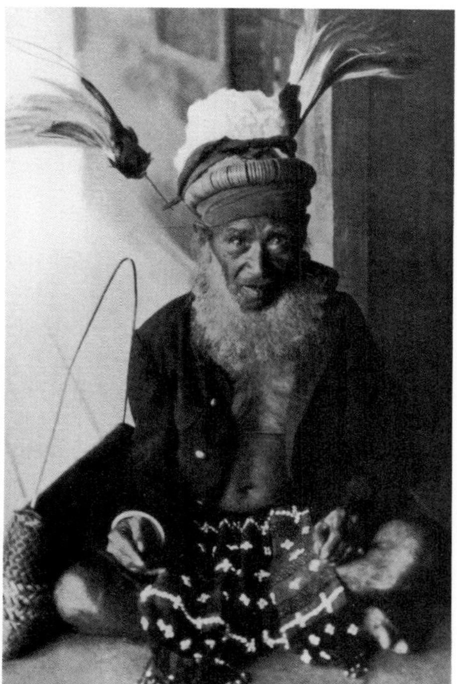

Fig. VIII.32 Elder in ceremonial dress, including a feather headdress, an imported jacket, and a locally manufactured shell-decorated loincloth, Tanimbar, before 1940. Drabbe 1940:fig. 64

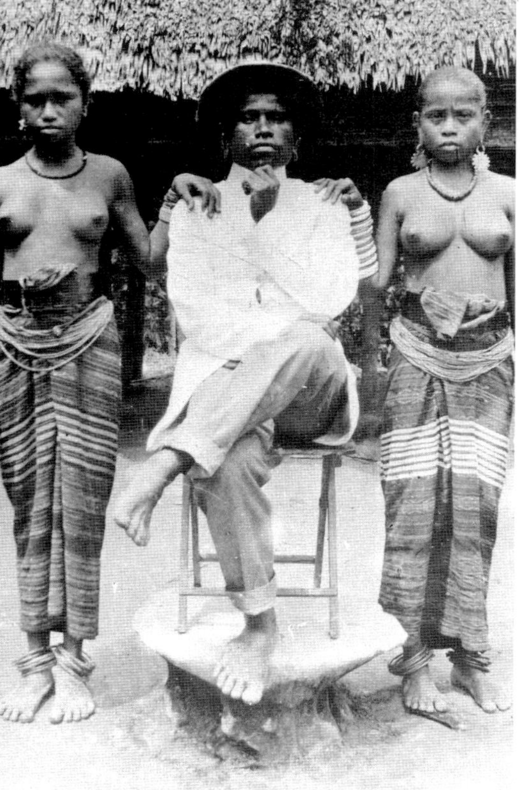

Fig. VIII.33 Two women wearing tube-skirts (*bakan maran*) and heirloom jewelry, posed beside a man in a colonial hat and jacket, Tanimbar, early 1900s. Courtesy Royal Tropical Institute, Tropenmuseum, The Netherlands.

central panel ornamented with brown pinstripes (see illustration in McKinnon 1989). Only the end bands are adorned with warp *ikat* patterns.

The second most valued type of Tanimbar tube-skirt is the *bakan maran* (Fig. VIII.34), characterized by bold dark and light stripes in the center and warp *ikat* end patterns including colored stripes called "rainbows" (McKinnon 1989:34–35). This type of textile always conforms to a certain compositional arrangement: the middle section on each side of the white-striped center includes three bands of geometrically patterned *ikat* separated by finely striped or *ikat* stippled bands. The end sections are separated from the middle sections by a solid black band. These geometric *ikat* end sections always include full or half "rainbows," bands of bright color, usually red and blue, which frame the geometric patterned bands. When worn in the traditional manner, the bright white stripes of the *bakan maran* skirt appear at the height of the wearer's lower hips or upper thighs (Fig. VIII.33).

Although female activities such as weaving and products such as textiles, in Tanimbar at least, are contrasted with male counterparts associated with danger and death, they are, in themselves, not considered sufficient to produce fertility in either the fields or the household. Rather, according to Moluccan cosmology, the creation of life emerges from the union of male and female forces, just as both types of objects must be present in the ritual gift exchange of a marriage alliance (Valeri 1980; McKinnon 1983, 1989; Rodgers 1985). As Valeri stresses when writing about marriage exchanges on Ceram, there is no local idea that valuables are paid in exchange for a wife, given that the different types of valuables given by the groom's and wife's families must be equal in monetary terms (1980:182). Rather they say that the process of negotiation and exchange of the two types of valuables gives them pleasure (Valeri 1980:191). Similarly, when some people of Tanimbar were asked why they bother to make these exchanges, which give them no real profit or accumulation of valuables, one answer given was that the exchanges are "tasty" (*manminak*), or aesthetically pleasing (McKinnon in press). Thus, it is not only the aesthetic productions themselves but also the social contexts of their use and transient ownership that are integral to Southeast Moluccan conceptions of their artworks.

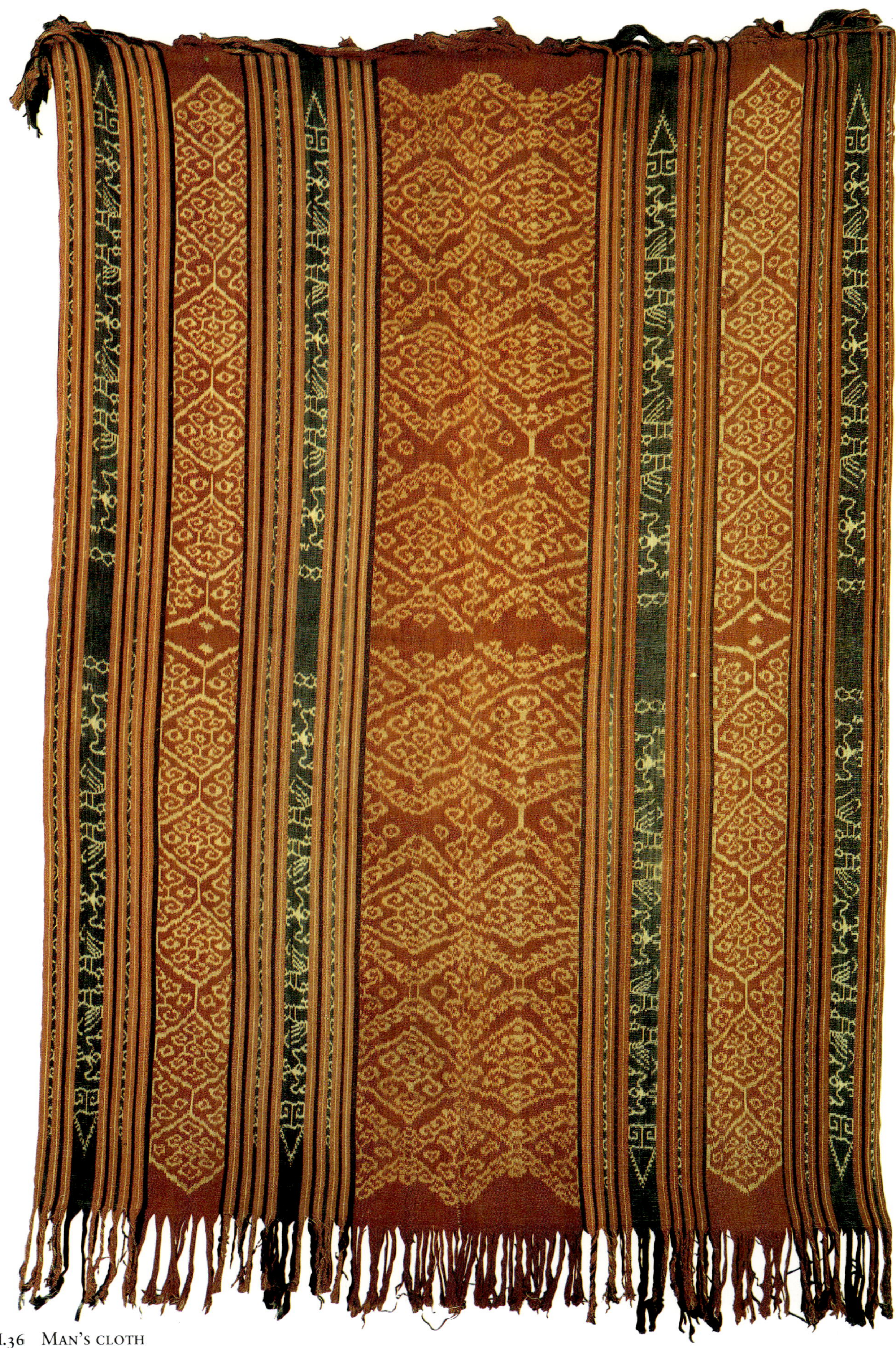

Fig. VIII.36 Man's cloth
Kisar, Southeast Moluccas
Cotton, 202.5 x 125
Thomas Murray

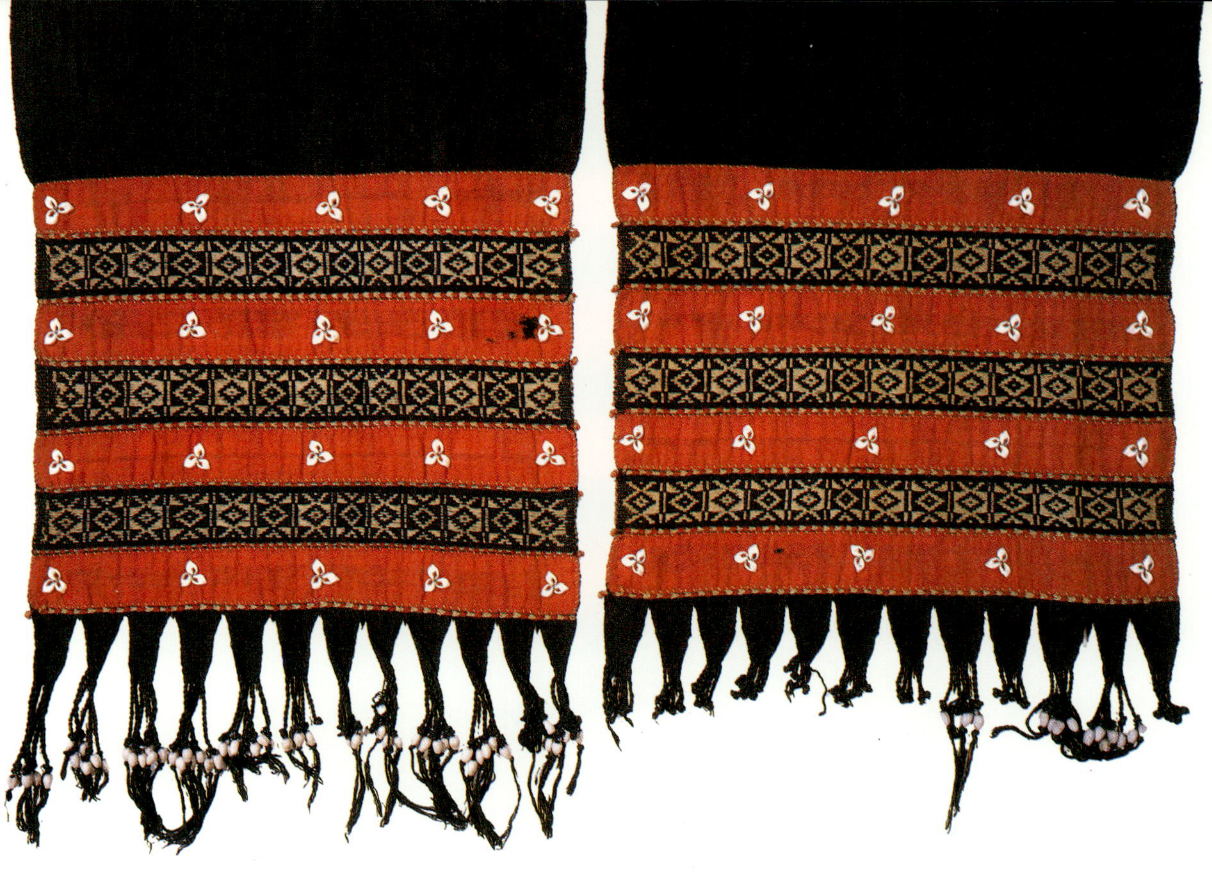

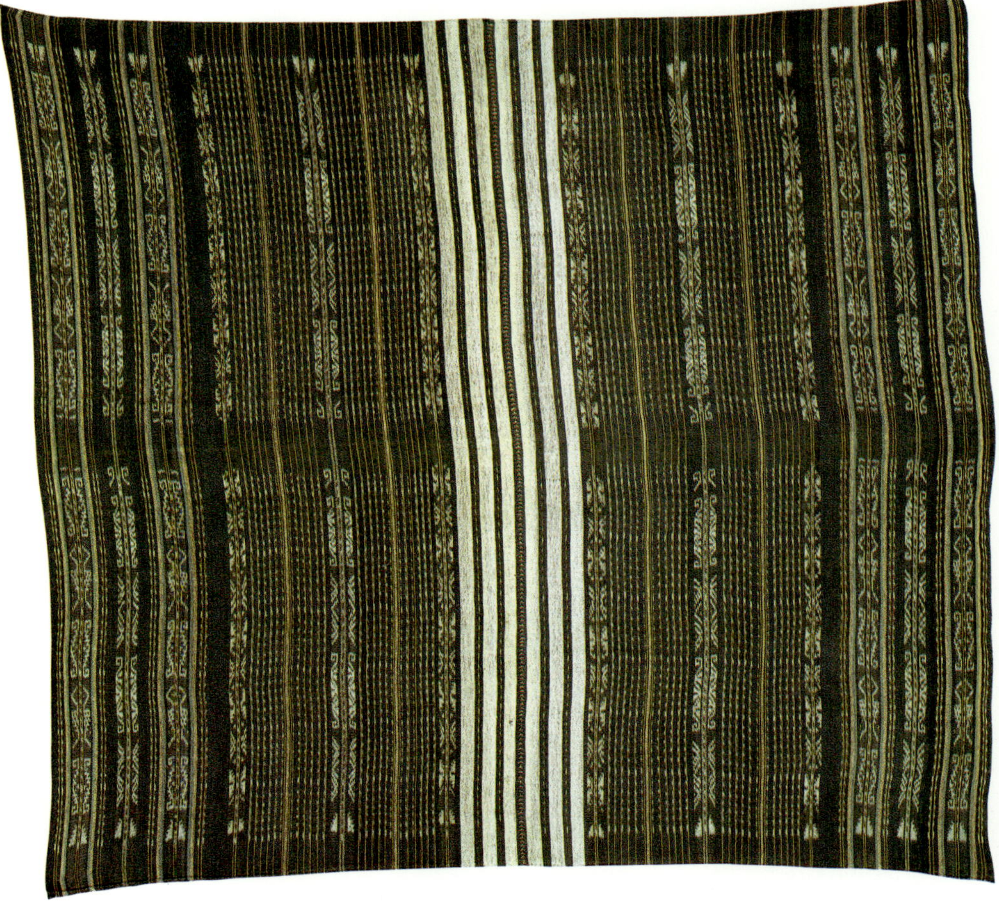

TOP
Fig. VIII.35 Man's loincloth, *eman*
Tanimbar, Southeast Moluccas
Cotton, shells, seeds, 32.5 x 392.8
Collection of John and Anne Summerfield

BOTTOM
Fig. VIII.34 Woman's tube-skirt, *bakan maran*
Tanimbar, Southeast Moluccas
Cotton, 137.6 x 121.2
Thomas Murray

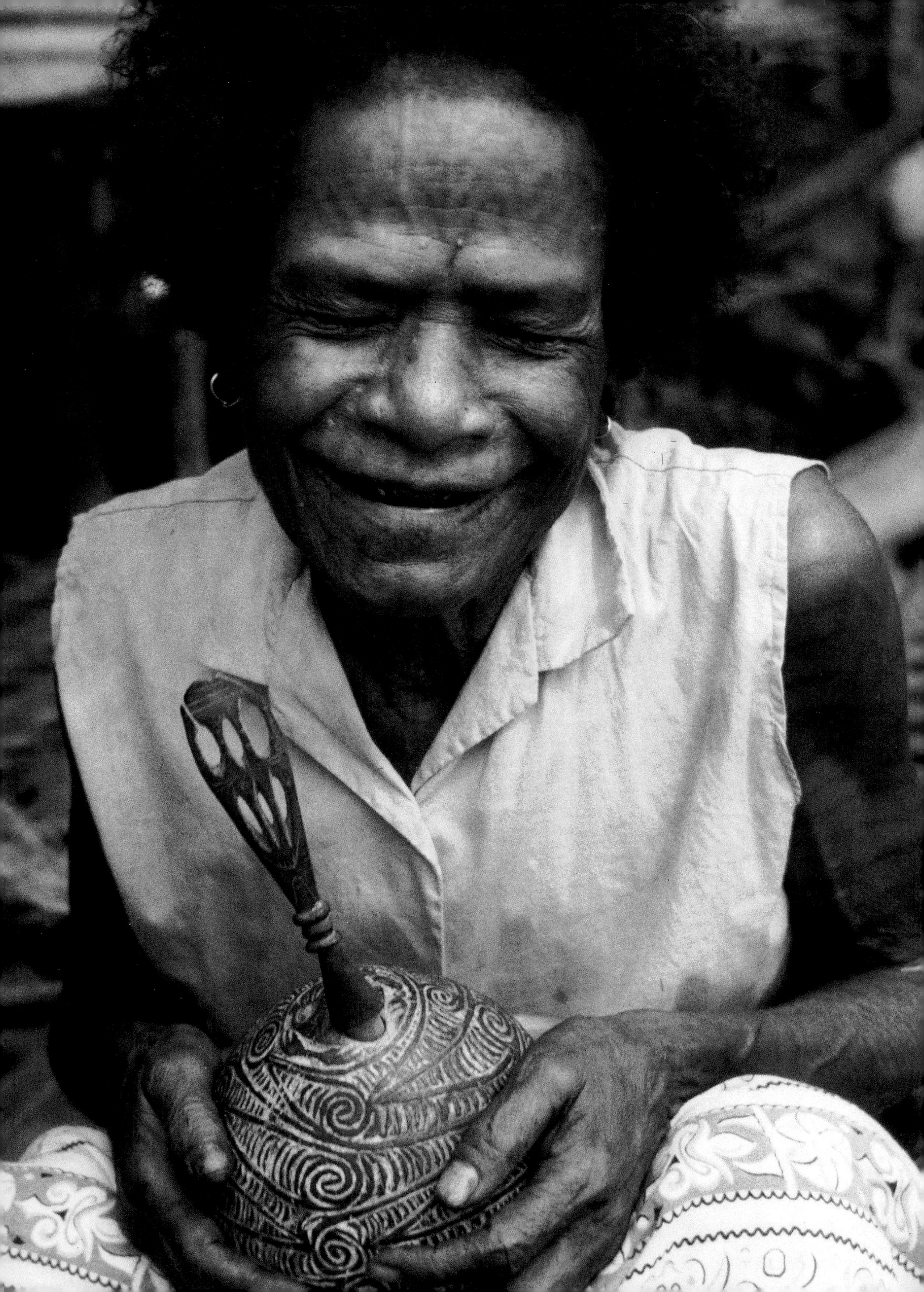

IX

North Coast of Irian Jaya

by Annamarie L. Rice

Fig. IX.1 Woman with a lime gourd made from coconut shell, a prerogative of certain older and important women, Jobe village, Lake Sentani, 1958. Jac. Hoogerbrugge

New Guinea, the main island of Melanesia, is situated between Micronesia to the north, Australia to the south, and greater Southeast Asia to the west. Irian Jaya, the western half of the island, covers 421, 841 square kilometers (162,873 square miles). The projected population of Irian Jaya for 1990 is 1,600,000 (Biro Pusat Statistik 1988:45). The word Irian is derived from the Biak word *irjan*, which means pretty, light, and emergent. The island is often said to be shaped like a bird; the upper northwest corner, which resembles the head, was called "Vogelkop" (bird head) by the Dutch and is now known as the "Kepala Burung" (bird's head) region. Like a bird's backbone, a mountain range, with several permanently snow-capped peaks, runs northwest to southeast along the center of the island.

The modern political history of Irian Jaya has been heavily influenced by foreign powers. The island has been visited by Chinese, Arabic, and Moluccan traders, as well as by the Portuguese, Spanish, and English. The Netherlands was the first European power, however, to attempt to gain political hegemony over the western half of the island. In an effort to expand resources for the Dutch East India Company and extend more political control over Indonesia, the Dutch built their first fort on Irian Jaya in 1828. This fort was abandoned in 1836 because of the harsh environment. It was not until Dutch government posts were built in Manokwari and Fak-Fak in 1898, Merauke in 1903, and Humboldt Bay in 1910, that Irian Jaya was considered to be under Dutch rule. Although they established forts, the impenetrability of the terrain kept the Dutch from moving deeply into the interior of the island, and so their real influence was limited.

During the Second World War, the Japanese invaded Irian Jaya but were ultimately expelled by the Allies, who placed it under Dutch administrative rule in 1945. In 1963, as part of the United Nations–sponsored Act of Free Choice, sovereignty of the area was transferred to the United Nations. In 1969 an indigenous Irian vote was held to determine whether Irian would become an

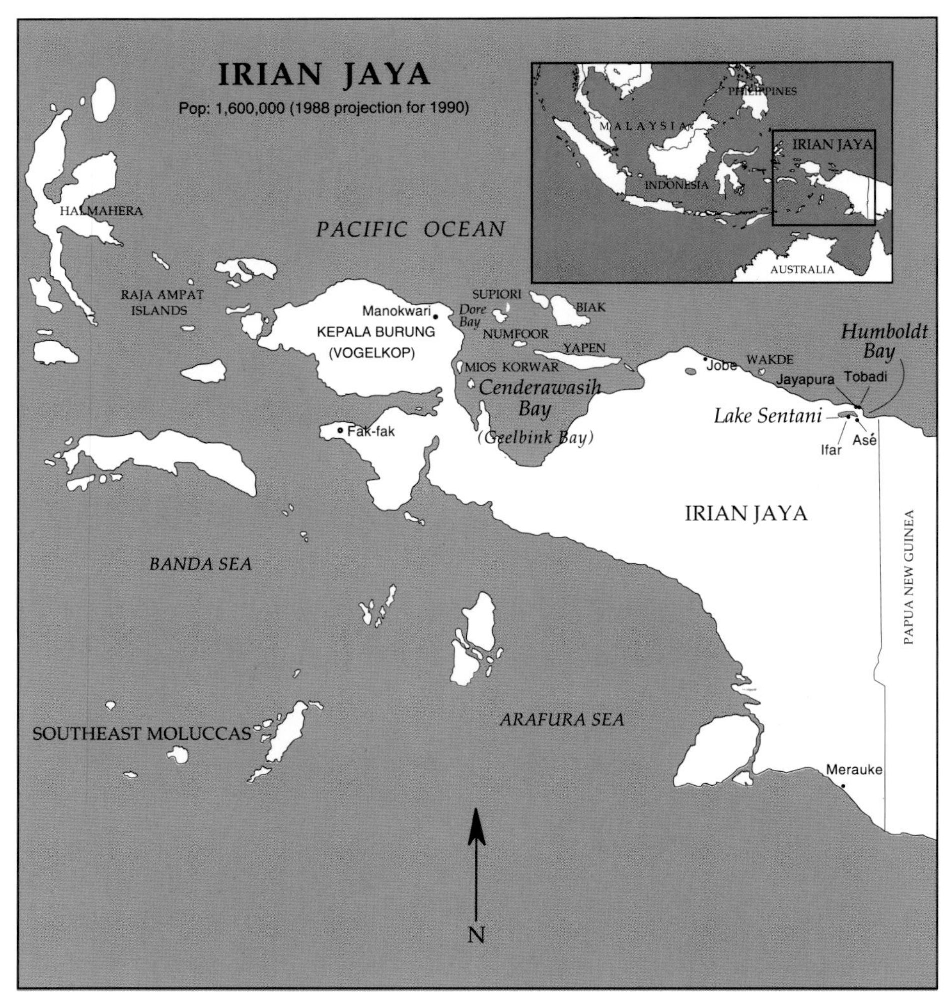

Fig. IX.2 Spatula
Dore Bay
Wood, 52 x 6 x 3.75
Department of Anthropology, Smithsonian Institution, 283926. Collected by W. L. Abbott. Accessioned in 1914.

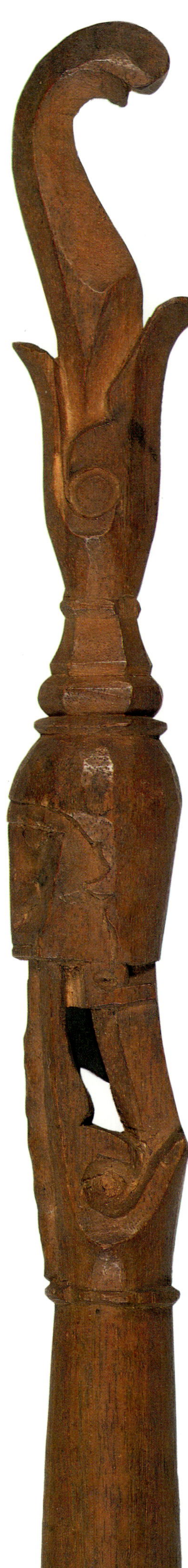

independent country or part of Indonesia. The outcome of this vote was that western Irian became part of the Republic of Indonesia and renamed Irian Jaya, "glorious Irian."

Archaeological evidence suggests that New Guinea was inhabited by 30,000 years ago (Bellwood 1979:63–64), and recent findings indicate that settlement may have occurred as early as 40,000 years ago (Groube 1986). The first migrants to the island were likely to have been speakers of Australoid languages. They were followed by several waves of non-Austronesian and Austronesian-language speakers (Wurm 1983:25). Today, the peoples of Irian Jaya speak either non-Austronesian or Austronesian languages. More non-Austronesian languages are spoken than Austronesian, with the Austronesian-language speakers settled mainly along the north coast (for further discussion of Austronesian and non-Austronesian languages see catalog chapter I). The language variations on New Guinea are greater than those in all of Island Southeast Asia, Micronesia, and Polynesia combined (Wurm 1983; personal communication, Stuart Kirsch 1990).

New Guinea has three ecological zones: coast, interior lowland, and highland. Subsistence strategies vary among these zones. Highland dwellers cultivate sweet potatoes and taro (a starchy tuberous root) and as a result have a more sedentary lifestyle, and population density is higher. Peoples of the interior lowland are dependent on sago palm, taro, and fishing, as well as hunting and-gathering. Peoples along the coasts depend upon sago and coconut palms, taro, pig and fish as well as maritime trade.

On the north coast of Irian Jaya, sago is the dietary staple. Sago is prepared by pounding and washing the pith of the sago palm (*Metroxylon* spp), and then it is either baked or made into pudding. This staple is augmented with tropical tubers, bananas, coconuts, sugar cane, pig, tree kangaroos, opossums, cassowary, bandicoots, field rats, and fish. The people of both Cenderawasih Bay and Lake Sentani have produced beautiful objects with which to prepare and serve these foods. These spatulas (Figs. IX.2, IX.4), are carved with anthropomorphic heads (a leitmotif of the region), which resemble those of the *korwar* ancestor figure. This long thin spatula (Fig. IX.2) terminates in a crook, used to hang it, which is an ingenious design of a tongue curving out of the mouth of an animal.

On Lake Sentani, carved plates were used to serve foods and also to carry food from private homes to the men's ceremonial house (Sande 1907:12). Large ceremonial plates (Fig. IX.6) were kept by the local headman for use at feasts to display pig's meat.

Carved hooks were used for the ritual presentation of food. On Lake Sentani on special occasions this hook (Fig. IX.3) was used to hang the first yields of the hunt or the harvest and other offerings to the local headman. The projecting hooks on this piece are carved with ancestor figures. Because this type of sacred hook was made to ensure prosperity, fertility, and peace, it had to be possessed by the headman. A human figure carved on the end of Fig. IX.5, for instance, was thought to represent fertility (Hoogerbrugge 1967:64–66). The s-shaped motif (seen on Fig. IX.3 and the back of Fig. IX.5) is distinctive of Lake Sentani art. The same design can also be seen on the plate (Fig. IX.6), the drum (Fig. IX.15), and the paddle (Fig. IX.28).

The peoples of Irian Jaya had no weaving tradition. Body adornment usually consisted of armbands, necklaces, or various types of headdresses and other decorations (see de Clercq and Schmeltz 1893:plates I-XIII). Women, however, sometimes wore barkcloth skirts. In the village of Asé on Lake Sentani, the production of barkcloth began with procuring a sapling about two meters long and twelve to fourteen centimeters in diameter. The top layer of bark was scraped off with a shell. The sapling was then beaten with a short piece of wood held at a 45-degree angle, which eventually separated the inner bark from the stem. The bark was cut longitudinally where it was the most knotty and the inside fibers were removed. The fiber was then placed on stones and beaten and

Fig. IX.3 SUSPENSION HOOK
Lake Sentani
Wood, 50.5 x 40.5 x 8.9
Museum Nasional Indonesia, Jakarta, 18063D

OPPOSITE LEFT

Fig. IX.5 HOOK
Lake Sentani
Wood, 53 x 10 x 9
Museum Nasional Indonesia, Jakarta, 18063F

OPPOSITE RIGHT

Fig. IX.6 Large ceremonial plate, Ifar village, Lake Sentani, 1958. Jac. Hoogerbrugge

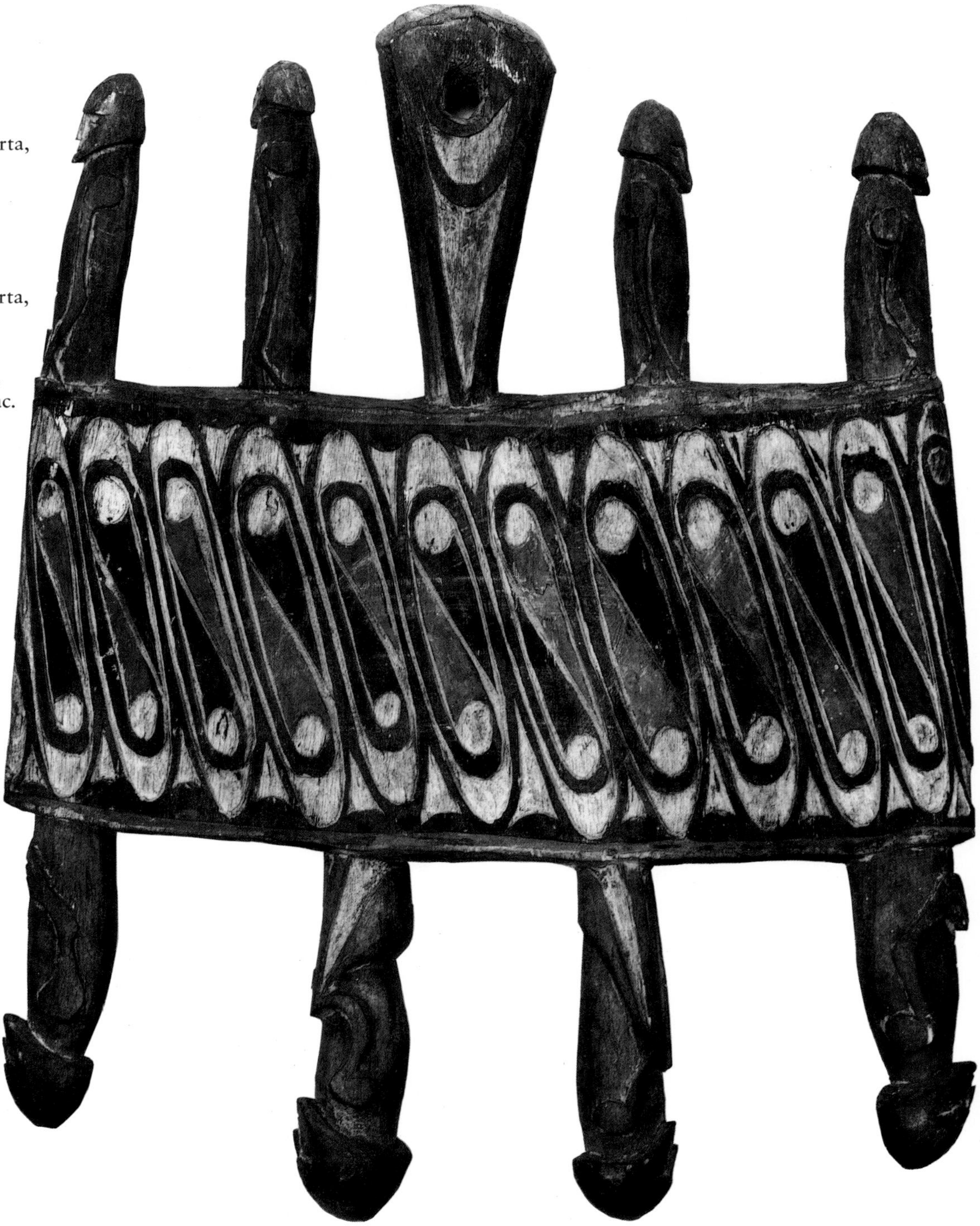

Fig. IX.4 SPATULA
Cenderawasih Bay
Wood, 49.3 x 5 x 13
Museum Nasional Indonesia, Jakarta, 7010

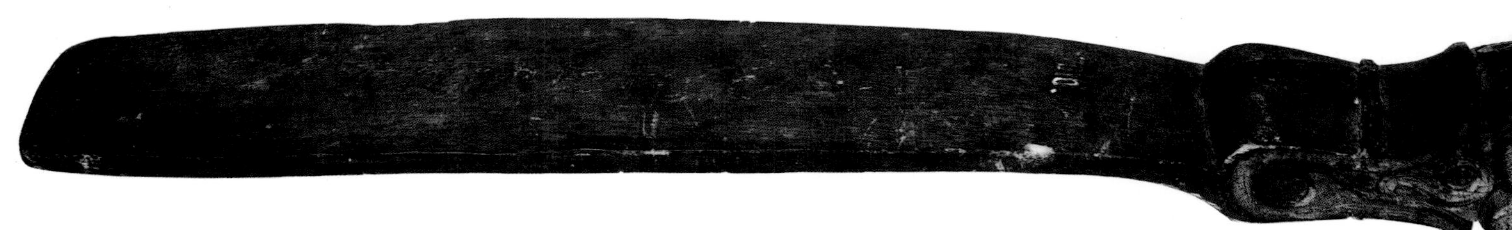

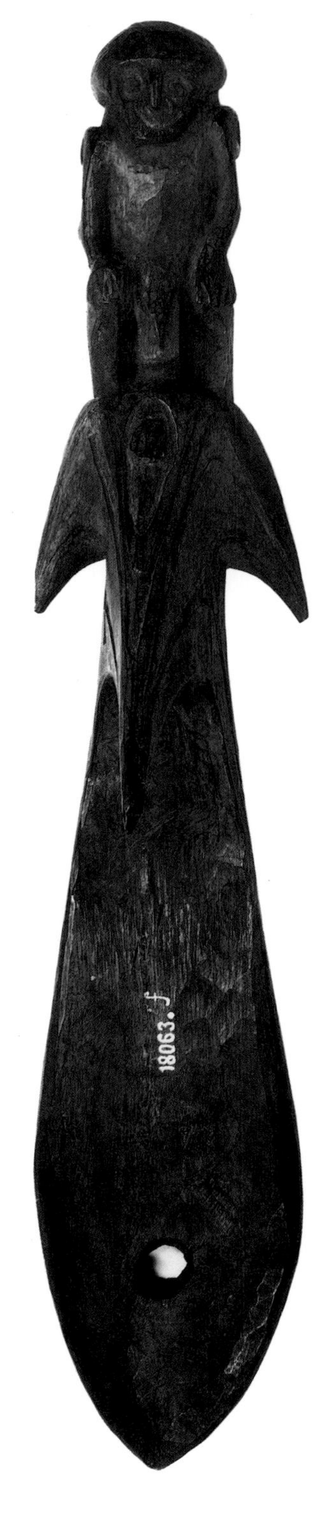

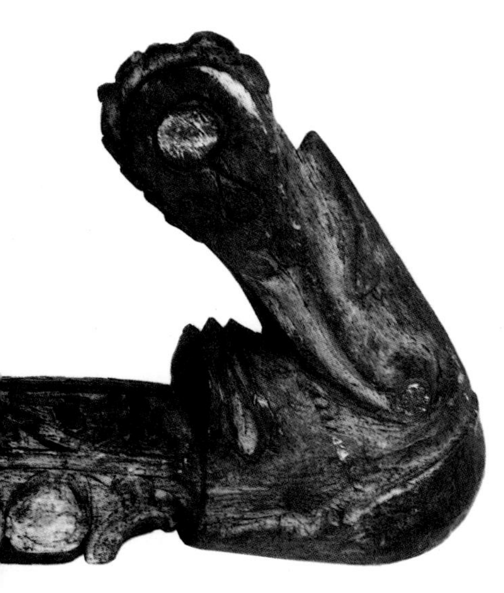

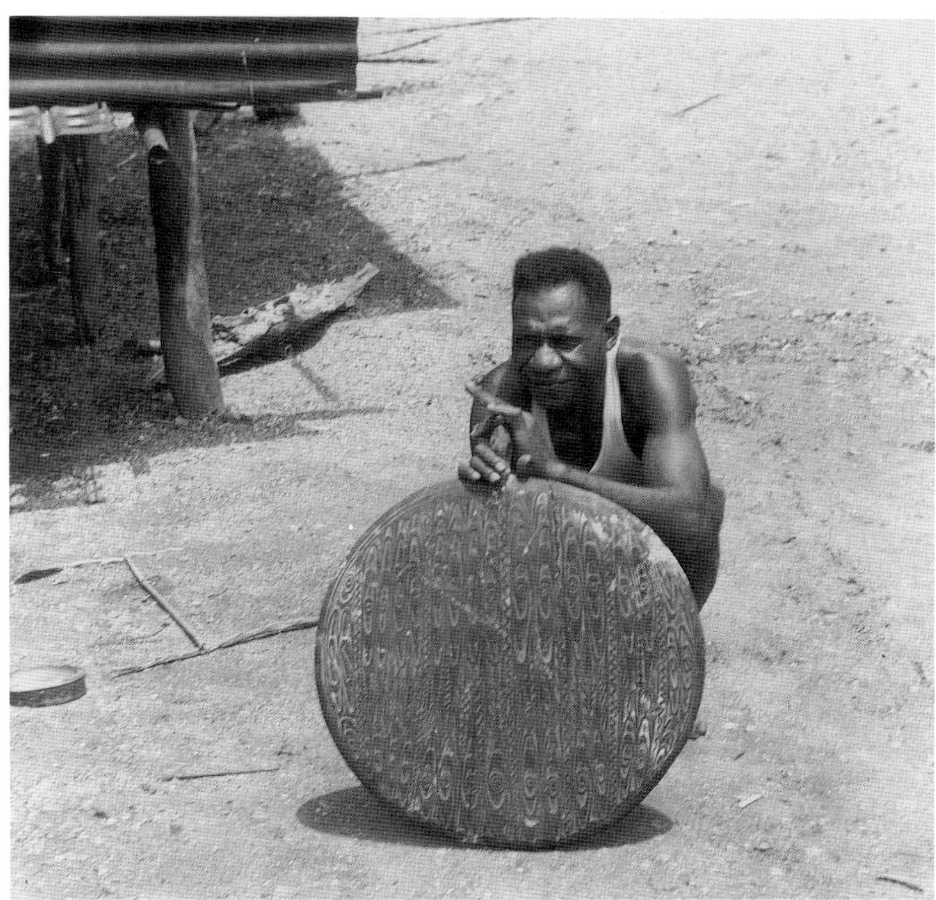

folded until it was thin and pliable. It was then soaked in water, wrung out by two women (one at each end), and hung to dry (Fig. IX.11; van der Sande 1907:234–235). Once dry, the barkcloth was ready for use or decoration.

Women were the fishers of Lake Sentani, which may account for the frequent depiction of aquatic life on barkcloth. The artist has creatively made use of a defect in the cloth (Fig. IX.7): the center around which the fish circle is a hole. On the left side of the cloth is a tree surrounded by bats. The center panel on this bark cloth (Fig. IX.8) contains frog and fish images. These cloths, painted freehand, would have been worn on ceremonial occasions or placed on the graves of women (Kooijman 1959:24; Meyn 1982).

The chewing of betel nut (a quid made from the leaf or fruit of the betel pepper, *Piper betel*, and the nut of the areca palm, *Areca catechu*, mixed with lime) is a social custom common throughout New Guinea. On Lake Sentani, most adults carry an incised gourd used to hold lime powder made from crushed or finely ground shells. Decorated gourds are traditionally crafted by specialists. After the stem is removed and the insides emptied and washed, the gourd is placed on a stick and dried in the sun. Designs are burnt onto the gourd using a strong leaf vein from the sago palm.

Men's lime gourds are long and thin (Fig. IX.9) and women's are short and squat (Fig. IX.1). The incised designs on the women's gourds are rubbed with lime, giving them a whitish appearance. The design on this gourd (Fig. IX.9) is called *waudjomo* (*wau* means cloud; *djomo* means to end in a point) because it resembles a cloud stretched over the horizon at sunset. This pattern may be used by any adult. Other types of motifs (Fig. IX.12) may only be used by men with high status, such as clan leaders or medicine men (Hoogerbrugge 1967: 53–62). Lime spatulas were used to remove lime from the gourd and also to cap it. The figures on this spatula (Fig. IX.9) are called "beads." Any member of the community may own spatulas with "bead" motifs. The figures on the other spatulas (Fig. IX.10) are referred to as *torèle uno* (human image) and are usually

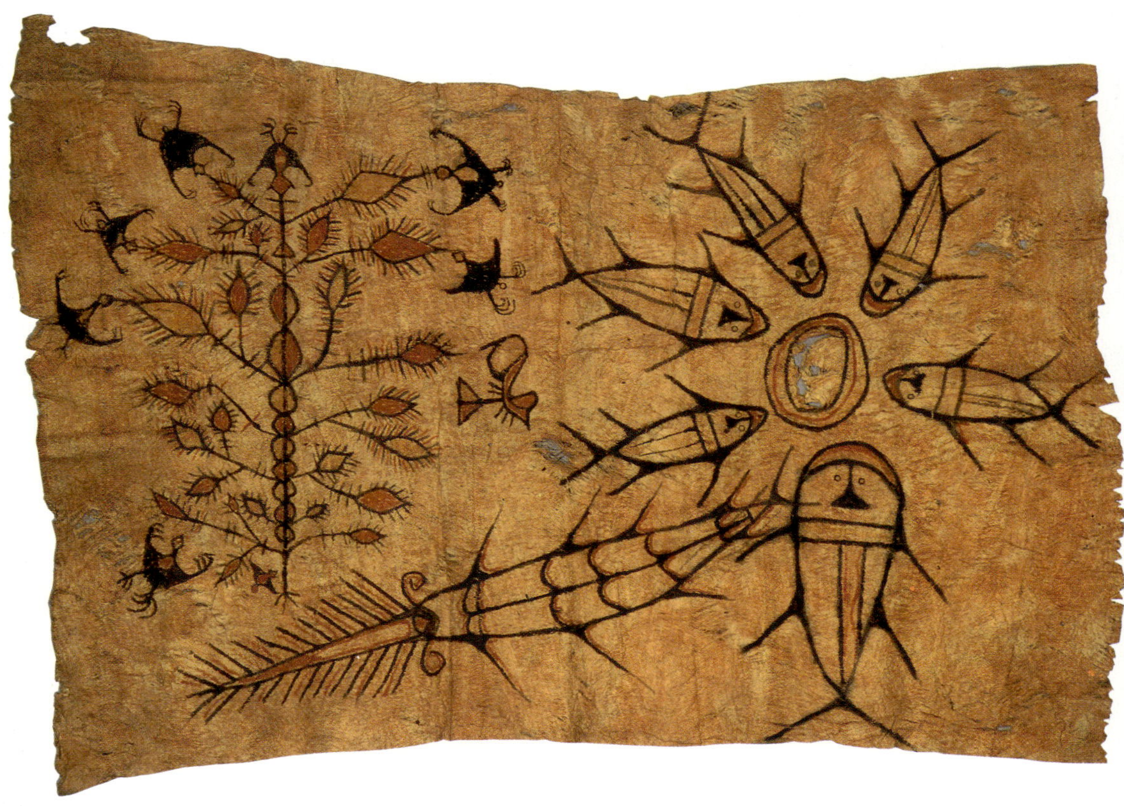

Fig. IX.7 BARKCLOTH
Lake Sentani
Tapa, paint, 127 x 90.5
Julius and Dorette
Fleischmann Collection.
Cincinnati Museum of Natural
History, A11357
J. and B. Schlessinger

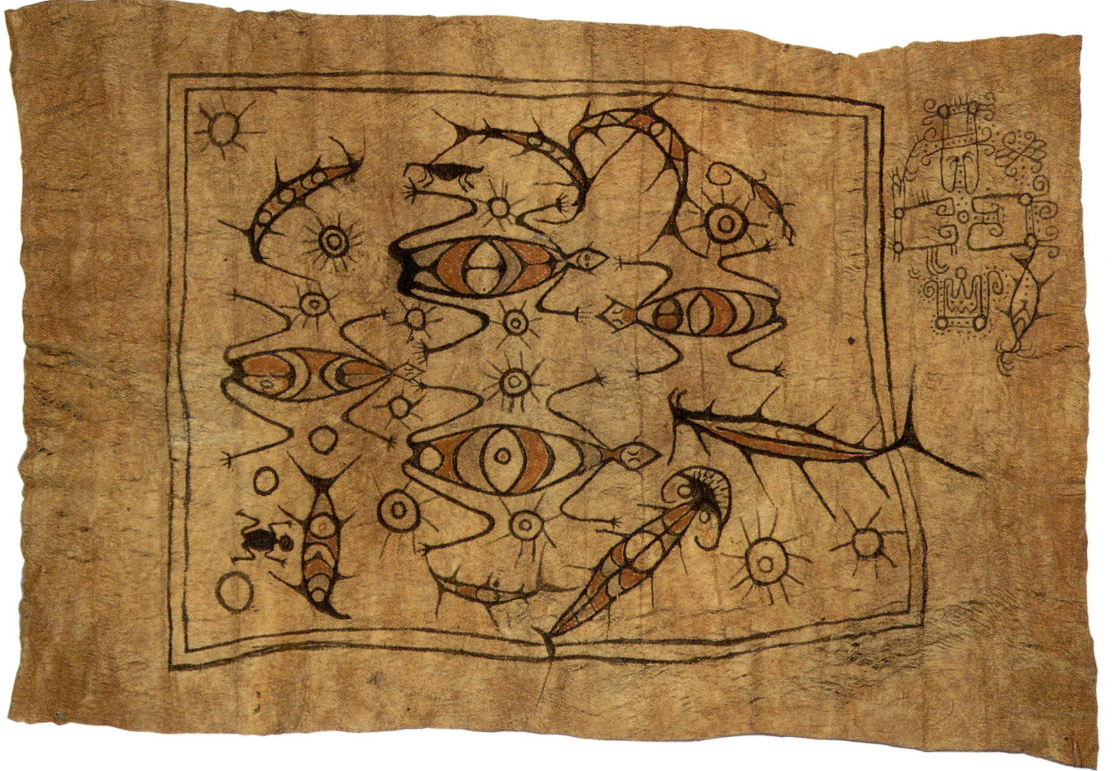

Fig. IX.8 BARKCLOTH
Lake Sentani
Tapa, paint, 144.5 x 98
Julius and Dorette
Fleischmann Collection.
Cincinnati Museum of Natural
History, A11384
J. and B. Schlessinger

OPPOSITE
LEFT
Fig. IX.9 LIME GOURD AND SPATULA
Lake Sentani Gourd, wood,
8 x 28 x 5.5
Department of Anthropology,
Smithsonian Institution,
283959a. Collected by
W. L. Abbott. Accessioned in
1914.

RIGHT
Fig. IX.10 LIME SPATULAS
Lake Sentani
Wood, 1.3 x 27.9 x 7.2;
2 x 26.3 x 2.4
Department of Anthropology,
Smithsonian Institution
283803 and 283959b.
Accessioned in 1914.

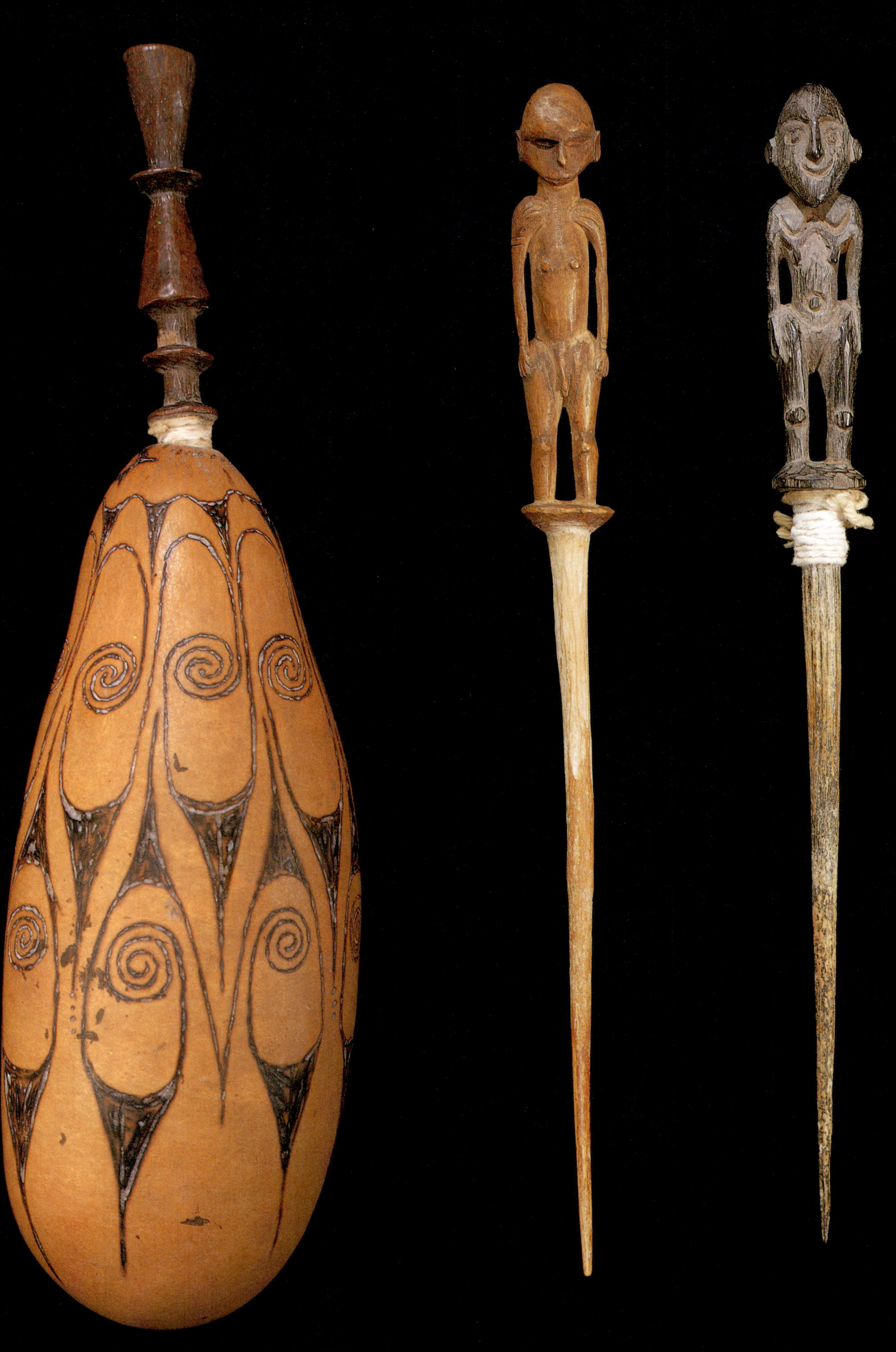

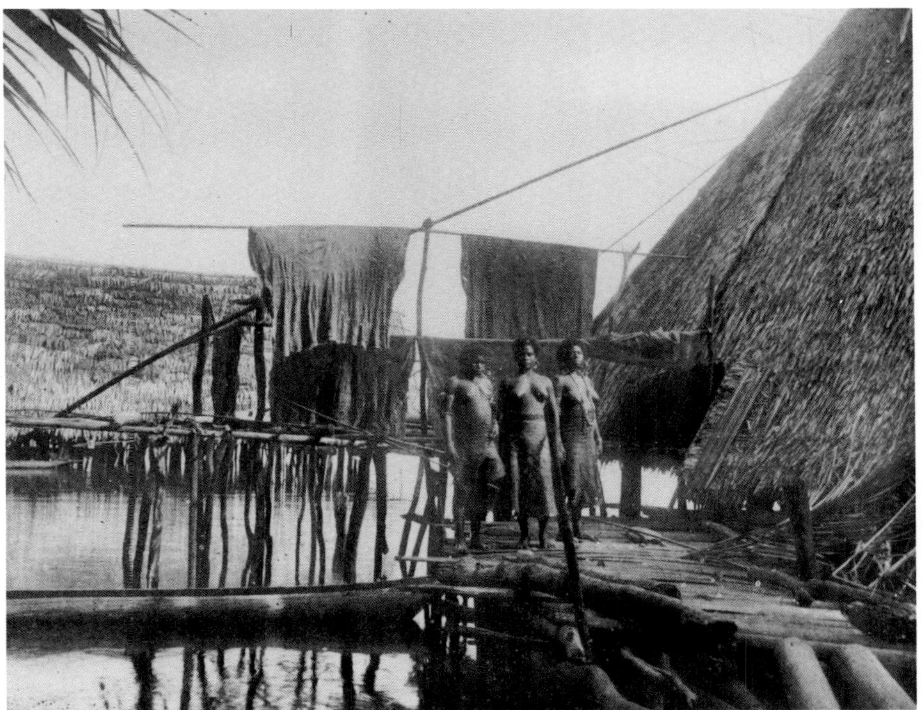

Fig. IX.11 Drying barkcloth, Asé village, Lake Sentani. van der Sande 1907:following p. 232

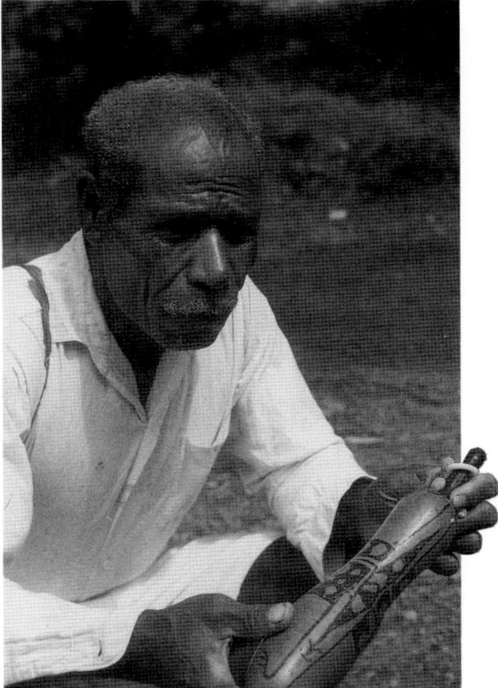

Fig. IX.12 Man with lime gourd, Jobe village, Lake Sentani, 1958. Jac. Hoogerbrugge

possessed by headmen, medicine men, or older male members of the community. Such human images are also carved on the tops of ceremonial staffs and house piles (for comparison see Kooijman 1959:23, 33–34).

For defensive reasons and because the marshy plains of the coast made inhospitable dwelling places, the majority of villages in Cenderawasih Bay, Humboldt Bay, and Lake Sentani traditionally consisted of houses built on piles over the water (Figs. IX.13, IX.14). Houses could hold up to one hundred people. There was a central hallway, or public room, where families cooked and socialized. Off this central hallway, each family had their own private room. The shore was reached either by plank bridge or boat. People traveled between settlements by boat. Today, as in other areas of Indonesia, most people live in single-family dwellings.

Social Life and Rituals of Initiation

Despite the existence of well-established trade routes and exchange systems throughout the island, groups on New Guinea tended to remain culturally isolated from each other because of warfare and such geographical barriers as impenetrable mountain terrain and unnavigable rivers. People rarely lived in groups of more than one thousand. Lineage and clan affiliation were generally traced through the male line. Social relations within New Guinea groups were fairly egalitarian. Political structure within the group was usually centered around one prominent male leader or headman. Males and females often were involved in different realms of social life. Women were responsible for the household, whereas men were more involved in politics and ceremonial life.

Male social life was traditionally centered around the men's ceremonial houses. The structure of such ceremonial houses, which are found all along the north coast of Irian Jaya, varied from region to region (Figs. IX.17–19). On Humboldt Bay and Lake Sentani, men gathered at these houses to discuss village affairs, politics, and lore. The male initiation ceremonies, one of the most impor-

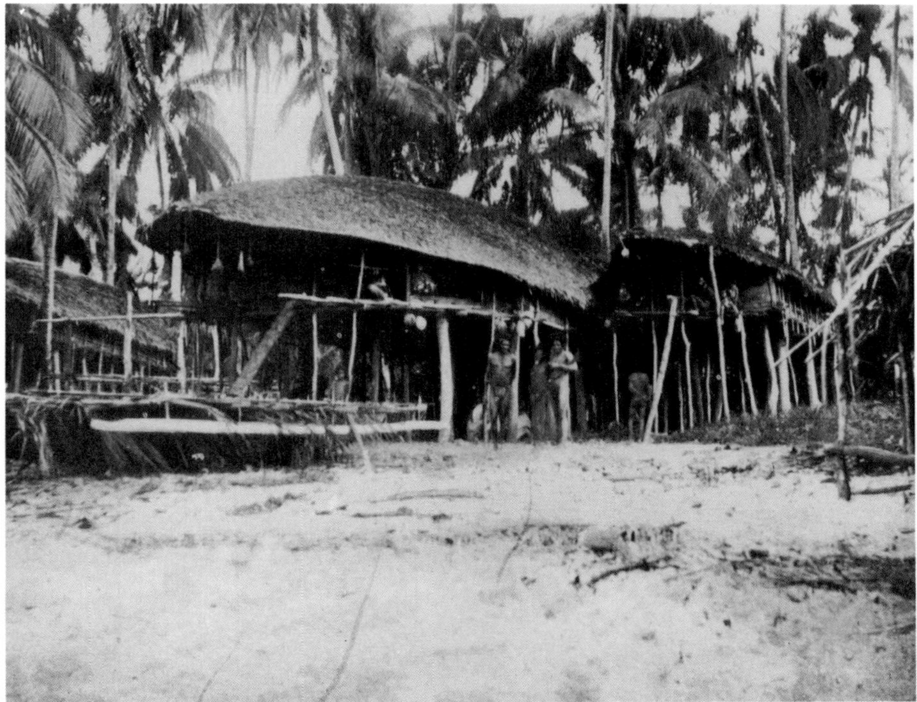

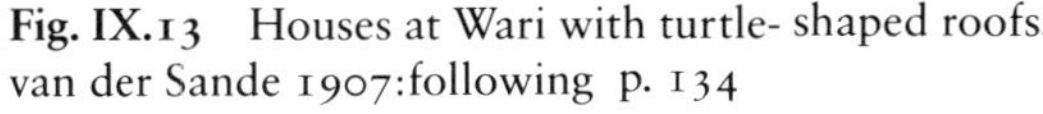

Fig. IX.13 Houses at Wari with turtle- shaped roofs. van der Sande 1907:following p. 134

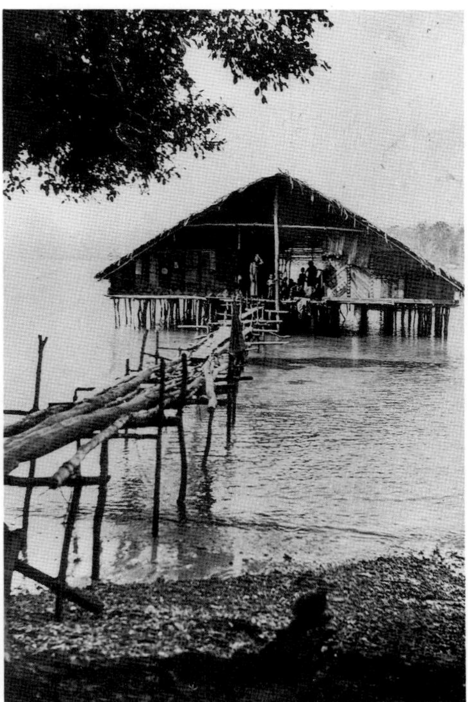

Fig. IX.14 House near Dore. Barbour 1908:479

tant events in a male's life, were held at these ceremonial houses. Adolescent boys were isolated in these structures and all the knowledge, both practical and esoteric, that they would need as adult members of the community was imparted to them.

In Humboldt Bay young men were first isolated from their families in a separate house before being brought to the ceremonial men's house (*karewari*) to undergo the initiation ritual. Large quantities of food, for both the men and spirits, were prepared by the women and brought to this house. When the village headman decided it was the proper time, the novices were rounded up and brought to the *karewari* where the initiation ceremonies began (Galis 1955:186–191).

Inside the *karewari* tutelage and care was provided by the elders. Special attention was usually given to a young man by his mother's brother, the representative of his mother's lineage. Initiates passed through periods of pain and deprivation to develop their strengths and focus their energies. For example, initiates had to sit or stand for long periods of time without moving, and they were not allowed to chew betel, smoke, speak, laugh, look directly at an elder, bathe, start a fire, make weapons, or have personal property. They had to let their hair grow, become accustomed to little food, play the flutes, and sing ritual songs. Initiates were taught social and religious law as well as the songs, stories, and myths of their tribe and clan. They learned to make nets, rope, ornaments, and to hunt and fish. They also received sexual training (Galis 1955:190–191). In some cases the initiation process was accompanied by ritualized homosexual acts between the initiates and elders, which involved imparting knowledge (as semen) from one generation to the next. Once these rituals ended, the "men" were reintroduced to society and the whole community held a great celebration, which included gift exchanges.

As early as the beginning of the twentieth century, the use of the male ceremonial houses began to decline because of opposition from missionaries,

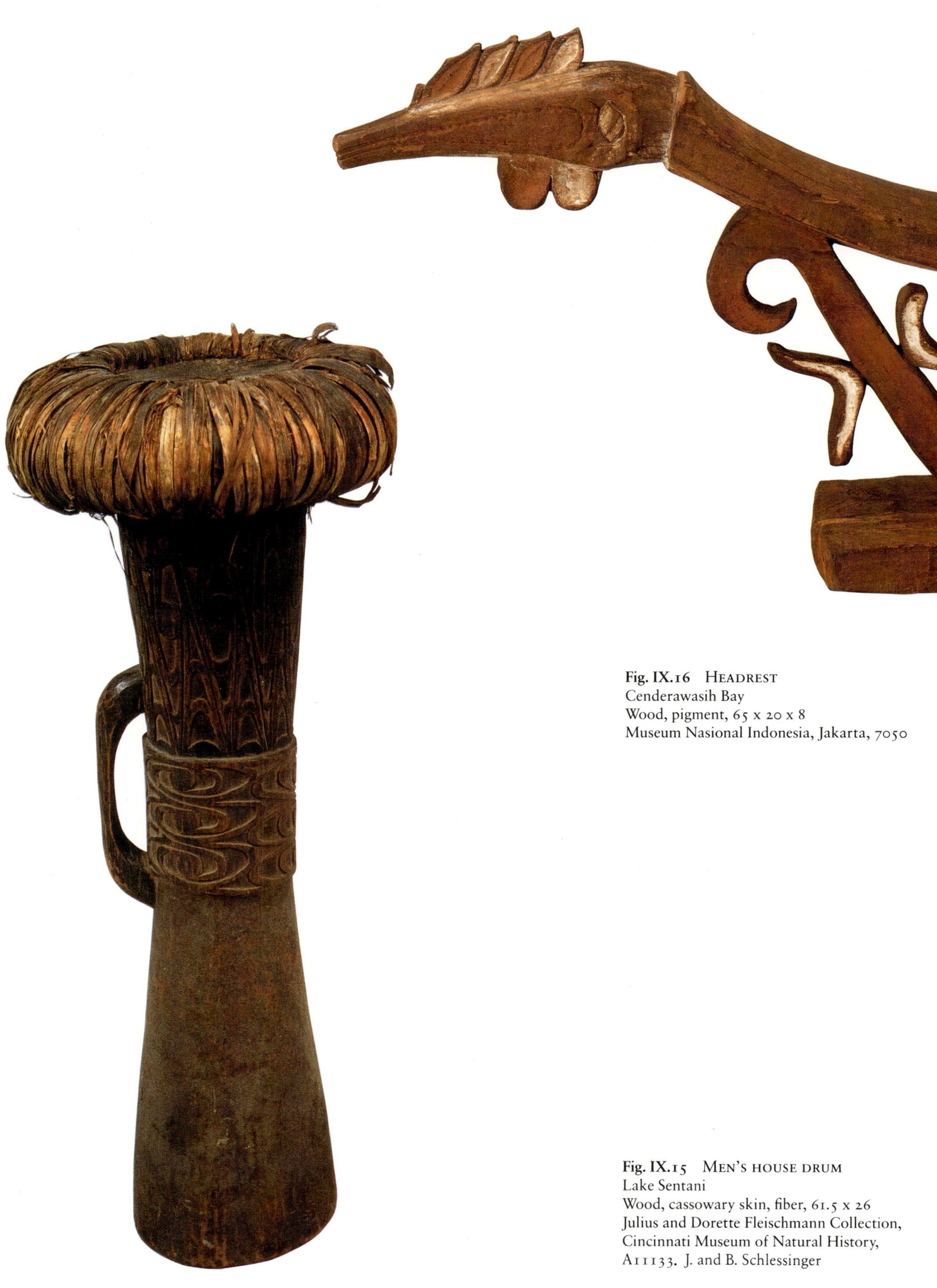

Fig. IX.16 HEADREST
Cenderawasih Bay
Wood, pigment, 65 x 20 x 8
Museum Nasional Indonesia, Jakarta, 7050

Fig. IX.15 MEN'S HOUSE DRUM
Lake Sentani
Wood, cassowary skin, fiber, 61.5 x 26
Julius and Dorette Fleischmann Collection,
Cincinnati Museum of Natural History,
A11133. J. and B. Schlessinger

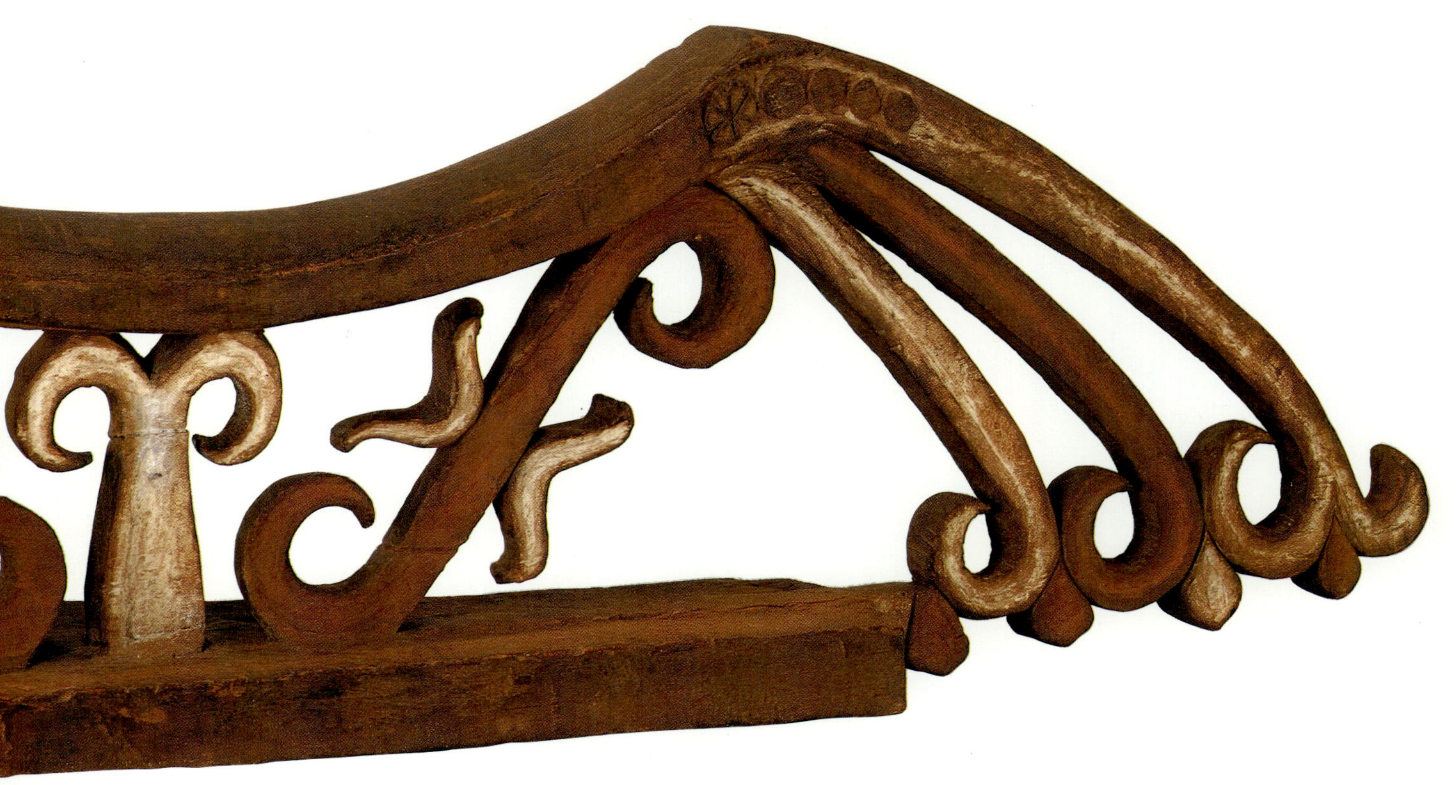

some individual Dutch officials, and increased contact with the outside world. When the photograph of the young men's house in Cenderawasih Bay was taken in 1903 (Fig. IX.17), people had begun to hold initiation ceremonies in private homes. The ceremonial house (Fig. IX.18), an excellent example of local design motifs and animal imagery (note especially the crocodile images carved on the house piles), was destroyed by the elders of the village after the missionary van Hasselt visited the island in the 1920s (van Hasselt 1926:131–137).

Ritual objects such as flutes, drums, ceremonial staffs and hoods, and skulls of animals that had been eaten during feasts, as well as objects of everyday use such as fishing nets, baskets, hooks, and headrests, were stored in the ceremonial men's house (Fig. IX.20). Flutes were among the most sacred items used by the men. Considered either feminine or masculine, they were always played together in pairs by specialists. Under no circumstances were the flutes to be blown by an uninitiated male or to be seen by a woman. Van der Sande writes, "the sound of the flutes gives to these objects their meaning; this sound often imitates the singing of birds, after which, in the case of some specimens, the flutes were named" (1907:296). The most important use of the flutes was during the male initiation ceremonies when the sound of the flute represented the voice of the presiding ancestor (Galis 1968–69). Flutes were also blown to announce the death of a prominent man and to announce that a celebration had been organized in the ceremonial house.

The sacred drums (seen hanging in Fig. IX.20) were used only for ceremonies inside the *karewari*. There are other types of drums, however, which could be used outside the ceremonial house, for instance, to summon people to a gathering. Drums were also used to announce the death of a high official. All drums on Lake Sentani have a carved center band, regardless of whether or not the rest of the body is carved (Fig. IX.15). This band is called a waistbelt (*jomalo*), the same name used for a waistbelt worn by the headman which is believed to have protective powers. A myth from Lake Sentani mentions the powers of these waistbelts: "each *ondoforo* [headman] wore . . . a waist-

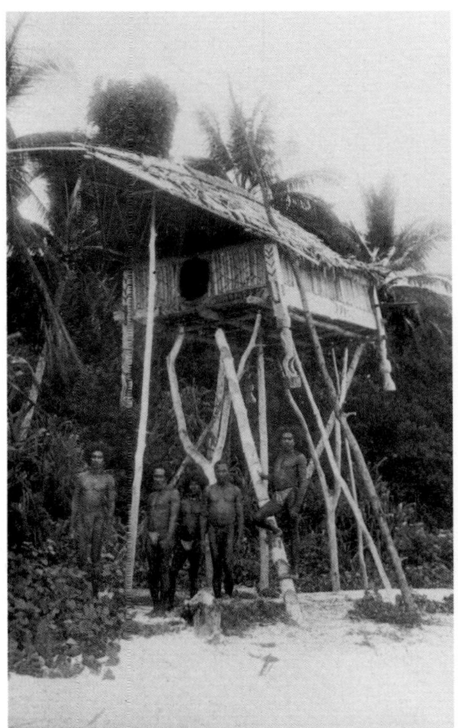

Fig. IX.17 Ceremonial house (*rum seram*) at Mios Korwar. van der Sande 1907:following p. 304

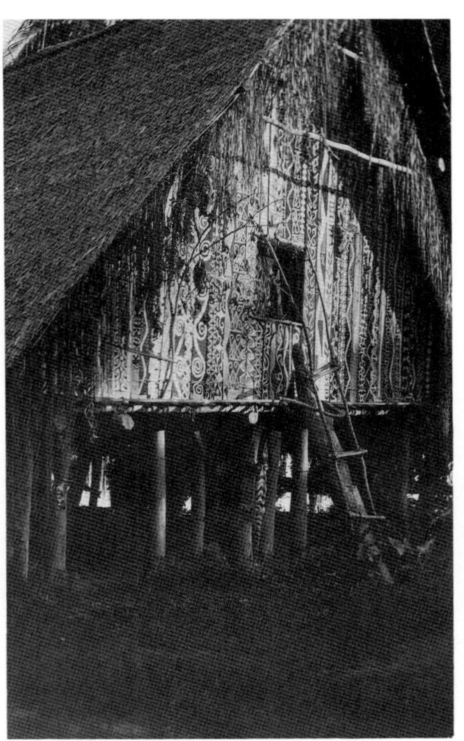

Fig. IX.18 Ceremonial house at Jamna. Barbour 1908:530

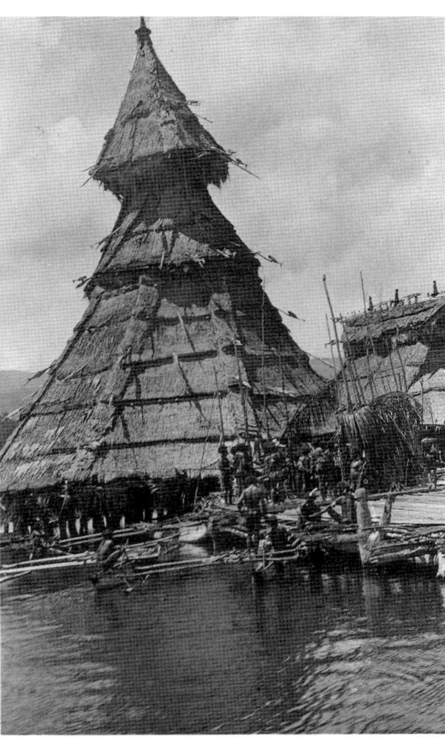

Fig. IX.19 Ceremonial house (*karewari*) at Tobadi. Barbour 1908:534

belt (*jomalo*) so that no arrows or knifes should strike him" (Hoogerbrugge 1967:13). The similarity in name implies a similarity in concept; the carved band on the drum may also offer protective power.

Headrests were one type of everyday object found in the men's ceremonial house. Used as pillows, they could be plain blocks of wood or elaborate supports carved with images of ancestor figures (see de Clercq and Schmeltz 1893:plate XVIII; van der Sande 1907:plate XVIII). Among the Waropen people of Cenderawasih Bay, headrests were also used in marriage exchange (Held 1957:109). This headrest (Fig. IX.16) displays a rooster, a common male motif throughout Indonesia.

The early descriptions of Irian Jaya tell us significantly less about the social life or life-cycle rites of women. Most of the early travelers or missionaries were men, who, therefore, had limited access to women's activities. It is known, however, that on Biak and Supiori in Cenderawasih Bay, all adolescent women went through a period of seclusion before they were married. Once this period of seclusion was over, they were called *insos* (*in* is a prefix for the feminine gender, *sos* means color). *Insos* is also the name of the period of seclusion itself. Jens reported that young women were isolated from one to four months in an area partitioned by mats in their parent's house. The richer the family, the longer the period of isolation. Before the adolescent girl entered the partitioned area, songs were sung to beseech the spirits not to lay any hindrances in the girl's way. An older woman, acting as guard, sat outside the partition and gave the girl food. While the girl sat in the partitioned area, she was forbidden to stretch out her legs, for this could incur the wrath of her ancestors and cause an illness or death in the family. At night, however, she was free to move as she pleased. For the first five or six nights her younger siblings were allowed to keep her company. During the following nights, room was made for her husband-to-be. The future husband was required to first purchase permission to enter the house from his in-laws. A poor man paid with an ax, a rich man with trade

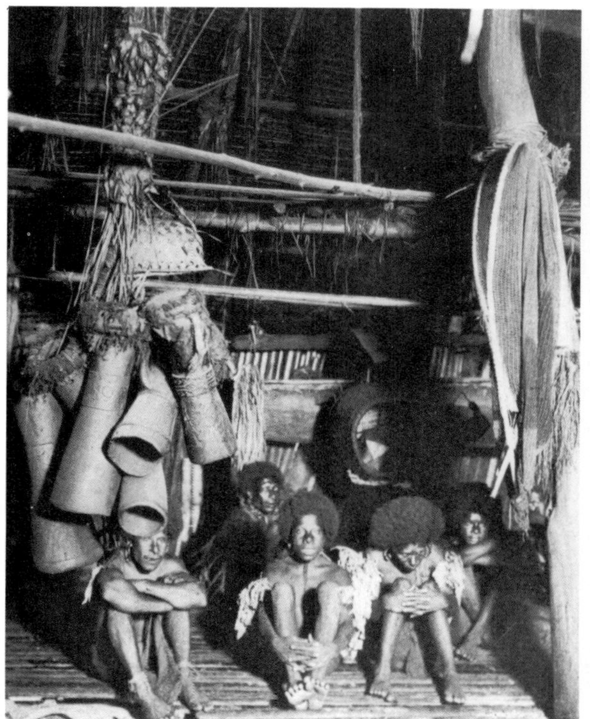

Fig. IX.20 Novices amidst items stored in the ceremonial house, Tobadi village, Humboldt Bay. van der Sande, 1907: following p. 292

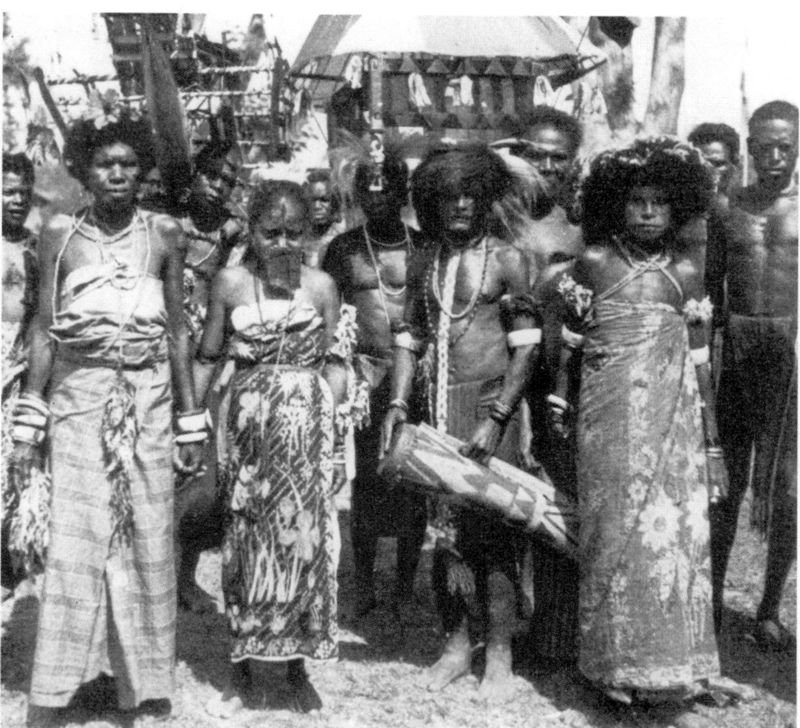

Fig. IX.21 A mock seclusion procession in Cenderawasih Bay, 1939. The cloth over the woman's mouth is thought to symbolize the period of isolation. Held 1951:199

goods such as blue cotton or plates. He paid these goods all at once and in turn received access to the girl's area for the rest of her seclusion. When the period of isolation was over, the marriage was considered final. When the woman emerged from her period of isolation, she wore swatches of blue cotton and a woven rope decorated with beads on her head. She was carried so that she would not come into contact with the ground, which was considered contaminated (Jens 1916:404–408). The accounts of early travelers or missionaries such as Jens were descriptive not analytic; therefore, this account raises as many questions as it answers. It does confirm that at least in Cenderawasih Bay, young women, like young men, had to go through some ceremonial process before they were considered full adult members of the community.

The Impact of Local Environment upon Cosmology, Myth, and Art

The people of New Guinea incorporated many elements of their environment, such as plants, animals, and natural forces such as wind, rain, thunder, and tides, into their cosmology, myth, and art. On the north coast of Irian Jaya, the constant proximity to and dependency on water for communication and trade as well as subsistence have lead to the frequent use of bird and fish motifs. These designs appear on both ceremonial and everyday objects and are incorporated into myths. The powerful role of these elements and the respect paid to them is described in the following passage from van Hasselt in which the wind is personified and its desires obeyed:

> When we passed the coast near Wariab and Sjeri . . . the Papuans extinguished all fires on the boat, as well as pipes and cigarettes. In short, everything burning was extinguished. In the distance there were three red hills and the Papuans said that in the middle of the hills there lived the "Wambraw," the mountain wind . . . and if the "Wambraw" saw fires it would become enraged, leave its hiding place, and destroy the boat in which the people had been so careless (van Hasselt 1926:35).

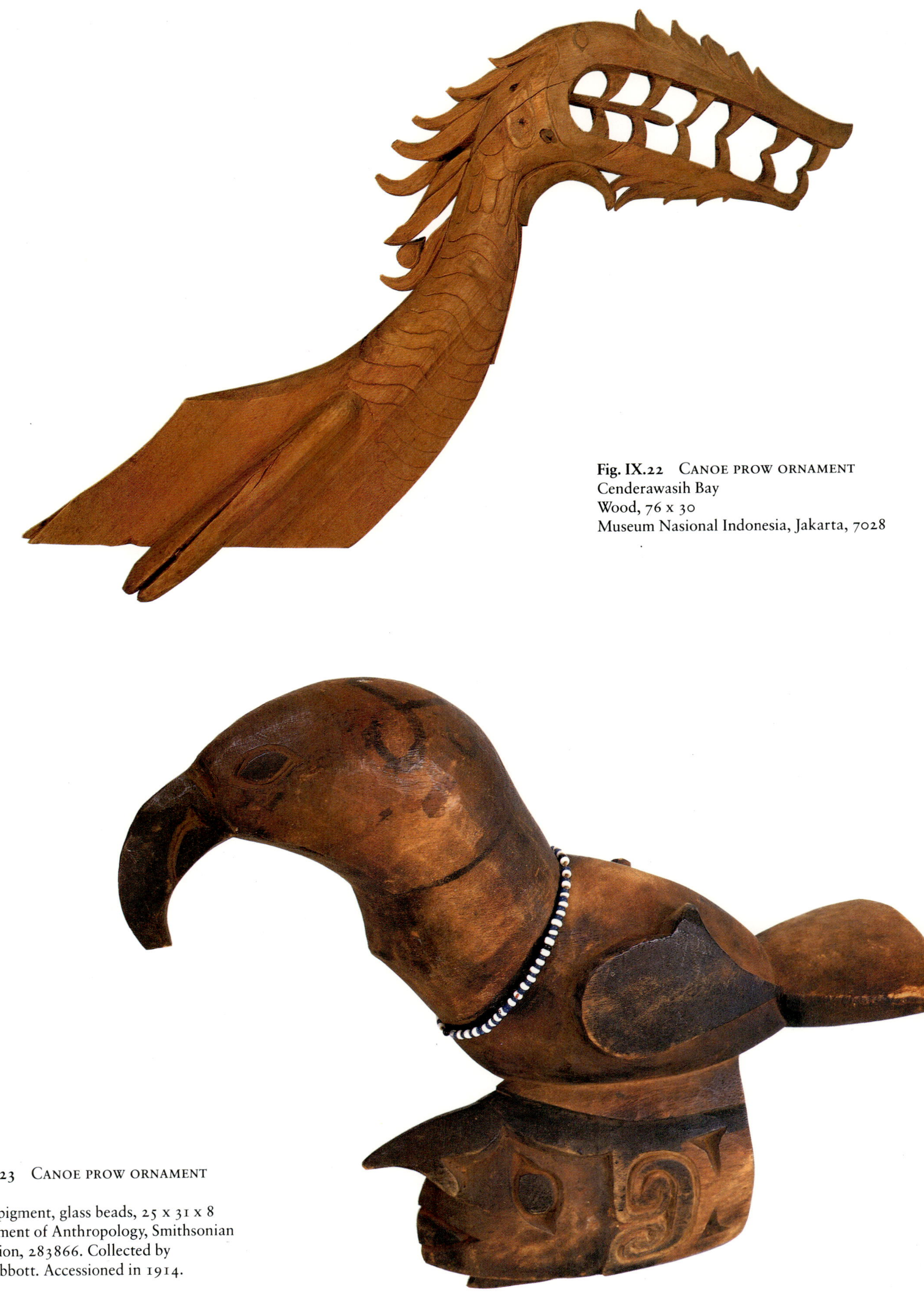

Fig. IX.22 CANOE PROW ORNAMENT
Cenderawasih Bay
Wood, 76 x 30
Museum Nasional Indonesia, Jakarta, 7028

Fig. IX.23 CANOE PROW ORNAMENT
Wakde
Wood, pigment, glass beads, 25 x 31 x 8
Department of Anthropology, Smithsonian Institution, 283866. Collected by W. L. Abbott. Accessioned in 1914.

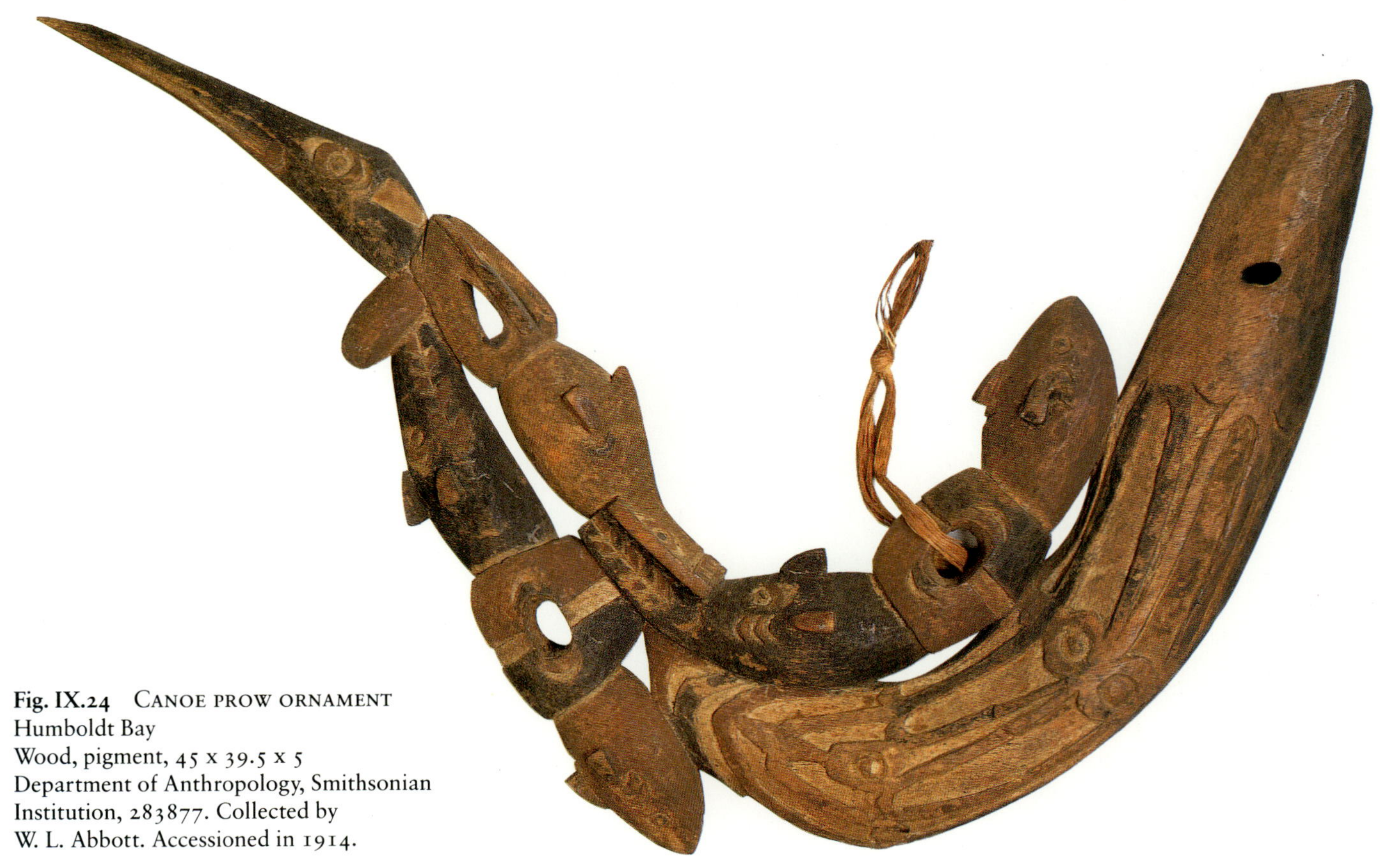

Fig. IX.24 CANOE PROW ORNAMENT
Humboldt Bay
Wood, pigment, 45 x 39.5 x 5
Department of Anthropology, Smithsonian Institution, 283877. Collected by W. L. Abbott. Accessioned in 1914.

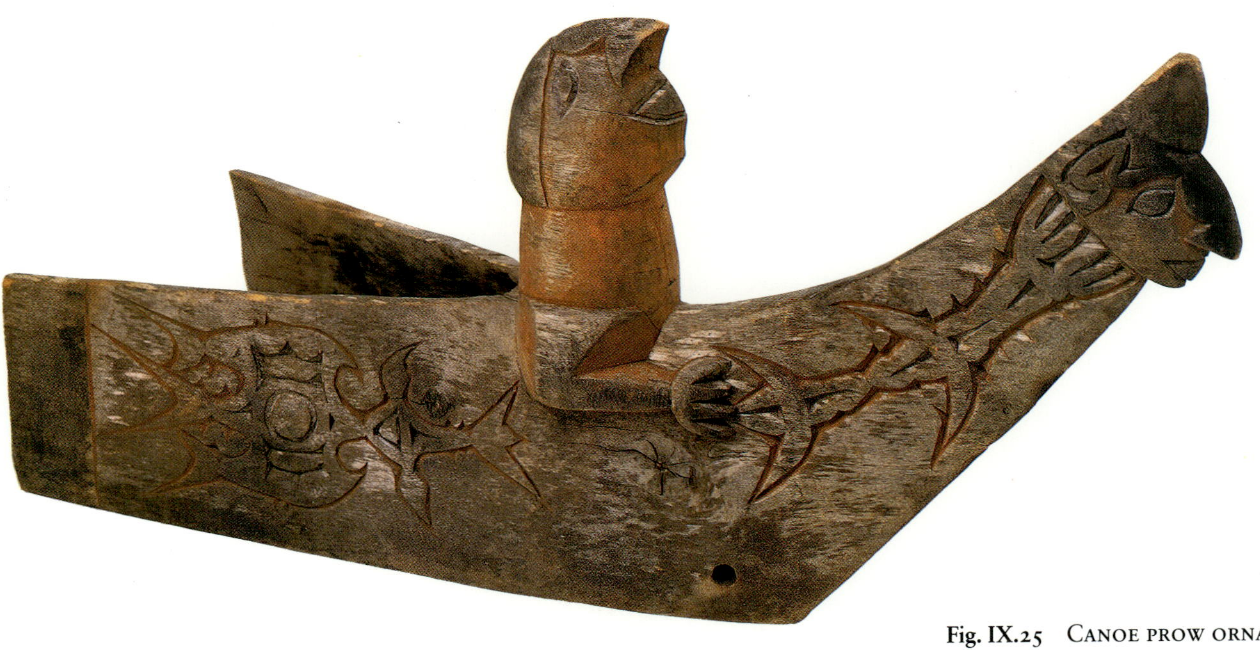

Fig. IX.25 CANOE PROW ORNAMENT
Wakde
Wood, pigment, 31.3 x 64 x 18.8
Department of Anthropology, Smithsonian Institution, 283879. Collected by W. L. Abbott. Accessioned in 1914.

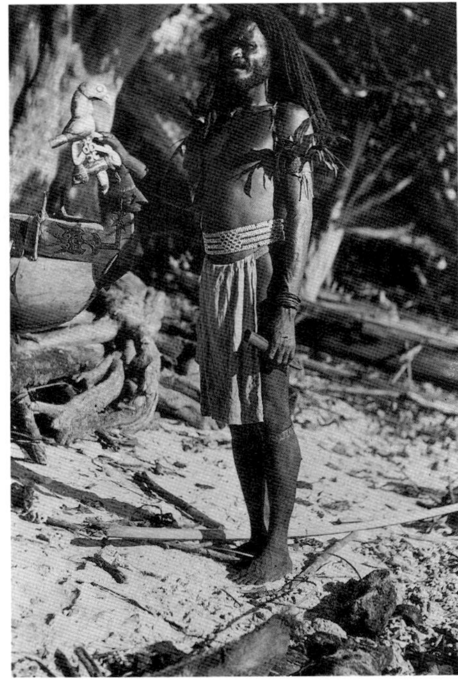

Fig. IX.26 A man from Jamna holds a prow ornament similar to the one seen in Fig. IX.23. The ornament on the boat is similar to the one seen in Fig. IX.25. Barbour 1908:531

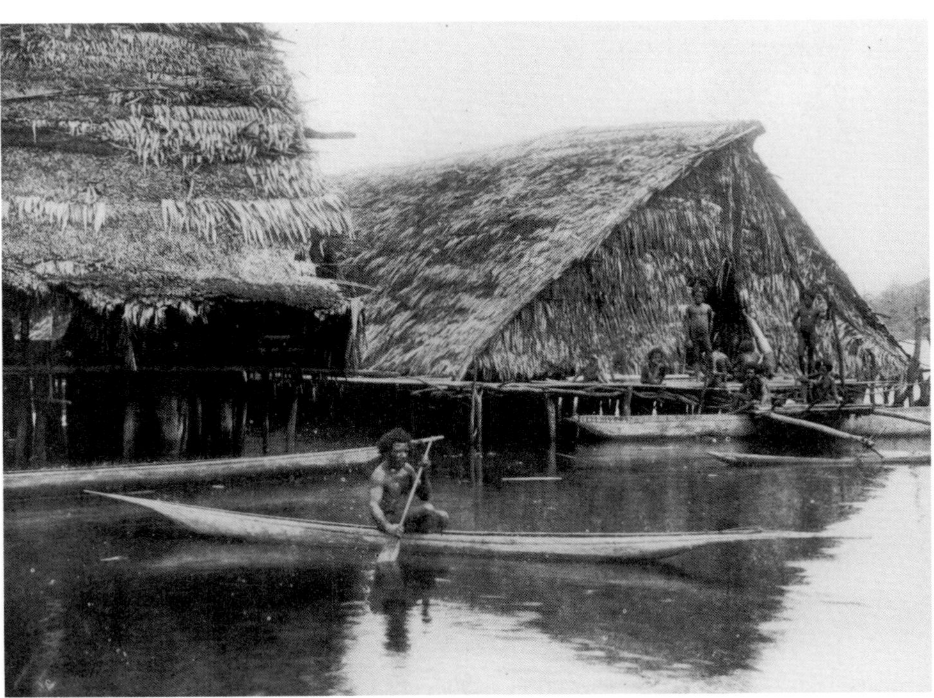

Fig. IX.27 Man rowing an *isja*, Lake Sentani. van der Sande 1907:following p. 200

In Humboldt Bay at the beginning of the fishing season, the "Lord of the Fishes" is beseeched during a special ceremony to offer his blessings for a successful catch (Galis 1955:106). Fish also provided omens:

> A dead fish drifting in front of the boat is a sign of impending danger should they continue; if seen on port side, it announces an impending death on the left side of the *perahu* [boat]; if seen on starboard side, it announces an impending death on the right side of the *perahu* (van Hasselt 1926:36).

The peoples of Cenderawasih Bay, Humboldt Bay, and Lake Sentani, all of which have *perahus* unique to their regions, exploited the marine environment for subsistence and traveled by water for trade. Many prow ornaments were decorated with bird, fish, and ancestor images, which offered guidance and protection. The finely carved image (Fig. IX.22) is a rooster or a stylized dragon. Its open scroll-like designs are reminiscent of work from the Moluccas, whose peoples were known to have visited the north coast of Irian Jaya by at least the sixteenth century. The bird (Fig. IX.23) has a beaded necklace atop an anthropomorphic head. Another prow ornament (Fig. IX.24) displays an array of intertwined aquatic and flying animals, and another (Fig. IX.25) includes a human figure riding in a ship.

Residents of Humboldt Bay make two types of boats. The men's boat (*wache*) has a single outrigger (a support extending from the main structure of the boat to help balance it) on the starboard side. The women's boat is a dugout without an outrigger.

On Lake Sentani, neither the men's boat (Fig. IX.27) nor the women's boat has an outrigger. Used for all activities, the *isja* is an extremely narrow boat designed for one man. Maneuvering this boat requires great balance and skill; therefore, miniature boats are built for little boys, with which they learn to maneuver at a young age (see film on New Guinea by Paul Wirz, Human Studies Film Archives, Smithsonian Institution). The *kaji* (Fig. IX.29) is a very long

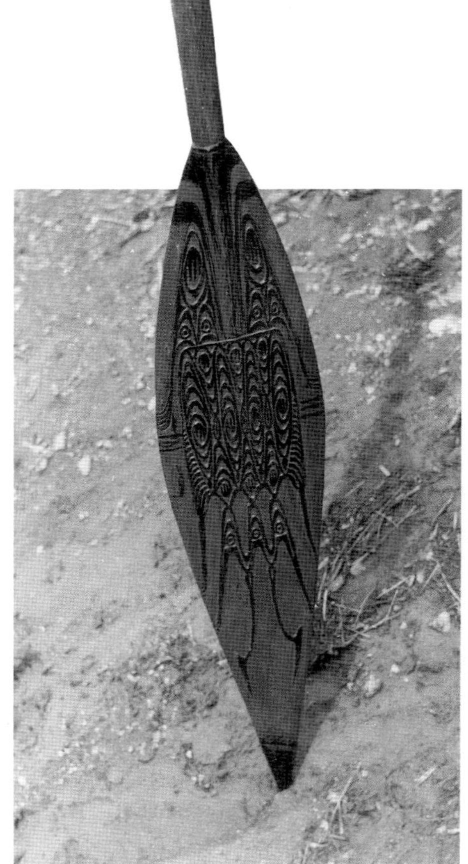

Fig. IX.28 Carved blade of a woman's paddle, Ifar village, Lake Sentani, 1957. Jac. Hoogerbrugge

dugout used by women for fishing or travel to the gardens. Women's paddles are carved with exquisite designs, while the men's are unadorned. The s-shaped design, which is distinctive of the Lake Sentani region, is seen again on this paddle (Fig. IX.28).

In Cenderawasih Bay both single and double outrigger boats were used. In Humboldt Bay, anyone could make a *perahu*, but in Cenderawasih Bay *parahus* were built either by specialists or sometimes by men from two patrilineally aligned clans who would join efforts to build and ornament a *perahu*. Among the Biak and Numfoor people of Cenderawasih Bay, the structure of a boat represents kinship structure. For instance, the seat in the middle of the boat was called *kèrèt* (a patrilineal clan). The shelters found in the middle of large *perahus* were called *èr* (the word used to indicate the four major groups that first settled Numfoor). The seats to the left and right along the sides of the boat were called *sim* (a patrilineal family unit). Moreover, where men stand in relation to the boat while building it and where they sit in it is also determined by their genealogy and clan affiliation. In Humboldt Bay, although the structure of the boat does not directly correspond to kinship structure, there is still a sense that the parts of the boat, like people, are related. For instance, the little planks at the ends of the boat were called the children of the larger boards running along the side of the boat (Galis 1955).

In addition to boats and prow ornaments, other objects are also carved with animal motifs. In Humboldt Bay, long poles with animal figures carved on the end (Figs. IX.34–37) were placed on the roof of the men's ceremonial house (Fig. IX.38) and on shelters built over graves. These ornaments are carved with various animals, including a skate (Fig. IX.34), birds (Figs. IX.36, IX.37), and a combination of pig and dog (Fig. IX.35). The s-shaped motifs also decorate the support under this animal (Fig. IX.35). All of these figures are colored red, white, and black, the most commonly used colors of the region.

Korwar: Ancestor Veneration

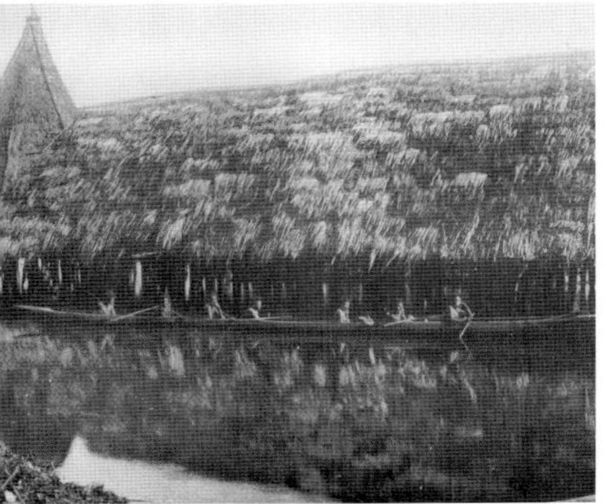

Fig. IX.29 Women setting off to garden in a *kaji*, Lake Sentani. van der Sande 1907:following p. 196

To show respect to their ancestors, the Biak of Cenderawasih Bay created ancestor figures (Figs. IX.30–32) from wood and, rarely, stone (Solheim 1979:326) and sometimes incorporated the skull of the deceased. These *korwar* were carved by family members after a relative's death or, in some cases, by the person himself before he died. The *korwar* functioned as a medium between the living and the dead. Stored either in the family house or at a grave site, *korwar* were often consulted as oracles before important undertakings:

> The *korwars* were consulted for rain or for help with fishing, to stave off evil, for advice on warfare, if the wind shall be propitious, if the rain shall soon stop, etc. On sea journeys a male figure is usually taken along and placed on the seat. A figure who has lost its power for whatever reason or who has deserted his worshippers is considered no longer useful and is thrown away (de Clercq and Schmeltz 1893:158).

When consulting a *korwar*, a priest tapped the figure against the ground until he fell into a trance and began to tremble. When asked questions, the priest answered in a strange tongue. After regaining consciousness, the priest interpreted the message from the *korwar* (van Baaren 1968:53). If the prediction was unfavorable, the expedition would be postponed and the *korwar* consulted again until it gave a favorable reply. If the *korwar* gave a favorable reply but the undertaking failed—for instance, if someone died or was injured, it was believed that the spirit of the ancestor had left the *korwar*, and the image might be destroyed (Solheim 1985:150). If an image was not destroyed, it would eventually be laid to rest at a grave site when its power was believed to be depleted.

Korwar were honored at various rituals: "During celebrations plates with food are set before the *korwars*, cigarettes are placed behind their ears, and other delicacies are offered them. This is done to placate the 'shadow' of the *korwar* so it will make sure all the members of the household have enough to

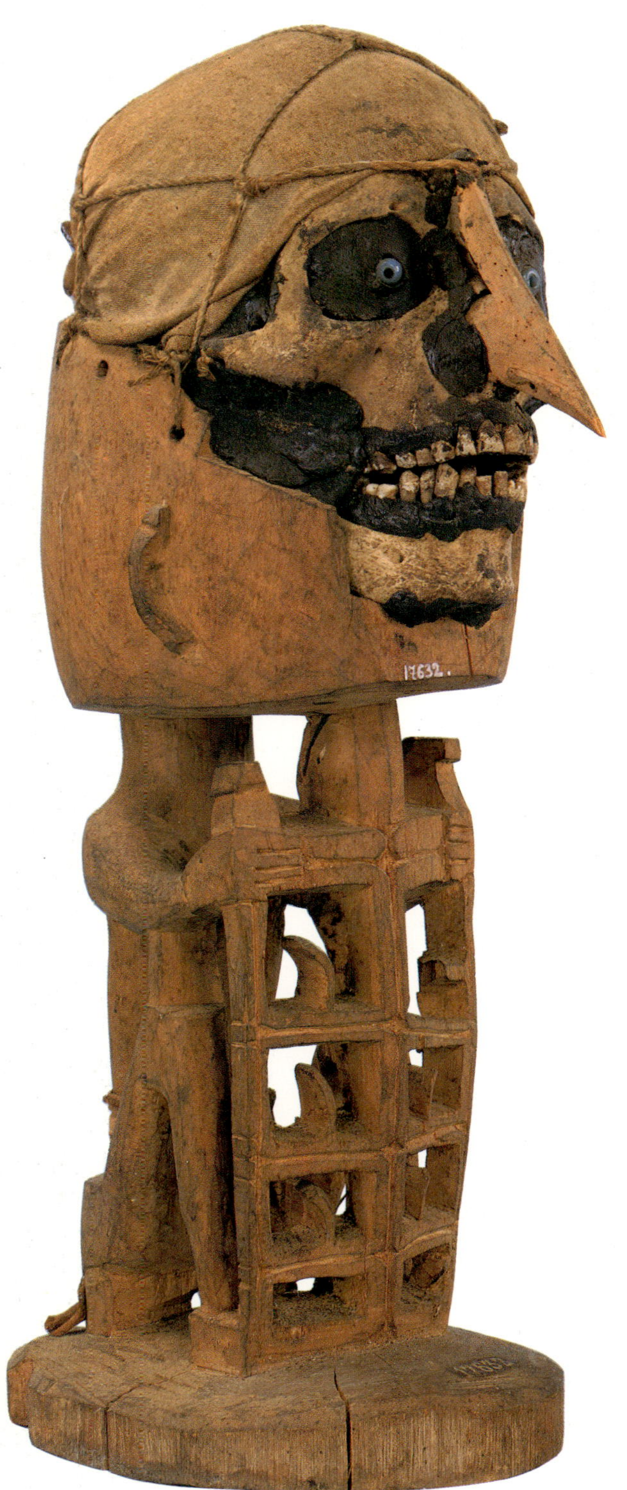

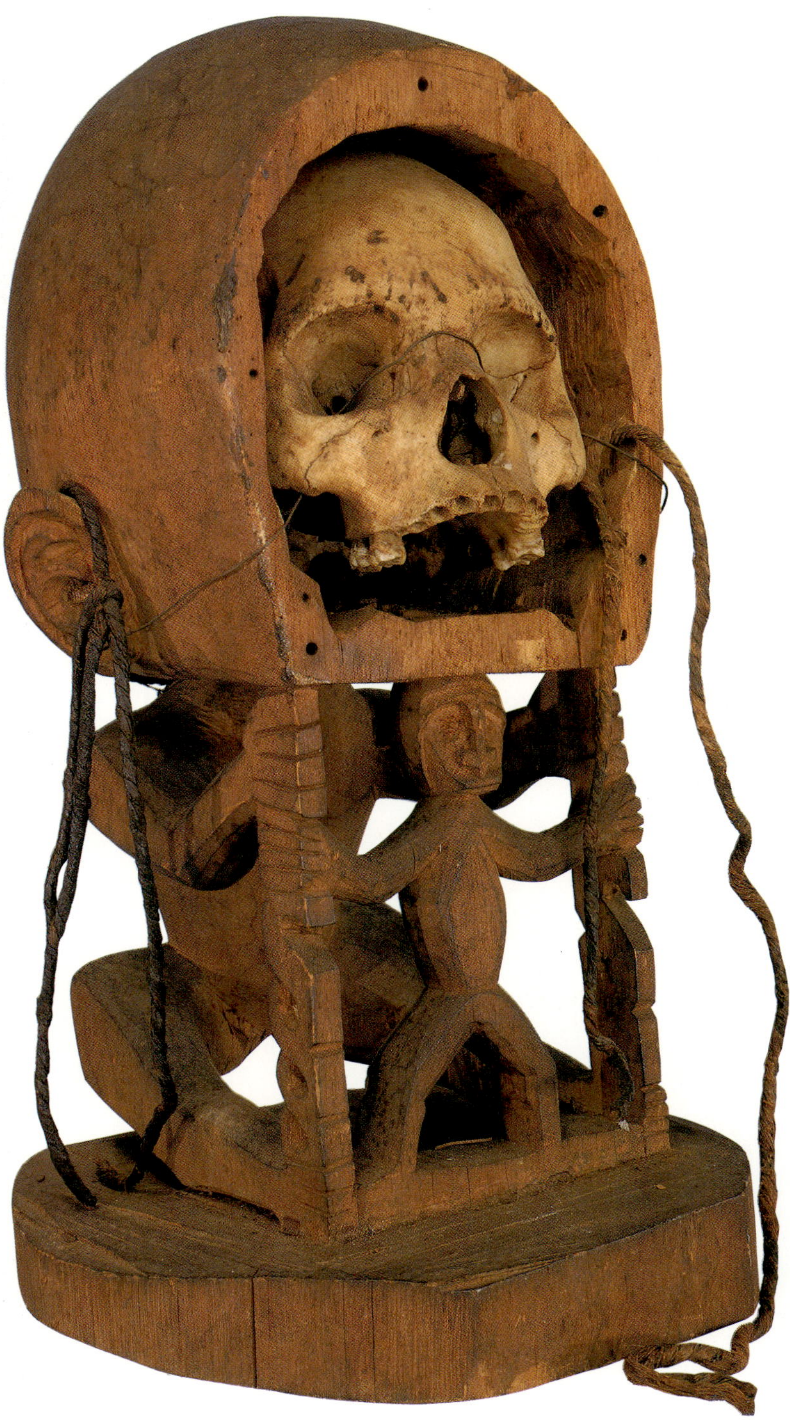

Fig. IX.30 ANCESTOR FIGURE, *KORWAR*
Cenderawasih Bay
Wood, cloth, human skull, glass beads,
48 x 17.5 x 26
Museum Nasional Indonesia, Jakarta, 17632.
Donated by W. K. H. F. de Bruijn in 1914.

Fig. IX.31 ANCESTOR FIGURE, *KORWAR*
Cenderawasih Bay
Wood, female human skull, twine,
41 x 23 x 25
Museum Nasional Indonesia, Jakarta, 6892

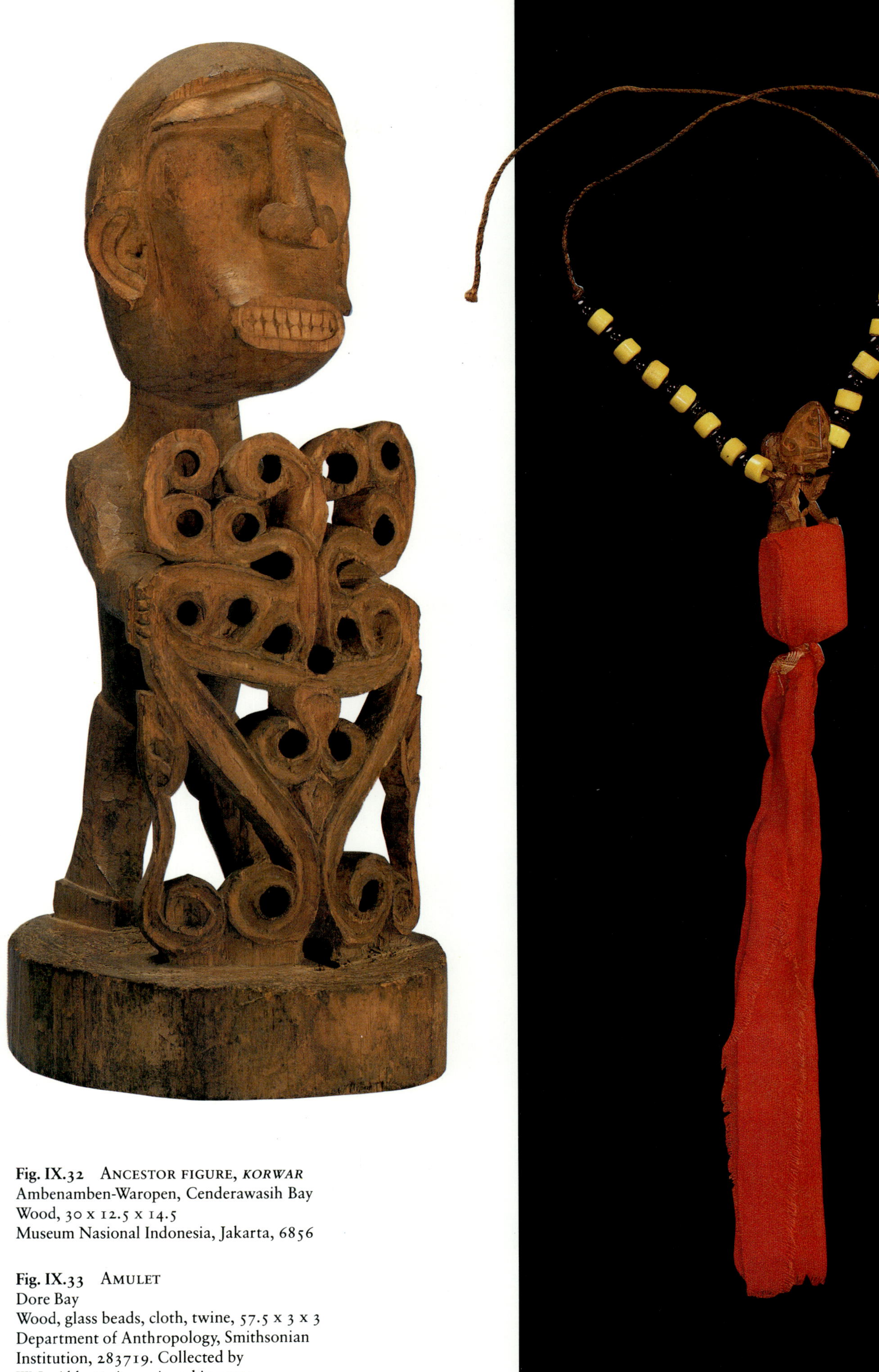

Fig. IX.32 Ancestor figure, *korwar*
Ambenamben-Waropen, Cenderawasih Bay
Wood, 30 x 12.5 x 14.5
Museum Nasional Indonesia, Jakarta, 6856

Fig. IX.33 Amulet
Dore Bay
Wood, glass beads, cloth, twine, 57.5 x 3 x 3
Department of Anthropology, Smithsonian Institution, 283719. Collected by W. L. Abbott. Accessioned in 1914.

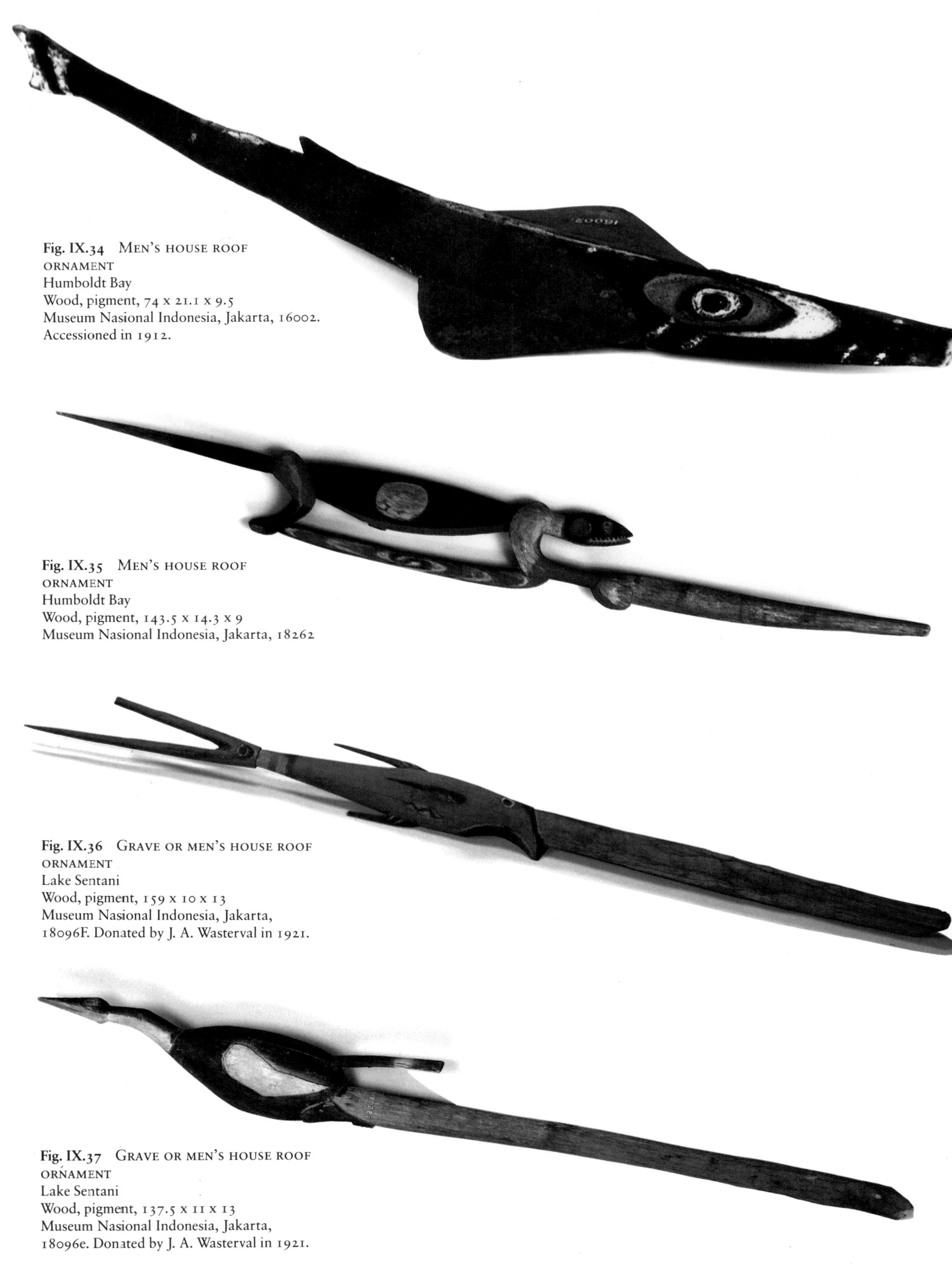

Fig. IX.34 MEN'S HOUSE ROOF ORNAMENT
Humboldt Bay
Wood, pigment, 74 x 21.1 x 9.5
Museum Nasional Indonesia, Jakarta, 16002.
Accessioned in 1912.

Fig. IX.35 MEN'S HOUSE ROOF ORNAMENT
Humboldt Bay
Wood, pigment, 143.5 x 14.3 x 9
Museum Nasional Indonesia, Jakarta, 18262

Fig. IX.36 GRAVE OR MEN'S HOUSE ROOF ORNAMENT
Lake Sentani
Wood, pigment, 159 x 10 x 13
Museum Nasional Indonesia, Jakarta, 18096F. Donated by J. A. Wasterval in 1921.

Fig. IX.37 GRAVE OR MEN'S HOUSE ROOF ORNAMENT
Lake Sentani
Wood, pigment, 137.5 x 11 x 13
Museum Nasional Indonesia, Jakarta, 18096e. Donated by J. A. Wasterval in 1921.

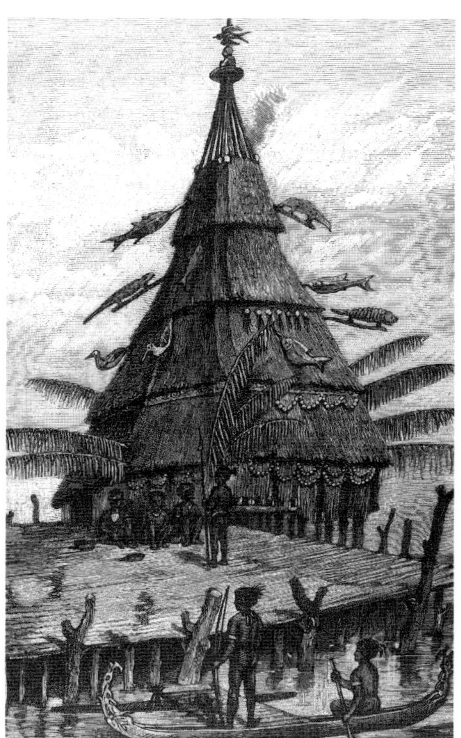

Fig. IX.38 Roof ornaments on the ceremonial house at Tobadi, Humboldt Bay. van Hasselt 1886–88:opposite p. 358

eat" (de Clercq and Schmeltz 1893:158). When a person dies, his soul goes immediately to heaven (*suruka*, probably from the Malay *surga*, heaven). However, a person's *nin* (shadow) remains on earth in proximity to the house until a *korwar* is made for it (van Balen 1886:557–558).

Some *korwar* are wrapped in cloth, which might have been done in imitation of an actual burial. Before interment, a corpse was ceremonially washed, wrapped in white cotton, covered in a mat, and then fastened with cords (van Hasselt 1930:259). The head of this *korwar* (Fig. IX.30) is similarly bound. Its eyes are blue trade beads of the same sort seen on the Flores ancestor figures (Fig. VII.15). The missing gums, cheeks, and eye sockets of the skull are filled in with putty. The ears are carved on the wooden holder supporting the head. A strip of faded red trade cloth is wrapped around its waist.

This *korwar* (Fig. IX.31) holds an interesting shield with a little human figure carved into it and incorporates the skull of a woman between the ages of eighteen and thirty-five (personal communication, Carol Butler and David Hunt 1990). Among the people of Roon, there was a specific ceremony for placing the skull into the *korwar*:

> While persons in the house are preparing for the nightly gathering, a group of men go to the *perahu* where the body lies and remove the skull, the first cervical vertebra, and the sternum. Once these bones are cleaned the latter two are taken home and given to the mother . . . who wraps them neatly in cloth and wears them around her neck during the period of mourning. The cervical vertebra is later used for divination (*kinsor*). A string is stuck through the projecting part of the vertebra and the vertebra is then held suspended between the thumb and finger of an outstretched hand. If the vertebra hangs still it is a good sign, if not, an unlucky sign. They do not return immediately to the house with the skull, instead they go into the woods and hang the skull from two crossed pieces of wood draped with sago fronds. After sundown, when all the friends have gathered, a group of men gather the skull and bring it in a basket underneath the back veranda (landward side) of the house, where the mother receives it through an opening in the floor because it may not be carried up the ladder. The mother . . . takes the skull first to the room where it is mourned over for some time. Thereafter, it is set in the wide central hall of the house where all the friends sit. Singing begins but without the accompaniment of the Papuan musical instruments. This singing is repeated the next night. . . . The *korwar* and the skull are then taken during low tide to land and the skull is placed in the *korwar*. . . . The *korwar* is now given a place in the house and is considered a member of the household (van Balen 1886:562–563).

Although different theories have been proposed (Feuilletau de Bruyn 1917; Serrurier 1898), none explains definitively why some *korwar* hold shields (Fig. IX.32). They may symbolize bravery (de Clercq and Schmeltz 1893:158) or represent spiritual protection. This unusual *korwar* figure (Fig. IX.32) is standing, not squatting as is most common, and the eyes appear as long slits squeezed shut. The open scroll-like pattern on the shield is similar to a type of carving seen in the Moluccas. De Clercq and Schmeltz also report that *korwar*-like wooden carvings are hung from the young men's houses (*rum seram*) in Cenderawasih Bay (Fig. IX.17).

Little charms with *korwar*-like amulets were worn for protection during warfare and travel and to attract women: "The talismans worn on a cord around the neck hang on the chest or down the back to bring luck during an attack as well as to offer protection against all conceivable evils. Young men also wear them down the back to attract a favored girl" (de Clercq and Schmeltz 1893:168). Pieces of magically powerful wood or root may also have been attached to the little wooden *korwar*-like faces; small slices of these substances would have been cut off and chewed with betel nut to offer protection during warfare. Sections of this wood or root could also have been burnt and then chewed to prevent rain during an attack. The *korwar*-like carvings on the charms are rarely if ever a direct representation of an ancestor (de Clercq 1893:176–177). The amulet (Fig. IX.33), wrapped in red trade cloth, is a port-

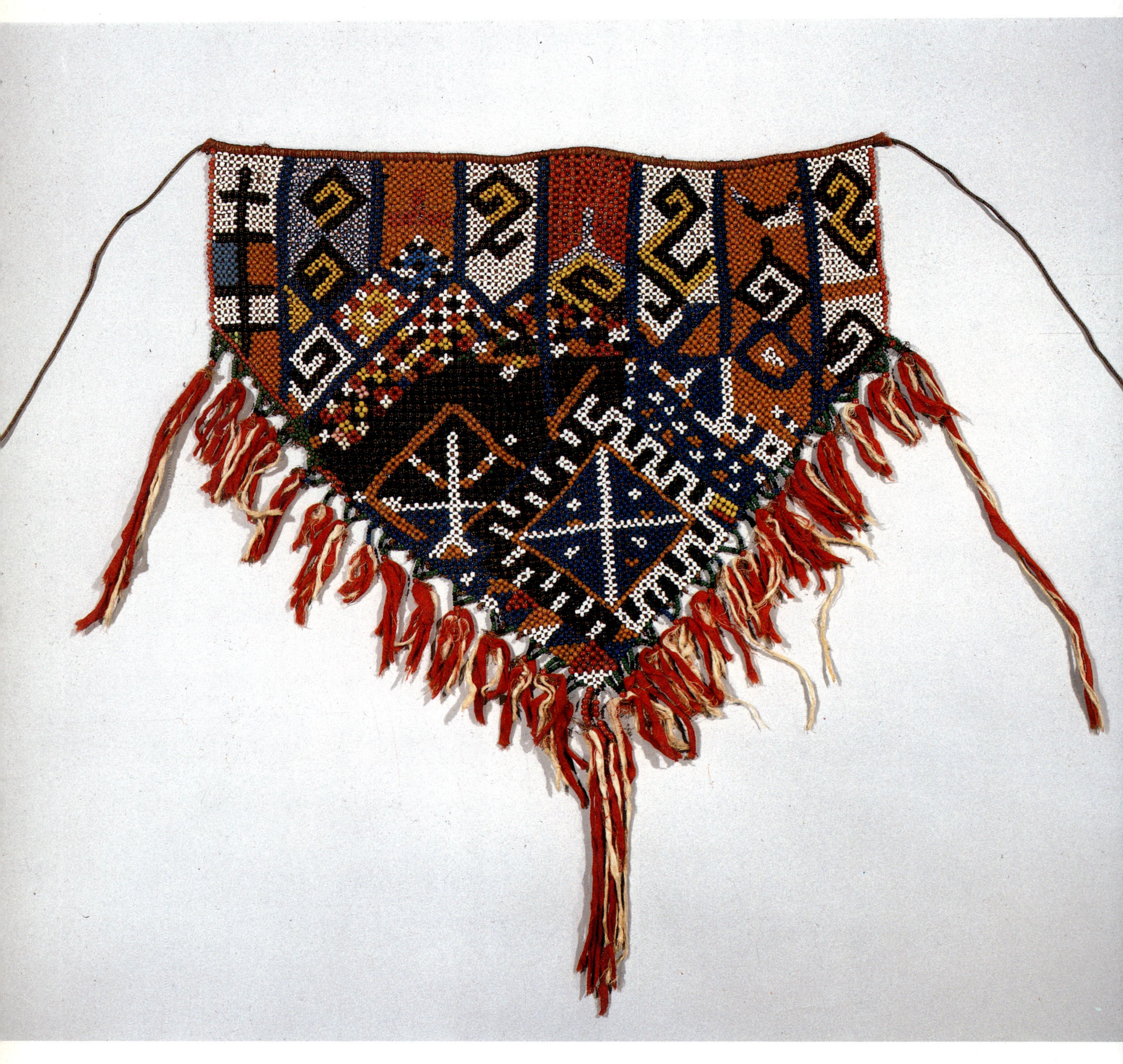

Fig. IX.39 Beaded apron
Manokwari
Glass beads, cotton, natural fiber thread,
53 x 43
Department of Anthropology, Smithsonian
Institution, 337454. Collected by
M. W. Stirling. Donated in 1927.

Fig. IX.40 Beaded apron
Cenderawasih Bay
Glass beads, cotton, natural fiber thread,
40.6 x 53.3
Thomas Murray

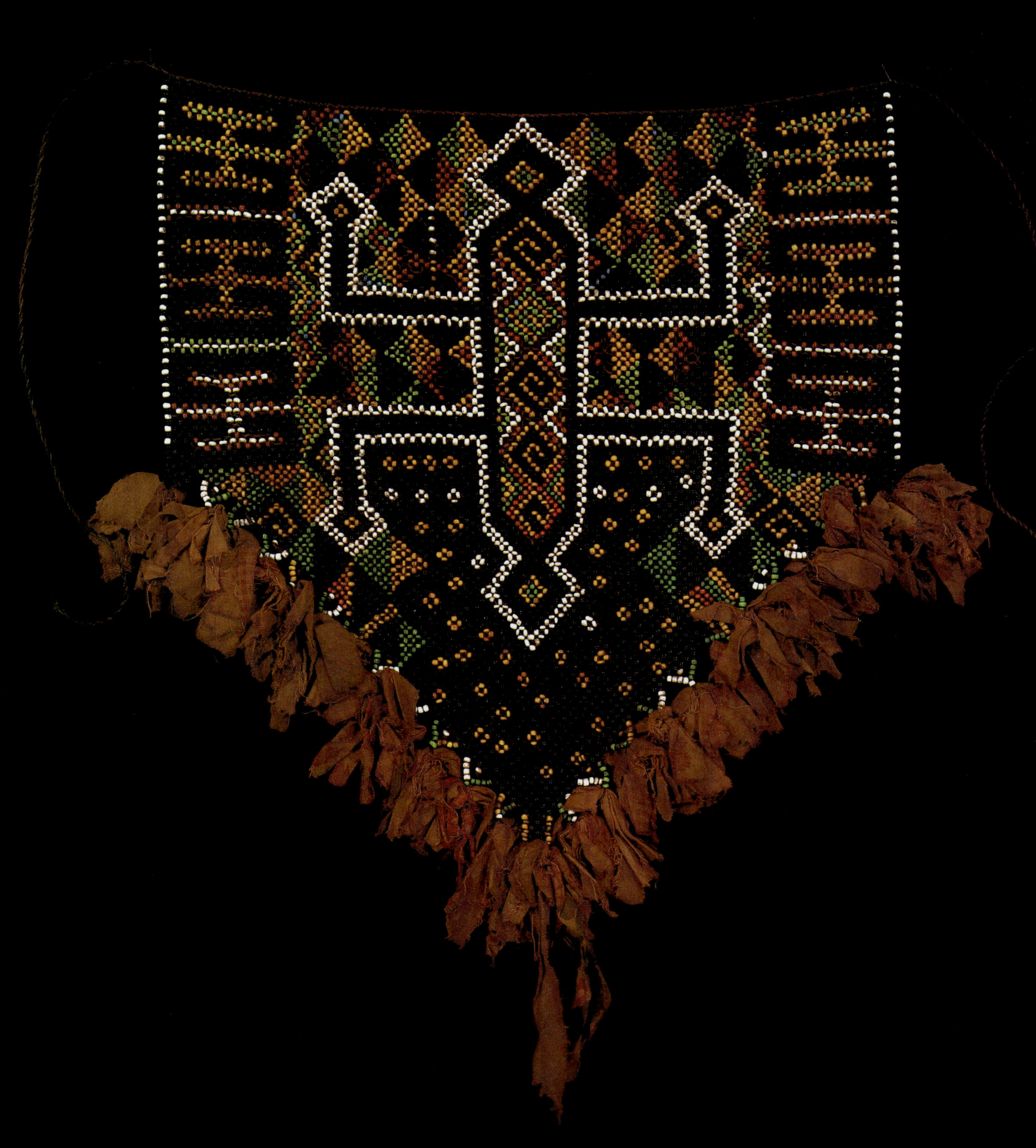

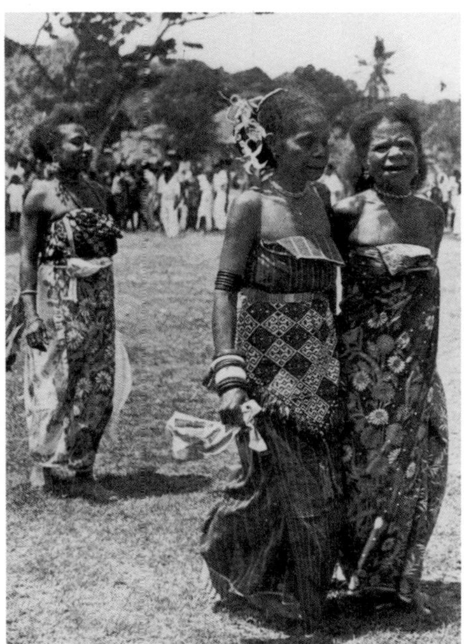

Fig. IX.41 Numfoor woman wearing a beaded apron over an imported sarong at a staged event, Cenderawasih Bay. Held 1940:143

able charm, believed to protect against such evils as malevolent spirits, unfavorable winds, illness, stranded boats, and bad luck in trade and fishing. Van der Sande points out that "teeth of crocodiles, nails from the claws of cassowaries, and similar objects also count as talismans, each for its particular purpose" (1907:303), although he does not describe these purposes.

Trade Goods and Their Role in Society

On the island of New Guinea, not only were trade routes between the peoples in the interior well established (Allen 1983) but for centuries the northern coastal peoples of Irian Jaya have engaged in active trade with the peoples of surrounding regions such as Melanesia and Indonesia. Local products, such as dammar, woods, birds of paradise and crowned pigeons, animal skins, dried fish, massooi bark (used to make pharmaceuticals), and sea cucumber (a delicacy), were exchanged with other Indonesian peoples for foreign items, such as metals, cotton fabrics, textiles (*kain timor*), glass beads, and porcelain. *Kain timor* was precious and was an important item of the bridewealth (van der Sande 1907:215). Red, white, and blue were the preferred colors for the cloth, perhaps because the hues closely resembled the most commonly used pigments of the area: red, white, and black. For part of the year, Moluccan traders settled on the north coast of Irian Jaya to wait out the monsoons, whose dangerous waves and currents made the waters difficult to navigate (Bink 1896). With them, the Moluccans brought the art of iron forging (Kamma and Kooijman 1973). The open scrollwork seen in Figs. IX.22 and IX.32, which resembles Moluccan designs, may have been learned from, or shared with, these traders.

Demand for these foreign goods enhanced the already-established trade systems between the peoples of the northern coast and those of the interior. The coastal people, who controlled trade along the coast, were able to charge exaggerated prices for foreign trade items in the interior. By this means, they could not only obtain necessary and exotic forest products from the interior but also increase their prestige and lure the peoples of the interior into relationships of economic dependency.

Such economic dependency also existed between the peoples of Humboldt Bay and Lake Sentani. In 1903 when van der Sande traveled to Humboldt Bay, his Humboldt Bay guide begged him not to trade modern commodities, such as knives and mirrors, at Asé village on Lake Sentani because these goods were not yet known in Humboldt Bay itself. Van der Sande concluded ". . . the natives from the interior or from the mountains are the sufferers, and are to a certain extent at the mercy of the inhabitants of the coast who fix the value of the productions and obtain great profits with little trouble" (1907:216). Meyer also states that the interior people were dependent on the coastal people (1875:28–29). Lake Sentani dwellers traded pig, sago, and lime gourds to the people at Humboldt Bay for smoked fish and valuable ancient beads, which were used in bridewealth and to increase prestige. These economic exchanges were accompanied by marriage exchanges: the Lake Sentani women were married to men from Humboldt Bay, where they were valued for their fishing skills.

Some of the most precious and valued objects to reach the north coast of Irian Jaya, mainly along ancient Chinese and Indian trade routes, were glass beads. These beads became integral for marriage gifts and the maintenance of prestige and were also used to mediate disputes. Local myths from both Humboldt Bay and Lake Sentani attribute the origin of beads to mythical bead trees supplied by the ancestors. According to legend, these bead trees, like the ancestors, came from the east. Because they were given by the ancestors, beads retain certain powers associated with the upper world, hence their prominent role in society. These two myths concern the origin of beads, the first from Humboldt Bay and the second from Lake Sentani:

> 1. The prize of the Itár people was their bead tree, whose fruit yielded beads. Because this tree was so fertile, Andjuwa decided to have sixteen boys and sixteen

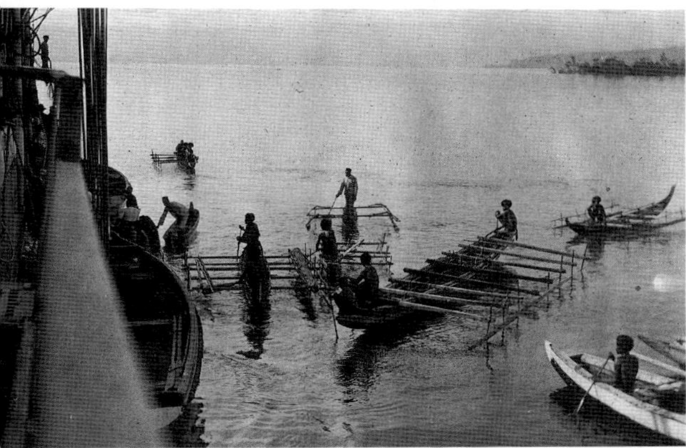

Fig. IX.42 Native traders approach a western ship, Cenderawasih Bay. Barbour 1908:545

girls guard the tree. Day and night they watched the tree to make sure that the fruit was not eaten by birds and the seeds deposited at another locale. The boys and girls fell in love with each other and they decided to run away and take the bead tree with them. They fled westward with the bead tree, a pig, a hunting dog, a drum, and sago plants. Eventually they disbanded settling in different areas, where they founded villages (Galis 1955:252).

2. When our forefathers still lived in the mountains to the east, they had a bead tree. When they moved from the east to the west they took with them their bead tree and planted it in the vicinity of Nafri on a hill. It was a large tree with beautiful flowers. After some time the area around the tree began to smell. It seemed that the tree was rotting and so they cut it down. When later generations were planting gardens they frequently found beads in the ground. They were the flowers from the bead tree of the ancestors (Hoogerbrugge 1967:51).

On Lake Sentani ancient glass beads were necessary for marriage. A bridewealth gift consisted of glass beads, stone axes, and in the case of the headman's sons, glass bracelets. When a young girl was promised to a family, the father of the groom-to-be gave the girl's father a yellow bead. In Humboldt Bay the bridewealth consisted of two stone axes and a quantity of antique beads, which the groom gave to the father-in-law. Half of the beads were then given to the mother-in-law and the rest were divided among the relatives of the bride.

On Lake Sentani, beads of a peculiar size, shape, or color were often believed to contain magic and could only be possessed by a headman or shaman, that is, someone mighty enough to control their power. Odd or uniquely shaped beads increased social status. On Lake Sentani and in other areas of the north coast of Irian Jaya, beads could even be used to pay compensation and settle disputes. They were also among the trade goods used by foreigners to purchase services from the local people. Bink relates: "The articles with which one can get the Sentaniers to do anything are blue and yellow bullet-shaped beads about the size of a pea; large oval yellow and blue beads, and especially large and small knives, axes, and hatchets" (1896:206).

Because of the scarcity and power of beads, they were also used to decorate ceremonial objects. The most elaborate examples of beaded objects are the beaded aprons from Cenderawasih Bay (Figs. IX.39, IX.40). Held believes these beaded aprons were originally manufactured by women on Yapen and then traded to other locations (1957:323). Little mention is made in the literature about how and by whom these objects were worn, but they may have been worn by men or women on ritual occasions. They have been seen worn by women during ritual dances with the apron fastened around the waist and the beaded section hanging over the backside (personal communication, Mrs. G. J. Held and Jac. Hoogerbrugge 1984). Records from the Museum Nasional Indonesia in Jakarta mention that they were worn by men during sago-cutting ceremonies and used as part of the bridewealth (Koleksi Pilihan:1984–85:553). Usually these beaded aprons are symmetrically designed. Although this apron (Fig. IX.39) is ornamented with typical design motifs, its asymmetric patterns are curious. The most notable feature is the diamond design in blue with a white cross in the center and a green-and-white border. These green-and-white figures are positive on one side of the diamond and negative on the other. This mirror imaging is common in Indonesian art. This apron (Fig. IX.40) is more symmetrically woven and portrays a lizard or frog. Both cloths are finished with strips of trade cloth.

Whatever their traditional use, beaded aprons are now worn by both men and women on special occasions. A photograph (Fig. IX.41), taken on the occasion of a feast in Manokwari village in August, 1939, when some Cenderawasih Bay groups and schools were invited to produce a show about their native customs, shows a Numfoor woman wearing a beaded apron (personal communication, Jac. Hoogerbrugge 1990).

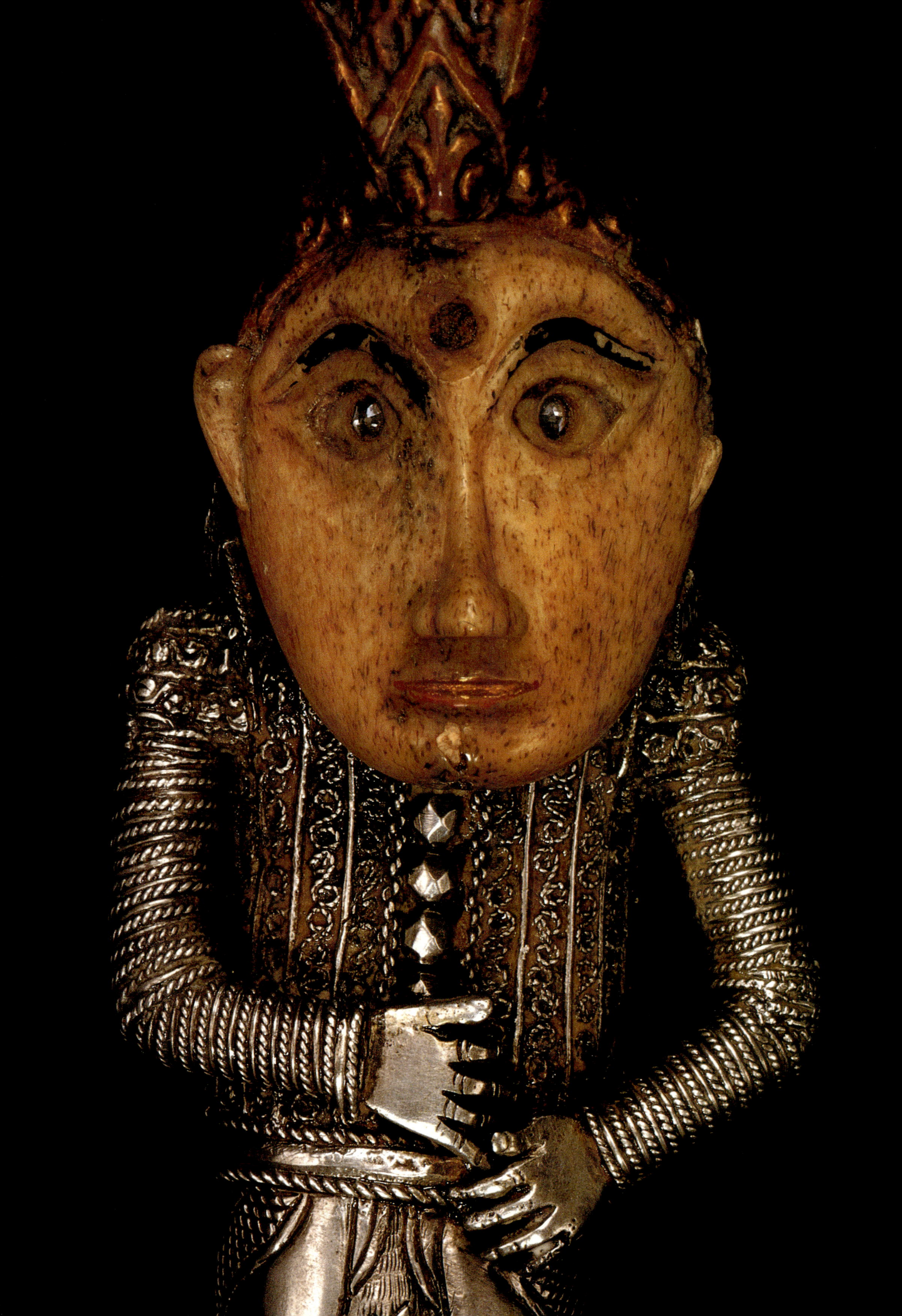

X

Courts of the Outer Islands

Fig. X.1 Human figure carved on the shaft of a dagger (detail of X.12).

THE EXTENSIVE SEA TRADE that developed along the routes between the Asian mainland and the Spice Islands of the Moluccas led to the formation of many coastal trading ports on the outer (as well as inner) islands. These ports attracted foreign traders by offering an array of products including gold, camphor, pepper, wood resins, honey, wax, pitch, sulphur, iron, cotton, rattan, spices, and foodstuffs (Ricklefs 1981: 18–19). Even though Indian, Chinese, and Javanese historical data regarding outer-island ports is sketchy prior to European colonization when foreign powers began systematically to compile documentation on Indonesia, the vastness of pre–sixteenth-century trade in the Indonesian archipelago can no longer be underestimated nor can there be any doubt about the Indonesians' active participation in this commerce as navigators (Taylor 1976). More than a mere way station between Europe and the Far East, these coastal centers were active participants in the trade that developed during the first millennium A.D. between the spice islands of the Moluccas, the Malaysian peninsula, India, China, Japan, Turkey and other Mediterranean ports, Arabia, and east Africa.

The ports of the Malay peninsula and the Indonesian archipelago flourished and declined as a result of fluctuating commercial hierarchies. Powerful centers holding monopolies over particular trade items extracted tribute from lesser ports for access to the foreign trade network. These smaller ports would store their inland goods at the major centers to await collection by the larger sea vessels of foreign traders. The traders at these smaller ports might, however, succeed in obtaining their own monopolies directly from the foreign merchants and thus might become the next predominant center.

After 100 A.D., some coastal trade centers—influenced by Indian traders and travelling religious scholars—developed into Hindu-Buddhist kingdoms. The exact dates and nature of the influences leading to these religious conversions accompanied by ideas regarding sacred kingship are largely unrecorded, but, generally speaking, delegates from foreign kingdoms interested in trade would enter a new area, offer exotic foreign goods, and look for an indigenous sov-

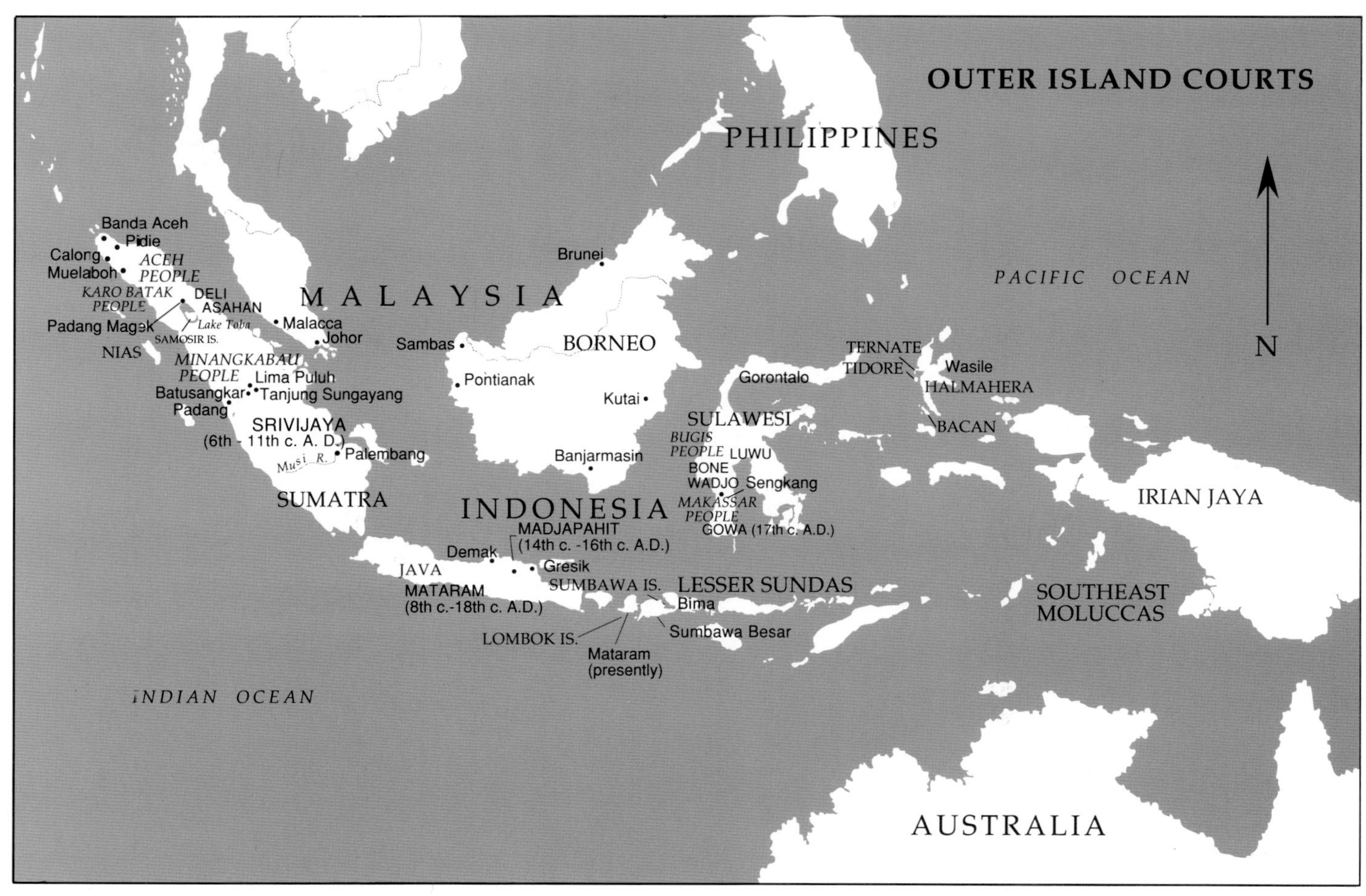

ereign. If one did not exist or if he would not cooperate, a rival local would be chosen and given some imported luxury items as an emblem of his ties to the greater power abroad. Successful trade with that community would increase the leader's wealth and ability to dominate in his own society. Moreover, his ability to invoke a charter of office from powerful foreign kings, or to invoke foreign gods, was often interpreted as a sign of his divine favor and preeminence. From the foreign kingdom's perspective, the value of installing a reliable local raja (Sanskrit word for "prince" or "chief") lay in the creation of a favorable climate for international trade. Although the terms "court" and "kingdom" invoke many meanings concerning statehood in the West, within the Malay context a kingdom (*kerajaan*) only means "having a raja" (Milner 1982:8–9). The central city of Southeast Asian courts served also as a sacred center, given that it housed the divine ruler (Anderson 1972; Tambiah 1976). Because power was an energy inferred from, but not created by, such concrete signs as wealth, actual political power was used to control and restrict access to the physical signs of spiritual potency such as sacred regalia (Errington 1989:10). Despite their claims to divine sovereignty, the rulers of the coastal courts led polities that were mostly small and shifting, dependent upon—and at pains to maintain—the allegiance of highland people associated with them through exchange relationships.

After 1300 A.D., when Muslim-controlled trade networks became more important than Hindu or Buddhist ones, the rajas of many small Hindu or Buddhist kingdoms converted to Islam, thereby becoming sultans (Arabic word for "sovereign" Fig. X.3). These emporia were characterized by so-called Malay court culture and are now populated by Malay or Islamic coastal peoples (Geertz 1963) who maintain ties to court culture though courts have now been abolished as political entities throughout the outer islands. The term "Malay" refers to a fluid coastal court culture (including its aesthetic aspects) more than a particular people because individuals often moved from an inland tribal area and thus became Malay or vice versa (Reid 1979:1).

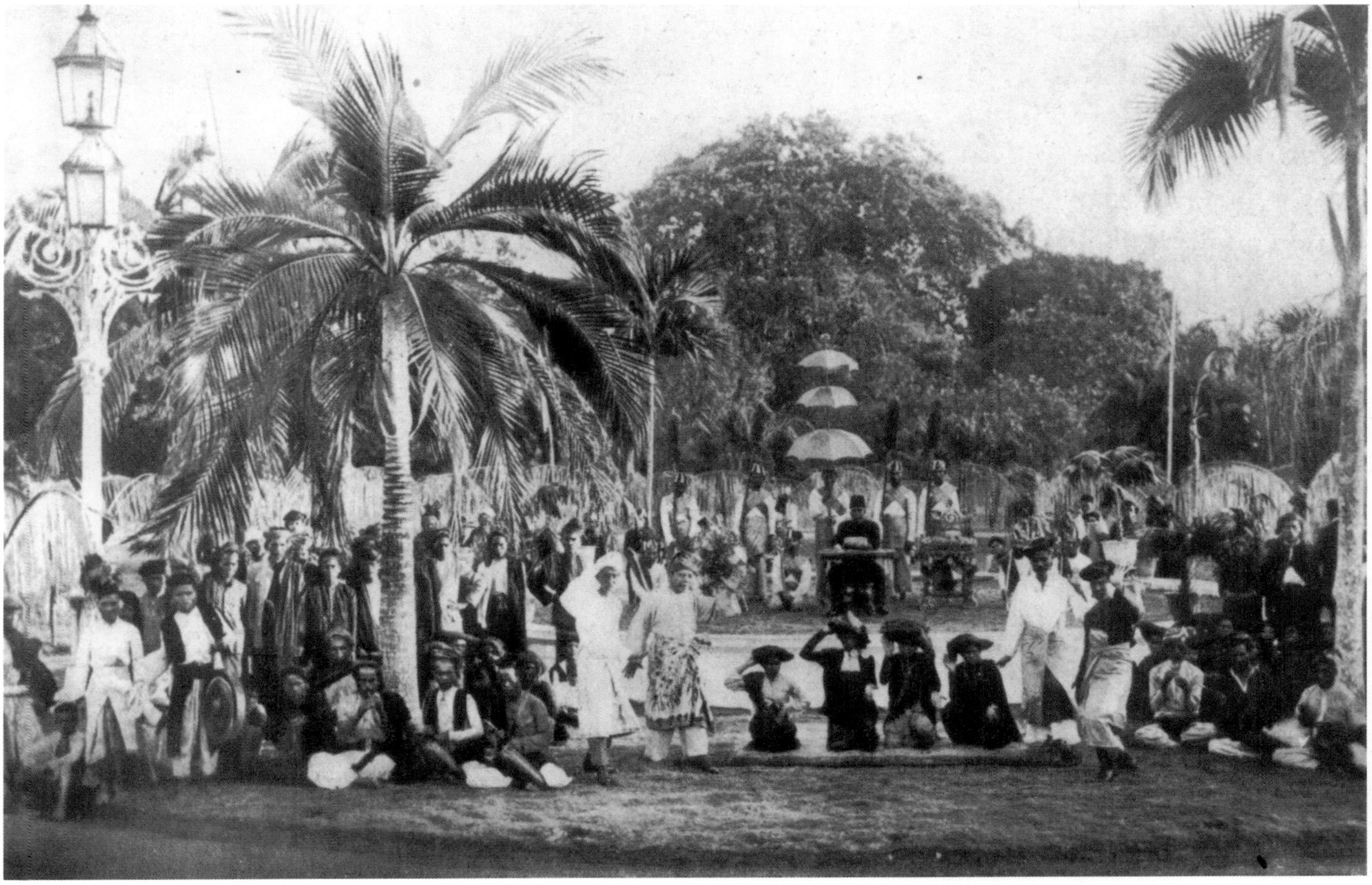

Fig. X.2 Wives of a Karo Batak headman dance with ritual specialists of the Sultan of Deli, North Sumatra, before 1900. van Eerde 1921:133. Courtesy Elsevier Press, Amsterdam.

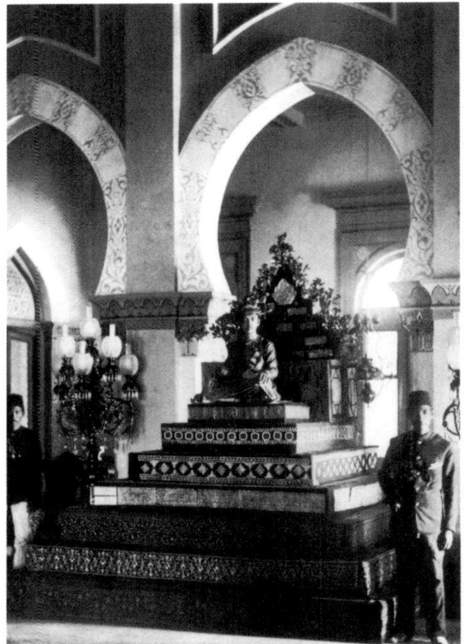

Fig. X.3 The Sultan of Deli on a raised throne, North Sumatra, before 1900. van Eerde 1921:251. Courtesy Elsevier Press, Amsterdam.

Ricklefs writes, "Europe was not the most advanced area of the world at the start of the fifteenth century. Nor was it the most dynamic. The major expanding force in the world was Islam; in 1453 the Ottoman Turks conquered Constantinople, and at the eastern end of the Islamic world the faith was spreading in Indonesia and the Philippines" (1981:20). By the sixteenth century, however, Portuguese and Dutch traders were also successfully competing in Malay trade. By the nineteenth century, the decorative arts of the Indonesian courts of the outer islands thus show a variety of Indian, Chinese, Middle Eastern, and European aesthetic influences. The particular courts whose artworks are discussed in this chapter, introduced here roughly from west to east, are merely a representative sample of the more numerous courts of varying sizes that developed throughout the archipelago between the sixth and twentieth centuries (see Fontein 1990; Jessup 1990 for more detailed studies of Indonesian court arts).

The history of the outer-island courts, like that of Java's courts, is largely a tale of foreign trade and political alliances. The most-sought-after trade items from Indonesia were spices: from the black pepper of Sumatra in the west to the cloves of the Moluccas in the east. Besides cloves, nutmeg, and mace (another product of the nutmeg tree), other spices generated income from the Moluccan region. The proceeds from trading in the outer islands may not have resulted in courts as famous or central as those in Java; they were, however, large enough to produce powerful coastal polities that rivalled European nations for military control of desirable ports and sea trade monopolies. Moreover, they developed unique styles of court artwork that integrated the techniques and designs of foreign lands with indigenous themes and motifs.

The outer-island courts not only traded with foreigners but they also developed systems of trade and cooperation with various other ethnic groups of the interior highlands on whom they were dependent for their continued supplies of forest products such as bamboo, rattan, tree resins, and medicinal plants. Highland and lowland polities exchanged not only natural resources and

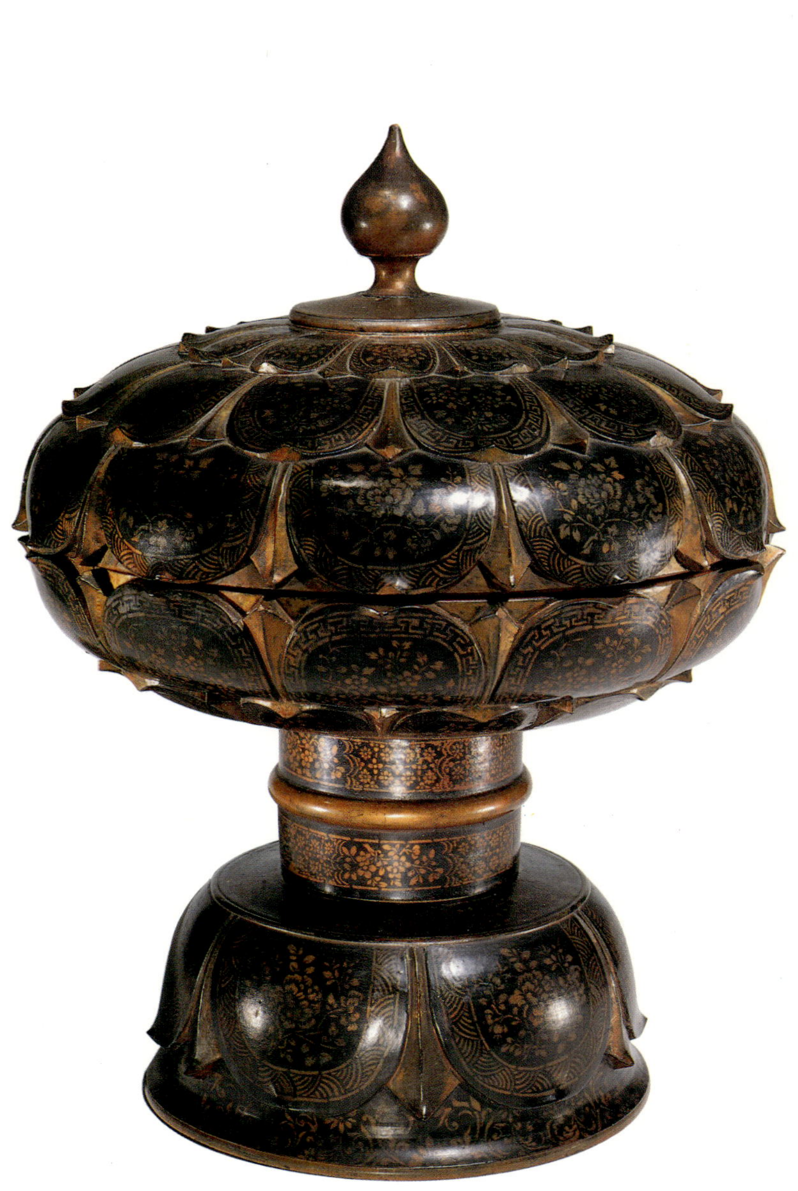

Fig. X.4 Box, *TENONG*
Palembang, South Sumatra
Lacquer, wood, gold leaf, pigment,
24.5 x 23.5
Museum Nasional Indonesia, Jakarta, 18865.
Accessioned in 1924.

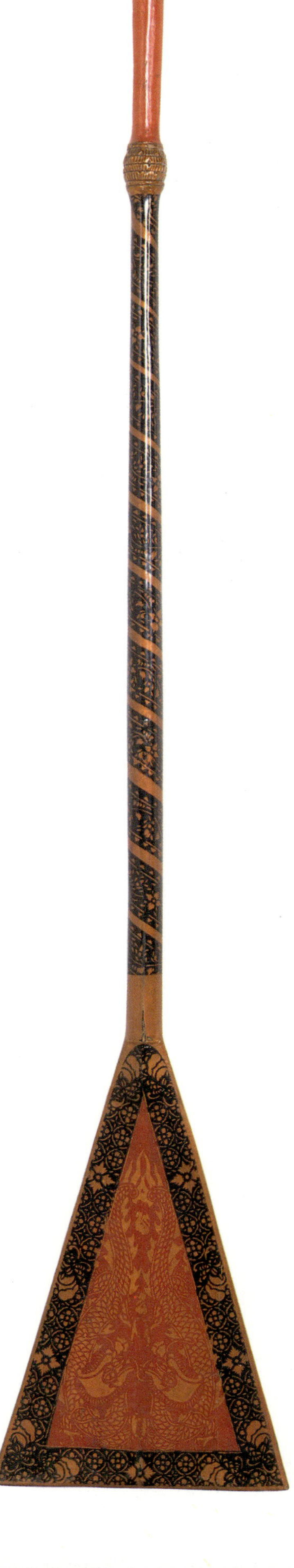

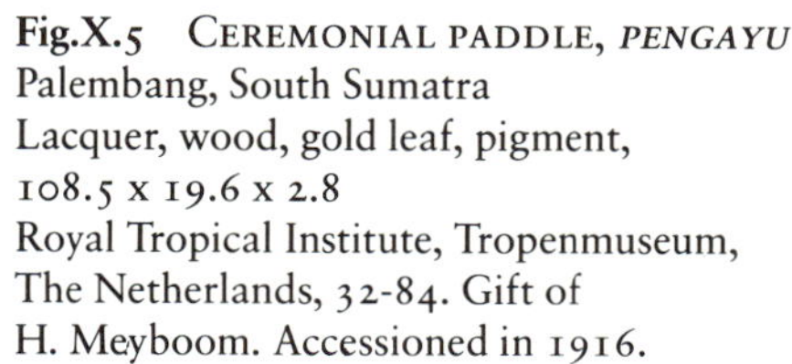

Fig.X.5 Ceremonial paddle, *PENGAYU*
Palembang, South Sumatra
Lacquer, wood, gold leaf, pigment,
108.5 x 19.6 x 2.8
Royal Tropical Institute, Tropenmuseum,
The Netherlands, 32-84. Gift of
H. Meyboom. Accessioned in 1916.

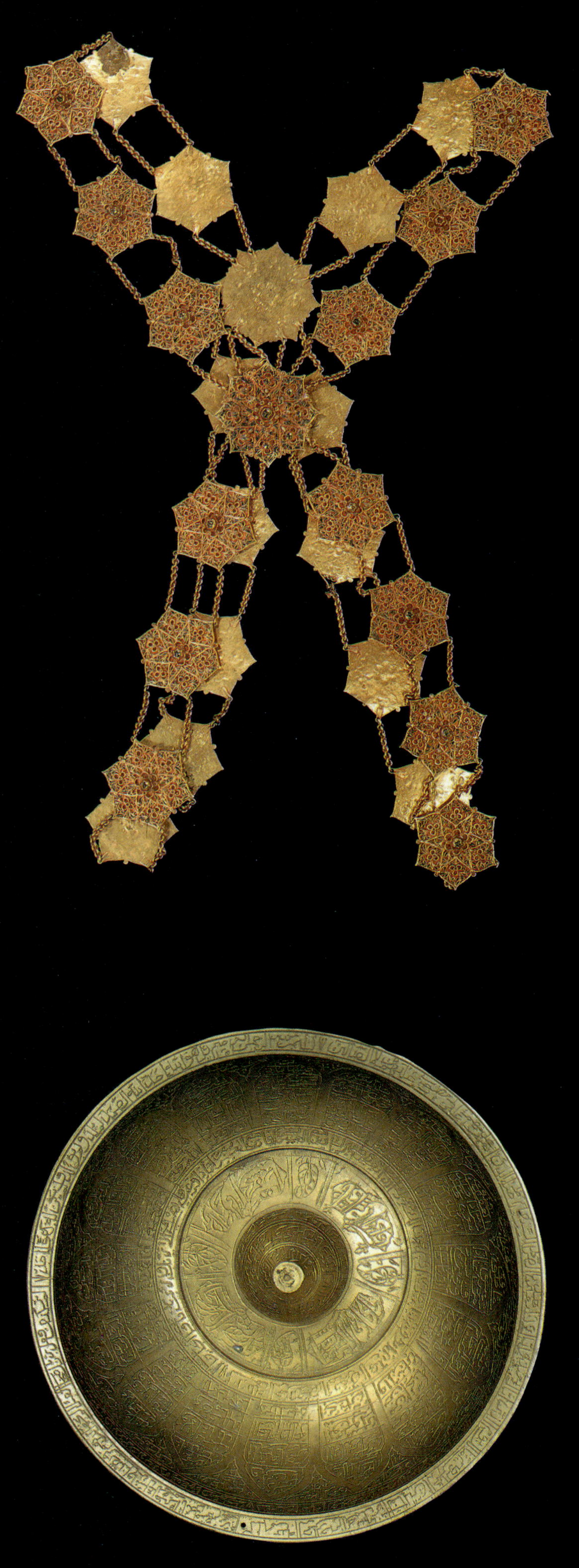

Fig. X.6 Bridal ornament, *simplaih meuëh*
Aceh, North Sumatra
Gold, enamel cloisonné, semiprecious stones, 48
Royal Tropical Institute, Tropenmuseum, The Netherlands, 1698-469. Accessioned in 1947.

Fig. X.7 Drinking bowl
Calong, Aceh, North Sumatra
Brass, 5 x 18.7
Royal Tropical Institute, Tropenmuseum, The Netherlands, 674-850

manufactured goods but also ritual knowledge, military assistance, and wives—all exchanges resulting in future obligations and debt repayment on both sides. The courts depended upon such links between highland exchange networks, which were based on indigenous standards of value, and foreign trade, which provided valuables to the local trade networks in exchange for surplus products (Barnes 1987:83). Intermarriage and gift exchange often took place between highland and lowland aristocracies to safeguard the prosperity and fertility of both communities. In some areas, shared mythologies, kinship relations, and attendance at each other's major rituals promoted interaction between coastal and inland communities. Their prior physical and spiritual claim on the land producing the desired resources was an important factor in establishing the inland group's partial superiority over the coastal traders (Condominas 1977). These relations between lowland court and highland chiefdoms continued to flourish until the twentieth century (Fig. X.2), and in some areas these relationships are recognized at the level of family ties even today. The spiritual powers of the ruling families and their sacred heirlooms have been maintained in social practice even though their political efficacy has dissipated.

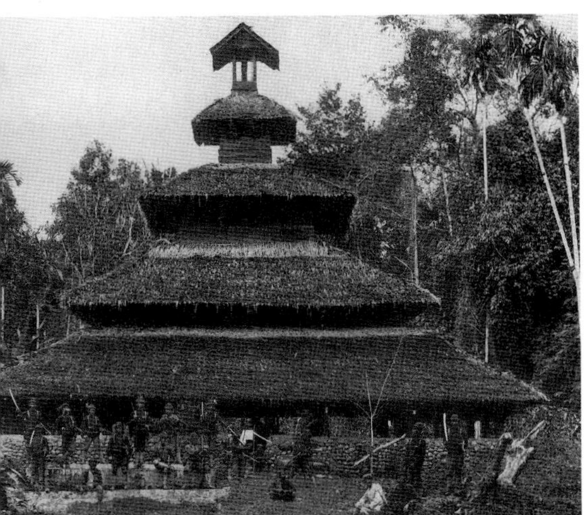

Fig. X.8 A mosque in Aceh, North Sumatra, before 1900. van Eerde 1921:75. Courtesy Elsevier Press, Amsterdam.

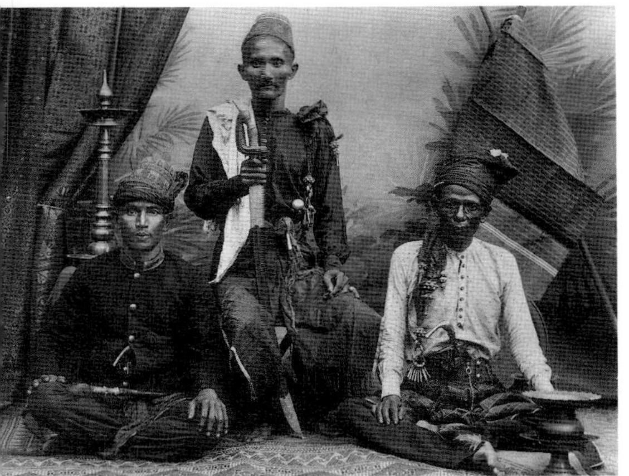

Fig. X.9 Three Aceh district leaders in ceremonial dress, Aceh, North Sumatra, circa 1900. Courtesy Rijksmuseum voor Volkenkunde, Leiden.

Sumatra

According to Chinese and early Malay records, a major center of maritime trade between the sixth and eleventh centuries A.D. was the east Sumatran kingdom of Srivijaya (Coedès 1968[1944]; Wolters 1967). By the seventh and eighth centuries, this kingdom, which was centered near present-day Palembang, possessed a large fleet of commercial ships and was governed by rulers practicing Mahayana Buddhism. The rapid expansion of Srivijaya in the fifth and sixth centuries was attributable to a booming economy fed by the Chinese fascination with such luxury items as gems, textiles, spices, and tree resins from Sassanid Persia. These Persian items were transported to China in Sumatran ships. Eventually these traders successfully increased their profits by replacing the desired Persian products with substitute items of Indonesian origin (Nicholl 1983). For example, tree resins from Persia coveted for Chinese medicines were replaced by camphor from Sumatra and Borneo, which was used to produce the same types of medicinal ointments.

The central power of the mercantile kingdom of Srivijaya fluctuated greatly according to the court's relationships with its various trading partners of the Sumatran interior and coasts (Wolters 1970; Hall 1976:5). Eventually leadership in trade was taken over by a series of other Malay court centers such as Melaka (called Malacca in the West and located in present-day Malaysia), and Johor (also on the Malaysian peninsula). Prior to the twentieth century, peoples and trade moved freely across the Strait of Malacca between what is now Sumatra and Peninsular Malaysia. In fact, some histories state that it was a prince of Palembang in Sumatra that founded the port of Melaka following a Majapahit kingdom attack on Palembang in 1377 (Ricklefs 1981:18). Melaka later gained power through Chinese alliances supporting the port's successful Asian trade.

Through centuries of intense Chinese-Sumatran contact during the first millennium A.D., the court arts of the Palembang region (see map 1), which reemerged as a prominent court some centuries after the eleventh-century decline of Srivijaya, developed a refined east Asian style. Lacquer-ware techniques were introduced by Chinese artisans. In the court city of Palembang, local Indonesian craftsmen produced objects of plaited bamboo, rattan, or wood, which were then painted and lacquered by Chinese artisans who had migrated to Sumatra (van Brakel et al. 1987:255). Sometimes a base coat of lacquer and ash was applied, to provide a smooth surface for the black or red paint. Next patterns in black india ink or gold leaf were applied, and then the whole object was coated with lacquer resin. Since lacquer coating is waterproof, the technique was suitable even for the production of ceremonial boat paddles for the royal court of Palembang. Oars similar to the one illustrated (Fig. X.5) were

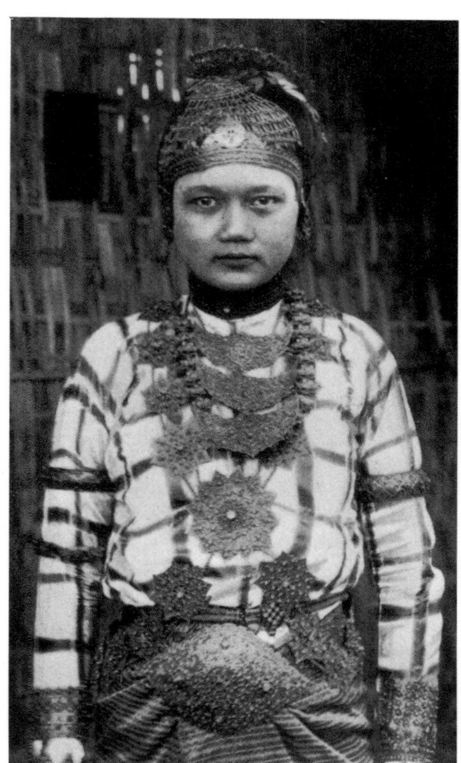

Fig. X.10 Bride wearing chest ornament (*simplaih*), Aceh, North Sumatra, before 1900. Jasper and Pirngadie 1927 (vol. 4): fig. 109

used by young unmarried girls of rank (Fig. X.13) when boating on the Musi River (van Brakel et al. 1987:274). The red and black floral designs and overall form of the paddle are characteristic of a recognizable coastal Malay aesthetic, which drew upon many shared Chinese, Indian, and Persian design patterns.

The Chinese-introduced lacquer-ware technique was also favored for ornamental boxes owned by aristocratic families and given as a dowry gift by the bride's family (van Brakel et. al. 1987:15, 262). Made in the late nineteenth or early twentieth century for the bridal chamber of a noble woman, the rounded section of this container (Fig. X.4) was used to store food. This type of container was sometimes stacked upon a second box intended to hold dowry textiles (Jessup 1990:218, 244). The lacquered container's lotus shape is a Chinese symbol of purity and regeneration. The minaret shape of the container may be traced to designs for embossed copper-alloy items produced in the Persian Gulf or Arabian Sea as early as the seventeenth century (personal communication, F. K. Lehman 1990). Craftsmen in China during subsequent centuries copied the form of such wares on demand for export, often adding more characteristically Chinese motifs in the surface adornment. Such mixed or evolving artisanry traditions were introduced to the Indonesian coastal courts by migrant artists from the Asian mainland.

Invasions from Hindu-Buddhist courts in Java and the Chola kingdom of southern India in 1025 further weakened Srivijaya's already declining mercantile dominance in favor of Javanese kingdoms such as Mataram I, whose Buddhist Sailendra dynasty built the monumental temple of Borobudur in Central Java (Wolters 1967). This kingdom came to be overshadowed by the Hindu Sanjaya dynasty, which was in turn eclipsed in the twelfth and thirteenth centuries by the kingdoms of Kediri and Singasari in eastern Java. The famed Majapahit empire (see Noorduyn 1975, 1978), which claimed many outer-island regions as its vassal states, arose in the latter half of the thirteenth century, peaked in the late fourteenth century under the sovereignty of Hayam Wuruk, but declined in the fifteenth or sixteenth century, probably under repeated attacks from such Islamic kingdoms as Demak in Java. Majapahit, both an inland agricultural kingdom as well as a maritime empire with considerable naval power, stands out in Indonesian memory for its magnificence and is to this day seen as having established political boundaries for the present Republic (Ricklefs 1981:16–17)

The history of Islam in Indonesia is often begun on the basis of records from Marco Polo's visit to Indonesia in 1292 that report only towns in Aceh as Muslim. However, Chinese and Arab reports note the presence of Islamic merchants in Asian markets well before the eleventh century; so, contact presumedly can be dated to an earlier period (Groeneveldt 1960; Wheatley 1961). The Portuguese traveller Tomé Pires observed between 1512 and 1515 that the rulers of northern and eastern Sumatra as far south as Palembang were Muslim, but those of the southern and western regions were not yet converted. In western Sumatra, only the king of Minangkabau and his immediate court followed Islam although reportedly the number of converts was increasing rapidly (Ricklefs 1981:6–7).

By the sixteenth century, Aceh was heavily supported by its religious and trading ally Turkey in attempts to overthrow the colonial Portuguese from the port of Melaka (in present-day Malaysia). That wealthy port kingdom was considered the strategic link between both Islamic and Portuguese ports on the island of Goa off the Indian subcontinent and the Orient. Fractious competition and changing alliances characterized the trade in gold, tree resins, and most importantly black pepper. According to Portuguese chronicles, the Aceh court of northern Sumatra "repeatedly received military support from the Turks in exchange for large consignments of pepper, which were traded and retraded via the Red Sea as far as Venice" (Teensma 1989:308). A report of 1582 urged Portugal's King Phillip II to invade Aceh to prevent the Indians from Gujarat and "Muslims from Mecca" from buying up the valuable Sumatran black pepper.

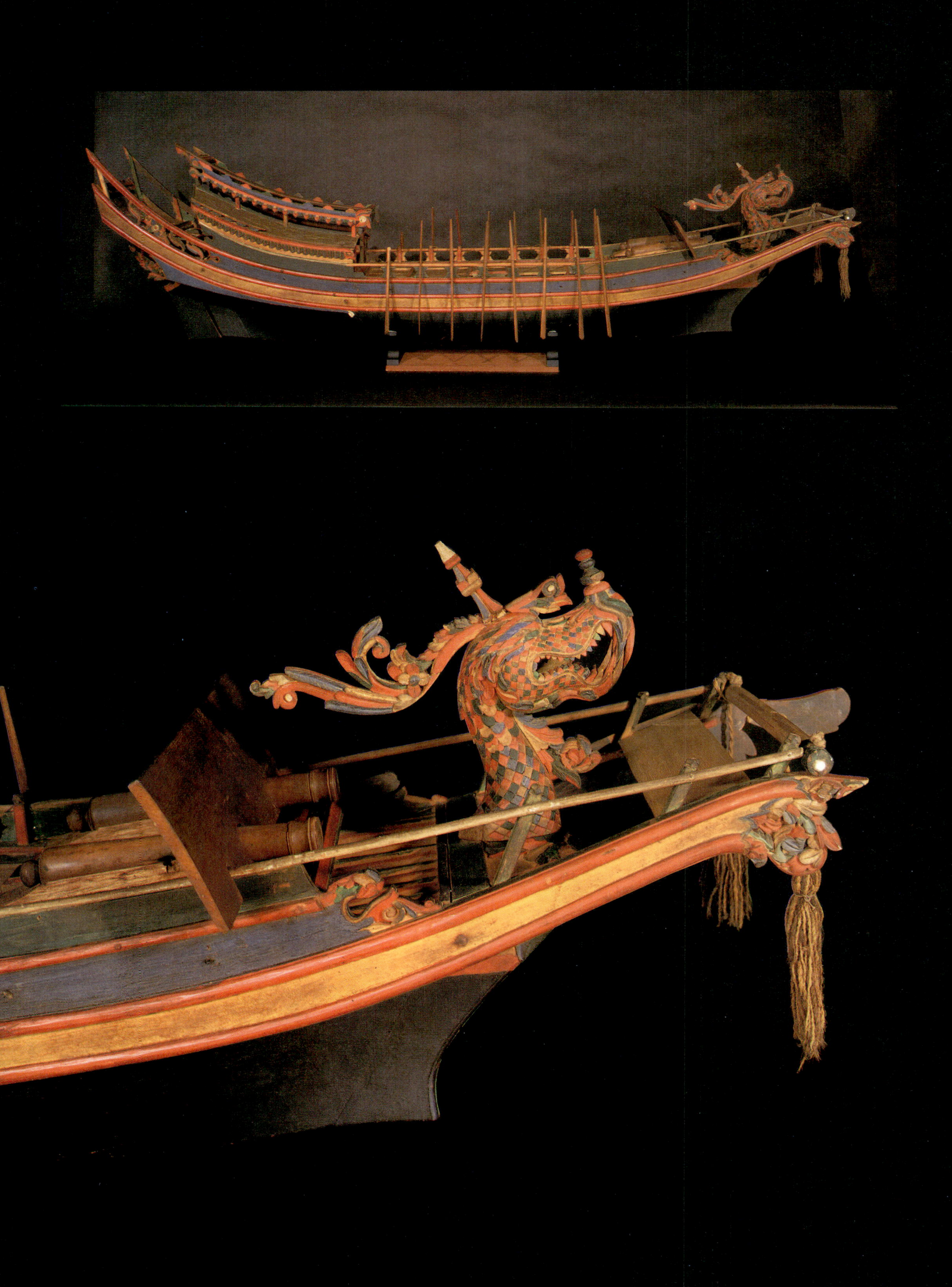

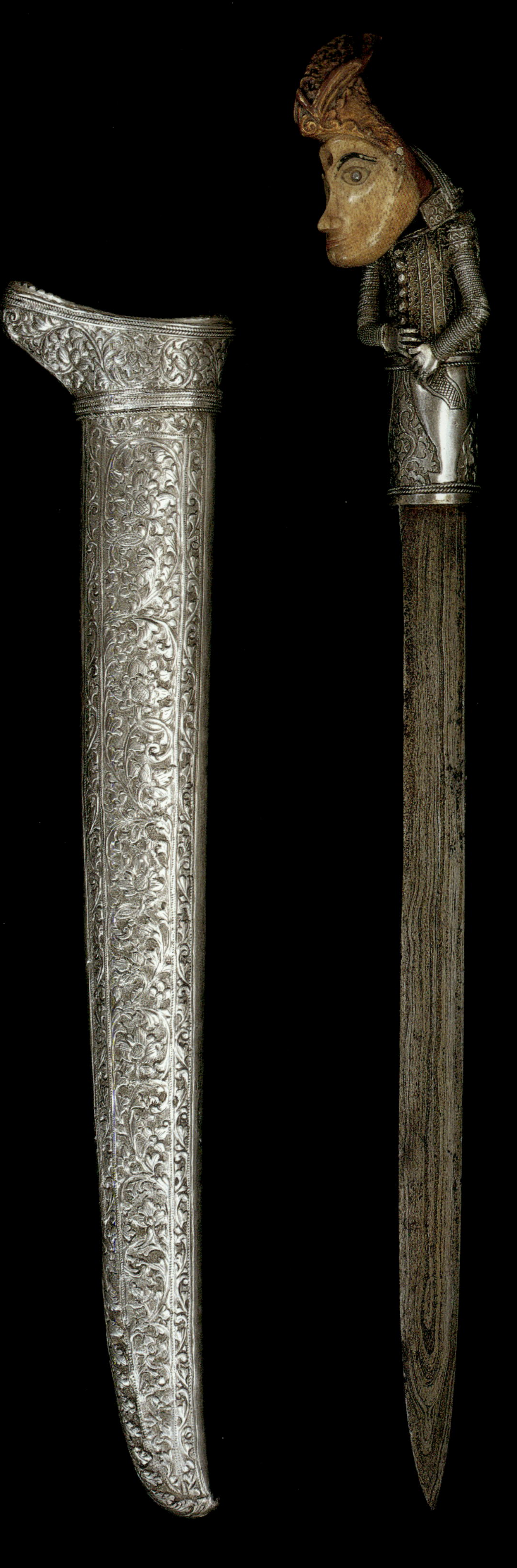

OPPOSITE
Fig. X.11 SHIP, *PERAHU LANCANG KUNING*
Asahan, North Sumatra
Wood, pigment, 63 x 212.5 x 47
Museum Nasional Indonesia, Jakarta, 828

Fig. X.11a Detail of Fig. X.11.

Fig. X.12 DAGGER AND SHEATH
Minangkabau, Lima Puluh village,
West Sumatra
Silver, iron, bone, pigment, 33 x 9 x 3.2
Museum Nasional Indonesia, Jakarta, 410

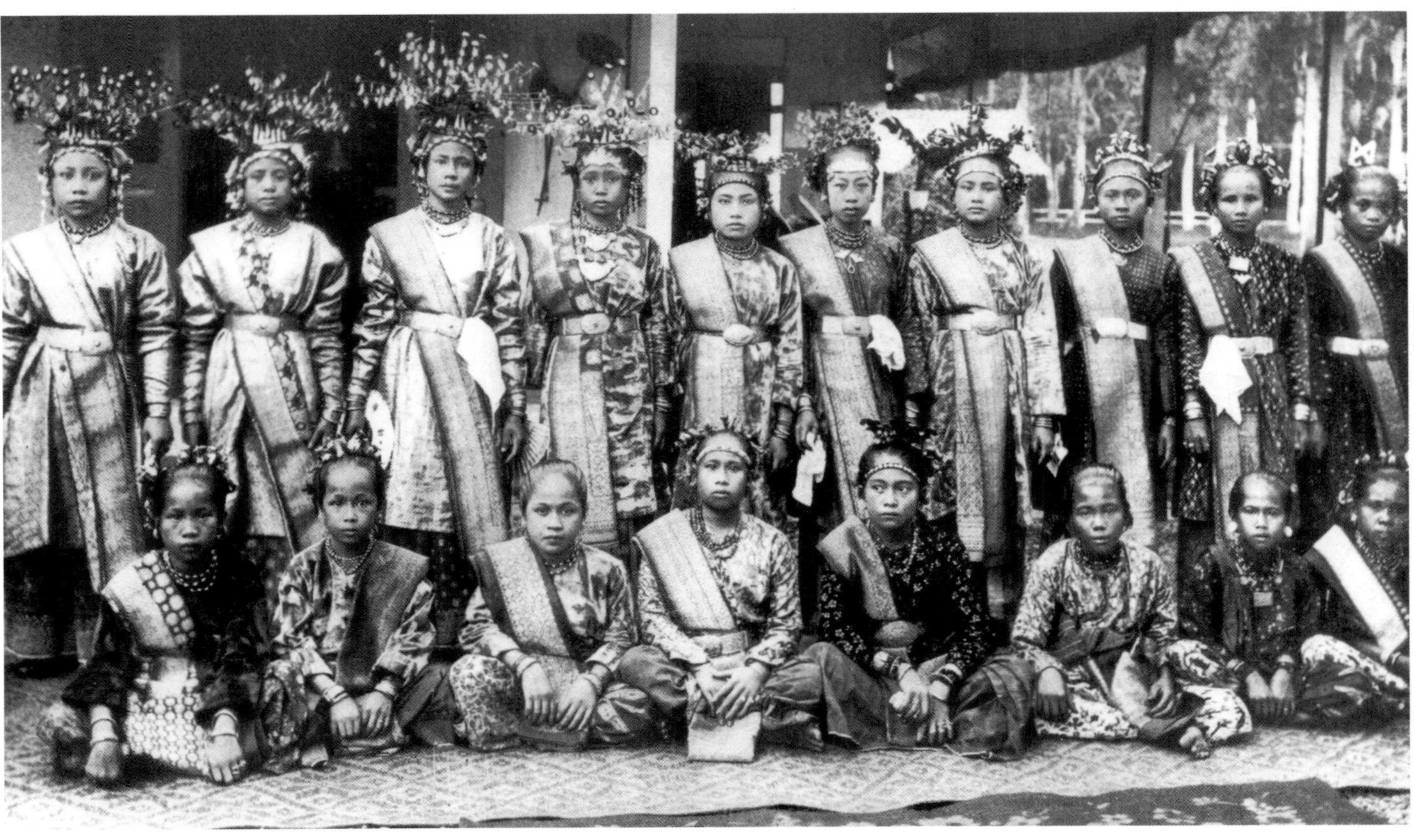

Fig. X.13 Young women in ceremonial dress, Palembang, South Sumatra, before 1900. van Eerde 1921:178. Courtesy Elsevier Press, Amsterdam.

Given the close trading relations between the kings of Aceh and the sultans of Turkey and Gujarat, Middle Eastern techniques and Islamic themes in Aceh court artwork were a symbol of these powerful foreign alliances and spiritual affiliation. Arabic calligraphy was used to ornament all types of objects including this brass bowl (Fig. X.7). Chapters 94, 97, 108, 109, 113 and 114 of the Koran are inscribed on the inside (personal communication, Wheeler Thackston 1990). The devout words on the bowl's inside rim are also from the Koran:

> God! there is no God but he, the living, the self-subsisting: neither slumber nor sleep seizeth him; to him belongeth whatsoever is in heaven and on earth. Who is he that can intercede with him but through his good pleasure. He knoweth that which is past and that which is to come unto them, and they shall not comprehend anything of his knowledge, but so far as he pleaseth. His throne is extended over heaven and earth, and the preservation of both is no burden unto him. He is the high and mighty (Koran, chapter II, verse 255, Wheeler Thackston, trans.).

The inner circle of the bowl contains invocations to God as provider of beneficial things and guarantor of success in important undertakings. The inside rim is inscribed with chapter I of the Koran. The upper part of the outside rim is an invocation of blessings upon the Prophet Muhammad, his daughter Fatima, her husband 'Ali, their sons Hasan and Husayn, and their descendants the Imams of the Shia. The rest of the outside is covered with invocations of attributes of God accompanied by assorted talismans (personal communication, Wheeler Thackston 1990). These passages from the Koran document the importance of Islam in Aceh courts since 1300 (Fig. X.8).

Brass (an alloy of copper and zinc) was preferred to bronze (an alloy of copper and tin) in Indonesia because of its greater availability and more golden color (van Brakel et al. 1987:257). The brass bowl was probably used during formal court ceremonies (Fig. X.9).

Aceh is also famous for its goldsmithing. Supported by mines located in the hills between Pidie and Muelaboh in the west, the Acehnese developed an

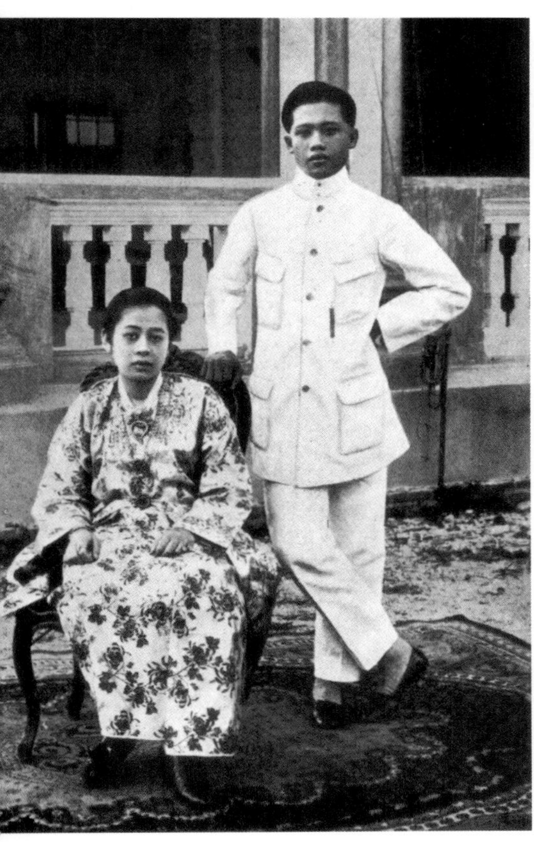

Fig. X.14 The daughter of the deceased Sultan of Asahan with the son of the regent of Asahan, North Sumatra, before 1900. van Eerde 1921:261. Courtesy Elsevier Press, Amsterdam.

early goldsmithing tradition (Leigh 1989:95). In the seventeenth century, the craftsmen of Sultan Iskander Muda were already famed for their production of gold jewelry and dagger hilts. Many of the finest Aceh artworks were consigned by the royal court and worn in annual processions that impressed foreign observers as well as court chroniclers with their opulence and grandeur (Reid 1988: 175–77). Even today the Acehnese value gold as ornamentation in both textiles and jewelry above all other types of ornamentation displayed in rituals (Leigh 1989:96). Symbolizing queens on their wedding day (Fig. X.10), brides, for example, are covered in gold supplementary weft cloths (*songket*), other precious textiles, and gold jewelry. The *simplaih* (Fig. X.6) is a crossbelt worn over the shoulders, with the ends hanging down both in the front and back. This *simplaih meuëh* is made of star-shaped pendants of red-stained gold adorned with cloisonné and semiprecious stone centers (van Brakel et al. 1987:274). Like crescent moons, stars are part of an artistic vocabulary derived from Muslim cultures from the Middle East.

By the sixteenth century, numerous Sumatran port cities besides Aceh, which controlled trade at the mouths of rivers serving as channels for the transport of goods to and from the interior, developed into small-scale Malay sultanates. Among these was Asahan, located east of the Batak region on the coast of North Sumatra. Reid writes, "The 'Malay' dynasties of East Sumatra were in fact molded from varied ethnic origins, with Batak, Minangkabau, Acehnese, and Indian elements predominating over the strictly Malay blood of Melaka and Johor" (Reid 1979:2). The ability of the Sumatran coastal courts to mediate with peoples of diverse ethnic groups for their mutual economic gain was the source of their political success. The rulers and vassals of the courts were therefore people whose livelihood and social status depended upon their access to sea trade and the ships that carried their trade goods.

Like other courts of both mainland and island Southeast Asia (Reid 1989: 175–80), Asahan engaged in yearly boat processions and ceremonies that proclaimed the power and divinity of the ruler. Although these boat ceremonies are still performed in many Muslim regions, their antecedents are Hindu and Buddhist. They were traditionally carried out (and are still today carried out in Thailand) at the October full moon, in association with Buddhist festivals. A stunning and elaborate royal barge procession was mounted in Bangkok in October 1957, for example, to celebrate the 2,500th birthday of the Buddha (Rongphim Krom Uthokkasat 1957). In the Buddhist Javanese kingdom of Majapahit, large ships came to be associated with the power and divine favor of the ruler (Jessup 1990:65). After the Islamization of coastal Sumatra and Borneo, ceremonial ships known as *perahu lancang kuning*, or yellow boats, continued to be displayed at yearly post-harvest ceremonies. Often, smaller ship models were used to present food offerings to the deities during these annual rituals. This ship model (Fig. X.11), probably commissioned for the Bataviaasch Genootschap Museum (now the Museum Nasional Indonesia, Jakarta), represented the ceremonial war ship owned by the ruling family of Asahan (Fig. X.14). The ship has a dragon figurehead (see also Figs. X.22, X.23) and the royal insignia of Asahan are depicted on the posts and masts.

The Minangkabau people of West Sumatra have followed Islam since the sixteenth century while also maintaining a traditional matrilineal social system. Important property such as houses, rice fields, lineage titles of honor, and familial affiliation pass according to female bloodlines, even though most formal political power is wielded by men, traditionally said to be the mother's brother at the household level and male lineage leaders at the community level (Abdullah 1966).

Foreign traders were attracted to the Minangkabau region because of its gold-producing areas in the central highlands. Hamka mentions a Chinese report stating that Arab traders were residing in western Sumatra as early as 674 A.D. (Hamka 1982:4). More reliable reports indicate that south Indian traders were established on the main trade route out of the central highlands by

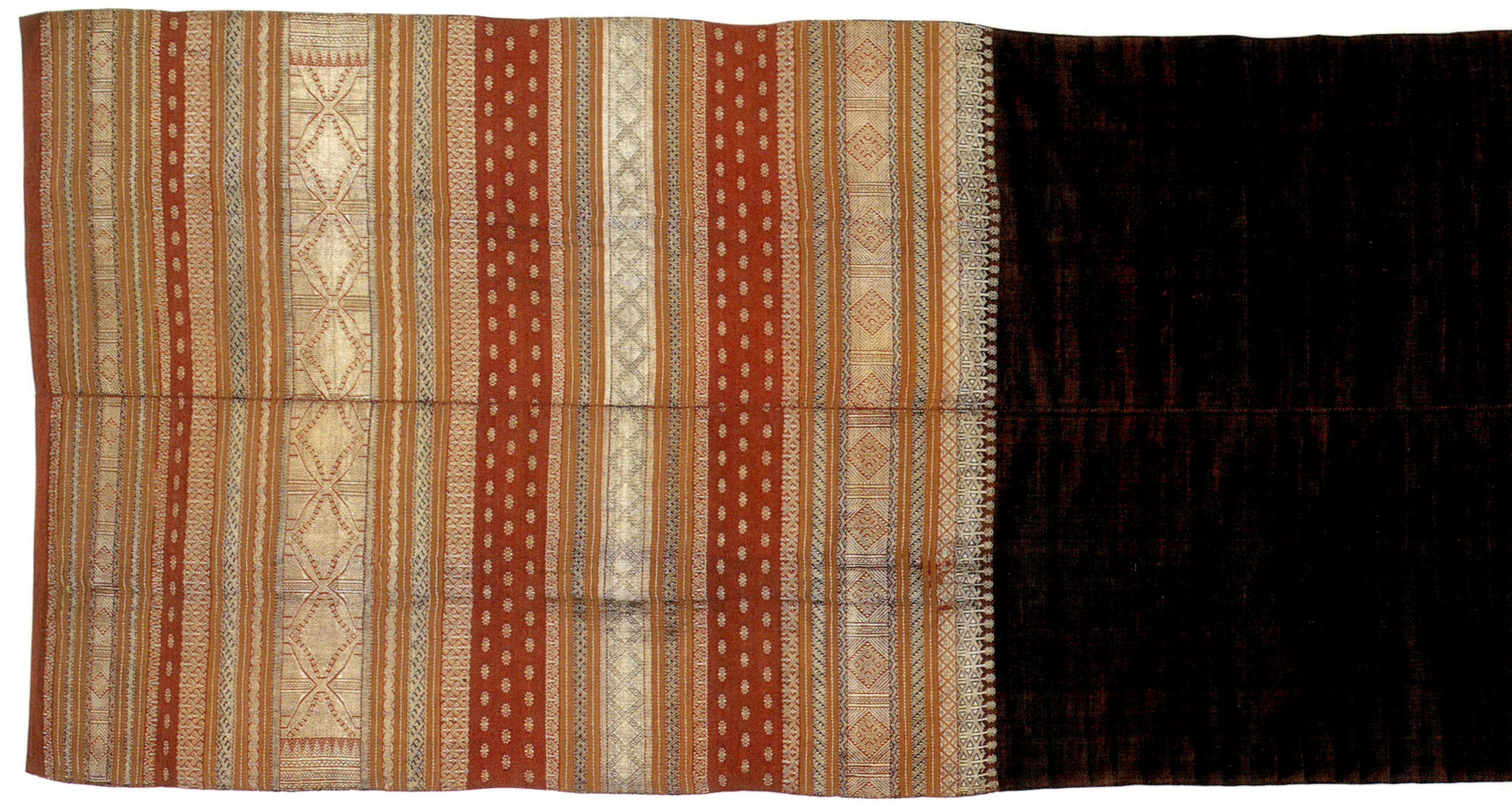

Fig.X.15 WOMAN'S CEREMONIAL HEADCLOTH, *TENGKULUAK*
Minangkabau, Padang Magek village,
West Sumatra
Silk, cotton, and gold yarns, 282 x 71.2
Collection of John and Anne Summerfield

Fig. X.16 A Minangkabau woman wears a *tengkuluak* headcloth representing buffalo horns, Batusangkar village, West Sumatra, 1987. Lucy A. Whalley

Fig. X.17 A traditional Minangkabau meeting house (*balai desa*) shows carving patterns similar to those in textiles designs, West Sumatra, 1970. Hijko Laeyendecker

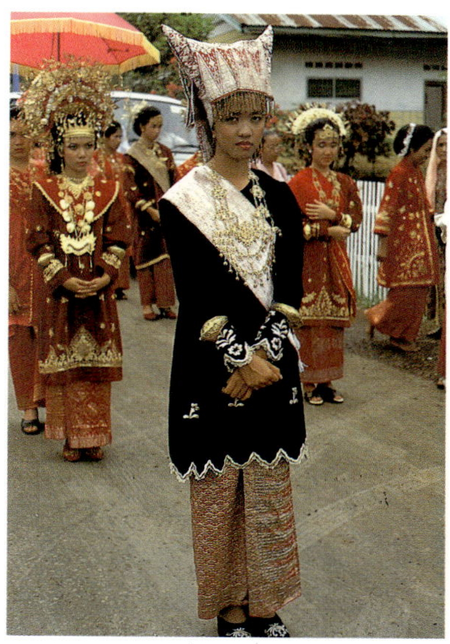

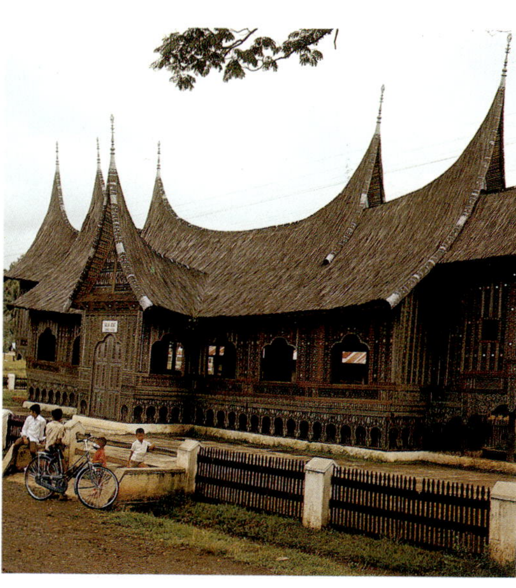

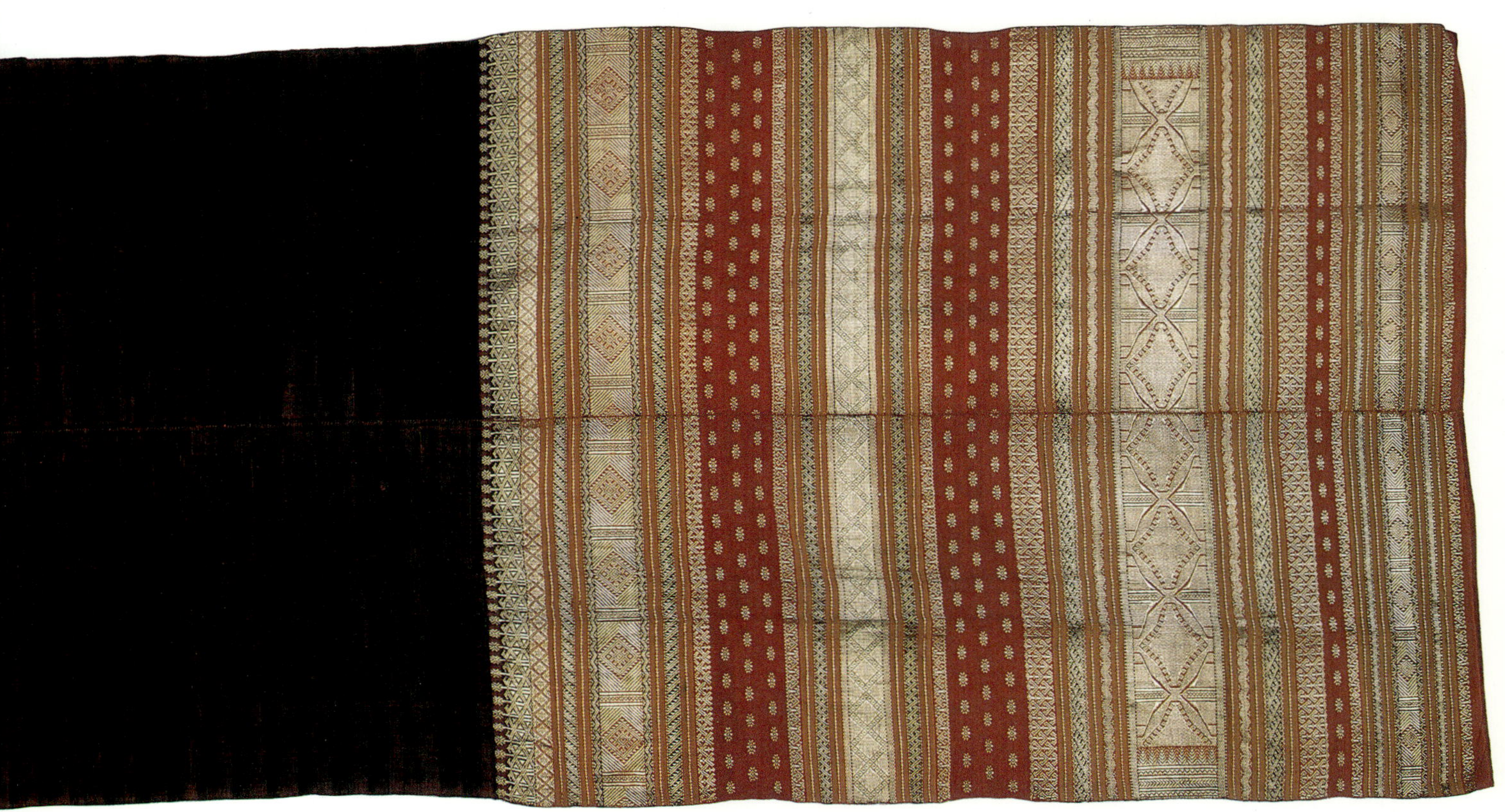

the twelfth or thirteenth centuries (Dobbin 1985). These Indians were increasingly attracted to the west coast of Sumatra once the mercantile kingdom of Srivijaya began to decline. Under the influence of Indian entrepreneurs, a local system of rajas was developed to control the movement of gold.

In 1347, a Sumatra-born aristocrat named Adityawarman raised at the Majapahit court established an independent Buddhist kingdom in the center of the gold-producing area. He reigned until 1375. Leading Minangkabau merchants on the coast acted as brokers between the foreign merchants and the upland suppliers. These middlemen were affiliated with Islam by the mid-sixteenth century, when Aceh was seeking to control the area and monopolize the Sumatran gold trade (Dobbin 1985:64). By the late sixteenth century, the Minangkabau people had developed a Muslim court center, and their leader emulated the courtly styles of the Malay kingdom of Melaka. By the time the gold mines were exhausted in the late eighteenth century, black pepper had become another prized trade commodity sought by both Acehnese and Dutch merchants.

Representatives from these various foreign court traditions introduced a Malay-influenced artistic style, as is shown by the intricate floral designs on the ceremonial dagger sheath (Fig. X.12). By the 1830s, certain villages near Bukittinggi were renowned for their gold and silver smiths who created filigree work in the form of flowers and foliage (Dobbin 1985:29–30). These smiths often migrated to the Sumatran coasts to work on gold ore that was gathered there for export. Goldsmithing was a small-scale, individualistic occupation. The artisan worked the entire piece from the ore, sold it himself, and even made his own iron tools. Often advances were required from patrons before commissioned pieces were completed. The original owner of a fine dagger such as the one in Fig. X.12 would probably have been a local raja or wealthy clan leader. Such items of regalia were usually thought to be invested with supernatural power, and the artisan would respect this power through proper rituals.

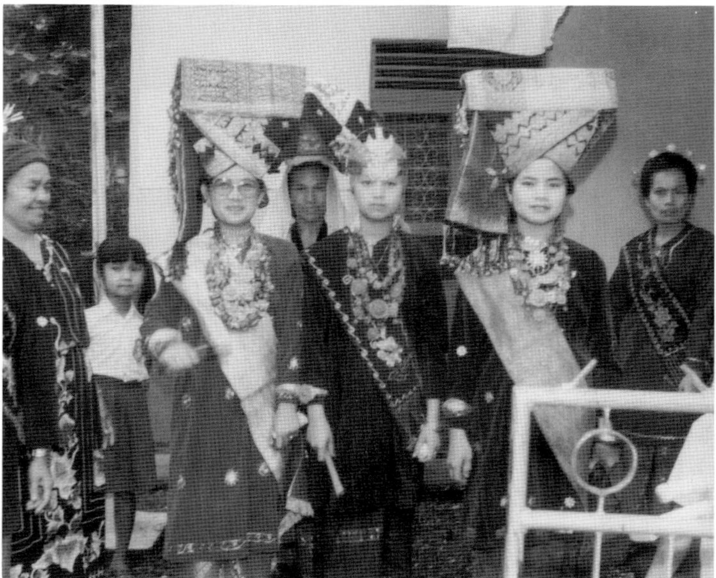

Fig.X.18 Minangkabau women wear headcloths as part of their ceremonial dress, Tanjung Sungayang, near Batusangkar village, West Sumatra. A. Sutan Madjo Indo

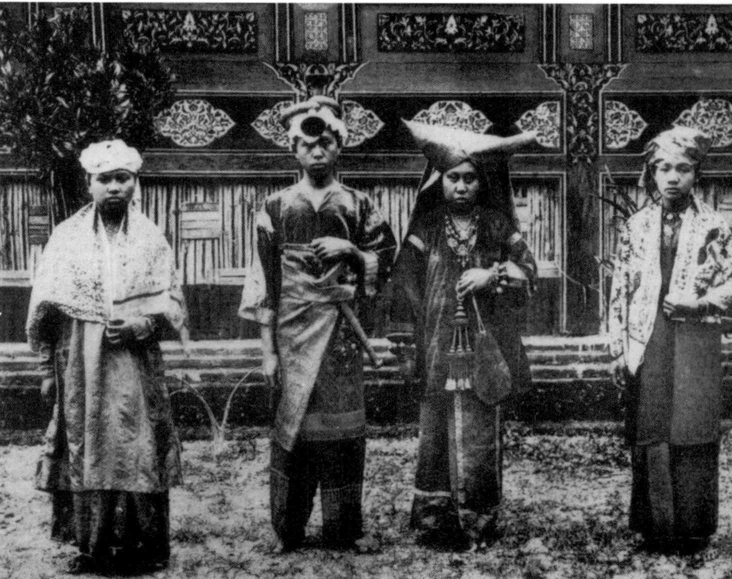

Fig. X.19 Minangkabau bride and groom in front of a traditional house with intricately carved boards, West Sumatra, early 1900s. Courtesy Koninklijke Nederlandse Toeristenbond ANWB, The Hague.

The Minangkabau kingdom declined by the early nineteenth century because its gold mines were exhausted and Muslim reformers forced the raja to flee. Valuables, however, remained in the hands of clan leaders who allowed them to be worn by relatives as sacred items of Minagkabau ceremonial dress (Fig. X.20). The silver-and-bone hilt represents a man in Minangkabau formal attire with a characteristic headdress. To produce the veined pattern (called *pamor*) on the blade, the artisan treated the nickel forged with iron with arsenic and lemon juice.

Textiles woven in the Minangkabau region of western Sumatra make sumptuous use of gold- and silver-wrapped threads patterned with supplementary weft. Such weaving materials were introduced by Arab and Indian merchants, who increasingly entered into the area in the fifteenth century after the fall of the Melaka kingdom. Very fine gold or silver wires were meticulously wrapped around silk or other natural fibers to create flexible gold threads that were inlaid over other warp threads to produce a luxurious pattern.

The headcloth (Fig. X.15) is an indispensable element of a Minangkabau woman's traditional dress at formal occasions when she represents her lineage. The cloth is folded to create a variety of forms: pointed, double-horned, or rectangular (Figs. X.16, X.18, X.19) according to regional traditions. The Minangkabau people commonly say that such a headcloth represents the weight of responsibility upon a woman who runs the family household (Kartiwa 1980:64). The motifs in the gold-patterned bands refer to proper behavior and ceremonial observance of a good Minangkabau community member (Sanday and Kartiwa 1984), as well as ceremonial foods and animals that embody such virtues as diligence or obedience (personal communication, Summerfield 1989). For example, the chain of diamonds seen in several bands is called *saik galamai*, a diamond-shaped cake that must be served at a ritual meal. The convex diamonds within rounded forms are called *kipang*, a ceremonial cake made with

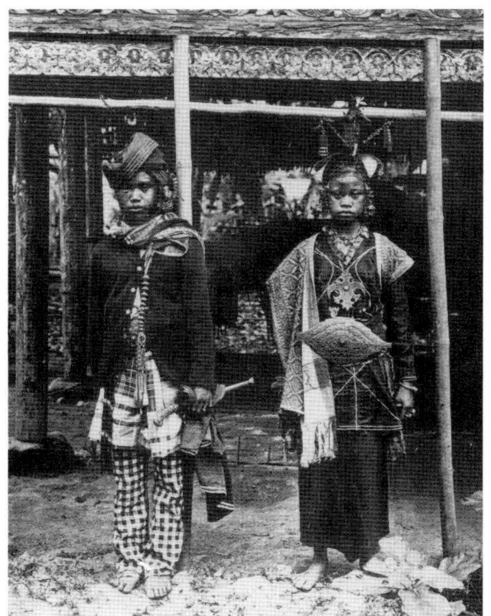

Fig. X.20 Minangkabau bride and groom with dagger in hand, West Sumatra, before 1910. Maass 1910

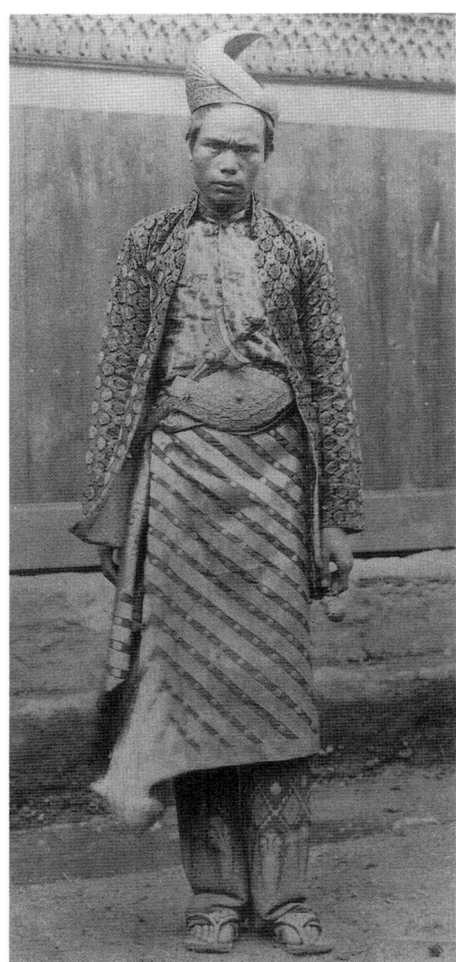

Fig.X.21 A Minangkabau bridegroom wears the traditional attire of a highland village, West Sumatra. Courtesy Rijksmuseum voor Volkenkunde, Leiden.

peanuts. Other motifs in the headcloth include *uleh*, caterpillars who after working hard in their youth turn into beautiful butterflies, and *itiek pulang petang*, ducks who always cooperate and return home in a straight line following their leader. Similar didactic motifs are carved by the Minangkabau on their traditional pointed-roof houses (Figs. X.17, X.19). Traditionally, the wealthier and the higher the status of the owner, the greater the number of designs carved on the outside panels.

Borneo

Archaeological evidence indicates that merchants from other parts of Asia were trading on the coasts of Borneo by the eleventh century A.D., if not before (Chin 1988:59). Exotic forest resources such as rhinoceros horn, hornbill ivory, swallows' nests, camphor, beeswax, and dammar resin were sought by the elites of China, India, and the Middle East. In exchange for these raw materials used for medicines, adornment, and delicacies, Borneo traders obtained ceramics, beads, bronzeware, and possibly luxury textiles. The finest of these imported objects, called *pesaka* ("heirloom"), were kept by the coastal courts. Other imports were traded to compensate the inland groups who collected the forest products and to tie them to the courts as regular trading partners and vassals.

The history of Borneo courts begins long before the establishment of the modern political borders that now divide the island into three different nations: Indonesia (Kalimantan), Malaysia (Sabah and Sarawak), and Brunei. Brunei, the major landfall between China and the spice islands, was the largest of the Borneo coastal courts, which also included the ports of Kutai, Banjarmasin, Pontianak, and Sambas—all located today in Indonesia. Like the coastal Sumatran courts described above, Brunei became a Hindu-Buddhist kingdom subsequent to contact with Indian and Chinese traders and religious teachers. A chronicle from the Borneo court of Kutai tells that the maharaja sultan was first consecrated as a cosmic ruler by a king of the Javanese empire of Majapahit (Hooykaas 1957). According to Brown, "many features of state ritual, custom, and mythology linked the ruler to an ultimate Hindu-Buddhist source of fertility: Indra, the god of the sky and the thunderbolt" (1988:47). Brunei myths relate how Brunei's coastal founders impregnated local women to produce prosperous coastal-interior unions. Given the concern of outer-island tribal societies with increasing their fertility and the widespread custom of creating political alliances through marital contracts, these stories are undoubtedly based on facts of political history.

Borneo's courts, like most early Southeast Asian states, were kingdoms defined by royal political centers, not by fixed geographical boundaries. Trading success alone perpetuated these alliances and prevented interior groups from uniting themselves under regional chiefs, because they looked to Malay court officials as political arbitrators.

By 1521, when Ferdinand Magellan's ships landed there, Brunei was a powerful Islamic sultanate controlling trade as far north as Manila and through much of northern and western Borneo (Brown 1988:46). Brunei and the other coastal courts such as Kutai and Banjarmasin maintained their central power by controlling trade flowing out of Borneo's numerous river mouths. Marine fleets were used both to defend the access points to interior resources and to convey these products to foreign trading partners. Sultans were known for their splendid royal ships, distinctively ornamented with dragon-headed prow ornaments, a symbol of supernatural and royal power throughout Southeast Asia and China (see Jessup 1990:61–69). Carved and painted prow ornaments (Figs. X.22, X.23) were made for royal boats owned by the rulers of Banjarmasin. Stylistically these boldly ornate carvings illustrate the influence of Chinese, Malay, and Javanese aesthetics in outer-island court artworks. Both dragons wear jewelled headdresses that are similar to those that bedeck many Javanese *wayang* puppets, and the headdress in Fig. X.23 is particularly complex, with a mythical *garuda* on the back side.

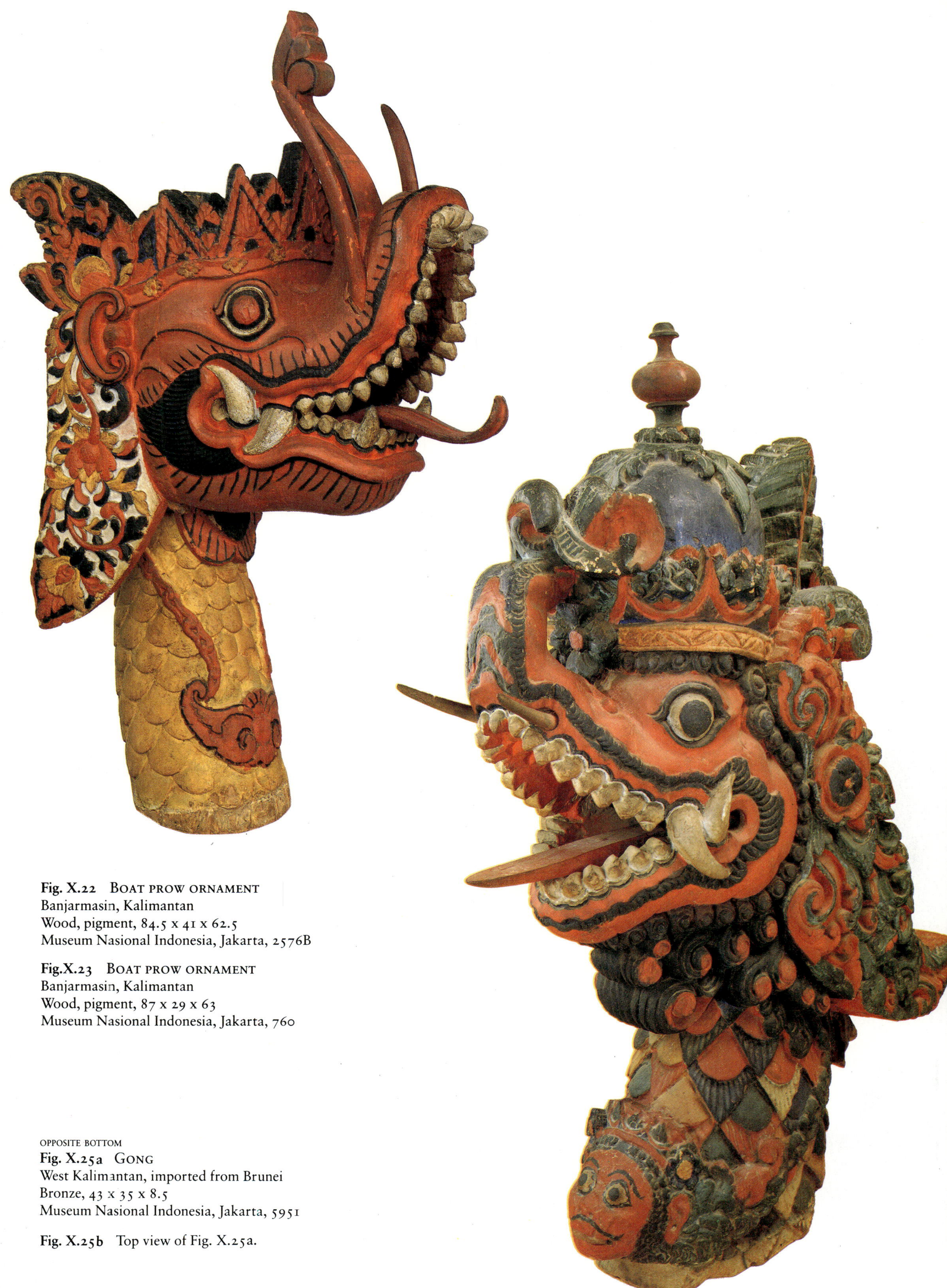

Fig. X.22 Boat prow ornament
Banjarmasin, Kalimantan
Wood, pigment, 84.5 x 41 x 62.5
Museum Nasional Indonesia, Jakarta, 2576B

Fig.X.23 Boat prow ornament
Banjarmasin, Kalimantan
Wood, pigment, 87 x 29 x 63
Museum Nasional Indonesia, Jakarta, 760

OPPOSITE BOTTOM
Fig. X.25a Gong
West Kalimantan, imported from Brunei
Bronze, 43 x 35 x 8.5
Museum Nasional Indonesia, Jakarta, 5951

Fig. X.25b Top view of Fig. X.25a.

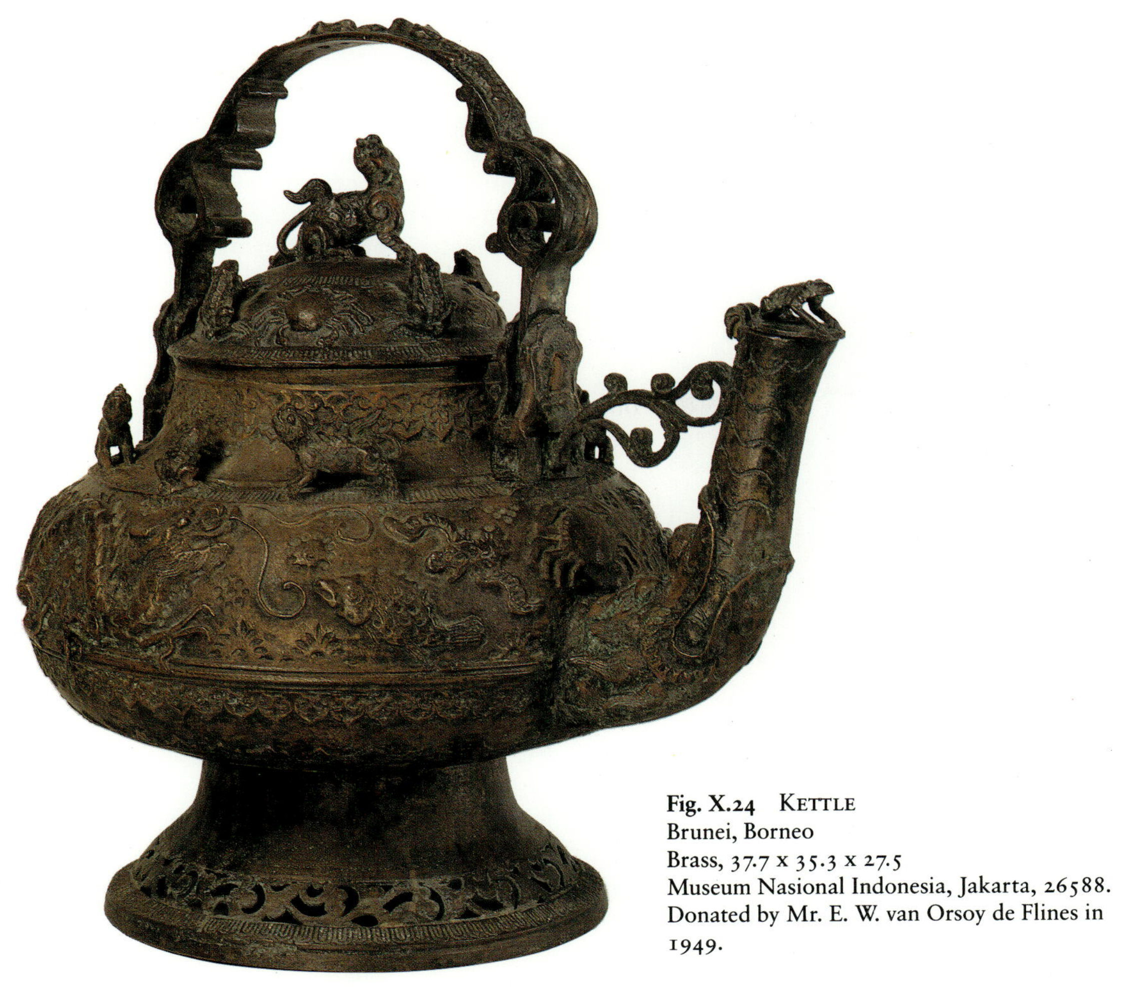

Fig. X.24 KETTLE
Brunei, Borneo
Brass, 37.7 x 35.3 x 27.5
Museum Nasional Indonesia, Jakarta, 26588.
Donated by Mr. E. W. van Orsoy de Flines in 1949.

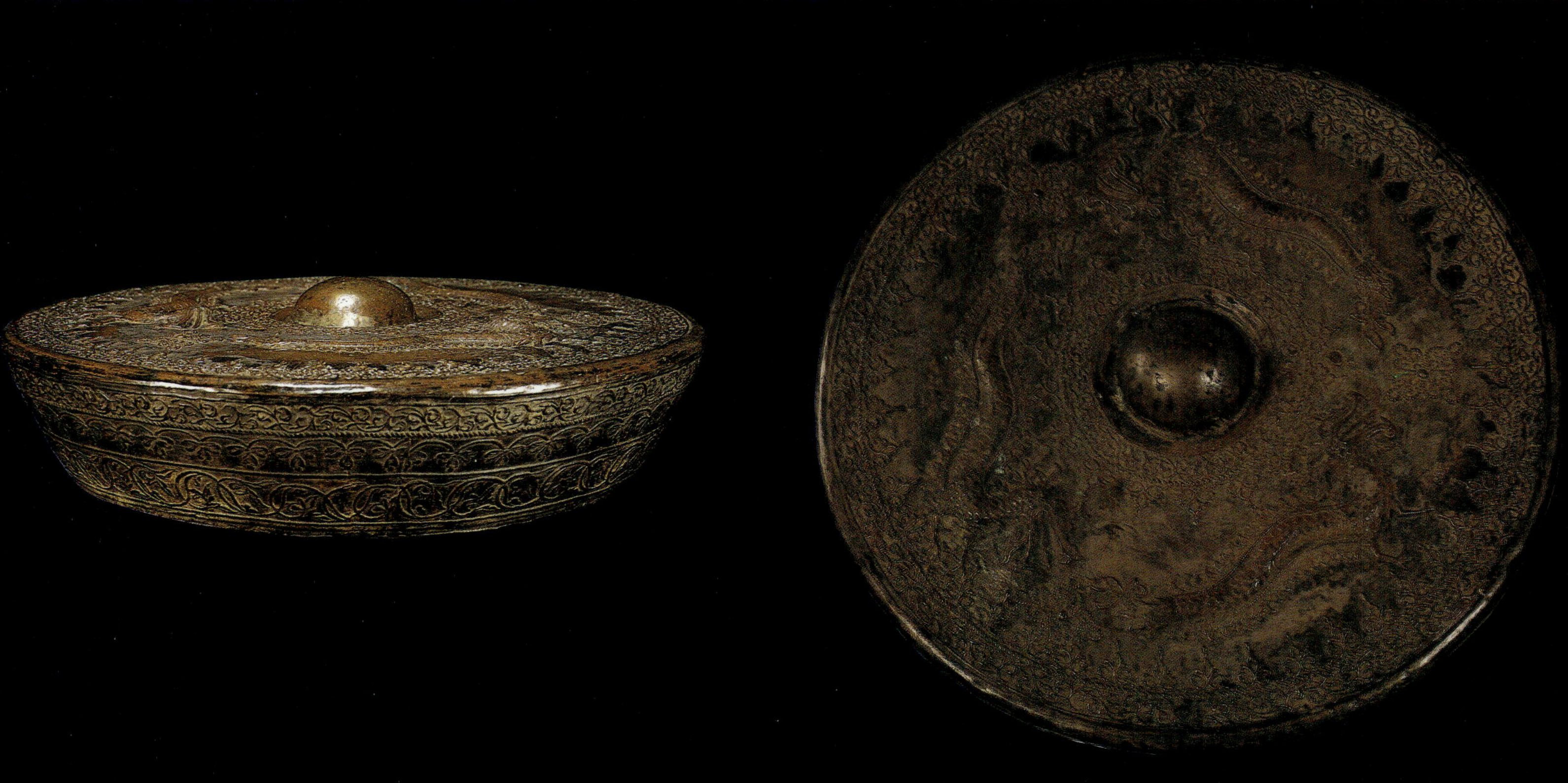

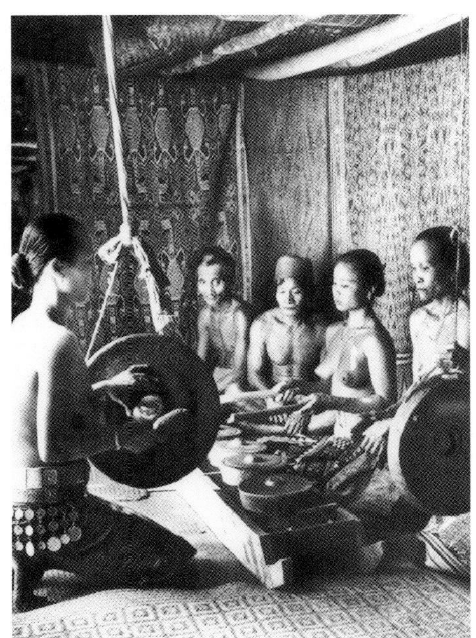

Fig. X.26 Iban Dayak woman plays brass gong, northern Borneo, before 1971. Hedda Morrison

The Chinese and other foreign techniques and motifs used in objects produced in or acquired by the coastal courts differentiated the artwork of the courts for the inland tribal groups, who saw these objects as exotic or even supernaturally empowered. For example, the kettle (Fig. X.24) is ornamented with *naga* dragons, emblems of supernatural power, and other Chinese-style animal figures. Such ceremonial vessels were used in Borneo courts to contain water or herbal tonics for members of the royal family.

The ritual dances and music of the Borneo courts, closely related to those of Javanese courts, impressed the inland peoples who traveled to the coast. Cast-bronze gongs (Fig. X.25) are a Chinese-influenced ceremonial item that spread far beyond the boundaries of the coastal courts to become valued heirlooms for the inland Dayak tribes. The use of these items by the Dayak for ritual purposes (Fig. X.26) led to increased demand and subsequent production of these objects—which further increased the coastal-inland trade. Between 1450 and 1680, gongs produced in China and Java were widely traded in Eastern Indonesia, Borneo, and the Philippines (Reid 1988:210). The extensive floral ornamentation on the sides and top of this gong (Fig. X.25) is characteristic of Indonesian rather than Chinese-produced gongs of this shape. Chinese gongs of this particular form were invariably plain (personal communication, F.K. Lehman 1990). The elaborate adornment on this Javanese gong includes Chinese-style encircling dragons motif, also seen on Chinese ceramics (Fig. 8), and often copied onto artworks of the outer islands.

Sulawesi and the Lesser Sundas

By the seventeenth century, three maritime kingdoms of southern Sulawesi—the Makassar kingdom of Gowa, and the Bugis kingdoms of Luwu and Bone—came to dominate eastern Indonesia. By the eighteenth century, the Bugis held power in Malay sultanates farther west such as Johor as well (Reid 1979:2). The Bugis and Makassar people were known throughout the archipelago as intrepid and professional warriors. There were even Bugis- and Makassar-written translations of Spanish and Portuguese manuscripts on gun manufacture (Ricklefs 1981: 45). Gowa, located near the present city of Ujung Pandang, was converted to Islam by its Makassar rulers in the early 1600s and proceeded to conquer and convert surrounding peoples. The court chroniclers listed only the great kingdoms of Aceh in northern Sumatra and Mataram in Java as friends or allies; all other neighboring regions were considered vassals. Sultan Hasanuddin of Gowa, for example, readily agreed to a request to send young women from his royal house to become wives of the Sultan of Mataram in Java (Andaya 1981:48).

Gowa's powerful trade relations with Java and European nations were reflected in Gowa's refined and opulent court tradition. The gold ornament (Fig. X.30), collected in South Sulawesi, closely resembles a type of earring (de Moor and Kal 1983:18) produced in the Majapahit Empire of central Java, which flourished between 1350 and 1500. It may have been imported from Java or produced by a local Sulawesi artisan knowledgeable in ancient court traditions and the technique of lost-wax casting. Details were added to the basic cast-gold shape of such ornaments through the techniques of engraving, cutting into the metal with a stylus, or chasing, stamping in a pattern with small chisels (van Brakel et al. 1987:251). A few such ornaments are now kept as sacred heirloom treasures by aristocratic families of coastal Sulawesi groups (Fig. X.36).

While seventeenth-century Gowa troops successfully conquered coastal regions in Sulawesi, eastern Borneo, Lombok, and the southern Moluccas, the Bugis kingdoms of southern Sulawesi retained their independence through a clever marriage and military alliance with Gowa and conversion to Islam (Noorduyn 1955:113; Andaya 1981:35–36). The Bugis of Luwu were great traders and seafarers of the archipelago (Fig. X.42), developing southern Sulawesi's earliest ties to faraway kingdoms in the Moluccas, Sumbawa, Java, and the Coromandel coast in India. Java, which produces no iron itself, was dependent on foreign metals for its sacred *kris*. Thus, it cultivated relations with the Bugis of Luwu in southern Sulawesi, which was an important resource area for iron

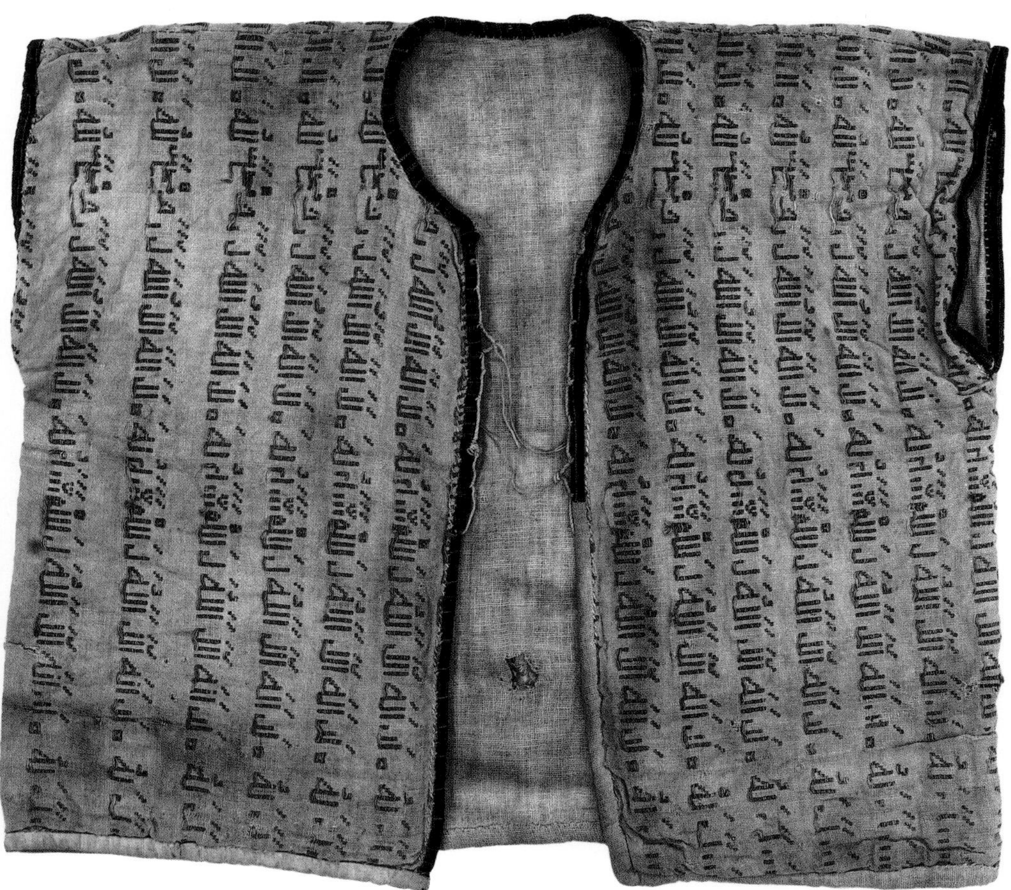

Fig. X.27 AMULET SHIRT
Lombok
Cotton, 45.5 x 51.3
Museum Negeri Nusa Tenggara Barat, Mataram, Lombok, 2351

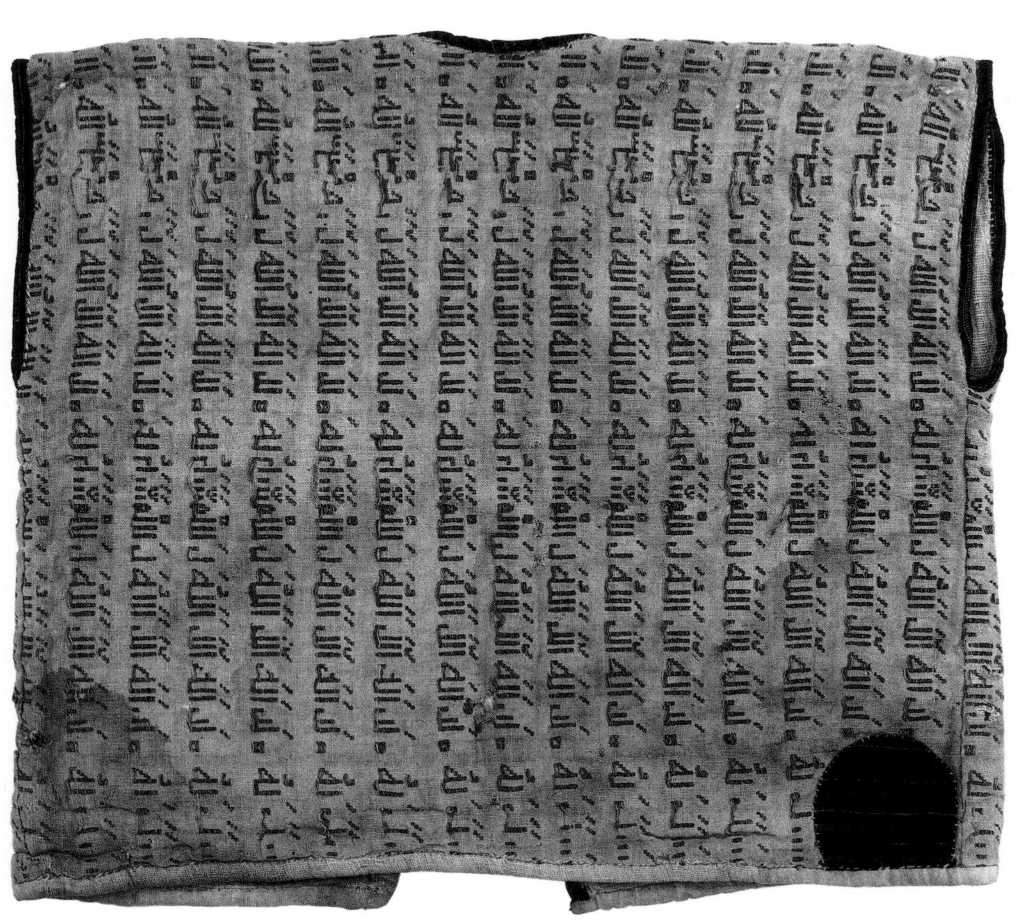

Fig. X.27a Back view of Fig. X.27.

Fig.X.28 SWORD, *KRIS*, AND SHEATH
Bugis, South Sulawesi
Wood, iron, gold, 48.2 x 14.5 x 7
Royal Tropical Institute, Tropenmuseum, The Netherlands, 1698-452. Accessioned in 1947

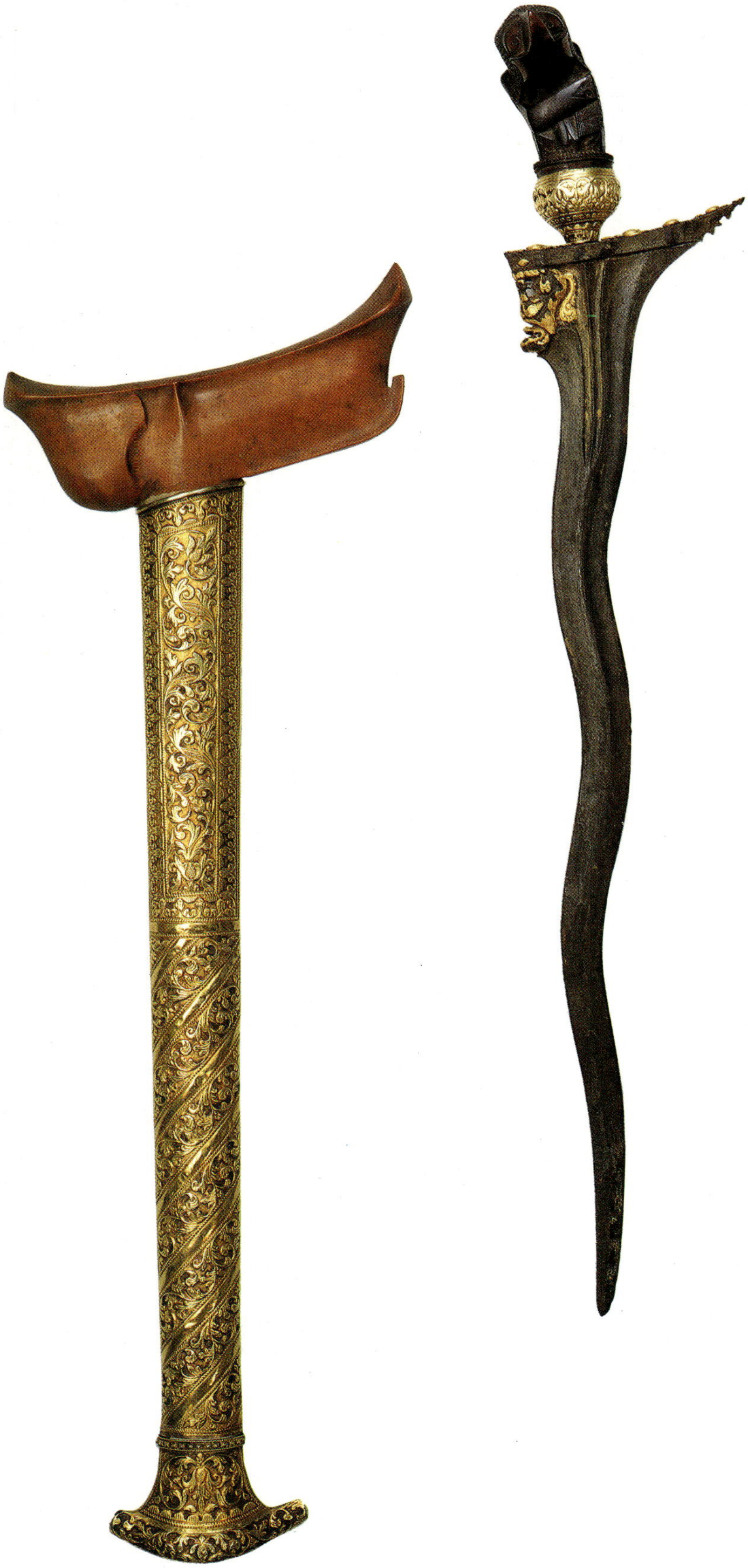

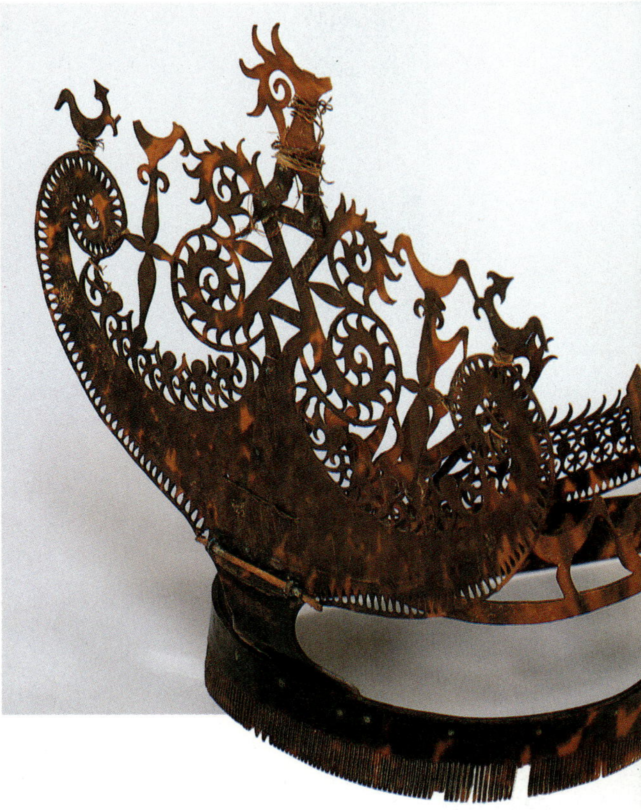

Fig. X.29 HEAD ORNAMENT
Gorontalo, North Sulawesi
Tortoise shell, 23 x 21 x 35.5
Museum Nasional Indonesia, Jakarta, 6497

OPPOSITE
Fig. X.30 EARRING
Makassar, collected in South Sulawesi
Gold, 3.6 x 2.8 x 2.5
Collection of Anita E. Spertus and Robert J. Holmgren, New York

Fig. X.31 BELT AND BUCKLE
Gorontalo, North Sulawesi
Copper alloy, cotton, bamboo, 31
Museum Nasional Indonesia, Jakarta, 6351

Fig. X.32 BELT BUCKLE
Lombok
Copper alloy, 15 x 6 x 4
Museum Negeri Nusa Tenggara Barat, Mataram, Lombok, 2527

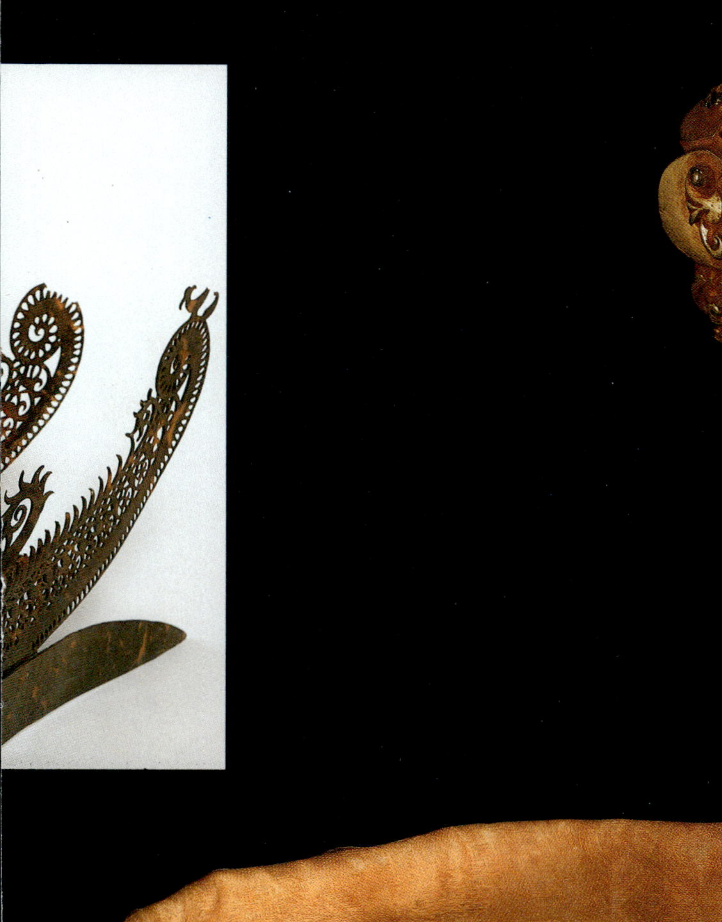

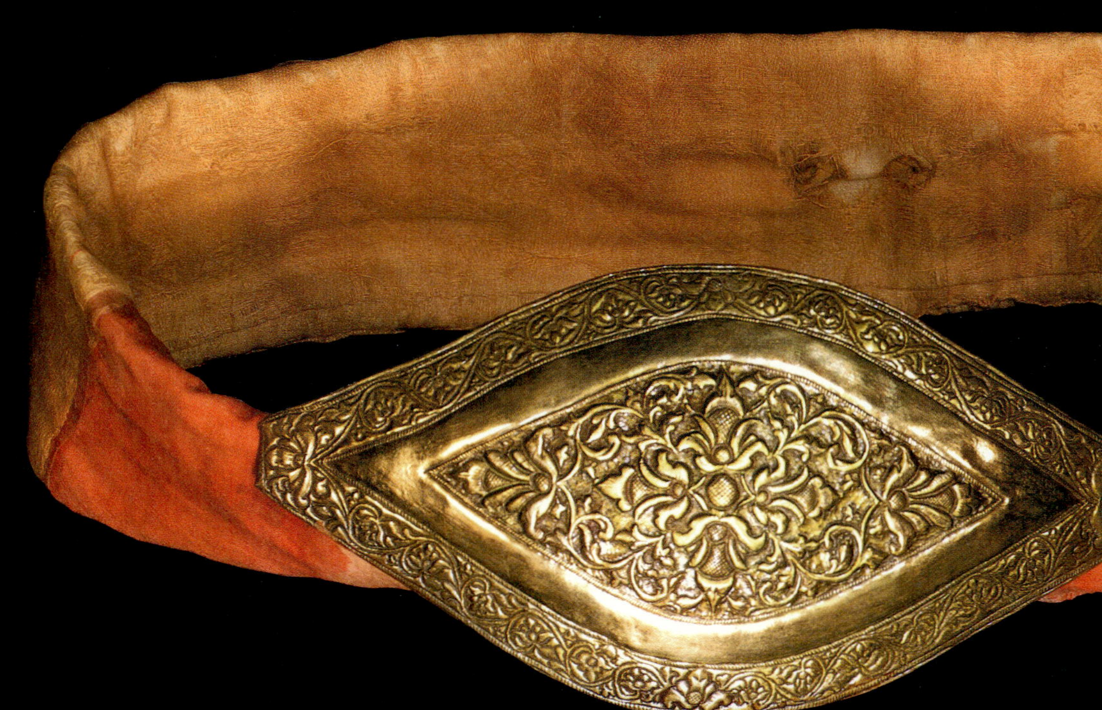

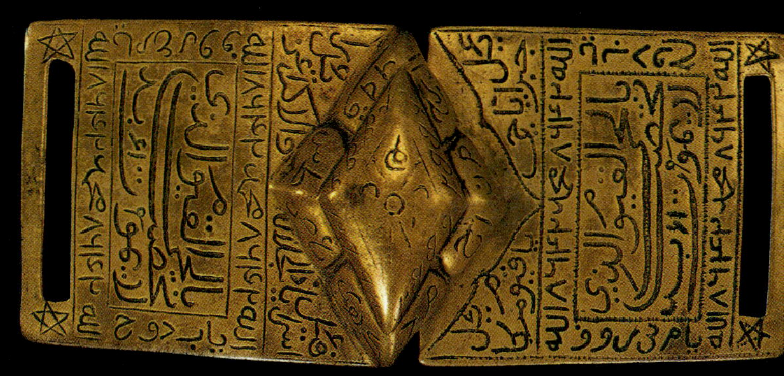

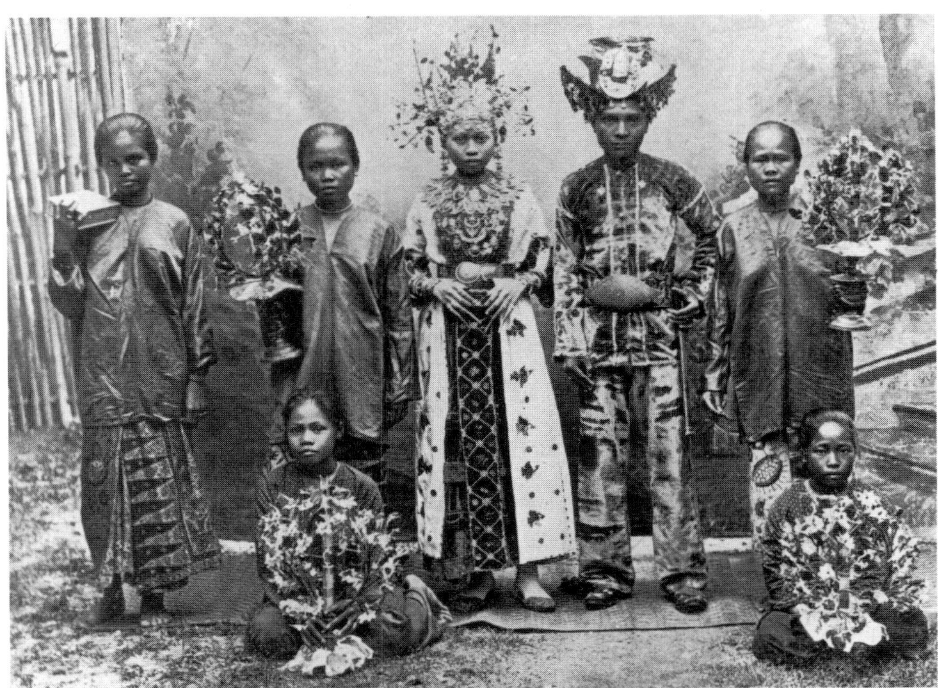

Fig. X.33 Gorontalo bridal pair, North Sulawesi, before 1921. van Eerde 1920:49. Courtesy Elsevier Press, Amsterdam.

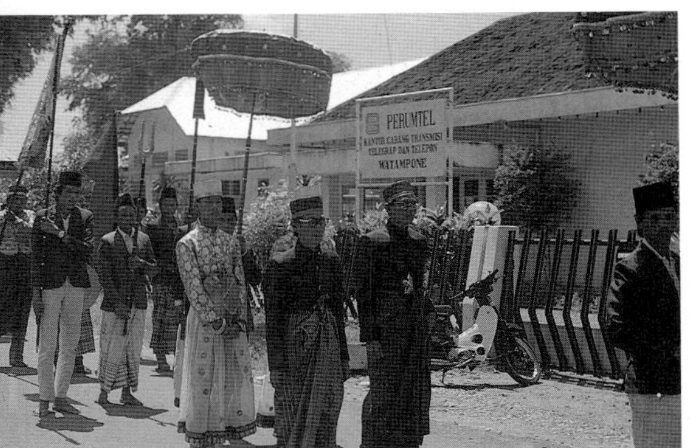

Fig. X.34 A Bugis ceremonial procession with men wearing *kris* and carrying umbrellas, Bone, South Sulawesi, 1988. David Brawn

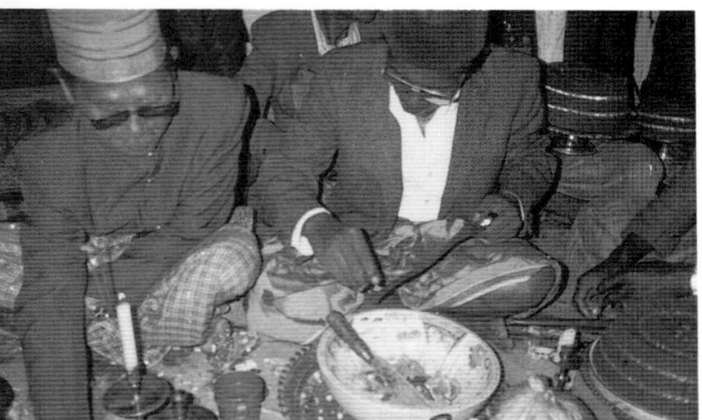

Fig. X.35 The blade of a sacred heirloom *kris* is ritually cleaned at a ceremony honoring a Bugis historical figure, Bone, South Sulawesi, 1988. David Brawn

mixed with nickel. Through centuries of contact, Bugis artisans emulated the refined sword-making techniques of the Javanese, who produced ritually empowered blades with the unusual nickel-iron construction recognized by the surface patterns called *pamor*.

For the Javanese, the *kris* is not only a weapon but also an object representing sacred and mystical concepts. The *kris* (Fig. X.28) was thought to be inhabited by a spirit suited to sword's owner, and the smith had to be able to control that supernatural power (Jessup 1990). The sheath is decorated with flowing floral patterns embossed in gold. The hilt is a stylized head of a sea bird, representing its owner's success at sea (Hamzuri 1984:38). The ridge at the base is typical of Sulawesi *kris*. Such sacred heirloom *kris* are now displayed to the public primarily at ceremonial occasions such as weddings and local processions celebrating historical traditions (Figs. X.34, X.35, X.37). On such occasions, *kris* and other heirloom objects signifying the power of aristocratic families are carried through the streets for display. The blades are sometimes ritually cleaned (Fig. X.35), and some heirlooms may be handled only by ritual specialists, such as the traditional male transvestite priests (*bissu*) of southern Sulawesi (Fig. X.37).

Some types of Indonesian court jewelry, displaying Malay or Chinese-Malay designs, were produced or worn in many different regions. The oversized, oval or eye-shaped silver belt buckle was one such type illustrating Malay-style floral motifs of Persian and Chinese influence (Fraser-Lu 1989). The belt buckle (Fig. X.31) was collected in the northern Sulawesi port of Gorontalo, which became a vassal port of the Bugis trading kingdom of southern Sulawesi. The buckle was worn for ceremonial attire at occasions such as weddings (Fig. X.33). Such buckles, however, were worn in many other outer-island court areas as well as part of the generalized Malay-style apparel (Fig. X.21).

Often court regalia of the outer islands imitated the form and designs of inner-island court jewelry (see Jessup 1990 for examples) but was manufactured of locally available materials. The outline of this unusual crown cut from a

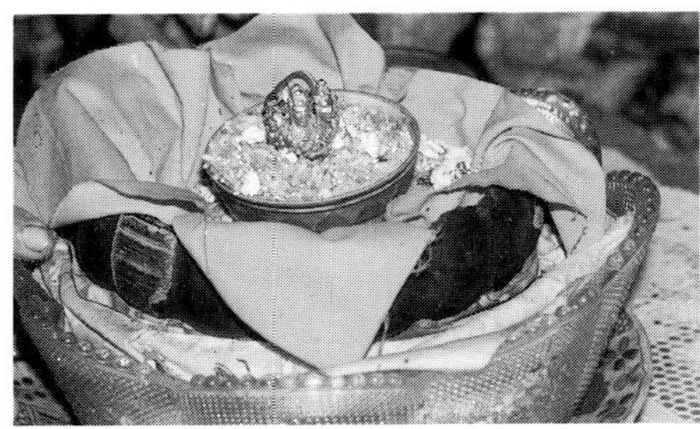

Fig.X.36 A gold ornament, similar to the one in Fig. X.30, is kept as sacred noble regalia by an aristocratic family in Sulawesi, 1986. Lorraine V. Aragon

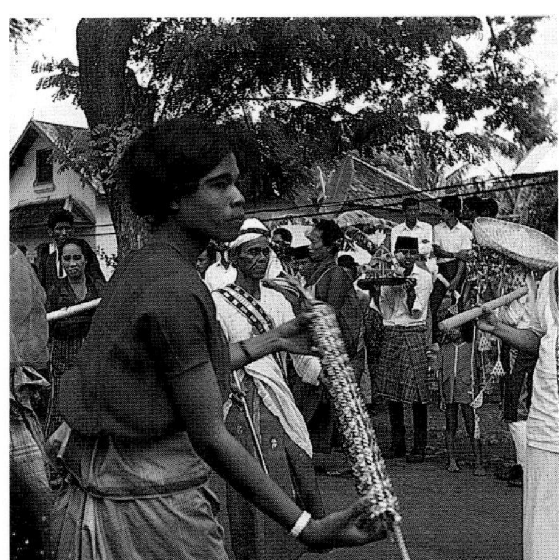

Fig. X.37 Transvestite priests (*bissu*) carry sacred Bugis regalia in ceremonial procession, South Sulawesi, 1963. Barbara Harvey

tortoise shell (Fig. X.29) may represent either a pair of animal horns or a ship, with small bird images floating across the top. The smaller spiral motifs resemble a cut nautilus shell, a sight familiar to these seafaring peoples.

As early as the sixteenth century, the eastern Indonesian islands of Lombok Sumba, Timor, and Sumbawa were exporting fragrant sandalwood to the thriving trade port of Melaka (Ricklefs 1981:19). By the seventeenth centuries, the influence of southern Sulawesi kingdoms was strongly felt in certain coastal regions of the Lesser Sunda Islands. Although the western half of the island of Lombok was populated by Balinese migrants in the seventeenth and eighteenth centuries (van der Kraan 1980) and certain artwork of Lombok was influenced by Hindu Balinese (Fig. VII.51), the eastern half of Lombok was converted to Islam after being missionized by religious teachers from eastern Java and politically dominated by the Makassar kingdom of Gowa. As a source of foreign spiritual power, the calligraphy and design motifs of these Muslim kingdoms were adopted by artisans and traders in the peripheral regions. This shirt (Fig. X.27), meant to protect the wearer from harm, is embroidered with a repeated Arabic phrase that is part of the Muslim creed (*shehadah*), which says, "there is no God but Allah, and Mohammed is his Messenger."

The belt buckle (Fig. X.32), inscribed with Arabic script, also served as an amulet for the Muslim owner. The four letters on the outside margin, BDWH, are frequently used on Muslim talismans because this "word" is considered lucky. Such "words" are formed according to mystical rules (Canaan 1937: 91–92); Allah is inscribed on all corners followed by "8642," which is "BDWH" in a reverse spelling of the Abjad code (personal communication, Raymond Hebert). As the reverse of a combination of letters representing the first sequence of even numbers (2, 4, 6, 8), this "word" is considered lucky (Canaan 1937: 91–92). The name "Mohammed" is written near the center of the buckle. Inside the rectangle, there is an invocation to "The God who is eternal." The words around the diamond center are requests to the archangels Israfil, Jibra'il, and Mika'il to protect the owner of the buckle from 'Izra'il or Satan.

In the seventeenth century, there was a confrontation between Hindu Balinese and Muslim Makassar forces in the islands of Lombok and Sumbawa in the Lesser Sundas. By 1660, the two kingdoms of Bima and Sumbawa, both located on the island of Sumbawa, had been converted to Islam and were sending troops to support Gowa's struggles against Dutch incursions in eastern Indonesia (Andaya 1981:60). These Lesser Sunda coastal kingdoms were closely allied with the Muslim trading network of the outer-island kingdoms led by Makassar, Ternate, and Tidore in the Moluccas, which was being increasingly threatened by the Dutch East India Trading Company. In 1669, the Makassar sultan was thoroughly defeated by Dutch forces who then began to implement Dutch sovereignty in eastern Indonesia (Ricklefs 1981:62–63).

The artworks of the small courts in the Lesser Sundas variously reflect elements from indigenous tradition, contact with the Hindu Balinese, and contact with Muslim peoples, such as those from Makassar. Worn by a noble Sumbawa bridegroom, the fan-shaped form of the head ornament (Fig. X.38) imitates the shape of a lontar palm (*Borassus* sp.) frond. The silver ornament that faces front, called *kemang setangi*, was reserved for the possessions of Sumbawa aristocrats (Departemen Pendidikan dan Kebudayaan 1981–2:465). The fine silver craftsmanship of the bangles suggest Balinese influence (personal communication, J. Fox 1990) or at least the introduction of technical skills from another larger court such as Makassar. The name given to this Sumbawa headdress, *kasigar*, is an old Malay term cognate with *sigar*, the unmarried Lampung women's headdress, and *siga*, the term for a man's barkcloth headscarf in central Sulawesi.

The Northern Moluccas

Within the northern Moluccas, trade and the formation of court sultanates was intimately related to the foremost trade goods of that region: spices. The clove

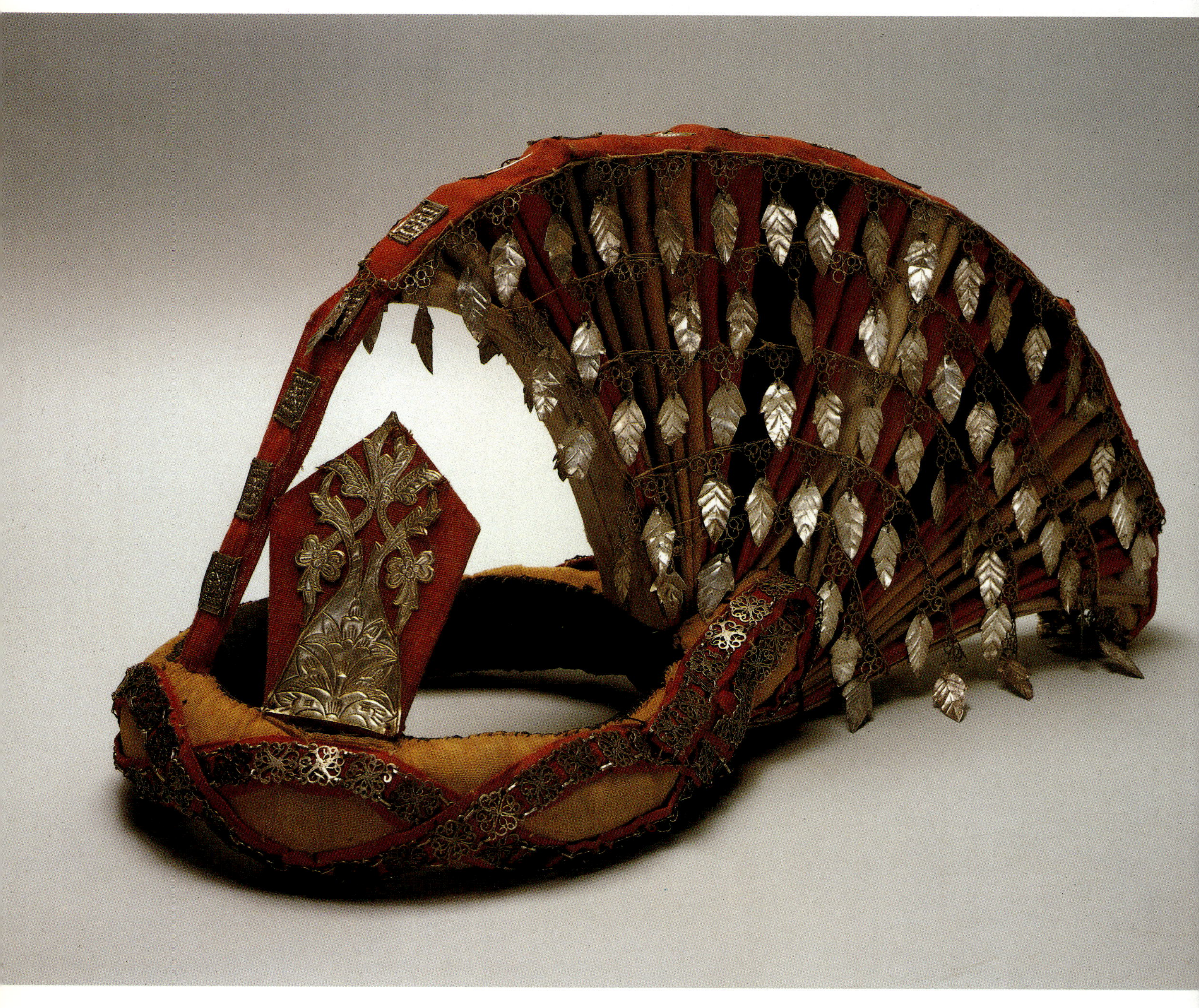

Fig. X.38 Head ornament, *kasigar*
Sumbawa
Cloth, silver, 40 x 22
Museum Negeri Nusa Tenggara Barat,
Mataram, Lombok, 1159

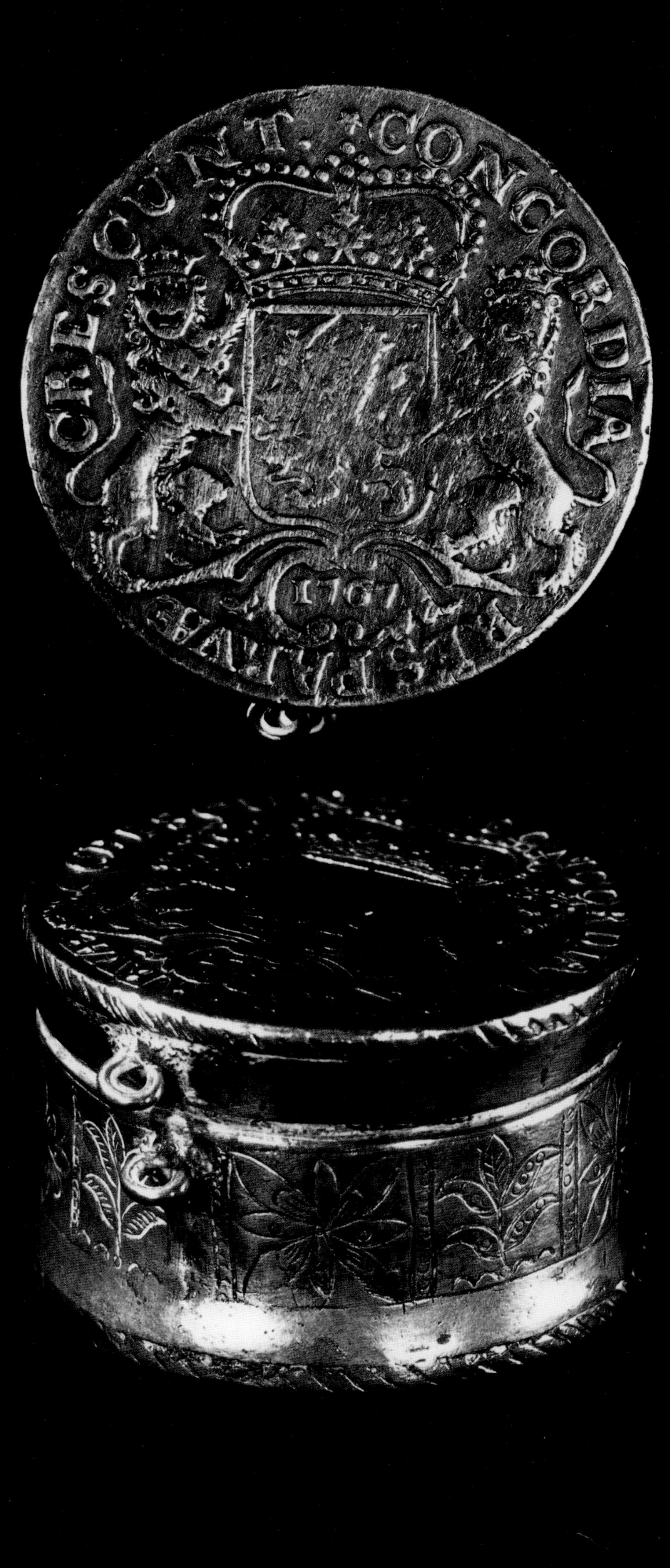

Fig. X.39 LIME CONTAINER, *O DOFAI MA NGI*
Halmahera, northern Moluccas
Silver, 2.2 x 4.5 x 4.2
Anonymous loan

Fig. X.39a Side view of Fig. X.39.

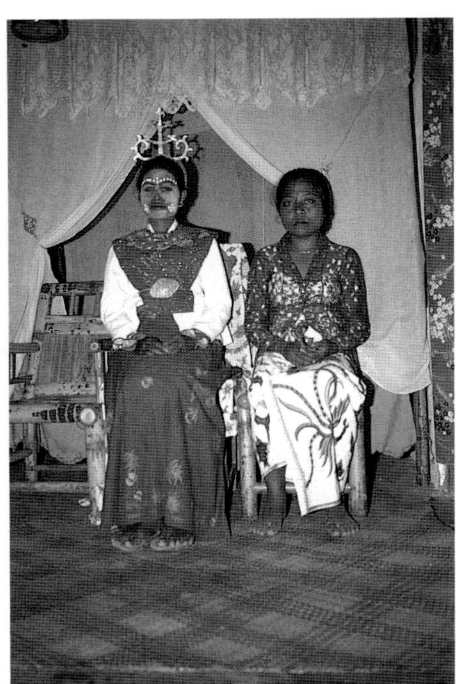

Fig. X.40 A Tobelo bride is being honored or "displayed" (*imiteru*) at her husband's family home on the evening of her wedding, Wasile village, Halmahera, northern Moluccas, 1978. Paul M. Taylor

(*Syzygium aromaticum* Kuntze) is indigenous only to this area, while nutmeg (*Myristica fragrans* Hout) has been exported from the northern Moluccas throughout recorded history. The clove tree and nutmeg tree evolved in this region, where local languages relate thêm to their wild antecedents (see, e.g., Taylor 1990:69–70). The antiquity of trade is better documented in this region than in any other area of Indonesia. Burkill (1966[1935]:1550) dates the introduction of nutmeg into Europe from the sixth century A.D. and also notes its apparent antiquity in southern Asia, where vocabularies throughout the region use the Sanskrit term for the spice. The antiquity of clove exportation from the northern Moluccas can clearly be traced to Roman times, for Pliny the Elder describes the clove in his writings of the first century A.D. (see Innes Miller 1969). The *Ramayana*, written about 200 B.C., also mentions cloves, and general references to unidentified spices occur in Egyptian, Chinese, Indian, and Mesopotamian sources. A recent archaeological find suggests that the clove trade to the West may in fact have begun much earlier, for a single clove has been found among charred plant remains on the floor of a burned pantry room at the Mesopotamian site of Terqa, in present-day Syria, dated to 1700 B.C. (Buccellati and Buccellati 1983).

Until the sixteenth century, clove production remained indigenous to the northern Moluccan region. As van Fraassen (1981) notes, "cloves existed for the outside world long before the Moluccas did," though foreign traders—indigenous ones for millennia, followed by other Asian traders, and then the Portuguese in 1512—followed the clove trail to its source in the northern Moluccas. Christopher Columbus, in fact, intended to reach the northern Moluccas by a roundabout route and found America by mistake.

The Portuguese built their first permanent Moluccan settlement on Ternate in 1522. From their base on Ternate they maintained their preeminence in the Moluccan spice trade throughout the sixteenth century. In general, periods of intense conflict with the Ternatese rulers and populace alternated with periods of peaceful cooperation, as Portuguese allied themselves with ambitious Ternatese individuals to extend their trade monopoly (van Fraassen 1981). When Tomé Pires visited Indonesia in the early 1500s, the Moluccan kings of Ternate, Tidore, and Bacan were already Muslim, a result of their long-distance spice trade to the west through the kingdom of Melaka (Ricklefs 1981:7). Some reports say that the Muslim religious leader (*wali*) Sunan Giri from the port of Gresik in eastern Java became the religious teacher of Zainal Abidin, the ruler of Ternate from 1486 to 1500.

In the early seventeenth century, Dutch traders competed heavily with the Muslim traders from western Indonesia. In 1605 the Netherlands succeeded in capturing the Portuguese forts on Ternate, in the northern Moluccas. By 1630 they had set up a rival port in Ambon, the central Moluccan town that was to become much later the capital of a united Moluccan province under the Dutch. In the seventeenth century, the Dutch allied themselves with the Ternatese in opposition to the Portuguese and Spanish—and also, from the Ternatese point of view, in opposition to the sultanate of Tidore (another small island sultanate to the south of Ternate). In effect, however, the ultimate goal of Dutch alliances was control of the spice trade, and this eventually brought them into conflicts with Moluccan rulers, including their former allies in Ternate. By the 1670s, the Dutch East India Company had made strategic alliances with the Bugis leader Arung Palakka leading to a Dutch conquest of the Makassar kingdom of Gowa as well as of both Muslim sultanates of Ternate and Tidore. During the seventeenth century, the Dutch were eventually able to expel all other European and Asian merchants from the Moluccan spice trade.

As part of the late seventeenth-century agreement between the defeated Ternatese sultan and the Dutch East India Company, no more cloves were grown in the northern Moluccas, and the clove trade was instead concentrated on islands around Ambon in the central Moluccas. In general, as van Fraassen writes (1981:11–12), the main goal of Dutch efforts throughout the eighteenth

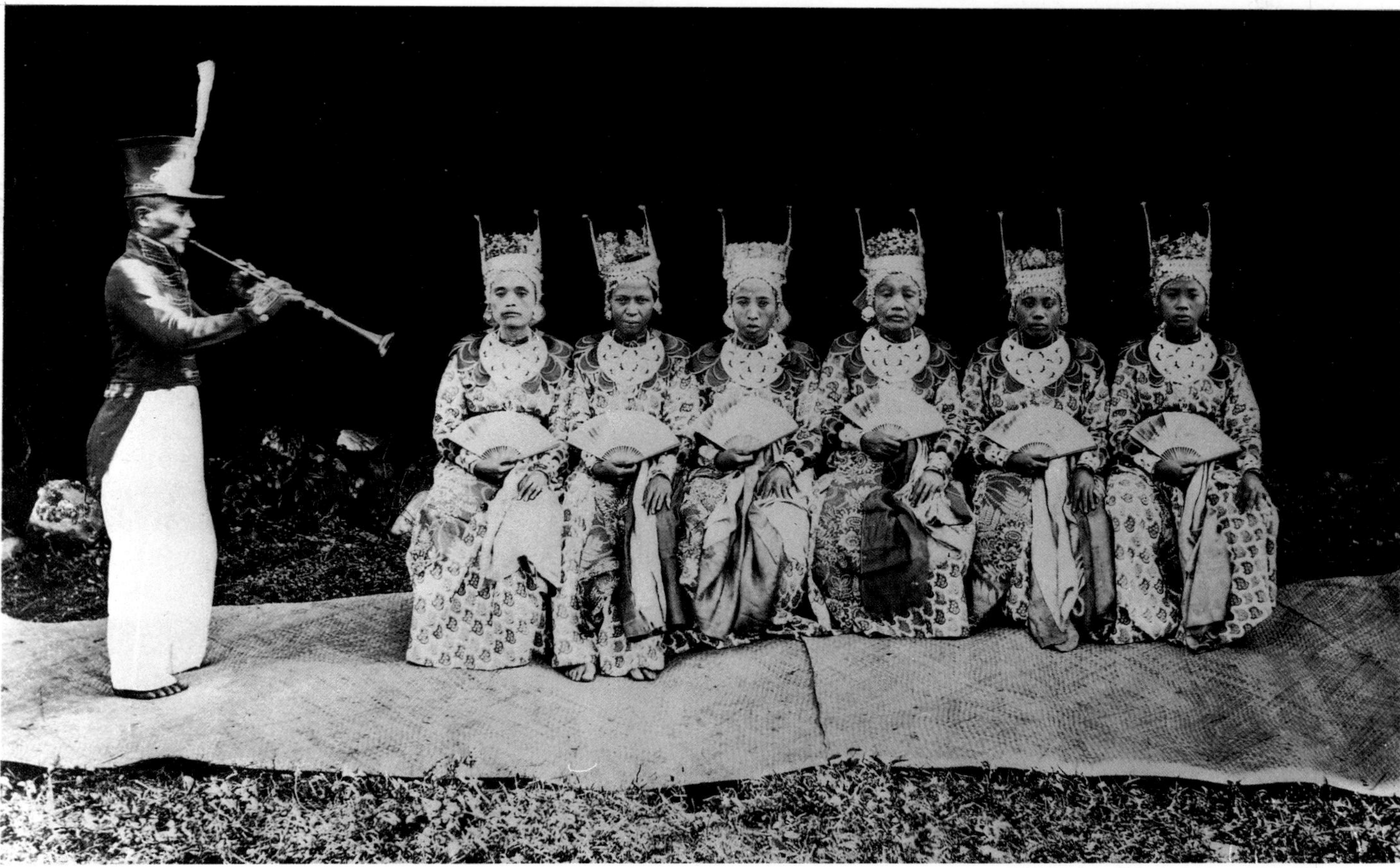

Fig. X.41 Dancers in formal court dress and a musician wearing apparel introduced during the Dutch colonial era, Ternate, northern Moluccas, early 1900s. Courtesy Royal Tropical Institute, Tropenmuseum, The Netherlands.

century was to isolate Ternate, Tidore, and other areas of the northern Moluccas from the outside world, and to destroy clove trees throughout the northern Moluccas in favor of the more easily policed regions of the central Moluccas, which the Dutch thoroughly controlled (see Hanna 1978 on the central Moluccan spice monopoly).

Unlike the courts considered previously, Ternate and the northern Moluccan courts had no hinterland on their own islands, since both Ternate and Tidore are tiny islands off the coast of Halmahera. Nevertheless, the valuable spice commodities they controlled gave them great importance to world trade and to European colonizers, and their navies assured tribute from the populations of much larger islands of the region. Ternate and Tidore divided sovereignty over Halmahera, while Ternate at times received tribute from the Sula Mangoli archipelago and elsewhere (see de Clercq 1890 and van Fraassen 1987 on the history of Ternate). Tidore laid claim to all of Irian Jaya. Though one can speculate on the structure of the northern Moluccan courts prior to European contact, that contact came early and with great force, broadly reducing the political power and economic base of the sultanates over time.

From the late seventeenth century onward, the Netherlands was more than just a competing commercial concern in eastern Indonesia; it was an imperial colonial force as well. During the eighteenth and nineteenth centuries, the Dutch colonial government did its best to retain Moluccan leaders who would cooperate fully with Dutch trading interests. To this end, gifts of European valuables, including coins and textiles, were provided to the cooperative courts. Van de Wall's (1922) description and catalog of regalia and other possessions in the sultan's palace on Ternate lists numerous gifts from Portuguese, Spanish, English, and Dutch monarchs, as well as gifts from other sultans and tribute from Ternate's dependencies on Halmahera and elsewhere.

The silver container (Fig. X.39) is a family heirloom from a Tobelo family on Halmahera, in a region associated with the court of Ternate (Fig. X.41).

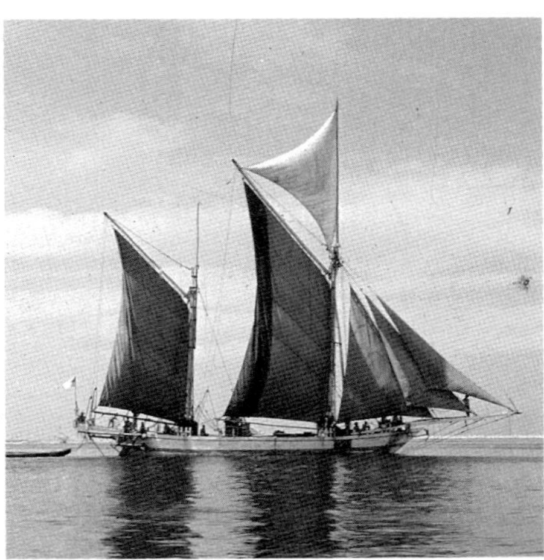

Fig. X.42 A traditional Bugis ship (*pinisi*) seen in the harbor of Ujung Pandang, South Sulawesi, 1963. Barbara Harvey

Dutch colonial coins dated 1707 and 1773 form the top and base of the container, and its sides are decorated with patterns of indigenous flowers. Such containers are used by Tobelo women to store powdered lime made from ground shells. The lime is added to betel-nut preparations and chewed as a mild stimulant. This silver lime container has aligned eyelets on the base and lid, through which a silver chain was passed. Such containers were often strung on the same chain with other silver feminine implements, such as a toothpick, a nosepick, and a pair of tweezers. A fine heirloom such as this would be worn on ceremonial occasions. On her wedding day, for example, a Tobelo bride is bedecked with heirloom jewelry and other female goods borrowed from her family or given to her as her dowry. Brought to her new husband's home, she is traditionally honored (*imiteru*, or "displayed") wearing her finest clothing and heirlooms for three successive evenings of feasting and dance. This custom continues today, often supplemented by cassette tape recordings, radio music, or traditional music played on electric guitars. The bride (Fig. X.40) sits motionless as her new in-laws and their guests celebrate. Her new sister-in-law (left) waits upon her and occasionally hangs a curtain between the bride and her admirers in order to adjust the bride's ornaments and posture if her motionless stance becomes difficult to maintain.

The courts in Indonesia's outer islands were trade emporia. Except for the spice monopoly controlled by Dutch after the seventeenth century, the trade in these emporia was always dominated by indigenous peoples exchanging Indonesian products and imported goods in local and international markets. Courts provided the entryway for foreign ideas, including the Hindu and Buddhist concepts of divine kingship around which Indonesian rulers originally organized courts, as well as the Islamic religion to which the court's rulers and populations converted.

Courts were also the avenue for introducing prestigious foreign artistic techniques and aesthetic motifs to the upriver or hinterland peoples. The people of a court's hinterlands, often called "dependents" of the court, stressed that they provided products as well as soldiers for the court in times of need. The dependancy was mutual, for a court required a hinterland. Even in antiquity, a court's role was to mediate between the populations of its hinterland and the bearers of international trade.

As elsewhere in the outer islands, the artworks produced in court societies served to honor ancestors, consolidate marriage alliances, link the people and their rulers to divine or spiritual forces, and affirm political power, social rank, and kin relationships. Courts developed from indigenous forms of Indonesian social organization combined with new ideas about statecraft and the divine role of the king or sultan. Similarly, court arts enriched by diverse foreign aesthetic ideas and techniques nonetheless express indigenous Indonesian themes. Court arts have also been understood and borrowed by artists and users of art in the many inland societies throughout the archipelago on which the courts have always depended.

References

Abdullah, Taufik
1966 "Adat and Islam: An Examination of Conflict in Minangkabau." *Indonesia* 2:1–24.

Adam, Tassilo
1919 *Tentoonstelling der Bataksche ethnografische verzameling en der fotografiën van Batakland en volk*. Deli (Sumatra): Delische Kunstkring.

Adams, Kathleen Marie
1984 "Come to Tana Toraja, 'Land of the Heavenly Kings'; Travel Agents as Brokers in Ethnicity." *Annals of Tourism Research* 11 (3):469–86.

1988 "Carving a New Identity: Ethnic and Artistic Change in Tana Toraja, Indonesia." Ph.D. dissertation, Univ. of Washington.

in press "More than an Icon of Identity: Torajan Art as Ethnic Weapon." In Ottenberg forthcoming.

Adams, Marie Jeanne
1969 *System and Meaning in East Sumba Textile Design: A Study in Traditional Indonesian Art*. New Haven: Yale Univ. Southeast Asian Studies.

1980 "Structural Aspects of East Sumbanese Art." In Fox 1980, 208–20.

Adhyatman, Sumarah
1983 *Keramik Mutakhir Bergaya Antik / Modern Ceramics in Antique Syle*. Jakarta: Himpunan Keramik Indonesia.

Adriani, Nicolaus
1928 *Bare'e-Nederlandsch Woordenboek Met Nederlandsch-Bare'e Register*. Leiden: E. J. Brill.

Adriani, Nicolaus, and Albertus C. Kruyt
1905 *Geklopte Boomschors als Kleedingstof op Midden-Celebes*. Leiden: E. J. Brill.

1912 *De Bare'e-Sprekende Toradja's van Midden-Celebes*. 3 vols. Batavia: Landsdrukkerij.

Aeckerlin, J. A.
1894 "De Pangkat Papadon in de Lampongsche Districten." *De Indische Gids* 16 (2):1532–42.

Albright Art Gallery
1948 *Indonesian Art*. New York: The Asia Institute.

Allen, Bryant
1983 "Human Geography of Papua New Guinea." *J. of Human Evolution* 12 (1):3–23.

Andaya, Leonard Y.
1981 *The Heritage of Arung Palakka*. Verhandelingen van het Koninklijk Instituut voor Taal-, Land-en Volkenkunde, 91. The Hague: Nijhoff.

Anderson, Benedict
1972 "The Idea of Power in Javanese Culture." In Holt et al. 1972, 1–69.

Appell, George N., ed.
1976 *The Societies of Borneo, Explorations in the Theory of Cognatic Social Structure*. Washington, D.C.: American Anthropological Association Special Publication no. 6.

Aragon, Lorraine V.
1990 "Barkcloth Production in Central Sulawesi: A Vanishing Textile Technology in Outer Island Indonesia." *Expedition* 32 (1):33–48.

in prep. "Divine Justice: Protestant Christianization and Reinterpreted Traditions in Central Sulawesi, Indonesia." Ph.D. dissertation, Univ. of Illinois.

Avé, J. B., and Victor T. King
1986 *People of the Weeping Forest: Tradition and Change in Borneo*. Leiden: National Museum of Ethnology.

van Baaren, Theodorus P.
1968 *Korwars and Korwar Style*. The Hague: Mouton and Co.

van Balen, J. A.
1886 "Iets over het Dodenfeest bij de Papoea's aan de Geelvinksbaai: Uitreksels uit een Brief van de Zendelingleeraar J. A. van Balen te Roon." *Tijdschrift voor Indische Taal-, Land- en Volkenkunde* 31:556–75.

Barbier, Jean Paul
1978 *Symbolique et motifs du sud de Nias*. Geneva: Musée Barbier-Mueller.

1983 *Tobaland: The Shreds of Tradition*. Geneva: Musée Barbier-Mueller.

1984 *Indonesian Primitive Art: Indonesia, Malaysia, the Philippines, from the Collection of the Barbier-Mueller Museum, Geneva*. Dallas: Dallas Museum of Art.

1988 "A Stone Rider of the Batak of Sumatra." In Barbier and Newton 1988, 50–65.

in press "The Responsible and the Irresponsible: Observations on the Destruction and Preservation of Indonesian Art." In Taylor in press b.

Barbier, Jean Paul, and Douglas Newton, eds.
1988 *Islands and Ancestors: Indigenous Styles of Southeast Asia*. New York: The Metropolitan Museum of Art.

Barbier-Mueller Museum
1988 *Yesterday, Today and Tomorrow: The Collections and Activities of the Barbier-Mueller Museum, 1977–1987*. Geneva: Musée Barbier-Mueller.

Barbour, Thomas
1908 "Notes on A Zoological Collecting Trip to Dutch New Guinea." *National Geographic* 19 (7):469–84.

1908 "Further Notes on Dutch New Guinea." *National Geographic* 18 (8):527–45.

Barnes, John Arundel
1971 *Three Styles in the Study of Kinship*. Berkeley and Los Angeles: Univ. of California Press.

Barnes, Robert H.
1974 *Kédang: A Study of the Collective Thought of an Eastern Indonesian People*. Oxford: Clarendon Press.

1987 Review of *Southeast Asia in the 9th to 14th Centuries*, edited by David G. Marr and A. C. Milner. *Canberra Anthropology* 10 (1):74–85.

Barnes, Ruth
1989a "Bridewealth Cloth of Lamalera." In Gittinger 1989, 43–56.

1989b *The Ikat Textiles of Lamalera: A Study of an Eastern Indonesian Weaving Tradition*. Leiden: E. J. Brill.

in press a "Patola in Southern Lembata." In *Proceedings of the Second Symposium on Indonesian Textiles, Köln 1985*, edited by K. von Welck. Cologne: Rautenstrauch-Joest Museum.

in press b " 'Without Cloth We Cannot Marry': The Textiles of Lamaholot in Transition." In Taylor in press b.

Barraud, C.
1979 *Tanebar-Evav: Une société de maisons tournées vers le large*. Cambridge: Cambridge Univ. Press.

Bartlett, Harley Harris
1973 *The Labors of the Datoe and Other Essays on the Bataks of Asahan (North Sumatra).* Michigan Papers on South and Southeast Asia, no. 5. Ann Arbor: Univ. of Michigan Press.

Bastiaans, J.
1939 "Batato's in het oude Gorontalo, in verband met den Gorontaleeschen staatsbouw." *Tijdschrift voor Indische Taal-, Land- en Volkenkunde* 79:23–72.

Bastin, John, and Bea Brommer
1979 *Nineteenth-Century Prints and Illustrated Books of Indonesia, with Particular Reference to the Print Collection of the Tropenmuseum, Amsterdam.* Utrecht: Spectrum.

Bataviaasch Genootschaap
1933 *Jaarboek Koninklijk Bataviaasch Genootschaap van Kunsten en Wetenschappen* Bandung: A. C. Nij and Co.

Bellwood, Peter
1979 *Man's Conquest of the Pacific: The Prehistory of Southeast Asia and Oceania.* New York: Oxford Univ. Press.
1985 *Prehistory of the Indo-Malaysian Archipelago.* Sydney: Academic Press Australia.

Bellwood, Peter, and Peter Koon
1989 " 'Lapita Colonists Leave Boat Unburned!' The Question of Lapita Links with Island Southeast Asia." *Antiquity* 63 (240):613–22.

Bernet Kempers, August J.
1978 *Monumental Bali: Introduction to Balinese Archaeology: Guide to the Monument.* The Hague: Van Goor.
1988 *The Kettledrums of Southeast Asia: A Bronze Age World and Its Aftermath.* Modern Quaternary Research in Southeast Asia, no. 10. Rotterdam: Balkema.

Best, Elsdon
"Did Polynesian Voyagers Know the Double Outrigger?" *J. of the Polynesian Society* 32:200–14.

Bertling, C. T.
1927 " 'Hampatongs' of 'Tempatongs' van Borneo." *Nederlandsch-Indië Oud & Nieuw* 12 (5):131–41, 179–92, 223–36.

Bezemer, T. J.
n.d. *Indonesian Arts and Crafts.* Amsterdam: J. M. Meulenhoff.

Bigalke, Terence
1981 "A Social History of 'Tana Toraja' 1870–1965." Ph.D. dissertation, Univ. of Wisconsin, Madison.

Bink, G. L.
1996 "Drie Maanden aan de Humboldtsbaai." *Tijdschrift van het Bataviaasch Genootschaap* 39:143–211.

Biro Pusat Statistik
1987–88 *Statistik Indonesia / Statistical Yearbook of Indonesia.* Jakarta.

Bolland, Rita
1970 "Three Looms for Tablet Weaving." *Tropical Man* 3:160–89.

Bolle, Lea
1988 "The Tugu of the Toba Batak: A Grave as a Monument and a Beacon." In Schefold et al. 1988, 30–36.

Bovill, Kathryn J.
1986 "Toba Batak Marriage and Alliance: Family Decisions in an Urban Context." Ph.D. dissertation, Univ. of Illinois.

van Brakel, J. H., B.A.P. van Duuren, H. J. Gortzak, W. H. Kal, and B. C. Meulenbeld
1987 *Budaya Indonesia: Kunst en Cultuur in Indonesië / Budaya Indonesia: Arts and Crafts in Indonesia.* Amsterdam: Tropenmuseum.

Brown, Donald E.
1988 "Tribe-Sultanate Relationships: Traditional Patterns of Rule in Brunei." *Expedition* 30 (1):45–50.

Bruner, Edward M.
1972 "Batak Ethnic Associations in Three Indonesian Cities." *Southwestern Journal of Anthropology* 28:207–29.
1973a "The Expression of Ethnicity in Indonesia." In Cohen 1973, 251–80.
1973b "Kin and Non-Kin." In *Urban Anthropology*, edited by A. Southall, 373–92. New York: Oxford Univ. Press.
1984 "The Symbolics of Urban Migration." In Maybury–Lewis 1984, 64–76.
1987 "Megaliths, Migration and the Segmented Self." In Carle 1987, 133–49.

Bruner, M., and Judith O. Becker, eds.
1979 *Art, Ritual, and Society in Indonesia.* Athens, OH: Ohio Univ. Center for International Studies

Buccellati, Giorgio, and Marilyn Kelly Buccellati
1983 "Terqa: The First Eight Seasons." *Les Annales archéologiques arabes syriennes: Revue d'archéologie et d'histoire* 32 (2):47–67.

Bühler, Alfred, and Eberhard Fischer
1979 *The Patola of Gujarat.* 2 vols. Basel: Krebs AG.

Bujono, Bambang
1979 "Ada Monumen Diganti Botol." *Majalah Tempo* (March 17, 1979):16–17.

Burkill, I. H.
1966 [1935] *A Dictionary of the Economic Products of the Malay Peninsula*, 2 vols. Kuala Lumpur: Ministry of Agriculture and Co-operatives.

Cameron, Elisabeth I.
1985a "Ancestor Motifs of the Paiwan." In Feldman 1985c, 161–70.
1985b "Ancestors and Living Men among the Batak." In Feldman 1985c, 79–100.

Cameron, Elisabeth I., and E. Sumnik-Dekovich
1985 "Magamaog: Benevolent Ancestor of the Yami." In Feldman 1985c, 171–74.

Canaan, Tewfik
1937 "The Decipherment of Arabic Magical Bowls." *Berytus Archeological Studies* 4:69–110.

Carle, R.
1987 *Cultures and Societies of North Sumatra.* Veröffentlichungen der Universität Hamburg, vol. 19. Berlin: Dietrich Reimer Verlag

ten Cate, W. C.
1922 "De Doodenpalen in de Onderafdeeling Melawi der Afdeeling Sintang van de Residentie Westerafdeeling van Borneo." *Tijdschrift voor Indische Taal-, Land- en Volkenkunde* 61:201–22. Batavia: Albrecht Co.

Cense, A. A.
1952 "Makassars-Boeginese Prauwvaart op Noord-Australie." *Bijdragen tot de Taal-, Land- en Volkenkunde van Nederlandsch-Indië* 108 (3):248–64.

Chin, Lucas
1988 "Trade Objects: Their Impact on the Cultures of the Indigenous Peoples of Sarawak, Borneo." *Expedition* 30 (1):59–64.

Chong Chin Seng
1987 *Traditional Melanau Woodcarving (Bilum) in Dalat, Sarawak.* Sarawak: Persatuan Kesusasteraan Sarawak.

de Clercq, F. S. A.
1990 *Bijdragen tot de Kennis der Residentie Ternate.* Leiden: E. J. Brill.

de Clercq, F. S. A., and J. D. E. Schmeltz
1893 *Ethnographische Beschrijving van de Westen Noordkust van Nederlandsch Nieuw-Guinea.* Leiden: P.W.M. Trap.

Clifford, James
1988 *The Predicament of Culture: Twentieth-Century Ethnography, Literature, and Art.* Cambridge: Harvard Univ. Press.

Coedès, G.
1968 [1944] *The Indianized States of Southeast Asia.* S. B. Cowing, trans. Honolulu: Univ. of Hawaii Press.

Cohen, A., ed.
1973 *Urban Ethnicity.* London: Tavistock.

Cole, Douglas
1985 *Captured Heritage: The Scramble for Northwest Coast Artifacts.* Seattle: Univ. of Washington Press.

Collins, G. E. P.
1937 *East Monsoon.* New York: Charles Scribner's Sons.

Condominas, George
1977 "Pour une definition anthropologique du concept d'espace social." *Asie du Sud-est et Monde Insulindien* 8 (2):5–54.

Coomaraswamy, Ananda K.
1965 *History of Indian and Indonesian Art.* New York: Dover Publications, Inc.

Coville, Elizabeth
1988 " 'A Single Word Brings to Life': The Maro Ritual in Tana Toraja (Indonesia)." Ph.D. dissertation, Univ. of Chicago.
1989 "Centripetal Ritual in a Decentered World: Changing Maro Performances in Tana Toraja." In Russell and Cunningham 1989, 103–31.

Crystal, Eric
1977 "Tourism in Toraja (Sulawesi, Indonesia)." In *Hosts and Guests: The Anthropology of Tourism* edited by Valene L. Smith, 109–25. Philadelphia: Univ. of Pennsylvania Press.
1979 "Mountain Ikats and Coastal Silks: Traditional Textiles in South Sulawesi." In Fischer 1979, 53–62.
1985 "The Soul that is Seen: The *Tau Tau* as Shadow of Death, Reflection of Life in Toraja Tradition." In Feldman 1985c, 129–46.
1989 "Myth, Symbol and Function of the Toraja House." *Traditional Dwellings and Settlements Review* 1 (1):7–17.
in press "Rape of the Ancestors." In Taylor in press b.

Cummins, J. S.
1962 *The Travels and Controversies of Friar Domingo Navarrete 1618–1686*, 2 vols. Cambridge: Hakluyt Society for Cambridge Univ. Press.

Cunningham, Clark E.
1958 *The Postwar Migration of the Toba-Bataks*

to East Sumatra. New Haven: Yale Univ. Southeast Asian Studies, Cultural Report Series, no. 5.
1964 "Order in the Atoni House." *Bijdragen tot de Taal-, Land- en Volkenkunde* 120 (1):34–68.
1965 "Order and Change in an Atoni Diarchy." *Southwestern J. of Anthropology* 21:359–82.

Davenport, William H.
1988 "Introduction [to Special Issue on Borneo]." *Expedition* 30 (1):3–4.

Denslow, J. S., and C. Padoch, eds.
1988 *People of the Tropical Rain Forest*. Berkeley and Los Angeles: Univ. of California Press.

Departemen Pendidikan dan Kebudayaan
1981–82 *Katalog Koleksi Museum Negeri Nusa Tenggara Barat*. Mataram: Departemen Pendidikan dan Kebudayaan.

van Dijk, Toos, and Nico de Jonge
1980 *Ship Cloths of the Lampung South Sumatera*. Amsterdam: Galerie Mabuhay.
1990 "After Sunshine Comes Rain: A Comparative Analysis of Fertility Rituals in Marsela and Luang, South-East Moluccas." *Bijdragen Tot de Taal-, Land- en Volkenkunde* 146 (1):3–20.

Dobbin, Christine
1983 *Islamic Revivalism in a Changing Peasant Economy (Central Sumatra, 1784–1847)*. Scandinavian Institute of Asian Studies Monograph Series, no. 47. London: Curzon Press.

Domeny de Rienzi, Gregoire Louis
1836 *Océanie ou cinquième partie du monde. Revue géographique et ethnographique de la Malaisie, de la Micronésie, de la Polynésie et de la Mélanésie; offrant les résultats des voyages et des découvertes de l'auteur et de ses devanciers, ainsi que ses nouvelles classifications et divisions de ces contrées*. Paris: Firmin Didot.

Douwes Dekker, N. A.
1961 *Tanah Air Kita: A Book on the Country and People of Indonesia*. The Hague: W. Van Hoeve, Ltd.

Drabbe, P.
1923 "De Heidensche Huwelijk op Tanimbar." *Bijdragen tot de Taal-, Land- en Volkenkunde van Nederlandsch-Indië* 79 (4):546–68.
1940 "Het Leven van den Tanémbarees: Ethnografische Studie over het Tanémbareesche Volk." *Internationales Archiv für Ethnographie*, supplement to vol. 37.

Drake, Richard Allen
1988 "Ibanic Textile Weaving: Its Enchantment in Social and Religious Practices." *Expedition* 30 (1):29–36.

DuBois, Cora
1944 *The People of Alor*. Minneapolis: Univ. of Minnesota Press.

Durdik, P.
1892 "Genees- en Verloskunde bij de Niassers." *Geneeskundig Tijdschrift van Nederlandsch-Indië* 22:243–75.

van Eerde, J. C., ed.
1920–21 *De Volken van Nederlandsch-Indië*, 2 vols. Amsterdam: Elsevier.

Ellis, George R.
1980 "The Art of the Toraja." *Arts of Asia* 10(5):94–107.

Elmberg, John-Erik
1968 *Balance and Circulation: Aspects of Tradition and Change among the Mejprat of Irian Barat*. Stockholm: Ethnographical Museum, Monograph Series, no. 12.

Erb, Maribeth
1988 "Flores: Cosmology, Art and Ritual." In Barbier and Newton 1988, 106–19.

Errington, Shelly
1989 *Meaning and Power in a Southeast Asian Realm*. Princeton: Princeton Univ. Press.
in press "Afterword: A Meta-Mega Story About Indonesian 'Arts' in Jeopardy." In Taylor in press b.

Feldman, Jerome
1977 "The Architecture of Nias, Indonesia with Special Reference to Bawömataluo Village." Ph.D. dissertation, Columbia Univ.
1979 "The House as World in Bawömataluo, South Nias." In Bruner and Becker 1979, 127–89.
1983 "The High Tigers in South Nias, Indonesia." *Empirical Studies in the Arts* 1 (2):143–56.
1985a "Ancestors in the Art of Indonesia and Southeast Asia." In Feldman 1985c, 35–44.
1985b "Ancestral Manifestations in the Art of Nias Island." In Feldman 1985c, 45–78.
1988 "The Seat of the Ancestors in the Homeland of the Nias People." In Barbier and Newton 1988, 34–49.
1989 "Ceremonial Attire in Nias." In Gittinger 1989, 199–212.
in press "The Adaptation of Indigenous Forms to Western Taste: The Case of Nias." In Taylor in press b.
———, ed.
1985c *The Eloquent Dead: Ancestral Sculpture of Indonesia and Southeast Asia*. Los Angeles: UCLA Museum of Cultural History.

Feuilletau de Bruyn, W.K.H.
1917 "De Schouten Eilanden." *Tijdschrift voor het Binnenlandsch Bestuur* 51:385–88.

Fischer, H. Th.
1938 " 'Masculine' and 'Feminine' Presents." *Man* 38 (181):158–59.

Fischer, H. W.
1909 "Nias." Leiden: *Catalogus van 'sRijks Ethnographisch Museum*, 23 vols. In Vol. 4:1–81,199–222.

Fischer, Joseph
1990 *Modern Indonesian Art: Three Generations of Tradition and Change 1945–1990*. New York and Jakarta: Festival of Indonesia/Panitia KIAS.

Fischer, J., ed.
1979 *Threads of Tradition: Textiles of Indonesia and Sarawak*. Berkeley and Los Angeles: Univ. of California Press.

Fontein, Jan
1990 *The Sculpture of Indonesia*. Washington, D. C.: The National Gallery of Art; New York: Harry N. Abrams, Inc.

Forth, Gregory L.
1981 *Rindi: An Ethnographic Study of a Traditional Domain in Eastern Sumba*. Verhandelingen van het Koninklijk Instituut Voor Taal-, Land- en Volkenkunde, no. 93. The Hague: Nijhoff.

Fox, James J.
1971 "Semantic Parallelism in Rotinese Ritual Language." *Bijdragen Tot de Taal-, Land- en Volkenkunde* 127 (2):215–55.
1977 *Harvest of the Palm: Ecological Change in Eastern Indonesia*. Cambridge: Harvard Univ. Press.
1988 "Introduction." In Fox 1988, 1–28.
1989 "Category and Complement: Binary Ideologies and the Organization of Dualism in Eastern Indonesia." In Maybury-Lewis and Almagor 1989, 33–56.
———, ed.
1980 *The Flow of Life: Essays on Eastern Indonesia*. Cambridge: Harvard Univ. Press.
1988 *To Speak in Pairs: Essays on the Ritual Languages of Eastern Indonesia*. Cambridge Studies in Oral and Literate Cultures, vol. 15. Cambridge: Cambridge Univ. Press.

van Fraassen, Christiaan Frans
1981 "A Historical Introduction to the Literature." In Polman 1981, 1–37.
1987 "Ternate, de Molukken en de Indonesische Archipel: Van Soa-Organisatie en Vierdeling: Een Studie van Traditionele Samenleving en Cultuur in Indonesië." Ph.D. dissertation, Leiden University.

Fraser, D., ed.
1966 *The Many Faces of Primitive Art*. Englewood Cliffs, NJ: Prentice Hall.

Fraser-Lu, Sylvia
1988 *Handwoven Textiles of South-East Asia*. Singapore: Oxford Univ. Press.
1989 *Silverware of South-East Asia*. Images of Asia Series. Oxford: Oxford Univ. Press.

Frazer, J. K.
1890 *The Golden Bough: A Study of Comparative Religion*, 2 vols. London: MacMillan and Co.

Freeman, J. D.
1970 *Report on the Iban*. New York: The Athlone Press.
1979 "Severed Heads That Germinate." In Hook 1979, 233–46.

Galis, Klaas Wilhelm
1955 *Papua's van de Humboldt-Baai: Bijdrage tot een Ethnografie*. The Hague: J. N. Voorhoeve.
1963 "De Biak-Noemfoorse Prauw." *Kultuurpatronen. Bulletin Ethnografisch Museum, Delft* 5–6:120–42.
1968–69 "Nogmaals Sentani." *Kultuurpatronen. Bulletin Ethnografisch Museum, Delft* 10–11:59–96.

Ganjing, Augustine Anggat
1988 *Basic Iban Design: An Introduction*. Gana Ngadi, trans. Kuala Lumpur: Ministry of Education.

Geertz, Clifford
1966 [1963] *Agricultural Involution: The Processes of Ecological Change in Indonesia*. Berkeley and Los Angeles: Univ. of California Press.

Geertz, Hildred
1963 "Indonesian Cultures and Communities." In McVey 1963, 24–96.

Geirnaert, Danielle C.
1983 "Ask Lurik Why Batik: A Structural Analysis of Textiles and Classifications (Central Java)." In *The Future of Structuralism—Papers of IUAES Intercongress, Amsterdam, 1981*, edited by J. G. Oosten and A. de Ruijter, 155–99. Amsterdam: Göttingen.

1989a "Textiles of West Sumba: The Lively Renaissance of an Old Tradition." In Gittinger 1989, 57–79.

1989b "The Pogo Nauta Ritual in Laboya (West Sumba): Of Tubers and Mamuli." In *Rituals and Socio-cosmic Order in Eastern Indonesian Societies*, edited by C. Barraud and J. D. M. Platenkamp, *Bijdragen tot de Taal-, Land- en Volkenkunde* 145 (4):445–3.

Gerbrands, A. A.
1983 "Speigelen, uitklappen en omkeren: een aspect van ethnocommunicatie." In *Liber Memorialis Prof. Dr. P.J. Vandenhoute*, 511–50. Ghent: Seminarie voor Etnische Kunst.

Geurtjens, H.
1910 "Le cérémonial des voyages aux îles Kei." *Anthropos* 5:334–58.

1921 *Uit een vreemde wereld, of het leven en streuen der inlanders op de Kei-eilanden.* 's-Hertogenbosch: Teulings' Uitgevers-Maatschappij.

1941 *Zijn Plaats Onder de Zon.* Roermond-Maaseik: J. J. Romen and Zonen.

Gittinger, Mattiebelle
1972 "A Study of the Ship Cloths of South Sumatra: Their Design and Usage." Ph.D. dissertation, Columbia Univ.

1975 "Selected Batak Textiles." *Textile Museum Journal* 4 (2):13–29.

1976 "The Ship Textiles of South Sumatra: Functions and Design System." *Bijdragen tot de Taal-, Land- en Volkenkunde* 132 (2–3):207–27.

1979 *Splendid Symbols: Textiles and Tradition in Indonesia.* Washington, D.C.: Textile Museum.

1989 "A Reassessment of the Tampan of South Sumatra." In Gittinger 1989, 225–39.

———, ed.
1980 *Indonesian Textiles, Irene Emery Roundtable on Museum Textiles, 1979 Proceedings*, Washington, D. C.: Textile Museum.

1989 *To Speak With Cloth: Studies in Indonesian Textiles.* Los Angeles: UCLA Museum of Cultural History.

Glover, I. C.
1979 "The Late Prehistoric Period in Indonesia." In Smith and Watson 1979, 167–84.

Goloubew, V.
1929 "L'age du bronze au Tonkin." *Bulletin de l'Ecole Française d'Extrême-Orient* 29:1–46.

Graburn, Nelson H. H.
1976 *Ethnic and Tourist Arts: Cultural Expressions from the Fourth World.* Berkeley and Los Angeles: Univ. of California Press.

Green, R. C.
1979 "Early Lapita Art from Polynesia and Island Melanesia: Continuities in Ceramic, Barkcloth, and Tattoo Decorations." In Mead 1979, 13–31.

1982 "Models for the Lapita Cultural Complex." *New Zealand Journal of Archaeology* 4:7–19.

Griffiths, Michael
1989 *Indonesian Eden: Aceh's Rainforest.* n.p.: Mobil Services Co., Ltd.

Groeneveldt, W. P.
1960 *Historical Notes on Indonesia and Malaya Compiled from Chinese Sources.* Jakarta: Bhratara.

Groube, Les
1986 "A 40,000 Year-Old Human Occupation Site at Huon Peninsula, PNG." *Nature* 324 (4):453–56.

Grubauer, Albert
1913 *Unter Kopfjägern in Central-Celebes; Ethnologische Streifzüge in Südost- und Central-Celebes von Professor Albert Grubauer.* Leipzig: R. Voigtlanders.

Gwatkin, Nina Wade-Dalton
1986 *Scenes for a Raja: Study of an Indian Kalamkari Found in Indonesia.* Museum of Cultural History Monograph Series, no. 27. Los Angeles: UCLA Museum of Cultural History.

ter Haar, B.
1948 *Adat Law in Indonesia.* Translated, edited and with an introduction by E. A. Hoebel and A. A. Schiller. New York: Institute of Pacific Relations.

Hackmack, Adolf
1973 *Chinese Carpets and Rugs.* New York: Dover Publications.

Haddon, Alfred C., and James Hornell
1975 *Canoes of Oceania.* Honolulu: Bishop Museum Press.

Haddon, Alfred C., and Laura E. Start
1936 *Iban or Sea Dayak Fabrics and Their Patterns.* Cambridge: Cambridge Univ. Press.

Hale, Horatio
1968 [1846] *Ethnography and Philology. United States Exploring Expedition, during the years 1838, 1839, 1840, 1841, 1842. Under the command of Charles Wilkes, U.S.N.* Ridgewood, NJ: Gregg Press.

Hall, Kenneth R.
1976 "An Introductory Essay on Southeast Asian Statecraft in the Classical Period." In Hall and Whitmore 1976, 1–24.

1985 *Maritime Trade and State Development in Early Southeast Asia.* Honolulu: Univ. of Hawaii Press.

Hall, Kenneth R., and John K. Whitmore, eds.
1976 *Explorations in Early Southeast Asian History: The Origins of Southeast Asian Statecraft.* Michigan Papers on South and Southeast Asia, no. 11. Ann Arbor: Univ. of Michigan Press.

Hamka
1982 *Ayaku: Riwayat Hidup Dr. H. Abdul Karim Amrullah dan Perjuangan Kaum Agama di Sumatera.* Jakarta: Umminda.

Hämmerle, P. Johannes M.
1984 "Die Megalithkultur im Susua Gomo-Gebiet, Nias." *Anthropos* 79:587–625.

1986 *Famatö Harimao: Pesta Harimao—Fondrakö—Börönadu dan Kebudayaan Lainnya di Wilayah Maenamölö, Nias Selatan.* Teluk Dalam: Abidin Medan.

Hamilton, Roy W.
1989 "Textiles of the Ende-Lio Region of Flores Island, Indonesia." M.A. thesis, Univ. of Washington.

1990 "Local Textile Trading Systems in Indonesia: An Example from Flores." Paper delivered at the 1990 Symposium of the Textile Society of America, Washington, D.C.

Hamzuri
1984 *Keris.* Jakarta: Jambatan.

Hanna, Willard A.
1978 *Indonesian Banda: Colonialism and its Aftermath in the Nutmeg Islands.* Philadelphia: Institute for the Study of Human Issues.

Harrisson, Barbara
1963 *Orang-utan.* New York: Doubleday.

Harrisson, Tom
1972 "The Borneo Stone Age—In the Light of Recent Research." *Sarawak Museum Journal* 20 (40–41):385–412.

van Hasselt, F. J. F.
1926 *In het Land van de Papoea's.* Utrecht: Kemmink en Zoon.

1930 "Or, mana, for en verwante begrippen bij de Papoea's voornamelijk van Noemfoorschen stam." *Mededeelingen, Tijdschrift voor Zendingswetenschappen* 74:235–62.

van Hasselt, J. L.
1886–88 "Eenige Aanteekeningen aangaande de Bewoners der N. Westkust van Nieuw Guinea, Meer Bepaaldelijk den Stam der Noefoorezen." *Tijdschrift voor Indische Taal-, Land- en Volkenkunde* 31:576–593, 32:261–272.

van Heekeren, H. R.
1958 *The Bronze-Iron Age of Indonesia.* The Hague: Nijhoff.

Heger, F.
1902 *Alte Metalltrommeln aus Südost-Asien.* 2 vols. Leipzig: K. von Hiersemann.

Heine Geldern, R.
1947 "The Drum Named Makalamau." *India Antiqua* [special issue]: 167–79. Leiden: E. J. Brill.

1966 "Some Tribal Art Styles of Southeast Asia: An Experiment in Art History." In Fraser 1966, 165–221.

1972 [1935] "The Archaeology and Art of Sumatra." In Loeb 1972 [1935], 305–31.

Held, Gerrit Jan
1940 "Slangfiguren in het Initiatie-Ritueel in de Geelvinkbaai." *Cultureel Indië*, vol. 2:138–47. Leiden: E. J. Brill.

1951 *De Papoea, Cultuurimprovisator.* The Hague and Bandung:N. V. Uitgeverij W. van Hoeve.

1957 *The Papuas of Waropen.* The Hague: Nijhoff.

Helfrich, O. L.
1889 "Bijdragen tot de Geographische, Geologische en Ethnographische Kennis der Afdeeling Kroë." *Bijdragen tot de Taal-, Land- en Volkenkunde van Nederlandsch-Indië* 38:515–629.

Heppell, Michael
1989 "Whither Dayak Art?" *The Sarawak Museum Journal* 40 (61, new series):75–91.

van Heurn, F. C.
1929 *De Olifanten van Sumatra.* The Hague: Gerretsen.

Heyne, K.
1950 *De Nuttige Planten van Indonesië*, 2 vols. The Hague: van Hoeve.

Hicks, David
1976 *Tetum Ghosts and Kin: Fieldwork in an Indonesian Community.* Palo Alto: Mayfield.

1988 "Art and Religion on Timor." In Barbier and Newton 1988, 138–51.

Higham, C. F. W.
1983 "The Ban Chiang Culture in Wider Perspective." *Proceedings of the British Academy* 69:229–61.

Hingmann, John J., ed.
1970 *Handbook of Social and Cultural Anthro-*

pology. Chicago: Rand McNally College Publishing.

Hissink, I.

1904 "Het Pepadonwezen en zijne Attributen in Verband met de Oude Staatkundige Indeeling in Marga's en het Huwelijks-en Erfrecht in de Afdeeling Toelang Bawang, de Lampongsche Districten." *Tijdschrift van het Bataviaasch Genootschap* 47:69–167.

1912 "Nota van Toelichting Betreffende de Zelfbestuurende Landschappen Paloe, Dolo, Sigi en Biromaroe." *Tijdschrift voor Indische Taal-, Land- en Volkenkunde* 54:58–128.

Ho, Chuimei

1988 *Minnan Blue-and-white Wares: An Archaeological Survey of Kiln Sites of the 16th-19th Centuries in Southern Fujian, China*. Oxford: B.A.R. International Series 428.

Hogbin, Ian, and L. R. Hiatt, eds.

1966 *Readings in Australian and Pacific Anthropology*. Melbourne: Melbourne Univ. Press.

Holmgren, Robert J., and Anita Spertus

1980 "Tampan Pasisir: Pictoral Documents of an Ancient Indonesian Coastal Culture." In Gittinger 1980, 157–98.

1989 *Early Indonesian Textiles from Three Island Cultures*. New York: The Metropolitan Museum of Art.

Holt, Claire

1971 "Dances of Sumatra and Nias." *Indonesia* 11:1–21.

Holt, C., B. Anderson, and J. Siegel, eds.

1972 *Culture and Politics in Indonesia*. Ithaca: Cornell Univ. Press

Honigmann, John J.

1973 *Handbook of Social and Cultural Anthropology*. Chicago: Rand McNally Co.

de Hoog, J.

1959 "Nieuwe Methoden en Inzichten ter Bestudering van de Funktionele Betekenis der Beelden in Het Indonesisch-Melanesisch Kultuurgebied." *Kultuurpatronen. Bulletin Ethnografisch Museum—Delft* 1:1–98.

Hoogerbrugge, Jac.

1967 "Sentani-Meer, Mythe en Ornament." *Kultuurpatronen. Bulletin Ethnografisch Museum—Delft* 9:4–91.

Hook, R. H., ed.

1979 *Fantasy and Symbol*. London: Academic Press.

van der Hoop, A. N. J. Th. à Th.

1940 "De Megalithische Hoofdenzetel Oorsprong van den Lampongschen Pepadon?" *Tijdschrift voor Indische Taal-, Land- en Volkenkunde* 80:60–77.

Hooykaas, Jacoba

1957 "Upon a White Stone Under a Nagasari Tree." *Bijdragen tot de Taal-, Land- en Volkenkunde van Nederlandsch-Indië* 113 (4):324–40.

Horridge, G. Adrian

1978 *The Design of Planked Boats of the Moluccas*. Maritime Monographs and Reports, no. 38. Basildon, England: Trustees of the National Maritime Museum.

1979 *The Konjo Boatbuilders and the Bugis Prahus of South Sulawesi*. Maritime Monographs and Reports, no. 40. Basildon, England: Trustees of the National Maritime Museum.

1987 *Outrigger Canoes of Bali and Madura, Indonesia*. Bishop Museum Special Publication 77. Honolulu: Bishop Museum Press.

Horst, D. W.

1993 *De Rum-Serams op Nieuw-Guinea of het Hinduïsme in het Oosten van Onzen Archipel*. Leiden: E. J. Brill.

Hose, C.

1988 [1926] *Natural Man, A Record from Borneo*. Singapore: Oxford Univ. Press.

Hose, C., and W. McDougall

1912 *The Pagan Tribes of Borneo: a Description of Their Physical, Moral, and Intellectual Condition, with Some Discussion of Their Ethnic Relations*, 2 vols. London: MacMillan and Co.

Hoskins, Janet

1988 "Arts and Cultures of Sumba." In Barbier and Newton 1988, 20–137.

Hough, Walter

1932 "The Buffalo Motive in Middle Celebes Decorative Design." *Proceedings of the United States National Museum, Smithsonian Institution, Washington, D.C.* 79 (29):1–8.

Hutterer, Karl L.

1977 *Economic Exchange and Social Interaction in Southeast Asia: Perspectives from Prehistory, History, and Ethnography*. Michigan Papers on South and Southeast Asia, no. 13. Ann Arbor: Univ. of Michigan Press.

1982 *Interaction between Tropical Ecosystems and Human Foragers: Some General Considerations*. Honolulu: Working Paper, Environment and Policy Institute, The East-West Center, April 1982.

1988 "The Prehistory of the Asian Rain Forests." In Denslow and Padoch 1988, 63–72.

Innes Miller, J.

1969 *The Spice Trade of the Roman Empire, 29 B.C. to A.D. 641*. Oxford: Clarendon Press.

Ishige, Naomichi, ed.

1980 "The Galela of Halmahera: A Preliminary Survey." *Senri Ethnographical Studies*, no. 7. Osaka: National Museum of Ethnology.

Jager Gerlings, Johannes Hendrik

1952 *Sprekende Weefsels: Studie over Onstaan en Betekenis van Weefsels van Enige Indonesische Eilanden*. Amsterdam: Scheltens and Giltay.

Jasper, J. E., and Mas Pirngadie

1912–30 *De Inlandsche Kunstnijverheid in Nederlandsch-Indië*, 5 vols. Vol. 1. *Het vlechtwerk*, 1912. Vol. 2. *De weefkunst*, 1912. Vol. 3. *De batikkunst*, 1916. Vol. 4. *De goud-en zilversmeedkunst*, 1927. Vol. 5. *De bewerking van niet-edele metalen (koperbewerking en pamorsmeedkunst)*, 1930. The Hague: Mouton and Co.

Jens, Fr. Joh.

1916 "Het Insos- en het K'Bor-feest op Biak en Soepiori." *Bijdragen tot de Taal-, Land- en Volkenkunde van Nederlandsch-Indië* 72 (3–4):404–411.

Jessup, Helen I.

1990 *Court Arts of Indonesia*. New York: The Asia Society Galleries and Harry N. Abrams, Inc.

Jessup, Timothy T., and Andrew P. Vayda

1988 "Dayaks and Forests of Interior Borneo." *Expedition* 30 (1):5–17.

de Jonge, Nico

1989 "Aboard in Babar." In Schefold et al. 1989, 136–45.

de Josselin de Jong, P.E., ed.

1983 *Structural Anthropology in the Netherlands*. Koninklijk Instituut voor Taal-, Land- en Volkenkunde, Translation Series 17. Dordrecht: Foris Publications.

1984 *Unity in Diversity: Indonesia as a Field of Anthropological Study*. Verhandelingen van het Koninklijk Instituut voor Taal-, Land- en Volkenkunde, no. 103. Dordrecht: Foris Publications.

de Josselin de Jong, P.E., and Erik Schwimmer, eds.

1982 *Symbolic Anthropology in the Netherlands*. Verhandelingen van het Koninklijk Instituut voor Taal-, Land- en Volkenkunde, no. 95. The Hague: Nijhoff.

Kadang, K.

1960 *Ukiran Rumah Toradja*. Jakarta: Dinas Penerbitan Balai Jakarta.

Kamma, Freerk C.

1970 "A Spontaneous 'Capitalist' Revolution in the Western Vogelkop Area of West Irian." In *Anniversary Contributions to Anthropology: Twelve Essays*, edited by Leiden Ethnological Society, 132–42. Leiden: E. J. Brill.

Kamma, Freerk C., and Simon Kooijman

1973 "Romawa Forja Child of the Fire: Iron Working and the Role of Iron in West New Guinea (West Irian)." *Mededelingen van het Rijksmuseum voor Volkenkunde*, no. 18. Leiden: E. J. Brill

Kammerer, Cornelia Ann

1986 "Gateway to the Akha World: Kinship, Ritual, and Community among Highlanders of Thailand." Ph.D. dissertation, Univ. of Chicago.

Kartiwa, Suwati

1980 "The Social Function of the Kain Songket Minangkabau." In Gittinger 1980, 56–80.

1982 *Songket Indonesia*. Jakarta: Museum Nasional Indonesia.

1983 *Kain Tenun Donggala*. Palu, Sulawesi Tengah: Donggala Press.

Kaudern, Walter

1925–44 *Ethnographical Studies in Celebes. Results of the Author's Expedition to Celebes, 1917–1920*, 6 vols. Vol. 1. *Structures and Settlements in Central Celebes*, 1925. Vol. 2. *Migrations of the Toradja in Central Celebes*, 1925. Vol. 3. *Musical Instruments in Celebes*, 1927. Vol. 4. *Games and Dances in Celebes*. 1929. Vol. 5. *Megalithic Finds in Central Celebes*, 1938. Vol. 6. *Art in Central Celebes*, 1944. Göteborg: Elanders Bokytryckeri Aktiebolag.

1940 "The Noble Families or Maradika of Kulawi, Central Celebes." *Etnologiska Studier*, vol. 11.

Keane, Webb

1988 "Shadows of Men and Spirits: Mamuli of Sumba." *Tribal Art/Art Tribal* (2):1–15.

Kennedy, Raymond

1934 "Bark-Cloth in Indonesia." *J. of the Polynesian Society* 43 (4):229–43.

Keraf, Gregorius

1983 "Economy and Social Change in Lamalera, Indonesia." Unpublished Social Science Research Council Project Report.

Khan Majlis, Brigitte
1984 *Indonesische Textilien.* Cologne: Rautenstrauch-Joest-Museum für Volkerkunde.

King, Victor T.
1989 "Introduction." In Tillema 1989, 1–27.
———, ed.
1978 *Essays on Borneo Societies.* Oxford: Oxford Univ. Press.

Kipp, Rita Smith
1983 "A Political System of Highland Sumatra, or Rethinking Edmond Leach." In Kipp and Kipp 1983, 125–38.

Kipp, Rita S., and Richard Kipp, eds.
1983 *Beyond Samosir: Recent Studies of the Batak Peoples of Sumatra.* Athens: Ohio Univ. Papers in International Studies, Southeast Asia Series, no. 62.

Kipp, Rita Smith, and Susan Rodgers, eds.
1987 *Indonesian Religions in Transition.* Tucson: Univ. of Arizona Press.

Kirch, Patrick V.
1988a "Problems and Issues in Lapita Archaeology." In Kirch and Hunt 1988, 157–65.
1988b "The Talapakemalai Lapita Site and Oceanic Prehistory." *National Geographic Research* 4 (3):328–42.

Kirch, Patrick V., and Terry L. Hunt, eds.
1988 *Archaeology of the Lapita Cultural Complex: A Critical Review.* Seattle: Thomas Burke Memorial Washington State Museum.

Kis-Jovak, Jowa I., Hetty Nooy-Palm, Reimar Schefold, and Ursula Schulz-Dornburg
1988 *Banua Toraja: Changing Patterns in Architecture and Symbolism among the Sa'dan Toraja, Sulawesi Indonesia.* Amsterdam: Royal Tropical Institute.

Kleiwig de Zwaan, J. P.
1922 "Deux singuliers fétiches de l'île de Nias." *Revue d'Anthropologie* 32:342–46.
1923 "Een Paar Beeldjes uit Midden-Celebes." *Nederlandsch Tijdschrift voor Geneeskunde* 67 (16):1–3.
1930 "L'île de Nias et ses habitants." *Revue d' Anthropologie* 40:116–38.
1955 "Merkwaardige fetish-beelden van het eiland Nias." *Mens en Maatschappij* 30:170–74.

van Koenigswald, G. H. R.
1961 "Opmerkingen over Chineesche en Indonesische Invloeden op de Kunst van Nieuw-Guinea." *Kultuurpatronen. Bulletin Ethnografisch Museum, Delft* 3–4:124–40.

Koentjaraningrat
1975 *Anthropology in Indonesia: A Bibliographical Review.* Koninklijk Instituut voor Taal-, Land- en Volkenkunde Bibliographical Series, no. 8. The Hague: Nijhoff.
1984 *Kebudayaan, Mentalitas dan Pembangunan.* Jakarta: Gramedia.

Koleksi Pilihan
1980–86 *Koleksi Pilihan Museum Nasional / Selected Collection of The National Museum,* 3 vols. Jakarta: Proyek Pengembangan Museum Nasional.

Koloniaal Museum
1912 *Gids voor de bezoekers van het Koloniaal Museum te Haarlem, tevens beknopte handleiding bij de schoolverzamelingen.* Amsterdam: de Bussy.

Kooijman, Simon
1955 *De Kunst van Nieuw-Guinea.* The Hague: Servire.
1959 *The Art of Lake Sentani.* New York: The Museum of Primitive Art.
1963 "Ornamented Bark-cloth in Indonesia." *Mededelingen van het Rijksmuseum voor Volkenkunde, Leiden,* no. 16. Leiden: E. J. Brill.
1972 "Tapa in Polynesia." *Bishop Museum Bulletin,* no. 234. Honolulu: Bishop Museum Press.

Korn, V. E.
1953 "Batakse Offerande." *Bijdragen tot de Taal-, Land- en Volkenkunde van Nederlandsch-Indië* 109 (2):97–127.

Koubi, Jeannine
1979 "Le malade, le mort et son 'double' visible en pays Toradja, Sulawesi, Indonesie." In *Les hommes et la mort: rituels funéraires à travers le monde,* edited by Jean Guiart le Sycamore, 160–70. Paris: Musée National d'Histoire Naturelle.

van der Kraan, Alfons
1980 *Lombok: Conquest, Colonization and Underdevelopment, 1870–1940.* Singapore: Heinemann Educational Books.

van der Kroef, J. M.
1954 "Dualism and Symbolic Antithesis in Indonesian Society." *American Anthropologist* 56:847–62.

Krohn, William O.
1927 *In Borneo Jungles.* London: Gay & Hancock, Ltd.

Kruyt, Albertus C.
1938 *De West-Toradja's op Midden-Celebes,* 4 vols. Amsterdam: Uitgave van de N.V. Noord-Hollandsche Uitgevers-Maatschappij.

Kuipers, Joel
1988 "The Pattern of Prayer in Weyéwa." In Fox 1988, 104–28.

Laiya, Sitasi Z., Siswanto Zagötö, Happy Laiya, Selamat Zagötö, and Amita Zagötö,
1985 *Kamus Nias-Indonesia.* Jakarta: Departemen Pendidikan dan Kebudayaan, Pusat Pebinaan den Pengembangan Bahasa.

Langewis, Laurens, and Frits A. Wagner
1964 *Decorative Art in Indonesian Textiles.* Amsterdam: van der Peet.

Leach, Edmund R.
1954 *Political Systems of Highland Burma.* Cambridge: Harvard Univ. Press.

Lebar, Frank M., ed.
1972 *Indonesia, Andaman Islands, and Madagascar. Ethnic Groups of Insular Southeast Asia,* 2 vols. New Haven: Human Relations Area Files Press.

Lehman, F. K.
1963 *The Structure of Chin Society.* Urbana: Univ. of Illinois Press.

Leigh, Barbara
1989 *Hands of Time: The Crafts of Aceh / Tangan-tangan Trampil: Seni Kerajinan Aceh.* Jakarta: Penerbit Djambatan.

van Leur, J. C.
1960 *Indonesian Trade and State Development in Early Southeast Asia.* Honolulu: Univ. of Hawaii Press.

Lévi-Strauss, Claude
1963 [1958] *Structural Anthropology.* Translated by C. Jacobson and B. G. Schoepf. New York: Basic Books.
1979 *La voie des masques.* Paris: Plon.

Liebert, Gösta
1976 *Iconographic Dictionary of the Indian Religions: Hinduism-Buddhism-Jainism.* Leiden: E. J. Brill.

Loeb, Edwin Meyer
1972 [1935] *Sumatra: Its History and People.* Singapore: Oxford Univ. Press.

Lubis, A. Makti, S. Jusuf, T. M. Butar-butar, and M. Malau
1986 *Kalender Peramalan Batak.* Medan: Departemen Pendidikan dan Kebudayaan, Proyek Pengembangan Permuseuman Sumatera-Utara.

Lumholtz, Karl Sofus
1921 *Through Central Borneo: An Account of Two Years' Travel in the Land,* 2 vols. London: T. F. Unwin.

Maass, Alfred
1910 *Durch Zentral-Sumatra.* Berlin: Wilhelm Süsserott.

MacCormack, Carol, and Marilyn Strathern, eds.
1980 *Nature, Culture and Gender.* Cambridge: Cambridge Univ. Press.

Macknight, Campbell
1969 "The Sea Voyages of Eastern Indonesia." *Hemisphere* 13 (4):7–14.

Manguin, P.
1986 "Shipshape Societies: Boat Symbolism and Political Systems in Insular Southeast Asia." In Marr and Milner 1986.

Maquet, Jacques
1986 *The Aesthetic Experience: An Anthropologist Looks at the Visual Arts.* New Haven and London: Yale Univ. Press.

Marr, D., and A. Milner, eds.
1986 *Southeast Asia in the 9th to 14th Centuries.* Singapore: Institute of Southeast Asian Studies, Australian National Univ.

Marshall, Wolfgang
1976 *Der Berg des Herrn der Erde.* Munich: Deutscher Taschenbuch Verlag.

Mason, Otis
1908 "Vocabulary of Malaysian Basketwork: A Study in the W. L. Abbott Collections." *Proceedings of the U.S. National Museum* 35 (1631):1–51, plates 1–17.

Masyhuda, Mashuddin
1982–83 *Katalogus Koleksi, Museum Negeri, Sulawesi Tengah.* Palu: Museum Negeri Sulawesi Tengah.

Maybury-Lewis, D., ed.
1984 *The Prospects for Plural Societies,* Washington, D.C.: American Anthropological Association

Maybury-Lewis, David, and Uri Almagor, eds.
1989 *The Attraction of Opposites: Thought and Society in the Dualistic Mode.* Ann Arbor: Univ. of Michigan Press.

McCormack, W. C., and S. A. Wurm, eds.
1978 *Approaches to Language: Anthropological Issues.* The Hague: Mouton and Co.

McKinnon, Susan M.
1983 "Hierarchy, Alliance, and Exchange in the Tanimbar Islands." Ph.D. dissertation, Univ. of Chicago.
1987 "The House Altars of Tanimbar: Abstraction and Ancestral Presence." *Art Tribal/ Tribal Art* (1):3–16.
1988 "Tanimbar Boats." In Barbier and Newton 1988, 152–169.

1989 "Flags and Half-Moons: Tanimbarese Textiles in an 'Endangered' System of Valuables." In Gittinger 1989, 27–42.

in press *The Spear's Legacy: Hierarchy, Gender, and Exchange in the Tanimbar Islands.* Madison: Univ. of Wisconsin Press.

McNeely, Jeffrey A., and Paul Spencer Wachtel
1988 *Soul of the Tiger: Searching for Natural Answers in Exotic Southeast Asia.* New York: Doubleday.

McVey, Ruth, ed.
1963 *Indonesia.* New Haven: Southeast Asia Studies, Yale Univ. and Human Relations Area Files Press.

Mead, S. M., ed.
1979 *Exploring the Visual Art of Oceania.* Honolulu: Univ. of Hawaii Press.

Mendröfa, W.
1982 *Kamus Bahasa Nias Indonesia / Li Niha ba Li Indonesia.* Serie B Medan: Usaha Pagi Jaya.

Metcalf, Peter
1982 *A Borneo Journey into Death: Berawan Eschatology from its Rituals.* Philadelphia: Univ. of Pennsylvania Press.

Meyer, A. B.
1875 "Notizen über Glauben und Sitten der Papúas des Mafoor'schen Stammes auf Neu-Guinea." *Jahresberichte des Vereins für Erdkunde zu Dresden* 12:23–39.

Meyn, Susan L.
1982 *Black Island Paradise: Life in Melanesia.* Cincinnati: Cincinnati Museum of Natural History.

Milner, A. C.
1982 *Kerajaan: Malay Political Culture on the Eve of Colonial Rule.* Tucson: Association for Asian Studies and Univ. of Arizona Press.

Modigliani, Elio
1890 *Un Viaggio a Nias di Elio Modigliani.* Milan: Fratelli Treves.

Moerdowo
1958 *Reflections on Indonesian Arts and Culture.* Surabaya: Permata.

de Moor, Maggie, and Wilhelmina H. Kal
1983 *Indonesische Sieraden.* Amsterdam: Tropenmuseum.

Moss, Laurence A.G.
1986 *Art of the Lesser Sunda Islands: A Cultural Resource at Risk.* San Francisco: San Francisco Craft and Folk Art Museum.

in press "International Art Collecting, Tourism, and a Tribal Region in Indonesia." In Taylor in press b.

MvVR [Museum voor Volkenkunde, Rotterdam]
1988 *Expressions of Belief: Masterpieces of African, Oceanic, and Indonesion Art from the Museum voor Volkenkunde, Rotterdam.* New York: Rizzoli.

Needham, Rodney
1962 *Structure and Sentiment: A Test Case in Social Anthropology.* Chicago: Univ. of Chicago Press.

Neill, Wilfred T.
1973 *Twentieth-Century Indonesia.* New York: Columbia Univ. Press.

Newton, Douglas
1988 "Reflections in Bronze: Lapita and Dongson Art in the Western Pacific." In Barbier and Newton 1988, 10–23.

Nicholl, Robert
1983 "Brunei Rediscovered: A Survey of Early Times." *Journal of Southeast Asian Studies* 14 (1):32–45.

Nicholson, Julia
1988 *Traditional Indian Arts of Gujarat.* Leicestershire Museums Publications, no. 95. Leicester, England: Leicestershire Museums.

Niessen, Sandra A.
1982 "Descent Versus Exchange in the Batak *Tunggal Panaluan* Myth." Working Paper, no. 28. Leiden: Univ. of Leiden Institute of Cultural and Social Sciences.

1984 "Textiles are Female but What is Femaleness? Toba Batak Textiles in the Indonesian Field of Ethnological Study." In de Josselin de Jong 1984, 63–83.

1985 *Motifs of Life in Toba Batak Text and Textiles.* Dordrecht, Holland, and Cinnaminson, NJ: Foris Publications.

1988 "Modigliani's Batak Textiles: Evaluation of a Collection." *Archivio per L'Antropologia e la Etnologia* 118:57–91.

Nieuwenhuis, A. W.
1904–07 *Quer Durch Borneo*, 2 vols. Leiden: E. J. Brill.

Noorduyn, J.
1955 *Een Achttiende-eeuwse Kroniek van Wadjo': Buginese Historiographie.* The Hague: H. L. Smits

1975 "The Eastern Kings in Majapahit." *Bijdragen tot de Taal-, Land- en Volkenkunde* 131 (4):479–89.

1978 "Majapahit in the Fifteenth Century." *Bijdragen tot de Taal-, Land- en Volkenkunde* 134 (2–3):207–74.

Nooy-Palm, C. H. M.
1969 "Dress and Adornment of the Sa'dan-Toradja (Celebes, Indonesia)." *Tropical Man* 1969 (2):162–94.

1975a "Introduction to the Sa'dan Toraja People and Their Country." *Archipel* 10:53–92.

1975b *De Karbouw en de Kandaure.* Delft: Ethnographisch Museum Nusantara.

1979 *The Sa'dan-Toraja: A Study of Their Social Life and Religion.* Vol. 1. *Organization, Symbols and Beliefs.* Verhandelingen van het Koninklijk Instituut voor Taal, Land- en Volkenkunde, no. 87. The Hague: Nijhoff.

1986 *The Sa'dan-Toraja: A Study of Their Social Life and Religion.* Vol. 2. *Rituals of the East and West.* Verhandelingen van het Koninklijk Instituut voor Taal, Land- en Volkenkunde, no. 118. Dordrecht: Foris Publications.

1988 "The Mamasa and Sa'dan Toraja of Sulawesi." In Barbier and Newton 1988, 86–105.

1989 "The Sacred Cloths of the Toraja: Unanswered Questions." In Gittinger 1989, 163–80.

van Nouhuys, J. W.
1921 "Een Autochthon Weefgebied in Midden-Celebes." *Nederlandsch-Indië Oud en Nieuw* 6:237–43.

1925 "Was-batik in Midden-Celebes." *Nederlandsch-Indië Oud en Nieuw* 10:110–22.

Oliver, Douglas L.
1989 *The Pacific Islands.* 3d rev. ed. Honolulu: Univ. of Hawaii Press.

Ong, Eric
1988 *Pua: Iban Weavings of Sarawak.* Kuching: Society Atelier Sarawak.

Onvlee, L.
1949 "Naar Aanleiding van de Stuwdam in Mangili (Opmerkingen Over de Sociale Structuur van Oost-Soemba)." *Bijdragen Tot de Taal-, Land- en Volkenkunde van Nederlandsch-Indië* 105:445–59.

Ormeling, Ferdinand Jan
1955 *The Timor Problem: A Geographical Interpretation of an Underdeveloped Island.* Groningen: Wolters.

Ottenberg, Simon, ed.
forthcoming *Ethnicity in the Arts.*

Padoch, Christine
1988 "Agriculture in Interior Borneo: Shifting Cultivation and Alternatives." *Expedition* 30 (1):18–28.

Pakan, Priyanti
1977 "Orang Toraja: Identitas, Klasifikasi dan Lokasi." *Berita Antropologi* 9 (32–33):21–49.

Patanne, E. P.
1971 "Early Voyages in South-East Asia." *Hemisphere* 15 (9):30–35.

Pelzer, Karl J.
1963 "Physical and Human Resource Patterns." In McVey 1963, 1–23.

Perelaer, M. T. H.
1983 *Nederlandsch-Indië: De Buitenbezittingen.* Leiden: A. W. Sijthoff.

Pickering, Charles
1872 *The Races of Man and Their Geographical Distribution.* London: Bell & Daldy.

Polman, K.
1981 *The North Moluccas: An Annotated Bibliography.* Koninklijk Instituut voor Taal-Land-, en Volkenkunde, Bibliographical Series, no 11. The Hague: Nijhoff.

Price, Sally
1989 *Primitive Art in Civilized Places.* Chicago: The Univ. of Chicago Press.

Randhawa, M. S.
1963 "The Cult of Trees and Tree-worship in Buddhist-Hindu Sculpture." *Roopa-Lekha* (New Delhi) 33 (1):1–42.

Rassers, W. H.
1982 [1959] *Panji, the Culture Hero, A Structural Study of Religion in Java.* The Hague: Nijhoff.

Reid, Anthony
1979 *The Blood of the People: Revolution and the End of Traditional Rule in Northern Sumatra.* Oxford: Oxford Univ. Press.

1988 *Southeast Asia in the Age of Commerce 1450–1680.* Vol. 1. *The Lands Below the Winds.* New Haven: Yale Univ. Press.

Reid, Anthony, and Lance Castles, eds.
1975 *Pre-Colonial State Systems in Southeast Asia: The Malay Peninsula, Sumatra, Bali-Lombok, South Celebes.* Monographs of the Malaysian Branch of the Royal Asiatic Society, no. 6. Kuala Lumpur: Percetakan Mas Sdn. Bhd.

Renes, P. B.
1983 "Circular Connubium in the Leti Archipelago." In de Josselin de Jong 1983, 225–30.

Revel-Macdonald, Nicòle
1978 "La danse des 'hudoq,' (Kalimantan Timur)." *Objets et Mondes* 18 (1–2):31–44.

1988 "The Dayak of Borneo: On the Ancestors, the Dead and the Living." In Barbier and Newton 1988, 66–85.

Ricklefs, M. C.
1981 *A History of Modern Indonesia, c. 1300 to the Present*. Bloomington: Indiana Univ. Press.

Rodgers, Susan
1981 "Adat, Islam and Christianity in a Batak Homeland." Papers in International Studies, Southeast Asia Series, no. 57. Athens: Ohio Univ. Press.
1985 *Power and Gold: Jewelry from Indonesia, Malaysia, and the Philippines*. Geneva: Musée Barbier-Mueller.

Rongphim Krom Uthokkasat
1957 *Anuson ngan phutthaphayuhayattra thang chonlamak, nai kanchalong 25 phutthasattawat, 14 Phr tsaphakhom 2500*. Bangkok: Rongphim Krom Uthokkasat, 2500.

de Roo van Alderwelt, J.
1990 "Eenige Mededeelingen over Soemba." *Tijdschrift voor Indisch Taal-, Land- en Volkenkunde* 33:565–95.

Rouffaer, G.
1911 "Zeldzame Gouden Memoeli van Soemba." *Notulen van de Algemeene en Directievergaderingen van het Bataviaasch Genootschap van Kunsten en Weterschappen* 49 (appendix 2):29–31.

Roth, Henry Ling
1910 *Oriental Silverwork: Malay and Chinese*. London: Truslove and Hanson, Ltd.

Russell, Susan, and Clark E. Cunningham, eds.
1989 *Changing Lives, Changing Rites: Ritual and Social Dynamics in Philippine and Indonesian Uplands*. Michigan Studies of South and Southeast Asia, no. 1. Ann Arbor: Univ. of Michigan.

Sahlins, Marshall D.
1963 "Poor Man, Rich Man, Big-Man, Chief: Political Types in Melanesia and Polynesia." *Comparative Studies in Society and History* 5:285–300.

Sanday, Peggy R., and Suwati Kartiwa
1984 "Cloth and Custom in West Sumatra: The Codification of Minangkabau Worldview." *Expedition* 26 (4):13–29.

van der Sande, G. A. J.
1907 "Ethnography and Anthropology." *Nova Guinea*, vol. 3. Leiden: E. J. Brill.

Sandin, Benedict
1977 *Gawai Burong: the Chants and Celebrations of the Iban Bird Festival*. Pinang: Penerbit Universiti Sains Malaysia.

Sarasin, Paul, and Fritz Sarasin
1905 *Reisen in Celebes Ausgeführt in den Jahren 1893–1896 und 1902–1903*, 2 vols. Weisbaden: Kreidel.

Schärer, H.
1963 *Ngaju Religion: The Conception of God among a South Borneo People*. The Hague: Nijhoff.
1987 *Schatten van het Museum voor Volkenkunde*. Amsterdam: Meulenhoff/Landshoff.

Scheffler, Harold W.
1973 "Kinship, Descent, and Alliance." In Honigmann 1970, 747–93.

Schefold, Reimar
1988 "Mentawai: A Cosmos as Network of the Souls." In Schefold et al. 1988, 12–21.

Schefold, Reimar, Vincent Dekker, and Nico de Jonge, eds.
1988 *Indonesia in Focus*. Meppel, The Netherlands: Edu'Actief Publishing Company.

Schnitger, F. M.
1939 *Forgotten Kingdoms in Sumatra*. Leiden: E. J. Brill.

Schröder, E. E. W. Gs
1917 *Nias: Ethnographische, Geographische en Historische Aanteekeningen en Studiën*, 2 vols. Leiden: E. J. Brill.

Schuh, Gotthard
1943 *Eilanden der Goden*. Amsterdam: Elsevier.

Schulte Nordholt, H. G.
1971 *The Political System of the Atoni of Timor*. The Hague: Nijhoff.

Sellato, Bernard
1989 *Hornbill and Dragon*. Jakarta: Elf Aquitaine Indonésie.

Serrurier, L.
1898 "Die Korware oder Ahnenbilder Neu Guineas. Ein Beitrag zur Geschichte der bildenden Kunst." *Tijdschrift voor Indische Taal-, Land- en Volkenkunde* 1898:287–316.

Simkin, Tom, and Richard S. Fiske
1983 *Krakatau 1883: The Volcanic Eruption and Its Effects*. Washington, D.C.: Smithsonian Institution Press.

Singarimbun, Masri
1975 *Kinship, Descent and Alliance among the Karo Batak*. Berkeley and Los Angeles: Univ. of California Press.

Sitepu, Andrianus G.
1980 *Mengenal Seni Kerajinan Tradisional Karo*. Medan: Departemen Pendidikan dan Kebudayaan.

Smith, R. B., and W. Watson, eds.
1979 *Early South East Asia*. New York: Oxford Univ. Press.

Solheim, Wilhelm G.
1975 "Reflections on the New Data of Southeast Asian Prehistory: Austronesian Origins and Consequence." *Asian Perspectives* 18:146–60.
1979 "Irian Jaya Origins." *Australian Natural History* 19 (10):324–27.
1985 "Korwar of the Biak." In Feldman 1985c, 147–60.

Solyom, Garrett, and Bronwen Solyom
1978 *The World of the Javanese Keris*. Honolulu: East-West Center.

Spencer, J. E.
1966 *Shifting Cultivation in Southeast Asia*. University of California Publications in Geography, vol. 19. Berkeley and Los Angeles: Univ. of California Press.

Spriggs, M.J.T.
1984 "The Lapita Cultural Complex: Origins, Distribution, Contemporaries, and Successors." *J. of Pacific History* 19:202–23.

Steedly, Mary Margaret
1989 "Innocence as Authority: Shifting Gender Roles in Karo Curing Ritual." In Russell and Cunningham 1988, 133–66.

Steinhart, W. L.
1938 *Niassche Priesterlitanieën*. Verhandelingen van het Koninklijk Bataviaasch Genootschap van Kunsten en Wetenschappen, vol. 74 (1). Bandung: A. C. Nix & Co.
1937 *Niassche Teksten*. Verhandelingen van het Koninklijk Bataviaasch Genootschap van Kunsten en Wetenschappen, vol. 73. Bandung: A. C. Nix & Co.

Stöhr, W., ed.
1982 *Art of the Archaic Indonesians*. Dallas: Dallas Museum of Fine Arts.

Strathern, Marilyn
1988 *The Gender of the Gift: Problems with Women and Problems with Society in Melanesia*. Berkeley and Los Angeles: Univ. of California Press.

Sulaiman, Kalpana
1990 "Ancient Sculptures of Nias." *Arts of Asia* 20 (1):92–102.

Sumnik-Dekovich, Eugenia
1985 "The Significance of Ancestors in The Arts of the Dayak of Borneo." In Feldman 1985c, 101–28.

Suzuki, Peter
1958 *Critical Survey of Studies on the Anthropology of Nias, Mentawei and Enggano*. Koninklijk Instituut voor Taal-, Land- en Volkenkunde Bibliographic Series, vol. 3. The Hague: Nijhoff.
1959 "The Religious System and Culture of Nias, Indonesia." Ph.D. dissertation, Leiden Univ.

Tambiah, S. J.
1976 *World Conqueror and World Renouncer*. Cambridge: Cambridge Univ. Press.

Tana Toraja Dalam Angkat
1983 *Tana Toraja Dalam Angkat*. Ujung Pandang: Kantor Statistik, Daerah Tingkat I Sulawesi Selatan.

Taylor, Keith
1976 "Madagascar in the Ancient Malayo-Polynesian Myths." In Hall and Whitmore 1976, 25–60.

Taylor, Paul Michael
1985 "The Indonesian Collections of William Louis Abbott (1860–1936): Invitation to a Research Resource at the Smithsonian Institution." *Council for Museum Anthropology Newsletter* 9 (2):5–14.
1988 "From *mantra* to *mataráa*: Opacity and Transparency in the Language of Tobelo Magic and Medicine (Halmahera Island, Indonesia)." *Social Science and Medicine* 27 (5):425–36.
1990 *The Folk Biology of the Tobelo People: A Study in Folk Classification*. Smithsonian Contributions to Anthropology, vol. 34. Washington, D.C.: Smithsonian Institution Press.
in press a "The 'Nusantara' Concept of Culture: Local Traditions and National Identity as Expressed in Indonesia's Museums." In Taylor in press b.

———, ed.
in press b *Fragile Traditions: Indonesian Art in Jeopardy*.

Team Prasurvey Propinsi Sulteng
1973 *Peninggalan Nasional de Sulawesi Tengah*. Palu, Sulawesi: Team Prasurvey Kebudayaaan Propinsi Sulawesi Tengah.

Teensma, B. N.
1989 "An Unknown Portuguese Text on Sumatra from 1582." *Bijdragen tot de Taal-, Land- en Volkenkunde* 145 (2–3):308–23.

Terrell, John
1986 *Prehistory in the Pacific Islands: A Study of Variation in Language, Customs, and Human Biology*. Cambridge: Cambridge Univ. Press.

Thomas, J. W., and E. A. Taylor Weber
1987 *Niasch-Maleisch-Nederlandsch Woordenboek*. Jakarta: Landsdrukkerij.

Tichelman, G. L.
1939 "The Batak Magic Wand." In Schnitger 1939, 109–31.
1940a "Het Snel-Motief op Toradja-Foejas." *Cultureel Indië*, April: 113–18.
1940b "Het Snelmotief op een Badjoa-Hoed (Celebes)." *Cultureel Indië*, Dec:278–79.
1953 "Quelques données sur la crosse sacerdotale des Bataks." *Ethnos* 1953 (1–2):7–20.
1960 "De Bronzen Ethnografica van het Sentanimeer-Gebied." *Kultuurpatronen. Bulletin Ethnografisch Museum, Delft* 2:33–45.

Tillema, Hendrik Freerk
1989 *A Journey Among the People of Borneo in Word and Picture.* Edited and with an introduction by Victor T. King, under the auspices of the Rijksmuseum voor Volkenkunde, Leiden. Singapore and New York: Oxford Univ. Press.

Tobing, Philip O. L.
1956 *The Structure of the Tobak-Batak Belief in the High God*. Amsterdam: Jacob van Campen.

Traube, Elizabeth G.
1980 "Mambai Rituals of Black and White." In Fox 1980, 290–314.
1986 *Cosmology and Social Life: Ritual Exchange among the Mambai of East Timor*. Chicago: Univ. of Chicago Press.

University of California Irvine
1967 *Melanesian Art*. Irvine: Univ. of California.

Vatter, Ernst
1932 *Ata Kiwan: Unbekannte Bergvölker im Tropischen Holland*. Leipzig: Bibliographisches Institut A.G. [Indonesian translation: *Ata Kiwan*, S.D. Syah, trans. Jakarta: Nusa Indah, 1984.]
1934 "Der Schlangendrache auf Alor und verwandte Darstellungen in Indonesien, Asien und Europa." *Jahrbuch für Prähistorische und Ethnographische Kunst* 9:119–48.

Vayda, Andrew
1976 *War in Ecological Perspective: Persistence, Change, and Adaptive Processes in Three Oceanian Societies*. New York: Plenum.

van der Veen, H.
1924 "Aanteekeningen bij het Artikel van A. C. Kruyt 1923/4." *Tijdschrift voor Indische Taal-, Land- en Volkenkunde* 63:356–68.
1929 "Nota Betreffende de Grenzen van de Sa'danse Taalgroep en het Haar Aanverwante Taalgebied." *Tijdschrift voor Indische Taal-, Land- en Volkenkunde* 69:50–97.
1965 *The Merok Feast of the Sa'dan Toradja*. The Hague: Nijhoff.
1966 *The Sa'dan Toradja Chant for the Deceased*. The Hague: Nijhoff.

Vergouwen, J. C.
1964 *The Social Organization and Customary Law of the Toba- Batak of Northern Sumatra*. Koninklijk Instituut voor Taal-, Land- en Volkenkunde Translation Series, no. 7. The Hague: Nijhoff.

Vion, Anne-Marie
1987 "Falsifications Indonésiennes." *Art Tribal/ Tribal Art* 2:16–19.

Visser, Leontine E.
1989 "Foreign Textiles in Sahu Culture." In Gittinger 1989, 81–90.

Vogelsanger, Cornelia
1980 "A Sight for the Gods: Notes on the Social and Religious Meaning of Iban Ritual Fabrics." In Gittinger 1980, 115–26.

Volkenkundig Museum Nusantara
1984 *Sieraden en Lichaamsversiering uit Indonesië*. Delft: Volkenkundig Museum Nusantara.

Volkman, Toby Alice
1985 *Feasts of Honor: Ritual and Change in the Toraja Highlands*. Chicago and Urbana: Univ. of Illinois Press.
1986 "Tourism and the Arts in Southern Sulawesi." *Cultural Survival* 6 (4):21–23.
1987 "Mortuary Tourism in Tana Toraja." In Kipp and Rodgers 1987.
1990 "Visions and Revisions: Toraja Culture and the Tourist Gaze." *American Ethnologist* 17 (1):91–110.

van Vollenhoven, Cornelis
1918–33 *Het Adatrecht van Nederlandsch-Indië*, 3 vols. Leiden: E. J. Brill.

Voorhoeve, P., and J. H. Neumann
1933 "De Bataks." In *Jaarboek van het Koninklijk Bataviaasch Genootschap van Kunsten en Wetenschappen*, 385–90. Bandung: A.C. Nix & Co.

Vroklage, B. A. G.
1952–53 *Ethnographie der Belu in Zentral-Timor*, 3 vols. Leiden: E. J. Brill.

van de Wall, V. I.
1922 "Het Museum Kedaton van Ternate: Korte beschrijving met catalogus." *Oudheidkundig Verslag* (1922):138–53.

Wallace, Alfred Russel
1962 [1869] *The Malay Archipelago*. New York: Dover Publications, Inc.

Waterson, Roxana
1988 "The House and the World: The Symbolism of Sa'dan Toraja House Carvings." *Res* 15:35–60.
1990 *The Living House: An Anthropology of Architecture in South-East Asia*. Singapore: Oxford Univ. Press.

Wheatley, Paul
1961 *The Golden Khersonese: Studies in the Historical Geography of the Malay Peninsula Before A.D. 1500*. Kuala Lumpur: Univ. of Malaya Press.

Whittier, Herbert L.
1973 "Social Organization and Symbols of Social Differentiation: An Ethnographic Study of the Kenyah Dayak of East Kalimantan (Borneo)." Ph.D. dissertation, Michigan State Univ.

Whittier, Herbert L., and Patricia R. Whittier
1988 "Baby Carriers: A Link Between Social and Spiritual Values Among the Kenyah Dayak of Borneo." *Expedition* 30 (1):51–58.

Wilcox, Harry
1949 *White Stranger: Six Moons in Celebes*. London: Collins Publishers.

Wolters, Oliver W.
1967 *Early Indonesian Commerce: A Study of the Origins of Srivijaya*. Ithaca: Cornell Univ. Press.
1970 *The Fall of Srivijaya in Malay History*. Ithaca: Cornell Univ. Press.
1982 *History, Culture and Region in Southeast Asian Perspectives*. Singapore: Institute of Southeast Asian Studies.

van Wouden, F. A. E.
1968 [1935] *Types of Social Structure in Eastern Indonesia*. Koninklijk Instituut voor Taal-, Land- en Volkenkunde Translation Series, no. 11. The Hague: Nijhoff.

Wright, Leigh R.
1972 *Vanishing World: The Ibans of Borneo*. New York: Weatherhill.

Wurm, S. A.
1978 "The Emerging Linguistic Picture and Linguistic Prehistory of the Southwestern Pacific." In McCormack and Wurm 1978.
1982 *Papuan Languages of Oceania*. Tübingen: Gunter Narr Verlag.
1983 "Linguistic Prehistory in the New Guinea Area." *Journal of Human Evolution* 12:25–35.

Wurm, S. A., and S. Hattori
1983 *Language Atlas of the Pacific Area*, Part II. Canberra: Australian Academy of the Humanities.

Yamamoto, Yoshiko Miko
1986 "A Sense of Tradition—An Ethnographic Approach to Nias Material Culture." Ph.D. dissertation, Cornell Univ.

Zerner, Charles, and Toby Alice Volkman
1988 "The Tree of Desire: A Toraja ritual poem." In Fox 1988, 282–305.

Index

Figures incorporated with text of the same content are not cited separately. Figures are numbered only when two or more figures of different content appear on the same page. Maps are indicated by *m.* following the page number.

C

D

E

F

G

H

I

J

K

L

M

N

O

P

Q

R

S

T

U

V

W

Z